Business Organizations for Paralegals

Kathleen Mercer Reed
The University of Toledo Director of Paralegal Studies

Henry R. Cheeseman
University of Southern California Marshall School of Business

John J. Schlageter, III
The University of Toledo Paralegal Studies Program

Prentice Hall
Boston Columbus Indianapolis New York San Francisco Upper Saddle River
Amsterdam Cape Town Dubai London Madrid Milan Munich Paris Montreal Toronto
Delhi Mexico City São Paulo Sydney Hong Kong Seoul Singapore Taipei Tokyo

Editor in Chief: Vernon Anthony
Acquisitions Editor: Gary Bauer
Development Editor: Linda Cupp
Editorial Assistant: Tanika Henderson
Director of Marketing: David Gesell
Senior Marketing Manager: Leigh Ann Sims
Senior Marketing Assistant: Les Roberts
Project Manager: Holly Shufeldt
Senior Art Director: Jayne Conte
Cover Designer: Karen Noferi
Cover Art: Corbis
Full-Service Project Management and Composition: Chitra Ganesan/PreMediaGlobal
Printer/Binder: Edwards Brothers
Cover Printer: Lehigh-Phoenix Color
Text Font: 11/13 Goudy

Credits and acknowledgments borrowed from other sources and reproduced, with permission, in this textbook appear on the appropriate page within the text.

Library of Congress Cataloging-in-Publication Data
Reed, Kathleen Mercer.
Business organizations for paralegals / Kathleen Mercer Reed, Henry R. Cheeseman, John J. Schlageter, III.
p. cm.
Includes index.
ISBN-13: 978-0-13-510364-7
ISBN-10: 0-13-510364-9
1. Business enterprises—Law and legislation—United States. 2. Legal assistants—United States—Handbooks, manuals, etc. I. Cheeseman, Henry R. II. Schlageter, John J. III. Title.
KF1355.R44 2012
346.73'065—dc22

2011001681

10 9 8 7 6 5 4 3 2 1

Prentice Hall
is an imprint of

www.pearsonhighered.com

ISBN 10: 0-13-510364-9
ISBN 13: 978-0-13-510364-7

PREFACE

ABOUT THE BOOK

Business Organizations for Paralegals provides paralegal students with the opportunity to study the depth and breadth of business organizations while helping them develop high-level critical thinking skills, understand legal ethics, read about some of the country's most successful practicing paralegals, and create legal documents to get ready for their first day on the job.

This text contains a wide variety of exercises and applications that will ask students to apply concepts to situations that they will encounter in practice. One of the most exciting exercises takes students through the process of forming their own mock business. At the very beginning of the course, students will be asked to form a mock business, and then, as the course progresses, students will use that mock business as the basis for selected chapter assignments and exercises; to help them learn various aspects of business creation and operation in a hands-on way.

CHAPTER ORGANIZATION AND FEATURES

Each chapter of this textbook has in-depth business organizations coverage and provides numerous ways for students to improve their critical thinking skills.

Every chapter opens with a **Case Scenario**. This hypothetical case gives the student a real-world situation to consider as they read that particular chapter. Then, as a learning reinforcement, each chapter ends by revisiting that chapter's Case Scenario and asking questions about possible outcomes relating to that hypothetical case. To relate the hypothetical situation to the real-world, students are then given information on a *real* case that involves the same or similar facts, along with a case citation (in proper Blue Book format!) so that students can locate and read the real-life case. The purpose of the Case Scenario feature is to give the student a frame of reference as they read the chapter and provide for an end-of-chapter review of the material as well.

The **Chapter Objectives** feature encourages students to watch for particular concepts in the chapter. The feature also serves as a broad chapter outline and reinforces the learning outcomes for that chapter.

Key Terms in each chapter are bolded when first introduced and then are defined in the margin.

Important business organizations **Cases** are highlighted throughout each chapter. Some of these are U.S. Supreme Court cases, which may be "Landmark Cases," and some cases are from various state courts. All are real cases that illustrate and explain concepts covered in the chapter. While these cases are presented in a shorter format than the actual case opinion; the case citation is always given so that students can locate and read the case in its entirety. Case citations are also presented in the proper "Blue Book" format for consistency with the techniques the paralegal student has learned in their legal research courses.

Relevant **Laws** are provided in boxed features and in chapter discussions. As the student is reading along, the law that is referenced in the discussion is located right there. This cuts down on shuffling back and forth between chapter discussion and an appendix or outside resources. These boxes and discussions may include references to specific state law, websites with that information, or other places where the student can find additional information.

Exhibits help clarify legal formats and documents that may be foreign to students.

Concept Summaries appear periodically within each chapter to give students a chance to pause and be sure they have mastered the preceding material.

SPECIAL CHAPTER FEATURES

All of the special features of this textbook are designed to give the paralegal student an in-depth understanding of business organizations—and of the paralegal's role in this area of law.

Paralegal Perspective

One of the most interesting special features of this textbook is the "Paralegal Perspective." This feature will introduce the student to the "face" of paralegals working in many different areas of the law. Through articles they've written, paralegals explain how they work within the field of business organizations. Students will enjoy getting to know some of the country's most successful practicing paralegals. Students will enjoy getting to know these successful paralegals from all across the country.

The Ethical Paralegal

Several features focus on ethics and appropriate ethical conduct for a paralegal working in the area of business organizations. This includes a "Business Ethics" feature box and specific ethical situations and cases involving paralegals. These features enforce for the student the important concept that "ethics" is not just something contained in an ethics course.

Portfolio Exercises

The "Portfolio Exercises" contained in this textbook will accomplish several important things for the paralegal student. One is to inspire students to create various legal documents while in school—using the student's own mock business—so that students know how to create these documents their first day on the job. Equally as important is the student using the "Portfolio" feature as a tool that will help the student get the job in the first place. For students not familiar with a portfolio, the following paragraphs describe its purposes and features.

An employment portfolio is a collection of samples of a prospective employee's *best* work. Traditionally, the portfolio is arranged in an attractive binder or file folder. However, new technology and techniques are being applied to portfolios so that they can also be maintained on the web through companies such as *Epsilen* (an academic version of the social networks like Facebook and MySpace).

The point is that a portfolio represents the prospective employee's (in your case, the *paralegal's*) best organization, writing, and critical thinking skills. The portfolio presents the paralegal's abilities in a much stronger, more positive way than if the paralegal tried to describe to the employer the work he or she is capable of doing. By using a portfolio, the paralegal has concrete evidence of his or her abilities and talents. The portfolio builds confidence in the paralegal's skills, knowledge, and abilities in the prospective employer's mind. The portfolio can be an important tool to help the student get his or her first job as a paralegal.

Finally, many paralegal programs now require students to maintain a portfolio throughout their studies, with the completed portfolio being reviewed and graded in a capstone course. This "Portfolio" feature will provide tools for the student to complete such required portfolio assignments.

The portfolio exercises are designed so that each student uses his or her own mock business as the basis for completion of the exercises. This method of reinforcement will help students learn various aspects of business creation and operation in a more hands-on way.

BUILDING PARALEGAL SKILLS: END-OF-CHAPTER EXERCISES AND APPLICATIONS

End-of-chapter materials are always important in every textbook. In this textbook, exercises are designed to confirm that a student understands the concept, can apply it to real situations, and gets hands-on experience producing the types of documents he or she will work with in practice.

Each chapter in this textbook concludes with **Working the Web Internet Exercises and Case Questions**. This feature is especially important because of the many businesses we can view and contact online. In addition to increasing the student's knowledge of business organizations, these Internet exercises will help students increase their knowledge of locating and understanding relevant case law.

The **Chapter Review** in this textbook is different from the usual narrative style of summarizing a chapter into one or two paragraphs. Instead, the Chapter Review here reiterates all of the key points of the chapter. While not a substitute for *reading* the chapter, the Chapter Review is, in essence, a chapter outline. Students will find this outline to be an important reinforcement feature that students can use when studying for exams.

The **Test Review Terms and Concepts** is a compilation of all of the "Key Terms" defined in the margin throughout that chapter. This is another important reinforcement feature for the student.

The **Case Scenario Revisited** follows up on the Case Scenario from the beginning of the chapter. The students will have already considered a hypothetical case as they read the particular chapter. Now, the Case Scenario Revisited feature asks questions about possible outcomes relating to the hypothetical case. Students are given information on a real case involving the same or similar facts and are also given a case citation so that they can locate and read the real-life case. This feature provides the student with another type of end-of-chapter review of the material.

A number of **Critical Legal Thinking Cases** follows. These are real-life cases, carefully selected to expand on what the student has just learned and to help students apply legal theory to practical application. While these cases are presented in a short paragraph summary, the case citation is always given so that students can locate and read the case in its entirety. Case citations are presented in the proper "Blue Book" format for consistency with the techniques the paralegal student has learned in his or her legal research course. The questions at the end of each of these Critical Legal Thinking Cases are presented in a way to encourage the kind of critical thinking the paralegal needs on the job. Rather than asking the student a specific question about the case, these questions are designed to help the student learn the application of law to fact.

The **Business Ethics Cases** feature highlights real-life cases involving various ethical values and moral principles relating to the area of business organizations. These cases are presented not just to illustrate *legal* ethics, but also the ethical values that form a background for a practice in business organizations. While these cases are presented in a short paragraph summary, the case citation is always given so that students can locate and read the case in its entirety. Case citations are presented in the proper "Blue Book" format for consistency with the techniques the paralegal student has learned in his or her legal research course.

A detailed **Case Listing** makes the many important court cases provided through the textbook easy to locate. Case citations are presented in the proper "Blue Book" format for consistency with the techniques the paralegal student has learned in their legal research course.

SUPPLEMENTS

Resources for Students

Companion Website Access at **www.pearsonhighered.com/Reed**. This website contains an online study guide, including true/false and multiple-choice questions, PowerPoint presentations for each chapter, and the web exercises.

E-Book This text is also available in electronic format at **www.CourseSmart.com**.

Resources for Instructors

To access supplementary materials online, instructors need to request an instructor access code. Go to **www.pearsonhighered.com/irc**, where you can register for an instructor access code. Within 48 hours of registering, you will receive a confirming e-mail including an instructor access code. Once you have received your code, locate your text in the online catalog and click on the Instructor Resources button on the left side of the catalog product page. Select a supplement, and a log in page will appear. Once you have logged in, you can access instructor material for all Prentice Hall textbooks.

Instructor's Manual A comprehensive outline of each text chapter includes teaching suggestions for each chapter as well as key chapter objectives.

Pearson MyTest Electronic Testing Program Pearson MyTest is a powerful assessment generation program that helps instructors easily create and print quizzes and exams. Questions and tests can be authored online, allowing instructors ultimate flexibility and the ability to efficiently manage assessments anytime, anywhere. Educator access to MyTest is already included in Pearson's Instructor Resource Center (IRC) Educator suite. Simply go to **www.pearsonmytest.com** and log in with your existing IRC login name and password.

PowerPoint Presentation A ready-to-use PowerPoint slideshow designed for classroom presentation. Use it as-is or edit content to fit your individual classroom needs.

ACKNOWLEDGMENTS

To the Publishers at Pearson Prentice Hall:

The authors would like to acknowledge and thank the publishing team at Pearson Prentice Hall, particularly Gary Bauer and Linda Cupp for their support and expertise.

To the Reviewers:

Special thanks to the reviewers of this text:

Ronald L. Foster, Davenport University
Gary Laurie, Montclair State University
Lucy Michaud, Lincoln College of New England
Robert E. Mongue, The University of Mississippi

To Those Providing Invaluable Assistance:

The authors wish to acknowledge the invaluable assistance of the following:

Dawn Knisel for her amazing cite-checking work of every case in this textbook. This feature will show paralegal students the proper "Blue Book" format for this important legal writing technique.

Kelly Vogelsong for her help and support on many aspects of creating this textbook.

Butheina Hamdah ("student extraordinare") for all of her help and assistance from a student's perspective.

Paralegals from across the country who participated in the "Paralegal Perspective" feature. This feature puts a "face" on the practicing paralegal in the area of business organizations.

Personal Acknowledgements from the Authors:

Author Kathleen Mercer Reed wishes to acknowledge and thankher best friend and husband, Tom.

Author John J. Schlageter, III, wishes to acknowledge and thank: his wife, Amanda, and their children, Emma, Grace, and Jack, for their love and understanding while he worked on this project; his father, John J. Schlageter, Jr., his trusted career mentor who is always willing to share his knowledge and experience with him; and his Mother, Darla Schlageter, for always believing in him; his siblings Amy, Kelly, Jeff, Molly, and Joseph, extended family, friends, and colleagues for their advice, support, and encouragement; his paralegal students for their comments and contributions throughout his teaching career; and all those who have contributed to this endeavor.

ABOUT THE AUTHORS

KATHLEEN MERCER REED is the Chair of the Department of Undergraduate Legal Specialties and the Director of Paralegal Studies at The University of Toledo. The award-winning paralegal programs within her department hold prestigious American Bar Association approval and were named a "Program of Excellence" by the Ohio Board of Regents.

Professor Reed is a graduate of The University of Toledo, holding a Bachelor's of Science in Interdisciplinary Studies and an Associate Degree in Legal Assisting. She received her Juris Doctor from The University of Toledo College of Law and is a member of the State Bar of Ohio. She is a member of the Ohio State Bar Association, the Toledo Bar Association, and admitted to practice before the United States Supreme Court. She is the past president of the Paralegal Association of Northwest Ohio and the past chair of the Ohio State Bar Association's Paralegal Committee.

Professor Reed's legal experience includes employment with Hallett & Hallett Law Offices of Wauseon, Ohio; with The Honorable Richard L. Speer, United States Bankruptcy Judge in Toledo, Ohio; and with the law firm of Nathan & Roberts of Toledo, Ohio. She has been on the faculty at The University of Toledo since 1987, teaching in such areas as Legal Ethics, Litigation, Torts, and Civil Procedure. Professor Reed arranges and supervises over sixty internship placements every year. She was instrumental in developing one of the first paralegal courses in the country to be offered online, through distance education.

Professor Reed has written numerous articles on paralegal issues and has authored six paralegal textbooks in addition to this textbook and *Contract Law for Paralegals: Traditional and E-Contracts* published by Pearson Prentice Hall for Prentice Hall Publishing Company, which she also co-authored with Henry R. Cheeseman. She is also the author of a genealogy research book now in its third edition.

During her tenure at The University of Toledo, Kathleen has established two paralegal scholarship funds and arranged for the McQuade Endowment, a contribution that established and maintains The McQuade Courtroom in the Paralegal Studies Program. This high-tech courtroom is an integral part of teaching paralegals to use the technology important to today's practice of law.

Kathleen is married to Thomas Reed. The couple spends weekends at their cottage on Lake Gage in Northeast Indiana.

HENRY R. CHEESEMAN is clinical professor of Business Law, director of the Legal Studies Program, and co-director of the Minor in Business Law Program at the Marshall School of Business of the University of Southern California (USC), Los Angeles, California.

Professor Cheeseman earned a bachelor's degree in finance from Marquette University, both a master's in business administration (MBA) and a master's in business taxation (MBT) from the University of Southern California, a juris doctor (J.D.) degree from the University of California at Los Angeles School of Law, a master's of business administration with emphasis on law and economics from the University of Chicago, and a master's in law (L.L.M.) degree in financial institutions law from Boston University.

Professor Cheeseman has earned the "Golden Apple" Teaching Award on many occasions by having been voted by the students as the best professor at the

Marshall School of Business of the University of Southern California. He was named a fellow of the Center for Excellence in Teaching at the University of Southern California (USC) by the dean of the Marshall School of Business. The USC's Torch and Tassel Chapter of the Mortar Board has named Professor Cheeseman Faculty of the Month of USC.

Professor Cheeseman has co-authored another textbook for the paralegal market with Kathleen Mercer Reed—*Contract Law for Paralegals: Traditional and E-Contracts* published by Pearson Prentice Hall. He also writes leading business law and legal environment textbooks that are published by Prentice Hall. These include *Business Law: Legal Environment, Online Commerce, Business Ethics, and International Issues*; *Contemporary Business and Online Commerce Law*; *The Legal Environment of Business and Online Commerce*; *Essentials of Contemporary Business Law*; and *Introduction to Law: Its Dynamic Nature*.

Professor Cheeseman is an avid traveler and amateur photographer.

JOHN J. SCHLAGETER, III, is an associate lecturer at The University of Toledo in the Department of Undergraduate Legal Studies. In addition to teaching business organizations for the last eight years, throughout his thirteen-year teaching career, Lecturer Schlageter has taught many courses including: Business Law, Business Professionalism, Law Practice Management, Civil Procedure, Litigation, Contracts, and Introduction to Law.

Lecturer Schlageter has also completed Mediation Training by the International Academy of Dispute Resolution and has met all other requirements to become an authorized mediator of the Academy and has taught Mediation Topics and Techniques.

In addition, Lecturer Schlageter teaches Advocacy: Mock Trial and has coached The University of Toledo Mock Trial Team in performances at both regional and national competitions.

In all of his courses, Lecturer Schlageter incorporates the use of computers and legal software and enjoys integrating skills pertaining to the electronic courthouse and automated courtroom and presentation graphics.

Lecturer Schlageter is a graduate of the University of Cincinnati (BA) and The University of Toledo, College of Law. After earning his Juris Doctor (J.D.) degree, he was admitted to the Ohio and Michigan Bars, as well as the United States District Court, Northern District of Ohio and the United States District Court, Eastern District of Michigan. He is a member of the Toledo Bar Association, the Michigan State Bar Association, and the Michigan Trial Lawyers' Association.

Lecturer Schlageter maintains a law practice at the firm Shindler, Neff, Holmes, Schlageter & Mohler, LLP in Toledo, Ohio. He is experienced in the areas of general business, litigation, employment, franchise, estate planning, personal injury, and family law.

Lecturer Schlageter has repeatedly served as a guest speaker and has presented at various seminars on subjects including electronic discovery.

John, his wife Amanda, and their children Emma, Grace, and Jack reside in Sylvania, Ohio.

OVERVIEW OF BUSINESS ORGANIZATIONS

Breaking It Down—For Your Studies and Future Paralegal Career

There's no question. When confronted with the breadth and depth of business organizations, students can be overwhelmed. But, remember that the wide range of choices available to the entrepreneur is what makes the study of business organizations challenging—in a *good* way!—as well as fulfilling for those looking for success in their future paralegal career.

When beginning the study of business organizations, it is important for the paralegal student to understand that there are many different ways in which a business may be organized and operated in the United States. To break it down, you need to remember that the client/entrepreneur needs to find the best business organization for him or her if the client/entrepreneur is going to run a successful and productive endeavor.

Which form of business organization is selected depends on (A) the attributes or characteristics of the particular business type; and (B) the perceived advantages and disadvantages of that same business type.

(A) TYPES OF BUSINESS ORGANIZATIONS

The following business organizations are among those available for an entrepreneur to select. These are discussed in depth in this text:

1. Sole Proprietorship

In a sole proprietorship, the sole owner, known as the sole proprietor, owns all of the business assets and is the sole decision maker. Due to its ease of formation relative to other business forms, this form of enterprise is the most commonly selected form of business for new enterprises. The sole proprietor also owns all of the debts of the business and has unlimited personal liability for them which means that the proprietor's personal assets such as bank account funds, automobiles, and other assets can all be attached by creditors of the business. The sole proprietorship business does not file a tax return or pay income taxes separate from the proprietor. All profits and losses belong to the owner, who declares them on his or her individual tax return. This concept is called pass-through taxation. The sole proprietorship business dies with the proprietor, and the proprietorship business cannot be transferred to another owner. Sole proprietorships are discussed in Chapter 3.

2. General Partnership

In a general partnership, two or more persons co-own all of the business assets and share decision making, profits, and losses. Relative to other business forms, the general partnership is easily formed and is managed by mutual agreement. Although generally a written partnership is not required, for reasons discussed throughout the text, it is highly recommended that a written agreement be prepared and executed. General partners have unlimited personal liability for all business debts and obligations, and each partner is an agent of the partnership. General partnerships are subject to pass-through taxation. General partnerships are discussed in Chapter 4.

3. Limited Partnerships, Limited Liability Partnerships, and Limited Liability Limited Partnerships

A limited partnership is a type of investment vehicle created so persons can invest in a business enterprise and yet not have unlimited personal liability. A limited partnership is managed by one or more general partners, all of whom have unlimited personal liability for business debts and obligations. The limited partners may not manage or control this enterprise, and as long as they do not engage in active management, their liability is limited to the amount they invested in the business. Limited partnerships are more complex to form than general partnerships and can only be created by strict compliance with the pertinent state statutes. As with general partnerships, limited partnerships are subject to pass-through taxation.

The limited liability partnership form alters a basic principle of partnership law: Partners in this enterprise are not liable for the torts or acts of misconduct of their partners. In some states, the partners are not liable either for the torts of their partners or contractual obligations incurred by the entity or other partners. Ideally suited to legal, medical, and accounting practices, partners in one office are not liable for acts of partners in their office or a branch office simply because of the partner relationship. This form of business enterprise, which enjoys pass-through taxation and can be formed only through adherence to state statutes, combines some of the best features of partnerships and corporations.

The 2001 amendments to the Revised Uniform Limited Partnership Act permit a new form of entity called a limited liability limited partnership (LLLP). Like a limited partnership, an LLLP requires at least one general partner and at least one limited partner. However, the difference between a limited partnership and an LLLP is that in an LLLP, the general partners are not jointly and severally personally liable for the debts and obligations of the LLLP.

Limited partnerships, limited liability partnerships, and limited liability limited partnerships are discussed in Chapter 5.

4. Limited Liability Company

A limited liability company (LLC) can be created only by complying with pertinent state statutes. The owners of an LLC are called members, and almost all states now permit a one-member limited liability company. This business structure is said to be a hybrid between a partnership and a corporation, containing characteristics of both. Its primary characteristics are that its owners have limited liability (like shareholders in a corporation), and it has the pass-through or flow-through taxation of a partnership, meaning that all income earned by the entity is passed through to the owners, who pay taxes at whatever rate is applicable to them. Limited liability companies are discussed in Chapter 6.

5. Corporation

By far, the corporation is the most detailed of any of the business organizations the student will study in a number of chapters in this textbook. A corporation is created under state laws but may also be subject to federal law. The corporation is a separate legal entity from its shareholder owners. So, the corporation by itself may own property, enter into contracts, and sue and be sued just as an individual can. The amount of regulation with which the corporation must comply and how taxes are assessed all depend on the corporation type.

What is the corporation's purpose? Is the corporation expected to make a profit? Where will the corporation do business? Before forming the corporation, consider how the corporation is classified (note that more than one of the following will apply to the entrepreneur's future business).

- **Public** or **Private?**
  - **Public corporations** are created by the government to administer laws (such as the FDIC or a city that has been incorporated)
  - **Private corporations** are created by private persons for private purposes.
- **Profit** or **Nonprofit?**
  - Corporations **for profit** issue stock and expect to make a profit.
  - Corporations **not for profit** do not issue stock and do not expect to make a profit.
- **Domestic, Foreign,** or **Alien?**
  - A corporation is a **domestic corporation** in the state that has granted its charter.
  - A corporation is a **foreign corporation** in all the other states in which it does business.
  - A corporation domiciled in one country is an **alien corporation** in other countries in which it does business.
- **Publicly Traded** or **Closely Held?**
  - A **publicly traded corporation's** stock is sold to the public.
  - A **closely held corporation's** shareholders are usually family members and friends who are active in the business.
- **S Corporation** or **Professional Organization?**
  - Corporations meeting certain criteria may choose **S corporation** status, meaning they do not pay federal tax on income they earn; instead, their shareholders pay taxes on the income they receive.
  - A **professional organization** is formed for the purpose of practicing a profession, such as law, medicine, or accounting.
- **Parent** or **Subsidiary?**
  - A corporation creating *another* corporation is a **parent corporation**.
  - A **subsidiary corporation** is under the parent corporation's control, with the parent owning at least the majority of the shares of the corporation.

(B) ADVANTAGES/DISADVANTAGES TO CONSIDER IN THE SELECTION OF A BUSINESS ORGANIZATION

While a sole proprietorship may be ideal for one client, that type of business organization may be inappropriate for another. Determining which form of business enterprise is the most advantageous for a client involves careful consideration of a number of factors including the ease and cost of formation, the capital requirements of the business, the flexibility of management decisions, government restrictions, personal liability, and tax considerations.

1. Ease and Cost of Formation and Termination

The ease with which an enterprise can be formed and unformed, while others, such as limited partnerships and corporations, require compliance with state statutes and may be more expensive to organize, maintain and dissolve. Consideration should always be given as to how easy, expeditious, and expensive it is to begin and cease doing business.

2. Management

Some individuals prefer to manage their business themselves. For them, a sole proprietorship or general partnership may afford them the greatest ability to manage and control the enterprise. With this management and control, however, may come unlimited personal liability. Other individuals may prefer to invest in a business knowing their maximum potential loss as they enter the enterprise. For these individuals, limited partnerships or corporations may be ideal so long as they understand that their ability to influence and control the business is limited as well.

Chapter 12 discusses employment law, workers' compensation, occupational safety, overtime pay, government programs, immigration law, and other laws affecting employment. Chapter 13 explores employment law and more particularly the comprehensive set of federal and state laws that eliminated major forms of employment discrimination passed to guarantee equal employment opportunity to all employees and job applicants.

There are many different ways in the United States in which a business may be organized and operated. International and world trade law, important to both nations and businesses, is discussed in Chapter 14.

3. Liability and Financial Risk

The financial exposure an individual faces is one of the most critical factors to consider in selecting a form of business enterprise. As discussed in Chapters 1 and 2, businesses often act through designated individuals, called agents, to conduct their operations, and many legal relationships in business are governed by the law of agency. The acts of agents will bind the businesses they serve if the agent has either actual or apparent authority to act. Employees may or may not serve as agents. Some enterprises shield the individual from unlimited personal liability, while others expose the individual to greater risk. Clients must be fully informed of the potential liability consequences when selecting a particular form of business.

4. Continuity of Existence

Some business organizations, such as corporations, are capable of existing perpetually. Other forms of business enterprises do not have such continuity of existence. For example, a sole proprietorship generally terminates with the death of the sole proprietor, and limited liability companies are subject to a term of duration in a few states. Consideration should be given to the intended duration of the enterprise.

5. Transferability

Clients should consider the ease with which they can "get into" and "get out of" the business enterprise. It may be difficult to transfer out of a general partnership because the partnership agreement may severely restrict the ability of partners to transfer their interests. On the other hand, to get out of a corporation, one need only sell his or her stock to another. If clients foresee a need to liquidate their investment in an enterprise for a cash return, they should evaluate how easy or difficult it may be to transfer into and out of the enterprise.

6. Profits and Losses

While a sole proprietor maintains all profits, he or she is also solely liable for all losses. In a partnership, partners have the ability to bind each other, and thus, while a partner may be able to share a loss with a co-partner, the very reason the partner may have a loss is due to the co-partner's activities. Clients must carefully consider the division of profits and losses when evaluating the form of business enterprise to select.

7. Taxation

Clients should consider applicable tax requirements. For some, the individual tax rates may be best; for others, the corporate tax rates may yield the best advantages. Many business entities afford single or pass-through taxation, while corporations are burdened by double taxation.

GETTING STARTED EXERCISE

A Hands-On Method to Help Students Get the Most Out of This Textbook and Prepare for Their Paralegal Careers

Every day, entrepreneurs in this country and around the world create important new businesses that change the world. Those businesses hire employees, provide new products and services, and contribute to the growth of economies of countries. Just imagine what the world would look like if Bill Gates had never created his business!

By participating in this "Getting Started Exercise" and answering the questions below, you will get in touch with *your* inner entrepreneur to create a fictitious business. Why is this an important tool for getting the most out of this textbook and preparing for your paralegal career?

As you go through this business organizations course, your instructor may require you to complete portfolio exercises and other assignments that relate to your fictitious business. While completing those exercises and assignments, you will discover which one of the major forms of business organization—*sole proprietorship, general partnership, limited partnership, limited liability partnership, limited liability company*, or *corporation*—is the right business form for *your* fictitious business.

As you will see from the paralegals featured throughout this textbook, helping your attorney determine which business organization is right for the client is a critical skill needed for your professional career.

And, who knows? An extra benefit of creating your own fictitious business is that *you* might become the next Bill Gates!

1. What will be the name of the business you will form? ________________

   ____

2. Call the secretary of state in your state or visit its website and check to see whether your proposed name is available. If you made a phone call, what is the name of the person you spoke with?

   ____

3. Will you operate the business under any names other than the name indicated in your answer to question 1 above? If so, what names?

   ____

4. Briefly describe your business and the industry in which it will engage.

   ____

   ____

   ____

   ____

   ____

5. State whether your business will be selling, manufacturing, or purchasing anything. If so, explain.

____

____

____

____

____

6. State whether your business will be providing any type of service or services. If so, explain.

____

____

____

____

____

7. Other than yourself, how many other persons/entities, if any, will have an ownership interest in your business? What percentage of the total business will they own?

____

____

____

____

____

8. Who will conduct the day-to-day operations of your business?

____

____

____

9. How much time per week will you and the other owners (if any) be able to devote to your business?

____

____

____

10. What type of start-up expenses do you think you may incur in starting your business?

____

____

____

11. In which states will your business operate? ______________________

____

12. Where will any needed cash or start-up monies come from (e.g., family, your own funds, bank loans, another owner, etc.)?

____

____

____

____

13. Will your business have any employees?

____

TABLE OF CONTENTS

CHAPTER 4

CHAPTER 5

CHAPTER 6

CHAPTER 7

Corporate Formation and Financing 161

CHAPTER 8

Franchises and Special Forms of Businesses 207

CHAPTER 9

Corporate Governance and the Sarbanes-Oxley Act 239

CHAPTER 10

CHAPTER 11

CHAPTER 12

CHAPTER 13

CHAPTER 14

Appendix A

Appendix B

Appendix C

Appendix D

Appendix E

Appendix F

Appendix G

"Let every eye negotiate for itself, and trust no agent."

–William Shakespeare
Much Ado About Nothing

CHAPTER 1
Agency

CASE SCENARIO

The law firm where you work as a paralegal represents Renaldo, Inc., which does business as Baker Street. Renaldo, Inc., owns and operates a nightclub in Georgia. On the evening in question, plaintiff Ginn became "silly drunk" at the nightclub and was asked by several patrons and the manager to leave the premises. The police were called, and Ginn left the premises. When Ginn realized that his jacket was still in the nightclub, he attempted to reenter the premises. He was met at the door by the manager, who refused him admittance. When Ginn persisted, an unidentified patron, without the approval of the manager, pushed Ginn, who lost his balance and fell backward. To break his fall, Ginn put his hand against the door jamb. The unidentified patron slammed the door on Ginn's hand and held it shut for several minutes. Ginn, who suffered severe injuries to his right hand, sued the nightclub for damages.

CHAPTER OBJECTIVES

After studying this chapter, you should be able to:

1. Define *agency*.
2. Identify, define, and distinguish between employer–employee, principal–agent, and principal–independent contractor relationships.
3. Describe the types of authority an agent can have.
4. Describe the duties that principals and agents have to one another.
5. Describe how agencies are created and terminated.

INTRODUCTION TO AGENCY

> It isn't the people you fire who make your life miserable, it's the people you don't.
> Harvey MacKay

If businesspeople had to personally conduct all their business, the scope of their activities would be severely curtailed. Partnerships would not be able to operate, corporations could not act through managers and employees, and sole proprietorships would not be able to hire employees. The use of agents (or agency), which allows one person to act on behalf of another, solves this problem.

Examples: Examples of agency relationships include a salesperson selling goods for a store, an executive working for a corporation, a partner acting on behalf of a partnership, an attorney representing a client, a real estate broker selling a house, or even the President acting on behalf of the United States.

agency law
The large body of common law that governs agency; a mixture of contract law and tort law.

Agency is governed by a large body of common law known as **agency law**. The formation of agencies, the duties of principals and agents, and termination of agencies are discussed in this chapter.

PARALEGAL PERSPECTIVE

***Amy M. Frakes** is a Certified 6 Sigma Black Belt at Caterpillar Inc., a global Fortune 50, in Peoria, Illinois. She received a bachelor in legal studies from Saint Mary-of-the-Woods College and a master's in business from St. Ambrose University. She worked as a paralegal for four and a half years and is currently in Global Purchasing.*

What are your views on "agency" as it relates to your job? Working in a global organization leads to many challenges when dealing with agency situations. For example, when an employee who has not been granted a general power of attorney executes an agreement on behalf of Caterpillar, Caterpillar might still be obligated to act under the terms and conditions of the agreement. As a paralegal, it is always a good idea to schedule continuing education sessions to help educate employees on agency issues.

What are the most important paralegal skills needed in your job? The negotiation skills I learned during my practice as a paralegal in Caterpillar's Intellectual Property department were recognized by the Global Purchasing group as a much-needed skill set for becoming a buyer in 2001. The ability to negotiate, multi-task, and understand complex legal situations has been the strong foundation needed for continued success in global purchasing.

What is the academic background required for a paralegal entering your area of practice? Caterpillar prefers for paralegals to have at least a certificate. However, it is now common practice for most paralegals to have an associate or bachelor.

How is technology involved in your job? I spend a great deal of my time running spreadsheets and analyzing facts and data. Additionally, PowerPoint is a tool that I use on a day-to-day basis. As the Internet has improved for research capabilities, noting trends in the marketplace and completing research on competitors of current suppliers for price comparison, a greater amount of time is spent on fact finding.

What trends do you see in your area of practice that will likely affect your job in the future? As negotiations continue to become more and more intense between corporations, I believe the opportunity will increase for paralegals to take on roles outside of the legal arena and begin to assume leadership positions within various areas of disciplines.

What do you feel is the biggest issue currently facing the paralegal profession? During my past work as a paralegal, I felt the most common issue was understanding the difference between a paralegal and an administrative assistant. It seems today those stereotypes are beginning to change, but it is still a predominant school of thought.

What words of advice do you have for a new paralegal entering your area of practice? Be open to new areas of opportunity. You may think that you are limited to strictly working with attorneys; however, there are many fields in the marketplace that need the skills you will learn during your paralegal studies.

THE NATURE OF AGENCY

The majority of agency relationships are formed by the mutual consent of a principal and an agent. Section 1(1) of the ***Restatement (Second) of Agency*** defines **agency** as a **fiduciary relationship** "which results from the manifestation of consent by one person to another that the other shall act in his behalf and subject to his control, and consent by the other so to act." The *Restatement (Second) of Agency* is the reference source for the rules of agency. A party who employs another person to act on their behalf is called a **principal**. A party who agrees to act on behalf of another is called an **agent**. The principal–agent relationship is commonly referred to as an *agency*. This relationship is depicted in Exhibit 1.1. There are three players in every contract entered into by an agent on behalf of a principal: the principal, the agent, and the third party. As shown below, when an agent acts on behalf of a principal with a third party, there are two contracts that come into play, namely, the agency contract between the principal and the agent and the resulting contract between the principal and the third party.

agency
The principal–agent relationship; the fiduciary relationship "which results from the manifestation of consent by one person to another that the other shall act in his behalf and subject to his control, and consent by the other so to act" [*Restatement (Second) of Agency*].

fiduciary relationship
A relationship in which one person is under a duty to act for the benefit of another on matters within the scope of the relationship.

principal
A party who employs another person to act on his or her behalf.

agent
A party who agrees to act on behalf of another.

Exhibit 1.1 Principal–Agent Relationship

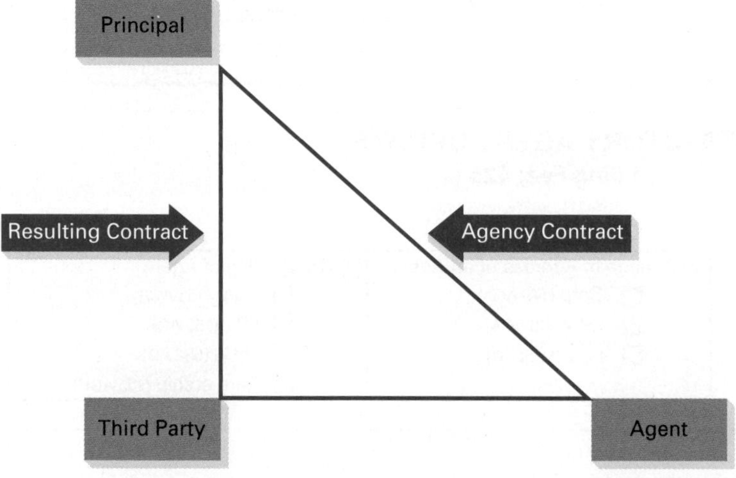

Persons Who Can Initiate an Agency Relationship

Any person who has the capacity to contract can appoint an agent to act on their behalf. For example, a business may appoint a statutory agent to receive legal notices on its behalf (see Exhibit 1.2). Generally, persons who lack contractual capacity, such as insane persons and minors, cannot appoint agents. However, the court can appoint legal guardians or other representatives to handle the affairs of insane persons, minors, and others who lack capacity to contract. With court approval, these representatives can enter into enforceable contracts on behalf of the persons they represent. A principal may appoint any person to act as an agent regardless of the person's mental capacity. The fact that an agent is incompetent will not affect the resulting contract but may have an effect on the underlying agency contract.

An agency can be created only to accomplish a lawful purpose. Agency contracts that are created for illegal purposes or are against public policy are void and unenforceable.

Example: A principal cannot hire an agent to kill another person.

Some agency relationships are prohibited by law.

Example: Unlicensed agents cannot be hired to perform the duties of certain licensed professionals (e.g., doctors, lawyers).

Principal–Agent Relationship

principal–agent relationship
A relationship formed when a principal hires an agent and gives that agent authority to act on his or her behalf.

A **principal–agent relationship** is formed when a principal (such as an employer) hires an agent (such as an employee) and gives that employee authority to act and enter into contracts on the principal's behalf. The extent of this authority is governed by any express agreement between the parties and implied from the circumstances of the agency.

Exhibit 1.2 Statutory Agent Form

Reset Form

THE SEAL OF THE SECRETARY OF STATE OF OHIO

Form 521 Prescribed by the:
Ohio Secretary of State

Central Ohio: (614) 466-3910
Toll Free: (877) SOS-FILE (767-3453)

www.sos.state.oh.us
Busserv@sos.state.oh.us

Expedite this form: (select one)
Mail form to **one** of the following:

○ Expedite — PO Box 1390, Columbus, OH 43216
***** Requires an additional fee of $100 *****

○ Non Expedite — PO Box 788, Columbus, OH 43216

STATUTORY AGENT UPDATE
Filing Fee: $25

(CHECK ONLY ONE (1) BOX)

(1) Subsequent Appointment of Agent	**(2)** Change of Address of an Agent	**(3)** Resignation of Agent
☐ Corp (165-AGS)	☐ Corp (145-AGA)	☐ Corp (155-AGR)
☐ LP (165-AGS)	☐ LP (145-AGA)	☐ LP (155-AGR)
☐ LLC (171-LSA)	☐ LLC (144-LAD)	☐ LLC (153-LAG)
		☐ Partnership (155-AGR)

Name of Entity ______________________

Charter, License or Registration No. ______________________

Name of Current Agent ______________________

Complete the information in this section if box (1) is checked

Name and Address of New Agent

____
Name of Agent

____
Mailing Address

______________ **Ohio** ______________
City State Zip Code

Complete the information in this section if box (1) is checked and business is an Ohio entity

ACCEPTANCE OF APPOINTMENT FOR DOMESTIC ENTITY'S AGENT

The Undersigned, ____________________________________, named herein as the
Name of Agent

Statutory agent for, ____________________________________,hereby acknowledges
Name of Business Entity

and accepts the appointment of statutory agent for said entity.

Signature: ____________________________
Statutory Agent

☐ **If the agent is an individual using a P.O. Box, the agent must check this box to confirm that the agent is an Ohio resident.**

Complete the information in this section if box (2) is checked

New Address of Agent ____________________________________
Mailing Address

____________	**Ohio**	____________
City	State	Zip Code

☐ **If the agent is an individual using a P.O. Box, check this box to confirm that the agent is an Ohio resident.**

Complete the information in this section if box (3) is checked

The agent of record for the entity identified on page 1 resigns as statutory agent.

Current or last known address of the entity's principal office where a copy of this Resignation of Agent was sent as of the date of filing or prior to the date filed.

____
Mailing Address

____________	**Ohio**	____________
City	State	Zip Code

By signing and submitting this form to the Ohio Secretary of State, the undersigned hereby certifies that he or she has the requisite authority to execute this document.

REQUIRED
Must be authenticated **(signed)** by an authorized representative **(See Instructions)**

________________________ ____________
Authorized Representative Date

____
Print Name

________________________ ____________
Authorized Representative Date

____
Print Name

Example: The president of a corporation usually has the authority to enter into major contracts on the corporation's behalf, and a supervisor on the corporation's assembly line may have the authority only to purchase the supplies necessary to keep the line running.

Employer–Employee Relationship

employer–employee relationship
A relationship that results when an employer hires an employee to perform some task or service but the employee has not been authorized to enter into contracts on behalf of his employer.

An **employer–employee relationship** exists when an employer hires an employee to perform some task or service but the employee has not been authorized to enter into contracts on behalf of his employer.

Example: A welder on General Motors Corporation's assembly line is employed in an employer–employee relationship if she is not authorized to enter into contracts on behalf of her employer. She has been employed to perform a task without being given agency authority.

An employee is an agent if he or she is empowered to enter into contracts on the employer's behalf.

Example: The welder in the previous example is an agent if she is given authority to enter into contracts on behalf of General Motors Corporation.

Principal–Independent Contractor Relationship

independent contractor
A person or business that is not an employee but is employed by a principal to perform a certain task on behalf of the principal.

professional agent
A person with considerable skill in his or her field.

Principals often employ outsiders—that is, persons and businesses that are not employees—to perform certain tasks on their behalf. These persons and businesses are called **independent contractors**.

Example: Doctors, dentists, consultants, stockbrokers, architects, certified public accountants, real estate brokers, and plumbers are examples of those in professions and trades who commonly act as independent contractors. An independent contractor who is a professional, such as a lawyer, is called a **professional agent**.

A principal can authorize an independent contractor to enter into contracts. Principals are bound by the authorized contracts of their independent contractors. For example, if a client authorizes an attorney to settle a case within a certain dollar amount and the attorney does so, the settlement agreement is binding.

Concept Summary

Kinds of Employment Relationships

Type of Relationship	Description
Principal–agent	The agent has authority to act on behalf of the principal, as authorized by the principal and implied from the agency. An employee is often the agent of his employer.
Employer–employee	An employee is hired to perform a task or service. An employee cannot enter into contracts on behalf of the employer.
Principal–independent contractor	An independent contractor conducts a transaction for the principal but is not subject to the control of the principal.

FORMATION OF AN AGENCY RELATIONSHIP

An agency and the resulting authority of an agent can arise in several ways, including express agency, implied agency, incidental authority, agency by ratification, and apparent agency. These types of agencies are discussed in the following sections.

Express Agency

Express agency is the most common form of agency. In an express agency, the agent has the authority to contract or otherwise act on the principal's behalf, as expressly stated in the agency agreement. In addition, the agent may also possess certain implied or apparent authority to act on the principal's behalf (as discussed later in this chapter).

express agency
An agency that occurs when a principal and an agent expressly agree to enter into an agency agreement with each other.

Express agency occurs when a principal and an agent expressly agree to enter into an agency agreement with each other. Express agency contracts can be either oral or written, unless the Statute of Frauds stipulates that they must be written. For example, in most states, a real estate broker's contract to sell real estate must be in writing.

If a principal and an agent enter into an **exclusive agency contract**, the principal cannot employ any agent other than the exclusive agent. If the principal does so, the exclusive agent can recover damages from the principal. If an agency is not an exclusive agency, the principal can employ more than one agent to try to accomplish a stated purpose. When multiple agents are employed, the agencies with all the agents terminate when any one of the agents accomplishes the stated purpose.

exclusive agency contract
A contract a principal and agent enter into that says the principal cannot employ any agent other than the exclusive agent.

In the following case, the court had to decide whether an agency had been created.

CASE 1.1 AGENCY

***Bosse v. Brinker Restaurant Corp.*, Opinion No. 89915, Docket No. 03-5064-A, 2005 Mass. LEXIS 372, at *1 (Super. Ct. August 1, 2005).**

"The evidence is insufficient to create a genuine issue whether Chili's appointed or authorized the patron to act as a posse to conduct the chase."

—Judge Sikora

Facts

Brendan Bosse and Michael Griffin were a part of a group of four teenagers eating a meal at a Chili's restaurant in Dedham, Massachusetts. Chili's is owned by Brinker Restaurant Corporation (collectively "Chili's"). The teenagers decided not to pay the $56 bill for their meal. They went out of the building, got in their car, and drove away, heading northward up Route 1.

A patron of the restaurant saw the teenagers leave without payment. He followed them in his white sport-utility vehicle (SUV). The teenagers saw him following them. A high-speed chase ensued through Dedham side streets. The patron used his cell phone to call the Chili's manager. The manager called 911 and reported the incident and the location of the car chase. The teenagers' car collided with a cement wall, and Bosse and Griffin were seriously injured. The Chili's patron drove past the crash scene and was never identified.

> The way to wealth is as plain as the way to market. It depends chiefly on two words, industry and frugality: that is, waste neither time nor money, but make the best use of both. Without industry and frugality nothing will do, and with them everything.
>
> Benjamin Franklin

Bosse and Griffin sued Chili's for compensatory damages for their injuries. The plaintiffs argued that the patron was an agent of Chili's, and therefore Chili's was liable to the plaintiffs, based on the doctrine of *respondeat superior*, which holds a principal liable for the acts of its agents. Chili's filed a motion for summary judgment, arguing that the patron was not its agent.

Issue

Was the restaurant patron who engaged in the high-speed car chase an agent of Chili's?

Language of the Court

The plaintiffs sue under the theory of respondeat superior. They contend that the Chili's patron converted to a Chili's servant; that he conducted the chase as an agent of the restaurant; and that the restaurant should be liable for the consequences of his negligent or reckless pursuit. An agency relationship will require three elements. Most obviously, Chili's must have consented to the action of the patron on its behalf. Second, Chili's must have retained control, or the right of control, over the physical conduct of the patron in the performance of the pursuit. Third, the conduct of the agent must serve the benefit or further the interest of the principal.

The evidence is insufficient to create a genuine issue whether Chili's appointed or authorized the patron to act as a posse to conduct the chase. No information indicates any preliminary communication between the patron and restaurant manager. The events were spontaneous and fast breaking. No member of Chili's house staff joined in the pursuit. The plaintiffs argue that Chili's effectively assented to an agency relationship by acceptance of the patron's reconnaissance reports during the course of the chase; and by failure to instruct him to break off the chase. That circumstance is not enough. The patron need not have been an agent to engage in that conduct. He was pursuing petty crime. Chili's was reporting the petty crime to the police. No information indicates that Chili's had any effective control over the patron. The dominant purpose of Chili's relay of the patron's reports to the police appears to have been the public interest in the apprehension of petty criminals and not the private recovery of the unpaid bill.

Decision

The superior court held that the restaurant patron who engaged in the high-speed chase in which the plaintiffs were injured was not an agent of Chili's restaurant. The superior court granted summary judgment to Chili's.

Case Questions

1. **Critical Legal Thinking** What does the doctrine of *respondeat superior* provide? Explain.
2. **Business Ethics** Why do you think the plaintiffs sued Chili's? Do you think they had a very good chance of winning the lawsuit against Chili's?
3. **Contemporary Business** Did the elements exist to make the restaurant patron an agent of Chili's restaurant? Explain. Is the restaurant patron liable?

CONTEMPORARY Environment

POWER OF ATTORNEY

A **power of attorney** is one of the most formal types of express agency agreements. It is often used by a principal to give an agent the power to sign legal documents, such as deeds to real estate, on behalf of the principal. There are two kinds of powers of attorney:

1. **General power of attorney**, which confers broad powers on the agent to act in any matters on the principal's behalf.
2. **Special power of attorney**, which limits the agent to those acts specifically enumerated in the agreement.

An agent with power of attorney is called an **attorney-in-fact** even though that person does not have to be a lawyer. Powers of attorney must be written. Usually, they must also be notarized. Often, a principal makes a power of attorney a **durable power of attorney**. A durable power of attorney remains effective if the principal is incapacitated.

power of attorney
An express agency agreement that is often used to give an agent the power to sign legal documents on behalf of the principal.

general power of attorney
A power of attorney that authorizes an agent to transact business for the principal.

special power of attorney
A power of attorney that limits the agent's authority to only a specified matter.

attorney-in-fact
Someone who is given authority through a power of attorney to do a particular act. An "attorney-in-fact" need not be a member of the legal profession.

durable power of attorney
A power of attorney that remains in effect during the grantor's incompetency.

Implied Agency

In many situations, a principal and an agent do not expressly create an agency. Instead, the agency is implied from the conduct of the parties. This type of agency is referred to as an **implied agency**. The extent of the agent's authority is determined from the facts and circumstances of the particular situation. Implied authority can be conferred by industry custom, prior dealing between the parties, the agent's position, acts deemed necessary to carry out the agent's duties, and other factors the court deems relevant. Implied authority cannot conflict with express authority or with stated limitations on express authority.

implied agency
An agency that occurs when a principal and an agent do not expressly create an agency, but it is inferred from the conduct of the parties.

Incidental Authority

Often, even an express agency agreement does not provide enough detail to cover contingencies that may arise in the future regarding the performance of the agency. In such a case, the agent possesses certain implied authority to act beyond his express agency powers. This authority is sometimes referred to as **incidental authority**. Certain emergency situations may arise in the course of an agency. If the agent cannot contact the principal for instructions, the agent has incidental emergency powers to take all actions reasonably necessary to protect the principal's property and rights.

incidental authority
Authority needed to carry out actual or apparent authority.

Example: A homeowner employs a real estate broker to sell his house. The real estate broker's express powers are to advertise and market the house for sale, show the house to prospective buyers, and accept offers from persons who want to purchase the house. The homeowner goes away on a month-long trip where he cannot be contacted. During this time, a water pipe breaks and begins to leak water in the house. The real estate broker has incidental authority to hire a plumber to repair the pipe to stop the water leak. The homeowner is responsible for paying for the repairs.

An agent's scope of employment was at issue in the following case.

CASE 1.2 SCOPE OF EMPLOYMENT

***Keating v. Goldick*, No. 00C-10-223 WCC, No. 01C-11-027 WCC, 2004 Del. LEXIS 102, at *1 (Super Ct. April 6, 2004).**

"There comes a point in every litigation where common sense will make some conclusions obvious."

—Judge Carpenter

Facts

Lapp Roofing and Sheet Metal Company, Inc., is an Ohio corporation headquartered in Dayton, Ohio. The company provides construction services in several states. Lapp Roofing sent James Goldick and other Lapp Roofing employees to work on a roofing project in Wilmington, Delaware. Lapp Roofing's company policy prohibited employees from driving company vehicles for personal purposes. Lapp Roofing entrusted Goldick, as job foreman, with a white Ford van to transport the workers to the job site and to provide transportation to meals and other necessities.

While in Wilmington, Goldick and another Lapp Roofing employee, James McNees, went to Gators Bar and Restaurant. Goldick, after eating and drinking for several hours, was ejected from the bar. Shortly thereafter, Goldick drove the company van onto the curb in front of the bar, striking two people in the parking lot and seven individuals on the curb outside the bar. Subsequently, the police stopped the van and apprehended Goldick. Goldick was arrested and pleaded guilty to criminal assault charges. Christopher M. Keating and the other injured individuals filed a personal injury lawsuit against Goldick and Lapp Roofing. Lapp Roofing defended, alleging that it was not liable because Goldick's negligent conduct was committed outside the scope of his employment.

> Shortly his fortune shall be lifted higher; True industry doth kindle honour's fire.
> William Shakespeare

Issue

Was Goldick's negligent conduct committed within the scope of his employment for Lapp Roofing?

Language of the Court

There comes a point in every litigation where common sense will make some conclusions obvious. If the injured plaintiffs were not involved in this litigation and were simply asked whether they believe that an individual who used an employer's truck late at night to go to a bar and consume alcohol was acting within the scope of that employer's employment, they would without hesitation say no. Logic and common sense would lead any reasonable person to the same conclusion.

One could argue that sending a work crew from Ohio with only a work truck as transportation would be sufficient deviation. To a degree, the court agrees this allows the range of covered conduct to be explained. Obviously a crew who is assigned for several days or weeks to a remote location will need to utilize the company vehicle to get meals or other necessities associated with that stay. Therefore, if this event had occurred as the employees were leaving Happy Harry's after they obtained a needed prescription or from Denny's Restaurant after a meal, the court believes these foreseeable and logical consequences of a lengthy stay away from home would bring the conduct within the scope of employment under the dual purpose rationale.

However, no reasonable person could conclude this limitation on available transportation would provide the mechanism to expand the coverage to a drunken brawl that occurred after hours and was unassociated with the employee's work or associated with his stay. Such conduct is so adverse to the employer that no conceivable benefit could be derived. It is completely unrelated to the employer's business and does not advance the work for which the employees were sent to this location. Here, Goldick used the van to go drinking with another employee and drove the van in the parking lot and on the curb injuring various individuals. No jury could reasonably conclude that Goldick's conduct was actuated, even in part, by a purpose to serve his employer. This incident did not occur during working hours and Goldick decided to go to Gators and become intoxicated for purely personal reasons and not to serve Lapp Roofing's interests whatsoever.

Decision

The superior court held that Goldick was not acting within the course and scope of his employment when his negligent conduct occurred. The superior court granted summary judgment to Lapp Roofing on this issue.

Case Questions

1. **Critical Legal Thinking** Define *scope of employment*. Why is this concept important in principal–agent relationships? Explain.
2. **Contemporary Business** Why was Lapp Roofing found not liable in this case? Explain. If the negligent conduct had occurred when Goldick was driving to a restaurant for a meal, would the decision have been the same?
3. **Business Ethics** Did Lapp Roofing act ethically in denying liability for the negligent conduct of one of its employees?

Agency by Ratification

Agency by ratification occurs when (1) a person misrepresents himself or herself as another's agent when in fact he or she is not and (2) the purported principal ratifies (accepts) the unauthorized act. In such cases, the principal is bound to perform, and the agent is relieved of any liability for misrepresentation.

agency by ratification
An agency that occurs when (1) a person misrepresents himself or herself as another's agent when in fact he or she is not and (2) the purported principal ratifies the unauthorized act.

Example: Emma sees a house for sale and thinks her friend Claire would want it. Emma enters into a contract to purchase the house from the seller and signs the contract as agent for Claire. Because Emma is not Claire's agent, Claire is not bound to the contract. However, if Claire agrees to purchase the house, there is an agency by ratification. The ratification "relates back" to the moment Claire entered into the contract. Upon ratification of the contract, Claire is obligated to purchase the house.

Apparent Agency

apparent agency (agency by estoppel)
Agency that arises when a principal creates the appearance of an agency that in actuality does not exist.

estopped
To stop or bar, impede.

Apparent agency (or **agency by estoppel**) arises when a principal creates the appearance of an agency that in actuality does not exist. Where an apparent agency is established, the principal is **estopped** (stopped) from denying the agency relationship and is bound to contracts entered into by the apparent agent while acting within the scope of the apparent agency. Note that the principal's actions—not the agent's—create an apparent agency.

Example: Horses, Inc., interviews Grace for a sales representative position. Grace, accompanied by Grace Ann, the national sales manager, visits retail stores located in the open sales territory. While visiting one store, Grace Ann tells the store manager, "I wish I had more sales reps like Grace." Nevertheless, Grace is not hired. If Grace later enters into contracts with the store on behalf of Horses, Inc., and Grace Ann has not controverted the impression of Grace she left with the store manager, the company will be bound to the contract.

Concept Summary

Formation of Agency Relationships

Type of Agency	Formation	Enforcement of the Contract
Express	Authority is expressly given to the agent by the principal.	Principal and third party are bound to the contract.
Implied	Authority is implied from the conduct of the parties, custom and usage of trade, or act incidental to carrying out the agent's duties.	Principal and third party are bound to the contract.
Incidental	Authority that is implied to act beyond express agency powers to take all actions reasonably necessary to protect the principal's property and rights.	Principal and third party are bound to the contract.
Apparent	Authority is created when the principal leads a third party to believe that the agent has authority.	Principal and third party are bound to the contract.
By ratification	Acts of the agent are committed outside the scope of their authority.	Principal and third party are not bound to the contract unless the principal ratifies the contract.

PRINCIPAL'S DUTIES

A principal owes certain duties to an agent. These duties are discussed in the following paragraphs.

Principal's Duty to Compensate

A principal owes a **duty to compensate** an agent for services provided. Usually, the agency contract (whether written or oral) specifies the compensation to be paid. The principal must pay this amount either upon the completion of the agency or at some other mutually agreeable time.

duty to compensate
A duty that a principal owes to pay an agreed-upon amount to the agent either upon the completion of the agency or at some other mutually agreeable time.

If there is no agreement as to the amount of compensation, the law implies a promise that the principal will pay the agent the customary fee paid in the industry. If the compensation cannot be established by custom, the principal owes a duty to pay the reasonable value of the agent's services. There is no duty to compensate a gratuitous agent. However, gratuitous agents who agree to provide their services free of charge may be paid voluntarily.

Certain types of agents traditionally perform their services on a **contingency-fee basis**. Under this type of arrangement, the principal owes a duty to pay the agent the agreed-upon contingency fee only if the agency is completed. Real estate brokers, finders, lawyers, and salespersons often work on a contingency-fee basis.

contingency-fee basis
A contractual arrangement whereby an attorney agrees to represent the client with the compensation to be a percentage of the amount recovered for the client.

Principal's Duties to Reimburse and to Indemnify

In carrying out an agency, an agent may spend his or her own money on the principal's behalf. Unless otherwise agreed, the principal owes a **duty to reimburse** the agent for all such expenses if they were (1) authorized by the principal, (2) within the scope of the agency, and (3) necessary to discharge the agent's duties in carrying out the agency.

duty to reimburse
A duty that a principal owes to repay money to the agent if the agent spent his or her own money during the agency on the principal's behalf.

Example: A principal must reimburse an agent for authorized business trips taken on the principal's behalf.

A principal also owes a **duty to indemnify** the agent for any losses the agent suffers because of the principal. This duty usually arises where an agent is held liable for the principal's misconduct.

duty to indemnify
A duty that a principal owes to protect the agent for losses the agent suffered during the agency because of the principal's misconduct.

Example: An agent enters into an authorized contract with a third party on the principal's behalf, the principal fails to perform on the contract, and the third party recovers a judgment against the agent. The agent can recover indemnification of this amount from the principal.

Principal's Duty to Cooperate

Unless otherwise agreed, a principal owes a **duty to cooperate** with and assist an agent in the performance of the agent's duties and the accomplishment of the agency.

duty to cooperate
A duty that a principal owes to cooperate with and assist the agent in the performance of the agent's duties and the accomplishment of the agency.

Example: Unless otherwise agreed, a principal who employs a real estate agent to sell her house owes a duty to allow the agent to show the house to prospective purchasers during reasonable hours.

■ AGENT'S DUTIES

An agent owes certain duties to a principal. These duties are discussed in the following paragraphs.

Agent's Duty to Perform

duty to perform
An agent's duty to a principal that includes (1) performing the lawful duties expressed in the contract and (2) meeting the standards of reasonable care, skill, and diligence implicit in all contracts.

An agent who enters into a contract with a principal has two distinct obligations: (1) to perform the lawful duties expressed in the contract and (2) to meet the standards of reasonable care, skill, and diligence implicit in all contracts. Collectively, these duties are referred to as the agent's **duty to perform**. Normally, an agent is required to render the same standard of care, skill, and diligence that a fictitious reasonable agent in the same occupation would render in the same locality and under the same circumstances.

Example: A general medical practitioner in a rural area would be held to the standard of a reasonable general medical practitioner in rural areas. The standard might be different for a general medical practitioner in a big city. In some professions, such as accounting, a national standard of performance (e.g., "generally accepted accounting principles") is imposed. If an agent holds himself or herself as possessing higher-than-customary skills, the agent is held to that higher standard of performance. For example, a lawyer who claims to be a specialist in securities law will be held to a reasonable specialist-in-securities-law standard.

An agent who does not perform his or her express duties or fails to use the standard degree of care, skill, or diligence is liable to the principal for breach of contract. An agent who has negligently or intentionally failed to perform properly is also liable in tort to the principal.

Agent's Duty to Notify

duty of notification
An agent's duty to notify the principal of information he or she learns from a third party or other source that is important to the principal. (Also referred to as *duty to notify*.)

imputed knowledge
Information that is learned by an agent that is attributed to the principal.

In the course of an agency, the agent usually learns information that is important to the principal. This information may come from third parties or other sources. The agent's duty to notify the principal of such information is called the **duty of notification**, *or duty to notify*. The agent is liable to the principal for any injuries resulting from a breach of this duty. Most information learned by an agent in the course of an agency is *imputed* to the principal **imputed knowledge**. This means that the principal is assumed to know what the agent knows This is so even if the agent does not tell the principal certain relevant information.

Agent's Duty to Account

duty to account
A duty that an agent owes to maintain an accurate accounting of all transactions undertaken on the principal's behalf. Also known as the *duty of accountability*.

Unless otherwise agreed, an agent owes a duty to maintain an accurate accounting of all transactions undertaken on the principal's behalf. This **duty to account** (sometimes called the **duty of accountability**) includes keeping records of all property and money received and expended during the course of the agency. A principal has a right to demand an accounting from the agent at any time, and the agent owes a legal duty to make the accounting. This duty also requires the agent to (1) maintain a separate account for the principal and (2) use the principal's property in an authorized manner.

Any property, money, or other benefit received by the agent in the course of an agency belongs to the principal. For example, all secret profits received by an agent are the property of the principal. If an agent breaches the agency contract, the principal can sue the agent to recover damages caused by breach. The court can impose a *constructive trust* for the benefit of the principal on any property purchased with secret profits.

TERMINATION OF AN AGENCY BY ACTS OF THE PARTIES

An agency contract is similar to other contracts in that it can be terminated by an act of the parties. Note that once an agency relationship is terminated, the agent can no longer represent the principal or bind the principal to contracts. The parties to an agency contract can terminate the agency contract either by agreement or by their actions. The four methods of termination of an agency relationship by acts of the parties are as follows:

1. ***Mutual agreement.*** As with any other contract, the parties to an agency contract can mutually agree to terminate their agreement. By doing so, the parties relieve each other of any further rights, duties, obligations, or powers provided for in the agency contract. Either party can propose the termination of an agency contract.
2. ***Lapse of time.*** Agency contracts are often written for a specific period of time. When this is the case, the agency terminates when the specified time period elapses. If an agency contract does not set forth a specific termination date, the agency terminates after a reasonable time has elapsed. The courts often look to the custom of an industry in determining the reasonable time for the termination of the agency.

   Example: A principal and an agent enter into an agency contract "beginning January 1, 2011, and ending December 31, 2014." The agency automatically terminates on December 31, 2014.
3. ***Purpose achieved.*** A principal can employ an agent for the time it takes to accomplish a certain task, purpose, or result. Such agencies automatically terminate when they are completed.

   Example: A principal employs a licensed real estate broker to sell his house. The agency terminates when the house is sold and the principal pays the broker the agreed-upon compensation.
4. ***Occurrence of a specified event.*** An agency contract can specify that the agency exists until a specified event occurs. The agency terminates when the specified event happens.

   Example: A principal employs an agent to take care of his dog until he returns from a trip. The agency terminates when the principal returns from the trip.

Notification Required at the Termination of an Agency

If an agency is terminated by agreement between the parties, the principal is under a **duty of notification of the termination of the agency to third parties.** Unless otherwise required, the notice can be from the principal or some other source (e.g., the agent). However, if an agency terminates by operation of law, there is no duty to notify third parties about the termination.

The termination of an agency extinguishes an agent's actual authority to act on the principal's behalf. However, if the principal fails to give the proper notice of termination to a third party, the agent still has apparent authority to bind the principal to contracts with these third parties. If this happens, the contract is enforceable against the principal. The principal's only recourse is against the agent to recover damages caused by these unauthorized contracts.

> The crowning fortune of a man is to be born to some pursuit which finds him employment and happiness, whether it be to make baskets, or broad swords, or canals, or statues, or songs.
>
> Ralph Waldo Emerson

The following notification requirements must be met:

- ***Parties who dealt with the agent.*** Direct notice of termination must be given to all persons with whom the agent dealt. Although the notice may be either written or oral, it is better practice to give written notice.
- ***Parties who have knowledge of the agency.*** The principal must give direct or constructive notice to any third party who has knowledge of the agency but with whom the agent has not dealt. Direct notice is often in the form of a letter. Constructive notice usually consists of placing a notice of the termination of the agency in a newspaper serving the relevant community. This notice is effective even against persons who do not see it.
- ***Parties who have no knowledge of the agency.*** Generally, a principal is not obligated to give notice of termination to strangers who have no knowledge of the agency. However, a principal who has given the agent written authority to act but fails to recover the writing upon termination of the agency may be liable to strangers who later rely on the writing and deal with the agent. The laws of most states provide that this liability can be avoided by giving constructive notice (e.g., newspaper announcement) of the termination of the agency.

Wrongful Termination of an Agency or Employment Contract

revocation of authority
Termination of authority.

renunciation of authority
The express or tacit abandonment of a right without transferring it to another.

wrongful termination
The termination of an agency contract in violation of the terms of the agency contract. The nonbreaching party may recover damages from the breaching party.

Generally, agency and employment contracts that do not specify a definite time for their termination can be terminated at will by either the principal or the agent, without liability to the other party. When a principal terminates an agency contract, it is called a **revocation of authority**. When an agent terminates an agency, it is called a **renunciation of authority**.

Unless an agency is irrevocable, both the principal and the agent have individual power to unilaterally terminate any agency contract. Note that having the power to terminate an agency agreement is not the same as having the right to terminate it. The unilateral termination of an agency contract may be wrongful. If a principal's or an agent's termination of an agency contract breaches the contract, the other party can sue for damages for **wrongful termination**.

CONTEMPORARY Environment

agency coupled with an interest
A special type of agency that is created for the agent's benefit and that the principal cannot revoke.

irrevocable
Not capable of being revoked or recalled.

AGENCY COUPLED WITH AN INTEREST

An **agency coupled with an interest** is a special type of agency relationship that is created for the agent's benefit. This type of agency is **irrevocable** by the principal (i.e., the principal cannot terminate it). An agency coupled with an interest is commonly used in security agreements to secure loans. An agency coupled with an interest is not terminated by the death or incapacity of either the principal or the agent. It terminates only when the agent's obligations are performed. However, the parties can expressly agree that an agency coupled with an interest is terminated.

Example: Heidi owns a piece of real estate. She goes to Wells Fargo Bank to obtain a loan on the property. The bank makes the loan but requires her to sign a security agreement (e.g., a mortgage) pledging the property as collateral for the loan. The security agreement contains a clause that appoints that bank as Heidi's agent and permits the bank to sell the property and recover the amount of the loan from the sale proceeds if she defaults on her payments. This agency is irrevocable by Heidi, the principal.

Example: A principal employs a licensed real estate agent to sell his house. The agency contract gives the agent an exclusive listing for three months. After one month, the principal unilaterally terminates the agency. The principal has the power to do so, and the agent can no longer act on behalf of the principal. However, because the principal did not have the right to terminate the contract, the agent can sue him and recover damages (i.e., lost commission) for wrongful termination.

> Most are engaged in business the greater part of their lives, because the soul abhors a vacuum and they have not discovered any continuous employment for man's nobler faculties.
>
> Henry David Thoreau

TERMINATION OF AN AGENCY BY OPERATION OF LAW

Agency contracts can be **terminated by operation of law** as well as by agreement. The five methods of terminating an agency relationship by operation of law are as follows:

termination by operation of law
An agency is terminated by operation of law, including: (1) death of the principal or agent, (2) insanity of the principal or agent, (3) bankruptcy of the principal, (4) impossibility of performance, (5) changed circumstances, and (6) war between the principal's and agent's countries.

1. **Death.** The death of either the principal or the agent terminates an agency relationship. This rule is based on the old legal principle that because a dead person cannot act, no one else can act for them. Note that an agency terminates even if one party is unaware of the other party's death. An agent's actions that take place after the principal's death do not bind the principal's estate.
2. **Insanity.** The insanity of either the principal or the agent generally terminates an agency relationship. A few states have modified this rule to provide that a contract entered into by an agent on behalf of an insane principal is enforceable if (1) the insane person has not been adjudged insane, (2) the third party does not have knowledge of the principal's insanity at the time of contracting, and (3) the enforcement of the contract will prevent injustice.
3. **Bankruptcy.** An agency relationship is terminated if the principal is declared bankrupt. Bankruptcy requires the filing of a petition for bankruptcy under federal bankruptcy law. With few exceptions, neither the appointment of a state court receiver nor the principal's financial difficulties or insolvency terminates the agency relationship. The agent's bankruptcy usually does not terminate an agency unless the agent's credit standing is important to the agency relationship.
4. **Changed circumstances.** An agency terminates when there is an unusual change in circumstances that would lead the agent to believe that the principal's original instructions should no longer be valid.

   Example: A principal employs a licensed real estate agent to sell a farm for $100,000. The agent thereafter learns that oil has been discovered on the property and makes it worth $1 million. The agency terminates because of this change in circumstances.

5. **War.** The outbreak of a war between the principal's country and the agent's country terminates an agency relationship between the parties. Such an occurrence usually makes the performance of the agency contract impossible.

Termination by Impossibility

termination by impossibility
When an agency relationship terminates because a situation arises that makes its fulfillment impossible.

An agency relationship terminates if a situation arises that makes its fulfillment impossible. The following circumstances can lead to **termination by impossibility**:

- The loss or destruction of the subject matter of the agency

  Example: A principal employs an agent to sell his horse, but the horse dies before it is sold. The agency relationship terminates at the moment the horse dies.

termination by acts of the parties
An agency is terminated by acts of the parties, including: (1) mutual agreement, (2) lapse of time, (3) achieving the purpose of the agency, and (4) the occurrence of a specified event.

- The loss of a required qualification

  Example: A principal employs a licensed real estate agent to sell her house, and the real estate agent's license is revoked. The agency terminates at the moment the license is revoked.

- A change in the law

  Example: A principal employs an agent to trap alligators. If a law is passed that makes trapping alligators illegal, the agency contract terminates when the law becomes effective.

Concept Review

Kinds of Employment Relationships

Type of Relationship	Description
Principal–agent	The agent has authority to act on behalf of the principal, as authorized by the principal and implied from the agency. An employee is often the agent of his employer.
Employer-employee	An employee is hired to perform a task or service. An employee cannot enter into contracts on behalf of the employer.
Principal-Independent Contractor	An independent contractor conducts a transaction for the principal but is not subject to the control of the principal.

Formation of Agency Relationships

Type of Agency	Formation	Enforcement of the Contract
Express	Authority is expressly given to the agent by the principal.	Principal and third party are bound to the contract.
Implied	Authority is implied from the conduct of the parties, custom and usage of trade, or act incidental to carrying out the agent's duties.	Principal and third party are bound to the contract.
Incidental	Authority that is implied to act beyond express agency powers to take all actions reasonably necessary to protect the principal's property and rights.	Principal and third party are bound to the contract.
By Ratification	Acts of the agent are committed outside the scope of their authority.	Principal and third party are not bound to the contract unless the principal ratifies the contract.
Apparent	Authority is created when the principal leads a third party to believe that the agent has authority.	Principal and third party are bound to the contract.

CHAPTER REVIEW

AGENCY, p. 1

The Nature of Agency

1. ***Agency***. Agency is a fiduciary relationship that results from the manifestation of consent by one person to act on behalf of another person, with that person's consent.
2. ***Parties***.
   a. ***Principal***. A principal is a party who employs another person to act on their behalf.
   b. ***Agent***. An agent is a party who agrees to act on behalf of another person.

Principal–Agent Relationship

In this type of relationship, an employer hires an employee and authorizes the employee to enter into contracts on the employer's behalf.

Employer–Employee Relationship

In this type of relationship, an employer hires an employee to perform some form of physical service. An employee is not an agent unless the principal authorizes the employee to enter into contracts on the principal's behalf.

Principal–Independent Contractor Relationship

In this type of relationship, a principal employs a person who is not an employee of the principal. The independent contractor has authority only to enter into contracts authorized by the principal.

FORMATION OF AN AGENCY RELATIONSHIP, p. 7

Express Agency

In an express agency, the principal and agent expressly agree in words to enter into an agency agreement. The agency contract may be oral or written, unless the Statute of Frauds requires it to be in writing.

Implied Agency

In an implied agency, the agency is implied (inferred) from the conduct of the parties.

Incidental Agency

Arises when there is implied authority to to act beyond express agency powers to take all actions reasonably necessary to protect the principal's property and rights.

Apparent Agency

Apparent agency arises when a principal creates the appearance of an agency that in actuality does not exist. Also called *agency by estoppel* or *ostensible agency*.

Agency by Ratification

Agency by ratification occurs when a person misrepresents himself of herself as another's agent when, in fact, he or she is not an agent, but the purported principal ratifies (accepts) the unauthorized act.

PRINCIPAL'S AND AGENT'S DUTIES, p. 13

Principal's Duties

Duty of compensation. A principal must pay the agent the agreed-upon compensation. If there is no agreement, the principal must pay what is customary in the industry or, if there is no custom, the reasonable value of the services.

Duties of reimbursement and indemnification. A principal must *reimburse* an agent for all expenses paid that were authorized by the principal, within the scope of the agency, and necessary to discharge the agent's duties. The principal must *indemnify* the agent for any losses suffered because of the principal's misconduct.

Duty of cooperation. A principal must cooperate with and assist the agent in the performance of the agent's duties and the accomplishment of the agency.

Agent's Duties

Duty of performance. An agent must perform the lawful duties expressed in the agency contract with reasonable care, skill, and diligence.

Duty of notification. An agent owes a duty to notify the principal of any information they learn that is important to the agency. Information learned by the agent in the course of the agency is *imputed* to the principal.

Duty of accountability. An agent must maintain an accurate accounting of all transactions undertaken on the principal's behalf. A principal may demand an accounting from the agent at any time.

TERMINATION OF AN AGENCY, p. 17

Termination by Acts of the Parties

The following *acts of the parties* terminate agency contracts:

1. ***Mutual agreement.*** Parties mutually agree to terminate an agency contract.
2. ***Lapse of time.*** The stipulated time period of the agency expires.
3. ***Purpose achieved.*** The stipulated purpose of the agency is achieved.
4. ***Occurrence of a specified event.*** The occurrence of a stipulated event happens.

Notification of Termination

If an agency is terminated by agreement between the parties, the principal must notify third parties as follows:

1. ***Parties who dealt with the agent.*** Direct notice must be given to these parties.
2. ***Parties who have knowledge of the agency.*** Direct or constructive (e.g., public notice in newspapers) notice must be given to these parties.
3. ***Parties who have no knowledge of the agency.*** No notice needs to be given to these parties.

If the proper notice of termination of an agency is not given, the agent has *apparent authority* to bind the principal to contracts.

The principal and agent both have the *power* to terminate an agency at any time. After termination, the agent can no longer act on behalf of the principal. The terminating party may not, however, have had the *right* to terminate the agency and may be held liable for damages caused by *wrongful termination* of the agency.

Irrevocable Agency

An *agency coupled with an interest* is a special type of agency that is irrevocable by the principal. This type of agency is commonly used in security interests to secure loans.

Wrongful Termination of an Agency Contract

If an agency is for an agreed-upon term or purpose, the *unilateral termination* of the agency contract by either the principal or the agent constitutes the *wrongful termination* of the agency. The breaching party is liable to the other party for damages caused by the breach.

Termination by Operation of Law

Agency contracts can be terminated by *operation of law*. This includes the following methods:

1. ***Death***. Either the principal or the agent dies.
2. ***Insanity***. Either the principal or the agent is insane.
3. ***Bankruptcy***. The principal is bankrupt.
4. ***Impossibility***. A situation arises that makes the performance of the agency contract impossible.
5. ***Changed circumstances***. An unusual circumstance would lead the agent to believe that the principal's original instructions are no longer valid.
6. ***War***. War breaks out between the principal's country and the agent's country.

Termination by Impossibility

Agency contracts can be terminated if a situation arises that makes its fulfillment impossible. The following circumstances can lead to termination by impossibility:

1. ***The loss or destruction of the subject matter of the agency***. A principal employs an agent to sell his horse, but the horse dies before it is sold.
2. ***The loss of a required qualification***. A principal employs a licensed real estate agent to sell her house, and the real estate agent's license is revoked.
3. ***A change in the law***. A principal employs an agent to trap alligators. If a law is passed that makes trapping alligators illegal, the agency contract terminates when the law becomes effective.

TEST REVIEW TERMS AND CONCEPTS

Agency 3
Agency by ratification 11
Agency coupled with an interest 16
Agency law 2
Agent 3
Apparent agency (agency by estoppel) 12

Attorney-in-fact 9
Contingency-fee basis 13
Durable power of attorney 9
Duty of notification (duty to notify) 14
Duty of notification of termination of an agency 15
Duty to account (duty of accountability) 14
Duty to compensate 13
Duty to cooperate 13
Duty to indemnify 13
Duty to perform 14
Duty to reimburse 13
Employer–employee relationship 6
Estopped 12
Exclusive agency contract 7
Express agency 7
Fiduciary relationship 3
General power of attorney 9
Implied agency 9
Imputed knowledge 14
Incidental authority 9
Independent contractor 6
Irrevocable 16
Power of attorney 9
Principal 3
Principal–agent relationship 4
Professional agent 6
Renunciation of authority 16
Restatement (Second) of Agency 3
Revocation of authority 16
Special power of attorney 9
Termination by acts of the parties 17
Termination by impossibility 17
Termination by operation of law 17
Wrongful termination 16

CASE SCENARIO REVISITED

Remember the case scenario at the beginning of the chapter involving Renaldo, Inc., and Ginn's injuries at the Baker Street nightclub? Is the unidentified patron (who pushed Ginn) an agent of the nightclub? What will happen if Ginn sues the nightclub for damages? To help you with your answers, see *Ginn v. Renaldo, Inc.*, 359 S.E.2d 390 (Ga. Ct. App. 1987).

PORTFOLIO EXERCISE

For the business you created at the beginning of the course, appoint an agent to receive all legal notices on behalf of your business by completing the statutory update form shown as Exhibit 1.2 or by going to the following website: http://www.sos.state.oh.us/SOS/businessServices/Filing%20Forms%20%20Fee%20Schedule/521.aspx

WORKING THE WEB INTERNET EXERCISES

Activities

1. See "Law About . . . Agency," at **www.law.cornell.edu/topics/agency.html**.
2. One way to create an agency is to execute a power of attorney. See **smallbiz.biz.findlaw.com/bookshelf/sblg/sblgchp13_f.html** for information.

CRITICAL LEGAL THINKING CASES

Case 1.1 Independent Contractor Mercedes Connolly and her husband purchased airline tickets and a tour package for a tour to South Africa from Judy Samuelson, a travel agent doing business as International Tours of Manhattan. Samuelson sold tickets for a variety of airline companies and tour operators, including African Adventurers, which was the tour operator for the Connollys' tour. Mercedes fell while trying to cross a 6-inch-deep stream while the tour group was on a walking tour to see hippopotami in a river at a game reserve. In the process, she injured her left ankle and foot. She sued Samuelson for damages. Is Samuelson liable? *Connolly v. Samuelson*, 671 F. Supp. 1312 (D. Kan. 1987).

Case 1.2 Contract Liability Leroy Behlman and eighteen other football fans from Connecticut and New York decided to attend the Super Bowl football game in New Orleans. They entered into contracts with Octagon Travel Center, Inc. (Octagon), a tour operator, and paid $399 each for transportation, lodging, and a ticket to the Super Bowl football game. They purchased the tour package through Universal Travel Agency, Inc. (Universal), a travel agency that acts as a broker for a number of airline companies and tour operators. The individual contracts, however, were between the football fans and Octagon. When they arrived in New Orleans, no tickets to the Super Bowl were forthcoming. Upon returning, they sued Universal for breach of contract. Is Universal liable? *Behlman v. Universal Travel Agency, Inc.*, 496 A.2d 962 (Conn. App. St. 1985).

Case 1.3 Power of Attorney As a result of marital problems, Howard R. Bankerd "left for the west," and Virginia Bankerd, his wife, continued to reside in their jointly owned home. Before his departure, Howard executed a power of attorney to Arthur V. King, which authorized King to "convey, grant, bargain, and/or sell" Howard's interest in the property. For the ensuing decade, Howard lived in various locations in Nevada, Colorado, and Washington but rarely contacted King. Howard made no payments on the mortgage, for taxes, or for maintenance or upkeep of the home.

Nine years later, Virginia, who was nearing retirement, requested King to exercise his power of attorney and transfer Howard's interest in the home to her. King's attempts to locate Howard were unsuccessful. He believed that Howard, who would then be 69 years of age, might be dead. King gifted Howard's interest in the property to Virginia, who sold the property for $62,500. Four years later, Howard returned and filed suit against King, alleging breach of trust and fiduciary duty. Is King liable? *King v. Bankerd*, 492 A.2d 608 (Md. 1985).

Case 1.4 Apparent Agency Robert Bolus was engaged in various businesses in which he sold and repaired trucks. He decided to build a truck repair facility in Bartonsville, Pennsylvania. Bolus contacted United Penn Bank (Bank) to obtain financing for the project and was referred to Emmanuel Ziobro, an assistant vice president. Ziobro orally agreed that Bank would provide funding for the project. He did not tell Bolus that he only had express authority to make loans of up to $10,000. After extending $210,000 in loans to Bolus, Bank refused to provide further financing. When Bolus defaulted on the loans, Bank pressed judgment against Bolus. Bank sought to recover Bolus's assets in payment for the loan. Bolus sued Bank for damages for breach of contract. Who wins? *Bolus v. United Penn Bank*, 525 A.2d 1215 (Pa. Super. Ct. 1987).

Case 1.5 Imputed Knowledge Iota Management Corporation entered into a contract to purchase the Bel Air West Motor Hotel in the city of St. Louis from Boulevard Investment Company. The agreement contained the following warranty: "Seller has no actual notice of any substantial defect in the structure of the Hotel or in any of its plumbing, heating, air-conditioning, electrical, or utility systems."

When the buyer inspected the premises, no leaks in the pipes were visible. Iota purchased the hotel for $2 million. When Iota removed some of the walls and ceilings during remodeling, it found evidence of prior repairs to leaking pipes and ducts, as well as devices for catching water (e.g., milk, cartons, cookie sheets, buckets). The estimate to repair these leaks was $500,000. Evidence at trial showed that Cecil Lillibridge, who was Boulevard's maintenance supervisor for the four years prior to the motor hotel's sale, had actual knowledge of these problems and had repaired some of the pipes. Iota sued boulevard to rescind the contract. Is boulevard liable? *Iota Management Corp. v. Boulevard Inv. Co.*, 731 S.W.2d 399 (Mo. Ct. App. 1987).

BUSINESS ETHICS CASES

Case 1.6 Business Ethics The Hagues, husband and wife, owned a 160-acre tract that they decided to sell. They entered into a listing agreement with Harvey C. Hilgendorf, a licensed real estate broker, which gave Hilgendorf the exclusive right to sell the property for a period of twelve months. The Hagues agreed to pay Hilgendorf a commission of 6 percent of the accepted sale price if a bona fide buyer was found during the listing period.

By letter five months later, the Hagues terminated the listing agreement with Hilgendorf. Hilgendorf did not acquiesce to the Hagues' termination, however. One month later, Hilgendorf presented an offer to the Hagues from a buyer willing to purchase the property at the full listing price. The Hagues ignored the offer and sold the property to another buyer. Hilgendorf sued the Hagues for breach of the agency agreement. Did the Hagues act ethically in this case? Who wins the lawsuit? *Hilgendorf v. Hague*, 293 N.W.2d 272 (Iowa 1980).

Case 1.7 Business Ethics Elizabeth Krempasky, who was 82 years old, owned a house and four certificates of deposit (CDs) at a bank. In her will, Krempasky devised her estate to her niece, Lydia Vrablova Wanamaker. Krempasky died while a patient at a hospital. Wanamaker, who was appointed executrix of the decedent's estate, could not find the CDs. Upon further inquiry, she discovered that the name of Anna A. Parana, an acquaintance of Krempasky's, had been added to the CDs on the day of the decedent's death. Evidence showed that (1) Parana prepared the forms necessary to authorize the bank to add her name to the CDs, (2) the decedent signed the forms on the day of her death sometime before dying at 2:45 P.M., and (3) Parana presented the authorization forms to the bank sometime between 3:00 P.M. and 4:00 P.M. on the same day. A transfer of CDs to joint tenancy is not effective until the bank officially makes the transfer on its records, which it did because it did not have notice of Krempasky's death. Wanamaker, as executrix of the decedent's estate, filed a petition requesting that the CDs be ordered returned to the decedent's estate. Is Anna Parana an agent of Elizabeth Krempasky? Did Parana act ethically in this case? *Estate of Krempasky*, 501 A.2d 681 (Pa. Super. Ct. 1985).

"The law, wherein, as in a magic mirror, we see reflected not only our lives but the lives of all men that have been! When I think on this majestic theme, my eyes dazzle."

—Oliver Wendell Holmes, Jr.

To the Suffolk Bar Association (1885)

Liability of Principals, Agents, and Independent Contractors

CHAPTER 2

CASE SCENARIO

You are a paralegal at a law firm that represents Ray Johnson. Ray and his 8-year-old son, David, were waiting for a "walk" sign before crossing a street in downtown Salt Lake City. A truck owned by Newspaper Agency Corporation (NAC) and operated by its employee, Donald Rogers, crossed the intersection and jumped the curb, killing David and injuring Ray. Before reporting for work on the evening of the accident, Rogers had consumed approximately seven mixed drinks containing vodka and had chugalugged a 27-ounce drink containing two mini-bottles of tequila. His blood alcohol content after the accident was 0.18 percent.

Evidence showed that the use of alcohol and marijuana was widespread at NAC and that the company made no effort to curtail such use. Evidence further showed that NAC vehicles were returned with beer cans in them and that, on one occasion, an NAC supervisor who had observed drivers smoking marijuana had told the drivers to "do it on the road."

CHAPTER OBJECTIVES

After studying this chapter, you should be able to:

1. Describe the duty of loyalty owed by an agent to a principal.
2. Identify and describe the principal's liability for the tortious conduct of an agent.
3. Describe the principal's and agent's liability to third parties on resulting contracts.
4. Describe how independent contractor status is created.
5. Describe the principal's liability for torts of an independent contractor.

INTRODUCTION TO LIABILITY OF PRINCIPALS, AGENTS, AND INDEPENDENT CONTRACTORS

Principals and agents owe certain duties to each other and are liable to each other for breaching these duties. When acting for the principal, an agent often enters into contracts and otherwise deals with third parties. Agency law has established certain rules that make principals, agents, and independent contractors liable to third persons for contracts and tortious conduct.

This chapter discusses the liability of principals, agents, and independent contractors to each other and to third parties.

PARALEGAL PERSPECTIVE

***Daniel J. Cooper** is a paralegal with Rexam Plastic Packaging in Perrysburg, Ohio. He received a bachelor's degree in history and a postbaccalaureate certificate in paralegal studies from the University of Toledo. He specializes in intellectual property and has been a paralegal for two years.*

How does your work as a paralegal relate to principals, agents, and agency law? In my work as a paralegal, I have found a basic understanding of agency law that facilitates efficient and effective cooperation with local outside counsel, as well as with the many foreign agents that hold power of attorney to act on behalf of the company.

What are the most important paralegal skills needed in your job? Critical thinking and reasoning skills, and definitely a very high level of detail-orientation are needed.

What is the academic background required for a paralegal entering your area of practice? A bachelor is preferred, and a paralegal certificate is required. Those who may be interested in intellectual property and in ultimately pursuing registration as a patent agent, or even as a patent attorney, should seek their bachelor in a science, technology, and/or engineering field.

How is technology involved in your job? Computer skills are essential—Microsoft Word and Excel in particular. We also manage an extensive online database that tracks all docketing events related to the prosecution of our large profile of patent and trademark cases.

What trends do you see in your area of practice that will likely affect your job in the future? I see a greater reliance on our online database as a tool for managing almost every aspect of patent and trademark prosecution. I also envision increased use of "Crystal Reports" software, and the expansion of our department into other areas besides intellectual property—such as contract/agreement review and litigation support.

What do you feel is the biggest issue currently facing the paralegal profession? I feel this is the continuing migration from paper-based to computer-based files and processes. I think this is perhaps a greater task in the legal profession—for so long bogged down in paper—than it is in any other. Secondly, I think there is also somewhat of an identity crisis within the paralegal profession involving bona fide paralegal tasks v. administrative tasks and the extent to which the latter is involved in the paralegal's job description. The role of the professional paralegal is definitely still evolving.

What words of advice do you have for a new paralegal entering your area of practice? For those still in school, visit the USPTO website for a listing of bachelor degrees requisite to becoming a patent agent or patent attorney. Interest in those fields may indicate an affinity towards practicing in the intellectual property field of law, and a degree in one of these fields can leave the door open for future advancement. Use the elective opportunities in your paralegal studies program to focus on corporate or business law as well as contracts.

For those actually entering the field of intellectual property, be prepared to be a part of a dynamic environment that allows you to work with inventors and their creative inventions as part of the new product innovation process. From there, you will be involved in the extensive prosecution process that brings these innovative designs and processes into the realm of legal protection in the United States, and likely throughout the world considering the global nature of most businesses today.

AGENT'S DUTIES TO THE PRINCIPAL

Because an agency relationship is based on trust and confidence, the agent owes a fiduciary duty to the principal. As a result, the agent owes the principal a **duty of loyalty** in all agency-related matters. Thus, an agent owes a fiduciary duty not to act adversely to the interests of the principal. If this duty is breached, the agent is liable to the principal. The most common types of breaches of loyalty by an agent are discussed in the following paragraphs.

agent's duty of loyalty
A fiduciary duty owed by an agent not to act adversely to the interests of the principal.

Self-Dealing

Agents are generally prohibited from undisclosed **self-dealing** with the principal.

self-dealing
If the director or officer engages in purchasing, selling, or leasing of property with the corporation, the contract must be fair to the corporation; otherwise, it is voidable by the corporation. The contract or transaction is enforceable if it has been fully disclosed and approved.

Example: A real estate agent who is employed to purchase real estate for a principal cannot secretly sell his own property to the principal. However, the deal is lawful if the principal agrees to buy the property after the agent discloses his ownership of the property.

Usurping an Opportunity

An agent cannot **usurp an opportunity** that belongs to the principal. A third-party offer to an agent must be conveyed to the principal. The agent cannot appropriate the opportunity for himself or herself unless the principal rejects it after due consideration. Opportunities to purchase real estate, businesses, products, ideas, and other property are subject to this rule.

usurping an opportunity
A director or officer steals a corporate opportunity for himself or herself.

Competing with the Principal

Agents are prohibited from **competing with the principal** during the course of an agency unless the principal agrees to the competition. The reason for this rule is that an agent cannot meet his or her duty of loyalty when his or her personal interests conflict with the principal's interests. If the parties have not entered into an enforceable covenant not to compete, the agent is free to compete with the principal when the agency has ended.

competing with the principal
A way in which an agent can breach his or her duty of loyalty.

Misuse of Confidential Information

In the course of an agency, the agent often acquires confidential information about the principal's affairs (e.g., business plans, technological innovations, customer lists, trade secrets). The agent is under a legal duty not to disclose or **misuse confidential information** either during or after the course of the agency. There is no prohibition against using general information, knowledge, or experience acquired during the course of the agency.

misuse of confidential information
An agent's unauthorized disclosure of confidential information about the principal's affairs (e.g., business plans, technological innovations, customer lists, trade secrets) acquired by the agent in the course of an agency.

Dual Agency

An agent cannot meet a duty of loyalty to two parties that have conflicting interests. **Dual agency** occurs when an agent acts for two or more different principals in the same transaction. This practice is generally prohibited unless all the parties involved in the transaction agree to it. If an agent acts as an undisclosed dual agent, the agent must forfeit all compensation received in the transaction. Some agents, such as middlemen and finders, are not considered dual agents. This is because they only bring interested parties together; they do not take part in any negotiations.

dual agency
Occurs when an agent acts for two or more different principals in the same transaction.

> If we are industrious, we shall never starve; for, at the workingman's house hunger looks in, but dares not enter. Nor will the bailiff or the constable enter, for industry pays debts, while despair increaseth them.
> Benjamin Franklin

TORT LIABILITY TO THIRD PARTIES

A principal and an agent are each personally liable for their own tortious conduct. The principal is liable for the tortious conduct of an agent who is acting within the scope of his or her authority. The agent, however, is liable for the tortious conduct of the principal only if the agent directly or indirectly participates in or aids and abets the principal's conduct.

The courts have applied a broad and flexible standard in interpreting scope of authority in the context of employment. Although other factors may also be considered, the courts answer the following questions to determine whether an agent's conduct occurred within the scope of his or her employment:

- Was the act specifically requested or authorized by the principal?
- Was it the kind of act that the agent was employed to perform?
- Did the act occur substantially within the time period of employment authorized by the principal?
- Did the act occur substantially within the location of employment authorized by the employer?
- Was the agent advancing the principal's purpose when the act occurred?

Where liability is found, tort remedies are available to the injured party. These remedies include recovery for medical expenses, lost wages, pain and suffering, emotional distress, and, in some cases, punitive damages. As discussed in the following paragraphs, the three main sources of tort liability for principals and agents are negligence, intentional torts, and misrepresentation.

Negligence

Principals are liable for the negligent conduct of agents acting within the scope of their employment. This liability is based on the common law doctrine of ***respondeat superior*** ("let the master answer"), which, in turn, is based on the legal theory of **vicarious liability** (liability without fault). In other words, the principal is liable because of his or her employment contract with the negligent agent, not because the principal was personally at fault.

The doctrine of **negligence** rests on the principle that if the principal expects to derive certain benefits from acting through others (i.e., an agent), that person should also bear the liability for injuries caused to third persons by the negligent conduct of an agent who is acting within the scope of his or her employment.

respondeat superior
A rule that says an employer is liable for the tortious conduct of its employees or agents while they are acting within the scope of its authority.

vicarious liability
Being responsible because someone else is responsible; indirect legal responsibility (e.g., an employer is liable for the negligence of his or her employee).

negligence
Tortious liability that a principal has to a third party for the actions of an agent acting within the scope of his or her employment and that constitutes a breach of duty of reasonable care, knowledge, skill, and judgment that the agent owes the third party. This liability is based on the common law doctrine of ***respondeat superior***.

frolic and detour
A situation in which an agent does something during the course of his or her employment to further his or her own interests rather than the principal's.

Frolic and Detour

Agents sometimes do things during the course of their employment to further their own interests rather than the principal's. For example, an agent might take a detour to run a personal errand while on assignment for the principal. This is commonly referred to as **frolic and detour**. Negligence actions stemming from frolic and detour are examined on a case-by-case basis. Agents are always personally liable for their tortious conduct in such situations. Principals are generally relieved of liability if the agent's frolic and detour is substantial. However, if the deviation is minor, the principal is liable for the injuries caused by the agent's tortious conduct.

The following case involves frolic and detour.

CASE 2.1 FROLIC AND DETOUR

***Siegenthaler v. Johnson Welded Prod., Inc.*, No. 2006-CA-16, 2006 Ohio LEXIS 5616, at *1 (Ct. App. Oct. 20, 2006).**

"No reasonable finder of fact could find from this evidence that Spires was subject to the direction and control of Johnson Welded Products as to the operation of his truck at the time of the collision, while he was on his way to a friend's house for lunch."

—Judge Fain

Facts

Jesse Spires was employed as a welder by Johnson Welded Products, Inc. Johnson Welded Products provides a lunchroom equipped with a microwave, refrigerator, and vending machine for sandwiches, snacks, and drinks. Spires worked a shift that ran from 3:15 P.M. until 12:15 A.M. One day at work, Spires was on his way to a friend's house for lunch during his lunch break, driving his own pickup truck, when he collided with Donald Siegenthaler, who was riding a motorcycle. The collision, which was the result of Spires's negligence, caused injury to Siegenthaler.

Siegenthaler sued Johnson Welded Products, alleging that Spires was an agent of Johnson Welded Products at the time of the accident and that Johnson Welded Products was vicariously liable under the doctrine of *respondeat superior*. Johnson Welded Products argued that Spires was on personal business when he caused the accident. The trial court granted Johnson Welded Products's motion for summary judgment. Siegenthaler appealed.

Issue

Was Spires an agent of Johnson Welded Products, acting within the scope of his employment, at the time of the accident that injured Siegenthaler?

Language of the Court

Under the doctrine of respondeat superior, an employer will be held liable for the negligent act of its employee if the employee was acting within the course and scope of his employment. No reasonable finder of fact could find from this evidence that Spires was subject to the direction and control of Johnson Welded Products as to the operation of his truck at the time of the collision, while he was on his way to a friend's house for lunch.

There is nothing in this record to suggest that Spires's contract of employment with Johnson Welded Products purported to give Johnson Welded Products the right to control the manner in which Spires would drive his own vehicle to or from work, and the only reasonable inference is that Johnson Welded Products had no right to control Spires's conduct in that matter. We can see no reason why Johnson Welded Products would have any desire to control the manner in which its employees drive to or from work.

Decision

The court of appeals held that Spires was not acting within his scope of employment when he collided with and injured Siegenthaler. The court of appeals affirmed the trial court's grant of summary judgment to Johnson Welded Products.

Case Questions

1. **Critical Legal Thinking** Describe the doctrine of *respondeat superior*. What does the doctrine of frolic and detour provide?
2. **Business Ethics** Could Siegenthaler recover from Spires? If so, under what legal theory? Did Siegenthaler act ethically in bringing this case against Johnson Welded Products?
3. **Contemporary Business** How important is the element of control in determining whether an employee is acting within the scope of his or her employment?

Coming and Going Rule

Under the common law, a principal is generally not liable for injuries caused by its agents and employees while they are on their way to or from work. This rule, called the **coming and going rule**, applies even if the principal supplies the agent's automobile or other transportation or pays for gasoline, repairs, and other automobile operating expenses. This rule is quite logical. Because principals do not control where their agents and employees live, they should not be held liable for tortious conduct of agents on their way to and from work.

coming and going rule
A rule that says a principal is generally not liable for injuries caused by its agents and employees while they are on their way to or from work.

In the following case, the court applied the coming and going rule.

CASE 2.2 Coming and Going Rule

***American, Nat'l Property & Casualty Co. v. Farah*, No. 06AP-197, 2006 Ohio LEXIS 5496, at *1 (Ct. App. Oct. 24, 2006).**

> *"Therefore, the trial court applied the coming and going rule and determined that Morgenstern was not in the course of his company's business at the time of the accident."*
>
> —Judge Klatt

Facts

Daniel J. Morgenstern was a licensed chiropractor, and owned and was the sole shareholder of Daniel J. Morgenstern, D.C., Inc., d.b.a. Morning Star Chiropractic. He treated patients in an office located in Gahanna, Ohio. One day, when he did not have any scheduled appointments, he planned on meeting his wife at her sister's house. Around 11:00 A.M., Morgenstern drove to a restaurant for lunch. After having lunch, he headed toward his sister-in-law's house. On the way, he stopped at a grocery store in Columbus, Ohio. After leaving the store, his lunch began to "weigh a little heavy" on his stomach, so he decided to go to his office to take some nutrients for his stomach. On the way, Morgenstern collided with Ayan Farah's automobile. Farah was seriously injured as a result of the collision. Farah sued Morgenstern personally as well as his company, alleging that Morgenstern's negligence caused her injuries and that the company was vicariously liable.

American National Property and Casualty Company (ANPAC) insured Morgenstern personally for $250,000 for liability and insured the company for $1 million for liability. ANPAC filed a declaratory judgment action to resolve its insurance liability. ANPAC conceded that Morgenstern's $250,000 personal liability automobile insurance policy provided Farah with coverage. ANPAC argued, however, that its $1 million commercial automobile policy on the company

> No nation was ever ruined by trade.
>
> Benjamin Franklin

did not cover Farah because Morgenstern was not acting in the scope of his employment when the accident happened. ANPAC argued that the coming and going rule protected it from liability. The trial court agreed with ANPAC and entered judgment in favor of ANPAC. Farah appealed.

Issue

Did the coming and going rule protect the company, and therefore ANPAC, from liability to Farah?

Language of the Court

> *In determining whether an employee has a fixed place of employment, and therefore is subject to the coming and going rule, courts have focused on when and where the employee commences his substantial employment duties. If an employee commences substantial employment duties only after arriving at a specific and identifiable work place designated by the employer, the employee has a fixed place of employment and the coming and going rule applies. In the case at bar, the trial court found that Morgenstern has a fixed place of employment. Therefore, the trial court applied the coming and going rule and determined that Morgenstern was not in the course of his company's business at the time of the accident. Consequently, there was no coverage under the company's commercial policy. We agree.*
>
> *In the normal context, an employee's commute to a fixed work site bears no meaningful relation to his employment contract and serves no purpose of the employer's business. Morgenstern was driving to his office primarily because he did not feel well. Simply because he was listening to an audiotape of his lecture notes at the time of the accident does not change the fundamental character of the drive to his office. In conclusion, Morgenstern was driving to his Gahanna office at the time of the accident. That office was a fixed place of employment for Morgenstern. Thus, under the coming and going rule, he was not in the course of his company's business when he collided with appellant. Accordingly, ANPAC's commercial policy does not provide Morgenstern with coverage.*

Decision

The court of appeals held that Morgenstern was not acting within the course of the company's business when he collided with Farah and that the coming and going rule applied. The court of appeals affirmed the trial court's judgment, which held that ANPAC's $1 million commercial policy insuring the company was not available to Farah's claims.

Case Questions

1. **Critical Legal Thinking** What does the coming and going rule provide? Explain. What is the public policy that supports the coming and going rule?
2. **Business Ethics** Did Morgenstern want to be found to have been acting within the scope of his company's employment when the accident happened? Why or why not? Was it unethical for ANPAC to deny coverage on its commercial insurance policy?
3. **Contemporary Business** Why did the injured victim, Farah, want Morgenstern to be found to be acting within the scope of the company's employment when the accident happened?

Dual-Purpose Mission

dual-purpose mission
An errand or another act that a principal requests of an agent while the agent is on his or her own personal business.

Sometimes, a principal requests that an agent run errands or conduct other acts on his or her behalf while the agent or employee is on personal business. In this case, the agent is on a **dual-purpose mission**. That is, the agent is acting partly for himself or herself and partly for the principal. Most jurisdictions hold both the principal and the agent liable if the agent injures someone while on such a mission.

Example: Suppose a principal asks an employee to drop off a package at a client's office on the employee's way home. If the employee negligently injures a pedestrian while on this dual-purpose mission, the principal is liable to the pedestrian.

Intentional Tort

intentional tort
A tort committed by someone acting with general or specific intent.

Intentional torts include such acts as assault, battery, false imprisonment, and other intentional conduct that causes injury to another person. A principal is not liable for the intentional torts of agents and employees that are committed outside the principal's scope of business.

Example: If an employee attends a sporting event after working hours and gets into a fight with another spectator at the event, the employer is not liable.

However, a principal is liable under the doctrine of vicarious liability for intentional torts of agents and employees committed within the agent's scope of employment. The courts generally apply one of the following tests in determining whether an agent's intentional torts were committed within the agent's scope of employment:

motivation test
A test that determines whether an agent's motivation in committing an intentional tort is to promote the principal's business; if so, the principal is liable for any injury caused by the tort.

- ***Motivation test.*** Under the **motivation test**, if the agent's motivation in committing an intentional tort is to promote the principal's business, the principal is liable for any injury caused by the tort. However, if an agent's motivation in committing the intentional tort is personal, the principal is not liable, even if the tort takes place during business hours or on business premises.

  Example: Under the motivation test, an employer—the principal—is not liable if his employee, who is motivated by jealousy, injures on the job someone who dated her boyfriend. Here, the motivation of the employee was personal and not for the promotion of the principal's business.

work-related test
A test that determines whether an agent committed an intentional tort within a work-related time or space; if so, the principal is liable for any injury caused by the agent's intentional tort.

- ***Work-related test.*** Some jurisdictions have rejected the motivation test as too narrow. These jurisdictions apply the **work-related test** instead. Under this test, if an agent commits an intentional tort within a work-related time or space—for example, during working hours or on the principal's premises—the principal is liable for any injuries caused by the agent's intentional torts. Under this test, the agent's motivation is immaterial.

  Example: Under the work-related test, an employer—the principal—is liable if his employee, who was motivated by jealousy, injures on the work premises and during work hours someone who dated her boyfriend. Here, the motivation of the employee is not relevant. What is relevant is that the intentional tort was committed on work premises and during the employee's work hours.

ETHICS SPOTLIGHT

INTENTIONAL TORT

Kenya Massey and her fiancée, Raymond Rodriquez, entered a Starbucks coffee shop in Manhattan, New York City. The couple ordered two beverages from Starbucks employee Okang Wilson and paid for the drinks. When Massey and Rodriquez moved toward the seating area while waiting for their drinks to be prepared, Karen Morales, the shift supervisor at the store, told Massey and Rodriquez that they could not sit down because the store was closing. Massey asked Morales what time the store closed, and Morales told her that it closed at 10:00. Massey pointed at a large digital clock across the street that read 9:52. Morales responded that it was 10:00 according to her watch and that she was closing the store.

Massey, who had not yet received her drinks, informed Morales that when she received her drinks, she and Rodriquez intended to sit and enjoy them at Starbucks. Morales instructed Starbucks employee Louis Suriel to cancel Massey's beverage order and refund Massey's money. Massey asked to speak with a manager. Morales identified herself as the manager and told Massey to "get a life." Massey insisted she was not leaving until she could file a complaint about Morales's behavior.

At that point, Starbucks employee Melissa Polanco became involved in the argument. She told Massey, "I get off at ten o'clock, and we can go outside." Rodriquez suggested to Massey that they leave voluntarily, and Massey agreed. Suriel apologized to them as Morales, Polanco, and Wilson held the door open for Massey and Rodriquez as they exited. The couple walked away from the store while Massey and the employees yelled profanities at each other.

As Massey continued to walk away, Polanco ran after and caught her and punched Massey in the face. Morales then jumped on Massey's back. Massey and Morales fell into a snow bank on the sidewalk, and a physical altercation ensued. A pedestrian passerby finally separated Massey and Morales. Massey's face was bleeding when she got up.

Massey pressed criminal charges against Morales and Polanco the next morning. Morales and Polanco each pleaded guilty to assault. All three Starbucks employees who were involved in the altercation—Morales, Polanco, and Wilson—were terminated by Starbucks. Massey sued Starbucks for damages for the injuries she suffered. Starbucks moved for summary judgment, alleging that the employees were not acting within the scope of their employment when they assaulted Massey.

The U.S. District Court held against Massey and granted Starbucks's motion for summary judgment. The court found that the Starbucks employees were acting outside the scope of their employment when they assaulted Massey on the street. The court stated:

> *Massey contends that because her assault was sparked by a dispute concerning whether the store should close, the employees were acting in an employment capacity even when they chased Massey down the street. Massey fails to consider that she suffered no damages as a result of the dispute, but only as a result of the assault. Thus, the question for this court is not whether employees were acting within the scope of their employment when they first began arguing with Massey. Rather, the question is whether they were acting within the scope of their employment when they assaulted her.*
>
> *While the dispute may have started when the employees were acting within the scope of employment; it ended in an assault that was clearly outside of that scope. In this case, the employees did not assault Massey as part of their job. They did not attack Massey on the sidewalk to remove her from the store at closing time, or for any other employment-related purpose. In fact, the employees deliberately waited until Massey had voluntarily left the store before they assaulted her.*

The U.S. District Court held that the Starbucks employees were not acting within the scope of their employment when they assaulted Massey. The U.S. District Court granted Starbucks's motion for summary judgment. *Massey v. Starbucks Corp.*, No. 03 Civ. 7279 (SAS), 2004 U.S. Dist. LEXIS 12993, at *1 (S.D.N.Y. July 12, 2004).

Business Ethics

1. Was it ethical for Starbucks Corporation to deny liability in this case? Why or why not?

Misrepresentation

intentional misrepresentation (fraud or deceit)
A deceit in which an agent makes an untrue statement that the agent knows is not true.

innocent misrepresentation
A false statement that the speaker or writer does not know is false; a misrepresentation that, though false, was not made fraudulently.

Intentional misrepresentations are also known as **fraud** or **deceit**. They occur when an agent makes statements that the agent knows are not true. An **innocent misrepresentation** occurs when an agent negligently makes a misrepresentation to a third party. A principal is liable for the intentional and innocent misrepresentations made by an agent acting within the scope of employment. The third party can either (1) rescind the contract with the principal and recover any consideration paid or (2) affirm the contract and recover damages.

Example: Assume that (1) a car salesman is employed as an agent to sell the principal's car and (2) the principal tells the agent that the car was repaired after it was involved in a major accident. If the agent intentionally tells the buyer that the car was never involved in an accident, the agent has made an intentional misrepresentation. Both the principal and the agent are liable for this misrepresentation.

Concept Summary

Tort Liability of Principals and Agents to Third Parties

Agent's Conduct	Agent Liable	Principal Liable
Negligence	Yes	The principal is liable under the doctrine of *respondeat superior* if the agent's negligent act was committed within the agent's scope of employment.
Intentional tort	Yes	*Motivation test*: The principal is liable if the agent's motivation in committing the intentional tort was to promote the principal's business.
	Yes	*Work-related test*: The principal is liable if the agent committed the intentional tort within work-related time and space.
Misrepresentation	Yes	The principal is liable for the intentional and innocent misrepresentations made by an agent acting within the scope of the agent's authority.

CONTRACT LIABILITY TO THIRD PARTIES

A principal who authorizes an agent to enter into a contract with a third party is liable on the contract. Thus, the third party can enforce the contract against the principal and recover damages from the principal if the principal fails to perform it. The agent can also be held liable on the contract in certain circumstances. Imposition of contract liability to third parties depends on whether the agency is classified as fully disclosed, partially disclosed, or undisclosed.

Fully Disclosed Agency

fully disclosed agency
An agency in which a contracting third party knows (1) that the agent is acting for a principal and (2) the identity of the principal.

A **fully disclosed agency** results if a third party entering into a contract knows (1) that the agent is acting as an agent for a principal and (2) the actual identity of the principal.[1] The third party has the requisite knowledge if the principal's identity is disclosed to the third party by either the agent or some other source.

In a fully disclosed agency, the contract is between the principal and the third party. Thus, the principal, who is called a fully disclosed principal, is liable on the contract. The agent, however, is not liable on the contract because the third party relied on the principal's credit and reputation when the contract was made. An agent is liable on the contract if he or she guarantees that the principal will perform the contract.

The agent's signature on a contract entered into on the principal's behalf is important. It can establish the agent's status and, therefore, the agent's liability. For instance, in a fully disclosed agency, the agent's signature must clearly indicate that he or she is acting as an agent for a specifically identified principal.

Nature seems to have taken a particular care to disseminate her blessings among the different regions of the world, with an eye to their mutual intercourse and traffic among mankind, that the nations of the several parts of the globe might have a kind of dependence upon one another and be united together by their common interest.
Joseph Addison

Examples: Examples of proper signatures for an agent include "Allison Adams, agent for Peter Perceival," "Peter Perceival, by Allison Adams, agent," and "Peter Perceival, by Allison Adams."

Example: Jack decides to sell his house and hires Mitchell, a real estate broker, to list and sell the house for a price of $1 million. They agree that Mitchell will disclose the existence of the agency and the identity of the principal to interested third parties. This is a fully disclosed agency. Mitchell shows the house to Kelsey, a prospective buyer, and discloses to Kelsey that he is acting as an agent for Jack. Kelsey makes an offer for the house at the $1 million asking price. Mitchell signs the contract with Kelsey on behalf of Jack by signing as agent for Jack. Jack is liable on the contract with Kelsey, but Mitchell is not liable on the contract with Kelsey.

Partially Disclosed Agency

A **partially disclosed agency** occurs if the agent discloses his or her agency status but does not reveal the principal's identity, and the third party does not know the principal's identity from another source. The nondisclosure may be because (1) the principal instructs the agent not to disclose the principal's identity to the third party or (2) the agent forgets to tell the third party the principal's identity. In this kind of agency, the principal is called a **partially disclosed principal**.

partially disclosed agency
An agency in which a contracting third party knows that the agent is acting for a principal but does not know the identity of the principal.

partially disclosed principal
A principal whose existence, but not actual identity, is revealed by the agent to a third party.

In a partially disclosed agency, both the principal and the agent are liable on a third-party contract.[2] This is because the third party must rely on the agent's reputation, integrity, and credit because the principal is unidentified. If the agent is made to pay the contract, the agent can sue the principal for indemnification. The third party and the agent can agree to relieve the agent's liability. A partially disclosed agency can be created either expressly or by mistake.

Example: A principal and an agent agree that the agent will represent the principal to purchase a business and that the agent will disclose the existence of the agency and the identity of the principal to third parties; this is a fully disclosed agency. Suppose the agent finds a suitable business for the principal and contracts to purchase the business on behalf of the principal, but the agent mistakenly signs the contract with the third party "Allison Adams, agent." This is a partially disclosed agency that occurs because of mistake. The principal is liable on the contract with the third party, and the agent is also liable.

Undisclosed Agency

An **undisclosed agency** occurs when a third party is unaware of either the existence of an agency or the principal's identity. The principal is called an undisclosed principal. Undisclosed agencies are lawful. They are often used when

undisclosed agency
An agency in which a contracting third party does not know of either the existence of the agency or the principal's identity.

the principal feels that the terms of the contract would be changed if the principal's identity were known. For example, a wealthy person may use an undisclosed agency to purchase property if he thinks that the seller would raise the price of the property if his identity were revealed.

In an undisclosed agency, both the principal and the agent are liable on the contract with the third party. This is because the agent, by not divulging that he or she is acting as an agent, becomes a principal to the contract. The third party relies on the reputation and credit of the agent in entering into the contract. If the principal fails to perform the contract, the third party can recover against the principal or the agent. If the agent is made to pay the contract, the agent can recover indemnification from the principal. An undisclosed agency can be created either expressly or by mistake.

Example: The Walt Disney Company wants to open a new theme park in Chicago but needs to first acquire land for the park. Disney employs an agent to work on its behalf to acquire the needed property, with an express agreement that the agent will not disclose the existence of the agency to a third-party seller. If a seller agrees to sell the needed land, and the agent signs her name "Allison Adams," without disclosing the existence of the agency, it is an undisclosed agency. Disney is liable on the contract with the third-party seller, and so is the agent.

implied warranty of authority
A warranty of an agent who enters into a contract on behalf of another party that the agent has the authority to do so.

ratification
A situation in which a principal accepts an agent's unauthorized contract.

Agent Exceeding the Scope of Authority

An agent who enters into a contract on behalf of another party impliedly warrants that the agent has the authority to do so. This is called the agent's **implied warranty of authority**. If the agent exceeds the scope of his or her authority, the principal is not liable on the contract unless the principal **ratifies** it. The agent, however, is liable to the third party for breaching the implied warranty of authority. To recover, the third party must show (1) reliance on the agent's representation and (2) ignorance of the agent's lack of status.

Concept Summary

Contract Liability of Principals and Agents to Third Parties

Type of Agency	Principal Liable	Agent Liable
Fully disclosed	Yes	No, unless the agent (1) acts as a principal or (2) guarantees the performance of the contract
Partially disclosed	Yes	Yes, unless the third party relieves the agent's liability
Undisclosed	Yes	Yes
Nonexistent	No, unless the principal ratifies the contract	Yes, the agent is liable for breaching the implied warranty of authority

INDEPENDENT CONTRACTOR

Principals often employ outsiders—that is, persons and businesses that are not employees—to perform certain tasks on their behalf. These persons and businesses are called **independent contractors**. The party that employs an independent contractor is called a *principal*.

independent contractor
One who is entrusted to undertake a specific project but who is left free to do the assigned work and to choose the method for accomplishing it.

Example: Lawyers, doctors, dentists, consultants, stockbrokers, architects, certified public accountants, real estate brokers, and plumbers are examples of people who commonly act as independent contractors.

Example: Gabrielle is a lawyer who has her own law firm and specializes in real estate law. Emma, a real estate developer, hires Gabrielle to represent her in the purchase of land. Emma is the principal, and Gabrielle is the independent contractor.

A principal–independent contractor relationship is depicted in Exhibit 2.1.

Factors for Determining Independent Contractor Status

Section 2 of the *Restatement (Second) of Agency* defines *independent contractor* as "a person who contracts with another to do something for him who is not controlled by the other nor subject to the other's right to control with respect to his physical conduct in the performance of the undertaking." Independent contractors usually work for a number of clients, have their own offices, hire employees, and control the performance of their work.

The crucial factor in determining whether someone is an independent contractor or an employee is the degree of control that the principal has over the agent. Critical factors in determining independent contractor status include:

- Whether the worker is engaged in a distinct occupation or an independently established business
- The length of time the agent has been employed by the principal
- The amount of time that the agent works for the principal

Exhibit 2.1 Principal-Agent Relationship

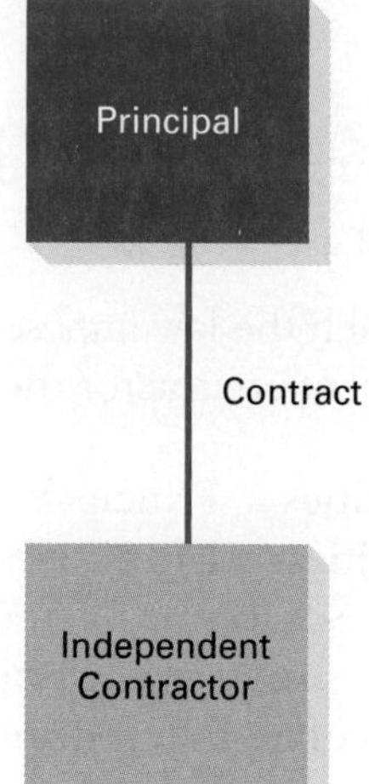

- Whether the principal supplies the tools and equipment used in the work
- The method of payment, whether by time or by the job
- The degree of skill necessary to complete the task
- Whether the worker hires employees to assist him or her
- Whether the employer has the right to control the manner and means of accomplishing the desired result

If an examination of these factors shows that the principal asserts little control, the person is an independent contractor. Substantial control indicates an employer–employee relationship. Labeling someone an independent contractor is only one factor in determining whether independent contractor status exists.

Liability for an Independent Contractor's Contracts

A principal can authorize an independent contractor to enter into contracts. Principals are bound by the authorized contracts of their independent contractors.

Example: A client hires a lawyer as an independent contractor to represent her in a civil lawsuit against a defendant to recover monetary damages. If the client authorizes the lawyer to settle a case within a certain dollar amount and the lawyer does so, the settlement agreement is binding.

If an independent contractor enters into a contract with a third party on behalf of the principal, without express or implied authority from the principal to do so, the principal is not liable on the contract.

Liability for an Independent Contractor's Torts

Generally, a principal is not liable for the torts of its independent contractors. Independent contractors are personally liable for their own torts. The rationale behind this rule is that principals do not control the means by which the results are accomplished.

Example: Grace hires Alexa, a lawyer and an independent contractor, to represent her in a court case. While driving to the courthouse to represent Grace at trial, Alexa negligently causes an automobile accident in which Abby is severely injured. Alexa is liable to Abby because she caused the accident. Grace is not liable to Abby because Alexa was an independent contractor when she caused the accident.

Exceptions in Which a Principal Is Liable for the Torts of an Independent Contractor

There are two exceptions in which the law imposes liability on a principal for the tortious conduct of an independent contractor the principal has hired:

inherently dangerous activity
An activity that can be carried out only by the exercise of special skill and care and that involves a grave risk of serious harm if done unskillfully or carelessly.

1. **Inherently dangerous activities.** Principals cannot avoid strict liability for **inherently dangerous activities** assigned to independent contractors. For example, the use of explosives, clearing of land by fire, and crop dusting involve special risks that are shared by the principal.
2. **Negligence in the selection of an independent contractor.** A principal who hires an unqualified or known dangerous person as an independent contractor is liable if that person injures someone while on the job.

ETHICS SPOTLIGHT

PRINCIPAL LIABLE FOR REPO MAN'S TORT

"The issue in this case is whether a secured creditor may avoid liability for breaches of the peace by using an independent contractor."

—*Judge Mauzy*

Yvonne Sanchez borrowed money from MBank El Paso (MBank) to purchase an automobile. She gave MBank a security interest in the vehicle to secure the loan. When Sanchez defaulted on the loan, MBank hired El Paso Recovery Service, an independent contractor, to repossess the automobile. The two men who were dispatched to Sanchez's house found the car parked in the driveway and hooked it to a tow truck. Sanchez demanded that they cease their efforts and leave the premises, but the men nonetheless continued with the repossession. Before the men could tow the automobile into the street, Sanchez jumped into the car, locked the doors, and refused to leave. The men towed the car at a high rate of speed to the repossession yard. They parked the car in the fenced repossession yard, with Sanchez inside, and padlocked the gate. Sanchez was left in the repossession lot with a Doberman Pinscher guard dog loose in the yard. Later, she was rescued by the police. The law prohibits the repossession of a vehicle if a breach of peace would occur. Sanchez filed suit against MBank, alleging that it was liable for the tortious conduct of El Paso Recovery Service. The trial court granted summary judgment to MBank, but the court of appeals reversed. MBank appealed.

The Supreme Court of Texas held that MBank, the principal, was liable for the tortious conduct of El Paso Recovery Service, an independent contractor. The court held that the act of repossessing an automobile from a defaulting debtor is an inherently dangerous activity and a nondelegable duty. The court concluded that El Paso Recovery Service had breached the peace in repossessing the car from Sanchez and caused her physical and emotional harm. The court held that MBank, the principal, could not escape liability by hiring an independent contractor to do this task. The court found MBank liable to Sanchez. *MBank El Paso, N.A. v. Sanchez*, 836 S.W.2d 151 (Tex. 1992).

Business Ethics

1. Did the independent contractor act responsibly in this case? Should the principal bank have been held liable in this case? Why or why not?

Concept Review

Tort Liability of Principals and Agents to Third Parties

Agent's Conduct	Agent Liable	Principal Liable
Negligence	Yes	The principal is liable under the doctrine of *respondeat superior* if the agent's negligent act was committed within the agent's scope of employment.
Intentional tort	Yes	*Motivation test*: The principal is liable if the agent's motivation in committing the intentional tort was to promote the principal's business.
	Yes	*Work-related test*: The principal is liable if the agent committed the intentional tort within work-related time and space.
Misrepresentation	Yes	The principal is liable for the intentional and innocent misrepresentations made by an agent acting within the scope of the agent's authority.

(continued)

Contract Liability of Principals and Agents to Third Parties

Type of Agency	Principal Liable	Agent Liable
Fully disclosed	Yes	No, unless the agent (1) acts as a principal or (2) guarantees the performance of the contract
Partially disclosed	Yes	Yes, unless the third party relieves the agent's liability
Undisclosed	Yes	Yes
Nonexistent	No, unless the principal ratifies the contract	Yes, the agent is liable for breaching the implied warranty of authority

CHAPTER REVIEW

AGENT'S DUTIES TO THE PRINCIPAL, p. 29

Duty of Loyalty

An agent owes a duty not to act adversely to the interests of the principal. The most common breaches of loyalty are the following:

1. ***Self-dealing.*** The agent cannot deal with the principal unless the agent's position is disclosed, and the principal agrees to deal with the agent.
2. ***Usurping an opportunity.*** An agent cannot usurp (take) an opportunity belonging to the principal as the agent's own.
3. ***Competing with the principal.*** An agent is prohibited from competing with the principal during the course of an agency unless the principal agrees.
4. ***Misuse of confidential information.*** An agent is under a legal duty not to disclose or misuse confidential information learned within the course of an agency.
5. ***Dual agency.*** An agent cannot act on behalf of two different principals in the same transaction unless the principals agree.

TORT LIABILITY TO THIRD PARTIES, p. 30

Tort Liability

A principal is liable for the *tortious conduct* of an agent who is acting within the *scope of the agent's authority*. Liability is imposed for misrepresentation, negligence, and intentional torts.

Negligence

A principal is liable for the negligent conduct of agents acting within the scope of their employment. Special negligence doctrines include:

1. ***Frolic and detour.*** A principal is generally relieved of liability if the agent's negligent act occurred on a substantial frolic and detour from the scope of employment.
2. ***Coming and going rule.*** A principal is not liable if the agent's tortious conduct occurred while on the way to or from work.
3. ***Dual-purpose mission.*** If an agent is acting on his or her own behalf and on behalf of the principal, the principal is generally liable for the agent's tortious conduct.

Intentional Tort

States apply one of the following rules to determine liability for intentional torts:

1. ***Motivation test.*** The principal is liable if the agent's intentional tort was committed to promote the principal's business.
2. ***Work-related test.*** The principal is liable if the agent's intentional tort was committed within a work-related time or space.

Agents are personally liable for their own tortious conduct.

Misrepresentation

A principal is liable for intentional and innocent misrepresentations made by an agent acting within the scope of the agent's employment.

CONTRACT LIABILITY TO THIRD PARTIES, p. 36

Fully Disclosed Agency

In fully disclosed agency, the third party entering into the contract knows that the agent is acting for a principal and knows the identity of the principal. The principal is liable on the contract; the agent is not liable on the contract.

Partially Disclosed Agency

In partially disclosed agency, the third party knows that the agent is acting for a principal but does not know the identity of the principal. Both the principal and the agent are liable on the contract.

Undisclosed Agency

In undisclosed agency, the third party does not know that the agent is acting for a principal. Both the principal and the agent are liable on the contract.

Agent Exceeding Scope of Authority

If the agent exceeds the scope of his or her authority, the principal is not liable on the contract unless the principal ratifies it.

INDEPENDENT CONTRACTOR, p. 39

Principal–Independent Contractor Relationship

In this type of relationship, a principal employs a person who is not an employee of the principal. The independent contractor has authority only to enter into contracts authorized by the principal.

Liability for an Independent Contractor's Contracts

Generally, principals are bound by the authorized contracts of their independent contractors.

Liability for an Independent Contractor's Torts

Generally, principals are not liable for the tortious conduct of independent contractors.

Exceptions in Which a Principal Is Liable for the Torts of an Independent Contractor

Exceptions to the rule are for:

1. Inherently dangerous activities
2. Negligence in selecting an independent contractor

Independent contractors are personally liable for their own torts.

TEST REVIEW TERMS AND CONCEPTS

Agent's duty of loyalty 29
Coming and going rule 32
Competing with the principal 29
Dual agency 29
Dual-purpose mission 34
Frolic and detour 30
Fully disclosed agency 36
Implied warranty of authority 38
Independent contractor 39
Inherently dangerous activity 40
Innocent misrepresentation 36
Intentional misrepresentation (fraud or deceit) 36
Intentional tort 34
Misuse of confidential information 29
Motivation test 34
Negligence 30
Partially disclosed agency 37
Partially disclosed principal 37
Ratification 38
Respondeat superior 30
Self-dealing 29
Undisclosed agency 37
Usurping an opportunity 29
Vicarious liability 30
Work-related test 34

CASE SCENARIO REVISITED

Remember the case scenario at the beginning of the chapter involving the injuries of Ray Johnson and the death of his son, David? What would happen if Ray sued Rogers and NAC for his physical injury and the wrongful death of his child, David? Is NAC liable? To help you with your answers, see *Johnson v. Rogers*, 763 P.2d 771 (Utah 1988).

PORTFOLIO EXERCISE

Describe in detail a situation wherein you anticipate your business acting as either an agent or a principal, being sure to identify the principal, agent, and third party.

WORKING THE WEB INTERNET EXERCISE

Activity

1. Agency law is very important and widely used in international business ventures. Search **google** to find how agency law is applied in other countries.

CRITICAL LEGAL THINKING CASES

Case 2.1 ***Fiduciary Duty*** After Francis Pusateri retired, he met with Gilbert J. Johnson, a stockbroker with E. F. Hutton & Co., Inc., and informed Johnson that he wished to invest in tax-free bonds and money market accounts. Pusateri opened an investment account with E. F. Hutton and checked a box stating that his objective was "tax-free income and moderate growth." During the course of a year, Johnson churned Pusateri's account to make commissions and invested Pusateri's funds in volatile securities and options. Johnson kept telling Pusateri that his account was making money, and the monthly statement from E. F. Hutton did not indicate otherwise. The manager at E. F. Hutton was aware of Johnson's activities but did nothing to prevent them. When Johnson left E. F. Hutton, Pusateri's account—which had been called the "laughingstock" of the office—had shrunk from $196,000 to $96,880. Pusateri sued E. F. Hutton for damages. Is E. F. Hutton liable? *Pusateri v. E.F. Hutton & Co.*, 180 Cal. App. 3d 247 (Cal. Ct. App. 1986).

Case 2.2 ***Fiduciary Duty*** Boettcher DTC Building Joint Venture (Boettcher) owned an office building in which it leased space to tenants. Harmon Wilfred, an independent leasing agent, contacted Boettcher on behalf of Landmark Associates (Landmark), which was interested in leasing office space in the Boettcher building. Wilfred represented Boettcher as a special agent in the transaction. Landmark executed a sixty-eight–month lease with Boettcher. Boettcher paid Wilfred a commission. Shortly thereafter, Landmark began negotiating with Boettcher for additional lease space. Landmark also contacted Wilfred to inquire about the availability of lease space in other buildings. When Wilfred found lease space for Landmark in another office building, Landmark vacated its premises at the Boettcher building and defaulted on its lease agreement. Boettcher sued Wilfred for damages, alleging that Wilfred had violated his fiduciary duty to Boettcher. Who wins? *Boettcher DTC Bldg. Joint Venture v. Wilfred*, 762 P.2d 788 (Colo. Ct. App. 1988).

Case 2.3 ***Duty of Loyalty*** Peter Shields was the president and a member of the board of directors of Production Finishing Corporation for seven years. The company provided steel polishing services. It did most, if not all, of the polishing work in the Detroit area, except for that of the Ford Motor Company. (Ford did its own polishing.) On a number of occasions, Shields discussed with Ford, on behalf of Production Finishing, the possibility of providing Ford's steel polishing services. When Shields learned that Ford was discontinuing its polishing operation, he incorporated Flat Rock Metal and submitted a confidential proposal to Ford that provided that he would buy Ford's equipment and provide polishing services to Ford. It was not until he resigned from Production Finishing that he informed the board of directors that he was pursuing the Ford business himself. Production Finishing sued Shields. Did Shields breach his fiduciary duty of loyalty to Production Finishing? Who wins? *Prod. Finishing Corp. v. Shields*, 405 N.W.2d 171 (Mich. Ct. App. 1987).

Case 2.4 *Independent Contractor* The Butler Telephone Company, Inc. (Butler), contracted with the Sandidge Construction Company to lay 18 miles of telephone cable in a rural area. In the contract, Butler reserved the right to inspect the work for compliance with the terms of the contract. Butler did not control how Sandidge performed the work. Johnnie Carl Pugh, an employee of Sandidge, was killed on the job when the sides to an excavation in which he was working caved in on top of him. Evidence disclosed that the excavation was not properly shored or sloped and that it violated general safety standards. Pugh's parents and estate brought a wrongful death action against Butler. Is Butler liable? *Pugh v. Butler Tel. Co.*, 512 So. 2d 1317 (Ala. 1987).

Case 2.5 *Personal Guaranty* Sebastian International, Inc. entered into a five-year lease to lease a building in Chatsworth, California. Just over two years later, with the consent of the master lessors, Sebastian sublet the building to West Valley Grinding, Inc. In conjunction with the execution of the sublease, the corporate officers of West Valley, including Kenneth E. Peck, each signed a guaranty of lease, personally ensuring the payment of West Valley's rental obligations. The guaranty contract referred to Peck in his individual capacity; however, on the signature line, he was identified as "Kenneth Peck, Vice President." Eight months later, West Valley went out of business, leaving twenty-four months remaining on the sublease. After unsuccessful attempts to secure another sublessee, Sebastian surrendered the leasehold back to the master lessors and brought suit against Peck to recover the unpaid rent. Peck argued that he was not personally liable because his signature was that of an agent for a disclosed principal and not that of a principal himself. Who wins? *Sebastian Int'l, Inc. v. Peck*, 195 Cal. App. 3d (Cal. Ct. App. 1987).

Case 2.6 *Contract Liability* G. Elvin Grinder of Marbury, Maryland, was a building contractor who, for years, did business as an individual and traded as "Grinder Construction." Grinder maintained an open account on his individual credit with Bryans Road Building & Supply Co., Inc. Grinder would purchase materials and supplies from Bryans on credit and later pay the invoices. G. Elvin Grinder Construction, Inc., a Maryland corporation, was formed, with Grinder personally owning 52 percent of the stock of the corporation. Grinder did not inform Bryans that he had incorporated, and he continued to purchase supplies on credit from Bryans under the name "Grinder Construction." Five years later, after certain invoices were not paid by Grinder, Bryans sued Grinder personally to recover. Grinder asserted that the debts were owed by the corporation. Bryans amended its complaint to include the corporation as a defendant. Who is liable to Bryans? *Grinder v. Bryans Road Bldg. & Supply Co.*, 432 A.2d 453 (Md. 1981).

Case 2.7 *Dual Agency* Chemical Bank was the primary bank for Washington Steel Corporation. As an agent for Washington Steel, Chemical Bank expressly and impliedly promised that it would advance the best interests and welfare of Washington Steel. During the course of the agency, Washington Steel provided the bank with comprehensive and confidential financial information, other data, and future business plans.

At some point during the agency, TW Corporation and others approached Chemical Bank to request a loan of $7 million to make a hostile tender offer for the stock of Washington Steel. Chemical Bank agreed and became an agent for

TW. Management at Chemical Bank did not disclose to Washington Steel its adverse relationship with TW, did not request Washington Steel's permission to act as an agent for TW, and directed employees of the bank to conceal from Washington Steel the bank's involvement with TW. After TW commenced its public tender offer, Washington Steel filed suit, seeking to obtain an injunction against Chemical Bank and TW. Who wins? *Washington Steel Corp. v. TW Corp.*, 465 F. Supp. 1100 (W.D. Pa. 1979).

Case 2.8 *Tort Liability* Intrastate Radiotelephone, Inc., was a public utility that supplied radiotelephone utility service to the general public for radiotelephones, pocket pagers, and beepers. Robert Kranhold, an employee of Intrastate, was authorized to use his personal vehicle on company business. One morning, when Kranhold was driving his vehicle to Intrastate's main office, he negligently struck a motorcycle being driven by Michael S. Largey, causing severe and permanent injuries to Largey. The accident occurred at the intersection where Intrastate's main office is located. Evidence showed that Kranhold acted as a consultant to Intrastate, worked both in and out of Intrastate's offices, had no set hours of work, often attended meetings at Intrastate's offices, and went to Intrastate's offices to pick things up or drop things off. Largey sued Intrastate for damages. Is Intrastate liable? *Largey v. Radiotelephone, Inc.*, 136 Cal. App. 3d 660 (Cal. Ct. App. 1982).

Case 2.9 *Tort Liability* Donnie Joe Jackson hired Ted Green to do some remodeling work on his house. Jackson never paid Green for his work, and a dispute arose as to how much was owed to Green. Jackson worked at the Higginbotham-Bartlett Lumber Company, a lumberyard where Green often purchased lumber and supplies. During the course of the following year, when Green went to the lumberyard to do business, Jackson verbally accosted him on at least three separate occasions. Each time, Green left the lumberyard. Green, accompanied by his son, made two trips to the facility. On the first trip, Jackson and Green had a verbal altercation. On the second trip, Jackson hit Green, knocking him unconscious and causing injuries. Green sued Jackson's employer for damages. Is the lumber company liable for the intentional tort of its agent? *Green v. Jackson*, 674 S.W.2d 395 (Tex. Ct. App. 1984).

BUSINESS ETHICS CASES

Case 2.10 *Business Ethics* William Venezio, a real estate broker, conducted his business under the trade name King Realty and had properly filed the required name certificate in the Schenectady County clerk's office. King Realty entered into a contract to purchase property located in the town of Rotterdam, Schenectady County, from Ermino Bianchi. Venezio signed the end of the contract "King Realty for Customer." Four days later, King Realty entered into a contract to sell the property to Mario Attanasio. However, Bianchi refused to sell the property to King Realty, alleging that because the original contract had failed to adequately identify the purchaser, there was not a binding contract. Venezio, d.b.a. King Realty, brought an action for specific performance against Bianchi. Was it ethical for Bianchi to try to back out of the contract? Can King Realty, as an agent for a partially disclosed principal, enforce the contract against Bianchi? *Venezio v. Bianchi*, 508 N.Y.S.2d 349 (N.Y. App. Div. 1986).

Case 2.11 ***Business Ethics*** National Biscuit Company (Nabisco) is a corporation that produces and distributes cookies and other food products to grocery stores and other outlets across the nation. Nabisco hired Ronnell Lynch as a cookie salesman-trainee and eventually assigned Lynch to his own sales territory. Lynch's duties involved making sales calls, taking orders, and making sure that shelves of stores in his territory were stocked with Nabisco products. During the first two months, Nabisco received numerous complaints from store owners in Lynch's territory that Lynch was overly aggressive and was taking for Nabisco products shelf space that was reserved for competing brands.

One day, after having been in his territory for two months, Lynch visited a grocery store that was managed by Jerome Lange. Lynch was there to place previously delivered merchandise on the store's shelves. An argument developed between Lynch and Lange. Lynch became very angry and started swearing. Lange told Lynch to stop swearing or leave the store because children were present. Lynch became uncontrollably angry and went behind the counter and dared Lange to fight. When Lange refused to fight, Lynch proceeded to viciously assault and batter Lange, causing severe injuries. When Lange sued Nabisco, Nabisco denied liability. Was it ethical for Nabisco to deny liability in this case? Do you think the prior complaints against Lynch had any effect on the decision reached in this case? Is Nabisco liable for the intentional tort (assault and battery) of its employee Ronnell Lynch? *Lange v. Nat'l Biscuit Co.*, 211 N.W.2d 783 (Minn. 1973).

ENDNOTES

1. *Restatement (Second) of Agency*, Section 4.
2. *Restatement (Second) of Agency*, Section 321.

"The merchant has no country."

—Thomas Jefferson

Entrepreneurships and Sole Proprietorships

CHAPTER 3

CASE SCENARIO

You are a paralegal at a law firm representing the estate of Stephen Ross. Before Mr. Ross passed away, he was a sole proprietor in an insurance business named Ross Insurance. Ross Insurance sold life insurance policies. Ross Insurance indicated to clients that the contributions to these life insurance plans were "tax deductible," even though there was no such indication from the Internal Revenue Service (IRS). After Ross's death, one of the insurance clients, John Borah, was audited by the IRS and was assessed fines and penalties for claiming tax deductions on the life insurance contributions.

CHAPTER OBJECTIVES

After studying this chapter, you should be able to:

1. Define *sole proprietorship*.
2. Describe the advantages of a sole proprietorship.
3. Describe the disadvantages of a sole proprietorship.
4. Describe how a sole proprietorship is formed.
5. Describe the liability of a sole proprietor.
6. Explain how a sole proprietorship is taxed.
7. Describe how a sole proprietorship can be terminated.

PARALEGAL PERSPECTIVE

Katherine A. Manns *is a paralegal with Fisher Price, Inc., in East Aurora, New York. She received her associate of applied science in Paralegal Studies from Hilbert College and Bachelors in Legal Studies from State University of New York at Buffalo. She has been working as a paralegal for twenty-three years and specializes in intellectual property, advertising, copyright, and trademarks.*

Do you think that paralegals have a role in entrepreneurship and business creation? Participating in a new business creation is a common activity among U.S. workers over the course of their careers. In recent years, it has been documented that self-employment is a major driver of economic growth in both the United States and Western Europe. As part of the legal team, paralegals are preventing entrepreneurs from making corporate mistakes during the incorporation process and intellectual property mistakes such as failing to register trademarks or patents.

What are the most important paralegal skills needed in your job? The most important skills an in-house corporate paralegal should possess are well-defined organizational skills; the ability to communicate clearly and concisely in written form and verbally; and the ability to change direction quickly and often.

What is the academic background required for a paralegal entering your area of practice? Four-year degree is required, preferably in the Paralegal Studies field.

How is technology involved in your job? Databases are a key to keeping organized in this specialty area (and many others I've dabbled in). Trying to clear advertisement spots for reuse or track terms and conditions of various licenses we have with third parties for use [of] their copyrights and trademarks would be extremely difficult without them. Also, the added ease of being able to communicate with third parties from other countries is much easier via e-mail and video conferencing; travel budgets have been greatly reduced or in some cases eliminated.

What trends do you see in your area of practice that will likely affect your job in the future? On the license spectrum, I can see third parties trying to make the most of their property by being very selective in the choices they make to license their marks, making sure they partner with a company that will increase their visibility and value. The same would hold true for companies that license to use those marks; they will be more selective in the companies they partner with, making sure they get the most for their dollar.

I also see those same companies working much harder on the front end of their advertising productions so that they get the most rights or a total buy out of rights for future use/reuse so the spots can be used for multiple venues and the reuse fees for talent and music are minimized. Pay for it once and use it until it doesn't work for them.

What do you feel is the biggest issue currently facing the paralegal profession? I believe this is the economy. Employees are asked to do more with less and in the legal field that may mean that the associates will continue to be required to maintain a high level of billable hours, which in turn will drain billable work from the paralegals. There will also be a trend for corporate clients to try and keep more work in-house or, if not, certainly limit the amount they will be billed by a private firm.

What words of advice do you have for a new paralegal entering your area of practice? Do well academically! Take extra courses offered in subjects like computers, online research, and foreign language. There are many others seeking that "golden" job, so it's important to position yourself as the best and most flexible candidate.

Once you have landed the job, never be afraid to ask questions up front. You need to be crystal clear about what is expected of you and what the end result should be. Speed is not always a plus in the legal field, especially if you have to go back and do something over because you didn't get a crucial piece of information from the beginning.

INTRODUCTION TO ENTREPRENEURSHIPS AND SOLE PROPRIETORSHIPS

A person who wants to start a business must decide whether the business should operate as one of the major forms of business organization—*sole proprietorship, general partnership, limited partnership, limited liability partnership, limited liability company*, or *corporation*—or under other available legal business forms. The selection depends on many factors, including the ease and cost of formation, the capital requirements of the business, the flexibility of management decisions, government restrictions, personal liability, tax considerations, and the like.

This chapter discusses entrepreneurship and sole proprietorship. General and limited partnership, corporation, limited liability company, limited liability partnership, franchise, and other forms of business are discussed in the following chapters.

ENTREPRENEURSHIP

An **entrepreneur** is a person who forms and operates a business. An entrepreneur may start a business by himself or co-found a business with others. Most businesses started by entrepreneurs are small, although some grow into substantial organizations. For example, Bill Gates started Microsoft Corporation, which grew into the giant software and Internet company. Michael Dell started Dell Computers as a mail-order business; it has become a leader in computer sales. Every day, entrepreneurs in this country and elsewhere around the world create new businesses that hire employees, provide new products and services, and contribute to the growth of economies of countries.

entrepreneur
A person who forms and operates a new business either by himself or herself or with others.

Entrepreneurial Forms of Conducting Business

Entrepreneurs contemplating starting a business have many options when choosing the legal form in which to conduct the business. Each of these forms of business has advantages and disadvantages for the entrepreneurs. The major forms for conducting businesses and professions are:

- Sole proprietorship
- General partnership
- Limited partnership
- Limited liability partnership
- Limited liability company
- Corporation

Certain requirements must be met to form and operate each of these forms of business. These requirements are discussed in this chapter and other chapters that follow.

SOLE PROPRIETORSHIP

A **sole proprietorship** is the simplest form of business organization. By definition, there can be only one owner of a sole proprietorship, and the owner of the business, the **sole proprietor**, *is* the business. There is no separate legal entity. Sole proprietorships are the most common form of business organization in the United States. Many small businesses—and a few large ones—operate in this way.

sole proprietorship
A form of business in which the owner is actually the business; the business is not a separate legal entity.

sole proprietor
An owner; one who runs a business.

CONTEMPORARY Environment

ENTREPRENEURSHIP: THE FOUNDING OF FACEBOOK

In 2004, Facebook was launched from a dorm room at Harvard University. Facebook was the brainchild of Mark Zuckerberg, a Harvard student, computer science major Andrew McCollum, and roommates Dustin Moskovitz and Chris Hughes. At first, Facebook became successful at Harvard University, with two-thirds of its students signing up in the first several weeks. The program was then spread to Stanford, Yale, and Columbia, and then to other universities.

The online social networking website became an instant success with the college crowd, and within a year, it had spread to thousands of campuses. Facebook then became popular among others, including high school students, geographical networks, and most other young people. Facebook allows a user to create a profile and post messages and photos for their friends to view—all for free. With more than eighty million users worldwide, Facebook has become the most popular website for uploading photos. More than one-half of its users return to it daily.

Facebook provides a limited and closed network. Membership can be gained only by entering an e-mail address; in addition, only individuals specifically tagged as friends are allowed to see that person's profile. Thus, Facebook is a "walled garden" in which users can post pictures and text, knowing that the general public—parents, teachers, employers, or potential employers—cannot view the content. This creates a sense of privacy and has distinguished Facebook from other social networks, such as MySpace, that allow users to communicate more freely. However, most users do not realize that this "wall" does not include Facebook itself. The Facebook licensing agreement gives Facebook royalty-free, perpetual, and irrevocable rights to the content posted by the users.

In 2004, Zuckerberg's Harvard classmates Divya Narendra, Cameron Winklevoss, and Tyler Winklevoss filed a lawsuit against him. They claimed that they hired Zuckerberg to finish the source code for their website, ConnectU, and that he stole their idea and source code. Their lawsuit asserted breach of contract, misappropriation of trade secrets, and copyright infringement, and the plaintiffs sought monetary damages. Zuckerberg denied their claims. A California judge has approved the settlement of the claims.

Mark Zuckerberg, the mythic entrepreneur, has been dubbed the youngest Internet billionaire. Facebook now offers one of the most lucrative venues for advertising on the Internet, and it has drawn the interest of several potential buyers.

> It has been uniformly laid down in this Court, as far back as we can remember, that good faith is the basis of all mercantile transactions.
>
> Justice Buller
> Salomons v. Nissen (1788)

Advantages of a Sole Proprietorship

There are several major advantages to operating a business as a sole proprietorship. They include the following:

- Forming a sole proprietorship is, comparatively speaking, easy and does not cost a lot.
- The owner has the right to make all management decisions concerning the business, including those involving hiring and firing employees.
- The sole proprietor owns all of the business and has the right to receive all of the business's profits.
- Operation as a sole proprietorship may be advantageous under federal and state tax laws.

Disadvantages of a Sole Proprietorship

There are important disadvantages to this business form, too. For example, the sole proprietor's access to the capital is limited to personal funds plus any loans the sole proprietor can obtain, and the sole proprietor is legally responsible for the business's contracts and the torts the sole proprietor or any of his or her employees commit in the course of employment. In addition, sole proprietors—as with all business owners—must pay self-employment tax.

Formation of a Sole Proprietorship

When compared with other business forms, creating or forming a sole proprietorship is easy. There are no formalities, and no federal or state government approval is required for formation. However, governments require all businesses, including sole proprietorships, to obtain licenses and/or permits to do business within certain industries. For example, before a restaurant owner may commence doing business, a license from the health department approving the kitchen equipment, fire department clearance for an exit system, a liquor license from the state liquor control commission, and a sales tax license may be necessary. An occupational license is necessary for certain industries such as insurance. If no other form of business organization is chosen and there is only one owner, the business is by default a sole proprietorship.

If a sole proprietor would like to hire one or more employees, the proprietor must obtain a tax identification number from the IRS. Generally, a sole proprietor should file only one Form SS-4 and needs only one employment identification number (EIN) regardless of the number of businesses operated as a sole proprietorship or trade names under which a business operates. However, if the proprietorship incorporates or enters into a partnership, a new EIN is required (see Form SS-4, Exhibit 3.1).

CONTEMPORARY Environment

d.b.a.—DOING BUSINESS AS

A sole proprietorship can operate under the name of the sole proprietor or a **trade name**. For example, an author of this book can operate as a sole proprietorship under the name "Henry R. Cheeseman" or under a trade name such as "The Big Cheese." Operating under a trade name is commonly designated as **d.b.a. (doing business as)** (e.g., Henry R. Cheeseman, doing business as "The Big Cheese").

Most states require all businesses that operate under a trade name to file a **fictitious business name statement** (or **certificate of trade name**) with the appropriate government agency (*see Form 534A Name Registration, Exhibit 3.2*).

The statement must contain the name and address of the applicant, the trade name, and the address of the business. Most states also require notice of the trade name to be published in a newspaper of general circulation serving the area in which the applicant does business.

These requirements are intended to disclose the real owner's name to the public. Noncompliance can result in a fine. Some states prohibit violators from maintaining lawsuits in the state's courts.

trade name
A name used in trade to designate a particular business.

doing business as (d.b.a.)
The act of operating under a trade name.

fictitious business name statement (certificate of trade name)
A statement that most states require businesses operating under a trade name to file.

Exhibit 3.1 Form SS-4

Form **SS-4** (Rev. January 2010) Department of the Treasury Internal Revenue Service

Application for Employer Identification Number

(For use by employers, corporations, partnerships, trusts, estates, churches, government agencies, Indian tribal entities, certain individuals, and others.)

▶ See separate instructions for each line. ▶ Keep a copy for your records.

OMB No. 1545-0003

EIN

Type or print clearly.

1 Legal name of entity (or individual) for whom the EIN is being requested

2 Trade name of business (if different from name on line 1) | 3 Executor, administrator, trustee, "care of" name

4a Mailing address (room, apt., suite no. and street, or P.O. box) | 5a Street address (if different) (Do not enter a P.O. box.)

4b City, state, and ZIP code (if foreign, see instructions) | 5b City, state, and ZIP code (if foreign, see instructions)

6 County and state where principal business is located

7a Name of responsible party | 7b SSN, ITIN, or EIN

8a Is this application for a limited liability company (LLC) (or a foreign equivalent)? . . . . ☐ Yes ☐ No

8b If 8a is "Yes," enter the number of LLC members . . . . ▶

8c If 8a is "Yes," was the LLC organized in the United States? . . . . ☐ Yes ☐ No

9a **Type of entity** (check only one box). **Caution.** If 8a is "Yes," see the instructions for the correct box to check.

☐ Sole proprietor (SSN) ________
☐ Partnership
☐ Corporation (enter form number to be filed) ▶________
☐ Personal service corporation
☐ Church or church-controlled organization
☐ Other nonprofit organization (specify) ▶________
☐ Other (specify) ▶

☐ Estate (SSN of decedent) ________
☐ Plan administrator (TIN) ________
☐ Trust (TIN of grantor) ________
☐ National Guard ☐ State/local government
☐ Farmers' cooperative ☐ Federal government/military
☐ REMIC ☐ Indian tribal governments/enterprises
Group Exemption Number (GEN) if any ▶

9b If a corporation, name the state or foreign country (if applicable) where incorporated | State | Foreign country

10 **Reason for applying** (check only one box)

☐ Started new business (specify type) ▶ ________
☐ Hired employees (Check the box and see line 13.)
☐ Compliance with IRS withholding regulations
☐ Other (specify) ▶

☐ Banking purpose (specify purpose) ▶________
☐ Changed type of organization (specify new type) ▶________
☐ Purchased going business
☐ Created a trust (specify type) ▶________
☐ Created a pension plan (specify type) ▶________

11 Date business started or acquired (month, day, year). See instructions.

12 Closing month of accounting year

13 Highest number of employees expected in the next 12 months (enter -0- if none). If no employees expected, skip line 14.

Agricultural	Household	Other

14 If you expect your employment tax liability to be $1,000 or less in a full calendar year **and** want to file Form 944 annually instead of Forms 941 quarterly, check here. (Your employment tax liability generally will be $1,000 or less if you expect to pay $4,000 or less in total wages.) If you do not check this box, you must file Form 941 for every quarter. ☐

15 First date wages or annuities were paid (month, day, year). **Note.** If applicant is a withholding agent, enter date income will first be paid to nonresident alien (month, day, year) . . . . ▶

16 Check **one** box that best describes the principal activity of your business. ☐ Health care & social assistance ☐ Wholesale-agent/broker
☐ Construction ☐ Rental & leasing ☐ Transportation & warehousing ☐ Accommodation & food service ☐ Wholesale-other ☐ Retail
☐ Real estate ☐ Manufacturing ☐ Finance & insurance ☐ Other (specify)

17 Indicate principal line of merchandise sold, specific construction work done, products produced, or services provided.

18 Has the applicant entity shown on line 1 ever applied for and received an EIN? ☐ Yes ☐ No
If "Yes," write previous EIN here ▶

Third Party Designee

Complete this section **only** if you want to authorize the named individual to receive the entity's EIN and answer questions about the completion of this form.

Designee's name | Designee's telephone number (include area code) ( )

Address and ZIP code | Designee's fax number (include area code) ( )

Under penalties of perjury, I declare that I have examined this application, and to the best of my knowledge and belief, it is true, correct, and complete.

Name and title (type or print clearly) ▶ | Applicant's telephone number (include area code) ( )

Applicant's fax number (include area code) ( )

Signature ▶ Date ▶

For Privacy Act and Paperwork Reduction Act Notice, see separate instructions. Cat. No. 16055N Form **SS-4** (Rev. 1-2010)

Exhibit 3.2 Form 534A Name Registration

Reset Form

Form 534A Prescribed by the:
Ohio Secretary of State

Central Ohio: (614) 466-3910
Toll Free: (877) SOS-FILE (767-3453)

www.sos.state.oh.us
Busserv@sos.state.oh.us

Expedite this form: (select one)
Mail form to **one** of the following:

○ Expedite — PO Box 1390, Columbus, OH 43216

***** Requires an additional fee of $100 *****

○ Non Expedite — PO Box 670, Columbus, OH 43216

NAME REGISTRATION
Filing Fee $50

(CHECK ONLY ONE (1) BOX)

☐ Trade Name (167-RNO) Date of first use: ______	☐ Fictitious Name (169-NFO)

Name being registered or reported: ____________________

Name of the Registrant: ____________________

NOTE: If the registrant is a foreign corporation licensed in Ohio under an assumed name, provide the assumed name and the name as registered in its jurisdiction of formation.

The Registrant is a(n): (Check only one (1) box)

- ☐ Individual
- ☐ Partnership
  Registration # , if any ______
- ☐ Limited Partnership
  Registration # ______
  If foreign, Jurisdiction of Formation ______
- ☐ Limited Liability Partnership
  Registration # ______
  If foreign, Jurisdiction of Formation ______
- ☐ Limited Liability Company
  Registration # ______
  If foreign, Jurisdiction of Formation ______
- ☐ Ohio Corporation
  Charter # ______
- ☐ Foreign Corporation
  Ohio license # ______
  Jurisdiction of Formation ______
- ☐ Unincorporated Association
- ☐ Professional Association
- ☐ Other

Exhibit 3.2 *(Continued)*

All registrants must complete the information in this section

Business address:

Mailing Address

City State Zip Code

The general nature of the business conducted by the registrant:

Complete the information in this section if registrant is a partnership not registered in Ohio

Provide the name and address of at least one general partner:

Name	Address

NOTE: Pursuant to OAG 89-081, if a general partner is a foreign corporation, it must be licensed to transact business in Ohio; if a general partner is a foreign corporation licensed in Ohio under an assumed name, please provide the assumed name and the name as registered in its jurisdiction of formation.

By signing and submitting this form to the Ohio Secretary of State, the undersigned hereby certifies that he or she has the requisite authority to execute this document.

REQUIRED
Must be authenticated **(signed)** by the registrant or an authorized representative

Signature Date

Print Name

Signature Date

Print Name

Exhibit 3.2 *(Continued)*

Instructions for Name Registration

This form should be used to register a trade name or report the use of a fictitious name.

To register a trade name, please select box 1. Pursuant to Ohio Revised Code §1329.01 (B) (4), please provide the date on which the registrant first used the trade name, which must be prior to the date of filing. Examples of "use" include opening a business account in the trade name, placing the trade name on products, advertisements using the trade name or business cards and letterhead.

To report the use of a fictitious name, please select box 2. Pursuant to Ohio Revised Code §1329.01 (D), any person who does business under a fictitious name not registered as a trade name must report the use of that name to the Secretary of State.

Name Being Registered or Reported
State the trade name or fictitious name to be registered or reported. Pursuant to Ohio Revised Code §1329.02 a trade name cannot indicate or imply that the registrant is incorporated unless the registrant is incorporated. Specifically, only a corporate can file a trade name which includes entity words such as: "company," "co.," "corporation," "corp.," incorporated," or "inc."

Registrant Information
Check the appropriate box to identify the type of entity registering the trade name or reporting the fictitious name. Complete the appropriate information on the lines provided for the specific entity type. If the entity is registered with our office, it must provide the charter/registration/license number. If the entity is incorporated in another jurisdiction, list the jurisdiction of formation and Ohio charter/registrations/license number.

State the name of the registrant on the line provided. If the registrant is a foreign corporation licensed in Ohio under an assumed name, the assumed name must be provided as well as the corporation's name as registered in the jurisdiction of formation.

Provide the complete business address of the registrant.

Information if Registrant is a General Partnership
Pursuant to Ohio Revised Code § 1329.01 (B) (1) (a), if the registrant is a general partnership, please provide the registration number assigned to the partnership by our office. If the general partnership is not registered in our office, please provide the name and address of at least one general partner.

Additional Provisions
If the information you wish to provide for the record does not fit on the form, please attach additional provisions on a single-sided, 8 1/2 x 11 sheet(s) of paper.

Signature(s)
After completing all information on the filing form, please make sure that the form is signed by an authorized representative.

****NOTE: Our office cannot file or record a document that contains a social security number or tax identification number. Please do not enter a social security number or tax identification number, in any format, on this form.**

Exhibit 3.3 Sole Proprietorship

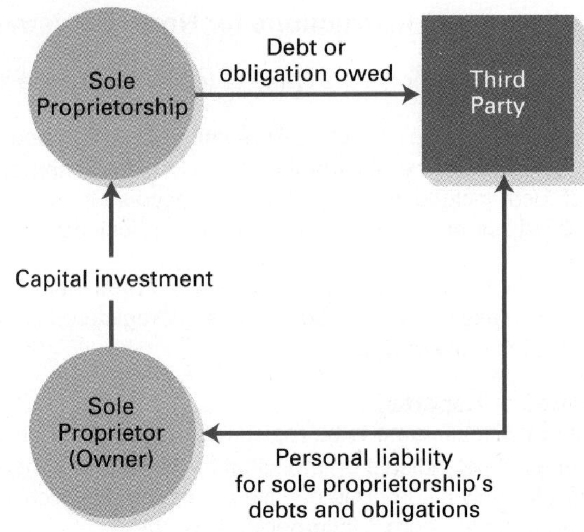

Personal Liability of Sole Proprietors

unlimited personal liability
A type of liability that allows creditors of a sole proprietor to recover claims against the business from the sole proprietor's personal assets (e.g., home, automobile, bank accounts).

A sole proprietor bears the risk of loss of the business; that is, the owner will lose his or her entire capital contribution if the business fails. In addition, the sole proprietor has **unlimited personal liability**. (see Exhibit 3.3) Therefore, creditors may recover claims against the business from the sole proprietor's personal assets (e.g., home, automobile, bank accounts).

Example: Jack opens a sporting goods store called "The Sports Store" and operates it as a sole proprietorship. Jack files the proper statement and publishes the necessary notice of the use of the trade name. Jack contributes $25,000 of his personal funds to the business and borrows $100,000 from a bank in the name of the business. Assume that after several months, Jack closes the business because it is unsuccessful. At the time it is closed, the business has no assets, owes the bank $100,000, and owes rent, trade credit, and other debits of $25,000. Here, Jack, the sole proprietor, is personally liable to pay the bank and all the debts of the sole proprietorship from his personal assets.

In the following case, the court had to decide the liability of a sole proprietor.

CASE 3.1 Sole Proprietorship

***Vernon v. Schuster*, d/b/a Diversity Heating and Plumbing, 688 N.E.2d 1172 (Ill. 1997).**

"It is well settled that a sole proprietorship has no legal identity separate from that of the individual who owns it."

—Judge Freeman

Facts

James Schuster was a sole proprietor doing business as (d.b.a.) "Diversity Heating and Plumbing." Diversity Heating was in the business of selling, installing, and servicing heating and plumbing systems. George Vernon and others (Vernon) owned a building that needed a new boiler. Vernon hired Diversity Heating to install a new boiler in the building. Diversity Heating installed the boiler and gave a warranty that the boiler would not crack for ten years. Four years later, James Schuster died. On that date, James's son, Jerry Schuster, inherited his father's business and thereafter ran the business as a sole proprietorship under the d.b.a "Diversity Heating and Plumbing." One year later, the boiler installed in Vernon's building broke and could not be repaired. Vernon demanded that Jerry Schuster honor the warranty and replace the boiler. When Jerry Schuster refused to do so, Vernon had the boiler replaced at a cost of $8,203 and sued Jerry Schuster to recover this amount for breach of warranty. The trial court dismissed Vernon's complaint, but the appellate court reinstated the case. Jerry Schuster appealed to the Supreme Court of Illinois.

Issue

Is Jerry Schuster liable for the warranty made by his father?

Language of the Court

Common identity of ownership is lacking when one sole proprietorship succeeds another. It is well settled that a sole proprietorship has no legal identity separate from that of the individual who owns it. The sole proprietor may do business under a fictitious name if he or she chooses. However, doing business under another name does not create an entity distinct from the person operating the business. The individual who does business as a sole proprietor under one or several names remains one person, personally liable for all his or her obligations. There is generally no continuity of existence because on the death of the sole proprietor, the sole proprietorship obviously ends.

In this case, therefore, it must be remembered that "Diversity Heating" has no legal existence. Diversity Heating was only a pseudonym for James Schuster. Once he died, Diversity Heating ceased to exist. Now, Diversity Heating is only a pseudonym for the defendant, Jerry Schuster. Once sole proprietor James Schuster died, he could not be the same sole proprietor as defendant Jerry Schuster who became a sole proprietor after his father's death. James Schuster and Jerry Schuster, one succeeding the other, cannot be the same entity. Even though defendant Jerry Schuster inherited Diversity Heating from his father, defendant would not have continued his father's sole proprietorship, but rather would have started a new sole proprietorship.

Decision

The Supreme Court of Illinois held that Jerry Schuster, as a sole proprietor, was not liable for the warranty previously made by his father, who was also a sole proprietor. The court reversed the decision of the appellate court.

Case Questions

1. **Critical Legal Thinking** Is a sole proprietorship a separate legal entity? Explain.
2. **Business Ethics** Did Jerry Schuster act unethically by failing to honor the warranty made by his father?
3. **Contemporary Business** What are the benefits and detriments of operating a sole proprietorship?

> Fraud is infinite in variety; sometimes it is audacious and unblushing; sometimes it pays a sort of homage to virtue, and then it is modest and retiring; it would be honesty itself, if it could only afford it.
>
> Lord MacNaghten
> Reddaway v. Banham (1896)

Taxation of a Sole Proprietorship

A sole proprietorship is not a separate legal entity, so it does not pay taxes at the business level. Instead, the earnings and losses from a sole proprietorship are reported on the sole proprietor's personal income tax filing. A sole proprietorship business earns income and pays expenses during the course of operating the business. A sole proprietor has to file tax returns and pay taxes to state and federal governments. For federal income tax purposes, a sole proprietor must prepare a personal income tax Form 1040 U.S. Individual Income Tax Return and report the income or loss from the sole proprietorship on the sole proprietor's personal income tax form (see Exhibit 3.4). The income or loss from the sole proprietorship is reported on Schedule C (Profit or Loss from Business), which must be attached to the taxpayer's Form 1040 (see Exhibit 3.5).

Sole proprietors must also pay self-employment (SE) tax, a Social Security and Medicare tax primarily for individuals who work for themselves. It is similar to the Social Security and Medicare taxes withheld from the pay of most wage earners.

SE tax is figured using Schedule SE (Form 1040). Social Security and Medicare taxes of most wage earners are figured by their employers. The SE tax rate is currently 15.3 percent. The rate currently consists of two parts: 12.4 percent for Social Security (old-age, survivors, and disability insurance) and 2.9 percent for Medicare (hospital insurance).

Termination of a Sole Proprietorship

Like the formation process, termination of the sole proprietorship is easy. There are no formalities, and no federal or state government approval is required for termination. The proprietor may simply cease doing business. However, care should be taken to notify third parties of the termination so as to avoid apparent authority and the creation of agency by estoppel. In addition, any agency that issued a license, permit, or identification number should be notified of the termination.

Concept Review

Sole Proprietorships

Definition	A sole proprietorship is the simplest form of business. The owner of the business, the sole proprietor, is the business. There is no separate legal entity.
Formation	There are few, if any, legal formalities required to form a sole proprietorship. If the sole proprietor hires employees, operates a regulated business, uses a trade name, or does business in other states, there may be laws that impose duties or responsibilities.
Management	The sole proprietor makes all management decisions.
Liability	Because the sole proprietor is the sole owner, he or she faces unlimited liability. The sole proprietor faces the legal responsibility for all losses or liabilities incurred by the business. If the business fails, the sole proprietor is personally liable for all debts to creditors.
Taxation	Income or loss for a sole proprietor is treated as individual income or loss and taxed as such.
Termination	The sole proprietorship terminates by law upon the death of the owner.

Exhibit 3.4 Form 1040

Form **1040** Department of the Treasury—Internal Revenue Service
U.S. Individual Income Tax Return 2009 (99) IRS Use Only—Do not write or staple in this space.

For the year Jan. 1–Dec. 31, 2009, or other tax year beginning , 2009, ending , 20 OMB No. 1545-0074

Label (See instructions on page 14.) **Use the IRS label.** Otherwise, please print or type.

LABEL HERE

Your first name and initial	Last name	**Your social security number**
If a joint return, spouse's first name and initial	Last name	**Spouse's social security number**
Home address (number and street). If you have a P.O. box, see page 14.	Apt. no.	▲ You **must** enter your SSN(s) above. ▲
City, town or post office, state, and ZIP code. If you have a foreign address, see page 14.		Checking a box below will not change your tax or refund.

Presidential Election Campaign ▶ Check here if you, or your spouse if filing jointly, want $3 to go to this fund (see page 14) ▶ ☐ **You** ☐ **Spouse**

Filing Status

Check only one box.

1 ☐ Single
2 ☐ Married filing jointly (even if only one had income)
3 ☐ Married filing separately. Enter spouse's SSN above and full name here. ▶
4 ☐ Head of household (with qualifying person). (See page 15.) If the qualifying person is a child but not your dependent, enter this child's name here. ▶
5 ☐ Qualifying widow(er) with dependent child (see page 16)

Exemptions

6a ☐ **Yourself.** If someone can claim you as a dependent, **do not** check box 6a . . . . .
b ☐ **Spouse** . . . . .

Boxes checked on 6a and 6b

c **Dependents:**

(1) First name Last name	(2) Dependent's social security number	(3) Dependent's relationship to you	(4) ✓ if qualifying child for child tax credit (see page 17)
			☐
			☐
			☐
			☐

No. of children on 6c who:
• **lived with you**
• **did not live with you due to divorce or separation (see page 18)**
Dependents on 6c not entered above

If more than four dependents, see page 17 and check here ▶ ☐

d Total number of exemptions claimed . . . . . **Add numbers on lines above ▶**

Income

Attach Form(s) W-2 here. Also attach Forms W-2G and 1099-R if tax was withheld.

If you did not get a W-2, see page 22.

Enclose, but do not attach, any payment. Also, please use **Form 1040-V.**

7	Wages, salaries, tips, etc. Attach Form(s) W-2		7	
8a	**Taxable** interest. Attach Schedule B if required		8a	
b	**Tax-exempt** interest. **Do not** include on line 8a	8b		
9a	Ordinary dividends. Attach Schedule B if required		9a	
b	Qualified dividends (see page 22)	9b		
10	Taxable refunds, credits, or offsets of state and local income taxes (see page 23)		10	
11	Alimony received		11	
12	Business income or (loss). Attach Schedule C or C-EZ		12	
13	Capital gain or (loss). Attach Schedule D if required. If not required, check here ▶ ☐		13	
14	Other gains or (losses). Attach Form 4797		14	
15a	IRA distributions 15a	b Taxable amount (see page 24)	15b	
16a	Pensions and annuities 16a	b Taxable amount (see page 25)	16b	
17	Rental real estate, royalties, partnerships, S corporations, trusts, etc. Attach Schedule E		17	
18	Farm income or (loss). Attach Schedule F		18	
19	Unemployment compensation in excess of $2,400 per recipient (see page 27)		19	
20a	Social security benefits 20a	b Taxable amount (see page 27)	20b	
21	Other income. List type and amount (see page 29)		21	
22	Add the amounts in the far right column for lines 7 through 21. This is your **total income** ▶		22	

Adjusted Gross Income

23	Educator expenses (see page 29)	23		
24	Certain business expenses of reservists, performing artists, and fee-basis government officials. Attach Form 2106 or 2106-EZ	24		
25	Health savings account deduction. Attach Form 8889	25		
26	Moving expenses. Attach Form 3903	26		
27	One-half of self-employment tax. Attach Schedule SE	27		
28	Self-employed SEP, SIMPLE, and qualified plans	28		
29	Self-employed health insurance deduction (see page 30)	29		
30	Penalty on early withdrawal of savings	30		
31a	Alimony paid **b** Recipient's SSN ▶	31a		
32	IRA deduction (see page 31)	32		
33	Student loan interest deduction (see page 34)	33		
34	Tuition and fees deduction. Attach Form 8917	34		
35	Domestic production activities deduction. Attach Form 8903	35		
36	Add lines 23 through 31a and 32 through 35		36	
37	Subtract line 36 from line 22. This is your **adjusted gross income** ▶		37	

For Disclosure, Privacy Act, and Paperwork Reduction Act Notice, see page 97. Cat. No. 11320B Form **1040** (2009)

Exhibit 3.4 *(Continued)*

Form 1040 (2009) Page **2**

Tax and Credits

38	Amount from line 37 (adjusted gross income)	38
39a	Check if: ☐ **You** were born before January 2, 1945, ☐ Blind. ☐ **Spouse** was born before January 2, 1945, ☐ Blind. **Total boxes checked ▶ 39a**	
b	If your spouse itemizes on a separate return or you were a dual-status alien, see page 35 and check here ▶ 39b ☐	
40a	**Itemized deductions** (from Schedule A) **or** your **standard deduction** (see left margin)	40a
b	If you are increasing your standard deduction by certain real estate taxes, new motor vehicle taxes, or a net disaster loss, attach Schedule L and check here (see page 35) . ▶ 40b ☐	
41	Subtract line 40a from line 38	41
42	**Exemptions.** If line 38 is $125,100 or less and you did not provide housing to a Midwestern displaced individual, multiply $3,650 by the number on line 6d. Otherwise, see page 37	42
43	**Taxable income.** Subtract line 42 from line 41. If line 42 is more than line 41, enter -0-	43
44	**Tax** (see page 37). Check if any tax is from: a ☐ Form(s) 8814 b ☐ Form 4972	44
45	**Alternative minimum tax** (see page 40). Attach Form 6251	45
46	Add lines 44 and 45 ▶	46
47	Foreign tax credit. Attach Form 1116 if required — 47	
48	Credit for child and dependent care expenses. Attach Form 2441 — 48	
49	Education credits from Form 8863, line 29 — 49	
50	Retirement savings contributions credit. Attach Form 8880 — 50	
51	Child tax credit (see page 42) — 51	
52	Credits from Form: a ☐ 8396 b ☐ 8839 c ☐ 5695 — 52	
53	Other credits from Form: a ☐ 3800 b ☐ 8801 c ☐ ____ — 53	
54	Add lines 47 through 53. These are your **total credits**	54
55	Subtract line 54 from line 46. If line 54 is more than line 46, enter -0- ▶	55

Standard Deduction for—
- People who check any box on line 39a, 39b, or 40b **or** who can be claimed as a dependent, see page 35.
- All others:

Single or Married filing separately, $5,700

Married filing jointly or Qualifying widow(er), $11,400

Head of household, $8,350

Other Taxes

56	Self-employment tax. Attach Schedule SE	56
57	Unreported social security and Medicare tax from Form: a ☐ 4137 b ☐ 8919	57
58	Additional tax on IRAs, other qualified retirement plans, etc. Attach Form 5329 if required	58
59	Additional taxes: a ☐ AEIC payments b ☐ Household employment taxes. Attach Schedule H	59
60	Add lines 55 through 59. This is your **total tax** ▶	60

Payments

61	Federal income tax withheld from Forms W-2 and 1099 — 61	
62	2009 estimated tax payments and amount applied from 2008 return — 62	
63	Making work pay and government retiree credits. Attach Schedule M — 63	
64a	**Earned income credit (EIC)** — 64a	
b	Nontaxable combat pay election — 64b	
65	Additional child tax credit. Attach Form 8812 — 65	
66	Refundable education credit from Form 8863, line 16 — 66	
67	First-time homebuyer credit. Attach Form 5405 — 67	
68	Amount paid with request for extension to file (see page 72) — 68	
69	Excess social security and tier 1 RRTA tax withheld (see page 72) — 69	
70	Credits from Form: a ☐ 2439 b ☐ 4136 c ☐ 8801 d ☐ 8885 — 70	
71	Add lines 61, 62, 63, 64a, and 65 through 70. These are your **total payments** ▶	71

If you have a qualifying child, attach Schedule EIC.

Refund

Direct deposit? See page 73 and fill in 73b, 73c, and 73d, or Form 8888.

72	If line 71 is more than line 60, subtract line 60 from line 71. This is the amount you **overpaid**	72
73a	Amount of line 72 you want **refunded to you.** If Form 8888 is attached, check here ▶ ☐	73a
▶ b	Routing number ▶ c Type: ☐ Checking ☐ Savings	
▶ d	Account number	
74	Amount of line 72 you want **applied to your 2010 estimated tax** ▶ 74	

Amount You Owe

75	**Amount you owe.** Subtract line 71 from line 60. For details on how to pay, see page 74 ▶	75
76	Estimated tax penalty (see page 74) — 76	

Third Party Designee

Do you want to allow another person to discuss this return with the IRS (see page 75)? ☐ **Yes.** Complete the following. ☐ **No**

Designee's name ▶ Phone no. ▶ Personal identification number (PIN) ▶

Sign Here

Joint return? See page 15. Keep a copy for your records.

Under penalties of perjury, I declare that I have examined this return and accompanying schedules and statements, and to the best of my knowledge and belief, they are true, correct, and complete. Declaration of preparer (other than taxpayer) is based on all information of which preparer has any knowledge.

Your signature	Date	Your occupation	Daytime phone number
Spouse's signature. If a joint return, **both** must sign.	Date	Spouse's occupation	

Paid Preparer's Use Only

Preparer's signature	Date	Check if self-employed ☐	Preparer's SSN or PTIN
Firm's name (or yours if self-employed), address, and ZIP code		EIN	
		Phone no.	

Form **1040** (2009)

Exhibit 3.5 Schedule C

SCHEDULE C (Form 1040)
Department of the Treasury
Internal Revenue Service (99)

Profit or Loss From Business
(Sole Proprietorship)

▶ Partnerships, joint ventures, etc., generally must file Form 1065 or 1065-B.
▶ Attach to Form 1040, 1040NR, or 1041. ▶ See Instructions for Schedule C (Form 1040).

OMB No. 1545-0074
2009
Attachment Sequence No. **09**

Name of proprietor | **Social security number (SSN)**

A Principal business or profession, including product or service (see page C-2 of the instructions) | **B Enter code from pages C-9, 10, & 11** ▶

C Business name. If no separate business name, leave blank. | **D Employer ID number (EIN), if any**

E Business address (including suite or room no.) ▶
City, town or post office, state, and ZIP code

F Accounting method: **(1)** ☐ Cash **(2)** ☐ Accrual **(3)** ☐ Other (specify) ▶

G Did you "materially participate" in the operation of this business during 2009? If "No," see page C-3 for limit on losses ☐ **Yes** ☐ **No**

H If you started or acquired this business during 2009, check here . . . ▶ ☐

Part I Income

1	Gross receipts or sales. **Caution.** See page C-4 and check the box if: • This income was reported to you on Form W-2 and the "Statutory employee" box on that form was checked, or • You are a member of a qualified joint venture reporting only rental real estate income not subject to self-employment tax. Also see page C-3 for limit on losses. . . . ▶ ☐	1	
2	Returns and allowances	2	
3	Subtract line 2 from line 1	3	
4	Cost of goods sold (from line 42 on page 2)	4	
5	**Gross profit.** Subtract line 4 from line 3	5	
6	Other income, including federal and state gasoline or fuel tax credit or refund (see page C-4)	6	
7	**Gross income.** Add lines 5 and 6 ▶	7	

Part II Expenses. Enter expenses for business use of your home **only** on line 30.

8	Advertising	8		18	Office expense	18	
9	Car and truck expenses (see page C-4)	9		19	Pension and profit-sharing plans	19	
10	Commissions and fees	10		20	Rent or lease (see page C-6):		
11	Contract labor (see page C-4)	11		a	Vehicles, machinery, and equipment	20a	
12	Depletion	12		b	Other business property	20b	
13	Depreciation and section 179 expense deduction (not included in Part III) (see page C-5)	13		21	Repairs and maintenance	21	
				22	Supplies (not included in Part III)	22	
				23	Taxes and licenses	23	
				24	Travel, meals, and entertainment:		
				a	Travel	24a	
14	Employee benefit programs (other than on line 19)	14		b	Deductible meals and entertainment (see page C-6)	24b	
15	Insurance (other than health)	15		25	Utilities	25	
16	Interest:			26	Wages (less employment credits)	26	
a	Mortgage (paid to banks, etc.)	16a		27	Other expenses (from line 48 on page 2)	27	
b	Other	16b					
17	Legal and professional services	17					

28	**Total expenses** before expenses for business use of home. Add lines 8 through 27 ▶	28	
29	Tentative profit or (loss). Subtract line 28 from line 7	29	
30	Expenses for business use of your home. Attach **Form 8829**	30	
31	**Net profit or (loss).** Subtract line 30 from line 29. • If a profit, enter on both **Form 1040, line 12,** and **Schedule SE, line 2,** or on **Form 1040NR, line 13** (if you checked the box on line 1, see page C-7). Estates and trusts, enter on **Form 1041, line 3.** • If a loss, you **must** go to line 32.	31	

32 If you have a loss, check the box that describes your investment in this activity (see page C-7).
• If you checked 32a, enter the loss on both **Form 1040, line 12,** and **Schedule SE, line 2,** or on **Form 1040NR, line 13** (if you checked the box on line 1, see the line 31 instructions on page C-7). Estates and trusts, enter on **Form 1041, line 3.**
• If you checked 32b, you **must** attach **Form 6198.** Your loss may be limited.

32a ☐ All investment is at risk.
32b ☐ Some investment is not at risk.

For Paperwork Reduction Act Notice, see page C-9 of the instructions. Cat. No. 11334P **Schedule C (Form 1040) 2009**

Exhibit 3.5 (*Continued*)

Schedule C (Form 1040) 2009 Page **2**

Part III **Cost of Goods Sold** (see page C-8)

33 Method(s) used to value closing inventory: **a** ☐ Cost **b** ☐ Lower of cost or market **c** ☐ Other (attach explanation)

34 Was there any change in determining quantities, costs, or valuations between opening and closing inventory? If "Yes," attach explanation . . . ☐ **Yes** ☐ **No**

35	Inventory at beginning of year. If different from last year's closing inventory, attach explanation	35	
36	Purchases less cost of items withdrawn for personal use	36	
37	Cost of labor. Do not include any amounts paid to yourself	37	
38	Materials and supplies	38	
39	Other costs	39	
40	Add lines 35 through 39	40	
41	Inventory at end of year	41	
42	**Cost of goods sold.** Subtract line 41 from line 40. Enter the result here and on page 1, line 4	42	

Part IV **Information on Your Vehicle.** Complete this part **only** if you are claiming car or truck expenses on line 9 and are not required to file Form 4562 for this business. See the instructions for line 13 on page C-5 to find out if you must file Form 4562.

43 When did you place your vehicle in service for business purposes? (month, day, year) ▶ ____ / ____ / ____

44 Of the total number of miles you drove your vehicle during 2009, enter the number of miles you used your vehicle for:

a Business ____________ **b** Commuting (see instructions) ____________ **c** Other ____________

45 Was your vehicle available for personal use during off-duty hours? . . . ☐ **Yes** ☐ **No**

46 Do you (or your spouse) have another vehicle available for personal use?. . . ☐ **Yes** ☐ **No**

47a Do you have evidence to support your deduction? . . . ☐ **Yes** ☐ **No**

b If "Yes," is the evidence written? . . . ☐ **Yes** ☐ **No**

Part V **Other Expenses.** List below business expenses not included on lines 8–26 or line 30.

48 **Total other expenses.** Enter here and on page 1, line 27 . . . 48

Schedule C (Form 1040) 2009

PARALEGAL PRACTICE TOOL

SOLE PROPRIETORSHIP FORMATION CHECKLIST

1. Select a Name and an Assumed Name if desired.
2. Check with the secretary of state for the availability of the Assumed Name(s) and if necessary, draft, execute, and file a Certificate of Assumed Name.
3. Determine the desired Capital Contribution.
4. Determine a fiscal year.
5. Draft and execute any desired employment contracts.
6. Determine whether qualification in other states is desired.
7. Secure all state and local licenses required to operate the business and secure any necessary insurance coverage.
8. Draft, execute, and file Form SS-4 filed with the IRS for employer's identification number if the partnership will have employees.
9. Place the name of the proprietorship or trade name on all business material (e.g., letterhead, invoices, business cards, signs, contracts, etc.).

CHAPTER REVIEW

ENTREPRENEURSHIP, p. 53

Entrepreneurship

Entrepreneur. An entrepreneur is a person who forms and operates a new business.

FORMS OF CONDUCTING BUSINESS, p. 53

Entrepreneurs may choose to conduct business using any of the following forms:

1. Sole proprietorship
2. General partnership
3. Limited partnership
4. Limited liability partnership (LLP)
5. Limited liability company (LLC)
6. Corporation

Certain requirements must be met to form and operate each of these forms of business.

SOLE PROPRIETORSHIP, p. 53

Sole Proprietorship

Sole proprietorship is a form of business in which the owner and the business are one. The business is not a separate legal entity.

Advantages of a Sole Proprietorship include:

- Formation is comparatively easy and inexpensive.
- The owner can make all of the management decisions.
- The sole proprietor owns all of the business and has the right to receive all of the profits.
- Potential for favorable tax treatment.

Disadvantages of a Sole Proprietorship include:

- limited access to capital.
- unlimited personal liability for business obligations.
- proprietor must pay self-employment tax.

Formation of Sole Proprietorship

- There are no formalities, and no federal or state government approval is required for formation.
- May need to obtain licenses and/or permits to do business within certain industries.
- May need to obtain a tax identification number from the IRS.

Personal Liability of Sole proprietorship

A sole proprietor bears the risk of losing not only his or her entire capital contribution if the business fails, but also his or her personal assets (e.g., home, automobile, bank accounts) as well.

Taxation of Sole Proprietorship

- Earnings and losses are reported on the sole proprietor's personal income tax filing.
- For federal income tax purposes, a sole proprietor must prepare a personal income tax Form 1040 U.S. Individual Income Tax Return.
- Sole proprietors must also pay self-employment (SE) tax.

Termination of Sole proprietorship

- There are no formalities, and no federal or state government approval is required for termination.
- Care should be taken to notify third parties of the termination so as to avoid apparent authority and the creation of agency by estoppel.
- Any agency that issued a license, permit, or identification number should be notified of the termination.

1. ***d.b.a. (doing business as).*** A sole proprietorship can operate under the name of the sole proprietor or a *trade name*. Operating under a trade name is commonly designated as a *d.b.a.* (*doing business as*). If a trade name is used, a *fictitious business name statement* must be filed with the appropriate state government office.
2. ***Personal liability of sole proprietors.*** A sole proprietor is personally liable for the debts and obligations of the sole proprietorship.

TEST REVIEW TERMS AND CONCEPTS

d.b.a. (doing business as) 55
Entrepreneur 53
Entrepreneurship 53
Fictitious business name statement (certificate of trade name) 55
Sole proprietor 53
Sole proprietorship 53
Trade name 55
Unlimited personal liability 60

CASE SCENARIO REVISITED

Remember the case scenario at the beginning of the chapter involving Ross Insurance's false claims to clients that life insurance contributions were tax deductible? Now that Stephen Ross is deceased, would client John Borah prevail in a law suit against Ross Insurance as a sole proprietorship? How do the courts define a "sole proprietorship"? As a sole proprietorship, does Ross Insurance have an existence separate from Mr. Ross? To help you with your answers, see *Borah v. Monumental Life Ins. Co.*, 2005 WL 351040, 3 (E.D.Pa., 2005).

PORTFOLIO EXERCISE

Using the sample business you created at the beginning of the course, complete Form SS-4. This form is used to apply for the federal employer identification number and may be completed online at the Internal Revenue Service website. The site also provides downloadable statistics and information on taxation for sole proprietorships. See http://www.irs.gov.

WORKING THE WEB INTERNET EXERCISES

Activities

1. If a sole proprietor hires employees, a state employer identification number may be required. The website of the Federation of Tax Administrators provides links to the state tax agency of each state. See **http://www.taxadmin.org.**
2. Bplans.com is a site aimed at the individual interested in starting a business. It contains a large collection of free sample business plan outlines and helpful tools for managing one's business. See **http://www.bplans.com.**

CRITICAL LEGAL THINKING CASES

Case 3.1 ***Insurance Issues for Sole Proprietors*** On October 7, 1996, Shelly J. Koehlke-Stark, a sole proprietor, took out a general liability insurance policy for her business known as Clay Street Inn. The declarations page denoted the insured as "Shelly J. Koehlke-Stark d.b.a. Clay Street Inn." On February 11, 1997, Shelly changed her business from a sole proprietorship to a corporation. Shelly did not notify the insurance company of the change in business status. On May 16, 1998, a single car accident occurred while Jose Marta was driving a car owned by the business manager, Jennifer Koehlke. Jennifer sought to recover uninsured/underinsured motorist (UM/UIM) coverage through Clay Street's commercial general liability policy. The insurance company claimed that the policy required that it be notified of a change in Clay Street's business structure and the trial court agreed. Jennifer appealed. Was the trial court correct? *Koehlke v. Clay Street Inn, Inc.*, No. 2002-A-0108, 2003 Ohio LEXIS 4819 (Ct. App. Sept. 30, 2003).

Case 3.2 ***Fictitious Name*** Mildred Skolnick conducted a business as a sole proprietor using the unregistered fictitious name Monaco Bay Apartments. Richard A. Chaikin sued Mildred Skolnick, d/b/a Monaco Bay Apartments based on the allegation that Skolnick owned, operated, controlled or managed the Apartments. Skolnick denied that she owned, operated, controlled or managed the Apartments. Did Skolnick waive the right to defend herself against the claims brought by Chaikin by failing to register her fictitious name? *Chaikin v. Skolnick*, 201 So. 2d 588 (Fla. Dist. Ct. App. 1967).

Case 3.3 ***Trade Name*** The Oklahoma Presbyterian College for Girls and others entered into a construction contract with M. J. Gill who was doing business as M. J. Gill Construction Company. When construction was not completed timely, the college sued M. J. Gill Construction Company, as principal and National Surety Company, as a surety. Gill contended that the court never obtained jurisdiction over him because he was sued under his assumed name, M. J. Gill Construction Company. Was he correct? *National Surety Co. v. Oklahoma Presbyterian College for Girls*, 132 P. 652 (Okla. 1913).

Case 3.4 ***Sole Proprietor Legally Separate from Owner*** Glidden Co. sold 100 percent of its stock to an independent subsidiary and then paid unemployment compensation at a reduced tax rate applicable to "new employers." Four years later, the Department of Labor and Industry retroactively increased Glidden's unemployment compensation tax rate arguing that the employer never changed despite a change in ownership Glidden challenged the order, claiming that the stock sale constituted a transfer between employers pursuant to *43 P.S. Sec. 784(d)(1)(B)*. Was the Glidden stock sale considered a transfer of business to a new employer? Was Glidden entitled to a reduced tax rate for Pennsylvania unemployment compensation? *Glidden Co. v. Department of Labor and Indus.*, 700 A.2d 555 (Pa. Commw. Ct. 1997).

Case 3.5 ***Suing Owner Separate from Sole Proprietorship*** Cashco Oil Co. filed a multicount complaint against an owner, Edward L. Moses, Jr., et al., which constituted an individual, a number of affiliated corporations, and a Moses sole proprietorship. Under Illinois law, can a sole proprietorship be separately sued apart from the individual? *Cashco Oil Co. v. Moses*, 605 F. Supp. 70 (N.D. Ill, 1985).

BUSINESS ETHICS CASE

Case 3.6 ***Personal Liability of Sole Proprietor*** Kenneth and Cheryl Duval sought monetary damages against Midwest Auto City, Inc., claiming the dealership had sold them automobiles in which the odometers had been turned back, and sold the cars as having less mileage than they actually had. The buyers brought suit against the sellers and alleged violations of *15 U.S.C.S. Sec. 1984, 1985, 1986, and 1988*, all of which made it a crime to transfer a car with a turned back odometer. Does a problem with one or two sales alone constitute a conspiracy? In light of many other similar transactions, was there clear and convincing evidence of intent to defraud? *Duval v. Midwest Auto City, Inc.*, 425 F. Supp. 1381 (D. Neb. 1977).

"One of the most fruitful sources of ruin to a man of the world is the recklessness or want of principle of partners, and it is one of the perils to which every man exposes himself who enters into a partnership."

—Vice Chancellor Malins

Mackay v. Douglas, 14 L.R.-Eq. 106 (1872).

General Partnerships

CHAPTER 4

CASE SCENARIO

The law firm at which you work as a paralegal represents Thomas Smithson, a house builder and a small-scale property developer. Smithson decided that a certain tract of undeveloped land in Franklin, Tennessee, would be extremely attractive for development into a subdivision. Smithson contacted the owner of the property, Monsanto Chemical Company, and was told that the company would sell the property at the "right price."

Since Smithson did not have the funds with which to embark unassisted in the endeavor, he contacted Frank White, a local realtor. The two of them orally agreed to develop the property together, with White providing the funding and, in lieu of a financial investment, Smithson overseeing the engineering of the property.

Smithson recently discovered that White contacted Monsanto and purchased the property directly from that company. White then sold the property to a subdivision developer for an $184,000 profit. To date, White has refused to pay Smithson an equal share of the profits.

CHAPTER OBJECTIVES

After studying this chapter, you should be able to:

1. Define *general partnership,* and describe how general partnerships are formed.
2. Explain the contract and tort liability of partners.
3. Describe how a partnership is dissolved and terminated.

INTRODUCTION TO GENERAL PARTNERSHIPS

As set out in the last chapter, a person who wants to start a business must decide which of the major forms of business organization—*sole proprietorship*, *general partnership*, *limited partnership*, *limited liability partnerships*, *limited liability company*, and *corporation*—the business should operate as. The selection depends on many factors, including the ease and cost of formation, the capital requirements of the business, the flexibility of management decisions, government restrictions, personal liability, tax considerations, and the like.

This chapter discusses general partnerships. Limited partnerships, limited liability partnerships, and limited liability limited partnerships are discussed in the next chapter.

GENERAL PARTNERSHIP

general partnership
An association of two or more persons to carry on as co-owners of a business for profit [UPA Section 6(1)]. Also known as an *ordinary partnership*.

A **general partnership**, sometimes called an ordinary partnership, has been recognized since ancient times. The English common law of partnerships governed early U.S. partnerships. The individual states expanded the body of partnership law.

general partners
Persons liable for the debts and obligations of a general partnership. Also known simply as *partners*.

A general partnership, or partnership, is a voluntary association of two or more persons for carrying on a business as co-owners for profit. The formation of a partnership creates certain rights and duties among partners and with third parties. These rights and duties are established in the partnership agreement and by law. **General partners**, or **partners**, are personally liable for the debts and obligations of the partnership (see Exhibit 4.1).

PARALEGAL PERSPECTIVE

Trisha Husul *is a paralegal with the Roswell Park Cancer Institute Division of Health Research, Inc., in Buffalo, New York. She graduated with a bachelor's degree in paralegal studies from Hilbert College and specializes in contracts law. She has been working as a paralegal for eight years.*

How do you think paralegals may be asked to work within the area of general partnership? Paralegals may be asked to complete formation documents for several types of entities, including general partnerships. This may include assisting the attorney with drafting the partnership agreement for the client.

What are the most important paralegal skills needed in your job? Legal writing and editing skills, along with the ability to comprehend and negotiate contract terms, are foremost in this role. Precise language is key.

What is the academic background required for a paralegal entering your area of practice? A bachelor's degree is required, along with two years of full-time experience in a law firm, or in-house setting.

How is technology involved in your job? The majority of the work is done on the computer, mostly redlining changes to a document and e-mailing the other party. Communication with the other party to the contract and with in-house counsel is constant.

What trends do you see in your area of practice that will likely affect your job in the future? Researchers and pharmaceutical companies are making advances, and each new drug trial the institution participates in needs a contract. My workload steadily increases as developments in cancer research are made.

What do you feel is the biggest issue currently facing the paralegal profession? A formal paralegal education sets the foundation for a solid career in the legal field. The levels of paralegal education vary widely. It would be great for employers to recognize the difference among education levels and compensate accordingly.

Exhibit 4.1 General Partnership

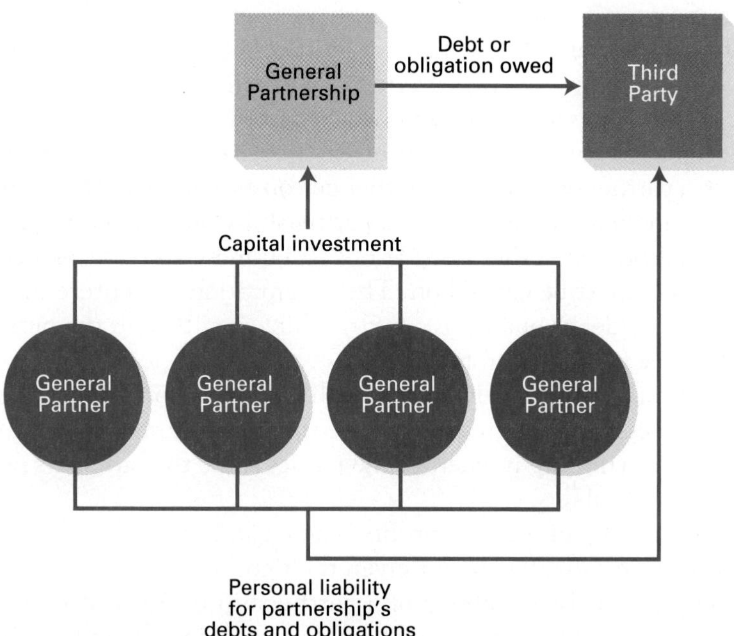

LANDMARK LAW

UNIFORM PARTNERSHIP ACT (UPA)

In 1914, the National Conference of Commissioners on Uniform State Laws (a group of lawyers, judges, and legal scholars) promulgated the Uniform Partnership Act (UPA). The UPA codifies partnership law. Its goal was to establish consistent partnership law that was uniform throughout the Unites States. The UPA has been adopted in whole or in part by forty-eight states, the District of Columbia, Guam, and the Virgin Islands. Because it is so important, the UPA forms the basis of the study of general partnerships in this chapter.

The UPA covers most problems that arise in the formation, operation, and dissolution of ordinary partnerships. Other rules of law or equity govern if there is no applicable provision of the UPA [UPA Section 5].

The original UPA treats partnerships as having both entity and aggregate characteristics. The *entity theory* of partnership, which considers partnerships as separate legal entities, allows for partnerships to hold title to personal and real property, transact business in the partnership name, and the like. The *aggregate theory* of partnership, which provides that the partnership is only an aggregation of the partners who transact business, allows for general partners to be personally liable for partnership obligations as discussed later in this chapter. The UPA has since adopted the *entity theory* of partnership. (See Appendix A for more detail on this act.)

General Partnership Name

An ordinary partnership can operate under the names of any one or more of the partners or under a fictitious business name. A partnership must file a fictitious business name statement—d.b.a. (doing business as)—with the appropriate government agency to operate under a trade name. The general partnership usually must publish a notice of the use of the trade name in a newspaper of general circulation where the partnership does business. The name selected by the partnership cannot indicate that it is a corporation (e.g., it cannot contain the term *Inc.*) and cannot be similar to the name used by any existing business entity.

Formation of a General Partnership

Uniform Partnership Act (UPA)
A model act that codifies partnership law. Most states have adopted the UPA in whole or in part.

A business must meet four criteria to qualify as a partnership under the **Uniform Partnership Agreement (UPA)** [UPA Section 6(1)]. It must be (1) an association of two or more persons (2) carrying on a business (3) as co-owners (4) for profit. A partnership is a voluntary association of two or more persons. All partners must agree to the participation of each co-partner. A person cannot be forced to be a partner or to accept another person as a partner. The UPA's definition of *person* includes natural persons, partnerships (including limited partnerships), corporations, and other associations. A business—a trade, an occupation, or a profession—must be carried on. The organization or venture must have a profit motive in order to qualify as a partnership, even though the business does not actually have to make a profit.

A general partnership may be formed with little or no formality. Co-ownership of a business is essential to create a partnership. The most important factor in determining co-ownership is whether the parties share the business's profits and management responsibility.

Receipt of a share of business profits is *prima facie* evidence of a partnership because nonpartners usually are not given the right to share in a business's profits. No inference of the existence of a partnership is drawn if profits are received in payment of (1) a debt owed to a creditor in installments or otherwise; (2) wages owed to an employee; (3) rent owed to a landlord; (4) an annuity owed to a widow, widower, or representative of a deceased partner; (5) interest owed on a loan; or (6) consideration for the sale of goodwill of a business [UPA Section 7]. An agreement to share losses of a business is strong evidence of a partnership.

The right to participate in the management of a business is important evidence for determining the existence of a partnership, but it is not conclusive evidence because the right to participate in management is sometimes given to employees, creditors, and others. It is compelling evidence of the existence of a partnership if a person is given the right to share in profits, losses, and management of a business.

The General Partnership Agreement

agreement
A mutual understanding between two or more persons about their relative rights and duties regarding past or future performances including course of dealing, usage of trade, and course of performance.

The **agreement** to form a partnership may be oral, written, or implied from the conduct of the parties. It may even be created inadvertently. No formalities are necessary, although a few states require general partnerships to file certificates of partnership with an appropriate government agency. Partnerships that exist for more than one year or are authorized to deal in real estate must be in writing under the Statute of Frauds.

It is a good practice for partners to put their partnership agreement in writing. A written document is important evidence of the terms of the agreement, particularly if a dispute arises among the partners.

partnership agreement
A written agreement that partners sign. Also called *articles of partnership*.

A written partnership agreement is called a **partnership agreement**, or **articles of partnership**. The parties can agree to almost any terms in their partnership agreement, except terms that are illegal. The articles of partnership can be short and simple or long and complex. If the agreement fails to provide for an essential term or contingency, the provisions of the UPA control. Thus, the UPA acts as a gap-filling device to the partners' agreement.

CASE 4.1 General Partnership

***Vohland v. Sweet*, 435 N.E. 2d 860 (Ind. Ct. App. 1982).**

Facts

Norman E. Sweet began working for Charles Vohland as an hourly employee at a garden nursery owned by Vohland in 1956, when he was a youngster. Upon completion of military service (from 1958 to 1960), Sweet resumed his former employment. In 1963, Charles Vohland retired, and his son Paul Vohland (Vohland) commenced what became known as Vohland's Nursery, the business of which was landscape gardening. Vohland purchased the interests of his brothers and sisters in the nursery. At that time, Sweet's status changed: He was to receive a 20 percent share of the net profit of the business after all expenses were paid, including labor, supplies, plants, and other expenses. Sweet contributed no capital to the enterprise. The compensation was paid on an irregular basis—every several weeks, Vohland and Sweet would sit down, compute the income received and expenses paid, and Sweet would be issued a check for 20 percent of the balance. No Social Security or income taxes were withheld from Sweet's checks.

It is when merchants dispute about their own rules that they invoke the law.
Judge Brett
Robinson v. Mollett (1875)

Vohland and Sweet did not enter into a written agreement. No partnership income tax returns were filed by the business. Sweet's tax returns declared that he was a self-employed salesman. He paid self-employment Social Security taxes. Vohland handled all the finances and books of the nursery and borrowed money from the bank solely in his own name for business purposes. Vohland made most of the sales for the business. Sweet managed the physical aspects of the nursery, supervised the care of the nursery stock, and oversaw the performance of the contracts for customers. Sweet testified that in the early 1970s, Vohland told him:

> *He was going to take me in and that I wouldn't have to punch a time clock anymore, that I would be on a commission basis and that I would be—have more of an interest in the business if I had an interest in the business. He referred to it as a "piece of the action."*

Vohland denied making this statement. Sweet brought this action for dissolution of the alleged partnership and for an accounting. He sought payment for 20 percent of the business's inventory. The trial court held in favor of Sweet and awarded him $58,733. Vohland appealed.

Issue

Did Vohland and Sweet enter into a partnership?

Court's Reasoning

Receipt by a person of a share of the profits is prima facie evidence that he or she is a partner in a business. Here, Sweet shared in the profits of the nursery. Although the parties called Sweet's sharing in the profits a "commission," the court stated that the term "when used by landscape gardeners and not lawyers, should not be restricted to its technical definition." The court found that the absence of a capital contribution by Sweet was not controlling and that his contribution of labor and skill would suffice.

Decision

The court of appeals held that partnership had been created between Vohland and Sweet. The court of appeals affirmed the decision of the trial court in favor of Sweet.

Case Questions

1. **Critical Legal Thinking** Do you think a partnership was formed in this case? Should all partnership agreements be required to be in writing?
2. **Business Ethics** Do you think either party acted unethically in this case?
3. **Contemporary Business** What are the economic consequences of founding a partnership?

Taxation of Partnerships

Partnerships do not pay federal income taxes. Instead, the income and losses of partnership flow onto and have to be reported on the individual partners' personal income tax returns. This is called "flow-through" taxation. However, a partnership has to file an information return with the government, telling the government how much income was earned or losses were incurred by the partnership. This way, the government tax authorities can trace whether partners are correctly reporting their income or losses. Form 1065 (see Exhibit 4.2) is an information return used to report the income, gains, losses, deductions, credits, etc., from the operation of a partnership. A partnership does not pay tax on its income but "passes through" any profits or losses to its partners. Partners must include partnership items on their tax returns.

Every domestic partnership must file Form 1065, unless it neither receives income nor incurs any expenditures treated as deductions or credits for federal income tax purposes. Each members pro rata share on the Schedule K-1 (see Exhibit 4.3).

RIGHTS OF GENERAL PARTNERS

The partners of a general partnership have certain rights. The rights of general partners are discussed in the following paragraphs.

Right to Participate in Management

In the absence of an agreement to the contrary, all partners have equal **rights to participate in management** (i.e., equal rights in the conduct and management of the partnership business). In other words, each partner has one vote, regardless of the proportional size of that partner's capital contribution or share in the partnership's profits. Under the UPA, a simple majority decides most ordinary partnership matters [UPA Section 18]. If the vote is tied, the action being voted on is considered to be defeated.

right to participate in management
A situation in which, unless otherwise agreed, each partner has a right to participate in the management of a partnership and has an equal vote on partnership matters.

Exhibit 4.2 Form 1065-U.S. Return of Partnership Income

Form **1065** Department of the Treasury Internal Revenue Service

U.S. Return of Partnership Income

For calendar year 2009, or tax year beginning ____________, 2009, ending ____________, 20____.

▶ See separate instructions.

OMB No. 1545-0099

2009

A Principal business activity	Use the IRS label. Otherwise, print or type.	Name of partnership	D Employer identification number
B Principal product or service		Number, street, and room or suite no. If a P.O. box, see the instructions.	E Date business started
C Business code number		City or town, state, and ZIP code	F Total assets (see the instructions) $

G Check applicable boxes: (1) ☐ Initial return (2) ☐ Final return (3) ☐ Name change (4) ☐ Address change (5) ☐ Amended return
(6) ☐ Technical termination - also check (1) or (2)

H Check accounting method: (1) ☐ Cash (2) ☐ Accrual (3) ☐ Other (specify) ▶

I Number of Schedules K-1. Attach one for each person who was a partner at any time during the tax year ▶

J Check if Schedules C and M-3 are attached . . . ☐

Caution. *Include **only** trade or business income and expenses on lines 1a through 22 below. See the instructions for more information.*

Income	1a	Gross receipts or sales	1a		
	b	Less returns and allowances	1b	1c	
	2	Cost of goods sold (Schedule A, line 8)		2	
	3	Gross profit. Subtract line 2 from line 1c		3	
	4	Ordinary income (loss) from other partnerships, estates, and trusts *(attach statement)*		4	
	5	Net farm profit (loss) *(attach Schedule F (Form 1040))*		5	
	6	Net gain (loss) from Form 4797, Part II, line 17 *(attach Form 4797)*		6	
	7	Other income (loss) *(attach statement)*		7	
	8	**Total income (loss).** Combine lines 3 through 7		8	
Deductions (see the instructions for limitations)	9	Salaries and wages (other than to partners) (less employment credits)		9	
	10	Guaranteed payments to partners		10	
	11	Repairs and maintenance		11	
	12	Bad debts		12	
	13	Rent		13	
	14	Taxes and licenses		14	
	15	Interest		15	
	16a	Depreciation *(if required, attach Form 4562)*	16a		
	b	Less depreciation reported on Schedule A and elsewhere on return	16b	16c	
	17	Depletion **(Do not deduct oil and gas depletion.)**		17	
	18	Retirement plans, etc.		18	
	19	Employee benefit programs		19	
	20	Other deductions *(attach statement)*		20	
	21	**Total deductions.** Add the amounts shown in the far right column for lines 9 through 20		21	
	22	**Ordinary business income (loss).** Subtract line 21 from line 8		22	

Sign Here

Under penalties of perjury, I declare that I have examined this return, including accompanying schedules and statements, and to the best of my knowledge and belief, it is true, correct, and complete. Declaration of preparer (other than general partner or limited liability company member manager) is based on all information of which preparer has any knowledge.

▶ Signature of general partner or limited liability company member manager ▶ Date

May the IRS discuss this return with the preparer shown below (see instructions)? ☐ Yes ☐ No

Paid Preparer's Use Only

Preparer's signature	Date	Check if self- employed ▶ ☐	Preparer's SSN or PTIN
Firm's name (or yours if self-employed), address, and ZIP code ▶			EIN ▶
			Phone no.

For Privacy Act and Paperwork Reduction Act Notice, see separate instructions. Cat. No. 11390Z Form **1065** (2009)

(continued)

Exhibit 4.2 *(Continued)*

Form 1065 (2009) Page **2**

Schedule A **Cost of Goods Sold** (see the instructions)

1	Inventory at beginning of year	1		
2	Purchases less cost of items withdrawn for personal use	2		
3	Cost of labor	3		
4	Additional section 263A costs (*attach statement*)	4		
5	Other costs (*attach statement*)	5		
6	**Total.** Add lines 1 through 5	6		
7	Inventory at end of year	7		
8	**Cost of goods sold.** Subtract line 7 from line 6. Enter here and on page 1, line 2	8		

9a Check all methods used for valuing closing inventory:

(i) ☐ Cost as described in Regulations section 1.471-3

(ii) ☐ Lower of cost or market as described in Regulations section 1.471-4

(iii) ☐ Other (specify method used and attach explanation) ▶ ____________

b Check this box if there was a writedown of "subnormal" goods as described in Regulations section 1.471-2(c) . . . ▶ ☐

c Check this box if the LIFO inventory method was adopted this tax year for any goods (*if checked, attach Form 970*) . . ▶ ☐

d Do the rules of section 263A (for property produced or acquired for resale) apply to the partnership? . . . . . ☐ **Yes** ☐ **No**

e Was there any change in determining quantities, cost, or valuations between opening and closing inventory? . . ☐ **Yes** ☐ **No**
If "Yes," attach explanation.

Schedule B **Other Information**

		Yes	No
1	What type of entity is filing this return? Check the applicable box: **a** ☐ Domestic general partnership **b** ☐ Domestic limited partnership **c** ☐ Domestic limited liability company **d** ☐ Domestic limited liability partnership **e** ☐ Foreign partnership **f** ☐ Other ▶ ____________		
2	At any time during the tax year, was any partner in the partnership a disregarded entity, a partnership (including an entity treated as a partnership), a trust, an S corporation, an estate (other than an estate of a deceased partner), or a nominee or similar person?		
3	At the end of the tax year:		
a	Did any foreign or domestic corporation, partnership (including any entity treated as a partnership), trust, or tax-exempt organization own, directly or indirectly, an interest of 50% or more in the profit, loss, or capital of the partnership? For rules of constructive ownership, see instructions. If "Yes," attach Schedule B-1, Information on Partners Owning 50% or More of the Partnership		
b	Did any individual or estate own, directly or indirectly, an interest of 50% or more in the profit, loss, or capital of the partnership? For rules of constructive ownership, see instructions. If "Yes," attach Schedule B-1, Information on Partners Owning 50% or More of the Partnership		
4	At the end of the tax year, did the partnership:		
a	Own directly 20% or more, or own, directly or indirectly, 50% or more of the total voting power of all classes of stock entitled to vote of any foreign or domestic corporation? For rules of constructive ownership, see instructions. If "Yes," complete (i) through (iv) below		

(i) Name of Corporation	**(ii)** Employer Identification Number (if any)	**(iii)** Country of Incorporation	**(iv)** Percentage Owned in Voting Stock

		Yes	No
b	Own directly an interest of 20% or more, or own, directly or indirectly, an interest of 50% or more in the profit, loss, or capital in any foreign or domestic partnership (including an entity treated as a partnership) or in the beneficial interest of a trust? For rules of constructive ownership, see instructions. If "Yes," complete (i) through (v) below		

(i) Name of Entity	**(ii)** Employer Identification Number (if any)	**(iii)** Type of Entity	**(iv)** Country of Organization	**(v)** Maximum Percentage Owned in Profit, Loss, or Capital

Form **1065** (2009)

Exhibit 4.2 *(Continued)*

Form 1065 (2009) Page **3**

		Yes	No
5	Did the partnership file Form 8893, Election of Partnership Level Tax Treatment, or an election statement under section 6231(a)(1)(B)(ii) for partnership-level tax treatment, that is in effect for this tax year? See Form 8893 for more details		
6	Does the partnership satisfy **all four** of the following conditions?		
a	The partnership's total receipts for the tax year were less than $250,000.		
b	The partnership's total assets at the end of the tax year were less than $1 million.		
c	Schedules K-1 are filed with the return and furnished to the partners on or before the due date (including extensions) for the partnership return.		
d	The partnership is not filing and is not required to file Schedule M-3		
	If "Yes," the partnership is not required to complete Schedules L, M-1, and M-2; Item F on page 1 of Form 1065; or Item L on Schedule K-1.		
7	Is this partnership a publicly traded partnership as defined in section 469(k)(2)?		
8	During the tax year, did the partnership have any debt that was cancelled, was forgiven, or had the terms modified so as to reduce the principal amount of the debt?		
9	Has this partnership filed, or is it required to file, Form 8918, Material Advisor Disclosure Statement, to provide information on any reportable transaction?		
10	At any time during calendar year 2009, did the partnership have an interest in or a signature or other authority over a financial account in a foreign country (such as a bank account, securities account, or other financial account)? See the instructions for exceptions and filing requirements for Form TD F 90-22.1, Report of Foreign Bank and Financial Accounts. If "Yes," enter the name of the foreign country. ▶ ______		
11	At any time during the tax year, did the partnership receive a distribution from, or was it the grantor of, or transferor to, a foreign trust? If "Yes," the partnership may have to file Form 3520, Annual Return To Report Transactions With Foreign Trusts and Receipt of Certain Foreign Gifts. See instructions		
12a	Is the partnership making, or had it previously made (and not revoked), a section 754 election?		
	See instructions for details regarding a section 754 election.		
b	Did the partnership make for this tax year an optional basis adjustment under section 743(b) or 734(b)? If "Yes," attach a statement showing the computation and allocation of the basis adjustment. See instructions		
c	Is the partnership required to adjust the basis of partnership assets under section 743(b) or 734(b) because of a substantial built-in loss (as defined under section 743(d)) or substantial basis reduction (as defined under section 734(d))? If "Yes," attach a statement showing the computation and allocation of the basis adjustment. See instructions.		
13	Check this box if, during the current or prior tax year, the partnership distributed any property received in a like-kind exchange or contributed such property to another entity (other than entities wholly-owned by the partnership throughout the tax year) . . . . . ▶ ☐		
14	At any time during the tax year, did the partnership distribute to any partner a tenancy-in-common or other undivided interest in partnership property?		
15	If the partnership is required to file Form 8858, Information Return of U.S. Persons With Respect To Foreign Disregarded Entities, enter the number of Forms 8858 attached. See instructions ▶ ______		
16	Does the partnership have any foreign partners? If "Yes," enter the number of Forms 8805, Foreign Partner's Information Statement of Section 1446 Withholding Tax, filed for this partnership. ▶ ______		
17	Enter the number of Forms 8865, Return of U.S. Persons With Respect to Certain Foreign Partnerships, attached to this return. ▶ ______		

Designation of Tax Matters Partner (see instructions)

Enter below the general partner designated as the tax matters partner (TMP) for the tax year of this return:

Name of designated TMP ▶		Identifying number of TMP ▶	
If the TMP is an entity, name of TMP representative ▶		Phone number of TMP ▶	
Address of designated TMP ▶			

Form **1065** (2009)

(continued)

Exhibit 4.2 *(Continued)*

Form 1065 (2009) Page **4**

Section		Schedule K — Partners' Distributive Share Items		Line	Total amount
Income (Loss)	1	Ordinary business income (loss) (page 1, line 22)		1	
	2	Net rental real estate income (loss) (*attach Form 8825*)		2	
	3a	Other gross rental income (loss)	3a		
	b	Expenses from other rental activities (*attach statement*)	3b		
	c	Other net rental income (loss). Subtract line 3b from line 3a		3c	
	4	Guaranteed payments		4	
	5	Interest income		5	
	6	Dividends: **a** Ordinary dividends		6a	
		b Qualified dividends	6b		
	7	Royalties		7	
	8	Net short-term capital gain (loss) (*attach Schedule D (Form 1065)*)		8	
	9a	Net long-term capital gain (loss) (*attach Schedule D (Form 1065)*)		9a	
	b	Collectibles (28%) gain (loss)	9b		
	c	Unrecaptured section 1250 gain (*attach statement*)	9c		
	10	Net section 1231 gain (loss) (*attach Form 4797*)		10	
	11	Other income (loss) (*see instructions*) Type ▶		11	
Deductions	12	Section 179 deduction (*attach Form 4562*)		12	
	13a	Contributions		13a	
	b	Investment interest expense		13b	
	c	Section 59(e)(2) expenditures: **(1)** Type ▶ **(2)** Amount ▶		13c(2)	
	d	Other deductions (*see instructions*) Type ▶		13d	
Self-Employment	14a	Net earnings (loss) from self-employment		14a	
	b	Gross farming or fishing income		14b	
	c	Gross nonfarm income		14c	
Credits	15a	Low-income housing credit (section 42(j)(5))		15a	
	b	Low-income housing credit (other)		15b	
	c	Qualified rehabilitation expenditures (rental real estate) (*attach Form 3468*)		15c	
	d	Other rental real estate credits (*see instructions*) Type ▶		15d	
	e	Other rental credits (*see instructions*) Type ▶		15e	
	f	Other credits (*see instructions*) Type ▶		15f	
Foreign Transactions	16a	Name of country or U.S. possession ▶			
	b	Gross income from all sources		16b	
	c	Gross income sourced at partner level		16c	
		Foreign gross income sourced at partnership level			
	d	Passive category ▶ **e** General category ▶ **f** Other ▶		16f	
		Deductions allocated and apportioned at partner level			
	g	Interest expense ▶ **h** Other ▶		16h	
		Deductions allocated and apportioned at partnership level to foreign source income			
	i	Passive category ▶ **j** General category ▶ **k** Other ▶		16k	
	l	Total foreign taxes (check one): ▶ Paid ☐ Accrued ☐		16l	
	m	Reduction in taxes available for credit (*attach statement*)		16m	
	n	Other foreign tax information (*attach statement*)			
Alternative Minimum Tax (AMT) Items	17a	Post-1986 depreciation adjustment		17a	
	b	Adjusted gain or loss		17b	
	c	Depletion (other than oil and gas)		17c	
	d	Oil, gas, and geothermal properties—gross income		17d	
	e	Oil, gas, and geothermal properties—deductions		17e	
	f	Other AMT items (*attach statement*)		17f	
Other Information	18a	Tax-exempt interest income		18a	
	b	Other tax-exempt income		18b	
	c	Nondeductible expenses		18c	
	19a	Distributions of cash and marketable securities		19a	
	b	Distributions of other property		19b	
	20a	Investment income		20a	
	b	Investment expenses		20b	
	c	Other items and amounts (*attach statement*)			

Form **1065** (2009)

Exhibit 4.2 *(Continued)*

Form 1065 (2009) Page **5**

Analysis of Net Income (Loss)

1	Net income (loss). Combine Schedule K, lines 1 through 11. From the result, subtract the sum of Schedule K, lines 12 through 13d, and 16l	1	

2 Analysis by partner type:	(i) Corporate	(ii) Individual (active)	(iii) Individual (passive)	(iv) Partnership	(v) Exempt organization	(vi) Nominee/Other
a General partners						
b Limited partners						

Schedule L **Balance Sheets per Books**

		Beginning of tax year		End of tax year	
	Assets	(a)	(b)	(c)	(d)
1	Cash				
2a	Trade notes and accounts receivable . . .				
b	Less allowance for bad debts				
3	Inventories				
4	U.S. government obligations				
5	Tax-exempt securities				
6	Other current assets (*attach statement*) . .				
7	Mortgage and real estate loans				
8	Other investments (*attach statement*) . . .				
9a	Buildings and other depreciable assets . .				
b	Less accumulated depreciation				
10a	Depletable assets				
b	Less accumulated depletion				
11	Land (net of any amortization)				
12a	Intangible assets (amortizable only) . . .				
b	Less accumulated amortization				
13	Other assets (*attach statement*)				
14	Total assets				
	Liabilities and Capital				
15	Accounts payable				
16	Mortgages, notes, bonds payable in less than 1 year				
17	Other current liabilities (*attach statement*) .				
18	All nonrecourse loans				
19	Mortgages, notes, bonds payable in 1 year or more				
20	Other liabilities (*attach statement*)				
21	Partners' capital accounts				
22	Total liabilities and capital				

Schedule M-1 **Reconciliation of Income (Loss) per Books With Income (Loss) per Return**

Note. Schedule M-3 may be required instead of Schedule M-1 (see instructions).

1	Net income (loss) per books		6	Income recorded on books this year not included on Schedule K, lines 1 through 11 (itemize):	
2	Income included on Schedule K, lines 1, 2, 3c, 5, 6a, 7, 8, 9a, 10, and 11, not recorded on books this year (itemize):		a	Tax-exempt interest $	
3	Guaranteed payments (other than health insurance)		7	Deductions included on Schedule K, lines 1 through 13d, and 16l, not charged against book income this year (itemize):	
4	Expenses recorded on books this year not included on Schedule K, lines 1 through 13d, and 16l (itemize):		a	Depreciation $	
a	Depreciation $				
b	Travel and entertainment $		8	Add lines 6 and 7	
			9	Income (loss) (Analysis of Net Income (Loss), line 1). Subtract line 8 from line 5 .	
5	Add lines 1 through 4				

Schedule M-2 **Analysis of Partners' Capital Accounts**

1	Balance at beginning of year . . .		6	Distributions: **a** Cash	
2	Capital contributed: **a** Cash . . .			**b** Property	
	b Property . .		7	Other decreases (itemize):	
3	Net income (loss) per books				
4	Other increases (itemize):				
			8	Add lines 6 and 7	
5	Add lines 1 through 4		9	Balance at end of year. Subtract line 8 from line 5	

Form **1065** (2009)

Exhibit 4.3 Form 1065 Schedule K-1

651109

☐ Final K-1 ☐ Amended K-1 OMB No. 1545-0099

Schedule K-1 (Form 1065) **2009**

Department of the Treasury
Internal Revenue Service

For calendar year 2009, or tax year beginning ________, 2009 ending ________, 20____

Partner's Share of Income, Deductions, Credits, etc.

► See back of form and separate instructions.

Part I Information About the Partnership

A Partnership's employer identification number

B Partnership's name, address, city, state, and ZIP code

C IRS Center where partnership filed return

D ☐ Check if this is a publicly traded partnership (PTP)

Part II Information About the Partner

E Partner's identifying number

F Partner's name, address, city, state, and ZIP code

G ☐ General partner or LLC member-manager ☐ Limited partner or other LLC member

H ☐ Domestic partner ☐ Foreign partner

I What type of entity is this partner? ________

J Partner's share of profit, loss, and capital (see instructions):

	Beginning	Ending
Profit	%	%
Loss	%	%
Capital	%	%

K Partner's share of liabilities at year end:

Nonrecourse . . . . $ ________
Qualified nonrecourse financing . $ ________
Recourse . . . . $ ________

L Partner's capital account analysis:

Beginning capital account . . . $ ________
Capital contributed during the year $ ________
Current year increase (decrease) . $ ________
Withdrawals & distributions . . $ (________)
Ending capital account . . . . $ ________

☐ Tax basis ☐ GAAP ☐ Section 704(b) book
☐ Other (explain)

M Did the partner contribute property with a built-in gain or loss?
☐ Yes ☐ No
If "Yes", attach statement (see instructions)

Part III Partner's Share of Current Year Income, Deductions, Credits, and Other Items

1	Ordinary business income (loss)	15	Credits
2	Net rental real estate income (loss)		
3	Other net rental income (loss)	16	Foreign transactions
4	Guaranteed payments		
5	Interest income		
6a	Ordinary dividends		
6b	Qualified dividends		
7	Royalties		
8	Net short-term capital gain (loss)		
9a	Net long-term capital gain (loss)	17	Alternative minimum tax (AMT) items
9b	Collectibles (28%) gain (loss)		
9c	Unrecaptured section 1250 gain		
10	Net section 1231 gain (loss)	18	Tax-exempt income and nondeductible expenses
11	Other income (loss)		
		19	Distributions
12	Section 179 deduction		
13	Other deductions	20	Other information
14	Self-employment earnings (loss)		

*See attached statement for additional information.

For IRS Use Only

For Paperwork Reduction Act Notice, see Instructions for Form 1065. Cat. No. 11394R Schedule K-1 (Form 1065) 2009

Right to Share in Profits

Unless otherwise agreed, the UPA mandates that a partner has the right to an equal share in the partnership's profits and losses [UPA Section 18(a)]. The right to share in the profits of the partnership is considered to be the right to share in the earnings from the investment of capital.

Right to Compensation and Reimbursement

Unless otherwise agreed, the UPA provides that no partner is entitled to compensation for their performance in the partnership's business [UPA Section 18(f)]. Under this rule, partners are not entitled to receive a salary for providing services to the partnership unless agreed to by the partners.

Under the UPA, it is implied that partners will devote full time and service to the partnership. Thus, unless otherwise agreed, income earned by partners from providing services elsewhere belongs to the partnership [UPA Section 21]. Partners sometimes incur personal travel, business, and other expenses on behalf of the partnership. A partner is entitled to **indemnification** (i.e., reimbursement) for such expenditures if they are reasonably incurred in the ordinary and proper conduct of the business [UPA Section 18(b)].

indemnification
The right of a partner to be reimbursed for expenditures incurred on behalf of the partnership.

Right to Return of Loans and Capital

A partner who makes a loan to the partnership becomes a creditor of the partnership. The partner is entitled to repayment of the loan, but this right is subordinated to the claims of creditors who are not partners [UPA Section 40(b)]. The partner is also entitled to receive interest from the date of the loan.

Upon termination of a partnership, the partners are entitled to have their capital contributions returned to them [UPA Section 18(a)]. However, this right is subordinated to the rights of creditors, who must be paid their claims first [UPA Section 40(b)].

Right to Information

Each partner has the right to demand true and full information from any other partner of all things affecting the partnership [UPA Section 20]. The corollary to this rule is that each partner has a duty to provide such information upon the receipt of a reasonable demand. The partnership books (e.g., financial records, tax records) must be kept at the partnership's principal place of business [UPA Section 19]. The partners have an absolute right to inspect and copy these records.

■ DUTIES OF GENERAL PARTNERS

General partners owe certain duties to each other and the partnership. The duties of partners are discussed in the following paragraphs.

fiduciary relationship
A relationship in which one person is under a duty to act for the benefit of another on matters within the scope of the relationship.

Duty of Loyalty

Partners are in a **fiduciary relationship** with one another. As such, they owe each other a **duty of loyalty**. This duty is imposed by law and cannot be waived. If there is a conflict between partnership interests and personal interests, the

duty of loyalty
A duty that a partner owes not to act adversely to the interests of the partnership.

partner must choose the interest of the partnership. Some basic forms of breach of loyalty involve:

self-dealing
If the directors or officers engage in purchasing, selling, or leasing of property with the corporation, the contract must be fair to the corporation; otherwise, it is voidable by the corporation. The contract or transaction is enforceable if it has been fully disclosed and approved.

- ***Self-dealing.*** **Self-dealing** occurs when a partner deals personally with the partnership, such as buying or selling goods or property to the partnership. Such actions are permitted only if full disclosure is made and consent of the other partners is obtained.

  Example: Dan is a partner in a partnership that is looking for a piece of real property on which to build a new store. Dan owns a desirable piece of property. To sell the property to the partnership, Dan must first disclose his ownership interest and receive his partners' consent.

usurping an opportunity
Stealing an opportunity for oneself.

- ***Usurping a partnership opportunity.*** A partner who is offered an opportunity on behalf of the partnership cannot **usurp the opportunity** for himself or herself. Thus, if a third party offers a business opportunity to a partner in his partnership status, the partner cannot take the opportunity for himself before offering it to the partnership. If the partnership rejects the opportunity, the partner is free to pursue the opportunity.

competing with the partnership
A way in which a partner in a partnership can breach his or her duty of loyalty.

- ***Competing with the partnership.*** A partner may not **compete with the partnership** without the permission of the other partners.

  Example: A partner of a general partnership that operates an automobile dealership cannot open a competing automobile dealership without their copartners' permission.

- ***Secret profits.*** Partners may not make **secret profits** from partnership business.

  Example: A partner who takes a kickback from a supplier has made a secret profit. The secret profit belongs to the partnership.

breach of confidentiality
A breach of fiduciary duty by a partner in a partnership to keep information confidential.

- ***Breach of confidentiality.*** Partners owe a duty to keep partnership information confidential by not committing a **breach of confidentiality**.

  Example: Trade secrets, customer lists, and other secret information are confidential. A partner who misuses this information—either by himself or by transferring the information to someone else—has **breached confidentiality**.

- ***Misuse of property.*** Partners owe a duty not to use partnership property for personal use.

A partner who breaches the duty of loyalty must disgorge any profits made from the breach to the partnership. In addition, the partner is liable for any damages caused by the breach.

Duty of Care

duty of care
The obligation partners owe to use the same level of care and skill that a reasonable person in the same position would use in the same circumstances. A breach of the duty of care is *negligence*.

A partner must use reasonable care and skill in transacting partnership business. The **duty of care** calls for the partners to use the same level of care and skill that a reasonable business manager in the same position would use in the same circumstances. Breach of the duty of care is negligence. A partner is liable to the partnership for any damages caused by his or her own negligence. The partners are not liable for honest errors in judgment.

Examples: Tina, Eric, and Brian form a partnership to sell automobiles. Tina, who is responsible for ordering inventory, orders large, expensive sport-utility vehicles (SUVs) that use a lot of gasoline. A war breaks out in the Middle East that interrupts the supply of oil to the United States. The demand for large SUVs drops substantially, and the partnership cannot sell its inventory. Tina is not liable because the duty of care was not breached.

Duty to Inform

Partners owe a **duty to inform** their co-partners of all information they possess that is relevant to the affairs of the partnership [UPA Section 20]. Even if a partner fails to communicate information to other partners, the other partners have **imputed knowledge** of all notices concerning any matters relating to partnership affairs. Knowledge is also imputed regarding information acquired in the role of partner that affects the partnership and should have been communicated to the other partners [UPA Section 12].

duty to inform
A duty a partner owes to inform his or her co-partners of all information he or she possesses that is relevant to the affairs of the partnership.

imputed knowledge
Knowledge attributed to a given person, especially because of the person's legal responsibility for another's conduct.

Example: Ted and Diane are partners. Ted knows that a piece of property owned by the partnership contains dangerous toxic wastes but fails to inform Diane of this fact. Even though Diane does not have actual knowledge of this fact, it is imputed to her.

Duty of Obedience

The **duty of obedience** requires partners to adhere to the provisions of the partnership agreement and the decisions of the partnership. A partner who breaches this duty is liable to the partnership for any damages caused by the breach.

duty of obedience
A duty that requires partners to adhere to the provisions of the partnership agreement and the decisions of the partnership.

Example: Emma, Grace, and Jack form a partnership to develop real property. Their partnership agreement specifies that acts of the partners are limited to those necessary to accomplish the partnership's purpose. Suppose Jack, acting alone, loses $100,000 of partnership funds in commodities trading. Jack is personally liable to the partnership for the lost funds because he breached the partnership agreement.

CONTEMPORARY Environment

RIGHT TO AN ACCOUNTING

Partners are not permitted to sue the partnership or other partners at law. Instead, they are given the right to bring an **action for an accounting** against other partners. An action for an accounting is a formal judicial proceeding in which the court is authorized to (1) review the partnership and the partners' transactions, and (2) award each partner his or her share of the partnership assets [UPA Section 24]. An action results in a money judgment for or against partners, according to the balance struck.

action for an accounting
A formal judicial proceeding in which the court is authorized to (1) review the partnership and the partners' transactions and (2) award each partner his or her share of the partnership assets.

■ LIABILITY OF GENERAL PARTNERS

Partners must deal with third parties in conducting partnership business. This often includes entering into contracts with third parties on behalf of the partnership. Partners, employees, and agents of the partnership sometimes injure third parties while conducting partnership business. Partners of a general partnership have personal liability for the contracts and torts of the partnership. Contract and tort liability of partnerships and their partners is discussed in the following paragraphs.

Tort Liability

While acting on partnership business, a partner or an employee of the partnership may commit a tort that causes injury to a third person. This tort could be caused by a negligent act, a breach of trust (such as embezzlement from a customer's account), breach of fiduciary duty, defamation, fraud, or another intentional tort. The partnership is liable if the act is committed while the person is acting within the ordinary course of partnership business or with the authority of their co-partners.

joint and several liability
Tort liability of partners together and individually. A plaintiff can sue one or more partners separately. If successful, the plaintiff can recover the entire amount of the judgment from any or all of the defendant-partners who have been found liable.

Under the UPA, partners are **jointly and severally liable** for torts and breaches of trust [UPA Section 15(a)]. This is so even if a partner did not participate in the commission of the act. This type of liability permits a third party to sue one or more of the partners separately. Judgment can be collected only against the partners who are sued. The partnership and partners who are made to pay **tort liability** may seek indemnification from the partner who committed the wrongful act. A release of one partner does not discharge the liability of other partners.

Example: Amanda, Barb, and Denise form a partnership. Denise, while on partnership business, causes an automobile accident that injures Catherine, a pedestrian. Catherine suffers $100,000 in injuries. Catherine, at her option, can sue Amanda, Barb, and Denise separately, or any two of them, or all of them.

The court applied the doctrine of joint and several liability in the following case.

CASE 4.2 Tort Liability of General Partners

Zuckerman v. Antenucci, 478 N.Y.S.2d 578 (N.Y. App. Div. 1984).

"A partnership is liable for the tortious act of a partner, and a partner is jointly and severally liable for tortious acts chargeable to the partnership."

—Judge Leviss

Facts

Jose Pena and Joseph Antenucci were both medical doctors who were partners in a medical practice. Both doctors treated Elaine Zuckerman during her pregnancy. Her son, Daniel Zuckerman, was born with severe physical problems. Elaine, as Daniel's mother and natural guardian, brought a medical malpractice suit against both doctors. The jury found that Pena was guilty of medical malpractice but that Antenucci was not. The amount of the verdict totaled $4 million. The trial court entered judgment against Pena but not against Antenucci. The plaintiffs made a posttrial motion for judgment against both defendants.

Issue

Is Antenucci jointly and severally liable for the medical malpractice of his partner, Pena?

Language of the Court

A partnership is liable for the tortious act of a partner, and a partner is jointly and severally liable for tortious acts chargeable to the partnership. When a tort is committed by the partnership, the wrong is imputable to all of the partners jointly and severally, and an action may be brought against all or any of them in their individual capacities or against the partnership as an entity. Therefore, even though the jury found that defendant Antenucci was not guilty of any malpractice in his treatment of the patient, but that defendant Pena, his partner, was guilty of malpractice in his treatment of the patient, they were then both jointly and severally liable for the malpractice committed by defendant Pena by operation of law.

Decision

The court held that both partners were jointly and severally liable for the judgment. The supreme court reversed the decision of the trial court and held that Antenucci was liable for the tort of his partner, Pena.

Case Questions

1. **Critical Legal Thinking** What is joint and several liability? How does it differ from joint liability?
2. **Business Ethics** Is it ethical for a partner to deny liability for torts of other partners?
3. **Contemporary Business** What types of insurance should a partnership purchase? Why?

joint liability
Liability of partners for contracts and debts of the partnership. A plaintiff must name the partnership and all of the partners as defendants in a lawsuit.

Contract Liability

As a legal entity, a partnership must act through its agents—that is, its partners. Contracts entered into with suppliers, customers, lenders, or others on the partnership's behalf are binding on the partnership. The Uniform Partnership Act permits a partnership to file a statement of partnership authority that identifies the partners authorized to perform certain acts. (See Exhibit 4.4.)

CASE 4.3 CONTRACT LIABILITY OF GENERAL PARTNERS

Edward A. Kemmler Memorial Foundation v. Mitchell, 584 N.E.2d 695 (Ohio 1992).

Facts

Clifford W. Davis and Dr. William D. Mitchell formed a general partnership to purchase and operate rental properties for investment purposes. The partnership purchased a parcel of real property from the Edward A. Kemmler Memorial Foundation (Foundation) on credit. Davis signed a $150,000 promissory note to the Foundation as "Cliff W. Davis, Partner." Prior to executing the note, Davis and Mitchell entered into an agreement that provided that only Davis, and not Mitchell, would be personally liable on the note to the Foundation. They did not inform the Foundation of this side agreement, however. When the partnership

Exhibit 4.4 Statement of Partnership Authority

GP-1

File # ______________________

Document # ______________________

State of California
Secretary of State

STATEMENT OF PARTNERSHIP AUTHORITY

A $70.00 filing fee must accompany this form.

IMPORTANT – Read instructions before completing this form.

This Space For Filing Use Only

PARTNERSHIP NAME

1. NAME OF PARTNERSHIP

OFFICE ADDRESSES (Do not abbreviate the city. Items 2 and 3 cannot be P.O. Boxes.)

2. STREET ADDRESS OF CHIEF EXECUTIVE OFFICE	CITY AND STATE		ZIP CODE
3. STREET ADDRESS OF CALIFORNIA OFFICE, IF ANY	CITY	STATE **CA**	ZIP CODE

NAMES & ADDRESSES OF PARTNERS (Complete Item 4 with the names and mailing addresses of all the partners (attach additional pages if necessary) **OR** leave Item 4 blank and proceed to Item 5. Any attachments to this document are incorporated herein by this reference.)

4. NAME	ADDRESS	CITY AND STATE	ZIP CODE
NAME	ADDRESS	CITY AND STATE	ZIP CODE
NAME	ADDRESS	CITY AND STATE	ZIP CODE

APPOINTED AGENT (If Item 4 was not completed, complete Item 5 with the name and mailing address of an agent appointed and maintained by the partnership who will maintain a list of the names and mailing addresses of all the partners. If Item 4 was completed, leave Item 5 blank and proceed to Item 6.)

5. NAME	ADDRESS	CITY AND STATE	ZIP CODE

AUTHORIZED PARTNERS (Enter the name(s) of all the partners authorized to execute instruments transferring real property held in the name of the partnership. Attach additional pages if necessary. Any attachments to this document are incorporated herein by this reference.)

6. PARTNER NAME:	PARTNER NAME:
PARTNER NAME:	PARTNER NAME:
PARTNER NAME:	PARTNER NAME:

ADDITIONAL INFORMATION

7. ADDITIONAL INFORMATION SET FORTH ON THE ATTACHED PAGES, IF ANY, IS INCORPORATED HEREIN BY THIS REFERENCE AND MADE PART OF THIS DOCUMENT.

EXECUTION (If additional signature space is necessary, the dated signature(s) with verification(s) may be made on an attachment to this document. Any attachments to this document are incorporated herein by this reference.)

8. I CERTIFY UNDER PENALTY OF PERJURY UNDER THE LAWS OF THE STATE OF CALIFORNIA THAT THE FOREGOING IS TRUE AND CORRECT OF MY OWN KNOWLEDGE.

SIGNATURE OF PARTNER	DATE	TYPE OR PRINT NAME OF PARTNER
SIGNATURE OF PARTNER	DATE	TYPE OR PRINT NAME OF PARTNER

GP-1 (REV 11/2006) APPROVED BY SECRETARY OF STATE

Clear Form Print Form

Exhibit 4.4 *(Continued)*

INSTRUCTIONS FOR COMPLETING THE STATEMENT OF PARTNERSHIP AUTHORITY (FORM GP-1)

For easier completion, this form is available on the Secretary of State's website at http://www.sos.ca.gov/business/ and can be viewed, filled in and printed from your computer. The completed form can be mailed to Secretary of State, Document Filing Support Unit, P.O. Box 944225, Sacramento, CA 94244-2250 or delivered in person to the Sacramento office, 1500 11th Street, 3rd Floor, Sacramento, CA 95814. If you are not completing this form online, please type or legibly print in black or blue ink. This form is only filed in the Sacramento office.

Statutory filing provisions are found in California Corporations Code section 16303. All statutory references are to the California Corporations Code, unless otherwise stated.

- Unless otherwise provided in the Partnership Agreement, a person who files a Statement of Partnership Authority (Form GP-1) pursuant to Section 16105 shall promptly send a copy of the statement to every non-filing partner and to any other person named as a partner in the statement. (Sections 16103(b)(1) and 16105(e).)

- In order for a statement to be effective for real estate transfers, a certified copy of the statement issued by the Secretary of State must be recorded in the office for recording transfers of real properly. (Section 16105(b).)

FEES: The fee for filing Form GP-1 is $70.00. There is an additional $15.00 special handling fee for processing a document delivered in person to the Sacramento office. The special handling fee must be remitted by separate check for each submittal and will be retained whether the document is filed or rejected. The preclearance and/or expedited filing of a document within a guaranteed time frame can be requested for an additional fee (in lieu of the special handling fee). Please refer to the Secretary of State's website at http://www.sos.ca.gov/business/precexp.htm for detailed information regarding preclearance and expedited filing services. The special handling fee or preclearance and expedited filing services are not applicable to documents submitted by mail. Check(s) should be made payable to the Secretary of State.

COPIES: The Secretary of State will certify two copies of the filed document(s) without charge, provided that the copies are submitted to the Secretary of State with the document(s) to be filed. Any additional copies submitted will be certified upon request and payment of the $8.00 per copy certification fee.

Complete Form GP-1 as follows:

Item 1. Enter the name of the partnership.

Item 2. Enter the complete street address, including the zip code, of the chief executive office of the general partnership. Please do not enter a P.O. Box or abbreviate the name of the city.

Item 3. Enter the complete street address of an office in California if the chief executive office entered in Item 2 is not located in California. Please do not enter a P.O. Box or abbreviate the name of the city.

Items 4 & 5. The partnership must provide either of the following: (Item 4) the names and mailing addresses of all of the partners; OR (Item 5) the name and mailing address of an agent appointed and maintained by the partnership to provide the names and mailing addresses of all the partners pursuant to the provisions of Section 16303(b). Attach additional pages, if necessary.

Item 6. Enter the names of all partners authorized to execute instruments transferring real property held in the name of the partnership. Attach additional pages, if necessary.

Item 7. Attach any other information to be included in the Statement of Partnership Authority, provided that the information is not inconsistent with law.

Item 8. Form GP-1 must be executed by at least two partners. (Section 16105(c).) If additional signature space is necessary, the signatures may be made on an attachment to the document.

Any attachments to Form GP-1 are incorporated by reference. All attachments should be 8 ½" x 11", one-sided and legible.

defaulted on the note, the Foundation sued the partnership and both partners to recover on the note. Mitchell asserted in defense that the side agreement with Davis relieved him of personal liability. The trial court found Davis and Mitchell jointly liable. The appellate court reversed, excusing Mitchell from liability. The Foundation appealed.

Issue

Are both partners, Davis and Mitchell, jointly liable on the note?

Court's Reasoning

The court stated the following legal principle:

> *Every partner is an agent of the partnership for the purpose of its business, and the act of every partner, including the execution in the partnership name of any instrument, for apparently carrying on in the usual way the business of the partnership of which he is a member binds the partnership, unless the partner so acting has in fact no authority to act for the partnership in the particular matter, and the person with whom he is dealing has knowledge of the fact that he has no such authority.*

The court stated that if a promissory note is executed in the name of the partnership, the partnership is bound, unless a contradictory agreement between the partners is known to the parties with whom they are dealing. The trial court found that the Foundation had no knowledge of the agreement between Davis and Mitchell regarding Mitchell's liability for the note.

> The partner of my partner is not my partner.
>
> Legal maxim

Decision

The Supreme Court of Ohio held that both partners were jointly liable on the note. The supreme court reversed the decision of the appellate court.

Case Questions

1. **Critical Legal Thinking** What is joint liability? Should one general partner be liable to pay a judgment against the partnership?
2. **Business Ethics** Should Davis and Mitchell have notified the Foundation of their side agreement?
3. **Contemporary Business** Is it financially dangerous to be a partner in a general partnership? Explain.

Under the UPA, partners are **jointly liable** for the contracts and debts of the partnership [UPA Section 15(b)]. This means that a third party who sues to recover on a partnership contract or debt must name all the partners in the lawsuit. If such a lawsuit is successful, the plaintiff can collect the entire amount of the judgment against any or all of the partners. If the third party's suit does not name all the partners, the judgment cannot be collected against any of the partners or the partnership assets. Similarly, releasing any partner from the lawsuit releases them all. A partner who is made to pay more than their proportionate share of contract liability may seek indemnification from the partnership and from those partners who have not paid their share of the loss.

Liability of Incoming Partners

A new partner who is admitted to a partnership is liable for the existing debts and obligations (antecedent debts) of the partnership only to the extent of their capital contribution. The incoming partner is personally liable for debts and obligations incurred by the partnership after becoming a partner.

Example: Bubble.com is a general partnership with four partners. On May 1, Helen is admitted as a new general partner by investing a $100,000 capital contribution. As of May 1, Bubble.com owes $800,000 of preexisting debt. After Helen becomes a partner, the general partnership borrows $1 million of new debt. If the general partnership goes bankrupt and out of business still owing both debts, Helen's capital contribution of $100,000 will go toward paying the $800,000 of existing debt owed by the partnership when she joined the partnership, but she is not personally liable for this debt. However, Helen is personally liable for the $1 million of unpaid debt that the partnership borrowed after she became a partner.

INTERNATIONAL LAW

Partnerships Outside the United States

The English forms of business organizations are essentially the same as those in the United States. Partnership law, in particular, is virtually identical. Thus, in both countries (and in countries following the English model), a partnership is an association of two or more persons carrying on a business with the intent to make a profit.

In the civil law countries, including France and Germany, every form of business organization, including a partnership, is a "company" (*société* in French, *Gesellschaft* in German). A French partnership, because it is a company, is considered as having separate legal or juridical personality independent from its partners and thus can own property or sue or be sued in its own name. In Germany, by comparison, a partnership does not have a separate juridical personality. Therefore, even though a German partnership is a company, the partners own the property, and the partners must sue or be sued.

Although partnerships are categorized as companies in both France and Germany, they remain associations of persons who have full individual liability for the actions of their company. Similarly, because they are associations, they must have two or more partners.

A specialized form of partnership, the limited partnership, is recognized in the civil law countries. At least one partner must be a general partner (with personal unlimited liability) and one must be a limited partner. In both France and Germany, persons can be either general or limited partners, but they cannot be both. In France, limited partners can participate in the internal administration of the partnership. In Germany, they can participate in internal administration and be given broad powers to deal with third parties on behalf of the partnership.

Germany recognizes another type of partnership, known as the silent partnership. This is a secret relationship between the partners that is unknown to third parties. The active partner conducts the business in their name alone, never mentioning the silent partner. So long as the silent partner's participation is not disclosed, the silent partner's risk is limited to the amount the partner invested.

DISSOLUTION OF A GENERAL PARTNERSHIP

The duration of a partnership can be a fixed term (e.g., five years) or until a particular undertaking is accomplished (e.g., until a real estate development is completed), or it can be an unspecified term. A partnership with a fixed duration is called a **partnership for a term**. A partnership with no fixed duration is called a **partnership at will**.

partnership for a term
A partnership created for a fixed duration.

partnership at will
A partnership created with no fixed duration.

The **dissolution** of a partnership is "the change in the relation of the partners caused by any partner ceasing to be associated in the carrying on of the business" [UPA Section 29]. A partnership that is formed for a specific time (e.g., five years) or purpose (e.g., the completion of a real estate development) dissolves automatically upon the expiration of the time or the accomplishment of the objective. Any partner of a partnership at will (i.e., one without a stated time or purpose) may rightfully withdraw and dissolve the partnership at any time.

dissolution
The change in the relation of the partners caused by any partner ceasing to be associated in the carrying on of the business [UPA Section 29].

Unless a partnership is continued, the **winding up** of the partnership follows its dissolution. The process of winding up consists of the liquidation (sale) of partnership assets and the distribution of the proceeds to satisfy claims against the partnership. The surviving partners have the right to wind up the partnership. If surviving partners perform the winding up, they are entitled to reasonable compensation for their services [UPA Section 18(f)].

winding up
The process of liquidating a partnership's assets and distributing the proceeds to satisfy claims against the partnership.

Wrongful Dissolution

A partner has the *power* to withdraw and dissolve the partnership at any time, whether it is a partnership at will or a partnership for a term. A partner who withdraws from a partnership at will has the *right* to do so and is therefore not liable for dissolving the partnership. A partner who withdraws from a partnership for a term prior to the expiration of the term does not have the right to dissolve the partnership. The partner's action causes a **wrongful dissolution** of the partnership. The partner is liable for damages caused by the wrongful dissolution of the partnership.

wrongful dissolution
A situation in which a partner withdraws from a partnership without having the right to do so at that time.

Notice of Dissolution

The dissolution of a partnership terminates the partners' actual authority to enter into contracts or otherwise act on behalf of the partnership. **Notice of dissolution** must be given to certain third parties. The degree of notice depends on the relationship of the third party with the partnership [UPA Section 35]:

notice of dissolution
The dissolution of a partnership terminates the partners' actual authority to enter into contracts or otherwise act on behalf of the partnership. A notice of dissolution must be given to certain third parties.

1. Third parties who have actually dealt with the partnership must be given **actual notice** (verbal or written) of dissolution or have acquired knowledge of the dissolution from another source.
2. Third parties who have not dealt with the partnership but have knowledge of it must be given either actual or constructive notice of dissolution. **Constructive notice** consists of publishing a notice of dissolution in a newspaper of general circulation serving the area where the business of the partnership was regularly conducted.
3. Third parties who have not dealt with the partnership and do not have knowledge of it do not have to be given notice.

actual notice
Notice given directly to, or received personally by, a party.

constructive notice
Usually written notice to a third party that is put into general circulation, such as in a newspaper.

If proper notice is not given to a required third party after the dissolution of a partnership, and a partner enters into a contract with the third party, liability may be imposed on the previous partners on the grounds of apparent authority.

Distribution of Assets

After partnership assets have been liquidated and reduced to cash, the proceeds are **distributed** to satisfy claims against the partnership. The debts are satisfied in the following order [UPA Section 40(b)]:

1. Creditors (except partners who are creditors)
2. Creditor-partners
3. Capital contributions
4. Profits

The partners can agree to change the priority of distributions among themselves. If the partnership cannot satisfy its creditors' claims, the partners are personally liable for the partnership's debts and obligations [UPA Sections 40(d), 40(f)]. After the proceeds are distributed, the partnership automatically terminates. Termination ends the legal existence of the partnership [UPA Section 30].

Continuation of a General Partnership After Dissolution

The surviving, or remaining, partners have the right to continue a partnership after its dissolution. It is good practice for the partners of a partnership to enter into a *continuation agreement* that expressly sets forth the events that allow for **continuation of the general partnership**, the amount to be paid outgoing partners, and other details.

continuation of a general partnership
Occurs when surviving or remaining partners exercise their right to continue the partnership after dissolution.

When a partnership is continued, the old partnership is dissolved, and a new partnership is created. The new partnership is composed of the remaining partners and any new partners admitted to the partnership. The creditors of the old partnership become creditors of the new partnership and have equal status with the creditors of the new partnership [UPA Section 41].

Liability of Outgoing Partners

The dissolution of a partnership does not of itself discharge the liability of outgoing partners for existing partnership debts and obligations. If a partnership is dissolved, each partner is personally liable for debts and obligations of the partnership that exist at the time of dissolution.

If a partnership is dissolved because a partner leaves the partnership, and the partnership is continued by the remaining partners, the outgoing partner is personally liable for the debts and obligations of the partnership at the time of dissolution. The outgoing partner is not liable for any new debts and obligations incurred by the partnership after the dissolution, as long as proper notification of their withdrawal from the partnership has been given to the creditor.

CONTEMPORARY Environment

RIGHT OF SURVIVORSHIP

A partner is a co-owner with the other partners of the specific partnership property as a **tenant in partnership** [UPA Section 25(1)]. This is a special legal status that exists only in a partnership. Upon the death of a partner, the deceased partner's right in specific partnership property vests in the remaining partner or partners; it does not pass to the deceased partner's heirs or next of

tenant in partnership
A special legal status that exists only in a partnership. Upon the death of a partner, the deceased partner's right in specific partnership property vests in the remaining partner or partners; it does not pass to the deceased partner's heirs or next of kin.

(continued)

right of survivorship
A joint tenant's right to succeed to the whole estate upon the death of the other joint tenant.

kin. This is called the **right of survivorship**. Upon the death of the last surviving partner, the rights in specific partnership property vest in the deceased partner's legal representative [UPA Section 25(2)(C)]. The *value* of the deceased partner's interest in the partnership passes to that partner's beneficiaries or heirs upon that partner's death, however.

Example: Amy, Eric, Kristi, Abby, and Jake form a general partnership to operate a new restaurant. After their first restaurant is successful, they expand until the partnership owns one hundred restaurants. At that time, Amy dies. None of the partnership assets transfer to Amy's heirs; for example, they do not get twenty of the restaurants. Instead, under the right of survivorship, they inherit Amy's *ownership interest*, and her heirs now have the right to receive Amy's one-fifth of the partnership's profits each year.

Concept Review

General Partnerships

Definition	An association of two or more persons to carry on as co-owners of a business for profit [UPA Section 6(1)]. Also known as an "ordinary partnership."
Formation	An agreement to form a partnership may be oral, written, or implied from the conduct of the parties. It may even be created inadvertently. No formalities are necessary in most states.
Management	All general partners may manage. Partners may also elect a manager.
Liability	Under the UPA, partners are *jointly and severally liable* for torts and breaches of trust; and *jointly liable* for contracts and debts of the partnership.
Taxation	Partnerships do not pay federal income taxes. Instead, the income and losses of the partnership flow onto and have to be reported on the individual partners' personal income tax returns.
Termination	The termination—or *dissolution*—of a partnership can occur automatically where a partnership is created for a specific time or accomplishment of an objective; or, if it is a "partnership at will," any partner can withdraw and dissolve the partnership at any time.

PARALEGAL PRACTICE TOOL

PARTNERSHIP FORMATION CHECKLIST

1. Select a Name and an Assumed Name, if desired.
2. Check with the secretary of state for the availability of the Assumed Name(s) and draft, execute, and file a Certificate of Assumed Name.
3. Determine the purpose(s) for which the partnership is to be formed (if other than general purposes of a partnership).
4. Determine the number and identity of partners.
5. Determine the number and identity of any desired managers.
6. Determine the desired Capital Contributions.
7. Determine a fiscal year.
8. Determine any restrictions on the transfer of a partnership interest.

9. Draft and execute a partnership agreement.
10. Draft and execute any desired employment contracts.
11. Determine whether qualification in other states is desired.
12. Secure all state and local licenses required to operate the business and secure any necessary insurance coverage.
13. Draft, execute, and file Form SS-4 filed with the IRS for employer's identification number if the partnership will have employees.
14. Place the name of the business or trade name on all partnership material (e.g., letterhead, invoices, business cards, signs, contracts, etc.).

CHAPTER REVIEW

GENERAL PARTNERSHIP, p. 74

General Partnership

1. ***General partnership.*** A general partnership is an association of two or more persons to carry on as co-owners of a business for profit [UPA § 6(1)].
2. ***Uniform Partnership Act (UPA).*** This model act codifies partnership law. Most states have adopted all or part of the UPA.
3. ***Partnership name.*** A general partnership can operate under the names of any one or more of the partners or under a fictitious business name.
4. ***Formation of a General Partnership.*** A business must meet four criteria to qualify as a partnership under the UPA [UPA Section 6(1)]. It must be (1) an association of two or more persons (2) carrying on a business (3) as co-owners (4) for profit.
5. ***The Partnership Agreement*** A partnership agreement establishes a general partnership. It sets forth the terms of the partnership.
6. ***Taxation of partnerships.*** Partnerships do not pay federal income taxes. The income and losses of a partnership flow onto individual partners' federal income tax returns.

Rights of General Partners

1. ***Right to Participate in management*** In the absence of an agreement to the contrary, each partner has one vote, regardless of the proportional size of that partner's capital contribution or share in the partnership's profits.
2. ***Right to Share in profits*** Unless otherwise agreed, the UPA mandates that a partner has the right to an equal share in the partnership's profits and losses [UPA Section 18(a)]. The right to share in the profits of the partnership is considered to be the right to share in the earnings from the investment of capital.
3. ***Right to Compensation and reimbursement*** Partners sometimes incur personal travel, business, and other expenses on behalf of the partnership. A partner is entitled to **indemnification** (i.e., reimbursement) for such expenditures if they are reasonably incurred in the ordinary and proper conduct of the business.
4. ***Right to return of loans and capital*** A partner who makes a loan to the partnership becomes a creditor of the partnership. The partner is entitled to repayment of the loan, but this right is subordinated to the claims of creditors who are not partners. Upon termination of a partnership, the partners are entitled to have their capital contributions returned to them. However, this right is subordinated to the rights of creditors, who must be paid their claims first.
5. ***Right to information*** Each partner has the right to demand true and full information from any other partner of all things affecting the partnership.

Duties of General Partners

1. ***Duty of loyalty.***
2. ***Partners are in a fiduciary relationship with one another.*** As such, they owe each other a duty of loyalty. Some basic forms of breach of loyalty involve: self-dealing, usurping a partnership opportunity, competing with the partnership, making secret profits from partnership business, breach of confidentiality and misuse of property. A partner who breaches the duty of loyalty must disgorge any profits made from the breach to the partnership. In addition, the partner is liable for any damages caused by the breach.
3. ***Duty of Care*** A partner must use reasonable care and skill in transacting partnership business. The duty of care calls for the partners to use the same level of care and skill that a reasonable business manager in the same position would use in the same circumstances. Breach of the duty of care is negligence.
4. ***Duty to Inform*** Partners owe a duty to inform their co-partners of all information they possess that is relevant to the affairs of the partnership
5. ***Duty of obedience*** The duty of obedience requires partners to adhere to the provisions of the partnership agreement and the decisions of the partnership. A partner who breaches this duty is liable to the partnership for any damages caused by the breach.

> The merchant has no country.
> Thomas Jefferson

Liability of General Partners

Partners of a general partnership have personal liability for the contracts and torts of the partnership. A new partner who is admitted to the partnership is liable for the existing debts and obligations (*antecedent debts*) of the partnership only to the extent of their capital contribution. The new partner is personally liable for debts and obligations incurred by the partnership after becoming a partner.

Dissolution of Partnerships

The dissolution of a partnership is a change in the relationship of the partners caused by any partner ceasing to be associated in the carrying on of the business [UPA § 29].

Wrongful Dissolution

Wrongful dissolution occurs when a partner withdraws from a partnership without having the *right* to do so at the time. The partner is liable for damages caused by the wrongful dissolution of the partnership.

Notice of Dissolution

1. ***Notice of dissolution to partners.*** Notice of dissolution must be given to all partners. If a partner who has not received notice of dissolution enters into a contract on behalf of the partnership in the course of partnership business, the contract is binding on all the partners.
2. ***Notice of dissolution to third parties.*** The following notice must be given to third parties when a partnership has been dissolved other than by operation of law:
   a. ***Actual notice.*** Actual notice must be given to third parties who have actually dealt with the partnership.
   b. ***Constructive notice.*** Constructive notice must be given to third parties who have not dealt with the partnership but have knowledge of it. Constructive notice is given by publishing a notice of dissolution in a

newspaper of general circulation serving the area where the business of the partnership is conducted.

c. ***No notice.*** Parties who have not dealt with the partnership and do not have knowledge of it do not have to be given notice.

Continuation of a Partnership After Dissolution

The surviving or remaining partners have the right to continue a partnership after dissolution. When a partnership is continued, the old partnership is dissolved and a new partnership is created.

1. ***Continuation agreement.*** This document expressly sets forth the events that allow for continuation of the partnership, the amount to be paid to outgoing partners, and other details.
2. ***Creditors' status.*** The creditors of the old partnership become creditors of the new partnership and have equal status with the creditors of the new partnership.
3. ***Liability of outgoing partners.*** An outgoing partner is liable for existing partnership debts unless the creditor, other partners, and the outgoing partner enter into an agreement that expressly relieves the outgoing partner of liability to the creditor.

TEST REVIEW TERMS AND CONCEPTS

CASE SCENARIO REVISITED

Remember the case scenario at the beginning of the chapter regarding the real estate partnership formed between Smithson and White? Because the agreement to purchase the Monsanto property for a subdivision development was not in writing, was a partnership formed? What recourse does Smithson have against White? Who wins? *Smithson v. White*, No. 87-380-II, 1988 Tenn. LEXIS 221, at *1 (Ct. App. May 4, 1988).

PORTFOLIO EXERCISE

For the business you created at the beginning of the semester, complete the Statement of Partnership Authority (see Exhibit 4.4) by going to the following website: **http://www.sos.ca.gov/business/gp/forms/gp-1.pdf**.

WORKING THE WEB INTERNET EXERCISES

Activities

1. Review the materials at **http://smallbiz.biz.findlaw.com/planning/index.html/planning/wa**. Compare this information with the text discussion of partnerships. Can you see why lawyers generally advise business clients *not* to do business in a partnership form?
2. A large, rambling, and self-consciously offbeat site is the Lectric Law Library, **www.lectlaw.com/bus.html**. There you will find a business law section with numerous items of interest, including an overview of (business) partnership law, with links to key primary and secondary sources.

CRITICAL LEGAL THINKING CASES

Case 4.1 General Partnership Richard Filip owned Trans Texas Properties (Trans Tex). Tracy Peoples was an employee of the company. In order to obtain credit to advertise in the *Austin American–Statesman* newspaper, which was owned by Cox Enterprises, Inc., Peoples completed a credit application that listed Jack Elliot as a partner in Trans Texas. Evidence showed that Elliot did not own an interest in Trans Texas and did not consent to or authorize Peoples to make this representation to Cox. Cox made no effort to verify the accuracy of the representation and extended credit to Trans Texas. When Trans Texas defaulted on payments owed Cox, Cox sued both Filip and Elliot to recover the debt. Is Elliot liable? *Cox Enter., Inc v. Filip*, 538 S.W.2d 836 (Tex. Ct. App. 1976).

Case 4.2 Tort Liability Charles Fial and Roger J. Steeby entered into a partnership called Audit Consultants to perform auditing services. Pursuant to the agreement, they shared equally the equity, income, and profits of the partnership. Originally, they performed the auditing services themselves, but as business increased, they engaged independent contractors to do some of the audit work. Fial's activities generated approximately 80 percent of the partnership's revenues. Unhappy with their agreement to divide the profits equally, Fial wrote a letter to Steeby seven years later, dissolving the partnership.

Fial asserted that the clients should be assigned based on who brought them into the business. Fial formed a new business called Audit Consultants of Colorado, Inc. He then terminated the original partnership's contracts with many clients and put them under contract with his new firm. Fial also terminated the partnership's contracts with the independent-contractor auditors and signed many of these auditors with his new firm. The partnership terminated about eleven months after Fial wrote the letter to Steeby. Steeby brought an action against Fial, alleging breach of fiduciary duty and seeking a final accounting. Who wins? *Steeby v. Fial*, 765 P.2d 1081 (Colo. Ct. App. 1988).

Case 4.3 Fiduciary Duty Edgar and Selwyn Husted, attorneys, formed Husted and Husted, a law partnership. Herman McCloud, who was the executor of his mother's estate, hired them as attorneys for the estate. When taxes were due on the estate, Edgar told McCloud to make a check for $18,000 payable to the Husted and Husted Trust Account and that he would pay the Internal Revenue Service (IRS) from this account. There was no Husted and Husted Trust Account. Instead, Edgar deposited the check into his own personal account and converted the funds to his own personal use. When Edgar's misconduct was uncovered, McCloud sued the law firm for conversion of estate funds. Is the partnership liable for Edgar's actions? *Husted v. McCloud*, 436 N.E.2d 341 (Ind. Ct. App. 1982).

Case 4.4 Tort Liability Thomas McGrath was a partner in the law firm Tarbenson, Thatcher, McGrath, Treadwell & Schoonmaker. One day, at approximately 4:30 P.M., McGrath went to a restaurant-cocktail establishment in Kirkland, Washington. From that time until about 1:00 A.M., he imbibed considerable alcohol while socializing and discussing personal and firm-related business. After 11:00 P.M., McGrath did not discuss firm business but continued to socialize and drink until approximately 1:45 A.M., when he and Fredrick Hayes, another bar patron, exchanged words. Shortly thereafter, the two encountered each other outside, and after another exchange, McGrath shot Hayes. Hayes sued McGrath and the law firm for damages. Who is liable? *Hayes v. Tarbenson, et al.*, 749 P.2d 178 (Wash. Ct. App. 1988).

Case 4.5 Notice of Dissolution Leonard Sumter, Sr., entered into a partnership agreement with his son, Michael T. Sumter, to conduct a plumbing business in Shreveport, Louisiana, under the name Sumter Plumbing Company. The father, on behalf of the partnership, executed a credit application with Thermal

Supply of Louisiana, Inc., for an open account to purchase supplies on credit. For the next four years, the Sumters purchased plumbing supplies from Thermal on credit and paid their bills without fail. Both partners and one employee signed for supplies at Thermal. In May 1980, the partnership was dissolved, and all outstanding debts to Thermal were paid in full. The Sumters did not, however, notify Thermal that the partnership had been dissolved.

A year later, the son decided to reenter the plumbing business. He used the name previously used by the former partnership, listed the same post office address for billing purposes, and hired the employee of the former partnership who signed for supplies at Thermal. The father decided not to become involved in this venture. The son began purchasing supplies on credit from Thermal on the open credit account of the former partnership. Thermal was not informed that the son was opening a new business. When the son defaulted on payments to Thermal, it sued the original partnership to recover the debt. Is the father liable for these debts? *Thermal Supply of La., Inc. v. Sumter*, 452 So. 2d 312 (La. Ct. App. 1984).

Case 4.6 Liability of General Partners Pat McGowan, Val Somers, and Brent Robertson were general partners of Vermont Place, a limited partnership formed for the purpose of constructing duplexes on an undeveloped tract of land in Fort Smith, Arkansas. The general partners appointed McGowan and his company, Advance Development Corporation, to develop the project, including contracting with materials people, mechanics, and other suppliers. None of the limited partners took part in the management or control of the partnership.

Eight months later, Somers and Robertson discovered that McGowan had not been paying the suppliers. They removed McGowan from the partnership and took over the project. The suppliers sued the partnership to recover the money owed them. The partnership assets were not sufficient to pay all their claims. Who is liable to the suppliers? *National Lumber Co. v. Advance Dev. Corp.*, 732 S.W.2d 840 (Ark. 1987).

BUSINESS ETHICS CASES

Case 4.7 Business Ethics Harriet Hankin, Samuel Hankin, Moe Henry Hankin, Perch P. Hankin, and Pauline Hankin, and their spouses, for many years operated a family partnership composed of vast real estate holdings. Some of the properties included restaurants, industrial buildings, shopping centers, golf courses, a motel chain, and hundreds of acres of developable ground, estimated to be worth $72 million. Because of family disagreement and discontent, the Hankin family agreed to dissolve the partnership. When they could not agree on how to liquidate the partnership assets, Harriet and Samuel (collectively called Harriet) initiated an equity action.

Based on assurances from Moe and Perch that they would sell the partnership assets as quickly as possible and at the highest possible price, the court appointed them as liquidators of the partnership during the winding-up period. Based on similar assurances, the court again appointed them liquidators for the partnership. But two years later, only enough property had been sold to retire the debt of the partnership. Evidence showed that Moe and Perch had not aggressively marketed the remaining properties and that Moe wished to purchase some of the properties for himself at a substantial discount from their estimated value. Six years and three appeals to the superior court later, Harriet brought an action seeking the appointment of a receiver to liquidate the remaining partnership assets.

Did the winding-up partners breach their fiduciary duties? Should the court appoint a receiver to liquidate the remaining partnership assets? Did Moe Henry Hankin act ethically in this case? *Hankin v. Hankin*, 493 A.2d 675 (Pa. 1985).

Case 4.8 Business Ethics John Gilroy, an established commercial photographer in Kalamazoo, Michigan, had a small contractual clientele of schools for which he provided student portrait photographs. Robert Conway joined Gilroy's established business, and they formed a partnership called "Skylight Studios." Both partners solicited schools with success, and gross sales, which were $40,000, increased every year and amounted to over $200,000 six years later.

Conway notified Gilroy that the partnership was dissolved. Gilroy discovered that Conway had closed up the partnership's place of business and opened up his own business, had purchased equipment and supplies in preparation for opening his own business and charged them to the partnership, had taken with him the partnership's employees and most of its equipment, had personally taken over business of some customers by telling them the partnership was being dissolved, and had withdrawn partnership funds for personal use. Gilroy sued Conway for an accounting, alleging that Conway had converted partnership assets. Did Conway act ethically in this case? Who wins? *Gilroy v. Conway*, 391 N.W.2d 419 (Mich. Ct. App. 1986).

"There are a great many of us who will adhere to that ancient principle that we prefer to be governed by the power of laws, and not by the power of men."

—***Woodrow Wilson***

Speech, September 25, 1912

Limited Partnerships

CHAPTER 5

CASE SCENARIO

The law firm at which you work as a paralegal represents Virginia Partners, Ltd. (Virginia Partners), a limited partnership organized under the laws of Florida. Virginia Partners conducted business in Kentucky but failed to register as a foreign limited partnership, as required by Kentucky law. Robert Day was a bystander observing acid being injected into an abandoned oil well by Virginia Partners. Day was tortiously and severely injured when a polyvinyl chloride (PVC) valve failed, causing a hose to rupture from its fitting and spray nitric acid on Day.

CHAPTER OBJECTIVES

After studying this chapter, you should be able to:

1. Define *limited partnership* and distinguish it from a *limited liability partnership* and a *limited liability limited partnership*.
2. Describe the process of forming a limited partnership.
3. Distinguish between limited and general partners.
4. Identify and describe the liability of general and limited partners.
5. Describe the process of dissolution and winding up of a limited partnership.

It is the privilege of a trader in a free country, in all matters not contrary to law, to regulate his own mode of carrying it on according to his own discretion and choice.

Baron Alderson
Hilton v. Eckersly (1855)

INTRODUCTION TO LIMITED PARTNERSHIPS

Limited partnerships are statutory creations that have been used since the Middle Ages. They include both general (manager) and limited (investor) partners. Today, all states have enacted statutes that provide for the creation of limited partnerships. In most states, these partnerships are called *limited partnerships* or special partnerships. Limited partnerships are used for such business ventures as investing in real estate, drilling oil and gas wells, investing in movie productions, and the like. In most states, the formation, operation, and termination of limited partnerships are regulated by the *Revised Uniform Limited Partnership Act (RULPA)*. Some limited partnerships qualify as *master limited partnerships* that are traded publicly. In addition, many states now permit the formation of a special form of partnership called a *limited liability limited partnership*.

This chapter discusses the formation, operation, and dissolution of limited partnerships. Master limited partnerships, limited liability partnership, and limited liability limited partnerships are also reviewed.

PARALEGAL PERSPECTIVE

Kelly J. Eckel *is the owner of a small business as an independent (self-employed) paralegal. She received an associate in paralegal studies from the University of Toledo and a bachelor of science in business management from the University of Phoenix. Her areas of specialization are litigation and case management, estate planning, LLC formation, notary services, pleading and discovery drafting/tracking/analyzing, and analyzing/summarizing medical records and depositions. She has been working as a paralegal for eleven years.*

What have you learned in your professional career as it relates to limited partnerships as a business organization? In order to encourage legal entrepreneurship and small business development and ownership, it has become increasingly important to limit the personal liability; and thus, minimize the exposure and loss of personal assets by the partners and/or investors. A limited partnership can help companies do this.

What are the most important paralegal skills needed in your job? Organization, prioritization, attention to detail, data management, written/verbal communication skills, and case management skills are critical to paralegals performing paralegal duties effectively.

What is the academic background required for a paralegal entering your area of practice? As we move toward such a competitive market, I believe a successful paralegal would need at least an associate degree.

How is technology involved in your job? I work primarily in a virtual environment, so technology is essential and imperative to the functioning of my business. Scanning, e-mail, Internet research, and word processing/computer software are vital to my business.

What trends do you see in your area of practice that will likely affect your job in the future? I believe the job market for independent paralegals is increasing as attorneys attempt to optimize cost effectiveness and paralegal efficiency. As attorneys recognize the prices of employing a full- or part-time paralegal (health insurance, fringe benefits, vacation, sick time, etc.), they will hopefully start looking towards freelance paralegals for specialized projects and case management.

What do you feel is the biggest issue currently facing the paralegal profession? I believe that the increase and attempt of institutions to offer six- or eight-week programs to accredit a paralegal and obtain a paralegal degree is hurting the reputation of paralegals that are educated by an American Bar Association–approved program or accredited colleges and universities.

What words of advice do you have for a new paralegal entering your area of practice? I think the most important piece of advice I could give is to recognize the importance of networking and staying active in the local and national paralegal associations. Networking has provided me with the majority of my clients and I have formed most of my professional relationships through networking with attorneys and paralegals in my community.

INTERNATIONAL LAW

Limited Partnerships Outside the United States

The limited partnership form of business is recognized outside the United States. As in the United States, at least one partner must be a general partner, and at least one partner must be a limited partner. Limited partners have limited liability for the debts and obligations of the partnership. In France, limited partners can participate in the internal administration of the limited partnership. In Germany, they can participate in the internal administration as well as deal with third parties on behalf of the limited partnership.

Germany recognizes a type of partnership called a "silent partnership." This is a secret relationship between the partners that is unknown to third parties. The active partner conducts the business in their name alone, never mentioning the silent partner. So long as the silent partner's participation is not disclosed, the silent partner's risk is limited to the amount the partner has invested.

ETHICS SPOTLIGHT

LIMITED PARTNER LIABLE ON PERSONAL GUARANTEE

> *"Stover had every reason to know that his unqualified signature on the documents would bind his personal credit as that of the general partner."*
>
> *–Judge Shangler*

Many small businesses, including limited partnerships, attempt to borrow money from banks or obtain credit from suppliers. Often these lenders require owners of partnerships and other small businesses to personally guarantee that they will repay the loan if the partnership or business does not. Consider the following case.

Linnane Magnavox Home Entertainment Center was a limited partnership that was organized under the law of Kansas. Paul T. Linnane was the sole general partner, and Richard Gale Stover was the limited partner. Stover was the "silent partner" who provided capital for the limited partnership. Stover took no part in the day-to-day management or control of the limited partnership. The limited partnership wanted to enter into a contract with General Electric Credit Corporation (GE Credit) whereby GE Credit would provide financing to the limited partnership. GE Credit refused to grant the credit to the limited partnership unless Stover, the limited partner, signed as the guarantor of the credit. It was not until Stover personally signed the credit agreement as the guarantor that GE Credit extended credit to the limited partnership.

When the limited partnership defaulted on the payment of the debt and Paul Linnane, the general partner, was adjudicated bankrupt, GE Credit sued Stover to recover the debt. The court of appeal held that Stover, the limited partner, was liable to pay the debts of the limited partnership to GE Credit. The court stated:

> *The question of decision as whether, for the purpose of the extension of credit to Linnane Magnavox, Stover put his personal assets at stake and GE Credit was therefore induced to extend its credit to the partnership. The evidence before the trial court was that GE Credit would have not extended credit to Linnane Magnavox had not Stover signed the credit agreement. Stover had every reason to know that his unqualified signature on the documents would bind his personal credit as that of the general partner.*

The court of appeals held that Stover was liable on his personal guarantee to GE Credit. *General Electric Credit Corps v Stover,* 708 S.W. 2d 355 (Ct. App. Mo. 1986).

Law and Ethics Questions

1. What is a personal guarantee? Why do lenders and other creditors often require personal guarantees?
2. **Ethics** Was it ethical for Stover to try to get out from his personal guarantee?

Web Exercises

1. WEB: Search the web to find the complete opinion of this case.
2. WEB: Use www.google.com to find an article on a case in which a person has been found liable on a personal guarantee. Read it.
3. WEB: Use www.google.com to find a copy of a personal guarantee.

LIMITED PARTNERSHIP

limited partnership
A type of partnership that has two types of partners: (1) general partners and (2) limited partners.

general partners
Partners in a limited partnership who invest capital, manage the business, and are personally liable for partnership debts.

limited partners
Partners in a limited partnership who invest capital but do not participate in management and are not personally liable for partnership debts beyond their capital contributions.

A **limited partnership**, or **special partnership**, has two types of partners: (1) **general partners**, who invest capital, manage the business, and are personally liable for partnership debts, and (2) **limited partners**, who invest capital but do not participate in management and are not personally liable for partnership debts beyond their capital contributions (see Exhibit 5.1).

A limited partnership must have one or more general partners and one or more limited partners [RULPA Section 101(7)]. There are no upper limits on the number of general or limited partners allowed in a limited partnership. Any person—including natural persons, partnerships, limited partnerships, trusts, estates, associations, and corporations—may be a general or limited partner. A person may be both a general partner and a limited partner in the same limited partnership.

Exhibit 5.1 Limited Partnership

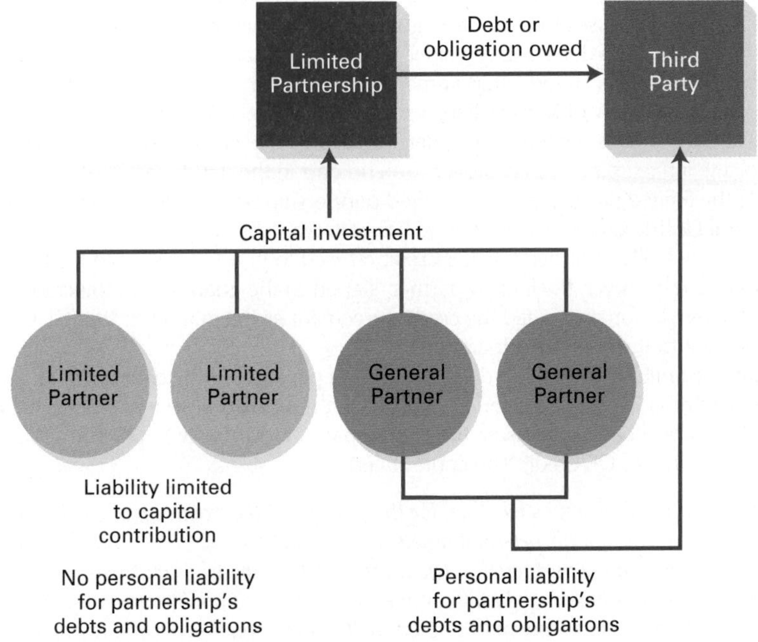

LANDMARK LAW

REVISED UNIFORM LIMITED PARTNERSHIP ACT

In 1916, the National Conference of Commissioners on Uniform State Laws, a group of lawyers, judges, and legal scholars, enacted the **Uniform Limited Partnership Act (ULPA)**. The ULPA contains a uniform set of provisions for the formation, operation, and dissolution of limited partnerships. Most states originally enacted this law.

In 1976, the National Conference of Commissioners on Uniform State Laws promulgated the **Revised Uniform Limited Partnership Act (RULPA)**, which provides a more modern, comprehensive law for the formation, operation, and dissolution of limited partnerships. This law supersedes the ULPA in the states that have adopted it. The RULPA provides the basic foundation for the discussion of limited partnership law in the following text. In 2001, certain **amendments** were made to the RULPA. The changes made by these amendments are noted in this chapter. (See Appendices B and C for more detail on these acts.)

The Revised Uniform Limited Partnership Act (RULPA) permits a corporation to be the sole general partner of a limited partnership. Where this is permissible, it affects the liability of the limited partnership. This is because the limited partners are liable only to the extent of their capital contributions, and the corporation acting as general partner is liable only to the extent of its assets.

Uniform Limited Partnership Act (ULPA)
A model law promulgated in 1916 for adoption by state legislatures to govern the relationship between the partners of a limited partnership.

Revised Uniform Limited Partnership Act (RULPA)
A 1976 revision of the ULPA that provides a more modern, comprehensive law for the formation, operation, and dissolution of limited partnerships.

Certificate of Limited Partnership

The creation of a limited partnership is formal and requires public disclosure. The entity must comply with the statutory requirements of the RULPA or other state statutes. Under the RULPA, two or more persons must execute and sign a **certificate of limited partnership** [RULPA Sections 201, 206]. The certificate must contain the following information:

certificate of limited partnership
A document that two or more persons must execute and sign that makes a limited partnership legal and binding.

- Name of the limited partnership
- General character of the business
- Address of the principal place of business and name and address of the agent to receive service of legal process
- Name and business address of each general and limited partner
- Latest date on which the limited partnership is to dissolve
- Amount of cash, property, or services (and description of property or services) contributed by each partner and any contributions of cash, property, or services promised to be made in the future
- Any other matters that the general partners determine to include

The certificate of limited partnership must be filed with the secretary of state of the appropriate state and, if required by state law, with the county recorder in the county or counties in which the limited partnership carries on business. The limited partnership is formed when the certificate of limited partnership is filed (see Exhibit 5.2).

Amendments to the Certificate of Limited Partnership

A limited partnership must keep its certificate of limited partnership current by filing necessary certificates of amendment at the same offices where the certificate of limited partnership is filed [RULPA Section 202(a)]. Such amendments

> It is the spirit and not the form of law that keeps justice alive.
> Earl Warren
> *The Law and the Future (1955)*

Exhibit 5.2 Certificate of Limited Partnership

Secretary of State
Limited Partnerships
1700 W. Washington Street, 7th Floor
Phoenix, Arizona 85007

Make Check Payable to:
Secretary of State
Fee: $10.00
Plus $3.00 per page
SUBMIT IN DUPLICATE
with a self-addressed, stamped envelope.

Secretary of State Use Only

Walk-in service: Phoenix: 1700 W. Washington, 1st Fl., Room 103
Tucson: 400 W. Congress, Ste. 252
Phone: (602) 542-6187 (800) 458-5842 (within Arizona)

All correspondence regarding this filing will be sent to the principal office identified below.

CERTIFICATE OF LIMITED PARTNERSHIP

A.R.S. § 29-308

Name of limited partnership (End the name with the words "Limited Partnership" or "L.P.")			
Arizona address of principal office (P.O. Box or C/O are unacceptable)	**City**	**State** Arizona	**Zip Code**
Name of agent for service of process		**Phone number (optional)**	
Arizona address of principal office (P.O. Box or C/O are unacceptable)	**City**	**State** Arizona	**Zip Code**
The name and business address of each general partner: (Attach additional sheets if necessary)			
Printed Name	**Signature**		
Address	**City**	**State**	**Zip Code**
Printed Name	**Signature**		
Address	**City**	**State**	**Zip Code**
The latest date on which the limited partnership is to dissolve, if any:	**Month/Day/Year**		

Any other matters: Please attach additional sheets

are filed to apprise creditors and others of current information regarding the limited partnership and its partners. A certificate of amendment must be filed within thirty days of the occurrence of the following events:

- A change in a partner's capital contribution
- The admission of a new partner
- The withdrawal of a partner
- The continuation of the business after a judicial decision dissolving the limited partnership after the withdrawal of the last general partner

Name of the Limited Partnership

The name of a limited partnership may not include the surname of a limited partner unless (1) it is also the surname of a general partner or (2) the business was carried on under that name before the admission of the limited partner [RULPA Section 102(2)]. A limited partner who knowingly permits his or her name to be used in violation of this provision becomes liable as a general partner to any creditors who extend credit to the partnership without actual knowledge of the limited partner's true status [RULPA Section 303(d)].

Other restrictions on the name of a limited partnership are that (1) the name cannot be the same as or deceptively similar to the names of corporations or other limited partnerships, (2) states can designate words that cannot be used in limited partnership names, and (3) the name must contain, without abbreviation, the words *limited partnership* [RULPA Section 102].

Capital Contributions

Under the RULPA, the capital contributions of general and limited partners may be in cash, property, services rendered, or promissory notes or other obligations to contribute cash or property or to perform services [RULPA Section 501]. A partner or creditor of a limited partnership may bring a lawsuit to enforce a partner's promise to make a contribution [RULPA Section 502(a)].

Defective Formation

Defective formation occurs when (1) a certificate of limited partnership is not properly filed, (2) there are defects in a certificate that is filed, or (3) some other statutory requirement for the creation of a limited partnership is not met. If there is a substantial defect in the creation of a limited partnership, persons who thought they were limited partners can find themselves liable as general partners.

defective formation
Occurs when (1) a certificate of limited partnership is not properly filed, (2) there are defects in a certificate that is filed, or (3) some other statutory requirement for the creation of a limited partnership is not met.

Partners who erroneously but in good faith believe they have become limited partners can escape liability as general partners by either (1) causing the appropriate certificate of limited partnership (or certificate of amendment) to be filed or (2) withdrawing from any future equity participation in the enterprise and causing a certificate showing this withdrawal to be filed. Nevertheless, the limited partner remains liable to any third party who transacts business with the enterprise before either certificate is filed if the third person believed in good faith that the partner was a general partner at the time of the transaction [RULPA Section 304].

Limited Partnership Agreement

Although not required by law, the partners of a limited partnership often draft and execute a **limited partnership agreement** (also called the **articles of limited partnership**) that sets forth the rights and duties of the general and limited partners; the terms and conditions regarding the operations, termination, and dissolution of the partnership; and so on. Where there is no such agreement, the certificate of limited partnership serves as the articles of limited partnership.

limited partnership agreement
A document that sets forth the rights and duties of general and limited partners; the terms and conditions regarding the operation, termination, and dissolution of a partnership; and so on.

It is good practice to establish voting rights in a limited partnership agreement or certificate of limited partnership. The limited partnership agreement can provide which transactions must be approved by which partners (i.e., general, limited, or both). General and limited partners may be given unequal voting rights.

> Let every nation know, whether it wishes us well or ill, that we shall pay any price, bear any burden, meet any hardship, support any friend, oppose any foe to assure the survival and the success of liberty.
>
> John F. Kennedy
> *Inaugural speech, January 20, 1961*

Share of Profits and Losses

A limited partnership agreement may specify how profits and losses from the limited partnership are to be allocated among the general and limited partners. If there is no such agreement, the RULPA provides that profits and losses from a limited partnership are shared on the basis of the value of each partner's capital contribution [RULPA Section 503].

Example: There are four general partners, each of whom contributes $50,000 in capital to the limited partnership, and four limited partners, each of whom contributes $200,000 capital. The total amount of contributed capital is $1 million. The limited partnership agreement does not stipulate how profits and losses are to be allocated. Assume that the limited partnership makes $3 million in profits. Under the RULPA, each general partner would receive $150,000 profit, and each limited partner would receive $600,000 profit.

Example: In the previous example, suppose that instead of making a profit, the limited partnership loses $3 million. The loss would be distributed based on the value of each partner's capital contribution. Each general partner would receive $150,000 loss and each limited partner would receive $600,000 loss.

Right to Information

Upon reasonable demand, each limited partner has the right to obtain from the general partners true and full information regarding the state of the business, the financial condition of the limited partnership, and so on [RULPA Section 305]. In addition, the limited partnership must keep the following records at its principal office:

- A copy of the certificate of limited partnership and all amendments thereto
- A list of the full name and business address of each partner
- Copies of effective written limited partnership agreements
- Copies of federal, state, and local income tax returns
- Copies of financial statements of the limited partnership for the three most recent years

Admission of a New Partner

Once a limited partnership has been formed, a new limited partner can be added only upon the written consent of all partners, unless the limited partnership agreement provides otherwise. New general partners can be admitted only with the specific written consent of each partner [RULPA Section 401]. A limited partnership agreement cannot waive the right of partners to approve the admission of new general partners. The admission is effective when an amendment of the certificate of limited partnership reflecting that fact is filed [RULPA Section 301].

Foreign Limited Partnership

domestic limited partnership
A limited partnership in the state in which it was formed.

foreign limited partnership
A limited partnership in all other states besides the one in which it was formed.

A limited partnership is a **domestic limited partnership** in the state in which it is organized. It is a **foreign limited partnership** in all other states. Under the RULPA, the law of the state in which the entity is organized governs its organization, its internal affairs, and the liability of its limited partners [RULPA Section 901].

Before transacting business in a foreign state, a foreign limited partnership must file an application for registration with that state's secretary of state. If the application conforms with that state's law, a **certificate of registration** permitting the foreign limited partnership to transact business will be issued [RULPA Section 902].

certificate of registration
A document that permits a foreign limited partnership to transact business in a state.

Once registered, a foreign limited partnership may use the courts of the foreign state to enforce its contracts and other rights. Failure to register neither impairs the validity of any act or contract of the unregistered foreign limited partnership nor prevents it from defending itself in any proceeding in the courts of the foreign state. However, unregistered foreign limited partnerships may not initiate litigation in the foreign jurisdiction. The limited partner's status is not affected by whether the limited partnership is registered or unregistered. For example, if a foreign limited partnership has failed to register in a foreign state and causes an injury to someone in that state, the limited partners are not personally liable [RULPA Section 907].

LIABILITY OF GENERAL AND LIMITED PARTNERS

The general partners of a limited partnership have **unlimited liability** for the debts and obligations of the limited partnerships. Thus, general partners have unlimited **personal liability** for the debts and obligations of the limited partnership. This liability extends to debts that cannot be satisfied with the existing capital of the limited partnership.

unlimited liability
General partners have unlimited personal liability for the debts and obligations of the limited partnership.

Generally, limited partners have **limited liability** for the debts and obligations of the limited partnership. Limited partners are liable only for the debts and obligations of the limited partnership up to their capital contributions, and they are not personally liable for the debts and obligations of the limited partnership.

CONTEMPORARY Environment

MASTER LIMITED PARTNERSHIP

One of the major drawbacks for investors who are limited partners in a limited partnership is that their investment usually is not liquid because there is no readily available market for buying and selling limited partnership interests. Certain limited partnerships can choose to be **master limited partnerships (MLPs)**. An MLP is a limited partnership whose limited partnership interests are traded on organized securities exchanges such as the New York Stock Exchange. An investment in an MLP is liquid because it can be sold on the stock exchange. Shares of ownership in MLPs are referred to as **units**.

master limited partnership (MLP)
A form of limited partnership that is listed on stock exchanges and is publicly traded to provide liquidity.

unit
A single thing of any kind; a fixed quantity.

By law, MLPs may engage in only certain businesses, such as petroleum and natural gas extraction, businesses involving pipelines for the transportation of natural resources, financial services, and some real estate enterprises. In most MLPs, a corporation remains the general partner of the MLP, and public investors are the limited partners. MLPs pay their investors quarterly required distributions (QRDs), similar to interest payments on bonds, at an amount stated in the investment contract.

There are tax benefits to owning a limited partnership interest in an MLP rather than owning corporate stock. MLPs pay no income tax; partnership income, and losses flow directly onto the individual partners' income tax returns. Profits and other distributions of MLPs also avoid the double taxation of corporate dividends. In addition, limited partners may deduct their prorated share of the MLP's depreciation on their personal tax returns. Thus, MLPs combine the liquidity of publicly traded securities and the tax benefits of limited partnerships.

> Four things belong to a judge: to hear courteously, to answer wisely, to consider soberly, and to decide impartially.
> Socrates

Example: Betty and Kate are the general partners of a limited partnership called Real Estate Development, Ltd. Kelly and Paula are limited partners of the limited partnership and have each invested $100,000 in the limited partnership. Real Estate Development, Ltd., borrows $2 million from City Bank. After six months, the limited partnership goes bankrupt, still owing City Bank $2 million. The limited partnership has spent all of its capital and is broke. In this case, the two limited partners each lose their $100,000 capital investment but are not personally liable for the $2 million debt owed by the limited partnership to City Bank. The two general partners, however, are each personally liable to City Bank for the limited partnership's unpaid $2 million loan to City Bank.

Participation in Management

Under partnership law, general partners have the right to manage the affairs of the limited partnership. On the other hand, as a trade-off for limited liability, limited partners give up their right to participate in the control and management of the limited partnership. This means, in part, that limited partners have no right to bind the partnership to contracts or other obligations.

Under the RULPA, a limited partner is liable as a general partner if the limited partner's participation in the control of the business is substantially the same as that of a general partner, but the limited partner is liable only to persons who reasonably believed the limited partner to be a general partner [RULPA Section 303(a)].

Permissible Activities of Limited Partners

The RULPA clarifies the types of activities that a limited partner may engage in without losing his or her limited liability. These activities include [RULPA Sections 303(b), 303(c)]:

- Being an agent, an employee, or a contractor of the limited partnership
- Being a consultant or an advisor to a general partner regarding the limited partnership
- Acting as a surety for the limited partnership
- Approving or disapproving an amendment to the limited partnership agreement
- Voting on the following partnership matters:
  a. The dissolution and winding up of the limited partnership
  b. The sale, transfer, exchange, lease, or mortgage of substantially all of the assets of the limited partnership
  c. The incurrence of indebtedness by the limited partnership other than in the ordinary course of business
  d. A change in the nature of the business of the limited partnership
  e. The removal of a general partner

limited liability of limited partners
The limited liability of limited partners of a limited partnership only up to their capital contributions to the limited partnership; limited partners are not personally liable for the debts and obligations of the limited partnership.

Example: John and Darla are investor limited partners in a limited partnership. At some time after they become limited partners, John and Darla think that the general partners are not doing a very good job at managing the affairs of the limited partnership, so they participate in the management of the limited partnership. While doing so, a bank loans $1 million to the limited partnership, believing that John and Darla are general partners because of their involvement in the management of the limited partnership. If the limited partnership defaults on the $1 million loan owed to the bank, John and Darla will be treated as general partners and will be held personally liable for the loan along with the general partners of the limited partnership.

personal liability of general partners
The unlimited personal liability of general partners of a limited partnership for the debts and obligations of the general partnership.

Example: Assume that in the previous example the general partners of the limited partnership vote to make John and Darla, limited partners, president and vice president of the limited partnership. John and Darla therefore have two distinct relationships with the limited partnership: first as investor limited partners and second as managers (president and vice president) of the limited partnership. In this case, John and Darla can lawfully participate in the management of the limited partnership without losing the limited liability shield granted by their limited partner status.

Liability on a Personal Guarantee

On some occasions, when limited partnerships apply for an extension of credit from a bank, a supplier, or another creditor, the creditor will not make the loan based on the limited partnership's credit history or ability to repay the credit. The creditor may require a limited partner to personally guarantee the repayment of the loan in order to extend credit to the limited partnership. If a limited partner personally guarantees a loan made by a creditor to the limited partnership and the limited partnership defaults on the loan, the creditor may enforce the **personal guarantee** and recover payment from the limited partner who personally guaranteed the repayment of the loan.

personal guarantee
Where a creditor may require a partner to personally guarantee the repayment of the loan in order to extend credit.

LIMITED LIABILITY PARTNERSHIP (LLP)

Many states have enacted legislation to permit the creation of **limited liability partnerships (LLPs)**. In an LLP, there does not have to be a general partner who is personally liable for the debts and obligations of the partnership. Instead, *all* partners are limited partners who stand to lose only their capital contribution if the partnership fails. None of the partners is personally liable for the debts and obligations of the partnership beyond their capital contribution (see Exhibit 5.3).

limited liability partnership (LLP)
A special form of partnership where all partners are limited partners and there are no general partners.

Exhibit 5.3 Limited Liability Partnership (LLP)

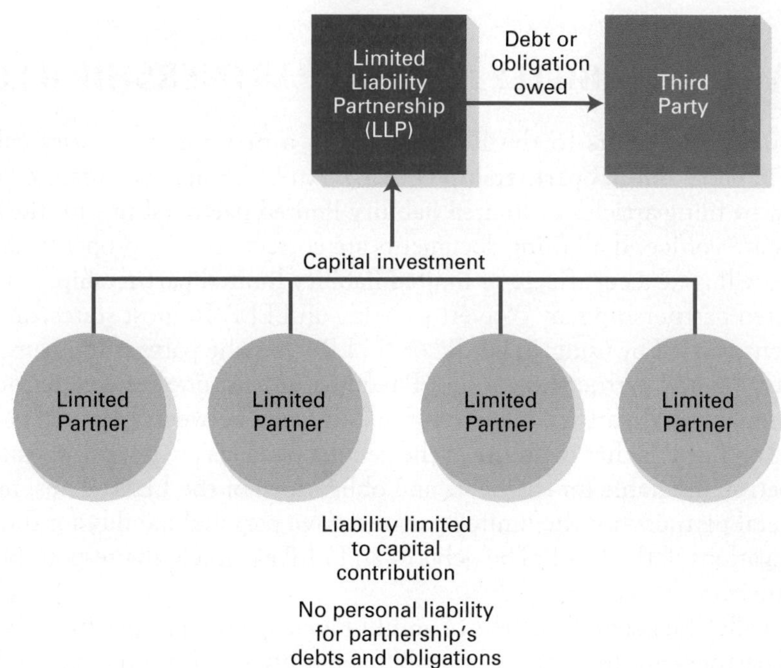

> A judge is a law student who marks his own examination papers.
> Henry Louis Mencken

In most states, the law restricts the use of LLPs to certain types of professionals, such as accountants, lawyers, and doctors. Nonprofessionals cannot use the LLP form of partnership. LLPs enjoy the "flow-through" tax benefit of other types of partnerships—that is, there is no tax paid at the partnership level, and all profits and losses are reported on the individual partners' income tax returns.

Example: Suppose Molly, Alex, Lauren, Allison, and Annie, all lawyers, form an LLP called MALAA LLP to provide legal services. While providing legal services to the LLP's client Multi Motors, Inc., Alex commits legal malpractice (negligence). This malpractice causes Multi Motors, Inc., a huge financial loss. In this case, Multi Motors, Inc., can sue and recover against Alex, the negligent party, and against MALAA LLP. Molly, Lauren, Allison, and Annie can lose their capital contribution in MALAA LLP but are not personally liable for the damages caused to Multi Motors, Inc. Alex is personally liable to Multi Motors, Inc., because he was the negligent party.

Articles of Limited Liability Partnership

articles of partnership
A written partnership agreement; a document that must be filed with the secretary of state to form a limited liability partnership.

An LLP is created formally by filing **articles of partnership** with the secretary of state of the state in which the LLP is organized. This is a public document. The LLP is a domestic LLP in the state in which it is organized. The LLP law of the state governs the operation of the LLP. An LLP may do business in other states, however. To do so, the LLP must register as a foreign LLP in any state in which it wants to conduct business.

LLP Liability Insurance

In most states, LLP law restricts the use of LLPs to certain types of professionals, such as accountants and lawyers. Many state laws require LLPs to carry a minimum of $1 million of liability insurance that covers negligence, wrongful acts, and misconduct by partners or employees of the LLP. This requirement guarantees that injured third parties will have compensation to recover for their injuries and is a trade-off for permitting partners to have limited liability.

LIMITED LIABILITY LIMITED PARTNERSHIP (LLLP)

limited liability limited partnership (LLLP)
A special type of limited partnership that has both general partners and limited partners where both the general and limited partners have limited liability and are not personally liable for the debts of the LLLP.

articles of limited liability limited partnership
A written partnership agreement; a document that must be filed with the secretary of state to form a limited liability limited partnership.

certificate of limited liability limited partnership
A document that is filed by an LLLP with the secretary of state's office to organize under state law.

The 2001 amendments to the RULPA permit a new form of entity called a **limited liability limited partnership (LLLP)**. An LLLP may be organized under state law by filing **articles of limited liability limited partnership** with the secretary of state's office. If all filing documents are correct and the proper fee is paid, the state will issue a **certificate of limited liability limited partnership**. An existing limited partnership may convert to being an LLLP. In most states, an LLLP must identify itself by using "L.L.L.P." or "LLLP" after the partnership name.

Like a limited partnership, an LLLP requires at least one general partner and at least one limited partner. However, the difference between a limited partnership and an LLLP is that in an LLLP, the general partners are not jointly and severally personally liable for the debts and obligations of the LLLP. Thus, neither the general partners nor the limited partners have personal liability for the debts and obligations of the LLLP. The debts of an LLLP are solely the responsibility of the partnership.

Typically, the general partners of an LLLP manage the partnership, while the limited partners are investors who only have a financial interest in the LLLP.

CONTEMPORARY Environment

ACCOUNTING FIRMS OPERATE AS LLPS

Prior to the advent of the limited liability partnership (LLP) form of doing business, accounting firms operated as general partnerships. As such, the general partners were personally liable for the debts and obligations of the general partnership. In large accounting firms, this personal liability was rarely imposed because the partnership usually carried sufficient liability insurance to cover most awards to third-party plaintiffs in lawsuits.

Under this system, when accounting firms were hit with large court judgments, the partners were personally liable. Many lawsuits were brought in conjunction with the failure of large commercial banks and other large firms that accountants had audited. Many of these firms failed because of fraud by their major owners and officers. The shareholders and creditors of these failed companies sued the auditors, alleging that the auditors had been negligent in not catching the fraud. Many juries agreed and awarded large awards against the accounting firms. Sometimes an accounting firm's liability insurance was not enough to cover a judgment, and personal liability was imposed on partners.

To address this issue, state legislatures created a new form of business, the LLP. This entity was particularly created for accountants, lawyers, and other professionals to offer their services under an umbrella of limited liability. The partners of an LLP have limited liability up to their capital contribution; the partners do not have personal liability for the debts and liabilities of the LLP, however.

Once LLPs were permitted by law, all of the "Big Four" accounting firms changed their status from general partnerships to LLPs. The signs and letterhead of each Big Four accounting firm prominently announce that the firm is an LLP. Many other accounting firms have also changed over to LLP status, as have many law firms.

Thus, a general partner can manage the affairs of the LLLP but not be personally responsible for the debts of the LLLP.

Many states currently offer the ability to form LLLPs. Other states are beginning to do so as well. An LLLP is a domestic LLLP in the state in which it is formed and a foreign LLLP in other states in which it operates. Because the LLLP is a new form of business, its use is not widespread. Most use of the LLLP form of business has been for real estate investments. Because the LLLP form of business is so new, there is very little case law in the area.

Concept Summary

Liability of Limited Partners of a Limited Partnership

General rule	Limited partners are not individually liable for the obligations of the partnership beyond the amount of their capital contribution.
Exceptions to the general rule	Limited partners are individually liable for the debts and obligations of the partnership in three situations:

(continued)

1. ***Defective formation.*** There has not been substantial compliance in good faith with the statutory requirements to create a limited partnership. *Exception:* Persons who erroneously believed themselves to be limited partners either (1) caused the appropriate certificate of limited partnership or amendment thereto to be filed or (2) withdrew from any future equity participation in the profits of the partnership and caused a certificate of withdrawal to be filed.
2. ***Participation in management.*** The limited partner participated in the management and control of the partnership. *Exception:* The limited partner was properly employed by the partnership as a manager or an executive.
3. ***Personal guarantee.*** The limited partner signed an enforceable personal guarantee to guarantee the performance of the limited partnership.

CONTEMPORARY Environment

CONTROL RULE

The general rule is that limited partners who take part in the management of the affairs of the limited partnership who have not been expressly elected to office to do so lose their limited liability shield and become general partners and are personally liable for the debts and obligations of the limited partnership.

The 2001 amendments to the RULPA make an important change to this "control rule." The new Section 303 eliminates this restriction and permits limited partners to participate in the management of a limited partnership without losing their limited liability shield. The limited liability partnership agreement can permit certain or all limited partners a say in how the partnership's business should be run. Section 303 places limited partners on par with shareholders of a corporation, members of a limited liability company (LLC), and the partners of a limited liability partnership (LLP) in terms of being able to participate in the management of the entity without becoming personally liable for the debts and obligations of the limited partnership.

States may adopt this change as part of their own limited liability partnership law.

DISSOLUTION OF A LIMITED PARTNERSHIP

dissolve
To terminate; bring to an end.

certificate of cancellation
A document that is filed with the secretary of state upon the dissolution of a limited partnership.

Just like a general partnership, a limited partnership may be **dissolved** and its affairs wound up. The RULPA establishes rules for the dissolution and winding up of limited partnerships. Upon the dissolution and the commencement of the winding up of a limited partnership, a **certificate of cancellation** must be filed by the limited partnership with the secretary of state of the state in which the limited partnership is organized [RULPA Section 203].

Causes of Dissolution

Under the RULPA, the following four events cause the dissolution of a limited partnership [RULPA Section 801]:

1. The end of the life of the limited partnership, as specified in the certificate of limited partnership (i.e., the end of a set time period or the completion of a project).
2. The written consent of all general and limited partners.
3. The withdrawal of a general partner. Withdrawal includes the retirement, death, bankruptcy, adjudged insanity, or removal of a general partner or the assignment by a general partner of their partnership interest. If a corporation or partnership is a general partner, the dissolution of the corporation or partnership is considered withdrawal.
4. The entry of a **decree of judicial dissolution**, which may be granted to a partner whenever it is not reasonably practical to carry on the business in conformity with the limited partnership agreement [RULPA Section 802] (e.g., if the general partners are deadlocked over important decisions affecting the limited partnership).

A limited partnership is not dissolved upon the withdrawal of a general partner if (1) the certificate of limited partnership permits the business to be carried on by the remaining general partner or partners or (2) within ninety days of the withdrawal, all partners agree in writing to continue the business (and select a general partner or partners, if necessary) [RULPA Section 801].

A lawyer with his briefcase can steal more than a hundred men with guns.

Mario Puzo
The Godfather

decree of judicial dissolution
A decree entered by a court that judicially dissolves a corporation on a specific date.

Winding Up

A limited partnership must **wind up** its affairs upon dissolution. Unless otherwise provided in the limited partnership agreement, the partnership's affairs may be wound up by the general partners who have not acted wrongfully or, if there are none, the limited partners. Any partner may petition the court to wind up the affairs of a limited partnership [RULPA Section 803]. A partner who winds up the affairs of a limited partnership has the same rights, powers, and duties as a partner winding up a general partnership.

winding up
The process by which a dissolved partnership's assets are collected, liquidated, and distributed to creditors, shareholders, and other claimants.

Distribution of Assets

After the assets of a limited partnership have been liquidated, the proceeds must be distributed. The RULPA provides the following order of distribution of partnership assets upon the winding up of a limited partnership [RULPA Section 804]:

1. *Creditors* of the limited partnership, including partners who are creditors (except for liabilities for distributions)
2. *Partners* with respect to:
   a. Unpaid distributions
   b. Capital contributions
   c. The remainder of the proceeds

The partners may provide in the limited partnership agreement for a different distribution among the partners, but the creditors must retain their first priority.

Concept Review

Limited Partnerships (LP), Limited Liability Partnerships (LLP), and Limited Liability Limited Partnerships (LLLP)

Definition	An association of two or more persons to carry on as co-owners of a business for profit having at least one general partner and at least one limited partner.
Formation	A certificate of limited partnership must be executed and filed with the secretary of state. If the limited partnership hires employees, operates a regulated business, uses a trade name, or does business in other states, there may be laws that impose duties or responsibilities. Articles of partnership may also be required.
Management	The general partners manage the business. Limited partners may not manage without losing their status as a limited partner.
Liability	Under the Uniform Partnership Act, partners are *jointly and severally liable* for torts and breaches of trust; and *jointly liable* for contracts and debts of the partnership. In many states, limited partnerships can elect the benefits of limited liability partnership or limited liability limited partnership status such that partners' liability for partnership obligations is limited.
Taxation	Partnerships do not pay federal income taxes. Instead, the income and losses of the partnership flow onto and have to be reported on the individual partners' personal income tax returns.
Termination	The termination–or *dissolution*–of a limited partnership can occur automatically where a partnership is created for a specific time or accomplishment of an objective; or, if a "partnership at will," any partner can withdraw and dissolve the partnership at any time. A certificate of cancellation must be filed with the secretary of state. Withdrawal of a limited partner does not cause a dissolution.

PARALEGAL PRACTICE TOOL

LIMITED PARTNERSHIP FORMATION CHECKLIST

1. Select a partnership Name and an Assumed Name, if desired. Consider filing an application for reservation of name to reserve the desired name.
2. Check with the secretary of state for the availability of the name(s) and, if desired, draft, execute, and file an Application to Reserve Name.
3. Designate a Registered Agent and Registered Office.
4. Determine the purpose(s) for which the limited partnership is to be formed (if other than general purposes of a limited partnership).
5. Determine the duration of the limited partnership.
6. Determine the number and identity of the general partners.
7. Determine the number and identity of the limited partners.
8. Determine the number and identity of any desired officers.
9. Determine the desired initial Capital Contributions.
10. Determine a fiscal year.
11. Determine any restrictions on the transfer of partnership interests.
12. Draft and execute a partnership agreement.
13. Draft and execute any desired employment contracts.
14. Determine whether qualification in other states is desired.

15. Secure all state and local licenses required to operate the business and secure any necessary insurance coverage.
16. Draft, execute, and file a Certificate of Limited Partnership and Certificate of Assumed Name (if desired) with the secretary of state.
17. Draft, execute, and file Form SS-4 filed with the IRS for employer's identification number if the limited partnership will have employees.
18. Place the name of the limited partnership or trade name on all partnership material (e.g., letterhead, invoices, business cards, signs, contracts, etc.).

CHAPTER REVIEW

LIMITED PARTNERSHIP, p. 108

Uniform Limited Partnership Act

1. ***Uniform Limited Partnership Act (ULPA).*** This 1916 model act contains a uniform set of provisions for the formation, operation, and dissolution of limited partnerships.
2. ***Revised Uniform Limited Partnership Act (RULPA).*** This 1976 revision of the ULPA provides a more modern comprehensive law for the formation, operation, and dissolution of limited partnerships.

Limited Partnerships

1. ***Limited partnership.*** This is a special form of partnership that has both limited and general partners.
   a. ***General partners.*** General partners in a limited partnership invest capital, manage the business, and are personally liable for partnership debts.
   b. ***Limited partners.*** Limited partners in a limited partnership invest capital but do not participate in management and are not personally liable for partnership debts beyond their capital contributions.
2. ***Corporation as sole general partner.*** A corporation may be the sole general partner of a limited partnership. Shareholders of corporations are liable only up to their capital contributions.

Formation of Limited Partnerships

1. ***Certificate of limited partnership.*** This certificate is a document that two or more persons must execute and sign that establishes a limited partnership. The certificate of limited partnership must be filed with the secretary of state of the appropriate state and may be amended from time to time.
2. ***Name of limited partnership.*** The name of a limited partnership may not include the surname of a limited partner unless (1) it is also the surname of a general partner or (2) the business was carried on under that name before the admission of the limited partner. Other restrictions on the name of a limited partnership are that (1) the name cannot be the same as or deceptively similar to the names of corporations or other limited partnerships, (2) states can designate words that cannot be used in limited partnership names, and (3) the name must contain, without abbreviation, the words *limited partnership*.
3. ***Capital contributions.*** Under the RULPA, the capital contributions of general and limited partners may be in cash, property, services rendered, or promissory notes or other obligations to contribute cash or property or to perform services.

4. ***Limited partnership agreement.*** This document sets forth the rights and duties of general and limited partners; the terms and conditions regarding the operation, termination, and dissolution of the partnership; and so on.
5. ***Defective formation.*** Defective formation occurs when (1) a certificate of limited partnership is not properly filed, (2) there are defects in a certificate that is filed, or (3) some other statutory requirement for the creation of a limited partnership is not met. A limited partner may be held liable as a general partner if the limited partnership is defectively formed.

Limited Partnership Agreement

A limited partnership agreement (also called articles of limited partnership) sets forth the rights and duties of the general and limited partners; the terms and conditions regarding the operations, termination, and dissolution of the partnership; and so on.

Share of Profits and Losses

Unless otherwise agreed, profits and losses from a limited partnership are shared on the basis of the value of the partner's capital contributions. A limited partner is not liable for losses beyond his or her capital contribution. The limited partnership agreement may specify how profits and losses are to be allocated among the general and limited partners.

Right to Information

Upon reasonable demand, each limited partner has the right to obtain from the general partners true and full information regarding the state of the business, the financial condition of the limited partnership, and so on.

Admission of a New Partner

Once a limited partnership has been formed, a new limited partner can be added only upon the written consent of all partners, unless the limited partnership agreement provides otherwise. A limited partnership agreement cannot waive the right of partners to approve the admission of new general partners.

Foreign Limited Partnership

A limited partnership is a foreign limited partnership in all state in which it was not organized. Before transacting business in a foreign state, a foreign limited partnership must be issued a certificate of registration.

LIABILITY OF GENERAL AND LIMITED PARTNERS, p. 113

Liability of General and Limited Partners

1. ***General partners.*** General partners of a limited partnership have *unlimited personal liability* for the debts and obligations of the limited partnership.
2. ***Limited partners.*** Limited partners of a limited partnership are liable only for the debts and obligations of the limited partnership up to their capital contributions.
3. ***Limited partners and management.*** Limited partners have no right to participate in the management of a partnership. A limited partner is *liable as a general partner* if his or her participation in the control of the business is substantially the same as that of a general partner, but the limited partner is liable only to persons who reasonably believed the limited partner to be a general partner. The RULPA clarifies the types of activities that a limited

partner may engage in without losing his or her limited liability. If a limited partner personally guarantees a loan made by a creditor to the limited partnership, and the limited partnership defaults on the loan, the creditor may recover payment from the limited partner who personally guaranteed the repayment of the loan.

LIMITED LIABILITY PARTNERSHIP (LLP), p. 115

Limited Liability Partnership

1. ***Limited liability partnership (LLP).*** The LLP is a relatively new form of business in which there does not have to be a general partner who is personally liable for debts and obligations of the partnership. All partners are limited partners and stand to lose only their capital contributions should the partnership fail. LLPs are formed by accountants and other professionals, as allowed by LLP law.
2. ***Partners.*** The partners are the owners of an LLP.
3. ***Articles of partnership.*** This is a document that the partners of an LLP must execute, sign, and file with the secretary of state of the appropriate state to form an LLP.
4. ***Taxation.*** An LLP does not pay federal income taxes unless it elects to do so. If an LLP is taxed as a partnership, the income and losses of the LLP flow onto individual partners' federal income tax returns.
5. ***LLP Liability Insurance.*** Many state laws require LLPs to carry a minimum of $1 million of liability insurance that covers negligence, wrongful acts, and misconduct by partners or employees of the LLP. This requirement guarantees that injured third parties will have compensation to recover for their injuries and is a trade-off for permitting partners to have limited liability.
6. ***Dissolution Of A Limited Partnership.*** The RULPA establishes rules for the dissolution and winding up of limited partnerships. Upon the dissolution and the commencement of the winding up of a limited partnership, a *certificate of cancellation* must be filed by the limited partnership with the secretary of state of the state in which the limited partnership is organized.

LIMITED LIABILITY LIMITED PARTNERSHIP (LLLP), p. 116

Limited Liability Limited Partnership

An LLLP is a special type of limited partnership that has both general partners and limited partners where both the general and limited partners have limited liability and are not personally liable for the debts of the LLLP.

TEST REVIEW TERMS AND CONCEPTS

Decree of judicial dissolution 119
Defective formation 111
Dissolve 118
Domestic limited partnership 112
Foreign limited partnership 112
General partner 108
Limited liability limited partnership (LLLP) 116
Limited liability of limited partners 114
Limited liability partnership (LLP) 115
Limited partner 108
Limited partnership (special partnership) 108
Limited partnership agreement (articles of limited partnership) 111
Master limited partnership (MLP) 113
Personal guarantee 115
Personal liability of general partners 114
Revised Uniform Limited Partnership Act (RULPA) 109
Uniform Limited Partnership Act (ULPA) 109
Unit 113
Unlimited liability 113
Winding up (wind up) 119

CASE SCENARIO REVISITED

Remember the case from the beginning of the chapter, where a bystander Day was sprayed with nitric acid, receiving severe injuries, at an abandoned oil well owned by Virginia Partners? If Day sued Virginia Partners and its limited partners to recover damages, are the limited partners liable? To help you with your answer, review the case *Virginia Partners, Ltd. v. Day*, 738 S.W.2d 837 (Ky. Ct. App. 1987).

PORTFOLIO EXERCISE

Using the sample limited partnership agreement that follows as a guide, draft a limited partnership agreement for the business you created at the beginning of the course.

WORKING THE WEB INTERNET EXERCISES

Activities

1. Study the provisions of the Uniform Limited Partnership Act at **www.law.upenn.edu/bll/ulc/ulpa/final2001.html**.
2. Check your state statute on LLPs. Are LLPs permitted in your jurisdiction? Are there any limitations on the type of businesses allowed to operate as an LLP? See "LII: Partnership Law" at **www.law.cornell.edu/topics/partnership.html**.

LIMITED PARTNERSHIP AGREEMENT

1. Introduction. This agreement of Limited Partnership dated January 2, 2011 by and between John Weston, Wai Chan, and Susan Martinez (General Partners) and Shari Berkowitz, Raymond Wong, and Harold Johnson (Limited Partners).

The General Partners and Limited Partners agree to form a Limited Partnership (Partnership) pursuant to the provisions of the California Revised Limited Partnership Act on the terms and conditions hereinafter set forth.

2. Name of Partnership. The name of the Partnership shall be "The Wilshire Investment Company, a California Limited Partnership." The business of the Partnership shall be conducted in that name.

3. Principal Place of Business. The principal office of the Partnership shall be at 4000 Wilshire Boulevard, Los Angeles, California 90010 or at such other place within California as may be determined from time to time by the General Partners.

4. Purpose of the Partnership. The Partnership shall be engaged in the business of buying, selling, and developing commercial and industrial real estate and such activities as are related or incidental thereto.

5. Agent for Service of Process. The name of the agent for service of process is Frederick Friendly, whose address is 2500 Century Park East, Suite 600, Los Angeles, California 90067.

6. Term of Partnership. The term of the Partnership shall commence on the date on which the Partnership's Certificate of Limited Partnership is filed by the Secretary of State of California and shall continue until it terminates in accordance with the provisions of this Agreement.

7. Certificate of Limited Partnership. The General Partners shall immediately execute a Certificate of Limited Partnership and cause that Certificate to be filed in the office of the secretary of state of California. The General Partners shall also record a certified copy of the Certificate in the office of the county recorder of every county in which the Partnership owns real property.

8. Members of the Partnership.

(a) The names and addresses of each original General Partner is as follows:

Name	Address
John Weston	500 Ocean Boulevard, Los Angeles, California
Wai Chan	700 Apple Road, Seattle, Washington
Susan Martinez	800 Palm Drive, Miami, Florida

(b) The names and addresses of each original Limited Partner is as follows:

Name	Address
Shari Berkowitz	700 Apple Street, New York, New York
Raymond Wong	900 Flower Avenue, San Francisco, California
Harold Johnson	300 Oil Field Road, Houston, Texas

9. General Partners' Capital Contributions. The General Partners shall make the following contributions to the Partnership's capital no later than January 2, 2011.

Cash

John Weston	$ 60,000

Property

Wai Chan	$ 30,000
Susan Martinez	$ 30,000

No interest will be paid on any balances in the General Partners' capital accounts.

10. Limited Partners' Capital Contributions. The Limited Partners shall make the following contributions to the Partnership's capital no later than January 2, 2011.

Cash

Shari Berkowitz	$100,000
Raymond Wong	$ 50,000
Harold Johnson	$ 50,000

No interest will be paid on any balances in the General Partners' capital accounts.

11. Additional Capital Contributions from Limited Partners. The General Partners may call for additional cash contributions to the Partnership's capital from the Limited Partners. The aggregate of all additional contributions made by the Limited Partners pursuant to this Paragraph shall not exceed 100 percent of the original capital contributions made by them pursuant to Paragraph 10 of this Agreement. Notice of the call shall be made by registered mail, return receipt requested, and shall be deemed made when posted. The Limited Partners's additional capital contribution must be made no later than 60 days following the call.

12. Division of Profits. Each Partner shall receive the following share of the net profits of the Partnership:

Partner	Percent
General Partners:	
John Weston	30%
Wai Chan	15%
Susan Martinez	15%
Limited Partners:	
Shari Berkowitz	20%
Raymond Wong	10%
Harold Johnson	10%

13. Sharing of Losses. Each Partner shall bear a share of the losses of the Partnership equal to the share of the profits to which he is entitled. The share of the losses of each Partner shall be charged against his contribution to the capital of the Partnership.

The Limited Partners will not be liable for any Partnership debts or losses beyond the amounts to be contributed to them pursuant to Paragraphs 10 and 11 of this Agreement.

After giving effect to the share of losses chargeable against the capital contributions of Limited Partners, the remaining Partnership losses shall be borne by the General Partners in the same proportions in which, between themselves, they are to share profits.

14. Management of Partnership. The General Partners shall have the sole and exclusive control of the Limited Partnership.

The General Partners shall have an equal voice in the management of the Partnership, and each shall devote his or her full time to the conduct of the Partnership's business.

The General Partners shall have the power and authority to take such action from time to time as they may deem to be necessary, appropriate, or convenient in connection with the management and conduct of the business and affairs of the Partnership, including, without limitation, the power to

(a) Acquire property, including real and personal property.

(b) Dispose of Partnership property.

(c) Borrow or lend money.

(continued)

(Continued)

(d) Make, deliver, or accept commercial paper.
(e) Pledge, mortgage, encumber, or grant a security interest in the Partnership properties as security for repayment of loans.
(f) Take any and all other action permitted by law that is customary in or reasonably related to the conduct of the Partnership business or affairs.

15. Limited Partners Not to Manage Business. The Limited Partners will not manage the business of the Partnership or assist in its management.

16. Partnership Books and Records. The Partnership books of account will be kept in accordance with generally accepted accounting principles. The books and supporting records will be maintained at the Partnership's principal office and will be examined by the Partnership's certified public accountants at least annually. The Partnership's fiscal year shall start on January 1 and close on December 31.

17. General Partner's Salaries. The General Partners shall each receive a salary of $60,000 per annum, payable in monthly installments, as compensation for managing the Partnership. No increases shall be made in the General Partners' salaries without the written consent of a majority of the Limited Partners.

18. Admission of New General Partners. No new General Partners will be admitted to the Partnership without the written consent of all the General Partners and Limited Partners as to both his or her admission and the terms on which the new General Partner is admitted.

19. Admission of New Limited Partners. No new Limited Partners will be admitted to the Partnership without the written consent of all the General Partners and Limited Partners as to both his or her admission and the terms on which the new Limited Partner is admitted.

20. No Sale or Assignment of, or Granting Lien on Partnership Interest by General Partner. Without the written consent of all the General Partners and Limited Partners, no General Partner shall assign, mortgage, or give a security interest in his or her Partnership interest.

21. Right of Limited Partner to Assign Partnership Interest or Substitute New Limited Partner. Upon 30 days' written notice to the General Partners, a Limited Partner can assign his or her interest in the Partnership's profits to a third party. Such assignment shall not constitute a substitution of the third party as a new Limited Partner in the place of the assignor. A Limited Partner may substitute a third party in his or her place as a new Limited Partner only with the consent in writing of all the General Partners and Limited Partners.

22. Effect of Death, Disability, or Retirement of a General Partner. The death, retirement, or permanent disability of a General Partner (the withdrawing General Partner) that makes it impossible for him or her to carry out his or her duties under this Agreement shall terminate the Partnership.

If a General Partner survives, the remaining General Partners may continue the Partnership business and may purchase the interest of the withdrawing General Partner in the assets and goodwill of the Partnership. The remaining General Partners have the option, exercisable by them at any time within 30 days after the date on which the withdrawing General Partner ceases to be a General Partner, to purchase the withdrawing General Partner's interest by paying to the person legally entitled thereto the value of that interest as shown on the lst regular accounting of the Partnership preceding the date on which the General Partner ceased to be General Partner, together with the full unwithdrawn portion of the withdrawing General Partner's interest by paying to the person legally entitled thereto the value of that interest as shown on the last regular accounting of the Partnership preceding the date on which the General Partner ceased to be General Partner, together with the full unwithdrawn portion of the withdrawing General Partner's distributive share of any net profits earned by the Partnership between the date of that accounting and the date on which the withdrawing General Partner ceased to be a General Partner of the Partnership.

23. Duties of Remaining Purchasing General Partners. Upon the purchase of a withdrawing General Partner's interest, the remaining General Partners shall assume all obligations of the Partnership and shall hold the withdrawing General Partner, the personal representative and estate of the withdrawing General Partner, and the property of the withdrawing General Partner free and harmless from all liability for those obligations.

The remaining General Partners shall immediately amend the Certificate of Limited Partnership and shall file such amendment with the office of the Secretary of State, and shall cause to be prepared, filed, served, and published all other notices required by law to protect the withdrawing General Partner or the personal representative and estate of the withdrawing General Partner from all liability for the future obligations of the Partnership business.

24. Effect of Death of Limited Partner or Substitution of Limited Partner. The death of a Limited Partner or the substitution of a new Limited Partner for a Limited Partner shall not affect the continuity of the Partnership of the conduct of its business.

25. Voluntary Dissolution. A General Partner may terminate the Partnership at any time upon 120 days written notice to each Limited Partner. Upon termination of the Partnership, it shall be liquidated in accordance with Paragraph 26 of this Agreement.

26. Liquidation of Partnership. If the Partnership is liquidated, its assets, including its goodwill and name, shall be sold in the manner designed to produce the greatest return. The proceeds of the liquidation shall be distributed in the following order:

(a) To creditors of the Partnership including Partners who are creditors to the extent permitted by law, in satisfaction of liabilities of the Partnership
(b) To Partners in payment of the balances in their income accounts
(c) To Partners in payment of the balances in their capital accounts
(d) To Partners in payment of the remainder of the proceeds

27. Certificate of Dissolution. Upon dissolution of the Partnership, the General Partners shall execute and file in the office of the secretary of state a Certificate of Dissolution. If dissolution occurs after a sole General Partner ceases to be General Partner, the Limited Partners conducting the winding up of the Partnership's affairs shall file the Certificate of Dissolution.

28. Entire Agreement. This Agreement contains the entire understanding among the Partners and supersedes any prior written or oral agreements between them respecting the subject matter contained herein. There are no representations, agreements, arrangements, or understandings, oral or written, between and among the Partners relating to the subject matter of this Agreement that are not fully expressed herein.

29. Controlling Law. This Agreement shall be interpreted under the law of the State of California. Further, each Partner consents to the jurisdiction of the courts of the State of California.

30. Service of Notices. Service of notice upon the Partnership will be made by registered or certified mail, return receipt requested, addressed to the Partnership's principal place of business.

Service of notice upon any or all Partners will be made by registered mail, return receipt requested, addressed to the addresses given in this Agreement or such other addresses as a Partner may from time to time give to the Partnership.

31. Severability. If any provisions of this agreement shall be declared by a court of competent jurisdiction to be invalid, void, or unenforceable, the remaining provisions shall continue in full force and effect.

32. Arbitration of Disputes. Any controversy concerning this Agreement will be settled by arbitration according to the rules of the American Arbitration Association, and judgment upon the award may be entered and enforced in any court.

____

General Partner　　　　Limited Partner

____

General Partner　　　　Limited Partner

CRITICAL LEGAL THINKING CASES

Case 5.1 *Liability of General Partners* Pat McGowan, Val Somers, and Brent Robertson were general partners of Vermont Place, a limited partnership formed for the purpose of constructing duplexes on an undeveloped tract of land in Fort Smith, Arkansas. The general partners appointed McGowan and his company, Advance Development Corporation, to develop the project, including contracting with materials people, mechanics, and other suppliers. None of the limited partners took part in the management or control of the partnership.

Eight months later, Somers and Robertson discovered that McGowan had not been paying the suppliers. They removed McGowan from the partnership and took over the project. The suppliers sued the partnership to recover the money owed them. The partnership assets were not sufficient to pay all their claims. Who is liable to the suppliers? *National Lumber Co. v. Advance Dev. Corp.*, 732 S.W.2d 840 (Ark. 1987).

Case 5.2 *Liability of Limited Partners* Union Station Associates of New London (USANL) was a limited partnership formed under the laws of Connecticut. Allen M. Schultz, Anderson Nolter Associates, and the Lepton Trust were limited partners. The limited partners did not take part in the management of the partnership. The National Railroad Passenger Association (NRPA) entered into an agreement to lease part of a railroad facility from USANL. NRPA sued USANL for allegedly breaching the lease and also named the limited partners as defendants. Are the limited partners liable? *National R.R. Passenger Ass'n v. Union Station Assoc. of New London*, 643 F. Supp. 192 (D.D.C. 1986).

Case 5.3 *Liability of Limited Partners* 8 Brookwood Fund (Brookwood) was a limited partnership that was formed to invest in securities. The original certificate of limited partnership was filed with the Westchester County, New York, clerk; it listed Kenneth Stein as the general partner and Barbara Stein as the limited partner. Within the next four months, additional investors joined Brookwood as limited partners. However, no certificate amending the original certificate was filed to reflect the newly admitted limited partners. The newly added partners conducted themselves at all times as limited partners.

The partnership purchased securities on margin (i.e., it borrowed a percentage of the purchase price of the securities) from the securities firms of Sloate, Weisman, Murray & Co., Inc. (Sloate), and Bear Stearns & Co., Inc. (Bear Stearns). One day, the stock market crashed, causing many of the securities that Brookwood had purchased to go down in value. The securities firms made margin calls on Brookwood to pay more money to cover the losses. When the margin calls were not met, Sloate and Bear Stearns immediately initiated arbitration proceedings to recover the balance of $1,849,183 allegedly due after Brookwood's accounts were liquidated. Nine days later, Brookwood filed a certificate amending the original certificate of limited partnership to reflect the recently added limited partners.

Upon receiving the notice of arbitration, the recently added limited partners renounced their interest in the profits of the limited partnership. Can these limited partners be held individually liable for the partnership debts owed to Sloate and Bear Stearns? *8 Brookwood Fund v. Bear Stearns & Co.*, 539 N.Y.S.2d 411 (N.Y. App. Div. 1989).

Case 5.4 *Liability of Partners* Raugust-Mathwig, Inc., a corporation, was the sole general partner of a limited partnership. Calvin Raugust was the major shareholder of this corporation. The three limited partners were (1) Cal-Lee Trust, (2) W.J. Mathwig, Inc., and (3) W.J. Mathwig, Inc., and Associates. All three of the limited partners were valid corporate entities. Although the limited partnership agreement was never executed and a certificate of limited partnership was not filed with the state, the parties opened a bank account and began conducting business.

John Molander, an architect, entered into an agreement with the limited partnership to design a condominium complex and professional office building to be located in Spokane, Washington. The contract was signed on behalf of the limited partnership by its corporate general partner. Molander provided substantial architectural services to the partnership, but neither project was completed because of a lack of financing. Molander sued the limited partnership, its corporate general partner, the corporate limited partners, and Calvin Raugust individually to recover payments allegedly due him. Against whom can Molander recover? *Molander v. Raugust-Mathwig, Inc.*, 722 P.2d 103 (Wash. Ct. App. 1986).

Case 5.5 *Limited Partnership* The Courts of the Phoenix was a limited partnership that owned a building that housed several racquetball and handball courts. William Reich was its general partner. Charter Oaks Fire Insurance Company (Charter Oaks) issued a fire insurance policy that insured the building. One day, a fire caused extensive damage to the building. When the Chicago fire department found evidence of arson, Charter Oaks denied the partnership's \$1.7 million-plus insurance claim. It reasoned that Reich had either set the fire or had arranged to have it set in order to liquidate a failing investment. Can the limited partnership recover on the fire insurance policy? *Courts of the Phoenix v. Charter Oaks Fire Ins. Co.*, 560 F. Supp. 858 (N.D. Ill. 1983).

Case 5.6 *Removal of General Partner* The Aztec Petroleum Corporation (Aztec) was the general partner of a limited partnership. The partnership agreement provided that it could be amended by a vote of 70 percent of the limited partnership units. More than 70 percent of these units voted to amend the partnership agreement to provide that a vote of 70 percent of the limited partnership units could remove the general partner and replace it with another general partner. Prior to this amendment, there had been no provision for the removal and substitution of a general partner. Texas law requires unanimous approval of new partners unless the partnership agreement provides otherwise.

When a vote was held, more than 70 percent of the limited partnership units voted to remove Aztec as the general partner and replace it with the MHM Company. Aztec challenged its removal. Who wins? *Aztec Petroleum Corp. v. MHM Co.*, 703 S.W.2d 290 (Tex. Ct. App. 1985).

Case 5.7 *Limited Partner's Interest* When the Chrysler Credit Corporation (Chrysler Credit) extended credit to Metro Dodge, Inc. (Metro Dodge), Donald P. Peterson signed an agreement, guaranteeing to pay the debt if Metro Dodge did not pay. When Metro Dodge failed to pay, Chrysler Credit sued Peterson on the guarantee and obtained a judgment of \$350,000 against him. After beginning collection efforts, Chrysler Credit learned through discovery that Peterson owned four limited partnership units in Cedar Riverside Properties, a limited partnership. Can Chrysler Credit charge Peterson's limited partnership interests? *Chrysler Credit Corp. v. Peterson*, 342 N.W.2d 170 (Minn. Ct. App. 1984).

BUSINESS ETHICS CASES

Case 5.8 ***Business Ethics*** Robert K. Powers and Lee M. Solomon were among other limited partners of the Cosmopolitan Chinook Hotel (Cosmopolitan), a limited partnership. Cosmopolitan entered into a contract to lease and purchase neon signs from Dwinell's Central Neon (Dwinell's). The contract identified Cosmopolitan as a "partnership" and was signed on behalf of the partnership, "R. Powers, President." At the time the contract was entered into, Cosmopolitan had taken no steps to file its certificate of limited partnership with the state, as required by limited partnership law. The certificate was not filed with the state until several months after the contract was signed. When Cosmopolitan defaulted on payments due under the contract, Dwinell's sued Cosmopolitan and its general and limited partners. Did the limited partners act ethically in denying liability on the contract? Are the limited partners liable? *Dwinnell's Cent. Neon v. Cosmopolitan Chinook Hotel*, 587 P.2d 191 (Wash. Ct. App. 1978).

Case 5.9 ***Business Ethics*** The Second Montclair Company was a limited partnership organized under the laws of Alabama to develop an office building called Montclair II in Birmingham. Joseph Cox, Sr., and F&S were general partners, each owning a one-third interest in the limited partnership. Eleven limited partners owned equal shares of the remaining one-third interest. Cox was the president of Cox Realty and Development Company (Cox Realty), which had its offices in Montclair II. Cox Realty managed Montclair II under a written agreement with the limited partnership. Evidence showed that Cox used assets of the limited partnership for personal use. F&S sued Cox, seeking dissolution and liquidation of the limited partnership and damages. Did Cox act ethically in this case? Should the limited partnership be dissolved? Should damages be awarded? *Cox v. F&S*, 489 So. 2d 516 (Ala. 1986).

"Justice is the end of government. It is the end of civil society. It ever has been, and ever will be pursued, until it be obtained, or until liberty be lost in the pursuit."

–James Madison

The Federalist, No. 51 (1788)

Limited Liability Companies

CHAPTER 6

CASE SCENARIO

The law office at which you work as a paralegal represents a company called "Ummmmm." Emma, Grace, and Jack formed "Ummmmm" as a member-managed limited liability company (LLC) to operate a spa in Santa Fe, New Mexico. Each member contributed $100,000 in capital to start "Ummmmm." Emma entered into a contract on behalf of "Ummmmm" in which she contracted to have a new hot tub installed at the spa by Hot Tubs, Inc., for $80,000. Hot Tubs, Inc., installed the hot tub and sent a bill for $80,000 to "Ummmmm." "Ummmmm" has failed to pay the bill.

CHAPTER OBJECTIVES

After studying this chapter, you should be able to:

1. Define *limited liability company (LLC)*.
2. Describe the process of organizing LLCs.
3. Describe the limited liability shield provided by LLCs.
4. Compare member-managed LLCs and manager-managed LLCs.
5. Determine when members and managers owe fiduciary duties of loyalty and care to an LLC.

PARALEGAL PERSPECTIVE

Jenni Losel *is a director of legal affairs with Meritain Health, Inc., a national health care company, in Amherst, New York. She received a bachelor in legal studies from Hilbert College and has been working as a paralegal for twelve years. Her areas of responsibility include litigation management, oversight of the appeals and subrogation departments, and general corporate matters.*

Why do you think it is important for paralegals to understand limited liability companies? Given the increasing popularity of this newer form of business organization, it is important for paralegal students who aspire to work in this area of the law to have a working knowledge of the characteristics and complexities of limited liability companies.

What are the most important paralegal skills needed in your job? Highly effective communication skills are very important, especially strong writing skills. Reading comprehension skills; analytical skills; organization and prioritization; and legal research are also key components.

What is the academic background required for a paralegal entering your area of practice? An associate in legal/paralegal studies is the minimum required for an entry level position, while a bachelor is preferred.

How is technology involved in your job? Proficiency in Microsoft Office is required, as well as Internet research and online legal research skills (such as Westlaw).

What trends do you see in your area of practice that will likely affect your job in the future? The continued rise in matters being litigated will increase the need for litigation management and also create an increased need to identify and control risk.

What do you feel is the biggest issue currently facing the paralegal profession? I feel that the biggest issue facing the paralegal profession is the lack of regulation to becoming a paralegal. In order to become a paralegal, there should be education standards and a license or certificate should be required, along with continuing education requirements. This would increase the parity and compensation for paralegals and also result in more respect for the profession.

What words of advice do you have for a new paralegal entering your area of practice? Maintain copies and/or notes of assignments you work on so that you can use them as a reference tool in the future. Be willing to think outside the box and draw from different sources in order to solve the problem, especially when assigned a task with which you are unfamiliar. Organization is critical to success.

INTRODUCTION TO LIMITED LIABILITY COMPANIES

Owners may choose to operate a business as a *limited liability company (LLC)*. The use of LLCs as a form of conducting business in the United States is of rather recent origin. In 1977, Wyoming was the first state in the United States to enact legislation creating an LLC as a legal form for conducting business. This new form of business received little attention until the early 1990s, when several more states enacted legislation to allow the creation of LLCs. The evolution of LLCs then grew at a blinding speed, with all the states having enacted LLC statutes by 1998. Most LLC laws are quite similar, although some differences do exist between these state statutes.

An LLC is an unincorporated business entity that combines the most favorable attributes of general partnerships, limited partnerships, and corporations. An LLC may elect to be taxed as a partnership, the owners can manage the business, and the owners have limited liability for debts and obligations of the partnership. Many entrepreneurs who begin new businesses choose the LLC as their legal form for conducting business.

> The great can protect themselves, but the poor and humble require the arm and shield of the law.
>
> Andrew Jackson

The formation and operation of LLCs and the liability of their owners are discussed in this chapter.

LIMITED LIABILITY COMPANY (LLC)

Limited liability companies (LLCs) are creatures of state law, not federal law. An LLC can only be created pursuant to the laws of the state in which the LLC is being organized. These statutes, commonly referred to as **limited liability company codes**, regulate the formation, operation, and dissolution of LLCs. The state legislature may amend its LLC statutes at any time. The courts interpret state LLC statutes to decide LLC and member disputes.

An LLC is a separate *legal entity* (or legal person) distinct from its members [ULLCA Section 201]. LLCs are treated as artificial persons who can sue or be sued, enter into and enforce contracts, hold title to and transfer property, and be found civilly and criminally liable for violations of law.

limited liability company (LLC)
An unincorporated business entity that combines the most favorable attributes of general partnerships, limited partnerships, and corporations.

limited liability company codes
Statutes that regulate the formation, operation, and dissolution of LLCs.

Taxation of LLCs

Under the Internal Revenue Code and regulations adopted by the Internal Revenue Service (IRS) for federal income tax purposes, an LLC is **taxed** as a partnership unless it elects to be taxed as a corporation. Thus, an LLC is not taxed at the entity level, but its income or losses "flow through" to the members' individual income tax returns. This avoids double taxation. Most LLCs accept the default status of being taxed as a partnership instead of electing to be taxed as a corporation. (See Exhibit 6.1.)

tax
A charge, usually monetary, imposed by the government on persons, entities, transactions, or property to yield public revenue.

Powers of an LLC

An LLC has the same **powers** as an individual to do all things necessary or convenient to carry on its business or affairs, including owning and transferring personal property; selling, leasing, and mortgaging real property; making contracts and guarantees; borrowing and lending money; issuing notes and bonds; suing and being sued; and taking other actions to conduct the affairs and business of the LLC [ULLCA Section 112].

powers of an LLC
An LLC has the same powers as an individual to do all things necessary or convenient to carry on its business or affairs

Uniform Limited Liability Company Act (ULLCA)
A model act that provides comprehensive and uniform laws for the formation, operation, and dissolution of LLCs.

FORMATION OF AN LLC

Most LLCs are organized to operate businesses, real estate developments, and such. Certain professionals, such as accountants, lawyers, and doctors, cannot operate practices as LLCs; instead, they can operate practices as limited liability partnerships (LLPs), which are discussed in Chapter 5.

LANDMARK LAW

UNIFORM LIMITED LIABILITY COMPANY ACT

In 1996, the National Conference of Commissioners on Uniform State Laws (a group of lawyers, judges, and legal scholars) issued the **Uniform Limited Liability Company Act (ULLCA)**. The ULLCA codifies LLC law. Its goal is to establish comprehensive LLC law that is uniform throughout the United States. The ULLCA covers most problems that arise in the formation, operation, and termination of LLCs. The ULLCA is not a law unless a state adopts it as its LLC statute. Many states have adopted all or part of the ULLCA as their LLC law. The ULLCA was revised in 2006, and this revision is called the Revised Uniform Limited Liability Company Act (RULLCA).

The ULLCA forms the basis of the study of limited liability companies in this chapter. (See Appendix C for more detail on this act.)

An LLC can be organized in only one state, even though it can conduct business in all other states. When choosing a state for organization, the members should consider the LLC codes of the states under consideration. For the sake of convenience, most LLCs, particularly small ones, choose as the state of organization the state in which the LLC will be doing most of its business.

When starting a new LLC, the organizers must choose a name for the entity. The name must contain the words *limited liability company* or *limited company* or the abbreviation *L.L.C.*, *LLC*, *L.C.*, or *LC*. *Limited* may be abbreviated as *Ltd.*, and *company* may be abbreviated as *Co.* [ULLCA Section 105(a)].

Exhibit 6.1 Entity Classification Election

Form **8832**
(Rev. February 2010)
Department of the Treasury
Internal Revenue Service

Entity Classification Election

OMB No. 1545-1516

Type or Print	Name of eligible entity making election	**Employer identification number**
	Number, street, and room or suite no. If a P.O. box, see instructions.	
	City or town, state, and ZIP code. If a foreign address, enter city, province or state, postal code and country. Follow the country's practice for entering the postal code.	

▶ Check if: ☐ Address change

1 **Type of election** (see instructions):

a ☐ Initial classification by a newly-formed entity. Skip lines 2a and 2b and go to line 3.
b ☐ Change in current classification. Go to line 2a.

2a Has the eligible entity previously filed an entity election that had an effective date within the last 60 months?

☐ **Yes.** Go to line 2b.
☐ **No.** Skip line 2b and go to line 3.

2b Was the eligible entity's prior election for initial classification by a newly formed entity effective on the date of formation?

☐ **Yes.** Go to line 3.
☐ **No.** Stop here. You generally are not currently eligible to make the election (see instructions).

3 Does the eligible entity have more than one owner?

☐ **Yes.** You can elect to be classified as a partnership or an association taxable as a corporation. Skip line 4 and go to line 5.
☐ **No.** You can elect to be classified as an association taxable as a corporation or disregarded as a separate entity. Go to line 4.

4 If the eligible entity has only one owner, provide the following information:
a Name of owner ▶ ------------------------------
b Identifying number of owner ▶ ------------------------------

5 If the eligible entity is owned by one or more affiliated corporations that file a consolidated return, provide the name and employer identification number of the parent corporation:
a Name of parent corporation ▶ ------------------------------
b Employer identification number ▶ ------------------------------

For Paperwork Reduction Act Notice, see instructions. Cat. No. 22598R Form **8832** (Rev. 2-2010)

(continued)

Exhibit 6.1 *(Continued)*

Form 8832 (Rev. 2-2010) Page **2**

6 Type of entity (see instructions):

a ☐ A domestic eligible entity electing to be classified as an association taxable as a corporation.
b ☐ A domestic eligible entity electing to be classified as a partnership.
c ☐ A domestic eligible entity with a single owner electing to be disregarded as a separate entity.
d ☐ A foreign eligible entity electing to be classified as an association taxable as a corporation.
e ☐ A foreign eligible entity electing to be classified as a partnership.
f ☐ A foreign eligible entity with a single owner electing to be disregarded as a separate entity.

7 If the eligible entity is created or organized in a foreign jurisdiction, provide the foreign country of organization ▶ ______________________

8 Election is to be effective beginning (month, day, year) (see instructions) . . . . ▶ ____________

9 Name and title of contact person whom the IRS may call for more information	10 Contact person's telephone number

Consent Statement and Signature(s) (see instructions)

Under penalties of perjury, I (we) declare that I (we) consent to the election of the above-named entity to be classified as indicated above, and that I (we) have examined this consent statement, and to the best of my (our) knowledge and belief, it is true, correct, and complete. If I am an officer, manager, or member signing for all members of the entity, I further declare that I am authorized to execute this consent statement on their behalf.

Signature(s)	Date	Title

Form **8832** (Rev. 2-2010)

Articles of Organization

Because LLCs are creatures of statute, certain formalities must be taken and statutory requirements must be met to form an LLC. Under the ULLCA, an LLC may be organized by one or more persons. Some states require at least two members to organize an LLC. In states where an LLC may be organized by only one member, sole proprietors can obtain the benefit of the limited liability shield of an LLC.

articles of organization
The formal documents that must be filed at the secretary of state's office of the state of organization of an LLC to form the LLC.

An LLC is formed by delivering **articles of organization** to the office of the secretary of state of the state of organization for filing. If the articles are in proper form, the secretary of state will file the articles. The existence of an LLC begins when the articles of organization are filed. The filing of the articles of organization by the secretary of state is conclusive proof that the organizers have satisfied all the conditions necessary to create the LLC [ULLCA Section 202]. Under the ULLCA, the articles of organization of an LLC must set forth [ULLCA Section 203]:

- The name of the LLC
- The address of the LLC's initial office
- The name and address of the initial agent for service of process
- The name and address of each organizer
- Whether the LLC is a term LLC and, if so, the term specified
- Whether the LLC is to be a manager-managed LLC and, if so, the name and address of each manager
- Whether one or more of the members of the LLC are to be personally liable for the LLC's debts and obligations

The articles of organization may set forth provisions from the members' operating agreement and any other matter not inconsistent with law. An article of organization form for use in the State of Michigan is set forth in Exhibit 6.2. An LLC can amend its articles of organization at any time by filing **articles of amendment** with the secretary of state [ULLCA Section 204].

articles of amendment
A document filed to effectuate an amendment or change to an LLC's articles of organization.

Duration of an LLC

at-will LLC
An LLC that has no specified term of duration.

term LLC
An LLC that has a specified term of duration.

An LLC is an **at-will LLC** (i.e., with no specified term) unless it is designated as a **term LLC** and the duration of the term is specified in the articles of organization [ULLCA Section 203(a)(5)]. The duration of a term LLC may be specified in any manner that sets forth a specific and final date for the dissolution of the LLC.

Examples: Periods specified as "50 years from the date of filing of the articles of organizations" and "the period ending January 1, 2050" are valid to create a term LLC.

Capital Contribution to an LLC

A member's capital contribution to an LLC may be in the form of money, personal property, real property, other tangible property, intangible property (e.g., a patent), services performed, contracts for services to be performed, promissory notes, or other agreements to contribute cash or property [ULLCA Section 401].

A member's obligation to contribute capital is not excused by the member's death, disability, or other inability to perform. If a member cannot make the required contribution of property or services, he or she is obligated to contribute money equal to the value of the promised contribution. The LLC or any creditor who extended credit to the LLC in reliance on the promised contribution may enforce the promised obligation [ULLCA Section 402].

> There shall be one law for the native and for the stranger who sojourns among you.
> Moses
> Exodus 12:49

Exhibit 6.2 Articles of Organization Form

BCS/CD-700 (Rev. 01/10)

MICHIGAN DEPARTMENT OF ENERGY, LABOR & ECONOMIC GROWTH
BUREAU OF COMMERCIAL SERVICES

Date Received	**(FOR BUREAU USE ONLY)**
	This document is effective on the date filed, unless a subsequent effective date within 90 days after received date is stated in the document.

Name		
Address		
City	State	ZIP Code

EFFECTIVE DATE:

Document will be returned to the name and address you enter above.
If left blank, document will be returned to the registered office.

ARTICLES OF ORGANIZATION
For use by Domestic Limited Liability Companies
(Please read information and instructions on reverse side)

Pursuant to the provisions of Act 23, Public Acts of 1993, the undersigned executes the following Certificate:

ARTICLE I

1. The name of the limited liability company is:

ARTICLE II

The purpose or purposes for which the limited liability company is formed is to engage in any activity within the purposes for which a limited liability company may be formed under the Limited Liability Company Act of Michigan.

ARTICLE III

The duration of the limited liability company if other than perpetual is:

ARTICLE IV

1. The street address of the location of the registered office is:

____, Michigan __________
(Street Address) (City) (Zip Code)

2. The mailing address of the registered office if different than above:

____, Michigan __________
(P.O. Box or Street Address) (City) (Zip Code)

3. The name of the resident agent at the registered office is:

ARTICLE V (Insert any desired additional provision authorized by the Act; attach additional pages if needed.)

Signed this__________ day of ______________________________, ________

By____
(Signature(s) of Organizer(s))

____
(Type or Print Name(s) of Organizer(s))

Exhibit 6.2 *(Continued)*

BCS/CD-700 (Rev. 01/10)

Name of person or organization remitting fees.

Preparer's Name ______________________

Business telephone number (   ) ______________________

INFORMATION AND INSTRUCTIONS

1. This form may be used to draft your Articles of Organization. A document required or permitted to be filed under the act cannot be filed unless it contains the minimum information required by the Act. The format provided contains only the minimal information required to make the document fileable and may not meet your needs. This is a legal document and agency staff cannot provide legal service.
2. Submit one original of this document. Upon filing, the document will be added to the records of the Bureau of Commercial Services. The original will be returned to your registered office address unless you enter a different address in the box on the front of this document.

   Since this document will be maintained on electronic format, it is important that the filing be legible. Documents with poor black or white contrast, or otherwise illegible, will be rejected.
3. This document is to be used pursuant to the provisions of Act 23, P.A. of 1993, by one or more persons for the purpose of forming a domestic limited liability company. **Use form BCS/CD 701 if the limited liability company will be providing services rendered by a dentist, an osteopathic physician, a physician, a surgeon, a doctor of divinity or other clergy, or an attorney-at-law.**
4. Article I - The name of a domestic limited liability company is required to contain one of the following words or abbreviations: "Limited Liability Company", "L.L.C.", "L.C.", "LLC", or "LC".
5. Article II- Under section 203(b) of the Act, it is sufficient to state substantially, alone or with specifically enumerated purposes, that the limited liability company is formed to engage in any activity within the purposes for which a limited liability company may be formed under the Act.
6. Article V - Section 401 of the Act specifically states the business shall be managed by members unless the Articles of Organization state the business will be managed by manager. If the limited liability company is to be managed by managers instead of by members, insert a statement to the effect in Article V.
7. This document is effective on the date endorsed "Filed" by the Bureau. A later effective date, no more than 90 days after the date of delivery, may be stated as an additional article.
8. The Articles must be signed by one or more persons organizing the Limited Liability Company. State name of the organizers signing beneath their signature.
9. If more space is needed, attach additional pages. All pages should be numbered.
10. **NONREFUNDABLE FEE:** Make remittance payable to the State of Michigan. Include limited liability name on check or money order....................**$50.00**

Submit with check or money order by mail:

Michigan Department of Energy, Labor & Economic Growth
Bureau of Commercial Services
Corporation Division
P.O. Box 30054
Lansing, MI 48909

To submit in person:

2501 Woodlake Circle
Okemos, MI
Telephone: (517) 241-6470

Fees may be paid by check, money order, VISA or MasterCard when delivered in person to our office.

MICH-ELF (Michigan Electronic Filing System):

First Time Users: Call (517) 241-6470, or visit our website at http://www.michigan.gov/corporations
Customer with MICH-ELF Filer Account: Send document to (517) 636-6437

DELEG is an equal opportunity employer/program. Auxiliary aids, services and other reasonable accommodations are available upon request to individuals with disabilities.

Certificate of Interest

An LLC's operating agreement may provide that a member's ownership interest may be evidenced by a **certificate of interest** issued by the LLC [ULLCA Section 501(c)]. The certificate of interest acts the same as a stock certificate issued by a corporation.

certificate of interest
A document that evidences a member's ownership interest in an LLC.

Operating Agreement

Members of an LLC may enter into an **operating agreement** that regulates the affairs of the company and the conduct of its business and governs relations among the members, managers, and company [ULLCA Section 103(a)]. The operating agreement may be amended by the approval of all members unless otherwise provided in the agreement. The operating agreement and amendments may be oral but are usually written.

operating agreement
An agreement entered into among members that governs the affairs and business of the LLC and the relations among members, managers, and the LLC.

Conversion of an Existing Business to an LLC

Many LLCs are formed by entrepreneurs to start new businesses. In addition, an existing business may want to convert to an LLC to obtain its tax benefits and limited liability shield. General partnerships, limited partnerships, and corporations may be converted to LLCs if the following requirements are met [ULLCA Section 902]:

- An **agreement of conversion** is drafted that sets forth the terms of the conversion.
- The terms of the conversion are approved by all of the parties or by the number or percentage of owners required for conversion.
- Articles of organization of the LLC are filed with the secretary of state. The articles must state that the LLC was previously another form of business and the prior business's name.

agreement of conversion
A document that states the terms for converting an existing business to an LLC.

The conversion takes effect when the articles of organization are filed with the secretary of state or at any later date specified in the articles of organization. When the conversion takes effect, all property owned by the prior business vests in the LLC, and all debts, obligations, and liabilities of the prior business become those of the LLC [ULLCA Section 903].

Dividing an LLC's Profits and Losses

Unless otherwise agreed, the ULLCA mandates that a member has the right to an equal share in the LLC's profits [ULLCA Section 405(a)]. This is a default rule that the members can override by agreement and is usually a provision in their operating agreement. In many instances, the members may not want the profits of the LLC to be shared equally. This would normally occur if the capital contributions of the members were unequal. If the members of an LLC want the profits to be divided in the same proportion as their capital contributions, that should be specified in the operating agreement.

Examples: Raymond and Francie form an LLC. Raymond contributes $75,000 capital, and Francie contributes $25,000 capital. They do not have an agreement as to how profits are to be shared. If the LLC makes $100,000 in profits, under the ULLCA, Raymond and Francie will share the profits equally—$50,000 each. To avoid this outcome, Raymond and Francie should agree in their operating agreement how they want the profits to be divided.

An economist's guess is liable to be as good as anybody else's.

Will Rogers

Losses from an LLC are shared equally unless otherwise agreed. Sometimes members will not want to divide losses equally and maybe not even in the same way as their capital contributions. If the LLC has chosen to be taxed as a partnership, the losses from an LLC flow to the members' individual income tax returns. Losses from an LLC can sometimes be offset against members' gains from other sources. Therefore, the members may want to agree to divide the losses so that the members who can use them to offset other income will receive a greater share of the losses.

Profits and losses from an LLC do not have to be distributed in the same proportion.

Example: A member who has the right to a 10 percent share of profits may be given, in the operating agreement, the right to receive 25 percent of the LLC's losses.

Distributional Interest

distributional interest
A member's ownership interest in an LLC that entitles the member to receive distributions of money and property from the LLC.

A member's ownership interest in an LLC is called a **distributional interest**. A member's distributional interest in an LLC is a personal property and may be transferred in whole or in part [ULLCA Section 501(b)]. Unless otherwise provided in the operating agreement, a transfer of an interest in an LLC does not entitle the transferee to become a member of the LLC or to exercise any right of a member. A transfer entitles the transferee to receive only distributions from the LLC to which the transferor would have been entitled [ULLCA Section 502]. A transferee of a distributional interest becomes a member of the LLC if it is so provided in the operating agreement or if all the other members of the LLC consent [ULLCA Section 503(a)].

Example: Jeff, Becky, Drew, and Mia are members of the Boston Tea Party LLC; each owns a one-fourth interest in the LLC, and the members agree to divide the distributions equally in one-fourth portions. The LLC's operating agreement does not provide that a transferee of a distributional interest will become a member. Jeff sells his one-fourth interest to Brutus. The members do not consent to allow Brutus to become a member. The LLC makes $100,000 in profits. Brutus is entitled to receive one-fourth of the distributions ($25,000). Brutus is not a member of the LLC, however.

A transferor who transfers his or her distributional interest is not released from liability for the debts, obligations, and liabilities of the LLC [ULLCA Section 503(c)].

■ LIABILITY OF AN LLC

An LLC is liable for any loss or injury caused to anyone as a result of a wrongful act or omission by a member, a manager, an agent, or an employee of the LLC who commits the wrongful act while acting within the ordinary course of business of the LLC or with authority of the LLC [ULLCA Section 302].

Morality cannot be legislated, but behavior can be regulated. Judicial decrees may not change the heart, but they can restrain the heartless.
Martin Luther King, Jr.
Strength to Love (1963)

Example: Emma, Grace, and Jack form SSS, LLC, to own and operate a business. Each member contributes $10,000 capital. While on LLC business, Jack drives his automobile and accidentally hits and injures Charlie. Charlie can recover damages for his injuries from Jack personally because he committed the negligent act. Charlie can also recover damages from SSS, LLC, because Jack was acting within the scope of the ordinary business of the LLC when the accident occurred. Emma and Grace have limited liability only up to their capital contributions in SSS, LLC.

CONTEMPORARY Environment

DREAMWORKS SKG, LLC

Steven Spielberg, Jeffrey Katzenberg, and David Geffen formed DreamWorks SKG, which is a major movie and recording production company. Spielberg's fame and money came from directing films, Katzenberg had been a leading executive at Disney, and Geffen had built and sold a major record company. These multimillionaire multimedia giants combined their talents to create a formidable entertainment company.

DreamWorks was formed as a Delaware LLC. The organizers chose to create an LLC because it is taxed as a partnership, the profits (or losses) flow directly to the owners, and like a corporation, the owners are protected from personal liability beyond their capital contributions.

DreamWorks issued several classes of interests. The three principals put up $100 million ($33.3 million each) for "SKG" stock, which grants the principals 100 percent voting control and 67 percent of the firm's profits. In addition, each principal has multiyear employment contracts plus other benefits.

DreamWorks raised the other $900 million of its $1 billion capital from other investors, who were to receive one-third of future profits. The other investors were issued the following classes of stock:

Class	Investments
A	Outside investors. Class A stock was sold to big investors with over $20 million to invest. Microsoft's cofounder, Paul Allen, purchased $500 million of Class A stock. Class A investors got seats on the board of directors.
S	Outside investors. Class S stock was issued for smallish, "strategic" investments with other companies for cross-marketing purposes.
E	Employees. Employees were granted the right to participate in an employee stock purchase plan.

Liability of Managers

Managers of LLCs are not personally liable for the debts, obligations, and liabilities of the LLC they manage [ULLCA Section 303(a)].

Example: An LLC that is engaged in real estate development hires Darla Goldstein, a nonmember, to be its president. While acting within the scope of her LLC authority, Darla signs a loan agreement whereby the LLC borrows $1 million from a bank to complete the construction of an office building. If the LLC subsequently suffers financial difficulty and defaults on the bank loan, Darla is not personally responsible for the loan. The LLC is liable for the loan, but Darla is not because she was acting as the manager of the LLC.

Members' Limited Liability

member
An owner of an LLC.

limited liability
The liability of LLC members for the LLC's debts, obligations, and liabilities only to the extent of their capital contributions.

The owners of LLCs are usually called **members**. The general rule is that members are not personally liable to third parties for the debts, obligations, and liabilities of an LLC beyond their capital contribution. Members are said to have **limited liability** (see Exhibit 6.3). The debts, obligations, and liabilities of an

Exhibit 6.3 Limited Liability Company (LLC)

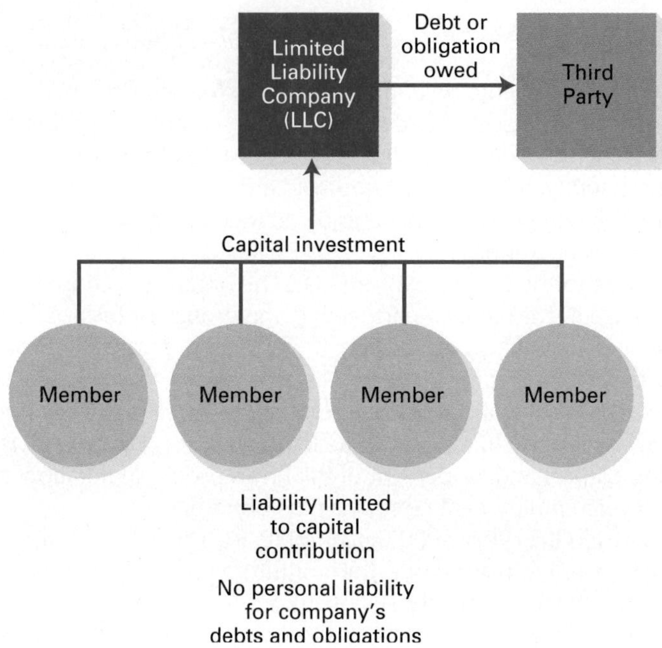

LLC, whether arising from contracts, torts, or otherwise, are solely those of the LLC [ULLCA Section 303(a)].

Example: Joe and Alyson form an LLC, and each contributes $25,000 in capital. The LLC operates for a period of time, during which it borrows money from banks and purchases goods on credit from suppliers. After some time, the LLC experiences financial difficulty and goes out of business. If the LLC fails with $500,000 in debts, each of the members will lose their capital contribution of $25,000 but will not be personally liable for the rest of the unpaid debts of the LLC.

The failure of an LLC to observe the usual company formalities is not grounds for imposing personal liability on the members of the LLC [ULLCA Section 303(b)]. For example, if the LLC does not keep minutes of the company's meetings, the members do not become personally liable for the LLC's debts.

In the following case, the court addressed the issue of the limited liability of a member of an LLC.

CASE 6.1 Limited Liability Company

***Siva v. 1138 LLC*, No. 06AP-959, 2007 Ohio LEXIS 4202, at *1 (Ct. App. Sept. 11, 2007).**

"Finally, the evidence did not show that Siva was misguided as to the fact he was dealing with a limited liability company."

—Judge Brown

Facts

Five members—Richard Hess, Robert Haines, Lisa Hess, Nathan Hess, and Zack Shahin—formed a limited liability company called 1138 LLC. Ruthiran Siva owned a commercial building located at 1138 Bethel Road, Franklin County, Ohio. Siva entered into a written lease agreement with 1138 LLC whereby 1138 LLC leased premises in Siva's commercial building for a term of five years at a monthly rental of $4,000. 1138 LLC began operating a bar on the premises. Six months later, 1138 LLC was in default and breach of the lease agreement. Siva sued 1138 LLC and Richard Hess to recover damages. Siva received a default judgment against 1138 LLC, but there was no money in 1138 LLC to pay the judgment. Hess, who had been sued personally, defended, arguing that as a member-owner of the LLC, he was not personally liable for the debts of the LLC. The trial court found in favor of Hess and dismissed Siva's complaint against Hess. Siva appealed.

It is the spirit and not the form of law that keeps justice alive.
Earl Warren
The Law and the Future (1955)

Issue

Is Richard Hess, a member-owner of 1138 LLC, personally liable for the debt owed by the LLC to Siva?

Language of the Court

Based upon the court's examination of the record, we find there was competent, credible evidence to support the trial court's determination. The evidence does not show that Hess purposely undercapitalized 1138 LLC, or that he formed the limited liability company in an effort to avoid paying creditors. According to Hess, the bar was never profitable. Based upon the evidence presented, a reasonable trier of fact could have concluded that 1138 LLC became insolvent due to unprofitable operations. Moreover, even if the record suggests poor business judgment by Hess, it does not demonstrate that he formed 1138 LLC to defraud creditors. Finally, the evidence did not show that Siva was misguided as to the fact he was dealing with a limited liability company. Siva's counsel drafted the lease agreement and Siva acknowledged at trial he did not ask any of the owners of 1138 LLC to sign the lease in an individual capacity.

Decision

The court of appeals held that Hess, as a member-owner of 1138 LLC, was not personally liable for the debt that the LLC owed to Siva. The court of appeals affirmed the decision of the trial court that dismissed Siva's complaint against Hess.

Case Questions

1. **Critical Legal Thinking** What is the liability of an LLC for its debts? What is the liability of a member-owner of an LLC for the LLC's debts? Explain.
2. **Business Ethics** Did Hess owe an ethical duty to pay the debt owed by 1138 LLC to Siva? Did Siva act ethically by suing Hess personally to recover the debt owed by the 1138 LLC?
3. **Contemporary Business** What should Siva have done if he wanted Hess to be personally liable on the lease? Explain.

Liability of Tortfeasors

tortfeasor
A person who intentionally or unintentionally (negligently) causes injury or death to another person. A tortfeasor is liable to persons he or she injures and to the heirs of persons who die because of his or her conduct.

A person who intentionally or unintentionally (negligently) causes injury or death to another person is called a **tortfeasor**. Tortfeasors are personally liable to persons they injure and to the heirs of persons who die because of the tortfeasors' conduct. This rule applies to members and managers of LLCs. Thus, if a member or a manager of an LLC negligently causes injury or death to another person, he or she is personally liable to the injured person or the heirs of the deceased person.

MANAGEMENT OF AN LLC

An LLC can be either a *member-managed LLC* or a *manager-managed LLC*. An LLC is a member-managed LLC unless it is designated as a manager-managed LLC in its articles of organization [ULLCA Section 203(a) (b)]. The distinctions between these two are as follows:

- ***Member-managed LLC.*** In this type of LLC, the members of the LLC have the right to manage the LLC.
- ***Manager-managed LLC.*** In this type of LLC, the members designate a manager or managers to manage the LLC, and by doing so, they delegate their management rights to the manager or managers, designated manager or managers have the authority to manage the LLC, and the members no longer have the right to manage the LLC.

A manager may be a member of an LLC or a nonmember. Whether an LLC is a member-managed or manager-managed LLC has important consequences on the right to bind the LLC to contracts and on determining the fiduciary duties owed by members to the LLC. These important distinctions are discussed in the paragraphs that follow.

MEMBER-MANAGED LLC

member-managed LLC
An LLC that has not designated that it is a manager-managed LLC in its articles of organization and is managed by its members.

In a **member-managed LLC**, each member has equal rights in the management of the business of the LLC, regardless of the size of the member's capital contribution. Any matter relating to the business of the LLC is decided by a majority vote of the members [ULLCA Section 404(a)].

Example: Emma, Grace, Jack, Amanda, and Charlie form North West.com, LLC. Amanda contributes $100,000 capital, and the other four members each contribute $25,000 capital. When deciding whether to add another line of products to the business, Jack, Amanda, and Charlie vote to add the line, and Emma and Grace vote against it. The line of new products is added to the LLC's business because three members voted yes, while two members voted no. It does not matter that the two members who voted no contributed $125,000 in capital collectively versus $75,000 in capital contributed by the three members who voted yes.

Manager-Managed LLC

manager-managed LLC
An LLC that has designated in its articles of organization that it is a manager-managed LLC and whose nonmanager members give their management rights over to designated managers.

In a **manager-managed LLC**, the members and nonmembers who are designated managers control the management of the LLC. The members who are not managers have no rights to manage the LLC unless otherwise provided in the operating agreement. In a manager-managed LLC, each manager has equal rights in the management and conduct of the company's business. Any matter related to the business of the LLC may be exclusively decided by the managers by a majority vote of the managers [ULLCA Section 403(b)]. A manager must be appointed by a vote of a majority of the members; managers may also be removed by a vote of the majority of the members [ULLCA Section 404(b)(3)].

Certain actions cannot be delegated to managers but must be voted on by all members of the LLC. These include (1) amending the articles of organization, (2) amending the operating agreement, (3) admitting new members, (4) consenting to dissolve the LLC, (5) consenting to merge the LLC with another entity, and (6) selling, leasing, or disposing of all or substantially all of the LLC's property [ULLCA Section 404(c)].

Laws too gentle are seldom obeyed; too severe, seldom executed.

Benjamin Franklin
Poor Richard's
Almanack (1756)

Concept Summary

Management of an LLC

Type of LLC	Description
Member-managed LLC	The members do not designate managers to manage the LLC. The LLC is managed by its members.
Manager-managed LLC	The members designate certain members or nonmembers to manage the LLC. The LLC is managed by the designated managers; nonmanager members have no right to manage the LLC.

Compensation and Reimbursement

A nonmanager member of an LLC is not entitled to compensation for services performed for the LLC (except for winding up the business of the LLC). Managers of an LLC, whether they are members or not, are paid compensation and benefits as specified in their employment agreements with the LLC [ULLCA Section 403(d)].

An LLC is obligated to reimburse members and managers for payments made on behalf of the LLC (e.g., business expenses) and to indemnify members and managers for liabilities incurred in the ordinary course of LLC business or in the preservation of the LLC's business or property [ULLCA Section 403(a)].

Agency Authority to Bind an LLC to Contracts

The designation of an LLC as member managed or manager managed is important in determining who has authority to bind the LLC to contracts. The following rules apply:

- ***Member-managed LLC.*** In a member-managed LLC, all members have agency authority to bind the LLC to contracts.

  Example: If Emma, Grace, and Jack form a member-managed LLC, each one of them can bind the LLC to a contract with a third party such as a supplier, purchaser, or landlord.

- ***Manager-managed LLC.*** In a manager-managed LLC, the managers have authority to bind the LLC to contracts, but generally, nonmanager members cannot bind the LLC to contracts.

Example: Emma, Grace, Jack, and Charlie form an LLC. They designate the LLC as a manager-managed LLC and name Amanda and John as the managers. Amanda, a manager, enters into a contract to purchase goods from a supplier for the LLC. Grace, a nonmanager member, enters into a contract to lease equipment on behalf of the LLC. The LLC is bound to the contract entered into by Amanda, a manager, but is not bound to the contract entered into by Grace, a nonmanager member.

An LLC is bound to contracts that members or managers have properly entered into on its behalf in the ordinary course of business [ULLCA Section 301].

Concept Summary

Agency Authority to Bind an LLC to Contracts

Type of LLC	Agency Authority
Member-managed LLC	All members have agency authority to bind the LLC to contracts.
Manager-managed LLC	The managers have authority to bind the LLC to contracts; generally, the nonmanager members cannot bind the LLC to contracts.

Duty of Loyalty Owed to an LLC

duty of loyalty
A duty owed by a member of a member-managed LLC and a manager of a manager-managed LLC to be honest in his or her dealings with the LLC and to not act adversely to the interests of the LLC.

A member of a member-managed LLC and a manager of a manager-managed LLC owe a *fiduciary* **duty of loyalty** to the LLC. This means that these parties must act honestly in their dealings with the LLC. The duty of loyalty includes the duty not to usurp the LLC's opportunities, make secret profits, secretly deal with the LLC, secretly compete with the LLC, or represent any interests adverse to those of the LLC [ULLCA Section 409(b)].

Example: Emma, Grace, Jack, and Charlie form the member-managed LLC Big.Business.com, LLC, which conducts online auctions over the Internet. Emma secretly starts a competing business to conduct online auctions over the Internet. Emma is liable for breaching her duty of loyalty to the LLC with Grace, Jack, and Charlie. Emma is liable for any secret profits she made, and her business will be shut down.

Example: In the preceding example, suppose that Emma, Grace, Jack, and Charlie designated their LLC as a manager-managed LLC and named Emma and Grace as managers. In this case, only the managers owe a duty of loyalty to the LLC, but nonmanager members do not. Therefore, Emma and Grace, the named managers, could not compete with the LLC; Jack and Charlie, nonmanager members, could compete with the LLC without any legal liability.

Limited Duty of Care Owed to an LLC

duty of care
A duty owed by a member of a member-managed LLC and a manager of a manager-managed LLC not to engage in (1) a known violation of law, (2) intentional conduct, (3) reckless conduct, or (4) grossly negligent conduct that injures the LLC.

A member of a member-managed LLC and a manager of a manager-managed LLC owe a *fiduciary* **duty of care** to the LLC not to engage in (1) a known violation of law, (2) intentional conduct, (3) reckless conduct, or (4) grossly negligent conduct that injures the LLC. A member of a member-managed LLC or a manager of a manager-managed LLC is liable to the LLC for any damages the LLC incurs because of such conduct.

This duty is a *limited duty of care* because it does not include ordinary negligence. Thus, if a covered member or manager commits an *ordinarily negligent* act that is not grossly negligent, they are not liable to the LLC.

Example: Amanda is a member of a member-managed LLC. While engaging in LLC business, Amanda is driving an automobile and accidentally hits Mara, a pedestrian, and severely injures her. Under agency theory, Mara sues the LLC and recovers $1 million in damages. If the court determines that Amanda was ordinarily negligent when she caused the accident—for example, she was driving the speed limit and did not see Mara because the sun was in her eyes—she will not be liable to the LLC for any losses caused to the LLC by her ordinary negligence. If instead the court determines that Amanda was driving 65 mph in a 35 mph zone and thus was grossly negligent, Amanda is liable to the LLC for the $1 million it was ordered to pay Mara.

No Fiduciary Duty Owed by a Nonmanager Member

A member of a manager-managed LLC who is not a manager owes no fiduciary duty of loyalty or care to the LLC or its other members [ULLCA Section 409(h)(1)]. Basically, a nonmanager member of a manager-managed LLC is treated equally to a shareholder in a corporation.

Example: Emma is a member of a thirty-person manager-managed LLC that is engaged in buying, developing, and selling real estate. Emma is not a manager of the LLC but is just a member-owner. If a third party approaches Emma with the opportunity to purchase a large and valuable piece of real estate that is ripe for development, and the price is below fair market value, Emma owes no duty to offer the opportunity to the LLC. She may purchase the piece of real estate for herself without violating any duty to the LLC.

DISSOLUTION OF AN LLC

Unless an LLC's operating agreement provides otherwise, a member has the *power* to withdraw from the LLC, whether it is an at-will LLC or a term LLC [ULLCA Section 602(a)]. The disassociation of a member from an at-will LLC is not wrongful unless the power to withdraw is eliminated in the operating agreement [ULLCA Section 602(b)]. The disassociation of a member from a term LLC before the expiration of the specified term is wrongful. A member who wrongfully disassociates himself or herself from an LLC is liable to the LLC and to the other members for any damages caused by the member's **wrongful disassociation** [ULLCA Section 602(c)].

wrongful disassociation
When a member withdraws from (1) a term LLC prior to the expiration of the term or (2) an at-will LLC when the operating agreement eliminates a member's power to withdraw.

A member's disassociation from an LLC terminates that member's right to participate in the management of the LLC, act as an agent of the LLC, or conduct the LLC's business [ULLCA Section 603(b)(3)]. Disassociation also terminates the disassociating member's duties of loyalty and care to the LLC [ULLCA Section 603(b)(3)].

Payment of Distributional Interest

If a member disassociates from an at-will LLC without causing a wrongful disassociation, the LLC must purchase the disassociated member's distributional interest [ULLCA Section 701(a)(1)]. The price and terms of a distributional interest may be fixed in the operating agreement [ULLCA Section 701(c)]. If the price is not agreed upon in the operating agreement, the LLC must pay the fair market value of the distributional interest.

If a member disassociates himself or herself from a term LLC, the LLC must only purchase the disassociating member's distributional interest on the expiration of the specified term of the LLC [ULLCA Section 701(a)(2)]. Any damages caused by wrongful withdrawal must be offset against the purchase price [ULLCA Section 701(f)].

Notice of Disassociation

For two years after a member disassociates himself or herself from an LLC that continues in business, the disassociating member has apparent authority to bind the LLC to contracts in the ordinary course of business except to parties who either (1) know of the disassociation or (2) are given notice of disassociation [ULLCA Section 703].

An LLC can give *constructive notice* of a member's disassociation by filing a **statement of disassociation** with the secretary of state, stating the name of the LLC and the name of the member disassociated from the LLC [ULLCA Section 704]. This notice is effective against any person who later deals with the disassociated member, whether the person was aware of the notice or not.

statement of disassociation
A document filed with the secretary of state that gives constructive notice that a member has disassociated from an LLC.

Example: Grace, Alexa, Holly, and Abby are members of a member-managed LLC that operates a gymnastics facility. Abby disassociates from the LLC. The LLC fails to file a statement of disassociation with the secretary of state. Although Abby has no express agency authority to bind the LLC to contracts because she is no longer a member of the LLC, Abby has apparent authority to bind the LLC to contracts in the ordinary course of business for two years after the disassociation or until the LLC files a statement of disassociation with the secretary of state. This does not apply to parties who are aware of Abby's disassociation with the LLC or those parties who are given notice of Abby's disassociation with the LLC.

Continuation of an LLC

At the expiration of the term of a term LLC, some of its members may want to continue the LLC. At the expiration of its term, a term LLC can be continued in two situations. First, the members of the LLC may vote prior to the expiration date to continue the LLC for an additional specified term. This requires the unanimous vote of all the members and the filing of an amendment to the articles of organization with the secretary of state, stating this fact. Second, absent the unanimous vote to continue the term LLC, the LLC may be continued as an at-will LLC by a simple majority vote of the members of the LLC [ULLCA Section 411(b)].

Winding Up an LLC's Business

winding up
The process by which a dissolved LLC's assets are collected, liquidated, and distributed to creditors, shareholders, and other claimants.

If an LLC is not continued, the LLC is wound up. The **winding up** of an LLC involves preserving and selling the assets of the LLC and distributing the money and property to creditors and members.

The assets of an LLC that is being dissolved must be applied to first pay off the creditors; thereafter, the surplus amount is distributed to the members in equal shares, unless the operating agreement provides otherwise [ULLCA Section 806]. It is good practice for members to specify in the operating agreement how distributions will be made to members. After dissolution and winding up, an LLC may terminate its existence by filing **articles of termination** with the secretary of state [ULLCA Section 805].

articles of termination
The documents that are filed with the secretary of state to terminate an LLC as of the date of filing or upon a later effective date specified in the articles.

CONTEMPORARY Environment

WHY OPERATE A BUSINESS AS A LIMITED LIABILITY COMPANY (LLC)?

Why should an LLC be used instead of an S corporation or a partnership? S corporations and partnerships are subject to many restrictions and adverse consequences that do not exist with an LLC. Some differences are as follows:

- S corporations cannot have shareholders other than estates, certain trusts, and individuals (who cannot be nonresident aliens). S corporations can have no more than seventy-five shareholders and one class of stock and may not own more than 80 percent of another corporation. LLCs have no such restrictions.
- In a general partnership, the partners are personally liable for the obligations of the partnership. Members of LLCs have limited liability.
- A limited partnership must have at least one general partner who is personally liable for the obligations of the partnership (although this partner can be a corporation). Limited partners are precluded from participating in the management of the business. An LLC provides limited liability to all members, even though they participate in management of the business.

INTERNATIONAL LAW

Limited Liability Companies in Foreign Countries

The United States did not invent the LLC as a form of business. An LLC form of business has been used in different countries of the world for a long time. The *limitada*, a form of business used in Latin America, has many similarities to the LLC. *Limitadas* have been used in Argentina, Brazil, Mexico, and other Latin American countries for a century. These entities share the features of limited liability of owners and centralized management with the LLC.

On the European continent, an equivalent form of business to the LLC has existed for centuries. In Spain, it was called the *sociedad de responsibilidades limitada*. Modern continental LLCs provide for limited liability of owners and centralized management. Germany was one of the last European countries to add the LLC as a form of business—one century ago. In England, an antecedent to the LLC, called the *stock company*, was developed around 1555. These companies, while technically partnerships, had limited liability of owners, free transferability of ownership interests, and centralized management similar to those of modern LLCs.

Concept Summary

Limited Liability Companies (LLC)

Definition	Unincorporated business entity that combines the most favorable attributes of general partnerships, limited partnerships, and corporations.
Formation	Formed by delivering articles of organization to the office of the secretary of state
Management	Each member has equal rights in the management of the business of the LLC. An LLC can be either a *member-managed LLC* or a *manager-managed LLC.*
Liability	Managers of LLCs are not personally liable for the debts, obligations, and liabilities of the LLC they manage. Members are not personally liable to third parties for the debts, obligations, and liabilities of an LLC beyond their capital contribution.
Taxation	An LLC is taxed as a partnership unless it elects to be taxed as a corporation. Thus, an LLC taxed as a partnership is not taxed at the entity level, but its income or losses "flow through" to the members' individual income tax returns.
Termination	After dissolution and winding up, an LLC may terminate its existence by filing articles of termination with the secretary of state.

PARALEGAL PRACTICE TOOL

LIMITED LIABILITY COMPANY FORMATION CHECKLIST

1. Select a company Name and an Assumed Name, if desired. Consider filing an application for reservation of name to reserve the desired name.
2. Check with the secretary of state for the availability of the name(s) and, if desired, draft, execute, and file an Application to Reserve Company Name.
3. Designate a Registered Agent and Registered Office.
4. Determine the purpose(s) for which the company is to be formed (if other than general purposes of a company).
5. Determine the duration of the company.
6. Determine which, if any, of the three corporate characteristics (centralized management, continuity of life, and free transferability of interests) are to be adopted.
7. Determine the number and identity of any desired managers.
8. Determine the number and identity of the members.
9. Determine the number and identity of any desired officers.
10. Determine the desired initial Capital Contributions.
11. Determine whether the company will be taxed as a partnership or a corporation and draft, execute, and file IRS Form 8832 if taxation as a corporation is desired.
12. Determine a fiscal year.
13. Determine any restrictions on the transfer of membership interests.
14. Draft and execute an operating agreement.
15. Draft and execute any desired employment contracts.
16. Determine whether qualification in other states is desired.
17. Secure all state and local licenses required to operate the business and secure any necessary insurance coverage.
18. Draft, execute, and file Articles of Organization and Certificate of Assumed Name (if desired) with the secretary of state.
19. Draft, execute, and file Form SS-4 filed with the IRS for employer's identification number if the corporation will have employees.
20. Place the name of the company or trade name on all company material (e.g., letterhead, invoices, business cards, signs, contracts, etc.).

CHAPTER REVIEW

LIMITED LIABILITY COMPANY (LLC), p. 133

Limited Liability Company (LLC)

An LLC is a special form of unincorporated business entity that combines the tax benefits of a partnership and limited liability attribute of a corporation.

1. ***Uniform Limited Liability Company Act (ULLCA).*** The ULLCA is a model act that provides comprehensive and uniform rules for the formation, operation, and dissolution of LLCs.
2. ***Taxation of LLCs.*** "Flow-through" taxation. For federal income tax purposes, an LLC is taxed as a partnership unless it elects to be taxed as a corporation.
3. ***Powers of an LLC.*** An LLC has the same powers as an individual to do all things necessary or convenient to carry on its business or affairs [ULLCA Section 112].

FORMATION OF AN LLC, p. 133

Articles of Organization

The articles of organization is a document that owners of an LLC must execute, sign, and file with the secretary of state of the appropriate state to form an LLC.

1. ***Name of an LLC.*** The name of an LLC must contain the words *limited liability company* or *limited company* or the abbreviation *L.L.C.*, *LLC*, *L.C.*, or *LC*. *Limited* may be abbreviated as *Ltd.*, and *company* may be abbreviated as *Co.*
2. ***Duration of an LLC.*** An LLC is an *at-will LLC* unless it is designated as a *term LLC* and the duration of the term is specified in the articles of organization.
3. ***Capital contribution to an LLC.*** A member's capital contribution to an LLC may be in the form of money, personal property, real property, other tangible property, intangible property (e.g., a patent), services performed, contracts for services to be performed, promissory notes, or other agreements to contribute cash or property.
4. ***Certificate of interest.*** The certificate of interest evidences a member's ownership interest in an LLC.
5. ***Operating agreement.*** An operating agreement is an agreement between members that governs the affairs and business of the LLC and relations among members, managers, and the LLC.
6. ***Conversion of an existing business to an LLC.*** An agreement of conversion is a document that sets forth the terms for converting general partnerships, limited partnerships, and corporations to an LLC.
7. ***Dividing an LLC's profits and losses.*** Unless otherwise agreed, the ULLCA mandates that a member has the right to an equal share in an LLC's profits and losses. Members may agree in an operating agreement how profits and losses of an LLC will be shared by the members.
8. ***Distributional interest.*** Distributional interest is a member's ownership interest in an LLC. This interest is personal property that may be transferred in whole or in part.

LIABILITY OF AN LLC, p. 140

Liability of an LLC

An LLC is liable for any loss or injury caused to anyone as a result of a wrongful act or omission by a member, a manager, an agent, or an employee of the LLC who commits the wrongful act while acting within the ordinary course of business of the LLC or with authority of the LLC.

Liability of Managers

Managers of LLCs are not personally liable for the debts, obligations, and liabilities of the LLC they manage. A member is personally liable for the debts of an LLC if he or she personally guarantees the repayment of the LLC's debts.

Members' Limited Liability

Members are liable for an LLC's debts, obligations, and liabilities only to the extent of their capital contributions. Members are not personally liable for the debts, obligations, and liabilities of the LLC.

Liability of Tortfeasor

1. ***Tortfeasor.*** A tortfeasor is a person who intentionally or unintentionally (negligently) causes injury or death to another person.
2. ***Liability of a tortfeasor.*** A member or manager of an LLC who intentionally or unintentionally (negligently) causes injury or death to another person is personally liable to the injured person or the heirs of a deceased person.

MANAGEMENT OF AN LLC, p. 144

Member-Managed LLC

In a member-managed LLC, the members have not designated managers to manage the LLC. A member-managed LLC is managed by its members.

Manager-Managed LLC

In a manager-managed LLC, the members have designated certain members or nonmembers to manage the LLC. A manager-managed LLC is managed by the designated managers; nonmanager members have no right to manage the LLC.

Compensation and Reimbursement

A nonmanager member of an LLC is not entitled to compensation for services performed for the LLC (except for winding up the business of the LLC). However, an LLC is obligated to reimburse members and managers for payments made on behalf of the LLC (e.g., business expenses).

Agency Authority to Bind an LLC to Contracts

1. ***Member-managed LLC.*** In a member-managed LLC, all members have agency authority to bind the LLC to contracts.
2. ***Manager-managed LLC.*** In a manager-managed LLC, the managers have authority to bind the LLC to contracts; the nonmanager members cannot bind the LLC to contracts.
3. ***LLC liability for contracts.*** An LLC is bound to contracts that members or managers have properly entered into on its behalf in the ordinary course of business or that the LLC has authorized.

Fiduciary Duties

1. ***Duty of loyalty.*** A member of a member-managed LLC and a manager of a manager-managed LLC owe a duty of care to the LLC. This means that these parties must act honestly in their dealings with the LLC. These parties are liable to the LLC for any secret profits made by them and damages caused to the LLC by a violation of their duty of loyalty.
2. ***Duty of care.*** A member of a member-managed LLC and a manager of a manager-managed LLC owe a duty of care to the LLC not to engage in:
   a. A known violation of law
   b. Intentional conduct
   c. Reckless conduct
   d. Grossly negligent conduct

A covered member or manager is liable to the LLC for any damages the LLC suffers because of such breaches of the duty of care.

3. ***Limited duty of care.*** A covered member or manager is not liable to the LLC for damages caused to the LLC because of their *ordinary negligence.*
4. ***No fiduciary duty owed by nonmanager member.*** A member of a manager-managed LLC who is not a manager owes no fiduciary duty of loyalty or care to the LLC.

DISSOLUTION OF AN LLC, p. 147

Disassociation from an LLC

1. ***Member's power to disassociate.*** Unless the operating agreement provides otherwise, members have the power to withdraw from both at-will and term LLCs.
2. ***Wrongful disassociation.***
   a. ***Term LLC.*** The disassociation of a member from a term LLC before the expiration of the specified term is wrongful.
   b. ***At-will LLC.*** The disassociation of a member from an at-will LLC is not wrongful unless the power to withdraw is eliminated in the operating agreement.
   c. ***Liability for wrongful disassociation.*** A member who wrongfully disassociates himself or herself from an LLC is liable to the LLC and to the other members for any damages caused by the member's wrongful disassociation.
3. ***Notice of disassociation.***
   a. ***Statement of disassociation.*** This document, filed with the secretary of state, states the name of the member disassociated from the LLC. This statement is *constructive notice* that is effective against persons, whether those persons are aware of the notice or not.
   b. ***Apparent authority.*** A disassociated member has apparent authority to bind an LLC to contracts in the ordinary course of business for two years after disassociation, unless either (1) the other party knew of the disassociation or (2) constructive notice of the disassociation was given.
4. ***Payment of Distributional Interest.*** If a member disassociates from an at-will LLC without causing a wrongful disassociation, the LLC must purchase the disassociated member's distributional interest. If a member disassociates himself or herself from a term LLC, the LLC must only purchase the disassociating member's distributional interest on the expiration of the specified term of the LLC.

5. ***Continuation of an LLC.*** At the expiration of a term LLC, the LLC can be continued by all or some of its members.
6. ***Winding up.*** If an LLC is not continued, an LLC's business is wound up. This consists of preserving and selling the assets of the LLC and distributing the money and property to creditors and members.

Limited Liability Companies in Foreign Countries

The United States did not invent the LLC as a form of business. An LLC form of business has been used in different countries of the world for a long time.

TEST REVIEW TERMS AND CONCEPTS

Agreement of conversion 139
Articles of amendment 136
Articles of organization 136
Articles of termination 149
At-will LLC 136
Certificate of interest 139
Distributional interest 140
Duty of care 146
Duty of loyalty 146
Limited liability 141
Limited liability company (LLC) 133
Limited liability company codes 133
Manager-managed LLC 144
Member 141
Member-managed LLC 144
Operating agreement 139
Powers of an LLC 133
Revised Uniform Limited Liability Company Act (RULLCA) 133
Statement of disassociation 148
Tax 133
Term LLC 136
Tortfeasor 144
Uniform Limited Liability Company Act (ULLCA) 133
Winding up 148
Wrongful disassociation 147

CASE SCENARIO REVISITED

Remember the case scenario at the beginning of the chapter where Emma, Grace, and Jack formed a spa called "Ummmmm" as a member-managed limited liability company (LLC). If Hot Tubs, Inc., sues "Ummmmm" to recover the $80,000 owed for a hot tub ordered by Emma, is "Ummmmm," the LLC, liable? Is Emma liable? On what premise do you base your answer? This is a hypothetical situation; see if you can find real-life cases that help you with your answer.

PORTFOLIO EXERCISE

For the business you created at the beginning of the course, complete the Articles of Organization (see Exhibit 6.2) by going to the following website: http://www.dleg.state.mi.us/bcsc/forms/corp/llc/700.pdf.

WORKING THE WEB INTERNET EXERCISES

Activities

1. Review business associations at jurist.law.pitt.edu/sg_bus.htm to determine why the LLC is an increasingly popular form of doing business.
2. Check your state statute on LLCs. How many persons are required to form an LLC? Visit the following website: www.4inc.com/llcfaq.htm.
3. For an overview of partnerships and LLCs in the context of a state law, see "Florida's New Partnership Law," at www.law.fsu.edu/journals/lawreview/issues/232/larson.html.

CRITICAL LEGAL THINKING CASES

Case 6.1 *Liability of Members* Renee, Amy, Mara, and Amanda form Microhard.com, LLC, a limited liability company, to sell computer hardware and software over the Internet. Microhard.com, LLC, hires Francie, a recent graduate of the University of Chicago and a brilliant software designer, as an employee. Francie's job is to design and develop software that will execute a computer command when the computer user thinks of the next command he or she wants to execute on the computer. Using Francie's research, Microhard.com, LLC, develops the Third Eye software program that does this. Microhard.com, LLC, sends Francie to the annual Comdex computer show in Las Vegas, Nevada, to unveil this revolutionary software. Francie goes to Las Vegas, and while there, she rents an automobile to get from the hotel to the computer show and to meet interested buyers at different locations in Las Vegas. While Francie is driving from her hotel to the site of the Comdex computer show, she negligently causes an accident in which she runs over Harold, a pedestrian.

Harold, who suffers severe physical injuries, sues Microhard.com, LLC, Francie, Renee, Amy, Mara, and Amanda to recover monetary damages for his injuries. Who is liable?

Case 6.2 *Liability of Members* Abigail, Ben, and Maggie each contribute $50,000 capital to form a limited liability company called Fusion Restaurant, LLC, which operates an upscale restaurant that serves "fusion" cuisine, combining foods from cultures around the world. Fusion Restaurant, LLC, as a business, borrows $1 million from Melon Bank for operating capital. Abigail, Ben, and Maggie are so busy cooking, serving, and running the restaurant that they forget to hold members' meetings, keep minute books, or otherwise observe any usual company formalities for the entire first year of business. After this one year of hard work, Fusion Restaurant, LLC, suffers financial difficulties and defaults on the $1 million bank loan from Melon Bank. Melon Bank sues Fusion Restaurant, LLC, Abigail, Ben, and Maggie to recover the unpaid bank loan. Who is liable?

Case 6.3 *Personal Guarantee* Darla, Amy, Kelly, and Molly form a limited liability company called Real Estate Developers, LLC. Each of the four owners contributes $50,000 capital to the LLC, and the LLC then purchases a 400-acre parcel of vacant land 75 miles from Toledo, Ohio. Real Estate Developers, LLC, wants to build a tract of homes on the site. The owners of Real Estate Developers, LLC, go to City Bank and ask to borrow $100 million to complete the development and construction of the homes. City Bank agrees to make the loan, but only if Darla agrees to personally guarantee the LLC's loan and give security for the loan by pledging her twelve-story penthouse in Manhattan, worth $100 million, as collateral for the loan. Darla agrees and signs the personal guarantee that pledges her penthouse as collateral for the loan; City Bank makes the $100 million loan to the LLC. Real Estate Developers, LLC, makes regular interest payments on the loan for one year and then defaults on the loan, with $100 million still owed to City Bank. At the time of default, Real Estate Developers, LLC's only asset is the 400-acre parcel of land that is still worth $150,000. City Bank sues Real Estate Developers, LLC, Darla, Amy, Kelly, and Molly to recover the amount of the unpaid loan. Who is liable to City Bank?

Case 6.4 *Member-Managed LLC* John, Jeff, and Joe form a limited liability company called Big Apple, LLC, to operate a bar in New York City. John, Jeff, and Joe are member-managers of the LLC. One of John's jobs as a member-manager is to drive the LLC's truck and pick up certain items of supply for the bar each Wednesday. On the way back to the bar one Wednesday after picking up the supplies for that week, John negligently runs over a pedestrian, Tilly Tourismo, on a street in Times Square. Tilly is severely injured and sues Big Apple, LLC, John, Jeff, and Joe to recover monetary damages for her injuries. Who is liable?

Case 6.5 *Manager-Managed LLC* Amanda, Emma, and Grace form Unlimited, LLC, a limited liability company that operates a chain of women's retail clothing stores that sell eclectic women's clothing. The company is a manager-managed LLC, and Amanda has been designated in the articles of organization filed with the secretary of state as the manager of Unlimited, LLC. Amanda sees a store location on Rodeo Drive in Beverly Hills, California, that she thinks would be an excellent location for an Unlimited store. Amanda enters into a five-year lease on behalf of Unlimited, LLC, with Landlord, Inc., the owner of the store building, to lease the store at $100,000 rent per year. While visiting Chicago, Grace sees a store location on North Michigan Avenue in Chicago that she thinks is a perfect location for an Unlimited store. Grace enters into a five-year lease on behalf of Unlimited, LLC, with Real Estate, Inc., the owner of the store building, to lease the store location at $100,000 rent per year. Is Unlimited, LLC, bound to either of these leases?

Case 6.6 *Division of Profits* Jack, Teddy, Braden, and Evan form a limited liability company called Millennium Foods, LLC, to operate an organic foods grocery store in Portland, Oregon. Jack and Teddy each contribute $25,000 capital, Braden contributes $50,000, and Evan contributes $100,000. The LLC's articles of organization are silent as to how profits and losses of the LLC are to be divided. The organic foods grocery store is an immediate success, and Millennium Foods, LLC, makes $200,000 profit the first year. Braden and Evan want the profits distributed based on the amount of the members' capital contribution. Jack and Teddy think the profits should be distributed equally. Who is correct?

Case 6.7 *Distributional Interest* Emma is one of five members of Blue Note, LLC, a limited liability company that operates a jazz club in New Orleans,

Louisiana. The LLC's operating agreement provides that Emma has the right to receive 20 percent of the LLC's profits. Emma also owns another business as a sole proprietorship and has taken out a $100,000 loan from River Bank to operate this other business. Emma defaults on her loan from River Bank, and River Bank sues Emma and obtains a charging order against Emma's ownership interest in Blue Note, LLC. What rights does River Bank have with regard to Blue Note, LLC, and Emma's interest in Blue Note, LLC?

Case 6.8 *Duty of Loyalty* Grace is a member and a manager of a manager-managed limited liability company called Movers & You, LLC, a moving company. The main business of Movers & You, LLC, is moving large corporations from old office space to new office space in other buildings. After Grace has been a member-manager of Movers & You, LLC, for several years, she decides to join her friend Keegan and form another LLC, called Keegan & Me, LLC. This new LLC provides moving services that move large corporations from old office space to new office space. Grace becomes a member-manager of Keegan & Me, LLC, while retaining her member-manager position at Movers & You, LLC. Grace does not disclose her new position at Keegan & Me, LLC, to the other members or managers of Movers & You, LLC. Several years later, the other members of Movers & You, LLC, discover Grace's other ownership and management position at Keegan & Me, LLC. Movers & You, LLC, sues Grace to recover damages for her working for Keegan & Me, LLC. Is Grace liable?

Case 6.9 *Duty of Care* Jack is a member of a member-managed limited liability company called Custom Homes, LLC. Custom Homes, LLC, is hired by an owner of a piece of vacant land located on Hilton Head Island, South Carolina, to build a new custom home on the site. Custom Homes, LLC, begins work on the house. Jack is responsible for making sure that flashing warning lights are placed in front of the house while it is being constructed to mark open holes in the ground and other dangerous conditions. One night, Jack leaves the site and forgets to place a flashing warning light marking a hole in front of the house that the LLC is building. That night, Kelsey, a neighbor who lives in one of the houses in the housing tract where the new house is being built, takes her dog for a walk. As Kelsey is walking by the unmarked area in front of the new house, she falls into the hole and is severely injured. Kelsey sues Custom Homes, LLC, to recover damages for her injuries. The jury finds that Jack was ordinarily negligent when he failed to place the flashing warning lights to mark the hole that Kelsey fell in and awards Kelsey $1 million for her injuries. Custom Homes, LLC, pays Kelsey the $1 million and then sues Jack to recover the $1 million. Is Jack liable?

BUSINESS ETHICS CASES

Case 6.10 *Business Ethics* Jake, Alex, Drew, and Jack want to start a new business that designs and manufactures toys for children. At a meeting in which the owners want to decide what type of legal form to use to operate the business, Drew states:

> *We should use a limited liability company to operate our business because this form of business provides us, the owners, with a limited liability shield, which means that if the business gets sued and loses, we the owners are not personally liable to the injured party except up to our capital contribution in the business.*

The others agree and form a limited liability company called Fuzzy Toys, LLC, to conduct the member-managed business. Each of the four owners contributes $50,000 as his capital contribution to the LLC. Fuzzy Toys, LLC, purchases $800,000 of liability insurance from Allied Insurance Company and starts business. Fuzzy Toys, LLC, designs and produces "Hank," a new toy male action figure. The new toy is an instant success, and Fuzzy Toys, LLC, produces and sells millions of these male action figures. After a few months, however, the LLC starts getting complaints that one of the parts of the male action figure is breaking off quite regularly, and some children are swallowing the part. The concerned member-managers of Fuzzy Toys, LLC, issue an immediate recall of the male action figure, but before all of the dolls are returned for a refund, Bo, a 7-year-old child, swallows the toy's part and is severely injured. Bo, through his mother, sues Fuzzy Toys, LLC, Allied Insurance Company, Jake, Alex, Drew, and Jack to recover damages for product liability. At the time of suit, Fuzzy Toys, LLC, has $200,000 of assets. The jury awards Bo $10 million for his injuries. Who is liable to Bo and for how much? How much does Bo recover? Did Jake, Alex, Drew, and Jack act ethically in setting up their toy business as an LLC? Explain.

Case 6.11 ***Business Ethics*** Matt, Ben, Caroline, and Maggie form iNet.com, LLC, a limited liability company. The four members are all Ph.D. scientists who have been working together in a backyard garage to develop a handheld wireless device that lets you receive and send e-mail, surf the Internet, use a word processing program that can print to any printer in the world, view cable television stations, and keep track of anyone you want anywhere in the world, as well as zoom in on the person being tracked without that person knowing you are doing so. This new device, called Eros, costs only $29 but makes the owners $25 profit per unit sold. The owners agree that they will buy a manufacturing plant and start producing the unit in six months. Maggie, who owns a one-quarter interest in iNet.com, LLC, decides she wants "more of the action" and soon, so she secretly sells the plans and drawings for the new Eros unit to a competitor for $100 million. The competitor comes out with exactly the same device, called Zeus, in one month and beats iNet.com, LLC, to market. The LLC, which later finds out about Maggie's action, suffers damages of $100 million because of Maggie's action. Is Maggie liable to iNet.com, LLC? Explain. Did Maggie act ethically in this case?

"A corporation is an artificial being, invisible, intangible, and existing only in the contemplation of law. Being the mere creature of the law, it possesses only those properties which the charter of its creation confers upon it, either expressly or as incidental to its very existence. These are such as supposed best calculated to effect the object for which it was created. Among the most important are immortality, and, if the expression may be allowed, individuality; properties by which a perpetual succession of many persons are considered as the same, and may act as a single individual."

–Chief Justice John Marshall

Dartmouth College v. Woodward, 17 U.S. 518 (1819).

Corporate Formation and Financing

CHAPTER 7

CASE SCENARIO

The law firm at which you work as a paralegal represents Leo V. Mysels, the president of Florida Fashions of Interior Design, Inc. (Florida Fashions). Florida Fashions is a Pennsylvania corporation and had never registered to do business in the state of Florida. While acting in the capacity of a salesman for the corporation, Mysels took an order for goods from Francis E. Barry. The transaction took place in Florida. Barry paid Florida Fashions for the goods ordered. Florida Fashions has failed to perform its obligations under the sales agreement.

CHAPTER OBJECTIVES

After studying this chapter, you should be able to:

1. Define *corporation* and list the major characteristics of a corporation.
2. Describe the process of forming a corporation.
3. Describe promoters' liability.
4. Define *common stock* and *preferred stock*.
5. Define *S corporation* and describe the tax benefits of this form of corporation.

PARALEGAL PERSPECTIVE

***Corry M. Baker** is an office administrator and OSBA-certified paralegal in the Toledo, Ohio office of Roetzel & Andress, LPA, a full-service, business law firm with eleven offices throughout Ohio, Florida, and Washington, D.C. She attended Rhodes State College and Bluffton University and received an associate in applied business and legal assisting as well as a bachelor in organizational management. She has been working as a paralegal for fourteen years. Some of her areas of specialization are corporate and business services; closely held and emerging businesses; and corporate governance, mergers, and acquisitions.*

Why do you think that corporation work is a good area for paralegals? Corporate formation and financing provide expansive opportunities for paralegals.

What are the most important paralegal skills needed for your job? The three most important skills in my job are what I call the ABC's of a paralegal: Focus your Attention to detail; an ability to think outside of the Box; and maintain efficient and effective Communication skills daily.

What is the academic background required for a paralegal entering your area of practice? My education in business, paralegal studies, and organizational management has assisted me to address many different problems. The skills gained through my education have been a great benefit to me.

How is technology involved in your job? Technology is an essential tool in my profession. It is an everyday necessity. Document management, case management, research, and other electronic-driven management programs are crucial when working as a paralegal.

What trends do you see in your area of practice that will likely affect your job in the future? Certification is the trend. Most states now require paralegal certification. Ohio has yet to adopt that law; however, the Ohio State Bar Association recently began offering a paralegal certification credentialing. I feel that this is just a precursor of new requirements that may be initiated in Ohio.

What do you feel is the biggest issue currently facing the paralegal profession? Due to the rise of malpractice coverage, many malpractice carriers are mandating paralegals to be college graduates and/or certified. Clients are interviewing potential legal counsel and requesting paralegals' credentials. As a result, I believe clients may deny paying for a paralegal who does not have the proper credentials and/or certifications.

What words of advice do you have for a new paralegal entering your area of practice? You need to be able to multitask, but make certain that you do not lose focus on the task at hand. Achieving an equal balance will keep you on your game and make you an asset to your firm.

INTRODUCTION TO CORPORATE FORMATION AND FINANCING

corporation
A fictitious legal entity that is created according to statutory requirements.

shareholder
A person who owns shares of stock in a corporation or joint-stock company.

general corporation statutes
Enacted by states to permit corporations to be formed without the separate approval of the legislature.

Corporations are the most dominant form of business organization in the United States, generating over 85 percent of the country's gross business receipts. Corporations range in size from one owner to thousands of owners. Owners of corporations are called **shareholders**.

Corporations were first formed in medieval Europe. Great Britain granted charters to certain trading companies from the 1500s to the 1700s. The English law of corporations applied in most of the colonies until 1776. After the Revolutionary War, the states of the United States developed their own corporation law.

Originally, corporate charters were individually granted by state legislatures. In the late 1700s, however, the states began enacting **general corporation statutes** that permitted corporations to be formed without the separate approval of the legislature. Today, most corporations are formed pursuant to general corporation laws of the states.

The formation and financing of corporations are discussed in this chapter.

NATURE OF THE CORPORATION

Corporations can be created only pursuant to the laws of the state of incorporation. These laws—commonly referred to as **corporations codes**—regulate the formation, operation, and dissolution of corporations. The state legislature may amend its corporate statutes at any time. Such changes may require a corporation's articles of incorporation to be amended.

corporations codes
State statutes that regulate the formation, operation, and dissolution of corporations.

The courts interpret state corporation statutes to decide individual corporate and shareholder disputes. As a result, a body of common law has evolved concerning corporate and shareholder rights and obligations.

The Corporation as a Legal "Person"

A corporation is a separate **legal entity** (or **legal person**) for most purposes. Corporations are treated, in effect, as artificial persons created by the state, which can sue or be sued in their own names, enter into and enforce contracts, hold title to and transfer property, and be found civilly and criminally liable for violations of law. Because corporations cannot be put in prison, the normal criminal penalty is the assessment of a fine, loss of a license, or another sanction. Corporations have unique characteristics, as discussed in the paragraphs that follow.

legal entity (legal person)
Legal existence; an entity other than a natural person that can function legally, sue, be sued, act through agents, and so on.

Limited Liability of Shareholders

As separate legal entities, corporations are liable for their own debts and obligations. Generally, the shareholders have only **limited liability**. That is, they are liable only to the extent of their capital contributions and do not have personal liability for the corporation's debts and obligations (see Exhibit 7.1).

Example: Kate and Betty form IT.com, Inc., a corporation, and each contributes $100,000 capital. The corporation borrows $1 million from State Bank. One year later, IT.com, Inc., goes bankrupt and defaults on the $1 million loan owed to

limited liability of shareholders
A general rule of corporate law that provides that, generally, shareholders are liable only to the extent of their capital contributions for the debts and obligations of their corporation and are not personally liable for the debts and obligations of the corporation.

Exhibit 7.1 Corporation

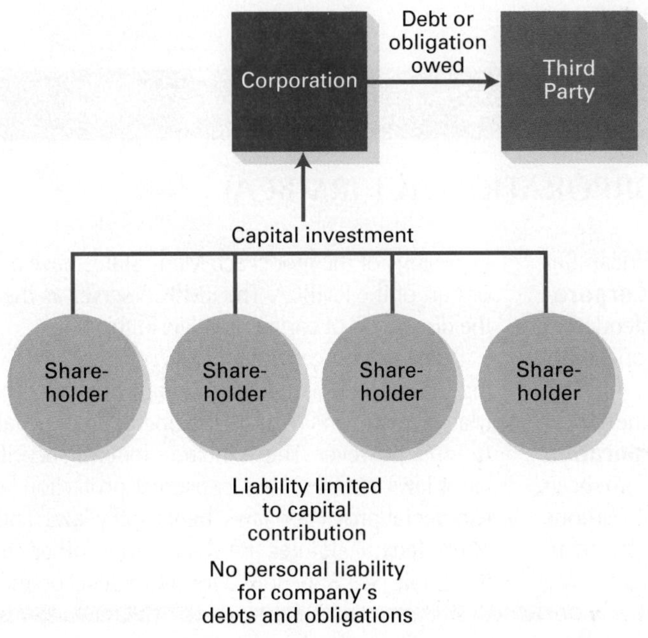

> They (corporations) cannot commit treason, nor be outlawed, nor excommunicated, for they have no souls.
> Lord Edward Coke
> *Reports (vol. V, Case of Sutton's Hospital)*

State Bank. At that time, IT.com, Inc., has only $50,000 in cash left, which State Bank recovers. Kate and Betty each lose their $100,000 capital contribution. However, Kate and Betty are not personally liable for the money still owed to State Bank. State Bank must absorb this loss.

Free Transferability of Shares

Corporate shares are freely transferable by a shareholder by sale, assignment, pledge, or gift unless they are issued pursuant to certain exemptions from securities registration. Shareholders may agree among themselves as to restrictions on the transfer of shares. National securities markets, such as the New York Stock Exchange and NASDAQ, have been developed for the organized sale of securities.

board of directors
A panel of decision makers, the members of which are elected by the shareholders.

officers
Employees of the corporation who are appointed by the board of directors to manage the day-to-day operations of the corporation.

Model Business Corporation Act (MBCA)
A model act drafted in 1950 that was intended to provide a uniform law for regulation of corporations.

Revised Model Business Corporation Act (RMBCA)
A 1984 revision of the MBCA that arranges the provisions of the act more logically, revises the language to be more consistent, and makes substantial changes in the provisions.

Perpetual Existence

Corporations exist in perpetuity unless a specific duration is stated in a corporation's articles of incorporation. The existence of a corporation can be voluntarily terminated by the shareholders. A corporation may be involuntarily terminated by the corporation's creditors if an involuntary petition for bankruptcy against the corporation is granted. The death, insanity, or bankruptcy of a shareholder, a director, or an officer of a corporation does not affect its existence.

Centralized Management

The **board of directors** makes policy decisions concerning the operation of a corporation. The members of the board of directors are elected by the shareholders. The directors, in turn, appoint corporate **officers** to run the corporation's day-to-day operations. Together, the directors and the officers form the corporate management.

LANDMARK LAW

REVISED MODEL BUSINESS CORPORATION ACT (RMBCA)

The Committee on Corporate Laws of the American Bar Association first drafted the **Model Business Corporation Act (MBCA)** in 1950. The model act was intended to provide a uniform law regulating the formation, operation, and termination of corporations.

In 1984, the committee completely revised the MBCA and issued the **Revised Model Business Corporation Act (RMBCA)**. Certain provisions of the RMBCA have been amended since 1984. The RMBCA arranges the provisions of the act more logically, revises the language of the act to be more consistent, and makes substantial changes in the provisions of the model act. Many states have adopted all or part of the RMBCA. The RMBCA serves as the basis for the discussion of corporation law in this book.

There is no general federal corporations law governing the formation and operation of private corporations. Many federal laws regulate the operation of private corporations, however. These include federal securities laws, labor laws, antitrust laws, consumer protection laws, environmental protection laws, bankruptcy laws, and the like. These federal statutes are discussed in other chapters in this book. (See Appendix D for more detail on this act.)

Public and Private Corporations

Government-owned corporations (or **public corporations**) are formed to meet a specific governmental or political purpose. Public corporations are formed pursuant to state law. Most cities and towns are formed as corporations, as are most water, school, sewage, and park districts. Local government corporations are often called **municipal corporations**.

government-owned (public) corporation
A corporation whose shares are traded to and among the general public.

municipal corporation
A city, town, or other local political entity formed by charter from the state and having the autonomous authority to administer the state's local affairs; especially a public corporation created for political purposes and endowed with political powers to be exercised for the public good in the administration of local civil government.

Private corporations are formed to conduct privately owned business. They are owned by private parties, not by the government. They range from small one-owner corporations to large multinational corporations such as Microsoft Corporation, Starbucks Corporation, and Google, Inc.

Profit and Not-for-Profit Corporations

Private corporations can be classified as either for *profit* or *not-for-profit corporations*. **Profit corporations** are created to conduct a business for profit and can distribute profits to shareholders in the form of dividends. Most private corporations fit this definition.

private corporation
A corporation formed to conduct privately owned business.

Not-for-profit corporations are formed for charitable, educational, religious, or scientific purposes. Although not-for-profit corporations may make a profit, they are prohibited by law from distributing this profit to their members, directors, or officers. About a dozen states have enacted the **Model Nonprofit Corporation Act**, which governs the formation, operation, and termination of not-for-profit corporations. All other states have their own individual statutes that govern the formation, operation, and dissolution of such corporations.

profit corporation
A corporation created to conduct a business for profit that can distribute profits to shareholders in the form of dividends.

not-for-profit corporation
A corporation organized for some purpose other than making a profit.

Model Nonprofit Corporation Act
A model act governing the formation, operation, and termination of not-for-profit corporations.

Publicly Held and Closely Held Corporations

Publicly held corporations have many shareholders. Often, they are large corporations with hundreds or thousands of shareholders, and their shares are traded on organized securities markets. Wal-Mart Stores, Inc., General Motors Corporation, and IBM are examples of publicly held corporations. The shareholders rarely participate in the management of such corporations.

publicly held corporation
A corporation that has many shareholders and whose securities are often traded on national stock exchanges.

A **closely held corporation (or close corporation)**, on the other hand, is one whose shares are owned by a few shareholders who are often family members, relatives, or friends. Frequently, the shareholders are involved in the management of the corporation. The shareholders sometimes enter into buy-and-sell agreements that prevent outsiders from becoming shareholders.

closely held corporation
A corporation owned by one or a few shareholders; also known as a *close corporation*.

Professional Corporations

Professional corporations are formed by professionals such as lawyers, accountants, physicians, and dentists. The abbreviations **P.C. (professional corporation), and P.A. (professional association)** often identify professional corporations. Shareholders of professional corporations are often called *members*. Generally, only licensed professionals may become members.

professional corporation
A corporation formed by lawyers, doctors, or other professionals.

P.A. (Professional Association)
A group of professionals organized to practice their profession together, although not necessarily in corporate or partnership form.

All states permit the incorporation of professional corporations, although some states allow only designated types of professionals to incorporate. Professional corporations have normal corporate attributes and are formed like other corporations. Members of a professional corporation are not usually liable for the torts committed by the corporation's agents or employees. Some states impose liability on members for the malpractice of other members of the corporation.

Domestic, Foreign, and Alien Corporations

domestic corporation
A corporation in the state in which it was formed.

foreign corporation
A corporation in any state or jurisdiction other than the one in which it was formed.

A corporation is a **domestic corporation** in the state in which it is incorporated. It is a **foreign corporation** in all other states and jurisdictions.

Example: The Ford Motor Company, a major manufacturer of automobiles and other vehicles, is incorporated in Delaware. It is a domestic corporation in Delaware. The Ford Motor Company conducts business in Michigan, where its headquarters offices are located, and it distributes vehicles in Delaware as well as the other forty-nine states. The Ford Motor Company is a foreign corporation in these other forty-nine states.

certificate of authority
A document authenticating a notarized document that is being sent to another jurisdiction.

A state can require a foreign corporation to *qualify* to conduct intrastate commerce within the state. Where a foreign corporation is required to qualify to conduct intrastate commerce in a state, it must obtain a **certificate of authority** from the state [RMBCA Section 15.01(a)]. This requires the foreign corporation to file certain information with the secretary of state, pay the required fees, and appoint a registered agent for service of process.

Conduct that usually constitutes "doing business" includes maintaining an office to conduct intrastate business, selling personal property in intrastate business, entering into contracts involving intrastate commerce, using real estate for general corporate purposes, and the like. Activities that are generally *not* considered doing business within the state include maintaining, defending, or settling a lawsuit or an administrative proceeding; maintaining bank accounts; effectuating sales through independent contractors; soliciting orders through the mail; securing or collecting debts; transacting any business in interstate commerce; and the like [RMBCA Sections 15.01(b), 15.01(c)].

Conducting intrastate business in a state in which it is not qualified subjects a corporation to fines. In addition, the corporation cannot bring a lawsuit in the state, although it can defend itself against lawsuits and administrative proceedings brought by others [RMBCA Section 15.02].

alien corporation
A corporation that is incorporated in another country.

An **alien corporation** is a corporation that is incorporated in another country. In most instances, alien corporations are treated as foreign corporations.

Concept Summary

Types of Corporations

Type of Corporation	Description
Domestic	A corporation is a domestic corporation in the state in which it is incorporated.
Foreign	A corporation is a foreign corporation in states other than the one in which it is incorporated.
Alien	A corporation is an alien corporation in the United States if it is incorporated in another country.

PARALEGAL PERSPECTIVE

Gail L. Whaley, ACP, is an advanced certified paralegal with Eastman & Smith Ltd. in Toledo, Ohio. She received a Bachelor of Science degree in social science/education from Michigan State University and a postbaccalaureate certificate in paralegal studies from the University of Toledo. She specializes in business organizations and has been working as a paralegal for thirty-four years.

How or why is the paralegal important to the form and financing of a company? Successful business ventures begin with the creative genius of the entrepreneur, but it generally takes a diverse team to bring those dreams into reality, including the intrepid paralegal who focuses on the small details of the big picture.

What are the most important paralegal skills needed for your job? Thorough knowledge of business organization statutes and state corporation division practices; workplace organization and communication skills; aptitude for technology and ability to adapt software for use in a business organizations practice.

What is the academic background required for a paralegal entering your area of practice? A bachelor's degree is required, preferably a four-year degree in paralegal studies with coursework including business law and secured transactions, as well as workplace organization. It is also helpful to have an understanding of real estate principles and practice and estate planning since those areas frequently overlap with the business law practice. This is especially true in a firm that specializes in smaller, closely held business entities.

How is technology involved in your job? Use of technology has become a major part of my job—from the use of Word to draft documents, to Excel and Access for managing the hundreds of minute books and related stock and membership records maintained by our firm. Additionally, practice management and docket/calendaring systems have become an integral part of the workplace.

What trends do you see in your area of practice that will likely affect your job in the future? I see continued emphasis on technology to help streamline the process of keeping projects on track and furthering communication among various members of the office team. I also envision a need to supplement the traditional paralegal staff with persons whose primary function is to keep track of the docketing/calendar and database systems. It is nearly impossible to have an effective system for marshalling, maintaining, and communicating huge quantities of detailed information about each entity a firm represents without a computerized database system that ties into the firm's calendar/docket system.

What do you feel is the biggest issue currently facing the paralegal profession? With the advent of paralegal degree programs, graduate paralegals are capable of performing most of the tasks traditionally performed by new (and even some more-experienced) law school graduates. In the past few decades, there has been a great increase in the number of law schools, with the concomitant increase in new law school graduates seeking employment. I have observed that law school graduates are often hired to fill positions that paralegals have successfully filled in the past. Many employers, unfortunately, assume it is to their advantage to hire a lawyer rather than a paralegal. However, it has been my observation that they are often disappointed to find that the new lawyer does not have the training or focus necessary to successfully organize a project or systematize a practice area.

Also, lawyers typically do not know how to utilize a paralegal. Even now, most law schools do not include information in the curriculum on how to work with paralegals and other support staff. Attorneys tend to either treat the paralegal as a "junior lawyer" or as a secretary. If viewed as a "junior lawyer," there is a risk that the paralegal will not be properly supervised, which becomes an ethical concern. Some lawyers do not fully understand that they must take ultimate responsibility for the paralegal's work product and it is, therefore, to their advantage to invest the necessary time to ensure that any given project is properly managed. If viewed more as a clerical worker, paralegals are sometimes given mundane work that probably should not even be charged to the client. Too often, work performed by secretaries or "legal administrative assistants" is being billed to clients as bona fide paralegal work.

What words of advice do you have for a new paralegal entering your area of practice? Keep on top of new developments in the business laws of the states where your firm practices. Also, prepare yourself to become the central clearinghouse for your firm's state filings. Keep organized. Also, be prepared to advocate for your position and train lawyers, over and over, on how to utilize a paralegal. Otherwise, you are likely to be relegated to a less-than professional position within your firm or law department.

The corporation is, and must be, the creature of the state. Into its nostrils the state must breathe the breath of a fictitious life. . .

Frederic William Maitland
Introduction to Gierke, Political Theories of the Middle Ages

INCORPORATION PROCEDURE

Corporations are creatures of statute. Thus, the organizers of a corporation must comply with the state's corporations code to form a corporation. The procedure for *incorporating* a corporation varies somewhat from state to state and is discussed in the following paragraphs.

Selecting a State for Incorporating a Corporation

A corporation can be incorporated in only one state, even though it can do business in all other states in which it qualifies to do business. In choosing a state for incorporation, the incorporators, directors, and/or shareholders must consider the corporation law of the states under consideration.

For the sake of convenience, most corporations (particularly small ones) choose the state in which the corporation will be doing most of its business as the state for incorporation. Large corporations generally opt to incorporate in the state with the laws that are most favorable to the corporation's internal operations (e.g., Delaware).

Selecting a Corporate Name

When starting a new corporation, the organizers must choose a name for the entity. To ensure that the name selected is not already being used by another business, the organizers should do the following [RMBCA Section 4.01]:

- Choose a name (and alternative names) for the corporation. The name must contain the word *corporation*, *company*, *incorporated*, or *limited* or an abbreviation of one of these words (i.e., *Corp.*, *Co.*, *Inc.*, *Ltd.*).
- Make sure the name chosen does not contain any word or phrase that indicates or implies that the corporation is organized for any purpose other than those stated in the articles of incorporation. For example, a corporate name cannot contain the word *Bank* if it is not authorized to conduct the business of banking.
- Determine whether the name selected is federally trademarked by another company and is therefore unavailable for use. Trademark lawyers and specialized firms can conduct trademark searches for a fee.
- Determine whether the chosen name is similar to other nontrademarked names and is therefore unavailable for use. Lawyers and specialized firms can conduct such searches for a fee.
- Determine whether the name selected is available as a domain name on the Internet. If the domain name is already owned by another person or business, the new corporation cannot use this domain name to conduct e-commerce over the Internet. Therefore, it is advisable to select another corporate name.

Incorporators

One or more persons, partnerships, domestic or foreign corporations, or other associations may act as **incorporators** of a corporation [RMBCA Section 2.01]. An incorporator's primary duty is to sign the articles of incorporation. Incorporators often become shareholders, directors, or officers of the corporation.

incorporator
The person(s), partnership(s), or corporation(s) that is responsible for incorporation of a corporation.

INTERNET LAW AND ONLINE COMMERCE

Choosing a Domain Name

Most large corporations trademark their corporate names as well as the major brand names of their products and services. In addition, since the advent of the Internet, these corporations usually register the **domain name** of their trademarks and service marks to promote and conduct business over the World Wide Web. One such corporation that did so was Ticketmaster Corporation, which registered the name Ticketmaster as a mark with the U.S. Patent and Trademark Office and also registered the domain name *ticketmaster.com*.

Subsequently, a person named Brown registered three domain names—*urn2ticketmaster.com*, *urn2ticketmaster.net*, and *urn2ticketmaster.org*. Ticketmaster Corporation brought an arbitration proceeding against Brown in the World Intellectual Property Organization (WIPO), alleging a violation of the Uniform Domain Name Dispute Resolution Procedure (UDRP), by which all domain name registrants agree to abide. To recover or cancel a domain name under UDRP, the petitioner must prove that (1) the challenged domain name is identical or confusingly similar to its trademark or service mark, (2) the registrant of the domain name has no legitimate interest in the name, and (3) the domain name was registered in *bad faith*.

The arbitrator first found that the three domain names registered by Brown were confusingly similar to Ticketmaster's service mark and that the addition of the prefix "urn2" (pronounced "you are into") did nothing to reduce the domain names' similarity or confusion with Ticketmaster's famous mark. Second, the arbitrator held that Brown had no legitimate interest in the domain names. Third, the arbitrator found that Brown had acted in bad faith in registering the domain names. The arbitrator noted that Brown had offered to sell *urn2ticketmaster.com* to Ticketmaster Corporation and had made no use of any of the names. Accordingly, the arbitrator ordered that the three domain names be canceled. *Ticketmaster Corporation v. Brown*, WIPO, No. D2001-0716 (2001)

domain name
A unique name that identifies an individual's or company's website.

ETHICS SPOTLIGHT

PROMOTERS' LIABILITY

A **promoter** is a person who organizes and starts a corporation, finds the initial investors to finance the corporation, and so on. Promoters often enter into contracts on behalf of a corporation prior to its actual incorporation. **Promoters' contracts** include leases, sales contracts, contracts to purchase real or personal property, employment contracts, and the like. Promoters' liability and the corporation's liability on promoters' contracts follow these rules:

- If the corporation never comes into existence, the promoters have joint personal liability on the contract unless the third party specifically exempts them from such liability.
- If the corporation is formed, it becomes liable on a promoter's contract only if it agrees to become bound to the contract. A resolution of the board of directors binds the corporation to a promoter's contract.
- Even if the corporation agrees to be bound to the contract, the promoter remains liable on the contract unless the parties enter into a **novation**, a three-party agreement in which the corporation agrees to assume the contract liability of the promoter with the consent of the third party. After a novation, the corporation is solely liable on the promoter's contract.

promoter
A person who organizes and starts a corporation, negotiates and enters into contracts in advance of its formation, finds the initial investors to finance the corporation, and so forth.

promoters' contracts
A collective term for such things as leases, sales contracts, contracts to purchase property, and employment contracts entered into by promoters on behalf of the proposed corporation prior to its actual incorporation.

novation
The substitution by mutual agreement of one debtor for another or of one creditor for another, whereby the old debt is extinguished.

Articles of Incorporation

articles of incorporation
The basic governing document of a corporation. It must be filed with the secretary of state of the state of incorporation; also known as a *corporate charter*.

The **articles of incorporation (or corporate charter)** is the basic governing document of a corporation. It must be drafted and filed with, and approved by, the state before the corporation can be officially incorporated. Under the RMBCA, the articles of incorporation must include [RMBCA Section 2.02(a)]:

- The name of the corporation
- The number of shares the corporation is authorized to issue
- The address of the corporation's initial registered office and the name of the initial registered agent
- The name and address of each incorporator

The articles of incorporation may also include provisions concerning (1) the period of duration (which may be perpetual), (2) the purpose or purposes for which the corporation is organized, (3) limitation or regulation of the powers of the corporation, (4) regulation of the affairs of the corporation, or (5) any provision that would otherwise be contained in the corporation's bylaws.

Exhibit 7.2 illustrates sample articles of incorporation.

Exhibit 7.2 Articles Of Incorporation

ARTICLES OF INCORPORATION
OF
THE BIG CHEESE CORPORATION

ONE: The name of this corporation is:

THE BIG CHEESE CORPORATION

TWO: The purpose of this corporation is to engage in any lawful act or activity for which a corporation may be organized under the General Corporation Law of California other than the banking business, the trust company business, or the practice of a profession permitted to be incorporated by the California Corporations Code.

THREE: The name and address in this state of the corporation's initial agent for service of process is:

Nikki Nguyen, Esq.
1000 Main Street
Suite 800
Los Angeles, California 90010

FOUR: This corporation is authorized to issue only one class of shares which shall be designated common stock. The total number of shares it is authorized to issue is 1,000,000 shares.

FIVE: The names and addresses of the persons who are appointed to act as the initial directors of this corporation are:

Shou-Yi Kang	100 Maple Street Los Angeles, California 90005
Frederick Richards	200 Spruce Road Los Angeles, California 90006
Jessie Quian	300 Palm Drive Los Angeles, California 90007
Richard Eastin	400 Willow Lane Los Angeles, California 90008

SIX: The liability of the directors of the corporation from monetary damages shall be eliminated to the fullest extent possible under California law.

SEVEN: The corporation is authorized to provide indemnification of agents (as defined in Section 317 of the Corporations Code) for breach of duty to the corporation and its stockholders through bylaw provisions or through agreements with the agents, or both, in excess of the indemnification otherwise permitted by Section 317 of the Corporations Code, subject to the limits on such excess indemnification set forth in Section 204 of the Corporations Code.

IN WITNESS WHEREOF, the undersigned, being all the persons named above as the initial directors, have executed these Articles of Incorporation.

Dated: January 1, 2011

Amending the Articles of Incorporation

A corporation's articles of incorporation can be amended to contain any provision that could have been lawfully included in the original document [RMBCA Section 10.01]. Such an amendment must show that (1) the board of directors adopted a *resolution* recommending the amendment and (2) the shareholders voted to approve the amendment [RMBCA Section 10.03]. The board of directors of a corporation may approve an amendment to the articles of incorporation without shareholder approval if the amendment does not affect rights attached to shares [RMBCA Section 10.02]. After the shareholders approve an amendment, the corporation must file **articles of amendment** with the secretary of state of the state of incorporation [RMBCA Section 10.06].

articles of amendment
A document filed to effectuate an amendment or change to a corporation's articles of incorporation.

Corporate Status

The RMBCA provides that corporate existence begins when the articles of incorporation are filed. The secretary of state's filing of the articles of incorporation is *conclusive proof* that the corporation satisfied all conditions of incorporation. After that, only the state can bring a proceeding to cancel or revoke the incorporation or involuntarily dissolve the corporation. Third parties cannot thereafter challenge the existence of the corporation or assert its lack of existence as a corporation as a defense against the corporation [RMBCA Section 2.03]. The corollary to this rule is that failure to file articles of incorporation is conclusive proof of the nonexistence of a corporation.

Purpose of a Corporation

A corporation can be formed for any lawful purpose. Many corporations include a **general-purpose clause** in their articles of incorporation. Such a clause allows the corporation to engage in any activity permitted by corporation law. A corporation may choose to limit its purpose or purposes by including a **limited-purpose clause** in the articles of incorporation [RMBCA Section 3.01]. For example, a corporation may be organized "to engage in the business of real estate development."

general-purpose clause
A clause often included in the articles of incorporation that authorizes the corporation to engage in any activity permitted by corporation law.

limited-purpose clause
A clause often included in the articles of incorporation that authorizes the corporation to engage in limited activities permitted by corporation law.

Registered Agent

The articles of incorporation must identify a registered office with a designated **registered agent** (either an individual or a corporation) in the state of incorporation [RMBCA Section 5.01]. The registered office does not have to be the same as the corporation's place of business. A statement of change must be filed with the secretary of state of the state of incorporation if either the registered office or the registered agent is changed. Attorneys often act as the registered agents of corporations.

The registered agent is empowered to accept service of process on behalf of the corporation.

registered agent
A person or corporation that is empowered to accept service of process on behalf of a corporation.

Example: If someone is suing a corporation, the complaint and summons are served on the registered agent. If no registered agent is named or the registered agent cannot be found at the registered office with reasonable diligence, service may be made by mail or alternative means [RMBCA Section 5.04].

Corporate Bylaws

In addition to the articles of incorporation, corporations are governed by their **bylaws**. Either the incorporators or the initial directors can adopt the bylaws of the corporation. The bylaws are much more detailed than are the articles of

bylaws
A detailed set of rules adopted by the board of directors after a corporation is incorporated that contains provisions for managing the business and the affairs of the corporation.

incorporation. Bylaws may contain any provisions for managing the business and affairs of the corporation that are not inconsistent with law or the articles of incorporation [RMBCA Section 2.06]. They do not have to be filed with any government official. The bylaws are binding on the directors, officers, and shareholders of the corporation.

The bylaws govern the internal management structure of a corporation. For example, they typically specify the time and place of the annual shareholders' meeting, how special meetings of shareholders are called, the time and place of annual and monthly meetings of the board of directors, how special meetings of the board of directors are called, the notice required for meetings, the quorum necessary to hold a shareholders' or board meeting, the required vote necessary to enact a corporate matter, the corporate officers and their duties, the committees of the board of directors and their duties, where the records of the corporation are kept, directors' and shareholders' rights to inspect corporate records, the procedure for transferring shares of the corporation, and such.

Sample provisions of corporate bylaws are set forth in Exhibit 7.3.

The board of directors has the authority to amend the bylaws unless the articles of incorporation reserve that right for the shareholders. The shareholders of

Exhibit 7.3 Bylaws

BYLAWS
OF
THE BIG CHEESE CORPORATION

ARTICLE I Offices

Section 1. Principal Executive Office. The corporation's principal executive office shall be fixed and located at such place as the Board of Directors (herein called the "Board") shall determine. The Board is granted full power and authority to change said principal executive office from one location to another.

Section 2. Other Offices. Branch or subordinate offices may be established at any time by the Board at any place or places.

ARTICLE II Shareholders

Section 1. Annual Meetings. The annual meetings of shareholders shall be held on such date and at such time as may be fixed by the Board. At such meetings, directors shall be elected and any other proper business may be transacted.

Section 2. Special Meetings. Special meetings of the shareholders may be called at any time by the Board, the Chairman of the Board, the President, or by the holders of shares entitled to cast not less than ten percent of the votes at such meeting. Upon request in writing to the Chairman of the Board, the President, any Vice President or the Secretary by any person (other than the Board) entitled to call a special meeting of shareholders, the officer forthwith shall cause notice to be given to the shareholders entitled to vote that a meeting will be held at a time requested by the person or persons calling the meeting, not less than thirty-five nor more than sixty days after the receipt of the request. If the notice is not given within twenty days after receipt of the request, the persons entitled to call the meeting may give the notice.

Section 3. Quorum. A majority of the shares entitled to vote, represented in person or by proxy, shall constitute a quorum at any meeting of shareholders. If a quorum is present, the affirmative vote of a majority of the shares represented and voting at the meeting (which shares voting affirmatively also constitute at least a majority of the required quorum) shall be the act of the shareholders, unless the vote of a greater number or voting by classes is required by law or by the Articles, except as provided in the following sentence. The shareholders present at a duly called or held meeting at which a quorum is present may continue to do business until adjournment, notwithstanding the withdrawal of enough shareholders to leave less than a quorum, if any action taken (other than adjournment) is approved by at least a majority of the shares required to constitute a quorum.

ARTICLE III Directors

Section 1. Election and term of office. The directors shall be elected at each annual meeting of the shareholders, but if any such annual meeting is not held or the directors are not elected thereat, the directors may be elected at any special meeting of shareholders held for that purpose. Each director shall hold office until the next annual meeting and until a successor has been elected and qualified.

Section 2. Quorum. A majority of the authorized number of directors constitutes a quorum of the Board for the transaction of business. Every act or decision done or made by a majority of the directors present at a meeting duly held at which a quorum is present shall be regarded as the act of the Board, unless a greater number be required by law or by the Articles. A meeting at which a quorum is initially present may continue to transact business notwithstanding the withdrawal of directors, if any action taken is approved by at least a majority of the required quorum for such meeting.

Section 3. Participation in Meetings by Conference Telephone. Members of the Board may participate in a meeting through use of conference telephone or similar communications equipment, so long as all members participating in such meeting can hear one another.

Section 4. Action Without Meeting. Any action required or permitted to be taken by the Board may be taken without a meeting if all members of the board shall individually or collectively consent in writing to such action. Such consent or consents shall have the same effect as a unanimous vote of the Board and shall be filed with the minutes of the proceedings of the Board.

the corporation have the absolute right to amend the bylaws even though the board of directors may also amend the bylaws [RMBCA Section 10.20].

Corporate Seal

Most corporations adopt a **corporate seal** [RMBCA Section 3.02(2)]. Generally, the seal is a design that contains the name of the corporation and the date of incorporation. It is imprinted by the corporate secretary on certain legal documents (e.g., real estate deeds) that are signed by corporate officers or directors. The seal is usually affixed using a metal stamp.

corporate seal
A design containing the name of the corporation and the date of incorporation that is imprinted by the corporate secretary using a metal stamp on certain legal documents.

Organizational Meeting

An **organizational meeting** of the initial directors of a corporation must be held after the articles of incorporation are filed. At this meeting, the directors must adopt the bylaws, elect corporate officers, and transact such other business as may come before the meeting [RMBCA Section 2.05]. The last category includes such matters as accepting share subscriptions, approving the form of the stock certificate, authorizing the issuance of the shares, ratifying or adopting promoters' contracts, authorizing the reimbursement of promoters' expenses, selecting a bank, choosing an auditor, forming committees of the board of directors, fixing the salaries of officers, hiring employees, authorizing the filing of applications for government licenses to transact the business of the corporation, and empowering corporate officers to enter into contracts on behalf of the corporation. Exhibit 7.4 contains sample corporate resolutions from an organizational meeting of a corporation.

organizational meeting
A meeting that must be held by the initial directors of a corporation after the articles of incorporation are filed.

FINANCING THE CORPORATION: STOCK

A corporation needs to finance the operation of its business. The most common way to do this is by selling *equity securities* and *debt securities*. **Equity securities (or stocks)** represent ownership rights in the corporation. Equity securities can be *common stock* or *preferred stock*. These are discussed in the following paragraphs.

equity securities
Representation of ownership rights to a corporation; also called *stocks*.

Common Stock

Common stock is an equity security that represents the residual value of a corporation. Common stock has no preferences. That is, creditors and preferred shareholders must receive their required interest and dividend payments before common shareholders receive anything. Common stock does not have a fixed maturity date. If a corporation is liquidated, the creditors and preferred shareholders are paid the value of their interests first, and the common shareholders are paid the value of their interests (if any) last. Corporations may issue different classes of common stock [RMBCA Sections 6.01(a), 6.01(b)].

common stock
A type of equity security that represents the *residual* value of a corporation.

Persons who own common stock are called **common stockholders**. A common stockholder's investment in the corporation is represented by a **common stock certificate**. Common stockholders have the right to elect directors and to vote on mergers and other important matters. In return for their investment, common stockholders receive **dividends** declared by the board of directors.

common stockholder
A person who owns common stock.

common stock certificate
A document that represents the common shareholder's investment in the corporation.

dividend
A distribution of profits of the corporation to shareholders.

Exhibit 7.4 Minutes Of An Organizational Meeting

MINUTES OF FIRST MEETING
OF
BOARD OF DIRECTORS
OF
THE BIG CHEESE CORPORATION
January 2, 2011
10:00 A.M.

The Directors of said corporation held their first meeting on the above date and at the above time pursuant to required notice.

The following Directors, constituting a quorum of the Board of Directors, were present at such meeting:

Shou-Yi Kang
Frederick Richards
Jessie Quian
Richard Eastin

Upon motion duly made and seconded, Shou-Yi was unanimously elected Chairman of the meeting and Frederick Richards was unanimously elected Secretary of the meeting.

1. Articles of Incorporation and Agent for Service of Process

The Chairman stated that the Articles of Incorporation of the Corporation were filed in the office of the California Secretary of State. The Chairman presented to the meeting a certified copy of the Articles of Incorporation. The Secretary was directed to insert the copy in the Minute Book. Upon motion duly made and seconded, the following resolution was unanimously adopted:

RESOLVED, that the agent named as the initial agent for service of process in the Articles of Incorporation of this corporation is here by confirmed as this corporation's agent for the purpose of service of process.

2. Bylaws

The matter of adopting Bylaws for the regulation of the affairs of the corporation was next considered. The Secretary presented to the meeting a form of Bylaws, which was considered and discussed. Upon motion duly made and seconded, the following recitals and resolutions were unanimously adopted:

WHEREAS, there has been presented to the directors a form of Bylaws for the regulation of the affairs of this corporation; and

WHEREAS, it is deemed to be in the best interests of this corporation that said Bylaws be adopted by this Board of Directors as the Bylaws of this corporation;

NOW, THEREFORE, BE IT RESOLVED, that Bylaws in the form presented to this meeting are adopted and approved as the Bylaws of this corporation until amended or repealed in accordance with applicable law.

RESOLVED FURTHER, that the Secretary of this corporation is authorized and directed to execute a certificate of the adoption of said Bylaws and to enter said Bylaws as so certified in the Minute Book of this corporation, and to see that a copy of said Bylaws is kept at the principal executive or business office of this corporation in California.

3. Corporate Seal

The secretary presented for approval a proposed seal of the corporation. Upon motion duly made and seconded, the following resolution was unanimously adopted:

RESOLVED, that a corporate seal is adopted as the seal of this corporation in the form of two concentric circles, with the name of this corporation between the two circles and the state and date of incorporation within the inner circle.

4. Stock Certificate

The Secretary presented a proposed form of stock certificate for use by the corporation. Upon motion duly made and seconded, the following resolution was unanimously adopted:

RESOLVED, that the form of stock certificate presented to this meeting is approved and adopted as the stock certificate of this corporation.

The secretary was instructed to insert a sample copy of the stock certificate in the Minute Book immediately following these minutes.

5. Election of officers

The Chairman announced that it would be in order to elect officers of the corporation. After discussion and upon motion duly made and seconded, the following resolution was unanimously adopted:

RESOLVED, that the following persons are unanimously elected to the offices indicated opposite their names

Title	Name
Chief Executive Officer	Shou-Yi Kang
President	Frederick Richards
Secretary and Vice President	Jessie Quian
Treasurer	Richard Eastin

There being no further business to come before the meeting, on motion duly made, seconded and unanimously carried, the meeting was adjourned.

CONTEMPORARY Environment

CLOSE CORPORATION ELECTION UNDER STATE CORPORATION LAW

Many of the formal rules in state corporation statutes are designed to govern the management of large, publicly held corporations. These rules may not be relevant for regulating the management of *close corporations*—that is, corporations formed by entrepreneurs with few shareholders who often work for the corporation and manage its day-to-day operations.

The **Model Statutory Close Corporation Supplement** (**Supplement**) was added to the RMBCA to permit entrepreneurial corporations to choose to be close corporations under state law. Only corporations with fifty or fewer shareholders may elect statutory close corporation (SCC) status. To choose this status, two-thirds of the shares of each class of shares of the corporation must approve the election. The articles of incorporation must contain a statement that the corporation is a statutory close corporation, and the share certificates must conspicuously state that the shares have been issued by a statutory close corporation.

A close corporation may dispense with some of the formalities of operating a corporation. For example, if all the shareholders approve, a close corporation may operate without a board of directors, and the articles of incorporation should contain a statement to that effect. The powers and affairs of the corporation are then managed by the shareholders. A close corporation need not adopt bylaws if the provisions required by law to be contained in bylaws are contained in the articles of incorporation or a shareholders' agreement.

A statutory close corporation need not hold annual shareholders' meetings unless one or more shareholders demand in writing that such meetings be held. The shareholders may enter into a shareholders' agreement about how the corporation will be managed. In effect, the shareholders can treat the corporation as a partnership for governance purposes [Supp. Section 20(b)(3)]. Selecting statutory close corporation status does not affect the limited liability of shareholders [Supp. Section 25].

model statutory close corporation supplement
Provisions added to RMBCA to permit entrepreneurial corporations to choose to be close corporations under state law.

Preferred Stock

Preferred stock is an equity security that is given certain *preferences and rights over common stock* [RMBCA Section 6.01(c)]. The owners of preferred stock are called **preferred stockholders**. Preferred stockholders are issued **preferred stock certificates** to evidence their ownership interest in the corporation.

Preferred stock can be issued in classes or series. One class of preferred stock can be given preference over another class of preferred stock. Like common stockholders, preferred stockholders have limited liability. Preferred stockholders generally are not given the right to vote for the election of directors or such. However, they are often given the right to vote if there is a merger or if the corporation has not made the required dividend payments for a certain period of time (e.g., three years).

Preferences of preferred stock must be set forth in the articles of incorporation. Preferred stock may have any or all of the preferences or rights discussed in the following paragraphs.

preferred stock
A type of equity security that is given certain preferences and rights over common stock.

preferred stockholder
A person who owns preferred stock.

preferred stock certificate
A document that represents a shareholder's investment in preferred stock in the corporation.

Dividend Preference

dividend preference
The right to receive a fixed dividend at stipulated periods during the year (e.g., quarterly).

fixed dividend
Where the dividend rate is usually set at a percentage of the initial offering price.

A **dividend preference** is the right to receive a **fixed dividend** at set periods during the year (e.g., quarterly). The dividend rate is usually a set percentage of the initial offering price.

Example: A stockholder purchases $10,000 of a preferred stock that pays an 8 percent dividend annually. The stockholder has the right to receive $800 each year as a dividend on the preferred stock.

Liquidation Preference

liquidation preference
The right to be paid a stated dollar amount if a corporation is dissolved and liquidated.

The right to be paid before common stockholders if the corporation is dissolved and liquidated is called a **liquidation preference**. A liquidation preference is normally a stated dollar amount.

Example: A corporation issues a preferred stock that has a liquidation preference of $200. This means that if the corporation is dissolved and liquidated, the holder of each preferred share will receive at least $200 before the common shareholders receive anything. Note that because the corporation must pay its creditors first, there may be insufficient funds to pay this preference.

Cumulative Dividend Right

cumulative preferred stock
Stock for which any missed dividend payments must be paid in the future to the preferred shareholders before the common shareholders can receive any dividends.

arrearages
Unpaid debts.

noncumulative preferred stock
Preferred stock that must receive dividends in full before common shareholders may receive any dividend.

Corporations must pay a preferred dividend if they have the earnings to do so. **Cumulative preferred stock** provides that any missed dividend payments must be paid in the future to the preferred shareholders before the common shareholders can receive any dividends. The amount of unpaid cumulative dividends is called dividend **arrearages**. Usually, arrearages can be accumulated for only a limited period of time (e.g., three years).

With **noncumulative preferred stock**, there is no right of accumulation. In other words, the corporation does not have to pay any missed dividends.

Example: The WindSock Corporation issues cumulative preferred stock that requires the payment of a quarterly dividend of $1.00 per share. The WindSock Corporation falls behind with six quarterly payments—$6.00 per share of preferred stock. The next quarter, the corporation makes a profit of $7.00 per share. The corporation must pay the $6.00 per share of arrearages to the preferred shareholders plus this quarter's payment of $1.00 per share. Thus, the common shareholders receive nothing.

Right to Participate in Profits

participating preferred stock
Stock that allows the preferred stockholder to participate in the profits of the corporation along with the common stockholders.

nonparticipating preferred stock
Preferred stock that does not give the shareholder the right to additional earnings—usually surplus common stock dividends—beyond those stated in the preferred contract.

Participating preferred stock allows a preferred stockholder to participate in the profits of the corporation along with the common stockholders. Participation is in addition to the fixed dividend paid on preferred stock. The terms of participation vary widely. Usually, the common stockholders must be paid a certain amount of dividends before participation is allowed. **Nonparticipating preferred stock** does not give the holder a right to participate in the profits of the corporation beyond the fixed dividend rate. Most preferred stock falls into this category.

Conversion Right

convertible preferred stock
Stock that permits the preferred stockholders to convert their shares into common stock.

Convertible preferred stock permits the preferred stockholders to convert their shares into common stock. The terms and exchange rate of the conversion are established when the shares are issued. The holders of convertible preferred stock usually exercise this option if the corporation's common stock significantly increases in value. Preferred stock without a conversion feature is called **nonconvertible preferred stock**. Nonconvertible stock is more common than convertible stock.

nonconvertible preferred stock
A security (bond or preferred stock) that may be exchanged by the owner for another security, especially common stock from the same company at a fixed price on a specified date.

Redeemable Preferred Stock

Redeemable preferred stock (or callable preferred stock) permits a corporation to redeem (i.e., buy back) the preferred stock at some future date. The terms of the redemption are established when the shares are issued. Corporations usually redeem the shares when the current interest rate falls below the dividend rate of the preferred shares. Preferred stock that is not redeemable is called **nonredeemable preferred stock**. Nonredeemable stock is more common than redeemable stock.

redeemable preferred stock
Stock that permits a corporation to buy back the preferred stock at some future date.

nonredeemable preferred stock
Preferred stock that is not redeemable.

Authorized, Issued, and Outstanding Shares

The number of shares provided for in the articles of incorporation is called **authorized shares** [RMBCA Section 6.01]. The shareholders may vote to amend the articles of incorporation to increase this amount. Authorized shares that have been sold by the corporation are called **issued shares**. Not all authorized shares have to be issued at the same time. Authorized shares that have not been issued are called **unissued shares**. The board of directors can vote to issue unissued shares at any time without shareholder approval.

A corporation is permitted to repurchase its shares [RMBCA Section 6.31]. Repurchased shares are commonly called **treasury shares**. Treasury shares cannot be voted by the corporation, and dividends are not paid on these shares. Treasury shares can be reissued by the corporation. The shares that are in shareholder hands, whether originally issued or reissued treasury shares, are called **outstanding shares**. Only holders of outstanding shares have the right to vote [RMBCA Section 6.03].

authorized shares
The number of shares provided for in the articles of incorporation.

issued shares
Shares that have been sold by a corporation.

unissued shares
Shares of a corporation that have been authorized but are not outstanding.

treasury shares
Shares of stock repurchased by the company itself.

outstanding shares
Shares of stock that are in shareholder hands.

Concept Summary

Types of Shares

Type of Share	Description
Authorized	Shares authorized in the corporation's articles of incorporation.
Issued	Shares sold by the corporation.
Treasury	Shares repurchased by the corporation. These shares do not have the right to vote.
Outstanding	Issued shares minus treasury shares. These shares have the right to vote.

Consideration to Be Paid for Shares

The RMBCA allows shares to be issued in exchange for any benefit to the corporation, including cash, tangible property, intangible property, promissory notes, services performed, contracts for services performed, or other securities of the cor-

CONTEMPORARY Environment

STOCK OPTIONS AND STOCK WARRANTS

Stock Warrants
A stock warrant is a stock option that is evidenced by a certificate.

Stock Options
A stock option gives the recipient the right to purchase shares of the corporation from the corporation at a stated price (called the *striking price*) for a specified period of time (called the *option period*).

A corporation can grant stock options (options) and **stock warrants** (warrants) that permit parties to purchase common or preferred shares at a certain price for a set time [RMBCA § 6.24].

A stock option gives the recipient the right to purchase shares of the corporation from the corporation at a stated price (called the *striking price*) for a specified period of time (called the *option period*). If the profitability of the corporation and the market value of its securities increase during the option period, the holder of the option is likely to *exercise the option*—that is, purchase the shares subject to the option. Stock options are nontransferable.

Corporations commonly grant stock options to top-level managers. Stock options are often issued to attract executive talent to work for the corporation. Shareholders sometimes criticize their corporations for being too generous in granting stock options.

A stock warrant is a stock option that is evidenced by a certificate. Warrants are commonly issued in conjunction with other securities. A warrant holder can exercise the warrant and purchase the common stock at the strike price anytime during the warrant period. Warrants can be transferable or nontransferable.

poration. In the absence of fraud, the judgment of the board of directors or shareholders as to the value of consideration received for shares is conclusive [RMBCA Sections 6.21(b), 6.21(c)].

FINANCING THE CORPORATION: DEBT SECURITIES

debt securities
Securities that establish a debtor–creditor relationship in which the corporation borrows money from the investor to whom a debt security is issued.

A corporation often raises funds by issuing debt securities [RMBCA Section 3.02(7)]. **Debt securities (also called fixed income securities)** establish a debtor–creditor relationship in which the corporation borrows money from the investor to whom the debt security is issued. The corporation promises to pay interest on the amount borrowed and to repay the principal at some stated maturity date in the future. The corporation is the *debtor*, and the holder is the *creditor*. The three classifications of debt securities—*debentures*, *bonds*, and *notes*—are discussed in the following paragraphs.

Debenture

debenture
A long-term unsecured debt instrument that is based on a corporation's general credit standing.

A **debenture** is a *long-term* (often thirty years or more), *unsecured* debt instrument that is based on a corporation's general credit standing. If the corporation encounters financial difficulty, unsecured debenture holders are treated as general creditors of the corporation (i.e., they are paid only after the secured creditors' claims are met).

Bond

bond
A long-term debt security that is secured by some form of collateral.

A **bond** is a *long-term* debt security that is *secured* by some form of *collateral* (e.g., real estate, personal property). Thus, bonds are the same as debentures except that they are secured. Secured bondholders can foreclose on the collateral in the event of nonpayment of interest, principal, or other specified events.

Note

A **note** is a *short-term* debt security with a maturity of five years or less. Notes can be either *unsecured* or *secured*. They usually do not contain a conversion feature. They are sometimes made redeemable.

note
A debt security with a maturity of five years or less.

Indenture Agreement

The terms of a debt security are commonly contained in a contract between the corporation and the holder; this contract is known as an **indenture agreement (or simply an indenture)**. The indenture generally contains the maturity date of the debt security, the required interest payment, the collateral (if any), rights to conversion into common or preferred stock, call provisions, any restrictions on the corporation's right to incur other indebtedness, the rights of holders upon default, and such. It also establishes the rights and duties of the indenture trustee. Generally, a trustee is appointed to represent the interest of the debt security holders. Bank trust departments often serve in this capacity.

indenture agreement
A contract between a corporation and a holder that contains the terms of a debt security.

Concept Summary

Debt Instruments

Debt Instrument	Description
Debenture	A *long-term, unsecured* debt instrument that is based on a corporation's general credit rating.
Bond	A *long-term* debt security that is *secured* by some form of property. The property securing the bond is called *collateral*. In the event of nonpayment of interest or principal or other specified events, bondholders can foreclose on and obtain the collateral.
Note	A *short-term* debt instrument with a maturity of five years or less. Notes can be either unsecured or secured.

CORPORATE POWERS

A corporation has the same basic rights to perform acts and enter into contracts as a physical person [RMBCA Section 3.02]. The express and implied powers of a corporation are discussed in the following paragraphs.

Express Powers

A corporation's **express powers** are found in (1) the U.S. Constitution, (2) state constitutions, (3) federal statutes, (4) state statutes, (5) articles of incorporation, (6) bylaws, and (7) resolutions of the board of directors. Corporation statutes normally state the express powers granted to the corporation.

express powers
Powers given to a corporation by (1) the U.S. Constitution, (2) state constitutions, (3) federal statutes, (4) state statutes, (5) articles of incorporation, (6) bylaws, and (7) resolutions of the board of directors.

Generally, a corporation has the power to purchase, own, lease, sell, mortgage, or otherwise deal in real and personal property; make contracts; lend money; borrow money; incur liabilities; issue notes, bonds, and other obligations; invest and reinvest funds; sue and be sued in its corporate name; make donations

court of chancery
Court that grants relief based on fairness; also called *equity court*.

CONTEMPORARY Environment

DELAWARE AND NEVADA CORPORATION LAW

The state of Delaware is the corporate haven of the United States. More than 50 percent of the publicly traded corporations in America, including 60 percent of the Fortune 500 companies, are incorporated in Delaware. In total, more than 500,000 business corporations are incorporated in Delaware. But why?

Remember that the state in which a corporation is incorporated determines the law that applies to the corporation: The corporations code of the state of incorporation applies to such things as election of directors, requirements for a merger to occur, laws for fending off corporate raiders, and such. So, even if a corporation does no business in Delaware, it can obtain the benefits of Delaware corporation law by incorporating itself in Delaware.

On the legislative side, Delaware has enacted the Delaware General Corporation Law. This law is the most advanced corporation law in the country, and the statute is particularly written to be of benefit to large corporations. For example, the Delaware corporations code provides for the ability of corporations incorporated in Delaware to adopt "poison pills" that make it virtually impossible for another company to take over a Delaware corporation unless the board of directors of the target corporation agrees and removes such poison pills. In addition, the legislature keeps amending the corporations code as the demands of big business warrant or need such changes. For instance, the legislature has enacted a state antitakeover statute that makes it legally impossible to take over a Delaware corporation unless the corporation's directors waive the state's antitakeover law and agree to be taken over.

On the judicial side, Delaware has a special court—the court of chancery—that hears and decides business cases. This court has been around for over two hundred years. During that time, it has interpreted Delaware corporation law favorably to large corporations in such matters as electing corporate boards of directors, eliminating negligence liability of outside directors, upholding the antitakeover provisions of the Delaware corporations code, and such. In addition, there are no emotional juries to worry about. The decisions of the chancery court are made by judges who are experts at deciding corporate law disputes. The court is known for issuing decisions favorable to large corporations as the court applies Delaware corporation law to decide disputes. Appeals from the court of chancery are brought directly to the Supreme Court of Delaware. Thus, Delaware courts have created a body of precedent of legal decisions that provides more assurance to Delaware corporations in trying to decide whether they will be sued and what the outcome will be if they do get sued.

The state of Delaware makes a substantial sum of money each year on fees charged to corporations incorporated within the state. Delaware is the "business state," providing advanced corporate laws and an expert judiciary for deciding corporate disputes.

The state of Nevada has become a state of choice for incorporation of corporations. The primary reason for incorporating in Nevada is tax: There are no state taxes on corporate income, franchises, or personal income; and for a Nevada resident, there is no state inheritance, gift, or estate tax. In addition, the Nevada corporations code makes it virtually impossible for creditors to ever reach the assets of shareholders of Nevada corporations. Nevada has also established a business court that has expert judges who hear only corporate and business matters. Nevada has taken a lead from Delaware and established itself as a business-friendly state. However, Nevada has aimed to attract smaller corporations, whereas Delaware still remains the choice of large, publicly held corporations.

for the public welfare or for charitable, scientific, or educational purposes; and the like. RMBCA Section 3.02 provides a list of express corporate powers.

Corporations formed under general incorporation laws cannot engage in certain businesses such as banking, insurance, or operation of public utilities. A corporation must obtain a corporate charter under special incorporation statutes and receive approval of special government administrative agencies before engaging in these businesses.

Implied Powers

Neither governing laws nor corporate documents can anticipate every act necessary for a corporation to carry on its business. **Implied powers** allow a corporation to exceed its express powers in order to accomplish its corporate purpose.

implied powers
Powers beyond express powers that allow a corporation to accomplish its corporate purpose.

Example: A corporation has implied power to open a bank account, reimburse its employees for expenses, engage in advertising, purchase insurance, and the like.

Ultra Vires Act

An act by a corporation that is beyond its express or implied powers is called an ***ultra vires* act**. The following remedies are available if an *ultra vires* act is committed:

***ultra vires* act**
An act by a corporation that is beyond its express or implied powers.

- Shareholders can sue for an injunction to prevent the corporation from engaging in the act.
- The corporation (or the shareholders, on behalf of the corporation) can sue the officers or directors who caused the act for damages.
- The attorney general of the state of incorporation can bring an action to enjoin the act or to dissolve the corporation [RMBCA Section 3.04].

TAXATION

A **C corporation** is a corporation that does not qualify to be or does not elect to be federally taxed as an S corporation. Any corporation with more than one hundred shareholders is automatically a C corporation for federal income tax purposes. A C corporation must pay federal income tax at the corporate level. In addition, if a C corporation distributes its profits to shareholders in the form of dividends, the shareholders must pay personal income tax on the dividends. This causes **double taxation**: one tax paid at the corporate level and another paid at the shareholder level. Form 1120 is used to report the income, gains, losses, deductions, and credits and to figure the income tax liability of a corporation.

C corporation
A corporation whose income is taxed through the corporation itself rather than through its shareholders.

double taxation
Taxing the same thing twice for the same purpose by the same taxing authority during identical taxation periods.

Congress enacted the **Subchapter S Revision Act** [26 U.S.C. Sections 6242 et seq.] to allow some corporations and their shareholders to avoid double taxation by electing to be S corporations.

If a corporation elects to be taxed as an **S corporation**, it pays no federal income tax at the corporate level. As in a partnership, the corporation's income or loss flows to the shareholders' individual income tax returns. Thus, this election is particularly advantageous if (1) the corporation is expected to have losses that can be offset against other income of the shareholders or (2) the corporation is expected to make profits and the shareholders' income tax brackets are lower

S Corporation
A corporation whose income is taxed through its shareholders rather than through the corporation itself. Only corporations with a limited number of shareholders can elect S corporation tax status under Subchapter S of the Internal Revenue Code.

> Did you ever expect a corporation to have a conscience, when it has no soul to be damned, and no body to be kicked?
> Lord Edward Thurlow, first Baron Thurlow

than the corporation's. Profits are taxed to the shareholders even if the income is not distributed. The shares retain other attributes of the corporate form, including limited liability.

Election to Be an S Corporation

Corporations that meet the following criteria can elect to be taxed as S corporations:

- The corporation must be a domestic corporation.
- The corporation cannot be a member of an affiliated group of corporations.
- The corporation can have no more than one hundred shareholders.
- Shareholders must be individuals, estates, or certain trusts. Corporations and partnerships cannot be shareholders.
- Shareholders must be citizens or residents of the United States. Nonresident aliens cannot be shareholders.
- The corporation cannot have more than one class of stock. Shareholders do not have to have equal voting rights.

An S corporation election is made by filing Form 2553 with the Internal Revenue Service (IRS). The election can be rescinded by shareholders who collectively own at least a majority of the shares of the corporation. However, if the election is rescinded, another S corporation election cannot be made for five years. Form 1120S is used to report the income, gains, losses, deductions, credits, and so on of a domestic corporation or other entity covered by an election to be an S corporation.

DISSOLUTION AND TERMINATION OF CORPORATIONS

The life of a corporation may be terminated voluntarily or involuntarily. The methods for dissolving and terminating corporations are discussed in the following paragraphs.

Voluntary Dissolution

voluntary dissolution
Dissolution of a corporation that has begun business or issued shares upon recommendation of the board of directors and a majority vote of the shares entitled to vote.

articles of dissolution
A document that a dissolving corporation must file with the appropriate governmental agency, usually the secretary of state, after the corporation has settled all its debts and distributed all its assets.

A corporation can be voluntarily dissolved. If the corporation has not commenced business or issued any shares, it may be dissolved by a vote of the majority of the incorporators or initial directors [RMBCA Section 14.01]. After that, the corporation can be voluntarily dissolved if the board of directors recommends dissolution and a majority of shares entitled to vote (or a greater number, if required by the articles of incorporation or bylaws) votes for dissolution as well [RMBCA Section 14.02].

For a **voluntary dissolution** to be effective, **articles of dissolution** must be filed with the secretary of state of the state of incorporation. A corporation is dissolved upon the effective date of the articles of dissolution [RMBCA Section 14.03]. See Exhibit 7.5.

Administrative Dissolution

administrative dissolution
Involuntary dissolution of a corporation that is ordered by the secretary of state if a corporation has failed to comply with certain procedures required by law.

The secretary of state can obtain **administrative dissolution** of a corporation if (1) it failed to file an annual report, (2) it failed for sixty days to maintain a registered agent in the state, (3) it failed for sixty days after a change of its registered

Exhibit 7.5 Articles Of Dissolution

D
PC

The Commonwealth of Massachusetts

William Francis Galvin
Secretary of the Commonwealth
One Ashburton Place, Boston, Massachusetts 02108-1512

FORM MUST BE TYPED **Articles of Voluntary Dissolution** FORM MUST BE TYPED
(General Laws Chapter 156D, Section 14.03; 950 CMR 113.41)

(1) Exact name of corporation: ______________________________

(2) Registered office address: ______________________________
(number, street, city or town, state, zip code)

(3) Date authorized: ______________________________
(month, day, year)

(4-5) Approved by:

(check appropriate box)

☐ the shareholders as required by G.L. Chapter 156D, Section 14.02.

The total number of votes entitled to be cast on the proposal to dissolve ____________________;
(number entitled to vote)

with____________ votes for and ____________ votes against the dissolution proposal; or
(number for dissolution) *(number against dissolution)*

____________ undisputed votes for dissolution; and the number cast was sufficient for approval.
(number of undisputed votes)

If voting by groups was required on the dissolution proposal, attach an additional sheet that states the total number of votes entitled to be cast by each voting group; and either the total number of votes cast for and against dissolution by each voting group; or the total of undisputed votes cast for dissolution by each group; and a statement that the number cast for dissolution was sufficient for approval.

OR

☐ a method or procedure specified in the articles of organization pursuant to G.L. Chapter 156D, Section 14.02.
Attach an additional sheet to set forth such method or procedure, together with sufficient information to establish that the corporation has complied therewith.

(6) The dissolution of the corporation shall be effective at the time and on the date approved by the Division, unless a later effective date not more than 90 days from the date and time of filing is specified:____________________

P.C.

c156ds1403950c11341 01/13/05

Signed by: ______________________________
(signature of authorized individual)

☐ Chairman of the board of directors,

☐ President,

☐ Other officer,

☐ Court-appointed fiduciary,

on this ____________ day of____________________ ,

Exhibit 7.5 *(Continued)*

COMMONWEALTH OF MASSACHUSETTS

William Francis Galvin
Secretary of the Commonwealth
One Ashburton Place, Boston, Massachusetts 02108-1512

Articles of Voluntary Dissolution
(General Laws Chapter 156D, Section 14.03; 950 CMR 113.41)

I hereby certify that upon examination of these articles of voluntary dissolution, duly submitted to me, it appears that the provisions of the General Laws relative to the organization of corporations have been complied with, and I hereby approve said articles; and the filing fee in the amount of $____________________ having been paid, said articles are deemed to have been filed with me this ____________ day of __________________, 2011, at _________ a.m./p.m.
time

Effective date: ______________________________________
(must be within 90 days of date submitted)

____
Examiner

WILLIAM FRANCIS GALVIN
Secretary of the Commonwealth

____
#A.R.

Filing fee: $100

TO BE FILLED IN BY CORPORATION
Contact Information:

____

____

____

Telephone: ______________________________________

Email: ____

Upon filing, a copy of this filing will be available at www.sec.state.ma.us/cor.
If the document is rejected, a copy of the rejection sheet and rejected document will be available in the rejected queue.

agent to file a statement of such change with the secretary of state, (4) it did not pay its franchise fee, or (5) the period of duration stated in the corporation's articles of incorporation has expired [RMBCA Section 14.20]. If the corporation does not cure the default within sixty days of being notified of it, the secretary of state issues a **certificate of dissolution** that dissolves the corporation [RMBCA Section 14.21].

certificate of dissolution
A document issued by a state authority (usually the secretary of state) certifying that a corporation is dissolved.

Judicial Dissolution

A corporation can be involuntarily dissolved by a judicial proceeding. **Judicial dissolution** can be instituted by the attorney general of the state of incorporation if the corporation (1) procured its articles of incorporation through fraud or (2) exceeded or abused the authority conferred on it by law [RMBCA Section 14.30(1)]. If a court judicially dissolves a corporation, it enters a **decree of dissolution** that specifies the date of dissolution [RMBCA Section 14.33].

judicial dissolution
Dissolution of a corporation through a court proceeding instituted by the state.

decree of dissolution
A decree entered by a court that judicially dissolves a corporation on a specific date.

Winding Up, Liquidation, and Termination

A dissolved corporation continues its corporate existence but may not carry on any business except as required to **wind up and liquidate** its business and affairs [RMBCA Section 14.05].

In a voluntary dissolution, the liquidation is usually carried out by the board of directors. If the dissolution is involuntary or the dissolution is voluntary but the directors refuse to carry out the liquidation, a court-appointed receiver carries out the winding up and liquidation of the corporation [RMBCA Section 14.32].

Termination occurs only after the winding up of the corporation's affairs, the liquidation of its assets, and the distribution of the proceeds to the claimants. The liquidated assets are paid to claimants according to the following priority: (1) expenses of liquidation and creditors according to their respective liens and contract rights, (2) preferred shareholders according to their liquidation preferences and contract rights, and (3) common stockholders.

The dissolution of a corporation does not impair any rights or remedies available against the corporation or its directors, officers, or shareholders for any right or claim existing or incurred prior to dissolution.

winding up and liquidation
The process by which a dissolved corporation's assets are collected, liquidated, and distributed to creditors, preferred shareholders, and common shareholders.

termination
The ending of a corporation that occurs only after the winding up of the corporation's affairs, the liquidation of its assets, and the distribution of the proceeds to the claimants.

Concept Review

Corporations

Definition	A separate legal entity (or legal person) treated, in effect, as artificial persons created by the state, which can sue or be sued in their own names, enter into and enforce contracts, hold title to and transfer property, and be found civilly and criminally liable for violations of law.
Formation	The organizers of a corporation must comply with the state's corporations code to form a corporation. The procedure for incorporating a corporation varies somewhat from state to state. Articles of incorporation (or corporate charter) is the basic governing document of a corporation. It must be drafted and filed with, and approved by, the state before the corporation can be officially incorporated.

(continued)

Management	The board of directors makes policy decisions concerning the operation of a corporation. The members of the board of directors are elected by the shareholders. The directors, in turn, appoint corporate officers to run the corporation's day-to-day operations. Together, the directors and the officers form the corporate management.
Liability	Generally, the shareholders have only limited liability. That is, they are liable only to the extent of their capital contributions and do not have personal liability for the corporation's debts and obligations.
Taxation	A C corporation must pay federal income tax at the corporate level. In addition, if a C corporation distributes its profits to shareholders in the form of dividends, the shareholders must pay personal income tax on the dividends. This causes double taxation. Form 1120 is used to report the income, gains, losses, deductions, and credits and to figure the income tax liability of a corporation. Form 1120S is used to report the income, gains, losses, deductions, credits, and so on of a domestic corporation or other entity covered by an election to be an S corporation.
Termination	The life of a corporation may be terminated voluntarily or involuntarily. A dissolved corporation continues its corporate existence but may not carry on any business except as required to wind up and liquidate its business and affairs. Termination occurs only after the winding up of the corporation's affairs, the liquidation of its assets, and the distribution of the proceeds to the claimants.

PARALEGAL PRACTICE TOOL

CORPORATION FORMATION CHECKLIST

1. Select a corporate Name and an Assumed Name if desired.
2. Check with the secretary of state for the availability of the name(s) and, if desired, draft, execute, and file an Application to Reserve Corporate Name.
3. Designate a Registered Agent and Registered Office.
4. Determine the duration and purpose(s) for which the corporation is to be formed (if other than general purposes of a corporation).
5. Determine the number and identity of incorporators.
6. Determine the number and identity of directors.
7. Determine the number and identity of officers.
8. Determine the desired authorized equity capitalization.
9. Secure stock subscription agreements.
10. Determine the actual equity and/or debt financing and which exemptions to federal and state law will apply.
11. Determine whether an S corporation election is desired.
12. Determine a fiscal year.
13. Determine any stock restrictions and/or designations.
14. Designate a date and time for an annual meeting of the board of directors and shareholders.
15. Draft and execute bylaws.
16. Draft and execute a shareholder agreement.
17. Draft and execute any desired employment contracts.
18. Determine whether qualification in other states is desired.
19. Secure all state and local licenses required to operate the business, and secure any necessary insurance coverage.
20. Draft, execute, and file Articles of Incorporation and Certificate of Assumed Name (if desired) with the secretary of state.
21. Draft, execute, and file S corporation election on Form 2553 with the Internal Revenue Service (IRS), if desired, within seventy-five days of beginning of taxable year.
22. Draft, execute, and file Form SS-4 filed with the IRS for employer's identification number if the corporation will have employees.
23. Draft and execute organizational meeting minutes.
24. Prepare a corporate minute book.
25. Place the name of the corporation or trade name on all corporate material (e.g., letterhead, invoices, business cards, signs, contracts).

CHAPTER REVIEW

NATURE OF THE CORPORATION, p. 163

Name of the Corporation

1. ***Corporation.*** A corporation is a legal entity created pursuant to the laws of the state of incorporation.
2. ***Corporations codes.*** State statutes govern the formation, operation, and dissolution of corporations.

The Corporation as a Legal "Person"

A corporation is a separate legal entity—an *artificial person*—that can own property, sue and be sued, enter into contracts, and such.

Characteristics of Corporations

1. ***Limited liability of shareholders.*** Shareholders are liable for the debts and obligations of the corporation only to the extent of their capital contributions.
2. ***Free transferability of shares.*** Shares of a corporation are freely transferable by shareholders unless they are expressly restricted.
3. ***Perpetual existence.*** Corporations exist in perpetuity unless a specific duration is stated in the corporation's articles of incorporation.
4. ***Centralized management.*** The *board of directors* of the corporation makes policy decisions for the corporation. Corporate *officers* appointed by the board of directors run the corporation's day-to-day operations. Together, the directors and officers form the corporation's management.

The Revised Model Business Corporation Act

1. ***Model Business Corporation Act (MBCA).*** This model act, drafted in 1950, was intended to provide a uniform law for the regulation of corporations.
2. ***Revised Model Business Corporation Act (RMBCA).*** RMBCA is a revision of the MBCA promulgated in 1984 that arranges the provisions of the model act more logically, revises the language to be more consistent, and makes substantial changes that modernize the provisions of the act.

Public and Private Corporations

1. ***Public corporation.*** A public corporation is a corporation formed to meet a specific governmental or political purpose; also called a *government-owned* corporation. *Municipal corporations* (i.e., cities) are an example.
2. ***Private corporation.*** A private corporation is a corporation formed to conduct privately owned businesses. It may be large or small.

Profit and Not-for-Profit Corporations

1. ***Profit corporation.*** A profit corporation is created to conduct a business for profit and can distribute profits to shareholders in the form of dividends.
2. ***Not-for-profit (nonprofit) corporation.*** A nonprofit corporation is formed to operate charitable institutions, colleges, universities, and other not-for-profit entities. There are no shareholders for these corporations.

Publicly Held and Closely Held Corporations

1. ***Publicly held corporation.*** A publicly held corporation has many shareholders, and its securities are often traded on national stock exchanges. General Motors Corporation is an example.
2. ***Closely held corporation.*** A closely held corporation is owned by one or a few shareholders. Examples are family-owned corporations. They are also called *close corporations*.

Professional Corporations

Professional corporations are formed by lawyers, doctors, and other professionals. Shareholders of professional corporations are usually called *members*. Members must be licensed to practice the profession for which the corporation is formed.

Domestic, Foreign, and Alien Corporations

1. ***Domestic corporation.*** A domestic corporation is a corporation in the state in which it is incorporated.
2. ***Foreign corporation.*** A foreign corporation is a corporation in any state other than the one in which it is incorporated. A domestic corporation often transacts business in states other than its state of incorporation; hence, it is a foreign corporation in these states. A foreign corporation must obtain a *certificate of authority* from these other states to transact intrastate business in those states.
3. ***Alien corporation.*** An alien corporation is a corporation that is incorporated in another country. Alien corporations are treated as foreign corporations for most purposes.

INCORPORATION PROCEDURE, p. 168

Incorporation Procedures

1. ***Incorporation.*** Incorporation is the process of incorporating (forming) a new corporation.
2. ***Corporations code.*** Corporations are creatures of statute; they can be formed only if certain statutory formalities contained in the state's corporations code are followed.

Selecting a State for Incorporating a Corporation

A corporation can be incorporated in only one state, although it can conduct business in other states.

Selecting a Corporate Name

A corporate name selected for a new corporation must be distinguishable from existing corporate names. A corporate name may be reserved for a limited period of time while the corporation is being formed.

Incorporators

Incorporators are the persons, partnerships, or corporations who are responsible for incorporating a new corporation.

Promoters' Liability

1. ***Promoter.*** A promoter is a person or persons who organize and start a corporation, negotiate and enter into contracts in advance of formation, find the initial investors to finance the corporation, and so forth.

2. ***Promoter's contract.*** A promoter's contract is entered into by a promoter on behalf of a proposed corporation prior to its actual incorporation. These contracts often include leases, sales contracts, contracts to purchase property, and so forth.
3. ***Liability of promoters for promoters' contracts.*** Promoters are personally liable for promoters' contracts unless (1) the corporation ratifies the contract as its own once it is formed and (2) the corporation, the promoter, and the third party with whom the contract is made enter into a *novation* agreement that expressly releases the promoter from liability.

Articles of Incorporation

The articles of incorporation is the basic governing document of a corporation. This document must be filed with the secretary of state of the state of incorporation. It is a public document. It is also called the *corporate charter*.

1. ***Information to be set forth in the articles of incorporation.*** The corporations code of each state sets out the information that must be included in the articles of incorporation. Additional information may be included in the articles of incorporation as deemed necessary or desirable by the incorporators.
2. ***Amending the articles of incorporation.*** The articles of incorporation can be amended to contain any provision that could have been lawfully included in the original articles of incorporation. After an amendment is approved by the shareholders, the corporation must file *articles of amendment* with the secretary of state in the state in which it is incorporated.

Corporate Status

RMBCA rule. The filing of the articles of incorporation is *conclusive proof* that a corporation exists. After that, only the state can challenge the status of the corporation; third parties cannot. Failure to file articles of incorporation is conclusive proof that the corporation does not exist; the state and third parties may challenge the existence of the corporation.

Other Issues Concerning Incorporation

1. ***Purpose of a corporation.*** A corporation can be formed for any lawful purpose. Corporations can limit the purposes of the corporation by including in the articles of incorporation a *limited-purpose clause* that stipulates the purposes and activities the corporation can engage in.
2. ***Registered agent.*** A new corporation must designate a person or corporation that is empowered to accept *service of process* on behalf of the corporation. A new designation must be made annually.

Corporate Bylaws

Bylaws are a detailed set of rules that are adopted by the board of directors after a corporation is formed; they contain provisions for managing the business and affairs of the corporation. This document does not have to be filed with the secretary of state.

Corporate Seal

A corporate seal is a design that contains the name of the corporation and the date of incorporation. It is imprinted, using a metal stamp containing the design, by the corporate secretary on certain legal documents.

Organization Meeting

An organization meeting must be held by the initial directors of a corporation after the articles of incorporation are filed. At this meeting, the directors adopt the bylaws, elect corporate officers, ratify promoters' contracts, adopt a corporate seal, and transact such other business as may come before the meeting.
Minutes. Minutes are the written recording of the actions taken by the directors at the organizational and other directors' meetings.

FINANCING THE CORPORATION: STOCK, p. 173

Financing the Corporation

Equity securities. These securities represent the ownership rights to the corporation. They are also called *stocks*. Equity securities consist of *common stock* and *preferred stock*.

Common Stock

Common stock is a type of equity security that represents the *residual value* of the corporation. Common stock has no preferences, and its shareholders are paid dividends and assets upon liquidation only after creditors and preferred shareholders have been paid.

1. ***Common stockholder.*** A common stockholder is a person who owns common stock.
2. ***Common stock certificate.*** A common stock certificate represents the common shareholder's investment in the corporation.

Preferred Stock

Preferred stock is a type of equity security that is given certain preferences and rights over common stock.

1. ***Preferred stockholder.*** A preferred stockholder is a person who owns preferred stock.
2. ***Preferred stock certificate.*** A preferred stock certificate represents the preferred stockholder's investment in the corporation.
3. ***Preferences and rights.*** Preferred stock may have any or all of the following preferences or rights:
   a. ***Dividend preference.*** This preference gives the right to receive a fixed dividend at stipulated periods during the year (e.g., quarterly).
   b. ***Liquidation preference.*** This preference gives the right to be paid a stated dollar amount if the corporation is dissolved and liquidated. The corporation must pay its creditors first, however.
   c. ***Cumulative dividend right.*** *Cumulative preferred stock* is stock that provides that any missed dividend payments must be paid in the future to the preferred shareholders before the common shareholders can receive any dividends.
   d. ***Right to participate in profits.*** *Participating preferred stock* is preferred stock that allows the stockholder to participate in the profits of the corporation along with the common stockholders on an expressly stated basis.
   e. ***Conversion right.*** *Convertible preferred stock* is preferred stock that permits stockholders to convert their shares into common stock at a stipulated conversion price.

4. ***Redeemable preferred stock.*** Redeemable preferred stock is preferred stock that may be bought back by the corporation at a specified price at some future date. This stock is also called *callable preferred stock.*

Authorized, Issued, and Outstanding Shares

1. ***Authorized shares.*** This is the number of shares provided for in the articles of incorporation. The shareholders may amend the articles of incorporation to increase this amount.
2. ***Issued shares.*** Issued shares are authorized shares that have been sold by the corporation.
3. ***Unissued shares.*** Unissued shares are authorized shares that have not been sold by the corporation.
4. ***Treasury shares.*** Treasury shares are issued shares that have been repurchased by the corporation. They may be resold by the corporation.
5. ***Outstanding shares.*** Outstanding shares are shares that are in shareholder hands, whether originally issued or reissued treasury shares. Only outstanding shares have the right to vote.

Consideration to Be Paid for Shares

Shares may be issued in exchange for any benefit to the corporation, including cash, tangible property, intangible property, promissory notes, services performed, contracts for services to be performed, or other securities of the corporation.

Stock Options and Stock Warrants

1. ***Stock option.*** A stock option is a nontransferable right to purchase shares of the corporation from the corporation at a stated price for a specific period of time.
   a. ***Striking price.*** The striking price is the stated price at which the stock may be bought at a future date.
   b. ***Option period.*** The option period is the specified period of time for exercising a stock option.
   c. ***Exercising the option.*** Exercising the option is the act of purchasing the shares subject to the option by the holder of the option. Stock options are usually granted to the management of a corporation.
2. ***Stock warrant.*** A stock warrant is a stock option that is represented by a certificate. Stock warrants are commonly issued in conjunction with another security. Warrants may be transferable or nontransferable.

FINANCING THE CORPORATION: DEBT SECURITIES, p. 178

Debt Securities

Debt securities establish a *debtor–creditor* relationship in which the corporation borrows money from the investor to whom the debt security is issued.

1. ***Debenture.*** A debenture is a *long-term unsecured* debt instrument that is based on the corporation's general credit rating.
2. ***Bond.*** A bond is a *long-term* debt security that is *secured* by some form of property. The property securing the bond is called *collateral.* In the event of nonpayment of interest or principal or other specified events, bondholders can foreclose on and obtain the collateral.
3. ***Note.*** A note is a *short-term* debt instrument with a maturity of five years or less. Notes can be either unsecured or secured.

4. ***Indenture agreement.*** The indenture agreement is the contract between the corporation and debt security holders, which contains the terms of the agreement between the corporation and the holders.

CORPORATE POWERS, p. 179

Corporate Powers

1. ***Express powers.*** A corporation has the express powers granted to it by the U.S. Constitution, state constitutions, federal statutes, state statutes (particularly the state's corporations code), articles of incorporation, bylaws, and resolutions of the board of directors.
2. ***Implied powers.*** Implied powers allow a corporation to accomplish its corporate purpose.

Ultra Vires Acts

Ultra vires acts are acts by a corporation that are beyond its express or implied powers.

Remedies. The following remedies are available if an *ultra vires* act is committed:

1. Shareholders can sue for an *injunction* to prevent the corporation from engaging in the act.
2. The corporation (or shareholders, on behalf of the corporation) can sue the officers and directors who caused the act for *damages*.
3. The attorney general of the state of incorporation can bring an action to enjoin the act or to dissolve the corporation.

TAXATION, p. 181

S Corporations

An S corporation is a corporation that has elected to be taxed as an S corporation for federal income tax purposes. An S corporation pays no federal income tax at the corporate level, and the S corporation's income or loss flows to the shareholders and must be reported on the shareholders' individual income tax returns. A corporation must meet certain requirements to elect to be an S corporation.

C Corporation

A C corporation is a corporation that either does not qualify to be an S corporation or elects not to be an S corporation. C corporations must pay federal income tax at the corporate level. If a C corporation distributes its profits to shareholders in the form of dividends, the shareholders must pay personal income tax on the dividends.

DISSOLUTION AND TERMINATION OF CORPORATIONS, p. 182

Voluntary Dissolution

Voluntary dissolution is dissolution of a corporation by the incorporators or initial directors if the corporation has not begun business or issued shares or by the majority vote of shareholders if the corporation has begun business or issued shares.

Articles of dissolution. This document is filed with the secretary of state of the state of incorporation when a corporation is voluntarily dissolved.

Administrative Dissolution

Administrative dissolution is involuntary dissolution of a corporation that is ordered by the secretary of state if the corporation has failed to comply with certain procedures required by law (e.g., failure to pay franchise tax).
Certificate of dissolution. This document is filed by the secretary of state when a corporation is administratively dissolved.

Judicial Dissolution

Judicial dissolution is dissolution of a corporation by a court proceeding instituted by:

1. ***The state.*** If the corporation (1) procured its articles of incorporation through fraud or (2) exceeded or abused the authority conferred upon it by law.
2. ***Decree of dissolution.*** Order issued by the court when a corporation has been judicially dissolved.

Winding Up, Liquidation, and Termination

1. ***Winding-up and liquidation.*** A dissolved corporation's assets are collected, liquidated, and distributed to creditors, shareholders, and other claimants.
2. ***Termination.*** The ending of a corporation occurs only after the winding up of the corporation's affairs, the liquidation of its assets, and the distribution of the proceeds and property to the claimants.

TEST REVIEW TERMS AND CONCEPTS

Corporation 162
Corporations code 163
Court of chancery 180
Cumulative preferred stock 176
Debenture 178
Debt securities (fixed income securities) 178
Decree of dissolution 185
Dividend preference 176
Dividends 173
Domain name 169
Domestic corporation 166
Double taxation 181
Equity securities (stocks) 173
Express powers 179
Fixed dividend 176
Foreign corporation 166
General corporation statutes 162
General-purpose clause 171
Government-owned (public) corporation 165
Implied powers 181
Incorporator 168
Indenture agreement (indenture) 179
Issued shares 177
Judicial dissolution 185
Legal entity (legal person) 163
Limited liability of shareholders 163
Limited-purpose clause 171
Liquidation preference 176
Model Business Corporation Act (MBCA) 164
Model Nonprofit Corporation Act 165
Model Statutory Close Corporation Supplement 175
Municipal corporation 165
Nonconvertible preferred stock 177
Noncumulative preferred stock 176
Nonparticipating preferred stock 176
Nonredeemable preferred stock 177
Note 179
Not-for-profit corporation 165
Novation 169
Officers 164
Organizational meeting 173
Outstanding shares 177
P.A. (professional association) 165
Participating preferred stock 176
P.C. (professional corporation) 165

Preferred stock 175
Preferred stock certificate 175
Preferred stockholder 175
Private corporation 165
Professional corporation 165
Profit corporation 165
Promoter 169
Promoters' contracts 169
Publicly held corporation 165
Redeemable preferred stock (callable preferred stock) 177
Registered agent 171
Revised Model Business Corporation Act (RMBCA) 164
S corporation 181
Shareholder 162
Stock option 178
Stock warrant 178
Termination 185
Treasury shares 177
Ultra vires act 181
Unissued shares 177
Voluntary dissolution 182
Winding up and liquidation 185

CASE SCENARIO REVISITED

Remember the case at the beginning of the chapter involving Florida Fashions? If a lawsuit is filed in this case, would that lawsuit be properly brought in Florida? What type of corporation is Florida Fashions in regard to the state of Pennsylvania and to the state of Florida? Can Florida Fashions defend itself in a lawsuit? To help you with your answer, see *Mysels v. Barry*, 332 So. 2d 38 (Fla. Dist. Ct. App. 1976).

PORTFOLIO EXERCISE

For the business you created at the beginning of the course, complete the Record of Proceedings of Incorporator, Share Subscriptions (as needed), Action by Written Consent of Shareholders in Lieu of First Meeting of Shareholders, Acceptance, Action by Written Consent of Directors in Lieu of First Meeting of Directors, and Stock Certificates (as necessary) printed in the following pages by filling in all blanks and/or modifying the minutes as appropriate. You will *not* be required to complete or attach to the minutes articles of incorporation, a code of regulations, or bylaws. [Note that the forms provided are for the State of Ohio. Depending upon your professor's instructions, use the Ohio forms that follow, or find the corresponding forms for your own state.]

RECORD OF PROCEEDINGS OF INCORPORATOR

On the ____th day of __________, 2011, desiring to form a corporation for profit in accordance with Chapter 1701, Ohio Revised Code, and under the corporation name, "______________" the undersigned did subscribe, as required by law, to Articles of Incorporation, which Articles of Incorporation, together with the Original Appointment of Agent and Receipt and Certificate of the Secretary of State of the State of Ohio were, on ______________, 2011, duly filed in the office of the Secretary of State of the State of Ohio at Columbus, Ohio, of the Records of Incorporation and Miscellaneous Filings and issued Charter Number 00000.

The original Articles of Incorporation and the Original Appointment of Agent, as filed and recorded in the office of the Secretary of State, together with the Receipt and Certificate of the Secretary of State, are attached hereto, made a part hereof and are marked Exhibit A.

The Incorporator then determined to fix the amount of consideration to be paid for the shares of common stock, ______________ (select *with par value* or *without par value*) of the Corporation and to adopt a plan to issue shares of common stock of the Corporation which qualify pursuant to Section 1244, Internal Revenue Code, in order to effectuate the offer, sale and issue of such shares in such a manner that the qualified Shareholders of the Corporation may receive the benefits of Section 1244. The Incorporator thereupon adopted the following plan:

1. It is hereby determined that this Corporation offer for sale and issue ______________ (____) shares of its common stock ______________ (select *with par value* or *without par value*) upon the terms and conditions set forth below.
2. It is further determined that the offer, sale and issue of such shares be effectuated in such a manner that qualified stockholders may receive the benefits of Section 1244 of the Internal Revenue Code.
3. The amount of consideration to be paid for said shares of common stock of the Corporation subscribed for prior to the first meeting of Shareholders be, and the same hereby is, fixed at ____ Dollar ($____) per share.
4. The following notation shall be made on each certificate evidencing shares of this Corporation issued pursuant to the foregoing plan:

   "This Certificate has been issued in accordance with Section 1244, Internal Revenue Code of 1954, as amended."

The Incorporator then received subscriptions for shares of common stock of the Corporation pursuant to the terms and conditions of the foregoing plan. Subscriptions were then received by the Incorporator, and such subscriptions are set forth in Exhibit B, attached hereto and made a part hereof.

____________________, 2011

____
(Signature of Incorporator)

EXHIBIT B

SUBSCRIPTION TO SHARES

of

____________________ CORPORATION

________________, 2011

________________, Ohio

(insert your city name)

I subscribe for ______________ (____) shares of common stock, (select *with par value* or *without par value*) of ______________. I agree to pay the sum of ______________ Dollars ($____) in cash when this subscription is accepted and a certificate for the shares is delivered to me.

I represent and warrant that I am a resident of the State of Ohio and that the shares of ______________ being purchased by me will be purchased for my own account, for investment and not for resale or redistribution, except in accordance with the Securities Act of 1933 and the rules and regulations of the Securities and Exchange Commission promulgated thereunder. I agree not to sell the shares unless they are registered under the securities laws or the sale is exempt from registration in the opinion of legal counsel for the corporation. I further agree that the certificate for said shares of ______________ shall bear the following legend:

"The securities represented by the within certificate have not been registered under the Securities Act of 1933, as amended, and may not be sold or transferred unless there is in effect with respect to said securities a registration statement pursuant to that Act, or unless the ______________ Corporation has received written opinion of counsel satisfactory to it that such sale or transfer is exempt from the registration requirement of that Act."

______________________ ______________________

Date (Signature of Subscriber)

ACTION BY WRITTEN CONSENT OF SHAREHOLDERS IN LIEU OF FIRST MEETING OF SHAREHOLDERS

-of-

____

__________________, 2011

__________________, Ohio
(insert your city name)

In lieu of the first meeting of Shareholders of _______________, the undersigned, being the owner(s) of all of the issued and outstanding shares of said Corporation and the only shareholder(s) who would be entitled to notice of a meeting of Shareholders held for the purpose of taking the action set forth below, do hereby, pursuant to ____________, authorize and take the following action and adopt the following resolutions:

RESOLVED, that the form of Code of Regulations attached hereto and marked "Exhibit A" be, and the same hereby is, adopted as the Code of Regulations of this Corporation;

RESOLVED, that the acts of the incorporator, as set forth in the record of the proceedings of the incorporator filed in the minute book of the corporation, be, and the same hereby are, in all respects approved and ratified.

RESOLVED, that the number of Directors of the Board of Directors of this Corporation be, and the same hereby is, fixed at _______________ (_____); and

RESOLVED FURTHER, that _______________ be and hereby is/are, nominated for the office of Director of this Corporation; and

RESOLVED FURTHER, that _______________ be, and hereby is/are, elected as a Director(s) of this Corporation, to serve until the next annual meeting of Shareholders, and until his successor is elected, or until his earlier resignation, removal from office or death.

____
(Signature of Shareholder)
Owning _______ Shares of Common Stock

____
(Signature of Shareholder)
Owning _______ Shares of Common Stock

____
(Signature of Shareholder)
Owning _______ Shares of Common Stock

ACCEPTANCE

______________, 2011

__________________, Ohio
(insert your city name)

The undersigned hereby accept(s) his/her/their election as a member/members of the Board of Directors of _______________ to serve until the next annual meeting of Shareholders and until their successors are duly elected or until their earlier resignation, removal from office or death, and the undersigned agree to faithfully perform the duties of said office.

________________ (Signature of Director)	________________ (Signature of Director)
________________ (Signature of Director)	________________ (Signature of Director)
________________ (Signature of Director)	________________ (Signature of Director)

ACTION BY WRITTEN CONSENT OF DIRECTORS
IN LIEU OF FIRST MEETING OF DIRECTORS

-of-

____

____________________, 2011

____________________, Ohio
(insert your city name)

The directors of _______________, acting by unanimous consent in accordance with the laws of the State of Ohio, hereby adopt the following resolutions:

RESOLVED, that the by-laws attached hereto shall be the by-laws of the corporation.

RESOLVED, that the actions of the Incorporator in taking subscriptions forshares of common stock, shares of common stock, _______________ (select *with par value* or *without par value*), of this Corporation on _______________, 2011 _______________, be and the same hereby are, ratified and confirmed; and

RESOLVED, that the actions of the Incorporator in accepting the subscriptions for shares of common stock of _______________ pursuant to the terms and conditions set forth in the subscription be, and the same hereby are, ratified and confirmed.

RESOLVED, that the Treasurer of this Corporation be, and he hereby is, authorized and directed to pay all fees, costs and expenses incurred in connection with the incorporation of this Corporation.

RESOLVED, that the form of definitive certificate for fully paid and nonassessable shares of common stock of this Corporation, which is attached to this Action by Written Consent as Exhibit A, be, and the same hereby is, authorized and approved as the form of certificate for the fully paid and non-assessable shares of common stock of this Corporation; and

RESOLVED, that the President and the Secretary or Assistant Secretary of this Corporation be, and they hereby are, authorized and directed to sign, issue and deliver certificates for shares of common stock to subscribers for shares of common stock of this corporation who have made payment for such shares.

RESOLVED, that the Secretary of this Corporation be, and he hereby is, authorized and directed to execute, acknowledge and file with the Division of Securities of the State of Ohio, on behalf of this Corporation, Form 3-0, Report of Sale of Equity Securities by a Corporation, if required, and to take such action and execute such documents as may be necessary.

RESOLVED, that the following individuals be, and they hereby are, elected to serve in the offices set forth opposite their respective names:

____________________ (Signature of President)	____________________ (Signature of Director)
____________________ (Signature of Secretary/Treasurer)	____________________ (Signature of Director)
	____________________ (Signature of Director)
	____________________ (Signature of Director)
	____________________ (Signature of Director)
	____________________ (Signature of Director)

[Front side of certificate]

EXHIBIT A

INCORPORATED UNDER THE LAWS
OF THE STATE OF OHIO

Certificate Number ______________ Shares ______________
(number of shares transferred)

THE ________ CORPORATION

AUTHORIZED SHARES
____ Shares of Common Stock
____ (select *with par value* or *without par value*)

THIS CERTIFIES THAT ______________ is the owner of ______________ (____) fully paid and ______________ (select *non-assessable* or *assessable*) shares of common stock, no par value, of ______________, transferable on the books of the Corporation by the holder hereof in person or by a duly authorized attorney upon surrender of this Certificate properly endorsed. This Certificate and the shares represented hereby are issued and shall be subject to the provisions of the Articles of Incorporation (as the same may be amended from time to time), the By-laws of the Corporation and any agreements referenced hereon, copies of which are on file at the office of the Corporation, to all of which the holder by acceptance hereof assents.

IN WITNESS WHEREOF, the said Corporation has caused this Certificate to be signed by its duly authorized officers at Toledo, Ohio.

(This Corporation has no seal.)

Dated: ______________2011____

____

______________________,
Secretary

______________,
President

This Certificate has been issued in accordance with Section 1244, Internal Revenue Code of 1954, as amended.

The securities represented by the within certificate have not been registered under the Securities Act of 1933, as amended, and may not be sold or transferred unless there is in effect with respect to said securities a registration statement pursuant to that Act or unless ______________ shall have received written opinion of counsel satisfactory to it that such sale or transfer is exempt from the registration requirement of that Act.

[Back side of certificate]

CERTIFICATE

FOR _____. SHARES

of

COMMON STOCK

of ____________________

____

ISSUED TO ____________________

____

DATED

____________________, 2011_____

The Company will mail to the holder of this Certificate, without charge, a statement of the express terms, if any, of the shares represented by the within certificate and of the other class or receipt of a written request for such express terms.

For Value Received, ____________________ hereby sell, assign and transfer unto

____

____

of the Shares represented by the within Certificate, and do hereby irrevocably constitute and appoint Attorney to transfer the said shares on the books of the within-named Corporation, with full power of substitution in the premises.

Dated: ____________________, 2011_____ Signed in the presence of:

____

(Signature of Witness)

WORKING THE WEB INTERNET EXERCISES

Activities

1. Create a hypothetical corporation by preparing articles of incorporation, bylaws, and a shareholder agreement, using forms suitable for your state. For a list of state corporation statutes, see **http://topics.law.cornell.edu/wex/table_corporations**.
2. Prepare minutes of the organizational meeting for your newly formed corporation. See FindLaw's compilation of state corporation and business forms at **www.findlaw.com/11stategov/indexcorp.html**.
3. Using your state's database of corporations, find the last field annual report of a local corporation and determine who the officers are and who is designated as the registered agent for service of process. See the "Legal Information Institute's Corporate Law Page" at **www.law.cornell.edu/topics/corporations.html**. See also "The Corporate Library" at **www.thecorporatelibrary.com**.
4. Assume that you have decided to form a nonprofit corporation. What other steps do you need to take to properly create such an entity? See "U.S. Incorporation and Nonprofits Online Directory; Charities, Secretary of State, Corporations Division, Foundation Directories, UCC, Trademarks 1996" at **www.internet-prospector.org/secstate.html**.

CRITICAL LEGAL THINKING CASES

Case 7.1 ***Legal Entity*** Jeffrey Sammak was the owner of a contracting business known as Senaco. Sammak decided to enter the coal reprocessing business. Sammak attended the "Coal Show" in Chicago, Illinois, at which he met representatives of the Deister Co., Inc. (Deister). Deister was incorporated under the laws of Pennsylvania. Sammak began negotiating with Deister to purchase equipment to be used in his coal reprocessing business. Deister sent Sammak literature, guaranteeing a certain level of performance for the equipment. Sammak purchased the equipment. After the equipment was installed, Sammak was dissatisfied with its performance. Sammak believed that Deister breached an express warranty and wanted to sue. Can a suit be brought against a corporation such as Deister? *Blackwood Coal v. Deister Co.*, 626 F. Supp. 727 (E.D. Pa. 1985).

Case 7.2 ***Limited Liability of Shareholders*** Joseph M. Billy was an employee of the USM Corporation (USM), a publicly held corporation. Billy was at work when a 4,600-pound ram from a vertical boring mill broke loose and crushed him to death. Billy's widow brought suit against USM, alleging that the accident was caused by certain defects in the manufacture and design of the vertical boring mill and the two moving parts directly involved in the accident, a metal lifting arm and the 4,600-pound ram. If Mrs. Billy's suit is successful, can the shareholders of USM be held personally liable for any judgment against USM? *Billy v. Consol. Mach. Tool Corp.*, 412 N.E.2d 934 (N.Y. 1980).

Case 7.3 ***Corporation*** William O'Donnel and Vincent Marino worked together as executives of a shipping container repair company known as Marine Trailers. Marine Trailers's largest customer was American Export Lines (American Export). When American Export became unhappy with the owners of Marine Trailers, it let O'Donnel and Marino know that if they formed their own company, American Exports would give them its business. O'Donnel and Marino decided to take American Exports's suggestion, and they bought the majority of shares of a publicly traded corporation known as Marine Repair Services, Inc. (Repair Services). O'Donnel and Marino operated Repair Services as a container repair company at the Port of New York. The company prospered, expanding to five other states and overseas. O'Donnel and Marino's initial $12,000 investment paid off. Ten years after buying the company, each man was earning over $150,000 a year in salary alone. What type of corporation is Repair Services? *O'Donnel v. Marine Repair Serv., Inc.*, 530 F. Supp. 1199 (S.D.N.Y. 1982).

Case 7.4 ***Corporation*** Hutchinson Baseball Enterprises, Inc. (Hutchinson, Inc.), was incorporated under the laws of Kansas. Among the purposes of the corporation, according to its bylaws, were to "promote, advance, and sponsor baseball, which shall include Little League and Amateur baseball, in the Hutchinson, Kansas, area." The corporation was involved in a number of activities, including leasing a field for American Legion teams, furnishing instructors as coaches for Little League teams, conducting a Little League camp, and leasing a baseball field to a local junior college for a nominal fee. Hutchinson, Inc., raised money through ticket sales to amateur baseball games, concessions, and contributions. Any profits were used to improve the playing fields. Profits were never distributed to the corporation's directors or members. What type of corporation is Hutchinson, Inc.? *Hutchinson Baseball Enter., Inc., v. Comm'r of Internal Revenue*, 696 F.2d 757 (10th Cir. 1982).

Case 7.5 *Corporation* Elmer Balvik and Thomas Sylvester formed a partnership, named Weldon Electric, for the purpose of engaging in the electrical contracting business. Balvik contributed $8,000 and a vehicle worth $2,000, and Sylvester contributed $25,000 to the partnership's assets. The parties operated the business as a partnership for several years and then decided to incorporate. Stock was issued to Balvik and Sylvester in proportion to their partnership ownership interests, with Sylvester receiving 70 percent and Balvik receiving 30 percent of the stock. Balvik and his wife and Sylvester and his wife were the four directors of the corporation. Sylvester was elected president of the corporation. Balvik was vice president. The corporation's bylaws stated that "sales of shares of stock by any shareholder shall be as set forth in a 'Buy Sell Agreement' entered into by the shareholders." What type of corporation is Weldon Electric? *Balvik v. Sylvester*, 411 N.W.2d 383 (N.D. 1987).

Case 7.6 *Corporation* Leo V. Mysels was the president of Florida Fashions of Interior Design, Inc. (Florida Fashions). Florida Fashions, which was a Pennsylvania corporation, had never registered to do business in the state of Florida. While acting in the capacity of a salesman for the corporation, Mysels took an order for goods from Francis E. Barry. The transaction took place in Florida. Barry paid Florida Fashions for the goods ordered. When Florida Fashions failed to perform its obligations under the sales agreement, Barry brought suit in Florida. What type of corporation is Florida Fashions in regard to the state of Pennsylvania and to the state of Florida? Can Florida Fashions defend itself in a lawsuit? *Mysels v. Barry*, 332 So. 2d 38 (Fla. Dist. Ct. App. 1976).

Case 7.7 *Promoters' Liability* The Homes Corporation (Homes), a closely held corporation whose sole stockholders were Jerry and Beverly Ann Allen, purchased 10 acres of real estate near Kahaluu on the island of Oahu, Hawaii. Homes made a down payment of $50,000. The Allens intended to obtain approval for a planned unit development (PUD) from the city and county of Honolulu and then develop the property with some sixty condominium townhouses. To further this project, the Allens sought an outside investor. Herbert Hadley, a real estate developer from Texas, decided to join the Allens' project. The two parties entered into an agreement whereby a new Hawaiian corporation would be formed to build the condominiums, with Handley owning 51 percent of the corporation's stock and the Allens the remaining 49 percent. The two parties began extensive planning and design of the project. They also took out a $69,500 loan from the Bank of Hawaii. After a year had gone by, Handley informed the Allens that he was no longer able to advance funds to the project. Soon thereafter, the city and county denied their PUD zoning application. The new corporation was never formed. Who is liable for the failed condominium project's contractual obligations? *Handley v. Ching*, 627 P.2d 1132 (Haw. Ct. App. 1981).

Case 7.8 *Promoters' Contracts* Martin Stern, Jr., was an architect who worked in Nevada. Nathan Jacobson asked Stern to draw plans for Jacobson's new hotel/casino, the Kings Castle at Lake Tahoe. Stern agreed to take on the project and immediately began preliminary work. At this time, Stern dealt directly with Jacobson who referred to the project as "my hotel." One month later, Stern wrote to Jacobson, detailing, among other things, the architect's services and fee. The two men subsequently discussed Stern's plans and set Stern's fee at $250,000. Three months later, Jacobson formed Lake Enterprises, Inc. (Lake Enterprises), a Nevada corporation of which Jacobson was the sole shareholder and president. Lake Enterprises was formed for the purpose of owning the new casino. During this period, Stern was paid monthly by checks drawn on an account belonging to another corporation controlled by Jacobson. Stern never agreed to contract with any of these corporations and always dealt exclusively with Jacobson. When Stern was not paid the full amount of his architectural fee, he sued Jacobson to recover. Jacobson claimed that he was not personally liable for any of Stern's fee because a novation had taken place. Who wins? *Jacobson v. Stern*, 605 P.2d 198 (Nev. 1980).

Case 7.9 *Preferred Stock* Commonwealth Edison Co. (Commonwealth Edison), through its underwriters, sold one million shares of preferred stock at an offering price of $100 per share. Commonwealth Edison wanted to issue the stock with a dividend rate of 9.26 percent, but its major underwriter, First Boston Corporation (First Boston), advised that a rate of 9.44 percent should be paid. According to First Boston, a shortage of investment funds existed, and a higher dividend rate was necessary for a successful stock issue. Commonwealth Edison's management was never happy with the high dividend rate being paid on this preferred stock. Nine months later, Commonwealth Edison's vice chairman was quoted in the report of the annual meeting of the corporation as saying, "we were disappointed at the 9.44 percent dividend rate on the preferred stock we sold last August, but we expect to refinance it when market conditions make it feasible." Commonwealth Edison, pursuant to the terms under which the stock was sold, bought back the one million shares of preferred stock at a price of $110 per share. What type of preferred stock is this? *Franklin Life Ins. Co. v. Commonwealth Edison Co.*, 451 F. Supp. 602 (S.D. Ill. 1978).

Case 7.10 *Debt Security* Financial Corporation of California (United Financial) was incorporated in the state of Delaware. United Financial owned the majority of a California savings and loan association as well as three insurance agencies. The next year, the original investors in United Financial decided to capitalize on an increase in investor interest in savings and loans. The first public offering of United Financial stock was made. The stock was sold as a unit, with 60,000 units being offered. Each unit consisted of two shares of United Financial stock and one $100, 5 percent interest-bearing debenture bond. This initial offering was a success. It provided $7.2 million to the corporation, of which $6.2 million was distributed as a return of capital to the original investors. What is the difference between the stock offered for sale by United Financial and the debenture bonds? *Jones v. H.F. Ahmanson & Co.*, 460 P.2d 464 (Cal. 1969).

BUSINESS ETHICS CASES

Case 7.11 Business Ethics John A. Goodman was a real estate salesman in the state of Washington. Goodman sold to Darden, Doman & Stafford Associates (DDS), a general partnership, an apartment building that needed extensive renovation. Goodman represented that he personally had experience in renovation work. During the course of negotiations on a renovation contract, Goodman informed the managing partner of DDS that he would be forming a corporation to do the work. A contract was executed in August between DDS and "Building Design and Development (In Formation), John A. Goodman, President." The contract required the renovation work to be completed by October 15. Goodman immediately subcontracted the work, but the renovation was not completed on time. DDS also found that the work that was completed was of poor quality.

Goodman did not file the articles of incorporation for his new corporation until November 1. The partners of DDS sued Goodman to hold him liable for the renovation contracts. Goodman denied personal liability. Was it ethical for Goodman to deny liability? Is Goodman personally liable? *Goodman v. Darden, Doman & Stafford Assoc.*, 670 P.2d 648 (Wash. 1983).

Case 7.12 *Business Ethics* Pursuant to a public offering, Knoll International, Inc. (Knoll), issued debentures to investors. The debentures bore interest at 8.125 percent; matured in thirty years; and were subordinated, convertible into common stock at the rate of each $19.20 of principal amount for one share of common stock, and redeemable. Section 8.08 of the indenture agreement provided that no debenture holder could sue unless the holders of 35 percent of the debentures requested the trustee to sue. The indenture also gave the trustee the authority to amend the indenture agreement.

Knoll was controlled through a series of subsidiaries by Knoll International Holdings, Inc. (Holdings), which, in turn, was controlled by Marshall S. Cogan. Four years later, Knoll merged into Holdings and paid its common shareholders $12 cash per share. Knoll and the indenture trustee executed a supplemental indenture that provided that each debenture holder would receive $12 cash for each $19.20 principal amount of debentures. Simons, a debenture holder who did not own 35 percent of the debentures, brought a suit against Knoll and Cogan. Does Knoll International, Inc., or Cogan owe a fiduciary duty to the debenture holders? Did Cogan breach an ethical duty to the debenture holders? *Simons v. Cogan*, 542 A.2d 785 (Del. Ch. 1987).

"It has been uniformly laid down in this Court, as far back as we can remember, that good faith is the basis of all mercantile transactions."

–Judge Buller

Salomons v. Nisson (1788)

Franchises and Special Forms of Businesses

CHAPTER 8

CASE SCENARIO

The law firm at which you work as a paralegal represents Libby-Broadway Drive-In, Inc. (Libby). Libby is a corporation licensed to operate a McDonald's fast-food franchise restaurant by the McDonald's System, Inc. (McDonald's). Libby was granted a license to operate a McDonald's in Cleveland, Ohio, and was granted an exclusive territory in which McDonald's could not grant another franchise. The area was described as "bound on the north by the south side of Miles Avenue, on the west and south side by Turney Road, on the east by Warrensville Center Road." McDonald's recently granted a franchise to another franchisee to operate a McDonald's restaurant on the west side of Turney Road.

CHAPTER OBJECTIVES

After studying this chapter, you should be able to:

1. Define *franchise* and describe the various forms of franchises.
2. Describe the rights and duties of the parties to a franchise agreement.
3. Identify the contract tort liability of franchisors and franchisees.
4. Define *licensing* and describe how trademarks and intellectual property are licensed.
5. Describe how international franchising, joint ventures, and strategic alliances are used in global commerce.

The jury, passing on the prisoner's life,
May, in the sworn twelve, have a thief or two
Guiltier than him they try.
William Shakespeare
Measure for Measure

INTRODUCTION TO FRANCHISES AND SPECIAL FORMS OF BUSINESSES

Franchising is an important method for distributing goods and services to the public. Originally pioneered by the automobile and soft drink industries, franchising today is used in many other forms of business. The 700,000-plus franchise outlets in the United States account for over 25 percent of retail sales and about 15 percent of the gross domestic product (GDP).

Special forms of business are used in domestic and international commerce. *Licensing* permits one business to use another business's trademarks, service marks, trade names, and other intellectual property in selling goods or services. *Joint ventures* allow two or more businesses to combine their resources to pursue a single project or transaction. *Strategic alliances* are often used to enter foreign markets.

This chapter discusses franchises, licensing, joint ventures, and strategic alliances used in domestic and international commerce.

PARALEGAL PERSPECTIVE

Linda C. Grummet *is a paralegal with the firm Elms Harmon Macchia, LLC, in San Antonio, Texas. She graduated from Texas State University–san Marcos with a master's in legal studies and a paralegal studies certificate. She has been working as a paralegal for six years.*

How or why do you think a paralegal is important in the areas of franchises and other special forms of business organizations? A paralegal's researching, drafting, and proofreading abilities are an integral part of the formation of franchise agreements.

What are the most important paralegal skills needed in your job? Skills needed in my job are research and investigative skills, writing and grammar skills, communication, organization, and attention to detail.

What is the academic background required for a paralegal entering your area of practice? A bachelor or paralegal certificate is required.

How is technology involved in your job? I frequently use legal research websites such as Westlaw in addition to the Secretary of State and State Comptroller's office websites to check for entity name availability and status. In addition, my job requires the daily use of technological systems such as word processing, e-mailing, printing, scanning, calendaring, and accessing a network database.

What trends do you see in your area of practice that will likely affect your job in the future? I see the trends of electronic filing of entity information documents and the growing implementation of paperless systems. Although the electronic filing of entity formation documents will provide more efficiency in the workplace, the use of paperless systems in maintaining corporate and company books is a challenge that will likely require the implementation of specific procedures for the archival of those documents.

What do you feel is the biggest issue currently facing the paralegal profession? I feel that this is the unauthorized practice of law. Since paralegals have direct client contact, they should be cautious when responding to a client's inquiry and never give legal advice. Although paralegals become proficient in using existing forms and have ease of access to those forms, thereby helping the efficiency of a paralegal, this can lead to serious consequences. The familiarity and frequent use of forms can lead a paralegal to give legal advice by explaining the steps involved in creating or terminating a business organization, interpreting the meaning of a legal document, or answering a client's question regarding the need for filing a particular form. Although a paralegal may be well versed in business organization and may know the answer to the client's question, in the absence of his or her supervising attorney, a paralegal must always inform a client that the paralegal cannot give legal advice and should refer the question to the supervising attorney.

What words of advice do you have for a new paralegal entering your area of practice? Become familiar with the rules of professional conduct published by the state bar. Also, when working with any business organization, always remember to check the entity's status with the Secretary of State, State Comptroller of Public Accounts, or other online legal research database to ensure its good standing.

FRANCHISE

A **franchise** is established when one party (the **franchisor**, or **licensor**) licenses another party (the **franchisee**, or **licensee**) to use the franchisor's trade name, trademarks, commercial symbols, patents, copyrights, and other property in the distribution and selling of goods and services. Generally, the franchisor and the franchisee are established as separate corporations. The term *franchise* refers to both the agreement between the parties and the franchise outlet.

There are several advantages to franchising. For example, the franchisor can reach lucrative new markets, the franchisee has access to the franchisor's knowledge and resources while running an independent business, and consumers are assured of uniform product quality.

A typical franchise arrangement is illustrated in **Exhibit 8.1**.

franchise
An arrangement that is established when one party (the *franchisor*) licenses another party (the *franchisee*) to use the franchisor's trade name, trademarks, commercial symbols, patents, copyrights, and other property in the distribution and selling of goods and services.

franchisor
One who grants a franchise.

franchisee
One who is granted a franchise.

Types of Franchises

There are four basic forms of franchises: (1) *distributorship franchise*, (2) *processing plant franchise*, (3) *chain-style franchise*, and (4) *area franchise*. They are discussed in the following paragraphs.

Distributorship Franchise

In a **distributorship franchise**, the franchisor manufactures a product and licenses a retail dealer to distribute a product to the public.

Example: Ford Motor Company manufactures automobiles and franchises independently owned automobile dealers (franchisees) to sell them to the public.

distributorship franchise
The franchisor manufactures a product and licenses a retail franchisee to distribute the product to the public.

Processing Plant Franchise

In a **processing plant franchise**, the franchisor provides a secret formula or the like to the franchisee. The franchisee then manufactures the product at its own location and distributes it to retail dealers.

Example: The Coca-Cola Corporation, which owns the secret formulas for making Coca-Cola and other soft drinks, licenses regional bottling companies to manufacture and distribute soft drinks under the "Coca-Cola" name and other brand names.

processing plant franchise
Where the franchisor provides a secret formula or the like to the franchisee. The franchisee then manufactures the product at its own location and distributes it to retail dealers.

Exhibit 8.1 Franchise

Chain-Style Franchise

chain-style franchise
The franchisor licenses the franchisee to make and sell its products or distribute services to the public from a retail outlet serving an exclusive territory.

In a **chain-style franchise**, the franchisor licenses the franchisee to make and sell its products or services to the public from a retail outlet serving an exclusive geographical territory. The product is made or the service provided by the franchise. Most fast-food franchises use this form.

Example: The Pizza Hut Corporation franchises independently owned restaurant franchises to make and sell pizzas to the public under the "Pizza Hut" name.

Area Franchise

area franchise
The franchisor authorizes the franchisee to negotiate and sell franchises on behalf of the franchisor.

In an **area franchise**, the franchisor authorizes the franchisee to negotiate and sell franchises on behalf of the franchisor. The area franchisee is called a subfranchisor (see Exhibit 8.2). An area franchise is granted for a certain designated geographical area, such as a state, a region, or another agreed-upon area. Area franchises are often used when a franchisor wants to enter a market in another country.

Example: If Starbucks wanted to enter the country of Vietnam to operate its coffee shops, it could grant an area franchise to a Vietnamese company, which would then choose the individual franchisees in that country.

State Disclosure Laws

Uniform Franchise Offering Circular (UFOC)
A uniform disclosure document that requires a franchisor to make specific presale disclosures to prospective franchisees.

Most states have enacted franchise laws that require franchisors to register and deliver disclosure documents to prospective franchisees. State franchise administrators developed a uniform disclosure document called the **Uniform Franchise Offering Circular (UFOC)**.

Exhibit 8.2 Area Franchise

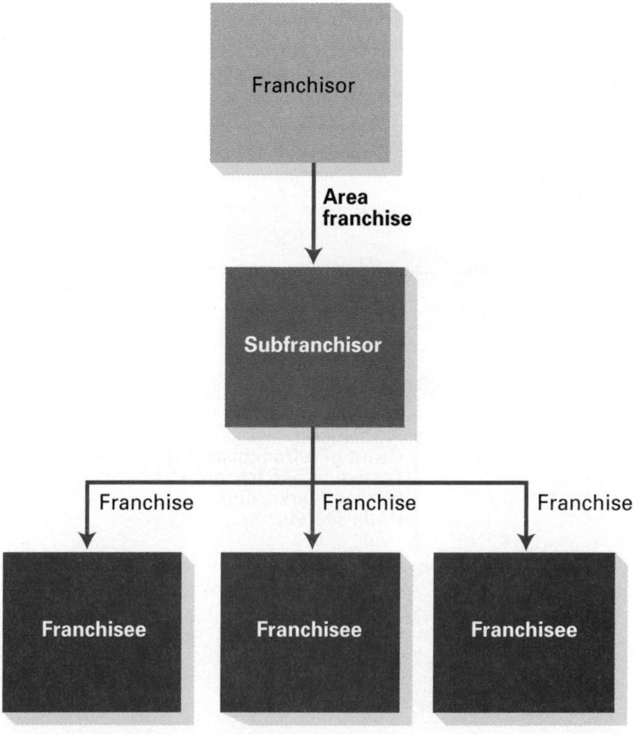

The UFOC and state laws require a franchisor to make specific presale disclosures to prospective franchisees. Information that must be disclosed includes a description of the franchisor's business, balance sheets and income statements of the franchisor for the preceding three years, material terms of the franchise agreement, any restrictions on the franchisee's territory, reasons permitted for the termination of the franchise, and other relevant information.

FTC Franchise Rule

The **Federal Trade Commission (FTC)**, a federal administrative agency, has adopted the **FTC franchise rule**. The FTC rule requires franchisors to make full *presale* disclosures nationwide to prospective franchisees.[1] The FTC does not require the registration of the disclosure document with the FTC prior to its use. The UFOC satisfies both state regulations and the FTC. The FTC rule requires the disclosures discussed in the following paragraphs.

Federal Trade Commission (FTC)
A federal government agency that is empowered to enforce federal franchising rules.

FTC franchise rule
A rule set out by the FTC that requires franchisors to make full presale disclosures to prospective franchisees.

Disclosure of Sales or Earnings Projections Based on Actual Data

If a franchisor makes sales or earnings projections for a potential franchise location that are based on the actual sales, income, or profit figures of an existing franchise, the franchisor must disclose the following:

- The number and percentage of its actual franchises that have obtained such results.
- A cautionary statement in at least 12-point boldface type that reads, "Caution: Some outlets have sold (or earned) this amount. There is no assurance you'll do as well. If you rely upon our figures, you must accept the risk of not doing so well."

> Whatever the human law may be, neither an individual nor a nation can commit the least act of injustice against the obscurest individual without having to pay the penalty for it.
> Henry David Thoreau

Disclosure of Sales or Earnings Projections Based on Hypothetical Data

If a franchisor makes sales or earnings projections based on hypothetical examples, the franchisor must disclose the following:

- The assumptions underlying the estimates.
- The number and percentage of actual franchises that have obtained such results.
- A cautionary statement in at least 12-point boldface print that reads, "Caution: These figures are only estimates of what we think you may earn. There is no assurance you'll do as well. If you rely upon our figures, you must accept the risk of not doing so well."

FRANCHISE AGREEMENT

A prospective franchisee must apply to the franchisor for a franchise. The franchise application often includes detailed information about the applicant's previous employment, financial and educational history, credit status, and so on.

If an applicant is approved, the parties enter into a **franchise agreement** that sets forth the terms and conditions of the franchise. Although some states permit oral franchise agreements, most have enacted Statute of Frauds that requires franchise agreements to be in writing. To prevent unjust enrichment, the courts occasionally enforce oral franchise agreements that violate the Statute of Frauds.

franchise agreement
An agreement that a franchisor and franchisee enter into that sets forth the terms and conditions of a franchise.

A franchise agreement often specifies the total investment that a franchisee must provide in order to be granted the franchise.

FTC notice
A statement required by the FTC to appear in at least 12-point boldface type on the cover of a franchisor's required disclosure statement to prospective franchisees.

CONTEMPORARY Environment

FTC FRANCHISE NOTICE

The FTC requires that the following statement, called the **FTC notice**, appear in at least 12-point boldface type on the cover of a franchisor's required disclosure statement to prospective franchisees:

> *To protect you, we've required your franchisor to give you this information.*
>
> *We haven't checked it, and don't know if it's correct. It should help you make up your mind. Study it carefully. While it includes some information about your contract, don't rely on it alone to understand your contract. Read all of your contract carefully. Buying a franchise is a complicated investment. Take your time to decide. If possible, show your contract and this information to an adviser, like a lawyer or an accountant. If you find anything you think may be wrong or anything important that's been left out, you should let us know about it. It may be against the law. There may also be laws on franchising in your state. Ask your state agencies about them.*

If a franchisor violates FTC disclosure rules, the wrongdoer is subject to an injunction against further franchise sales, civil fines, and an FTC civil action on behalf of injured franchisees to recover damages from the franchisor that were caused by the violation.

Topics Covered in a Franchise Agreement

Franchise agreements do not usually have much room for negotiation. Generally, the agreement is a standard form contract prepared by the franchisor. Franchise agreements cover the following topics:

- ***Quality control standards.*** The franchisor's most important assets are its name and reputation. The quality control standards set out in a franchise agreement—such as the franchisor's right to make periodic inspections of the franchisee's premises and operations—are intended to protect these assets. Failure to meet the proper standards can result in loss of the franchise.
- ***Training requirements.*** Franchisees and their personnel are usually required to attend training programs either on site or at the franchisor's training facilities.
- ***Covenant not to compete.*** Covenants not to compete prohibit franchisees from competing with the franchisor during a specific time and in a specified area after the termination of the franchise. Unreasonable (overextensive) covenants not to compete are void.
- ***Arbitration clause.*** Most franchise agreements contain an arbitration clause that provides that any claim or controversy arising from the franchise agreement or an alleged breach thereof is subject to arbitration. The U.S. Supreme Court has held such clauses to be enforceable.[2]
- ***Other terms and conditions.*** Capital requirements are included in a franchise agreement. Other terms and conditions may include restrictions on the use of the franchisor's trade name, trademarks, and logo; standards of

operation; duration of the franchise; record-keeping requirements; sign requirements; hours of operation; prohibition as to the sale or assignment of the franchise; conditions for the termination of the franchise; and other specific terms pertinent to the operation of the franchise and the protection of the parties' rights.

Sample provisions of a franchise agreement are set forth in **Exhibit 8.3**.

Franchise Fees

Franchise fees payable by the franchisee are usually stipulated in the franchise agreement. The franchisor may require the franchisee to pay any or all of the following fees:

- ***Initial license fee.*** An **initial license fee** is a lump-sum payment for the privilege of being granted a franchise.
- ***Royalty fees.*** A **royalty fee** is a fee for the continued use of the franchisor's trade name, property, and assistance that is often computed as a percentage of the franchisee's gross sales. Royalty fees are usually paid on a monthly basis.
- ***Assessment fee.*** An **assessment fee** is a fee for such things as advertising and promotional campaigns and administrative costs, billed either as a flat monthly or annual fee or as a percentage of gross sales.
- ***Lease fees.*** **Lease fees** are payment for any land or equipment leased from the franchisor, billed either as a flat monthly or annual fee or as a percentage of gross sales or other agreed-upon amount.
- ***Cost of supplies.*** **Cost of supplies** involves payment for supplies purchased from the franchisor.
- ***Consulting fees and other expenses.*** Many franchisors charge a monthly or annual fee for having experts from the franchisor help the franchisee to better conduct business.

Trademarks

A franchisor's ability to maintain the public's perception of the quality of the goods and services associated with its trade name, **trademarks**, and **service marks** is the essence of its success. The **Lanham Trademark Act**[3] provides for the registration of trademarks and service marks with the federal **Patent and Trademark Office (PTO)** in Washington, DC, by franchisors and others. Most franchisors license the use of their trade names, trademarks, and service marks and prohibit their franchisees from misusing these marks. Anyone who uses a mark without authorization may be sued for *trademark infringement*. The trademark holder can sue to recover damages and obtain an injunction prohibiting further unauthorized use of the mark.

Trade Secrets

Franchisors are often owners of **trade secrets**, including product formulas, business plans and models, and other ideas. Franchisors license and disclose many of their trade secrets to franchisees. The misappropriation of a trade secret is called **unfair competition**. The holder of the trade secret can sue the offending party for damages and obtain an injunction to prohibit further unauthorized use of the trade secret.

initial license fee
A lump-sum payment for the privilege of being granted a franchise.

royalty fee
Compensation for the use of property, expressed as a percentage of the receipts or as an account per unit produced; a payment made to an author or composer by a licensee, copyright holder, or assignee for each copy of their work sold; a payment made to an inventor for each article sold under their patent.

assessment fee
A fee for such things as advertising and promotional campaigns, administrative costs, and the like, billed either as a flat monthly or annual fee or as a percentage of gross sales.

lease fees
Payment for any land or equipment leased from the franchisor, billed either as a flat monthly or annual fee or as a percentage of gross sales or other agreed-upon amount.

cost of supplies
A franchise fee involving the payment for supplies purchased from the franchisor.

trademark or service mark
A distinctive mark, symbol, name, word, motto, or device that identifies the goods or services of a particular franchisor.

Lanham Trademark Act (as amended)
Federal statute that (1) establishes the requirements for obtaining a federal mark and (2) protects marks from infringement.

Patent and Trademark Office (PTO)
A federal administrative agency that reviews patent applications and grants patents.

trade secrets
Ideas that make a franchise successful but that do not qualify for trademark, patent, or copyright protection.

unfair competition
Competition that violates the law.

Exhibit 8.3 Sample Provisions of a Franchise Agreement

FRANCHISE AGREEMENT

Agreement, this 2nd day of January, 2010, between ALASKA PANCAKE HOUSE, INC., an Alaska corporation located in Anchorage, Alaska (hereinafter called the Company) and PANCAKE SYRUP COMPANY, INC., a Michigan corporation located in Detroit, Michigan (hereinafter called the Franchisee), for one KLONDIKE PANCAKE HOUSE restaurant to be located in the City of Mackinac Island, Michigan.

RECITALS

A. The Company is the owner of proprietary and other rights and interests in various service marks, trademarks, and trade names used in its business including the trade name and service mark "KLONDIKE PANCAKE HOUSE."

B. The Company operates and enfranchises others to operate restaurants under the trade name and service mark "KLONDIKE PANCAKE HOUSE" using certain recipes, formulas, food preparation procedures, business methods, business forms, and business policies it has developed. The Company has also developed a body of knowledge pertaining to the establishment and operation of restaurants. The Franchisee acknowledges that he does not presently know these recipes, formulas, food preparation procedures, business methods, or business policies, nor does the Franchisee have these business forms or access to the Company's body of knowledge.

C. The Franchisee intends to enter the restaurant business and desires access to the Company's recipes, formulas, food preparation procedures, business methods, business forms, business policies, and body of knowledge pertaining to the operation of a restaurant. In addition, the Franchisee desires access to information pertaining to new developments and techniques in the Company's restaurant business.

D. The Franchisee desires to participate in the use of the Company's rights in its service marks and trademarks in connection with the operation of one restaurant to be located at a site approved by the Company and the Franchisee.

E. The Franchisee understands that information received from the Company or from any of its officers, employees, agents, or franchisees is confidential and has been developed with a great deal of effort and expense. The Franchisee acknowledges that the information is being made available to him so that he may more effectively establish and operate a restaurant.

F. The Company has granted, and will continue to grant others, access to its recipes, formulas, food preparation procedures, business methods, business forms, business policies, and body of knowledge pertaining to the operation of restaurants and information pertaining to new developments and techniques in its business.

G. The Company has and will continue to license others to use its service marks and trademarks in connection with the operation of restaurants at Company-approved locations.

H. The Franchise Fee and Royalty constitute the sole consideration to the Company for the use by the Franchisee of its body of knowledge, systems, and trademark rights.

I. The Franchisee acknowledges that he received the Company's franchise offering prospectus at or prior to the first personal meeting with a Company representative and at least ten (10) business days prior to the signing of this Agreement and that he has been given the opportunity to clarify provisions he did not understand and to consult with an attorney or other professional advisor. Franchisee represents he understands and agrees to be bound by the terms, conditions, and obligations of this Agreement.

J. The Franchisee acknowledges that he understands that the success of the business to be operated by him under this Agreement depends primarily upon his efforts and that neither the Company nor any of its agents or representatives have made any oral, written, or visual representations or projections of actual or potential sales, earnings, or net or gross profits. Franchisee understands that the restaurant operated under this Agreement may lose money or fail.

AGREEMENT

Acknowledging the above recitals, the parties hereto agree as follows:

1. Upon execution of this Agreement, the Franchisee shall pay to the Company a Franchise Fee of $30,000 that shall not be refunded in any event.
2. The Franchisee shall also pay to the Company, weekly, a Royalty equal to eight (8%) percent of the gross sales from each restaurant that he operates throughout the term of this Agreement. "Gross sales" means all sales or revenues derived from the Franchisee's location exclusive of sales taxes.
3. The Company hereby grants to the Franchisee:
   a. Access to the Company's recipes, formulas, food preparation procedures, business methods, business forms, business policies, and body of knowledge pertaining to the operation of a restaurant.
   b. Access to information pertaining to new developments and techniques in the Company's restaurant business.
   c. License to use of the Company's rights in and to its service marks and trademarks in connection with the operation of one restaurant to be located at a site approved by the Company and the Franchisee.
4. The Company agrees to:
   a. Provide a training program for the operator of restaurants using the Company's recipes, formulas, food preparation procedures, business methods, business forms, and business policies. The Franchisee shall pay all transportation, lodging, and other expenses incurred in attending the program. The Franchisee must attend the training program before opening his restaurant.
   b. Provide a Company Representative that the Franchisee may call upon for consultation concerning the operation of his business.
   c. Provide the Franchise with a program of assistance that shall include periodic consultations with a Company Representative, publish a periodical advising of new developments and techniques in the Company's restaurant business, and grant access to Company personnel for consultations concerning the operation of his business.
5. The Franchisee agrees to:
   a. Begin operation of a restaurant within 365 days. The restaurant will be at a location found by the Franchisee and approved by the Company. The Company or one of its designees will lease the premises and sublet them to the Franchisee at cost. The Franchisee will then construct and equip his unit in accordance with Company specifications contained in the Operating Manual. Upon written request from the Franchisee, the Company will grant a 180-day extension that is effective immediately upon receipt of the request. Under certain circumstances, and at the sole discretion of the Company, the Company may grant additional time in which to open the business. In all instances, the location of each unit must be approved by the Company and the Franchisee. If the restaurant is not operating within 365 days, or within any approved extensions, this Agreement will automatically expire.
   b. Operate his business in compliance with applicable laws and governmental regulations. The Franchisee will obtain at his expense, and keep in force, any permits, licenses, or other consents required for the leasing, construction, or operation of his business. In addition, the Franchisee shall operate his restaurant in accordance with the Company's Operation Manual, which may be amended from time to time as a result of experience, changes in the law, or changes in the marketplace. The Franchisee shall refrain from conducting any business or selling any products other than those approved by the Company at the approved location.
   c. Be responsible for all costs of operating his unit, including but not limited to, advertising, taxes, insurance, food products, labor, and utilities. Insurance shall include, but not be limited to, comprehensive liability insurance including products liability coverage in the minimum amount of $1,000,000. The Franchisee shall keep these policies in force for the mutual benefit of the parties. In addition, the Franchisee shall save the Company harm from any claim of any type that arises in connection with the operation of his business.

INTERNATIONAL LAW

International Franchising

The international market presently offers a great opportunity for U.S. franchisors to expand their businesses. Many U.S. franchisors view international expansion as their number-one priority. However, in addition to providing lucrative new markets, international franchising also poses difficulties and risks.

The expansion into other countries through franchising means that U.S. franchisors can expand internationally without expending the huge capital investments that would otherwise be required if the franchisors tried to penetrate those markets with company-owned stores or branches. In addition, a foreign franchisee will have knowledge about the cultural and business traditions of the foreign country that the franchisor does not have. Consequently, the franchisee will be better able to serve the consumers and customers in the particular market.

Foreign franchising is not without difficulties, however. For example, the host country's laws may differ from U.S. laws. Foreign cultures may also require different advertising, marketing, and promotional approaches. In addition, the franchisor may be subjecting itself to government regulation in the host country. Finally, different dispute settlement procedures may be in place that will have to be used if there is a dispute between the U.S. franchisor and the foreign franchisee.

U.S. franchisors are expanding to Latin America, Asia, western and eastern Europe, and other areas of the world.

> The minute you read something that you can't understand, you can almost be sure that it was drawn up by a lawyer.
>
> Will Rogers

LIABILITY OF FRANCHISOR AND FRANCHISEE

If a franchise is properly organized and operated, the franchisor and franchisee are separate legal entities. Therefore, the franchisor deals with the franchisee as an *independent contractor*. Franchisees are liable on their own contracts and are liable for their own torts (e.g., negligence). Franchisors are liable for their own contracts and torts. Generally, neither party is liable for the contracts or torts of the other.

Example: Suppose that McDonald's Corporation, a fast-food restaurant franchisor, grants a restaurant franchise to Tina Corporation. Tina Corporation opens the franchise restaurant. One day, a customer at the franchise spills a chocolate shake on the floor. The employees at the franchise fail to clean up the spilled shake, and one hour later, another customer slips on the spilled shake and suffers severe injuries. The injured customer can recover damages from the franchisee, Tina Corporation, because it was negligent. It cannot recover damages from the franchisor, McDonald's Corporation.

Example: Suppose that in the preceding example, McDonald's Corporation, the franchisor, grants a franchise to Gion Corporation, the franchisee. McDonald's Corporation enters into a loan agreement with City Bank, whereby it borrows $100 million. Gion Corporation, the franchisee, is not liable on the loan. McDonald's Corporation, the franchisor and debtor, is liable on the loan.

In the case that follows, the court imposed liability on a franchisor for its own negligent conduct.

CASE 8.1 FRANCHISOR LIABILITY

Martin v. McDonald's Corp., 572 N.E.2d 1073 (Ill. App. Ct. 1991).

"The trial court correctly determined that McDonald's Corporation had a duty to protect plaintiffs Laura Martin, Maureen Kincaid, and Therese Dudek from harm."

—Judge McNulty

Facts

McDonald's Corporation (McDonald's) is a franchisor that licenses franchisees to operate fast-food restaurants and to use McDonald's trademarks and service marks. One such franchise, which was located in Oak Forest, Illinois, was owned and operated by McDonald's Restaurants of Illinois, the franchisee.

Recognizing the threat of armed robbery at its franchises, especially in the time period immediately after closing, McDonald's established a corporate division to deal with security problems at franchises. McDonald's prepared a manual for restaurant security operations and required its franchisees to adhere to these procedures.

Jim Carlson was the McDonald's regional security manager for the area in which the Oak Forest franchise was located. Carlson visited the Oak Forest franchise on October 31, to inform the manager of security procedures. He specifically mentioned these rules: (1) No one should throw garbage out the back door after dark, and (2) trash and grease were to be taken out the side glass door at least one hour prior to closing. During his inspection, Carlson noted that the locks had to be changed at the restaurant and an alarm system needed to be installed for the back door. Carlson never followed up to determine whether these security measures had been taken.

On the evening of November 29, a six-woman crew, all teenagers, was working to clean up and close the Oak Forest restaurant. Laura Martin, Therese Dudek, and Maureen Kincaid were members of that crew. A person later identified as Peter Logan appeared at the back of the restaurant with a gun. He ordered the crew to open the safe and get him the money and then ordered them into the refrigerator. In the course of moving the crew into the refrigerator, Logan shot and killed Martin and assaulted Dudek and Kincaid. Dudek and Kincaid suffered severe emotional distress from the assault.

Evidence showed that Logan had entered the restaurant through the back door. Trial testimony proved that the work crew used the back door exclusively, both before and after dark, and emptied garbage and grease through the back door all day and all night. In addition, there was evidence that the latch on the back door did not work properly. Evidence also showed that the crew had not been instructed about the use of the back door after dark, the crew had never received copies of the McDonald's security manual, and the required warning about not using the back door after dark had not been posted at the restaurant.

Martin's parents, Dudek, and Kincaid sued McDonald's to recover damages for negligence. The trial court awarded damages of $1,003,445 to the Martins for the wrongful death of their daughter and awarded $125,000 each to Dudek and Kincaid. McDonald's appealed.

Issue

Is McDonald's liable for negligence?

Language of the Court

> *The trial court correctly determined that McDonald's Corporation had a duty to protect plaintiffs Laura Martin, Maureen Kincaid, and Therese Dudek from harm. Although it did not specifically state that such duty was "assumed," there is ample support in case law and the facts of this case to support a determination that McDonald's Corporation voluntarily assumed a duty to provide security to plaintiffs and protect them from harm.*
>
> *Once McDonald's Corporation assumed the duty to provide security and protection to plaintiffs, it had the obligation to perform this duty with due care and competence, and any failure to do so would lead to a finding of breach of duty. Accordingly, there was ample evidence for the jury to determine that McDonald's had breached its assumed duty to plaintiffs.*

Decision

The appellate court held that McDonald's was negligent for not following up and making sure that the security deficiencies it had found at the Oak Forest franchise had been corrected. The appellate court affirmed the judgment of the trial court, holding McDonald's liable.

Case Questions

1. **Critical Legal Thinking** Should businesses be held liable for criminal actions of others? Why or why not?
2. **Business Ethics** Should McDonald's have denied liability in this case?
3. **Contemporary Business** What is the benefit to a franchisor of establishing and requiring its franchisees to adhere to security rules? Is there any potential detriment? Explain.

Apparent Agency

If a franchisee is the *actual* or *apparent agent* of the franchisor, the franchisor is responsible for the torts and contracts the franchisee committed or entered into within the scope of the agency. Actual agency is created when a franchisor expressly or implicitly makes a franchisee its agent. The franchisor is liable for the contracts entered into and torts committed by the franchisee while the franchisee is acting within the scope of the agency. Franchisors very seldom appoint franchisees as their agents.

Apparent agency is created when a franchisor leads a third person into believing that the franchisee is its agent. For example, a franchisor and franchisee who use the same trade name and trademarks and make no effort to inform the public of their separate legal status may find themselves in such a situation. However, mere use of the same name does not automatically make a franchisor liable for the franchisee's actions. The court's decision of whether an apparent agency has been created depends on the facts and circumstances of the case.

apparent agency
Agency that arises when a franchisor creates the appearance that a franchisee is its agent when, in fact, an actual agency does not exist.

CASE 8.2 FRANCHISOR AND APPARENT AGENCY

***Holiday Inns, Inc. v. Shelburne*, 576 So. 2d 322 (Fla. Dist. Ct. App. 1991).**

Facts

Holiday Inns, Inc. (Holiday Inns), is a franchisor that licenses franchisees to operate hotels using its trademarks and service marks. Holiday Inns licensed Hospitality Venture to operate a franchised hotel in Fort Pierce, Florida. The Rodeo Bar, which had a reputation as the "hottest bar in town," was located in the hotel.

The Fort Pierce Holiday Inn and Rodeo Bar did not have sufficient parking, so security guards posted in the Holiday Inn parking lot required Rodeo Bar patrons to park in vacant lots that surrounded the hotel but that were not owned by the hotel. The main duty of the guards was to keep the parking lot open for hotel guests. Two unarmed security guards were on duty on the night in question. One guard was drinking on the job, and the other was an untrained temporary fill-in.

The record disclosed that although the Rodeo Bar had a capacity of 240 people, the bar regularly admitted 270 to 300 people, with 50 to 75 people waiting outside. Fights occurred all the time in the bar and the parking lots, and often there were three or four fights a night. Police reports involving fifty-eight offenses, including several weapons charges and battery and assault charges, had been filed during the previous eighteen months.

On the night in question, the two groups involved in the altercation did not leave the Rodeo Bar until closing time. According to the record, these individuals exchanged remarks as they moved toward their respective vehicles in the vacant parking lots adjacent to the Holiday Inn. Ultimately, a fight erupted. The evidence shows that during the course of physical combat, Mr. Carter shot David Rice, Scott Turner, and Robert Shelburne. Rice died from his injuries.

Rice's heirs, Turner, and Shelburne sued the franchisee, Hospitality Venture, and the franchisor, Holiday Inns, for damages. The trial court found Hospitality Venture negligent for not providing sufficient security to prevent the foreseeable incident that took the life of Rice and injured Turner and Shelburne. The court also found that Hospitality Venture was the apparent agent of Holiday Inns and, therefore, Holiday Inns was vicariously liable for its franchisee's tortious conduct. Turner was awarded $3,825,000 for his injuries, Shelburne received $1 million, and Rice's interests were awarded $1 million. Hospitality Venture and Holiday Inns appealed.

Issue

Are the franchisee and the franchisor liable?

Court's Reasoning

A franchisee is always liable for its own tortious conduct. A franchisor may be held liable for the tortious conduct of a franchisee if the franchisee is the "apparent agent" of the franchisor. This "apparent agent" occurs when the franchisor misleads the public into believing that the franchise is really owned and operated by the franchisor, even though it is not. Here, the court held that Holiday Inns led the public into believing that its franchisees were part of the Holiday Inns system and not independently owned businesses. The trial court held that the Holiday Inns reservation system, as well as the signs at the Fort Pierce franchise hotel, gave this appearance to the public. Therefore, Holiday Inns was determined to be vicariously liable for the tortious conduct of its franchisee.

Decision

The court of appeals held that the franchisee was negligent and that the franchisee was the apparent agent of the franchisor. The court of appeals affirmed the judgment of the trial court.

Case Questions

1. **Critical Legal Thinking** What does the doctrine of apparent agency provide? How does it differ from actual agency?
2. **Business Ethics** Did Hospitality Venture act ethically in denying liability? Did Holiday Inns act ethically in denying liability?
3. **Contemporary Business** Why do you think the plaintiffs included Holiday Inns as a defendant in their lawsuit? Do you think the damages that were awarded were warranted?

TERMINATION OF A FRANCHISE

Most franchise agreements permit a franchisor to terminate the franchise for cause. For example, the continued failure of a franchisee to pay franchise fees or meet legitimate quality control standards would be deemed just cause. Unreasonably strict application of a just cause termination clause constitutes **wrongful termination**. A single failure to meet a quality control standard, for example, is not cause for termination.

wrongful termination
Termination of a franchise without just cause.

Termination-at-will clauses in franchise agreements are generally held to be void on the grounds that they are unconscionable. The rationale for this position is that the franchisee has spent time, money, and effort developing the franchise. If a franchise is terminated without just cause, the franchisee can sue the franchisor for wrongful termination. The franchisee can recover damages caused by the unlawful termination and recover the franchise.

Breach of the Franchise Agreement

A lawful franchise agreement is an enforceable contract. Each party owes a duty to adhere to and perform under the terms of the franchise agreement. If the agreement is breached, the aggrieved party can sue the breaching party for rescission of the agreement, restitution, and damages.

In the following case, the court held that a franchisor had properly terminated a franchisee.

ETHICS SPOTLIGHT

FRANCHISEE'S FRAUD CAUGHT

Baskin-Robbins Ice Cream Company (Baskin-Robbins) is a franchisor that has established a system of more than 2,700 franchise ice cream retail stores nationwide. The franchisees agree to purchase ice cream in bulk only from Baskin-Robbins or an authorized Baskin-Robbins source, to sell only Baskin-Robbins ice cream under the "Baskin-Robbins" trademarks, and to keep specific business hours. Franchisees agree to pay ice cream invoices to Baskin-Robbins when due. If ice cream invoices are not paid within seven days of delivery of the ice cream, payment by certified check is required. If such a check is not received, prepayment in cash is then required. If Baskin-Robbins must institute a lawsuit for a breach of the franchise agreement, the franchisee is required to pay all costs incurred by Baskin-Robbins if it is successful in the lawsuit.

Baskin-Robbins entered into a standard franchise agreement with D&L Ice Cream Company, Inc. (D&L), granting it a franchise to operate a retail ice cream store in Brooklyn, New York. During the course of the franchise, D&L consistently failed to maintain proper business hours and failed to pay ice cream invoices when due. Baskin-Robbins properly invoked its right to require payment by certified check. When such payment was not received, Baskin-Robbins required prepayment in cash for ice cream deliveries. In response, D&L purchased bulk ice cream from other manufacturers and sold it in its store under the "Baskin-Robbins" trademarks. Upon discovering this fact, Baskin-Robbins sent a notice of termination to D&L. D&L ignored the notice and continued to operate under the Baskin-Robbins store and sell other brands of ice cream in cups and containers bearing the Baskin-Robbins trademarks. Baskin-Robbins sued D&L for trademark infringement.

The court stated that the sale by a franchised licensee of unauthorized products—that is, products outside the scope of the license—is likely to confuse the public into believing that such products are in fact manufactured or authorized by the trademark owner, when in fact they are not. The court concluded that D&L had engaged in trademark infringement. The court held that Baskin-Robbins was entitled to a permanent injunction, to recover outstanding monies owed by D&L, to all profits made by D&L as a result of the trademark infringement, and to full costs and attorney's fees incurred in connection with this litigation. *Baskin-Robbins Ice Cream v. D&L Ice Cream Co., Inc.,* 576 F.Supp. 1055, Web 1983 U.S. Dist. Lexis 11057 (U.S. District Court for the Eastern District of New York).

Law and Ethics Questions

1. **Ethics** Did D&L act ethically in this case?
2. Do you think there was trademark infringement in this case?

Web Exercises

1. **Web** Search the web to find the complete opinion of this case.
2. **Web** Visit the website of the U.S. District Court for the Eastern District of New York, at www.nyed.uscourts.gov.

CASE 8.3 TERMINATION OF A FRANCHISE

***Dunkin' Donuts of Am., Inc. v. Middletown Donut Corp.,* 495 A.2d 66 (N.J. 1985).**

"A franchisee who gets caught with his hand in the proverbial cookie jar (or doughnut box, as the case may be) must suffer the known consequences."

—Judge Clifford

Facts

Dunkin' Donuts of America, Inc. (Dunkin' Donuts), is a franchisor that licenses franchised donuts shops throughout the United States. Gerald Smothergill, through two corporations, entered into franchise and lease agreements with

Dunkin' Donuts to operate Dunkin' Donuts franchise shops in Middletown and West Long Branch, New Jersey. Smothergill paid $115,000 for the two franchises. Under each franchise agreement, Smothergill was required to keep accurate sales records, pay a basic franchise fee of 4.9 percent of gross sales, and pay an advertising fee of 2 percent of gross sales. The lease agreements were conditioned on Smothergill's remaining a franchisee in good standing under the franchise agreements.

Subsequently, Dunkin' Donuts notified Smothergill that his franchise agreements were being terminated due to his intentional underreporting of gross sales. The termination notice provided an opportunity for Smothergill to cure the breach by making prompt payment of the amounts due. Smothergill made no attempt to cure and refused to abandon his Dunkin' Donuts shops. Dunkin' Donuts sued to enforce its claimed right of termination and to collect damages. The trial court permitted Dunkin' Donuts to terminate the franchise agreements. Smothergill appealed.

Issue

Did Dunkin' Donuts properly terminate the franchise agreements for cause?

Language of the Court

> *At the conclusion of the trial, the trial court found as fact that Smothergill had been guilty of substantial, intentional, and long-continued underreporting of gross sales at both of his Dunkin' Donuts stores. The court determined that Smothergill had failed to keep the financial records that were required under the franchise agreements and that the failure to keep records was not the result of carelessness or incompetence. Rather, Smothergill's delinquency in recordkeeping was part of a deliberate effort to underreport sales, which in turn would result in the underpayment of franchise fees, underpayment of advertising fund fees, underpayment of rental override charges, and evasion of federal and state taxes. In short, the trial court found as a fact that Smothergill was "guilty of unconscionable cheating."*
>
> *Dunkin' Donuts, as franchisor of a sizeable network of New Jersey franchises, has a real and legitimate interest in maintaining the integrity of its system. Other Dunkin' Donuts franchisees also have an interest in promoting honest reporting because a percentage of their reported gross sales are pooled in a common advertising fund that benefits all. To the extent that a franchisee such as Smothergill underreports gross sales, he cheats not only the franchisor but all other franchisees as well. Upon signing the Dunkin' Donuts franchise agreement, both franchisor and franchisee were aware of the rules of the game. Those rules seem fair. A franchisee who gets caught with his hand in the proverbial cookie jar (or doughnut box, as the case may be) must suffer the known consequences.*

Decision

The Supreme Court of New Jersey held that Smothergill had intentionally breached the franchise agreements and that Dunkin' Donuts had properly terminated Smothergill as a franchisee. The supreme court affirmed the trial court's decision, allowing Dunkin' Donuts to terminate the franchise agreements.

Case Questions

1. **Critical Legal Thinking** Should franchisors be permitted to terminate franchises at will? Or is the rule that permits franchisors to terminate franchises for cause a better rule? Explain.
2. **Business Ethics** Did Smothergill act ethically in this case?
3. **Contemporary Business** Do you think many franchisees "cheat" when franchise royalty fees are based on gross sales?

ETHICS SPOTLIGHT

HÄAGEN-DAZS ICE CREAM FRANCHISE

Franchise agreements are detailed documents that are carefully drafted to spell out the rights and duties of the parties. A franchisee must be careful to read and understand the terms of the agreement, as the following case demonstrates.

Reuben Mattus developed a "super premium" ice cream and named it "Häagen-Dazs" to give the product a Scandinavian flair. Mattus began selling Häagen-Dazs ice cream in prepackaged pints to small stores and delicatessens in the New York metropolitan area. Sales of the product were expanded into some grocery stores and other retail outlets.

Twenty years later, Mattus's daughter, Doris Mattus-Hurley, opened the first "Häagen-Dazs Shoppe" in Brooklyn Heights, New York. After this shop prospered, Mattus-Hurley began franchising other shops to independent franchisees throughout the country. Häagen-Dazs ice cream is manufactured, distributed, and franchised through a variety of corporate entities (collectively referred to as "Häagen-Dazs"). The franchise agreement grants a limited license to the franchisee to operate a single shop under the Häagen-Dazs trademark at a specific location for a specified term ranging from five to twelve years. The franchisee agrees to purchase all its ice cream from the franchisor at prices set by Häagen-Dazs.

Seven years after the Häagen-Dazs Company began granting franchises, the Pillsbury Company (Pillsbury), a diversified international food and restaurant company headquartered in Minneapolis, Minnesota, purchased the Häagen-Dazs Company, including its franchise operations. Pillsbury decided that it could maximize sales through methods of distribution that did not involve franchisees. Pillsbury substantially increased sales of Häagen-Dazs products to national grocery store chains, convenience stores such as 7-Eleven, and other retail outlets.

This change severely harmed sales at existing franchises. Franchisees located in many states sued Pillsbury, alleging breach of the franchise agreement. The plaintiffs claimed that the defendant breached the franchise agreement by distributing Häagen-Dazs ice cream through nonfranchised outlets that were not "upscale" and through mass distribution of prepackaged pints that competed with franchise outlet sales.

The U.S. District Court held that the express terms of the franchise agreement had not been violated. The franchise agreement expressly reserved the right of the franchisor to distribute Häagen-Dazs products "through not only Häagen-Dazs Shoppes, but through any other distribution method, which may from time to time be established." The court held that this language gave Pillsbury the right to aggressively distribute prepackaged pints of Häagen-Dazs ice cream through nonfranchise outlets even though that distribution adversely affected retail sales by franchisees. The U.S. District Court granted Pillsbury's motion for summary judgment. *Carlock v. Pillsbury Company*, 719 F.Supp. 791, Web 1989 U.S. Dist. Lexis 9370 (U.S. District Court for the District of Minnesota).

Law and Ethics Questions

1. **Ethics** Even though the express terms of the franchise agreement allowed Pillsbury to distribute Häagen-Dazs ice cream through nonfranchise outlets, do you think Pillsbury acted ethically in doing so?
2. **Ethics** Should franchise agreements include an implied covenant that requires a franchisor to act in good faith when dealing with franchisees? Would that have helped the franchisees in this case?

Web Exercises

1. **Web** Search the web to find the complete opinion of this case.
2. **Web** Visit the website of the U.S. District Court of Minnesota, at www.mnd.uscourts.gov.
3. **Web** Visit the website of Pillsbury Company at www.pillsbury.com. Can you find any information about Häagen-Dazs franchising?
4. **Web** Use www.google.com to find an article that discusses Häagen-Dazs franchise opportunities. Read it.
5. Web Use www.google.com to find a photo of a Häagen-Dazs franchise outlet.

LICENSING

Licensing is an important business arrangement in both domestic and international markets. **Licensing** occurs when one business or party that owns trademarks, service marks, trade names, and other intellectual property (the **licensor**) contracts to permit another business or party (the **licensee**) to use its trademarks, service marks, trade names, and other intellectual property in the distribution of goods, services, software, and digital information. A licensing arrangement is illustrated in **Exhibit 8.4**.

licensing
A business arrangement that occurs when the owner of intellectual property (the *licensor*) contracts to permit another party (the *licensee*) to use the intellectual property.

licensor
The owner of intellectual property or informational rights who transfers rights in the property or information to the licensee.

Example: The Walt Disney Company owns the merchandising rights to "Winnie the Pooh" stories and all the characters associated with the Winnie the Pooh stories. The Walt Disney Company enters into an agreement whereby it permits the Beijing Merchandising Company, a business formed under Chinese law, to manufacture and distribute a line of clothing, children's toys, and other items bearing the likeness of the Winnie the Pooh characters. This is a **license**. The Walt Disney Company is the licensor, and the Beijing Merchandising Company is the licensee.

licensee
The party who is granted limited rights in or access to intellectual property or informational rights owned by the licensor.

license
A contract that transfers limited rights in intellectual property and informational rights.

JOINT VENTURE

A **joint venture** is an arrangement in which two or more business entities combine their resources to pursue a single project or transaction. The parties to a joint venture are called joint venturers. Joint ventures resemble partnerships,

joint venture
An arrangement in which two or more business entities combine their resources to pursue a single project or transaction.

Exhibit 8.4 Licensing

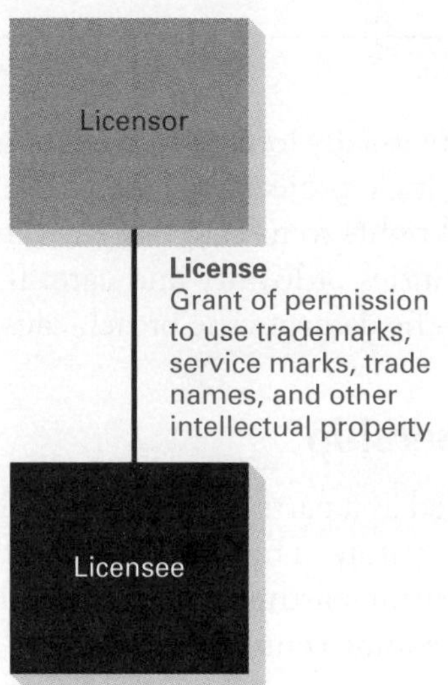

INTERNATIONAL LAW

Pokemon Licensing

The Japanese company Nintendo's animated Pokemon creatures have been a huge hit in Japan. In this role-playing game, children manipulate Pokemon characters with different stated strengths and weaknesses in a variant of the rock, paper, scissors game. The several hundred cute, gender-neutral characters, with such names as Pikachu, Piyo Piyo, Dalki, and Dragon Ball, show up in television (TV) cartoons and video games and on playing cards, book bags, and thousands of other items. Japenese children are crazy about acquiring the next Pokemon character.

But would American children buy into the oddly animated creatures and their interactive games? Nintendo had doubts and did not want to take the exporting risk directly. Up stepped Alfred Kahn and Thomas Kenney, both prior toy company executives, who formed 4Kids Entertainment, Inc., a U.S. Company. They approached Nintendo about bringing the Pokemon games and characters to the United States through the concept of licensing. After much negotiation, Nintendo agreed that 4Kids would be its licensing agent in the United States.

4Kids syndicated a Pokemon TV series, with episodes dubbed in English. Within four months, Pokemon was the top-rated syndicated kids' program in the United States. After this TV success, Nintendo released the first Pokemon video games in the United States, followed by trading cards, comic books, home videos, and compact discs. 4Kids has signed more than one hundred licensing deals for Pokemon, including deals with Hasbro toy company as its master toy licensee and TimeWarner for the Pokemon TV series. The Pokemon craze reached a fever pitch in the United States as it had in Japan.

The Pokemon invasion of the United States has reaped a plethora of royalties for Nintendo and its local entrepreneurs. The Pokemon sales have exceeded $1 billion in the United States, and 4Kids has earned up to $75 million, making its owners multimillionaires.

Web Exercises

1. **Web** Use www.google.com to find likenesses of several Pokemon characters.
2. **Web** Use www.google.com to find an article that discusses a licensing agreement. Read it.

except that partnerships are usually formed to pursue ongoing business operations rather than to focus on a single project or transaction. Unless otherwise agreed, joint venturers have equal rights to manage a joint venture. Joint venturers owe each other the fiduciary duties of loyalty and care. If a joint venturer violates these duties, it is liable for the damages the breach causes.

Joint Venture Partnership

joint venture partnership A partnership owned by two or more joint venturers that is formed to operate a joint venture.

If a joint venture is operated as a partnership, then each joint venturer is considered a partner of the joint venture. This is called a **joint venture partnership** (see Exhibit 8.5). In a joint venture partnership, each joint venturer is liable for the debts and obligations of the joint venture partnership.

Example: A new oil field is discovered in northern Canada. Two large oil companies, ChevronTexaco Corporation and ConocoPhillips Corporation, would each

Exhibit 8.5 Joint Venture Partnership

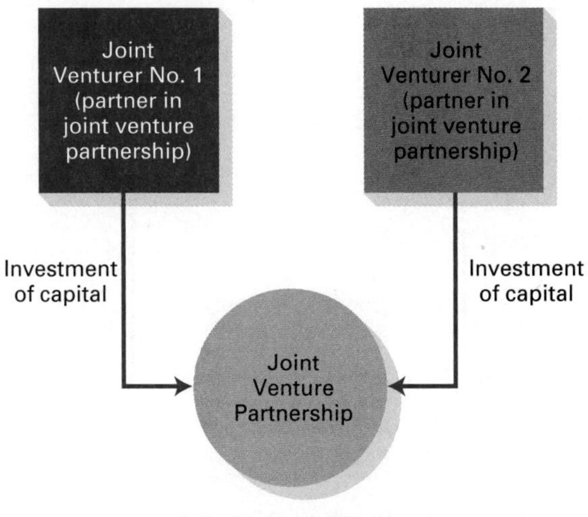

Joint Venturer No. 1 and Joint Venturer No. 2 are liable for the debts and obligations of the joint venture partnership

like to drill for oil there, but neither one has sufficient resources to do so alone. They join together to form a joint venture partnership, and each contributes $100 million capital to the joint venture. If the joint venture fails and the joint venture owes $1 billion to its creditors, which it cannot pay, ChevronTexaco and ConocoPhillips are each responsible for the joint venture's unpaid debts and obligations. This is because they are partners in the joint venture.

INTERNATIONAL LAW

A Starbucks U.S.–Chinese International Joint Venture

Starbucks has been a tremendous success in the United States. Beginning with a single outlet in Seattle, Washington, Starbucks Coffee Company has expanded Starbucks shops across the United States. The company expanded in the United States through company-owned stores.

When Starbucks wanted to enter overseas markets, however, it realized it could not expand solely through company-owned outlets. This was because (1) government restrictions in some countries prohibit 100 percent ownership of a business by a foreign investor and (2) the company lacked the business expertise and cultural knowledge necessary to enter many foreign markets. To enter foreign markets, Starbucks turned to joint ventures. For example, Starbucks is expanding its operations in China by using a 50-50 joint venture with Shanghai President Coffee Corporation, a Chinese company.

Web Exercises

1. **Web** Visit the website of Starbucks Corporation, at www.starbucks.com.
2. **Web** Use www.google.com to find an article that discusses the Starbucks–Shanghai President Coffee Corporation joint venture in China. Read it.
3. **Web** Use www.google.com to find an article that discusses the joint ventures Starbucks has made in other countries.

Exhibit 8.6 Joint Venture Corporation

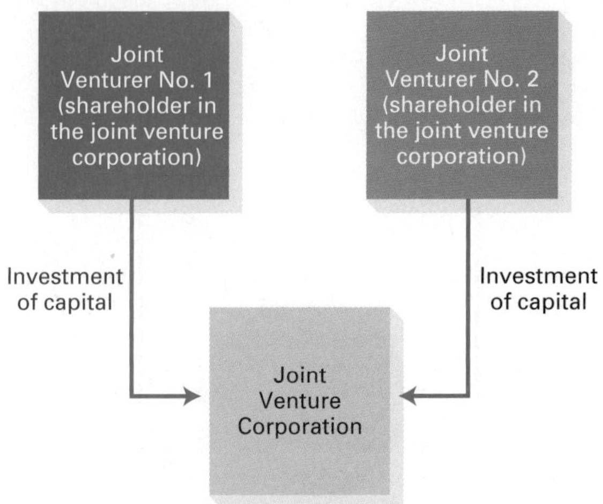

Joint Venture Corporation

joint venture corporation
A corporation owned by two or more joint venturers that is created to operate a joint venture.

In pursuing a joint venture, joint venturers often form a corporation to operate the joint venture. This is called a **joint venture corporation** (see Exhibit 8.6). The joint venturers are shareholders of the joint venture corporation. The joint venture corporation is liable for its debts and obligations. The joint venturers are liable for the debts and obligations of the joint venture corporation only up to their capital contributions to the joint venture corporation.

Example: Suppose that in the preceding example, ChevronTexaco Corporation and ConocoPhillips Corporation form a third corporation, called Canadian Imperial Corporation, to operate the joint venture. ChevronTexaco and ConocoPhillips each contribute $100 million capital to Canadian Imperial Corporation, and each becomes a shareholder of Canadian Imperial Corporation. If the joint venture fails and Canadian Imperial Corporation owes $1 billion to its creditors, which it cannot pay, ChevronTexaco and ConocoPhillips each loses its $100 million capital contribution but is not liable for any further unpaid debts or obligations of Canadian Imperial Corporation.

STRATEGIC ALLIANCE

strategic alliance
An arrangement between two or more companies in the same industry whereby they agree to ally themselves to accomplish a designated objective.

A **strategic alliance** is an arrangement between two or more companies in the same industry in which they agree to ally themselves to accomplish a designated objective. A strategic alliance allows the companies to reduce risks, share costs, combine technologies, and extend their markets. For example, companies often enter into strategic alliances when they decide to expand internationally into foreign countries.

Strategic alliances do not have the same protection as mergers, joint ventures, or franchising, and sometimes they are dismantled. Consideration must always be given to the fact that a strategic alliance partner is also a potential competitor.

PARALEGAL PERSPECTIVE

Mary Brownell *is a corporate paralegal with the in-house legal department at HCR Manor Care in Toledo, Ohio. She graduated with a postbaccalaureate certificate in paralegal studies from the University of Toledo. She specializes in the area of corporate transactions and has been working as a paralegal for over four years.*

Why or how do you think a paralegal is useful in a franchise situation? Paralegals perform the important function of monitoring a franchise's use of intellectual property.

What are the most important paralegal skills needed in your job? The most important paralegal skill my job requires is the ability to multitask. Each day I do a wide variety of tasks, so I need to be able to switch gears and prioritize. It is also necessary to pay attention to details so that my supervising attorneys do not have to go back and make a lot of corrections.

What is the academic background required for a paralegal entering your area of practice? My area of practice usually requires a four-year degree in paralegal studies, preferably from an ABA-approved school. My position at HCR requires the Certified Legal Assistant (CLA) certification through the National Association of Legal Assistants (NALA).

How is technology involved in your job? Technology has made corporate filings much easier. Most states accept filings electronically, which speeds up the process and allows me to quickly check the status of annual reports, assumed names, etc.

I maintain a web-based entity management system that tracks all of our corporate information (tax IDs, formation dates, directors and officers, etc.). This system gives employees throughout the company a quick, easy way to access up-to-date information. HCR uses an electronic case-management system and encrypts e-mails. We also have an e-discovery program in place to properly respond to discovery requests.

What trends do you see in your area of practice that will likely affect your job in the future? Corporate governance is a hot topic right now, with an increased focus on corporate compliance.

What do you feel is the biggest issue currently facing the paralegal profession? The economy. Many employers can't afford to send their paralegals for trainings or hire extra support staff, so job duties are increasing while compensation remains the same. In some extreme cases, paralegal positions are being eliminated, and attorneys are doing their own filings and research to save money.

What words of advice do you have for a new paralegal entering your area of practice? Take advantage of all training opportunities. Become a notary public. Join your local paralegal association to network with others in the profession. Never allow yourself to become stagnant; seek out opportunities to broaden your knowledge. Consider taking the certification exam through NALA or your state. Don't be afraid to ask questions. Develop forms and "cheat sheets" that you can refer to each time you do a similar task.

Concept Review

FRANCHISES

Definition	An arrangement that is established when one party licenses another party to use the franchisor's trade name, trademarks, commercial symbols, patents, copyrights, and other property in the distribution and selling of goods and services.
Formation	A franchise is established when one party (the franchisor, or licensor) licenses another party (the franchisee, or licensee) to use the franchisor's trade name, trademarks, commercial symbols, patents, copyrights, and other property in the distribution and selling of goods and services. Generally, the franchisor and the franchisee are established as separate corporations.
Liability	The franchisor deals with the franchisee as an *independent contractor*. Generally, neither party is liable for the contracts or torts of the other.

(continued)

Termination	Most franchise agreements permit a franchisor to terminate the franchise for cause. A lawful franchise agreement is an enforceable contract. Each party owes a duty to adhere to and perform under the terms of the franchise agreement. If the agreement is breached, the aggrieved party can sue the breaching party for rescission of the agreement, restitution, and damages.

INTERNET AND TECHNOLOGY

Strategic Internet Alliances in China

Leading Internet companies in the United States have eyed the China market for its tremendous growth potential. But China prohibits complete ownership of Internet companies in China by foreigners. In addition, the legendary Chinese "connections" method of conducting business places another hurdle in the way of foreign companies wishing to do business there. So what is the main way to tap into this Internet market? Strategic alliances.

A major strategic alliance by U.S. companies in China was their tie-in with and investment in China.com. China.com is a Chinese-language web portal backed by investments by U.S. companies Time Warner, Inc., Sun Microsystems, and Nortel Networks. China.com became China's largest Internet company when it went public. Intel Corp., another major U.S. company, has aligned itself with Sohu.com, a Chinese Internet company located in Beijing. CMGI Inc., a U.S. Internet holding company, has joined with Pacific Century Cyber-Works (PCCW), a Hong Kong company, to sell web content and e-commerce services to the exploding Chinese Internet market from its base in Hong Kong. The Chinese government has permitted these strategic alliances.

Based on the communist government's rules in China and a culture that favors business connections, U.S. Internet companies will continue to enter the Chinese Internet market through strategic alliances with Chinese Internet firms. These strategic alliances bring together the expertise of all the parties.

Web Exercises

1. **Web** Visit the website of China.com, at www.english.china.com.
2. **Web** Use www.google.com to find another example of a strategic alliance between companies from different countries.

CHAPTER REVIEW

FRANCHISE, p. 209

Franchise

A franchise is established when one party licenses another party to use the franchisor's trade name, trademarks, commercial symbols, patents, copyrights, and other property in the distribution and selling of goods and services.

1. ***Franchisor.*** The franchisor is the party who does the licensing in a franchise arrangement. Also called the *licensor*.

2. ***Franchisee.*** The franchisee is the party who is licensed by the franchisor in a franchise arrangement. Also called the *licensee.*

Types of Franchises

1. ***Distributorship franchise.*** The franchisor manufactures a product and licenses a retail franchisee to distribute the product to the public.
2. ***Processing plant franchise.*** The franchisor provides a secret formula or process to the franchisee, and the franchisee manufactures the product and distributes it to retail dealers.
3. ***Chain-style franchise.*** The franchisor licenses the franchisee to make and sell its products or distribute its services to the public from a retail outlet serving an exclusive territory.
4. ***Area franchise.*** The franchisor authorizes the franchisee to negotiate and sell franchises on behalf of the franchisor in designated areas. The area franchisee is called a *subfranchisor.*

State Disclosure Laws

Many states have enacted statutes that require franchisors to make specific presale disclosures to prospective franchisees. Some states use a uniform disclosure document called the *Uniform Franchise Offering Circular (UFOC).*

FTC Franchise Rule

The *FTC* requires franchisors to make presale disclosures to prospective franchisees. If the franchisor uses actual or hypothetical sales or income data in its sales materials, the franchisor must disclose assumptions underlying any estimates and how many franchises have obtained such results, and it must provide a mandated precautionary statement.

FRANCHISE AGREEMENT, p. 211

The Franchise Agreement

A franchise agreement is an agreement that the franchisor and franchisee enter into that sets forth the terms and conditions of the franchise (e.g., quality control standards, covenants not to compete). Common terms in a franchise agreement include:

1. Quality control standards
2. Training requirements
3. Covenant not to compete
4. Arbitration clause
5. Other terms and conditions

Franchise Fees

A franchisee may be required to pay any or all of the following franchise fees to the franchisor:

1. ***Initial license fee.*** This is a lump-sum payment for the privilege of being granted a franchise.
2. ***Royalty fee.*** This is a fee for the continued use of the franchisor's trade name, property, and assistance, and it is often computed as a percentage of the franchisee's gross sales.
3. ***Assessment fee.*** This is a fee for such things as advertising and promotional campaigns, administrative costs, and the like, billed either as a flat monthly or annual fee or as a percentage of gross sales.

4. ***Lease fees.*** These fees are payment for any land or equipment leased from the franchisor, billed either as a flat monthly or annual fee or as a percentage of gross sales or other agreed-upon amount.
5. ***Cost of supplies.*** These fees are payment for supplies purchased from the franchisor.

Trademarks

1. ***Trademarks and service marks.*** A distinctive mark, symbol, name, word, motto, or device may identify the goods or services of a particular franchisor.
2. ***Licensing of marks.*** A franchisor *licenses* the use of its trademarks and service marks to its franchisees in the franchise agreement.
3. ***Trademark infringement.*** Anyone who uses a mark without authorization from the franchisor may be sued for *trademark infringement*. The franchisor can recover damages and obtain an injunction prohibiting further unauthorized use of the mark.

Trade Secrets

1. ***Trade secrets.*** Trade secrets are ideas, formulas, and methods of doing business that make a franchise successful but do not qualify for trademark, patent, or copyright protection.
2. ***Misappropriation of trade secrets.*** Anyone who steals and uses a franchisor's trade secret is liable for misappropriation of a trade secret. The franchisor can recover damages and obtain an injunction prohibiting further unauthorized use of the trade secret.

LIABILITY OF FRANCHISOR AND FRANCHISEE, p. 215

Contract and Tort Liability

1. ***Liability.*** Franchisors and franchisees are liable for their own contracts and torts.
2. ***Independent contractor.*** An independent contractor is a separately organized and operated business that is not the agent of another party with whom it does business. This is the typical franchisor–franchisee arrangement. There is no agency relationship, so neither party is liable for the other's contracts or torts.
3. ***Actual agency.*** This arrangement occurs where a franchisor expressly or implicitly by its conduct makes a franchisee its agent. The franchisor is liable for the contracts entered into and torts committed by the franchisee while acting within the scope of the agency.
4. ***Apparent agency.*** This agency arises when a franchisor creates the appearance that a franchisee is its agent when in fact an actual agency does not exist. The franchisor is liable for the contracts entered into and torts committed by the franchisee acting as an apparent agent.

TERMINATION OF A FRANCHISE, p. 219

Termination of Franchises

Termination "for cause." Most franchise agreements and state and federal laws permit a franchisor to terminate the franchise "for cause" (e.g., nonpayment of franchise fees by the franchisee, continued failure of the franchisee to meet quality control standards).

Wrongful Termination

1. ***Termination at will.*** Most state and federal laws regulating franchising prohibit franchisors from terminating franchises at will. This is to prevent a franchisor from taking advantage of the good will developed at the franchise location by the franchisee.
2. ***Wrongful termination.*** If a franchisor terminates a franchise agreement without just cause, the franchisee can sue the franchisor for *wrongful termination*. The franchisee can recover damages caused by the wrongful termination and recover the franchise.

LICENSING, p. 223

Licensing

1. ***License.*** In a licensing arrangement, the owner of trademarks, service marks, trade names, and other intellectual property grants another party the right to use these in the manufacture and sale of goods, services, softwares, or digital information.
2. ***Licensor.*** The licensor is the party who grants the license.
3. ***Licensee.*** The licensee is the party to whom the license is granted.

JOINT VENTURE, p. 223

Joint Venture

1. ***Joint venture.*** A joint venture is an arrangement whereby two or more business entities combine their resources to pursue a single project or transaction.
2. ***Joint Venturer.*** A joint venturer is a party to a joint venture.

STRATEGIC ALLIANCE, p. 226

Strategic Alliance

1. ***Strategic alliance.*** A strategic alliance is an arrangement between two or more companies in the same industry whereby they agree to accomplish a designated objective.
2. ***International strategic alliance.*** A strategic alliance may be used by companies to enter a foreign market.

TEST REVIEW TERMS AND CONCEPTS

Franchise 209
Franchise agreement 211
Franchisee (licensee) 209
Franchisor (licensor) 209
FTC franchise rule 211
FTC notice 212
Initial license fee 213
Joint venture 223
Joint venture corporation 226
Joint venture partnership 224
Lanham Trademark Act 213
Lease fees 213
License 223
Licensee 223
Licensing 223
Licensor 223
Patent and Trademark Office (PTO) 213
Processing plant franchise 209
Royalty fee 213
Service mark 213
Strategic alliance 226
Trade secret 213
Trademark 213
Unfair competition 213
Uniform Franchise Offering Circular (UFOC) 210
Wrongful termination 219

CASE SCENARIO REVISITED

Remember the case at the beginning of the chapter where McDonald's granted a franchise to another franchisee—other than your law firm's client Libby—to operate a McDonald's restaurant on the west side of Turney Road. If Libby was to sue McDonald's, would the appropriate action be a breach of the franchise agreement. Would McDonald's be liable? To help you with your answer, see *Libby-Broadway Drive-In, Inc. v. McDonald's Sys., Inc.*, 391 N.E.2d 1 (Ill. App. Ct. 1979).

PORTFOLIO EXERCISE

For the business you created at the beginning of the course, draft a franchise agreement using Exhibit 8.3 as a guide. You may also choose to use any of the sample provisions of a franchise agreement.

WORKING THE WEB INTERNET EXERCISES

Activities

1. Review the FTC cases of alleged abusive practices of franchisors at **www.ftc.gov/bcp/franchise/1999-2000cases.htm**. How would you advise a franchisee client to protect against such practices? For information on federal law regarding franchising, see **www.ftc.gov/bcp/franchise/netfran.htm**.
2. Franchising makes extensive use of licensing of intellectual property, especially trademarks and trade secrets. Use the websites listed below to find examples of licensing agreements and the disputes that they can sometimes produce:
   - All About Trademarks, at www.ggmark.com
   - Intellectual Property Digital Library, at ipdl.wipo.int
   - JurisNotes.Com—A source for all aspects of intellectual property law, at www.jurisnotes.com

CRITICAL LEGAL THINKING CASES

Case 8.1 *Franchise Agreement* H&R Block, Inc. (Block), is a franchisor that licenses franchisees to provide tax preparation services to customers under the "H&R Block" service mark. June McCart was granted a Block franchise at 900 Main Street, Rochester, New York. For seven years, her husband, Robert, was involved in the operation of a Block franchise in Rensselaer, New York. After that, he assisted June in the operation of her Block franchise. All the McCarts' income during the time in question came from the Block franchises.

The Block franchise agreement that June signed contained a provision whereby she agreed not to compete (1) in the business of tax preparation (2) within 250 miles of the franchise (3) for a period of two years after the termination of the franchise. Robert did not sign the Rochester franchise agreement. Two years later, June wrote a letter to Block, giving notice that she was terminating the franchise. Shortly thereafter, the McCarts sent a letter to people who had been clients of the Rochester Block office, informing them that June was leaving Block and that Robert was opening a tax preparation service in which June would assist him. Block granted a new franchise in Rochester to another franchisee. It sued the McCarts to enforce the covenant not to compete against them. Who wins? *McCart v. H&R Block, Inc.*, 470 N.E.2d 756 (Ind. Ct. App. 1984).

Case 8.2 *Franchisor Disclosure* My Pie International, Inc. (My Pie), an Illinois corporation, was a franchisor that licensed franchisees to open pie shops under its trademark name. My Pie licensed thirteen restaurants throughout the country, including one owned by Dowmont, Inc. (Dowmont), in Glen Ellyn, Illinois. The Illinois Franchise Disclosure Act requires a franchisor that desires to issue franchises in the state to register with the state or qualify for an exemption from registration and to make certain disclosures to prospective franchisees. My Pie granted the license to Dowmont without registering with the state of Illinois or qualifying for an exemption from registration and without making the required disclosures to Dowmont. Dowmont operated its restaurant as a "My Pie" franchise for four years, and after that, it operated it under the name "Arnold's." Dowmont paid franchise royalty fees for the four years. My Pie sued Dowmont for breach of the franchise agreement to recover royalties it claimed were due from Dowmont. Dowmont filed a counterclaim, seeking to rescind the franchise agreement and recover the royalties it paid to My Pie. Who wins? *My Pie Int'l, Inc. v. Dowmont, Inc.*, 687 F.2d 919 (7th Cir. 1982).

Case 8.3 *Tort Liability* Georgia Girl Fashions, Inc. (Georgia Girl), was a franchisor that licensed franchisees to operate women's retail clothing stores under the "Georgia Girl" trademark. Georgia Girl granted a franchise to a franchisee to operate a store on South Cobb Drive in Smyrna, Georgia. Georgia Girl did not supervise or control the day-to-day operations of the franchisee. Melanie McMullan entered the store to exchange a blouse that she had previously purchased at the store. When she found nothing that she wished to exchange the blouse for, she began to leave the store. At that time, she was physically restrained and accused of shoplifting the blouse. McMullan was taken to the local jail, where she was held until her claim of prior purchase could be verified. The store then dropped the charges against her, and she was released from jail. McMullan filed an action against the store owner and Georgia Girl to recover damages for false imprisonment. Is Georgia Girl liable? *McMullan v. Georgia Girl Fashions, Inc.*, 348 S.E.2d 748 (Ga. Ct. App. 1986).

Case 8.4 *Tort Liability* The Seven-Up Company (Seven-Up) is a franchisor that licenses local bottling companies to manufacture, bottle, and distribute soft drinks using the "7-Up" trademark. The Brooks Bottling Company (Brooks) was a Seven-Up franchisee that bottles and sells 7-Up soft drinks to stores in Michigan. Under the franchise agreement, the franchisee was required to purchase the 7-Up syrup from Seven-Up, but it could purchase its bottles, cartons, and other supplies from independent suppliers if Seven-Up approved the design of these articles.

Brooks used cartons designed and manufactured by Olinkraft, Inc., using a design that Seven-Up had approved. Sharon Proos Kosters, a customer at a Meijer Thrifty Acres Store in Holland, Michigan, removed a cardboard carton containing six glass bottles of 7-Up from a grocery store shelf, put it under her arm, and walked toward the checkout counter. As she did so, a bottle slipped out of the carton, fell on the floor, and exploded, causing a piece of glass to strike Kosters in her eye as she looked down; she was blinded in that eye. Evidence showed that the 7-Up carton was designed to be held from the top and was made without a strip on the side of the carton that would prevent a bottle from slipping out if held underneath. Kosters sued Seven-Up to recover damages for her injuries. Is Seven-Up liable? *Kosters v. Seven-Up Co.*, 595 F.2d 347 (6th Cir. 1979).

Case 8.5 *Trademark* The Kentucky Fried Chicken Corporation (KFC) is the franchisor of Kentucky Fried Chicken restaurants. Franchisees must purchase equipment and supplies from manufacturers approved in writing by KFC. Equipment includes cookers, fryers, ovens, and the like; supplies include carry-out boxes, napkins, towelettes, and plastic eating utensils known as "sporks." These products are not trade secrets. KFC may not "unreasonably withhold" approval of any suppliers who apply and whose goods are tested and found to meet KFC's quality control standards. The ten manufacturers who went through KFC's approval process were approved. KFC also sells supplies to franchisees in competition with these independent suppliers. All supplies, whether produced by KFC or the independent suppliers, must contain "Kentucky Fried Chicken" trademarks.

Upon formation, Diversified Container Corporation (Diversified) began manufacturing and selling supplies to KFC franchisees without applying for or receiving KFC's approval. All the items sold by Diversified contained KFC trademarks. Diversified represented to franchisees that its products met "all standards" of KFC and that it sold "approved supplies." Diversified even affixed KFC trademarks to the shipping boxes in which it delivered supplies to franchisees. Evidence showed that Diversified products did not meet the quality control standards set by KFC. KFC sued Diversified for trademark infringement. Who wins? *Kentucky Fried Chicken Corp. v. Diversified Container Corp.*, 549 F.2d 368 (5th Cir. 1977).

Case 8.6 *Trademark* Ramada Inns, Inc. (Ramada Inns), is a franchisor that licenses franchisees to operate motor hotels using the "Ramada Inns" trademarks and service marks. In August, the Gadsden Motor Company (Gadsden), a partnership, purchased a motel in Attalla, Alabama, and entered into a franchise agreement with Ramada Inns to operate it as a Ramada Inns motor hotel. Five years later, the motel began receiving poor ratings from Ramada Inns inspectors, and Gadsden fell behind on its monthly franchise fee payments. Despite prodding from Ramada Inns, the motel never met the Ramada Inns operational standards again. One year later, Ramada Inns properly terminated the franchise agreement, citing quality deficiencies and Gadsden's failure to pay past-due franchise fees. The termination notice directed Gadsden to remove any materials or signs identifying the motel as a Ramada. Gadsden continued using Ramada Inns signage, trademarks, and service marks inside and outside the motel. In September, Ramada Inns sued Gadsden for trademark infringement. Who wins? *Ramada Inns, Inc. v. Gadsden Motel Co.*, 804 F.2d 1562 (11th Cir. 1986).

Case 8.7 *Termination of a Franchise* Kawasaki Motors Corporation (Kawasaki), a Japanese corporation, manufactures motorcycles that it distributes in the United States through its subsidiary, Kawasaki Motors Corporation, U.S.A. (Kawasaki USA). Kawasaki USA is a franchisor that grants franchises to dealerships to sell Kawasaki motorcycles. Kawasaki USA granted the Kawasaki Shop of Aurora, Inc. (Dealer), a franchise to sell Kawasaki motorcycles in Aurora, Illinois. The franchise changed locations twice. Both moves were within the 5-mile exclusive territory granted Dealer in the franchise agreement.

Dealer did not obtain Kawasaki USA's written approval for either move, as required by the franchise agreement. Kawasaki USA acquiesced to the first move but not the second. At the second new location, Dealer also operated Honda and Suzuki motorcycle franchises and was negotiating to operate a Yamaha franchise. The Kawasaki franchise agreement expressly permitted multiline dealerships. Kawasaki USA objected to the second move, asserting that Dealer had not received written approval for the move, as required by the franchise agreement. Evidence showed, however, that the real reason Kawasaki objected to the move was because it did not want its motorcycles to be sold at the same location as other manufacturers' motorcycles. Kawasaki terminated Dealer's franchise. Dealer sued Kawasaki USA for wrongful termination. Who wins? *Kawasaki Shop of Aurora, Inc. v. Kawasaki Motors Corp.*, 544 N.E.2d 457 (Ill. App. Ct. 1989).

BUSINESS ETHICS CASES

Case 8.8 ***Business Ethics*** Southland Corporation (Southland) owns the "7-Eleven" trademark and licenses franchisees throughout the country to operate 7-Eleven stores. The franchise agreement provides for fees to be paid to Southland by each franchisee based on a percentage of gross profits. In return, franchisees receive a lease of premises, a license to use the 7-Eleven trademark and trade secrets, advertising merchandise, and bookkeeping assistance. Vallerie Campbell purchased an existing 7-Eleven store in Fontana, California, and became a Southland franchisee. The franchise was designated #13974 by Southland. As part of the purchase, she applied to the state of California for transfer of the beer and wine license from the prior owner. Southland also executed the application. California approved the transfer and issued the license to "Campbell Vallerie Southland #13974."

An employee of Campbell's store sold beer to Jesse Lewis Cope, a minor who was allegedly intoxicated at the time. After drinking the beer, Cope drove his vehicle and struck another vehicle. Two occupants of the other vehicle, Denise Wickham and Tyrone Crosby, were severely injured, and a third occupant, Cedrick Johnson, was killed. Johnson (through his parents), Wickham, and Crosby sued Southland—but not Campbell—to recover damages. Is Southland legally liable for the tortious acts of its franchisee? Is it morally responsible? *Wickham v. Southland Corp.*, 213 Cal. Rptr. 825 (Cal. Ct. App. 1985).

Case 8.9 ***Business Ethics*** The Kentucky Fried Chicken Corporation (KFC), with its principal place of business in Louisville, Kentucky, is the franchisor of KFC restaurants. KFC's registered trademarks and service marks include "Kentucky Fried Chicken," "It's Finger Lickin' Good," and the portrait of Colonel Harlan Sanders. KFC grants licenses to its franchisees to use these marks in connection with the preparation and sale of "Original Recipe Kentucky Fried Chicken." Original Recipe Kentucky Fried Chicken, which is sold only by KFC franchisees, is prepared by a special cooking process featuring the use of a secret recipe seasoning known as "KFC Seasoning." This blend of seasoning was developed by KFC's founder, Colonel Harlan Sanders. As a condition of each franchise agreement, KFC requires that its franchisees use only KFC Seasoning in connection with the preparation and sale of Kentucky Fried Chicken.

KFC Seasoning is a trade secret. To make the seasoning, KFC has entered into contracts with two spice blenders, the John W. Sexton Company, Inc. (Sexton), and Strange Company (Strange). Each of these companies blends approximately one-half the spices of KFC Seasoning; neither has knowledge of the complete formulation of KFC Seasoning, and both entered into secrecy agreements to maintain the confidentiality of their formulations. After the seasoning is blended by Sexton and Strange, it is mixed together and sold directly to all KFC franchisees. KFC does not receive a royalty or other economic benefit from the sale of KFC Seasoning. KFC's relationship with Sexton and Strange has existed for more than twenty-five years; no other companies are licensed to blend KFC Seasoning.

Marion-Kay Company, Inc. (Marion-Kay), was a spice blender engaged in the manufacture of chicken seasoning known as "Marion-Kay Seasoning." Marion-Kay requested permission from KFC to sell its seasoning products to KFC franchisees. KFC refused the request. Four years later, KFC learned that Marion-Kay was supplying some KFC franchisees with Marion-Kay Seasoning and demanded it cease this practice. When Marion-Kay refused, KFC sued it for interference with contractual relations. Marion-Kay filed a counterclaim, alleging violation of antitrust law. Who wins? Was KFC justified in preventing Marion-Kay from blending its seasonings? Did Marion-Kay act ethically in selling seasoning to KFC franchisees? *KFC Corp. v. Marion-Kay Co.*, 620 F. Supp. 1160 (S.D. Ind. 1985).

ENDNOTES

1. 16 CFR Section 436.
2. Southland Corporation v. Keating, 465 U.S. 1, 104 S.Ct. 852, 79 L.Ed.2d 1, Web 1984 U.S. Lexis 2 (Supreme Court of the United States).
3. 15 U.S.C. Section 1114 et seq.

"Corporation: An ingenious device for obtaining individual profit without individual responsibility."

–Ambrose Bierce

The Devil's Dictionary

Corporate Governance and the Sarbanes-Oxley Act

CHAPTER 9

CASE SCENARIO

The law firm at which you work as a paralegal represents John Gibbons, William Smith, and Gerald Zollar, who are all shareholders in GRG Operating, Inc. (GRG). Zollar contributed $1,000 of his own funds so that the corporation could begin to do business. In exchange for this contribution, Gibbons and Smith both granted Zollar the right to vote their shares of GRG stock. They gave Zollar a signed form that stated that "Gibbons and Smith, for a period of 10 years from the date hereof, appoint Zollar as their proxy. This proxy is solely intended to be an irrevocable proxy." A year after the agreement was signed, Gibbons and Smith wanted to revoke their proxies.

CHAPTER OBJECTIVES

After studying this chapter, you should be able to:

1. Describe the functions of shareholders, directors, and officers in managing the affairs of a corporation.
2. Describe a director's and an officer's duty of care and the business judgment rule.
3. Describe a director's and an officer's duty of loyalty and how this duty is breached.
4. Define *piercing the corporate veil*, or *alter ego doctrine*.
5. Describe how the Sarbanes-Oxley Act affects corporate governance.

INTRODUCTION TO CORPORATE GOVERNANCE AND THE SARBANES-OXLEY ACT

Shareholders, directors, and officers have different rights in managing a corporation. The shareholders elect the directors and vote on other important issues affecting the corporation. The directors are responsible for making policy decisions and employing officers. The officers are responsible for the corporation's day-to-day operations.

As a legal entity, a corporation can be held liable for the acts of its directors and officers and for authorized contracts entered into on its behalf. The directors and officers of a corporation have certain rights and owe certain duties to the corporation and its shareholders. A director or an officer who breaches any of these duties can be held personally liable to the corporation, to its shareholders, or to third parties. Except in a few circumstances, shareholders do not owe a fiduciary duty to other shareholders or the corporation.

Following substantial corporate fraud in the 1990s and early 2000s, Congress enacted the *Sarbanes-Oxley Act of 2002*. This federal statute established rules to

PARALEGAL PERSPECTIVE

Karen Ferraro Brumit *is a PACE-registered paralegal with the Dayton office of Porter, Wright, Morris & Arthur, LLP, a large regional law firm. She received her associate in arts/liberal arts and associate in applied science/legal assisting from Sinclair Community College. She has been working as a paralegal for twenty-eight years and specializes in corporate and intellectual property.*

Why should a paralegal understand the area of corporate governance? To successfully assist business clients with their legal needs, corporate/business paralegals should never underestimate the implications associated with the failure to follow necessary and required corporate governance formalities.

What are the most important paralegal skills needed in your job? Knowledge of business organization law and trademark law, as well as familiarity with the various state and federal agencies that govern these areas are required. Having the social skills to work one on one with corporate and business clients is essential.

What is the academic background required for a paralegal entering your area of practice? A college degree in addition to a paralegal degree and experience in the business area are required.

How is technology involved in your job? Being fluent on the computer is essential. In addition to communicating with clients electronically on a daily basis, corporate/business paralegals must know how to electronically access and search public records wherever they are located and electronically investigate companies and individuals. The drafting of corporate documents and agreements is also essential. In addition, intellectual property paralegals must be familiar with the electronic filing of trademark applications and maintenance filings with the U.S. Patent and Trademark Office.

What trends do you see in your area of practice that will likely affect your job in the future? Business and corporate clients are increasingly monitoring the amount of legal fees they spend and are looking for ways to cut costs. Paralegals need to be able to accomplish their assigned tasks in a timely and cost-efficient manner. I see more and more clients requesting the services of a paralegal instead of an attorney whenever possible to keep legal fees under control, which means paralegals need to have advanced skills to assist clients.

What do you feel is the biggest issue currently facing the paralegal profession? The ongoing debate over the certification, licensing, and regulation of paralegals is an issue.

What words of advice do you have for a new paralegal entering your area of practice? Understand the complexities of each type of business organization and your role in creating and maintaining these entities. This means understanding the steps and documentation that go into the creation and maintenance of business entities as well as the people skills to create and maintain an ongoing relationship with the officers, directors, members, partners, and principals of those business entities.

improve corporate governance, prevent fraud, and add transparency to corporate operations. The Sarbanes-Oxley Act has ushered in a new era of corporate governance.

This chapter discusses the rights, duties, and liability of corporate shareholders, directors, and officers. It also discusses the provisions of the Sarbanes-Oxley Act.

SHAREHOLDERS

A corporation's **shareholders** own the corporation (see Exhibit 9.1). Nevertheless, they are not agents of the corporation (i.e., they cannot bind the corporation to contracts), and the only management duty they have is the right to vote on matters such as the election of directors and the approval of fundamental changes in the corporation.

shareholder
A person who owns shares of stock in a corporation or joint-stock company.

Shareholders' Meetings

Annual shareholders' meetings are held to elect directors, choose an independent auditor, and take other actions. These meetings must be held at the times fixed in the bylaws [RMBCA Section 7.01]. If a meeting is not held within either fifteen months of the last annual meeting or six months after the end of the corporation's fiscal year, whichever is earlier, a shareholder may petition the court to order the meeting held [RMBCA Section 7.03].

annual shareholders' meeting
A meeting of the shareholders of a corporation that must be held by the corporation to elect directors and to vote on other matters.

Special shareholders' meetings may be called by the board of directors, the holders of at least 10 percent of the voting shares of the corporation, or any other person authorized to do so by the articles of incorporation or bylaws (e.g., the president) [RMBCA Section 7.02]. Special meetings may be held to consider important or emergency issues, such as a merger or consolidation of the corporation with one or more other corporations, the removal of directors, amendment of the articles of incorporation, or dissolution of the corporation.

special shareholders' meetings
Meetings of shareholders that may be called to consider and vote on important or emergency issues, such as a proposed merger or amending the articles of incorporation.

Any act that can be taken at a **shareholders' meeting** can be taken without a meeting if all the corporate shareholders sign a written consent approving the action [RMBCA Section 7.04].

shareholders' meeting
A meeting held to elect directors, choose an independent auditor, and take other actions. These meetings must be held at the times fixed in the bylaws.

Exhibit 9.1 Shareholders

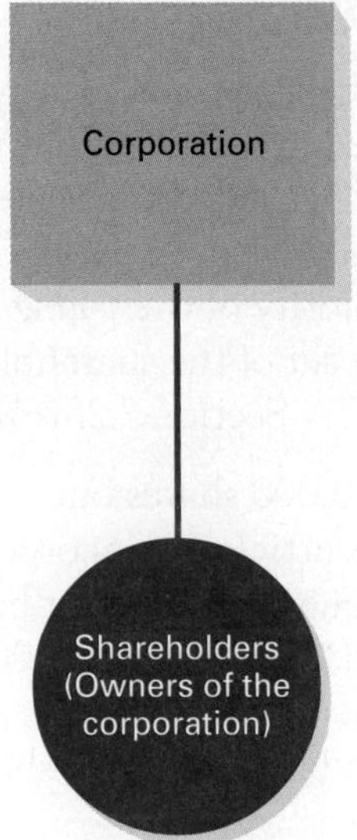

Notice of Shareholders' Meetings

notice of a shareholder's meeting
A corporation is required to give the shareholders written notice of the place, day, and time of annual and special meetings.

A corporation is required to give the shareholders written notice of the place, day, and time of annual and special meetings. For a special meeting, the purpose of the meeting must also be stated. Only matters stated in the **notice of a meeting** can be considered at the meeting. The notice, which must be given not less than ten days or more than fifty days before the date of the meeting, may be given in person or by mail [RMBCA Section 7.05]. If the required notice is not given or is defective, any action taken at the meeting is void.

Proxies

Shareholders do not have to attend a shareholders' meeting to vote. Shareholders may vote by *proxy*; that is, they can appoint another person (the proxy) as their agent to vote at a shareholders' meeting. The proxy may be directed exactly how to vote the shares or may be authorized to vote the shares at his or her discretion. Proxies may be in writing or posted online. The written document itself is called the **proxy** (or **proxy card**). Unless otherwise stated, a proxy is valid for eleven months [RMBCA Section 7.22].

proxy
A written document that a shareholder signs authorizing another person to vote his or her shares at the shareholders' meetings in the event of the shareholder's absence. Also called *proxy card*.

Voting Requirements

At least one class of shares of stock of a corporation must have voting rights. The Revised Model Business Corporation Act (RMBCA) permits corporations to grant more than one vote per share to some classes of stock and less than one vote per share to others [RMBCA Section 6.01].

Only shareholders who own stock as of a set date may vote at a shareholders' meeting. This date, which is called the **record date**, is set forth in the corporate bylaws. The record date may not be more than seventy days before the shareholders' meeting [RMBCA Section 7.07]. The corporation must prepare a shareholders' list that contains the names and addresses of the shareholders as of the record date and the class and number of shares owned by each shareholder. This list must be available for inspection at the corporation's main office [RMBCA Section 7.20].

record date
A date specified in corporate bylaws that determines whether a shareholder may vote at a shareholders' meeting.

Quorum and Vote Required

Unless otherwise provided in the articles of incorporation, if a majority of shares entitled to vote are represented at a meeting in person or by proxy, there is a **quorum** to hold the meeting. Once a quorum is present, the withdrawal of shares does not affect the quorum of the meeting [RMBCA Sections 7.25(a), 7.25(b)]. The affirmative *vote* of the majority of the *voting* shares represented at a shareholders' meeting constitutes an act of the shareholders for actions other than for the election of directors [RMBCA Section 7.25(c)].

quorum
The required number of shares that must be represented in person or by proxy to hold a shareholders' meeting. The RMBCA establishes a majority of outstanding shares as a quorum.

Example: A corporation has 20,000 shares outstanding. A shareholders' meeting is duly called to amend the articles of incorporation, and 10,001 shares are represented at the meeting. A quorum is present because a majority of the shares entitled to vote are represented. Suppose that 5,001 shares are voted in favor of the amendment. The amendment passes. In this example, just over 25 percent of the shares of the corporation bind the other shareholders to the action taken at the shareholders' meeting.

ETHICS SPOTLIGHT

CONTROLLING SHAREHOLDER'S BREACH OF FIDUCIARY DUTY

Shareholders usually do not owe a fiduciary duty to their fellow shareholders. However, many courts have held that a controlling shareholder does owe a fiduciary duty to monitor shareholders. A controlling shareholder is one who owns a sufficient number of shares to control the corporation effectively. This may or may not be majority ownership.

The courts have held that controlling shareholders breach their fiduciary duty to minority shareholders if they:

- Sell assets of the corporation and thereby cause an unusual loss to the minority shareholders.
- Sell corporate assets to themselves at less than fair market value.
- Sell controlling interest in the corporation to someone they know intends to loot the corporation and does.
- Take other action that oppresses the minority shareholders.

Law and Ethics Questions

1. **Ethics** Should controlling shareholders be held to a fiduciary duty to other shareholders? Why or why not?
2. Should all shareholders owe a fiduciary duty to each other? Discuss.

Straight (Noncumulative) Voting

Unless otherwise stated in a corporation's articles of incorporation, voting for the election of directors is by the **straight voting**, or **noncumulative voting**, method. This voting method is quite simple: Each shareholder votes the number of shares he or she owns on candidates for each of the positions open for election. Thus, a majority shareholder can elect the entire board of directors.

straight voting
A system in which each shareholder votes the number of shares he or she owns on candidates for each of the positions open. Also called *noncumulative voting*.

Example: A corporation has 10,000 outstanding shares. Erin owns 5,100 shares (51 percent), and Michael owns 4,900 shares (49 percent). Suppose that three directors of the corporation are to be elected from a potential pool of ten candidates. Erin casts 5,100 votes each for her three chosen candidates. Michael votes 4,900 shares for each of his three chosen candidates, who are different from those favored by Erin. Each of the three candidates whom Erin voted for wins, with 5,100 votes.

Supramajority Voting Requirement

The articles of incorporation or the bylaws of a corporation can require a greater than majority of the shares to constitute a quorum of the vote of the shareholders [RMBCA Section 7.27]. This is called a **supramajority voting requirement** (or **supramajority**). Such votes are often required to approve mergers, consolidation, the sale of substantially all the assets of a corporation, and such. To add a supramajority voting requirement, the amendment must be adopted by the number of shares of the proposed increase. For example, increasing a majority voting requirement to an 80 percent supramajority voting requirement would require an 80 percent affirmative vote.

supramajority voting requirement
A requirement that a greater than majority of shares constitutes a quorum of the vote of the shareholders. Also called *supermajority voting requirement*.

supramajority
Greater than the majority.

Voting Trusts

Sometimes shareholders agree in advance as to how their shares will be voted. A **voting trust** is an arrangement whereby shareholders transfer their stock

voting trust
An arrangement in which the shareholders transfer their stock certificates to a trustee who is empowered to vote the shares.

cumulative voting
A system in which a shareholder can accumulate all of his or her votes and vote them all for one candidate or split them among several candidates.

CONTEMPORARY Environment

CUMULATIVE VOTING

A corporation's articles of incorporation may provide for **cumulative voting** for the election of directors. Under this method, a shareholder can accumulate all of his or her votes and vote them all for one candidate or split them among several candidates. This means that each shareholder is entitled to multiply the number of shares he or she owns by the number of directors to be elected and cast the product for a single candidate or distribute the product among two or more candidates [RMBCA Section 7.28]. Cumulative voting gives a minority shareholder a better opportunity to elect someone to the board of directors.

Example: Suppose Emma owns 1,000 shares of a corporation. Assume that four directors are to be elected to the board. With cumulative voting, Emma can multiply the number of shares she owns (1,000) by the number of directors to be elected (four). She can cast all the resulting votes (4,000) for one candidate or split them among candidates as she determines.

Examples of cumulative voting are set forth in Exhibit 9.2.

Exhibit 9.2 Cumulative Voting

Formula for Cumulative Voting. A shareholder can use the following formula to determine whether or not he or she owns a sufficient number of shares to elect a director to the board of directors using cumulative voting:

$$\frac{S \times T}{D+1} + 1 = X$$

where X is the number of shares needed by a shareholder to elect a director to the board, S is the number of shares that actually vote at the shareholders' meeting, T is the number of directors the shareholder wants to elect, and D is the number of directors to be elected at the shareholders' meeting.

Example 1 Suppose there are 9,000 outstanding shares of a corporation. Shareholder 1 owns 1,000 shares, shareholder 2 owns 4,000 shares, and shareholder 3 owns 4,000 shares. Assume nine directors are to be elected to the board of directors. All the shares are voted. Under cumulative voting, does shareholder 1 have enough votes to elect a director to the board? The answer is yes:

$$\frac{9{,}000 \times 1}{9+1} + 1 = 901$$

Example 2 If a board of directors is divided into classes and elected by staggered elections, the ability of a minority shareholder to elect a director to the board is diminished. Suppose in Example 1 that the corporation staggered the election of the board of directors so that three directors are elected each year to serve three-year terms. How many shares would a shareholder have to own to elect a director to the board?

$$\frac{9{,}000 \times 1}{3+1} + 1 = 2{,}251$$

Because of the staggered election of the board of directors, shareholder 1 (who owns 1,000 shares) would not be able to elect a director to the board without the assistance of another shareholder.

certificates to a trustee. Legal title to these shares is held in the name of the trustee. In exchange, **voting trust certificates** are issued to the shareholders. The trustee of the voting trust is empowered to vote the shares held by the trust. The trust may either specify how the trustee is to vote the shares or authorize the trustee to vote the shares at his or her discretion. The members of the trust retain all other incidents of ownership of the stock. A voting trust agreement must be in writing and cannot exceed ten years. It must be filed with the corporation and is open to inspection by shareholders of the corporation [RMBCA Section 7.30].

voting trust certificate
A certificate issued by a voting trustee to the beneficial holders of shares held by the voting trust.

Shareholder Voting Agreements

Two or more shareholders may enter into an agreement that stipulates how they will vote their shares for the election of directors or other matters that require a shareholder vote. **Shareholder voting agreements** are not limited in duration and do not have to be filed with the corporation. They are specifically enforceable [RMBCA Section 7.31]. Shareholder voting agreements can be either revocable or irrevocable [RMBCA Section 7.22(d)].

shareholder voting agreement
An agreement between two or more shareholders that stipulates how they will vote their shares.

Right of First Refusal

Generally, shareholders have the right to transfer their shares. Shareholders may enter into agreements with one another to prevent unwanted persons from becoming owners of the corporation [RMBCA Section 6.27]. A **right of first refusal** is an agreement that shareholders enter into whereby they grant each other the right of first refusal to purchase shares they are going to sell. A selling shareholder must offer his or her shares for sale to the other parties to the agreement before selling them to anyone else. If the shareholders do not exercise their right of first refusal, the selling shareholder is free to sell his or her shares to another party. A right of first refusal may be granted to the corporation as well.

right of first refusal
An agreement that requires a selling shareholder to offer his or her shares for sale to the other parties to the agreement before selling them to anyone else.

Buy-and-Sell Agreement

Shareholders sometimes enter into a **buy-and-sell agreement** that requires selling shareholders to sell their shares to the other shareholders or to the corporation at the price specified in the agreement. The price of the shares is normally determined by a formula that considers, among other factors, the profitability of the corporation. The purchase of shares of a deceased shareholder pursuant to a buy-and-sell agreement is often funded by proceeds from life insurance.

buy-and-sell agreement
An agreement that requires selling shareholders to sell their shares to the other shareholders or to the corporation at the price specified in the agreement.

Preemptive Rights

The articles of incorporation can grant shareholders preemptive rights. **Preemptive rights** give existing shareholders the option of subscribing to new shares being issued by the corporation in proportion to their current ownership interests [RMBCA Section 6.30]. Such a purchase can prevent a shareholder's interest in the corporation from being *diluted.* Shareholders are given a reasonable period of time (e.g., thirty days) to exercise their preemptive rights. If a shareholder does not exercise his or her preemptive rights during this time, shares can then be sold to anyone.

preemptive rights
Rights that give existing shareholders the option of subscribing to new shares being issued in proportion to their current ownership interests.

Example: The ABC Corporation has 10,000 outstanding shares, and Grace owns 1,000 shares (10 percent). Assume that the corporation plans to raise more capital by issuing another 10,000 shares of stock. With preemptive rights, Grace must be offered the option to purchase 1,000 of the 10,000 new shares before they are offered to the public. If she does not purchase them, her ownership in the corporation will be diluted from 10 percent to 5 percent.

Right to Receive Information and Inspect Books and Records

annual report
A report provided to shareholders that contains a balance sheet, an income statement, and a statement of changes in shareholder equity.

Shareholders have the right to be informed about the affairs of the corporation. A corporation must furnish its shareholders with an **annual report** that contains a balance sheet, an income statement, and a statement of changes in shareholder equity [RMBCA Section 16.20].

Shareholders have an absolute *right to inspect* the shareholders' list, the articles of incorporation, the bylaws, and the minutes of shareholders' meetings held within the past three years. To inspect accounting and tax records, minutes of board and committee meetings, and minutes of shareholders' meetings held more than three years in the past, a shareholder must demonstrate a "proper purpose," such as deciding how to vote in a shareholder election, identifying fellow shareholders to communicate with them regarding corporate matters, investigating the existence of corporate mismanagement or improper action, and the like [RMBCA Section 16.02].

Dividends

dividend
A distribution of profits of the corporation to shareholders.

Profit corporations operate to make a profit. The objective of the shareholders is to share in those profits, either through capital appreciation, the receipt of dividends, or both. **Dividends** are paid at the discretion of the board of directors [RMBCA Section 6.40]. The directors are responsible for determining when, where, how, and how much will be paid in dividends. They may opt to retain the profits in the corporation to be used for corporate purposes instead of as dividends. This authority cannot be delegated to a committee of the board of directors or to officers of the corporation.

When a corporation declares a dividend, it sets a date, usually a few weeks prior to the actual payment, that is called the *record date*. Persons who are shareholders on that date are entitled to receive the dividend, even if they sell their shares before the payment date. Once declared, a cash or property dividend cannot be revoked. Shareholders can sue to recover declared but unpaid dividends.

Stock Dividends

stock dividend
Additional shares of stock distributed as a dividend.

Corporations may use additional shares of stock as a dividend. **Stock dividends** are not a distribution of corporate assets. They are distributed in proportion to the existing ownership interests of shareholders, so they do not increase a shareholder's proportionate ownership interest.

Example: Jack owns 1,000 shares (10 percent) of the 10,000 outstanding shares of ABC Corporation. If ABC Corporation declares a stock dividend of 20 percent, Jack will receive a stock dividend of 200 shares. He now owns 1,200 shares—or 10 percent—of a total of 12,000 outstanding shares.

Derivative Lawsuits

If a corporation is harmed by someone, the directors of the corporation have the authority to bring an action on behalf of the corporation against the offending party to recover damages or other relief. If the corporation fails to bring the lawsuit, shareholders have the right to bring the lawsuit on behalf of the corporation. This is called a **derivative action**, or **derivative lawsuit** [RMBCA Section 7.40].

derivative action (derivative lawsuit)
A suit by a beneficiary of a fiduciary to enforce a right belonging to the fiduciary; especially a suit asserted by a shareholder on the corporation's behalf against a third party (usually a corporate officer) because of the corporation's failure to take some action against the third party.

A shareholder can bring a derivative action if he or she (1) was a shareholder of the corporation at the time of the act complained of; (2) fairly and adequately represents the interests of the corporation; and (3) made a written demand upon the corporation to take suitable actions and either the corporation rejected the demand or ninety days have expired since the date of the demand.

To bring a derivative lawsuit, a shareholder usually must make a written demand upon the corporate directors to bring the lawsuit, and if the directors fail to bring the suit, then the shareholder may pursue the lawsuit on behalf of the corporation. Often, the third party who has damaged the corporation is one or more of the corporation's own directors or officers. For example, board members or officers, or both, may have committed fraud or otherwise stolen property from or misused property of the corporation. In this case, the written demand will be excused.

A derivative lawsuit will be dismissed by the court if either a majority of independent directors or a panel of independent persons appointed by the court determines that the lawsuit is not in the best interests of the corporation. This decision must be reached in good faith and only after conducting a reasonable inquiry.

If a shareholder's derivative action is successful, any award goes into the corporate treasury. The plaintiff-shareholder is entitled to recover payment for reasonable expenses, including attorneys' fees, incurred in bringing and maintaining the derivative action. Any settlement of a derivative action requires court approval.

CASE 9.1 DERIVATIVE LAWSUIT KAMEN V. KEMPER FINANCIAL SERVICES, INC.,

500 U.S. 90, (1991).

"Demand typically is deemed to be futile when a majority of the directors have participated in or approved the alleged wrongdoing."

—Justice Marshall

Facts

Jill S. Kamen was a shareholder of Cash Equivalent Fund, Inc. (Fund), a mutual fund that employed Kemper Financial Services, Inc. (Kemper), as its investment advisor. Kamen brought a derivative lawsuit on behalf of Fund against Kemper, alleging that Kemper violated fiduciary duties owed to Fund as imposed by the Investment Company Act of 1940 (Act), a federal statute. Kamen did not make a demand on Fund's board of directors to sue Kemper any earlier. She alleged that it would have been futile to do so because the directors were acting in a conspiracy with Kemper. The Act was silent as to the rule concerning derivative actions under the Act. The trial court granted Kemper's motion to dismiss the lawsuit. The court of appeals adopted a "universal demand rule" as part of the federal common law and affirmed. This rule requires that a shareholder always make a demand on the directors of a corporation before bringing a derivative lawsuit. Kamen appealed to the U.S. Supreme Court.

The law does not permit the stockholders to create a sterilized board of directors.
Justice Collins
Manson v. Curtis, 119 N.E. 559 (N.Y. 1918).

Issue

Should federal law adopt the universal demand rule for bringing derivative actions?

Language of the U.S. Supreme Court

The presumption that state law should be incorporated into federal common law is particularly strong in areas in which private parties have entered legal relationship with the expectation that their rights and obligations would be governed by state law standards. Corporation law is one such area. Corporations are creatures of state law, state law which is the font of corporate directors' powers. Consequently, we conclude that gaps in federal statutes bearing on the allocation of governing power within the corporation should be filled with state law.

The purpose of requiring a pre-complaint demand is to protect the directors' prerogative to take over the litigation or to oppose it. Thus, the demand requirement implements the basic principle of corporate governance that the decisions of a corporation—including the decision to initiate litigation—should be made by the board of directors or the majority of shareholders. To the extent that a jurisdiction recognizes the futility exception to demand, the jurisdiction places a limit upon the directors' usual power to control the initiation of corporate litigation. Demand typically is deemed to be futile when a majority of the directors have participated in or approved the alleged wrongdoing. Superimposing a rule of universal demand over the corporate doctrine of these States would clearly upset the balance that they have struck between the power of the individual shareholder and the power of the directors to control corporate litigation.

Decision

The U.S. Supreme Court refused to adopt the universal demand rule as federal common law but instead held that federal law should follow the appropriate state law concerning demands in derivative lawsuits if a federal statute is silent as to this issue. The U.S. Supreme Court reversed the decision of the U.S. Court of Appeals that had dismissed Kamen's lawsuit against Kemper.

Law and Ethics Questions

1. Which do you think is the better rule: the universal demand rule or the futility exception rule? Why?
2. **Ethics** Should Kamen have given the directors of Fund the opportunity to have sued Kemper before she did?
3. **Ethics** Do you think directors often engage in fraudulent conduct that harms the rights of shareholders?
4. **Ethics** Do you think that the possibility of derivative lawsuits makes directors and officers act more ethically?

Web Exercises

1. **Web** Web Search the web to find the complete opinion of this case.

2. **Web** Visit the website of the U.S. Supreme Court, at www.supremecourtus.gov and try to find documents that relate to this case.

3. **Web** Use www.google.com to find an article that discusses a recent derivative lawsuit. Read it.

Piercing the Corporate Veil

Shareholders of a corporation generally have **limited liability** (i.e., they are liable for the debts and obligations of the corporation only to the extent of their capital contribution), and they are not personally liable for the debts and obligations of the corporation. However, if a shareholder or shareholders dominate a corporation and use it for improper purposes, a court of equity can *disregard the corporate entity* and hold the shareholders of the corporation personally liable for the corporation's debts and obligations. This doctrine is commonly referred to as **piercing the corporate veil**. It is often resorted to by unpaid creditors who are trying to collect from shareholders a debt owed by the corporation. The piercing the corporate veil doctrine is also called the alter ego doctrine because the corporation becomes the *alter ego* of the shareholder.

limited liability
Liability that shareholders have only to the extent of their capital contribution. Shareholders are generally not personally liable for debts and obligations of the corporation.

piercing the corporate veil
A doctrine that says if a shareholder dominates a corporation and uses it for improper purposes, a court of equity can disregard the corporate entity and hold the shareholder personally liable for the corporation's debts and obligations. Also called the *alter ego doctrine*.

Courts will pierce the corporate veil if (1) the corporation has been formed without sufficient capital (i.e., *thin capitalization*) or (2) separateness has not been maintained between the corporation and its shareholders (e.g., commingling of personal and corporate assets, failure to hold required shareholders' meetings, failure to maintain corporate records and books). The courts examine this doctrine on a case-by-case basis.

The piercing the corporate veil doctrine was raised in the following case.

CASE 9.2 PIERCING THE CORPORATE VEIL

***Northeast Iowa Ethanol, LLC v. Drizin*, No. C03-2021, 2006 U.S. Dist. LEXIS 4828, at *1 (N.D. Iowa Feb. 7, 2006).**

"If capital is illusory or trifling compared with the business to be done and the risk of loss, this is a ground for denying the separate entity privilege."

—Judge Jarvey

Facts

Local farmers in Manchester, Iowa, decided to build an ethanol plant in the Manchester area. An ethanol plant produces ethanol and feed grain, which can be sold at a profit exceeding that of the sale of grain. After many meetings, the local farmers invested $2,365,000 for the project. The farmers formed Northeast Iowa Ethanol, LLC (Northeast Iowa), to hold the money and develop the project. William Ethanol Service agreed to invest $1 million, and North Central Construction agreed to invest $500,000. In all, $3,865,000 was raised for the construction of the ethanol plant. The funds were placed in an escrow account. The project needed another $20 million, for which financing needed to be secured.

Jerry Drizin formed Global Syndicate International, Inc. (GSI), a Nevada corporation, with $250 capital. GSI was formed for the purpose of assisting Northeast Iowa raise the additional financing for the project. Traditional financing from banks was not available for such a project, so Drizin looked for other sources of money. Drizin talked Northeast Iowa into transferring money to a bank in south Florida to serve as security for a possible loan. Drizin mixed those funds with his own personal funds. Through an array of complex transfers orchestrated by Drizin, all of the funds of Northeast Iowa were stolen. Drizin invested some funds in a worthless gold mine and lost the rest of the money in other worthless investments.

Plaintiff Northeast Iowa sued Drizin for civil fraud to recover its funds. Drizin defended, arguing that GSI was liable but that he was not liable because he was but a shareholder of GSI. The plaintiffs alleged that the doctrine of piercing the corporate veil applied and that Drizin was therefore personally liable for the funds.

Issue

Does the doctrine of piercing the corporate veil apply in this case, thus allowing the plaintiffs to pierce the corporate veil of GSI and reach shareholder Drizin for liability for civil fraud?

Language of the Court

In every financial scam like that perpetrated on the plaintiff here, there comes a point at which the victim must make an exceedingly quick decision and seemingly, the entire fate of the project depends on taking that leap of faith. From that point on, very bad things follow and only time will tell what they are.

Generally a corporation is a distinct entity from its shareholders. This distinction usually insulates shareholders from personal liability for corporate debts. However, this protection is not absolute. Personal liability may be imposed upon shareholders in "exceptional circumstances." The corporate veil may be pierced, for example, where the corporation is a mere shell, serving no legitimate business purpose, and used primarily as an intermediary to perpetuate fraud or promote injustice.

If a corporation lacks substantial capital such that it would not be able to meet its debts, this is a ground for denying the privilege of separate entity. If capital is illusory or trifling compared with the business to be done and the risk of loss, this is a ground for denying the separate entity privilege. Secondly, if corporate funds are not segregated, there is a strong inference that they are being used by the shareholders for their individual purposes. A major corporate officer cannot avoid liability by emulating the three fabled monkeys, "hearing, seeing and speaking no evil."

Without question, this case presents the "exceptional circumstance" warranting the piercing of GSI's corporate veil and finding Mr. Drizin personally liable for GSI's misdeeds, as the sole purpose of establishing GSI was to perpetuate fraud. GSI engaged in no legitimate business transactions whatsoever. The $250.00 initial capitalization of GSI is, in fact, "trifling compared with the business to be done and the risk of loss." GSI had no errors and omissions insurance. Mr. Drizin used GSI's accounts as his own, constantly transferring money from the GSI escrow account to his personal accounts for "reimbursement" and to other accounts for "safekeeping" and "diversification." And now, GSI is a defunct corporation. Justice and equity call for piercing the corporate veil.

Drizin's actions with respect to plaintiff's money were both outrageous and malicious. As a result of Drizin's tortious conduct, good people were hurt.

The evidence is clear, convincing, and satisfactory that punitive damages are appropriate in this case to punish Drizin and to deter others from engaging in similar conduct.

Decision

The U.S. District Court held that the corporate veil of GSI could be pierced to reach its shareholder Drizin. The court awarded the plaintiff compensatory damages of $3.8 million and punitive damages of $7.6 million against Drizin.

Case Questions

1. **Critical Legal Thinking** What is civil fraud? Explain. What does the doctrine of piercing the corporate veil provide? Explain.
2. **Business Ethics** Did Drizin act ethically in this case? Did the owners of Northeast Iowa have any responsibility for the losses they suffered in this case? Explain.
3. **Contemporary Business** Do you think that the plaintiff Northeast Iowa will recover on its $11.4 million judgment in this case?

INTERNET LAW AND ONLINE COMMERCE

Corporations Codes Recognize Electronic Communications

Most state corporations codes have been amended to permit the use of electronic communications to shareholders and among directors. For example, the Delaware General Corporation Law recognizes the following uses of electronic technology:

- Delivery of notices to shareholders may be made electronically if the shareholder consents to the delivery of notices in this form.
- Proxy solicitation for shareholder votes may be made by electronic transmission.
- The shareholders list of a corporation that must be made available during the ten days prior to a shareholders' meeting may be made available either at the principal place of business of the corporation or by posting the list on an electronic network.
- Shareholders who are not physically present at a meeting may be deemed present, participate in, and vote at the meeting by electronic communication; a meeting may be held solely by electronic communication, without a physical location.
- The election of directors of the corporation may be held by electronic transmission.
- Directors' actions by unanimous consent may be taken by electronic transmission.

The use of electronic transmissions, electronic networks, and communications by e-mail will make the operation and administration of corporate affairs more efficient.

PARALEGAL PERSPECTIVE

Lynn M. Floeter is a senior paralegal with Associated Banc-Corp, a national banking corporation, in Milwaukee, Wisconsin. She received her associate of applied science in paralegal studies from Finger Lakes Community College. She has been a paralegal for nine years and specializes in corporate law.

Why do you think it is important for a paralegal to be aware of the rules regarding corporate governance? The Sarbanes-Oxley Act of 2002 outlines the duties that must be adhered to by companies so that they are in compliance with the laws and regulations affecting the reliability of financial information that the company and its subsidiaries report to the public. There are major penalties for failure to comply. It is important for paralegals working in the area of corporate governance to be up to date on the latest regulations, so that they can be a knowledgeable resource [and so] that others working on a company's business can come to the paralegal for their assistance in reporting.

What are the most important paralegal skills needed in your job? The most important skills of this job (and of any job) are to know what is expected of you, be organized, be prepared for changes in the request, be familiar with the subject matter you are working on, and if not sure of something, ask questions—do not assume anything. In this job in particular, I have to be familiar with the phrases and terminology used in commercial mortgage loan documents. Additionally, it is necessary to have skills to perform unlimited amounts of research, usually online, in the areas of human resources and employment law.

What is the academic background required for a paralegal entering your area of practice? While practical experience is always best, this job requires a paralegal degree or certification.

How is technology involved in your job? We use technology in all aspects of this position. Our calendaring and e-mail is all in electronic format. All research is performed in the Internet, and one must be familiar with the different legal research resources.

What trends do you see in your area of practice that will likely affect your job in the future? In any position in the law department of a large corporation, there will always be work. The present economic situation is a big factor in the commercial loan sector, and there are going to be customers finding themselves in difficult financial situations that will require some sort of negation when it comes to their loans. Likewise, there will always be employees that feel discriminated against or unjustly treated in one way or another, either in the present job or after they have been terminated. Customers will find something to complain about when they feel they have been treated unfairly, and when money is tight, people usually try to find a way to get it somewhere—either by threat or suit. Unfortunately, the law department usually sees the down side to the situation rather than the upside.

What do you feel is the biggest issue currently facing the paralegal profession? I do not think there are enough competent, qualified paralegals working or recognized in their field. Many are not familiar with all the opportunities there are for work in areas unrelated to small practice law firms.

What words of advice do you have for a new paralegal entering your area of practice? Be good at what do you, be informed, be organized, and be respectful of the attorney you work for. He or she is the one with the law degree and spent all those years in law school and in practice. Be considerate of your colleagues. You never know when you will need their help on a project, and it is easier to ask someone you get along with than someone you can barely speak to. Most important, be willing to learn something new every day.

BOARD OF DIRECTORS

board of directors
A panel of decision makers who are elected by the shareholders.

The **board of directors** of a corporation is elected by the shareholders of the corporation. The board of directors is responsible for formulating *policy decisions* that affect the management, supervision, control, and operation of the corporation (see Exhibit 9.3) [RMBCA Section 8.01]. Such policy decisions include deciding the business or businesses in which the corporation should be engaged, selecting and removing the top officers of the corporation, determining the capital structure of the corporation, declaring dividends, and the like.

The board may initiate certain actions that require shareholders' approval. These actions are initiated when the board of directors adopts a *resolution* that

Exhibit 9.3 Board of Directors

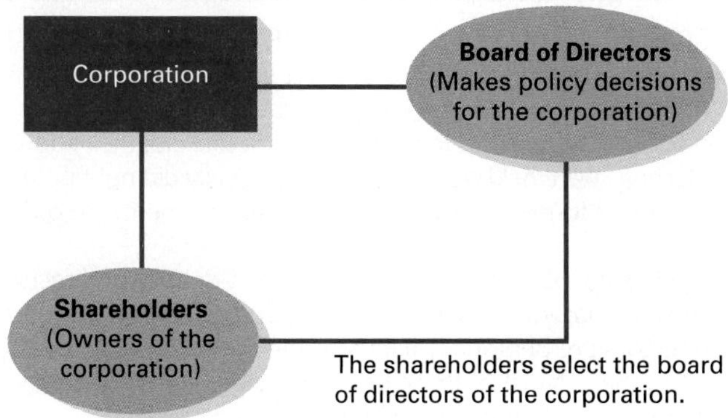

approves a transaction and recommends that it be submitted to the shareholders for a vote. Examples of such transactions include mergers, sale of substantially all of the corporation's assets outside the course of ordinary business operations, amendment of the articles of incorporation, and voluntary dissolution of the corporation.

Corporate directors are required to have access to the corporation's books and records, facilities, and premises, as well as any other information that affects the operation of the corporation. This right of inspection is absolute. It cannot be limited by the articles of incorporation, the bylaws, or board resolution.

Compensating Directors

Originally, it was considered an honor to serve as a director. No payment was involved. Today, directors are often paid an annual retainer and an attendance fee for each meeting attended. Unless otherwise provided in the articles of incorporation, the directors are permitted to fix their own compensation [RMBCA Section 8.11].

Selecting Directors

Boards of directors are typically composed of inside and outside directors. An **inside director** is a person who is also an officer of the corporation. For example, the president of the corporation often sits as a director of the corporation.

inside director
A member of the board of directors who is also an officer of the corporation.

An **outside director** is a person who sits on the board of directors of a corporation but is not an officer of that corporation. Outside directors are often officers and directors of other corporations, bankers, lawyers, professors, and others. Outside directors are often selected for their business knowledge and expertise.

outside director
A member of a board of directors who is not an officer of the corporation.

There are no special qualifications that a person must meet to be elected a director of a corporation. A director need not be a resident of the state of incorporation of the corporation or a shareholder of the corporation. The articles of incorporation or bylaws may prescribe qualifications for directors, however [RMBCA Section 8.02].

A board of directors can consist of one or more individuals. The number of initial directors is fixed by the articles of incorporation. This number can be amended in the articles of incorporation or the bylaws. The articles of incorporation or bylaws can establish a variable range for the size of the board of directors. The exact number of directors within the range may be changed from time to time by the board of directors or the shareholders [RMBCA Section 8.03].

ETHICS SPOTLIGHT

OUTSIDE DIRECTORS RELIEVED OF LIABILITY FOR ORDINARY NEGLIGENCE

In the past, being made a member of a board of directors of a corporation was considered to be an honor. Many persons outside the company, such as lawyers, doctors, businesspeople, professors, and others, were asked to sit on boards because of their knowledge, expertise, or contacts. Meetings were held once a month and usually did not take a lot of time, and votes were often just a formality to "rubber stamp" management's preordained decisions.

Things changed as an explosion of lawsuits against boards of directors occurred, brought by disgruntled shareholders, bondholders, and others. Under normal corporate laws, directors are personally liable for their intentional or negligent conduct that causes harm to others. Most of these lawsuits alleged that directors were negligent in one regard or another, and juries often agreed.

Inside directors—directors who are also executives of the corporation—remained on boards because of their vested interests, and their liability as officers would remain anyway. But "outside directors"—the directors from outside the company—began fleeing from corporations and refusing to accept nominations to boards of directors. The honor of sitting on a board of directors became a liability, and all of a board member's personal assets—house, investments, and bank accounts—were at risk.

In response to this situation, the Delaware legislature enacted a statute that provided that an outside director of a Delaware corporation cannot be held liable for ordinary negligence. Thus, this statute overrode the common law of negligence as it applied to outside directors. The law was hailed as a landmark, and many major corporations that were not already incorporated in Delaware abandoned their current states of incorporation and reincorporated there.

Many other states have enacted similar statutes. The RMBCA contains a similar provision [RMBCA Section 2.02(b)(4)]. The main features of these statutes are that they:

- Apply to outside directors but not to inside directors.
- Relieve liability for ordinary negligence but not for intentional conduct, recklessness, or gross negligence.
- Do not apply to violations of federal and state securities law.

Law and Ethics Questions

1. Should outside directors be relieved of ordinary negligence liability? Why or why not?
2. **Ethics** Do you think outside directors will act more or less carefully if they are relieved of liability for ordinary negligence?
3. Will more persons be willing to serve as outside directors of corporations under the new law?

Concept Summary

Classification of Directors

Classification	Description
Inside director	A person who is also an officer of the corporation
Outside director	A person who is not an officer of the corporation

Term of Office

The term of a director's office expires at the next annual shareholders' meeting following their election, unless terms are staggered [RMBCA Section 8.05]. The RMBCA allows boards of directors that consist of nine or more members to be divided into two or three classes (each class to be as nearly equal in number as possible) that are elected to serve *staggered terms* of two or three years [RMBCA Section 8.06]. The specifics of such an arrangement must be outlined in the articles of incorporation.

Example: Suppose a board of directors consists of nine directors. The board can be divided into three classes of three directors each, each class to be elected to serve a three-year term. Only three directors of the nine-member board would come up for election each year. This nine-member board could also be divided into two classes of five and four directors, each class to be elected to a two-year term.

Vacancies on a board of directors can occur because of death, illness, the resignation of a director before the expiration of his or her term, or an increase in the number of positions on the board. Such vacancies can be filled by the shareholders or the remaining directors [RMBCA Section 8.10].

Meetings of the Board of Directors

The directors of a corporation can act only as a board. They cannot act individually on the corporation's behalf. Every director has the right to participate in any meeting of the board of directors. Each director has one vote. Directors cannot vote by proxy.

Regular meetings of a board of directors are held at the times and places established in the bylaws. Such meetings can be held without notice. The board can call **special meetings** as provided in the bylaws [RMBCA Section 8.20(a)]. Special meetings are usually convened for such reasons as issuing new shares, considering proposals to merge with other corporations, adopting maneuvers to defend against hostile takeover attempts, and the like. The board of directors may act without a meeting if all the directors sign written consents that set forth the actions taken. The RMBCA permits meetings of the board to be held via conference calls [RMBCA Section 8.20(b)].

regular meeting of a board of directors
A meeting held by the board of directors at the time and place established in the bylaws.

special meeting of a board of directors
A meeting of the board of directors that may be called for such reasons as issuing new shares, considering proposals to merge with other corporations, adopting maneuvers to defend against hostile takeover attempts, and the like.

Quorum and Voting Requirement

A simple majority of the number of directors established in the articles of incorporation or bylaws usually constitutes a **quorum** for transacting business. However, the articles of incorporation and the bylaws may increase this number. If a quorum is present, the approval or disapproval of a majority of the quorum binds the entire board. The articles of incorporation or the bylaws can require a greater than majority of directors to constitute a quorum of the vote of the board [RMBCA Section 8.24].

quorum
The number of directors necessary to hold a board meeting or transact business of the board.

■ CORPORATE OFFICERS

A corporation's board of directors has the authority to appoint the officers of the corporation. The **corporate officers** are elected by the board of directors at such time and by such manner as prescribed in the corporation's bylaws. The directors

corporate officers
Employees of a corporation who are appointed by the board of directors to manage the day-to-day operations of the corporation.

ETHICS SPOTLIGHT

SARBANES-OXLEY ACT IMPOSES DUTIES ON AUDIT COMMITTEE

During the late 1990s and early 2000s, many corporations engaged in accounting fraud to report inflated earnings or to conceal losses. It was often management who perpetrated this accounting fraud, which was not detected by the board of directors. Sometimes members of the board of directors conspired or participated in the accounting fraud. In response, Congress enacted the federal *Sarbanes-Oxley Act of 2002*, which placed certain responsibilities on a corporation's **audit committee**.

audit committee
A committee appointed by the board of an organization, especially a corporation, to oversee the financial reporting process, select an independent auditor, and receive the audit.

A public company must have an audit committee. Members of the audit committee must be members of the board of directors and must be independent—that is, not employed by or receive compensation from the company or any of its subsidiaries for services other than as a board member and member of the audit committee. These board members are called *outside* board members because they are not employees (e.g., president, chief executive officer) of the corporation. At least one member of the audit committee must be a financial expert, based on either education or prior experience, who is able to understand generally accepted accounting principles, preparation of financial statements, and audit committee functions.

The audit committee is responsible for the appointment of, payment of compensation for, and oversight of public accounting firms employed to audit the company. The audit committee must preapprove all audit and permissible nonaudit services to be performed by a public accounting firm. The audit committee has authority to employ independent legal counsel and other advisors.

The Sarbanes-Oxley Act requires public companies to establish and maintain adequate internal controls and procedures for financial reporting. The act requires a public company to prepare an assessment of the effectiveness of its internal controls at the end of each fiscal year. These internal audits are supervised by the audit committee.

Business Ethics

1. Do you think there is very much fraud by boards of directors in managing corporations? Will the requirement of having only independent outside directors on the audit committee help prevent accounting fraud? Explain.

can delegate certain management authority to the officers of the corporation (see Exhibit 9.4).

At a minimum, most corporations have the following officers: a president, one or more vice presidents, a secretary, and a treasurer. The bylaws or the board of directors can authorize duly appointed officers the power to appoint assistant officers. The same individual may simultaneously hold more than one office in

Exhibit 9.4 Corporate Officers

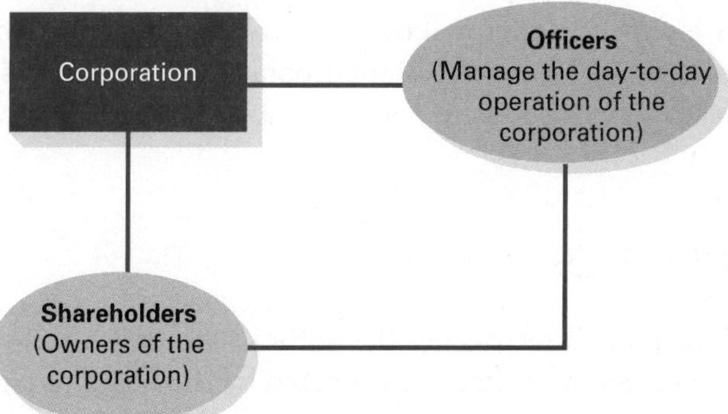

CONTEMPORARY Environment

COMMITTEES OF THE BOARD OF DIRECTORS

In the current complex business world, the demands on directors have increased. To help handle this increased workload, boards of directors have turned to creating committees of their members to handle specific duties. Board members with special expertise or interests are appointed to the various committees.

Unless the articles of incorporation or bylaws provide otherwise, the board of directors may create committees of the board and delegate certain powers to those committees [RMBCA Section 8.25]. All members of these committees must be directors. An act of a committee pursuant to delegated authority is the act of the board of directors.

Committees commonly appointed by the board of directors include the following:

- ***Executive committee.*** The executive committee has authority to (1) act on certain matters on behalf of the board during the interim period between board meetings and (2) conduct preliminary investigations of proposals on behalf of the full board. Most members of the committee are inside directors because it is easiest for them to meet to address corporate matters.
- ***Audit committee.*** The audit committee hires independent public accountants and supervises the audit of the financial records of the corporation.
- ***Nominating committee.*** The nominating committee nominates the management slate of directors to be submitted for shareholder vote.
- ***Compensation committee.*** The compensation committee approves management compensation, including salaries, bonuses, stock option plans, fringe benefits, and such.
- ***Investment committee.*** The investment committee is responsible for investing and reinvesting the funds of the corporation.
- ***Litigation committee.*** The litigation committee reviews and decides whether to pursue requests by shareholders for the corporation to sue persons who have allegedly harmed the corporation.

The following powers cannot be delegated to committees but must be exercised by the board itself: (1) declaring dividends, (2) initiating actions that require shareholders' approval, (3) appointing members to fill vacancies on the board, (4) amending the bylaws, (5) approving a plan of merger that does not require shareholder approval (short-form merger), and (6) authorizing the issuance of shares.

the corporation [RMBCA Section 8.40]. The duties of each officer are specified in the bylaws of the corporation.

An officer of a corporation may be removed by the board of directors. The board only has to determine that the best interests of the corporation will be served by such removal [RMBCA Section 8.43(b)]. Officers who are removed in violation of an employment contract can sue the corporation for damages.

Agency Authority of Officers

Officers and agents of a corporation have such authority as may be provided in the bylaws of the corporation or as determined by resolution of the board of directors [RMBCA Section 8.41]. Because they are agents, officers have authority, implied authority, and apparent authority to bind a corporation to contracts.

A corporation can *ratify* an unauthorized act of a corporate officer or agent. For example, suppose an officer acts outside the scope of his or her employment and enters into a contract with a third person. If the corporation accepts the benefits of the contract, it has ratified the contract and is bound by it. Officers are liable on an unauthorized contract if the corporation does not ratify it.

Concept Summary

Management of a Corporation

Group	Function
Shareholders	Owners of the corporation. They vote on the directors and other major actions to be taken by the corporation.
Board of directors	Responsible for making policy decisions and employing the major officers for the corporation. It may initiate certain actions that require shareholders' approval.
Officers	Responsible for the day-to-day operation of the corporation, including acting as agents for the corporation, hiring other officers and employees, and the like.

FIDUCIARY DUTY: DUTY OF OBEDIENCE

duty of obedience
A duty that directors and officers of a corporation have to act within the authority conferred upon them by state corporations codes, the articles of incorporation, the corporate bylaws, and the resolutions adopted by the board of directors.

The directors and officers of a corporation must act within the authority conferred upon them by the state's corporations code, the articles of incorporation, the corporate bylaws, and the resolutions adopted by the board of directors. This duty is called the **duty of obedience**. Directors and officers who either intentionally or negligently act outside their authority are personally liable for any resultant damages caused to the corporation or its shareholders.

Example: Suppose the articles of incorporation of a corporation authorize the corporation to invest in real estate only. If a corporate officer invests corporate funds in the commodities markets, the officer is liable to the corporation for any losses suffered.

FIDUCIARY DUTY: DUTY OF CARE

fiduciary duties
The duties of obedience, care, and loyalty owed by directors and officers to their corporation and its shareholders.

duty of care
A duty of corporate directors and officers to use care and diligence when acting on behalf of the corporation.

The directors and officers of a corporation owe certain **fiduciary duties** when making decisions and taking action on behalf of the corporation. One such duty is the **duty of care**. The duty of care requires corporate directors and officers to use *care and diligence* when acting on behalf of the corporation. To meet this duty of care, the directors and officers must discharge their duties (1) in good faith, (2) with the care that an *ordinary prudent person* in a like position would use under similar circumstances, and (3) in a manner they reasonably believe to be in the best interests of the corporation [RMBCA Sections 8.30(a), 8.42(a)].

A director or an officer who breaches the duty of care is personally liable to the corporation and its shareholders for any damages caused by the breach. Such breaches, which are normally caused by **negligence**, often involve a director's or an officer's failure to (1) make a reasonable investigation of a corporate matter, (2) attend board meetings on a regular basis, (3) properly supervise a subordinate who causes a loss to the corporation through embezzlement and such, or (4) keep adequately informed about corporate affairs. The courts examine breaches on a case-by-case basis.

negligence
Failure of a corporate director or officer to exercise the duty of care while conducting the corporation's business.

The Business Judgment Rule

The determination of whether a corporate director or officer has met his or her duty of care is measured as of the time the decision is made; the benefit of hindsight is not a factor. Therefore, the directors and officers are not liable to the corporation or its shareholders for honest mistakes of judgment. This is called the **business judgment rule**. Were it not for the protection afforded by the business judgment rule, many high-risk but socially desirable endeavors might not be undertaken.

business judgment rule
A rule that says directors and officers are not liable to the corporation or its shareholders for honest mistakes of judgment.

Example: After conducting considerable research and investigation, the directors of a major automobile company decide to produce large and expensive sport utility vehicles (SUVs). Three years later, when the SUVs are introduced to the public for sale, few of them are sold because of the public's interest in buying smaller, less expensive automobiles due to an economic recession and an increase in gasoline prices. Because this was an honest mistake of judgment on the part of corporate management, their judgment is shielded by the business judgment rule.

The court had to decide whether directors were protected by the business judgment rule in the following classic case.

CASE 9.3 Duty of Care

***Smith v. Van Gorkom*, 488 A.2d 858 (Del. 1985).**

"In the specific context of a proposed merger of a domestic corporation, a director has a duty, along with his fellow directors, to act in an informed and deliberate manner in determining whether to approve an agreement of merger."

—Judge Horsey

Facts

Trans Union Corporation (Trans Union) was a publicly traded, diversified holding company that was incorporated in Delaware. Its principal earnings were generated by its railcar leasing business. Jerome W. Van Gorkom was a Trans Union officer for more than twenty-four years, its chief executive officer for more than seventeen years, and the chairman of the board of directors for two years. Van Gorkom, a lawyer and certified public accountant, owned 75,000 shares of Trans Union. He was approaching 65 years of age and mandatory retirement. Trans Union's board of directors was composed of ten members—five inside directors and five outside directors.

Van Gorkom decided to meet with Jay A. Pritzker, a well-known corporate takeover specialist and a social acquaintance of Van Gorkom's, to discuss the possible sale of Trans Union to Pritzker. Van Gorkom met Pritzker at Pritzker's home on Saturday. He did so without consulting Trans Union's board of directors. At this meeting, Van Gorkom proposed a sale of Trans Union to Pritzker at a price of $55 per share. The stock was trading at about $38 in the market. On Monday, Pritzker notified Van Gorkom that he was interested in the $55 cash-out merger proposal. Van Gorkom, along with two inside directors, privately met with Pritzker on Tuesday and Wednesday. After meeting with Van Gorkom on Thursday, Pritzker notified his attorney to begin drafting the merger documents.

On Friday, Van Gorkom called a special meeting of Trans Union's board of directors for the following day. The board members were not told the purpose of the meeting. At the meeting, Van Gorkom disclosed the Pritzker offer and described its terms in a twenty-minute presentation. Neither the merger agreement nor a written summary of the terms of agreement was furnished to the directors. No valuation study as to the value of Trans Union was prepared for the meeting. After two hours, the board voted in favor of the cash-out merger with Pritzker's company at $55 per share for Trans Union's stock. The board also voted not to solicit other offers. The merger agreement was executed by Van Gorkom during Saturday evening at a formal social event he hosted for the opening of the Chicago Lyric Opera's season. Neither he nor any other director read the agreement prior to its signing and delivery to Pritzker.

> The director is really a watch-dog, and the watch-dog has no right, without the knowledge of his master, to take a sop from a possible wolf.
>
> Lord Justice Bowen
> *North Australian Territory v. Goldsborough*, 61 L.T. 716 (1890).

Trans Union's board of directors recommended that the merger be approved by its shareholders and distributed proxy materials to the shareholders, stating that the $55 per share price for their stock was fair. In the meantime, Trans Union's board of directors took steps to dissuade two other possible suitors who showed an interest in purchasing Trans Union. On February 10, 1981, 69.9 percent of the shares of Trans Union stock was voted in favor of the merger. The merger was consummated.

Alden Smith and other Trans Union shareholders sued Van Gorkom and the other directors for damages, alleging that the defendants were negligent in their conduct in selling Trans Union to Pritzker. The Delaware court of chancery held in favor of the defendants. The plaintiffs appealed.

Issue

Did Trans Union's directors breach their duty of care?

Language of the Court

In the specific context of a proposed merger of a domestic corporation, a director has a duty, along with his fellow directors, to act in an informed and deliberate manner in determining whether to approve an agreement of merger. The directors (1) did not adequately inform themselves as to Van Gorkom's role in forcing the sale of the company and in establishing the per share purchase price; (2) they were uninformed as to the intrinsic value of the company and (3) given these circumstances, at a minimum, they were grossly negligent in approving the sale of the company upon two hours' consideration, without prior notice, and without the exigency of a crisis or emergency.

Without any documents before them concerning the proposed transaction, the members of the board were required to rely entirely upon Van Gorkom's 20-minute oral presentation of the proposal. No written summary of the terms of the merger was presented; the directors were given no documentation to *support the adequacy of $55 price per share for sale of the company; and the board had before it nothing more than Van Gorkom's statement of his understanding of the substance of an agreement that he admittedly had never read or that any member of the board had ever seen. Thus, the record compels the conclusion that the board lacked valuation information to reach an informed business judgment as to the fairness of $55 per share for sale of the company. We conclude that Trans Union's board was grossly negligent in that it failed to act with informed reasonable deliberation in agreeing to the Pritzker merger proposal.*

Decision

The Supreme Court of Delaware held that the defendant directors had breached their duty of care. The supreme court reversed the judgment of the court of chancery and remanded the case to the court of chancery to conduct an evidentiary hearing to determine the fair value of the shares represented by the plaintiffs' class. If that value was higher than $55 per share, the difference was to be awarded to the plaintiffs as damages.

Case Questions

1. **Critical Legal Thinking** Describe the fiduciary duty of care owed by directors and officers. What does the business judgment rule provide? Explain.
2. **Business Ethics** Do you think Van Gorkom and the other directors had the shareholders' best interests in mind? Explain.
3. **Contemporary Business** What type of liability exposure is there for being a member of a board of directors? Explain.

Reliance on Others

Corporate directors and officers usually are unable to personally investigate every corporate matter brought to their attention. Under the RMBCA, directors and officers are entitled to rely on information, opinions, reports, or statements, including financial statements and other financial data, prepared or presented by [RMBCA §§ 8.30(b) and 8.42(b)]:

- Officers and employees of the corporation whom the director believes are reliable and competent in the matter presented.
- Lawyers, public accountants, and other professionals as to any matters that the director believes to be within their professional or expert competence.
- A committee of the board of directors upon which the director does not serve as to matters within the committee's designated authority and which committee the director reasonably believes to merit confidence.

A director is not liable if such information is false, misleading, or otherwise unreliable unless he or she has knowledge that would cause such reliance to be unwarranted [RMBCA §§ 8.30(c) and 8.42(c)]. The degree of an officer's reliance on such sources is more limited than that given to directors because they are more familiar with corporate operations.

> History suggests that capitalism is a necessary condition for political freedom.
> Milton Friedman

FIDUCIARY DUTY: DUTY OF LOYALTY

duty of loyalty
A duty that directors and officers have not to act adversely to the interests of the corporation and to subordinate their personal interests to those of the corporation and its shareholders.

Directors and officers of a corporation owe a fiduciary duty to act honestly. This duty, called the **duty of loyalty**, requires directors and officers to subordinate their personal interests to those of the corporation and its shareholders. Justice Benjamin Cardozo defined the duty of loyalty as follows:

> *[A corporate director or officer] owes loyalty and allegiance to the corporation—a loyalty that is undivided and an allegiance that is influenced by no consideration other than the welfare of the corporation. Any adverse interest of a director [or officer] will be subjected to a scrutiny rigid and uncompromising. He may not profit at the expense of his corporation and in conflict with its rights; he may not for personal gain divert unto himself the opportunities that in equity and fairness belong to the corporation.*
>
> *Many forms of conduct permissible in a workaday world for those acting at arm's length are forbidden to those bound by fiduciary ties. Not honesty alone, but the punctilio of an honor the most sensitive, is then the standard of behavior. As to this there has developed a tradition that is unbending and inveterate.*[1]

If a director or an officer breaches their duty of loyalty and makes a secret profit on a transaction, the corporation can sue the director or officer to recover the secret profit. Some of the most common breaches of the duty of loyalty are discussed in the following paragraphs.

Usurping a Corporate Opportunity

usurping a corporate opportunity
When a director or officer steals a corporate opportunity for himself or herself.

Directors and officers may not personally usurp (steal) a corporate opportunity for themselves. **Usurping a corporate opportunity** constitutes a violation of a director's or an officer's duty of loyalty. If usurping is proven, the corporation can (1) acquire the opportunity from the director or officer and (2) recover any profits made by the director or officer.

The following elements must be shown to prove usurping:

- The opportunity was presented to the director or officer in their corporate capacity.
- The opportunity is related to or connected with the corporation's current or proposed business.
- The corporation has the financial ability to take advantage of the opportunity.
- The corporate officer or director took the corporate opportunity for himself or herself.

However, the director or officer is personally free to take advantage of a corporate opportunity if it was fully disclosed and presented to the corporation and the corporation rejected it.

Self-Dealing

Under the RMBCA, a contract or transaction with a corporate director or officer is voidable by the corporation if it is unfair to the corporation [RMBCA Section 8.31]. Contracts of a corporation to purchase property from, sell property to, or make loans to corporate directors or officers where the directors or officers have not disclosed their interest in the transaction are often voided under this standard. In the alternative, the corporation can affirm the contract and recover any profits from the **self-dealing** employee. Contracts or transactions with corporate directors or officers are enforceable if their interest in the transaction has been disclosed to the corporation and the disinterested directors or the shareholders have approved the transaction.

self-dealing
If the directors or officers engage in purchasing, selling, or leasing of property with the corporation, the contract must be fair to the corporation; otherwise, it is voidable by the corporation. The contract or transaction is enforceable if it has been fully disclosed and approved.

Competing with the Corporation

Directors and officers cannot engage in activities that **compete with the corporation** unless full disclosure is made and a majority of the disinterested directors or shareholders approve the activity. The corporation can recover any profits made by non-approved competition and any other damages caused to the corporation.

competing with a corporation
A way in which a corporate officer or director can breach his or her duty of loyalty.

Making a Secret Profit

If a director or an officer breaches his or her duty of loyalty and makes a secret profit on a transaction, the corporation can sue the director or officer to recover the secret profit.

Example: Maxine is the purchasing agent for the Roebolt Corporation. Her duties require her to negotiate and execute contracts to purchase office supplies and equipment for the corporation. Assume that Bruce, a computer salesperson, pays Maxine a $10,000 kickback to purchase from him computers needed by the Roebolt Corporation. The Roebolt Corporation can sue and recover the $10,000 secret profit from Maxine.

CONTEMPORARY Environment

STATES ENACT CONSTITUENCY STATUTES

Under the classical theory of the corporation, the board of directors owe a fiduciary duty to act in the best interest of the shareholders of the corporation. The rights of other constituents—such as employees, bondholders and creditors, and suppliers and customers—exist by contract, period.

In recent years, more than thirty states have enacted constituency statutes that allow directors to consider constituents other than shareholders when making decisions. Constituency statutes recognize the complex nature of the modern corporation and the modern view that shareholders are not the only "owners" of corporations. These statutes acknowledge the rights of a variety of participants, including lenders, employees, managers, suppliers, distributors, customers, and the local communities in which corporations are located.

For example, Minnesota adopted the following statute:

> *In discharging the duties of the position of director, a director may, in considering the best interests of the corporation, consider the interests of the corporation's employees, customers, suppliers, and creditors, the economy of the state and nation, community and societal considerations, and the long-term as well as short-term interests of the corporation and its shareholders, including the possibility that these interests may be best served by the continued independence of the corporation. [Minn. Stat. § 302A.251(5)]*

Most constituency statutes are permissive, not mandatory. That is, directors may take into account non-stockholder interests but are not required to do so.

CRIMINAL LIABILITY

Corporate directors, officers, employees, and agents are personally liable for the crimes they commit while acting on behalf of the corporation. Criminal law sanctions include fines and imprisonment.

Under the law of agency, a corporation is liable for the crimes committed by its directors, officers, employees, or agents while acting within the scope of their employment. Because a corporation cannot be placed in prison, the criminal penalty imposed on a corporation is usually the assessment of a monetary fine or the loss of some legal privilege (such as a license).

Many states' attorney generals have aggressively pursued criminal cases against corporate officers and directors in recent years. The attorney general of New York has been a leading force in bringing cases against fraudulent officers and directors. The U.S. Department of Justice brings criminal cases against officers and directors for violating federal statutes, such as securities law, racketeering laws, and other federal statutes.

Concept Summary

Fiduciary Duties of Corporation Directors and Officers

Duty	Description	Violation
Duty of obedience	Duty to act within the authority given by state corporations codes, articles of incorporation, the corporate bylaws, and resolutions adopted by the board of directors.	Acts outside the corporate officer's or director's authority.
Duty of care	Duty to use care and diligence when acting on behalf of the corporation. This duty is discharged if an officer or a director acts: 1. In good faith 2. With the care that an ordinary prudent person in a like position would use under similar circumstances 3. In a manner he or she reasonably believes to be in the best interests of the corporation	Acts of negligence and mismanagement. Such acts include failure to: 1. Make a reasonable investigation of a corporate matter 2. Attend board meetings on a regular basis 3. Properly supervise a subordinate who causes a loss to the corporation 4. Keep adequately informed about corporate matters 5. Take other actions necessary to discharge duties
Duty of loyalty	Duty to subordinate personal interests to those of the corporation and its shareholders.	Acts of disloyalty. Such acts include unauthorized: 1. Self-dealing with the corporation 2. Usurping of a corporate opportunity 3. Competition with the corporation 4. Making of secret profit that belongs to the corporation

CONTEMPORARY environment

INDEMNIFICATION AND D&O INSURANCE PROTECTION

Directors and officers of corporations are sometimes personally named in lawsuits that involve actions they have taken on behalf of the corporation. Such lawsuits are often brought by disgruntled shareholders or third parties who claim they have suffered damages because of the director's or officer's negligence or other conduct.

Directors and officers can protect themselves against personal liability by making sure the corporation does the following:

- ***Purchase directors' and officers' liability insurance (D&O insurance).*** Corporations can purchase D&O insurance from private insurance companies by paying an annual premium for the insurance. The insurance company is required to defend a corporate director or officer who has been sued in their corporate capacity. The insurance company is also required, subject to the terms of the insurance coverage, to pay the litigation costs incurred in defending the lawsuit (e.g., attorneys' fees, court costs) and any judgments or settlement costs. Most D&O policies contain deductible clauses and maximum coverage limits [RMBCA § 8.57].
- ***Provide indemnification.*** Corporations may provide that directors and officers who are sued in their corporate capacities will be indemnified by the corporation for the costs of the litigation as well as any judgments or settlements stemming from the lawsuit. Indemnification means that the corporation—and not the director or officer personally—pays these costs. The RMBCA provides that a court may order indemnification if a director or an officer is found to be fairly and reasonably entitled to such indemnification [RMBCA § 8.54 and 8.56(1)].

SARBANES-OXLEY ACT

During the late 1990s and early 2000s, the U.S. economy was wracked by a number of business and accounting scandals. Companies such as Enron, Tyco, and WorldCom engaged in fraudulent conduct, leading to many corporate officers being convicted of financial crimes. Many of these companies went bankrupt, causing huge losses to their shareholders, employees, and creditors. Boards of directors were complacent, not keeping a watchful eye over the conduct of their officers and employees.

In response, Congress enacted the federal **Sarbanes-Oxley Act** of 2002. This act establishes far-reaching rules regarding corporate governance. The goals of the Sarbanes-Oxley Act are to improve corporate governance rules, eliminate conflicts of interest, and instill confidence in investors and the public that management will run public companies in the best interests of all constituents. Excerpts from the Sarbanes-Oxley Act are set forth as Appendix E to this book.

Sarbanes-Oxley Act
A federal act that imposes new rules that affect public accountants. The act created the Public Company Accounting Oversight Board (PCAOB); requires public accounting firms to register with the PCAOB; separates audit services and certain nonaudit services provided by accountants to clients; requires an audit partner of the accounting firm to supervise an audit and approve an audit report prepared by the firm and requires a second partner of the accounting firm to review and approve the audit report; and prohibits employment of an accountant by a previous audit client for certain positions for a period of one year following the audit.

ETHICS SPOTLIGHT

SARBANES-OXLEY ACT IMPROVES CORPORATE GOVERNANCE

The Sarbanes-Oxley Act has changed the rules of corporate governance in important respects. Several major provisions of the act regarding corporate governance are discussed in the following paragraphs.

CEO and CFO Certification

The chief executive officer (CEO) and chief financial officer (CFO) of a public company must file a statement accompanying each annual and quarterly report, certifying that the signing officer has reviewed the report; that, based on the officer's knowledge, the report

(continued)

> The increase of a great number of citizens in prosperity is a necessary element to the security, and even to the existence, of a civilized people.
> Eugene Buret

does not contain any untrue statement of a material fact or omit to state a material fact that would make the statement misleading; and that the financial statement and disclosures fairly present, in all material aspects, the operation and financial condition of the company. A knowing and willful violation is punishable by up to twenty years in prison and a fine up to $5 million.

Reimbursement of Bonuses and Incentive Pay

If a public company is required to restate its financial statements because of material noncompliance with financial reporting requirements, the CEO and CFO must reimburse the company for any bonuses, incentive pay, or securities trading profits made because of the noncompliance.

Prohibition on Personal Loans

The act prohibits public companies from making personal loans to their directors or executive officers.

Tampering with Evidence

The act makes it a crime for any person to knowingly alter, destroy, mutilate, conceal, or create any document to impair, impede, influence, or obstruct any federal investigation. A violation is punishable by up to twenty years in prison and a monetary fine.

Bar from Acting as an Officer or a Director

The Securities and Exchange Commission (SEC), a federal government agency, may issue an order prohibiting any person who has committed securities fraud from acting as an officer or a director of a public company.

Although the Sarbanes-Oxley Act applies only to public companies, private companies and nonprofit organizations are also influenced by the act's accounting and corporate governance rules.

Business Ethics

1. Will the CEO and CFO certification requirement reduce corporate fraudulent conduct? Explain. Will the Sarbanes-Oxley Act encourage more ethical behavior from corporate officers and directors?

Concept Review

Classification of Directors

Classification	Description
Inside director	A person who is also an officer of the corporation
Outside director	A person who is not an officer of the corporation

Management of a Corporation

Group	Function
Shareholders	Owners of the corporation. They vote on the directors and other major actions to be taken by the corporation.
Board of directors	Responsible for making policy decisions and employing the major officers for the corporation. It may initiate certain actions that require shareholders' approval.
Officers	Responsible for the day-to-day operation of the corporation, including acting as agents for the corporation, hiring other officers and employees, and the like.

Fiduciary Duties of Corporation Directors and Officers

Duty	Description	Violation
Duty of obedience	Duty to act within the authority given by state corporations codes, articles of incorporation, the corporate bylaws, and resolutions adopted by the board of directors.	Acts outside the corporate officer's or director's authority.
Duty of care	Duty to use care and diligence when acting on behalf of the corporation. This duty is discharged if an officer or a director acts: 1. In good faith 2. With the care that an ordinary prudent person in a like position would use under similar circumstances 3. In a manner he or she reasonably believes to be in the best interests of the corporation	Acts of negligence and mismanagement. Such acts include failure to: 1. Make a reasonable investigation of a corporate matter 2. Attend board meetings on a regular basis 3. Properly supervise a subordinate who causes a loss to the corporation 4. Keep adequately informed about corporate matters 5. Take other actions necessary to discharge duties
Duty of loyalty	Duty to subordinate personal interests to those of the corporation and its shareholders.	Acts of disloyalty. Such acts include unauthorized: 1. Self-dealing with the corporation 2. Usurping of a corporate opportunity 3. Competition with the corporation 4. Making of secret profit that belongs to the corporation

> It appears to me that the atmosphere of the temple of Justice is polluted by the presence of such things as companies.
>
> Lord Justice James
> *Wilson v. Church*, 11 Ch. D. 576 (1879).

CHAPTER REVIEW

SHAREHOLDERS, p. 241

Rights of Shareholders

Ownership rights. Shareholders of a corporation own the corporation.

Shareholders' Meetings

1. ***Annual shareholders' meeting.*** This meeting of the shareholders of a corporation must be held annually by the corporation to elect directors and vote on other matters.
2. ***Special shareholders' meeting.*** This meeting of shareholders may be called to consider and vote on important or emergency matters, such as a proposed merger or amending the articles of incorporation.
3. ***Notice of shareholders' meetings.*** The corporation must notify shareholders of the place, day, and time of annual and special shareholder meetings. If the required notice is not given or is defective, any action taken at the meeting is void.

Proxies

1. ***Proxy.*** Shareholders may appoint another person (the *proxy*) as their agent to vote their shares at shareholders' meetings.
2. ***Proxy card.*** A proxy card is a written document that a shareholder signs that authorizes another person to vote the shareholder's shares at a shareholders' meeting.

Voting Requirements

1. ***Record date.*** The record date is a date specified in the corporate bylaws that determines whether a shareholder may vote at a shareholders' meeting. Only persons who are shareholders on the record date are permitted to vote at the meeting.
2. ***Shareholders' list.*** This list contains the names and addresses of the shareholders as of the record date and the class and number of shares owned by each shareholder. This list must be made available to all shareholders.
3. ***Quorum.*** A quorum is the required number of shares that must be represented in person or by proxy to hold a shareholders' meeting. The RMBCA establishes a majority of outstanding shares as a quorum.
4. ***Vote required for elections other than for directors.*** The affirmative vote of the *majority* of the voting shares represented at a shareholders' meeting constitutes an act of the shareholders for actions other than for the elections of directors.
5. ***Voting methods for electing directors:***
   a. ***Straight (noncumulative) voting.*** Unless otherwise stated, each shareholder votes the number of shares he or she owns on candidates for each of the positions open for election. The candidate(s) with the most votes wins the open position(s).
   b. ***Cumulative voting.*** The articles of incorporation may provide for cumulative voting. Under this method, a shareholder is entitled to multiply the number of shares he or she owns by the number of directors to be elected and cast the product for a single candidate or distribute the product among two or more candidates.
6. ***Supramajority voting requirement.*** The articles of incorporation or bylaws can require a greater than majority of shares to constitute quorum or the vote of the shareholders (e.g., 80 percent). Also called *supermajority voting requirement.*

Voting Agreements

1. ***Voting trust.*** In this arrangement, participating shareholders transfer their shares to a trustee who is then empowered to vote the shares held by the trust. Shareholders are issued *voting trust certificates* that evidence their interest in the trust.
2. ***Shareholder voting agreements.*** These agreements are between two or more shareholders, who agree on how they will vote their shares. Voting agreements are enforceable.

Right to Transfer Shares

Shareholders have the right to transfer their shares. Shareholders can enter into the following agreements to restrict the transfer of shares:

1. ***Right of first refusal.*** This agreement requires the selling shareholder to offer his or her shares for sale to the other parties to the agreement before selling them to anyone else.

2. ***Buy-and-sell agreement.*** This agreement requires selling shareholders to sell their shares to the other shareholders or to the corporation at the price specified in the agreement.

Preemptive Rights

These rights give existing shareholders the option of subscribing to new shares being issued by the corporation in proportion to their current ownership interest.

Right to Receive Information and Inspect Books and Records

1. ***Annual financial statement.*** A corporation must furnish its shareholders with an annual *financial statement* containing a balance sheet, an income statement, and a statement of changes in shareholder equity.
2. ***Inspection rights.*** Shareholders have the *absolute right to* inspect the shareholders' list, the articles of incorporation, the bylaws, and the minutes of shareholders' meetings held within the past three years. They have the right to inspect accounting and tax records, minutes of board of directors and committee meetings, and minutes of shareholders' meetings held more than three years in the past if they demonstrate a *proper purpose*.

Directors' Authority to Pay Dividends

1. ***Dividends.*** The board of directors has the *discretion* to pay *dividends* to shareholders.
2. ***Record date.*** When a corporation declares a dividend, it sets a date, usually a few weeks prior to the actual payment, that establishes the *record date* for payment of the dividend. Shareholders as of that date will be paid the dividend.
3. ***Stock dividends.*** Additional shares of stock may be issued to the shareholders as a dividend. They are paid in proportion to the existing ownership interests of shareholders so they do not increase a shareholder's proportionate ownership interest.

Derivative Lawsuits

A shareholder may bring a derivative lawsuit on behalf of the corporation against an offending party who has injured the corporation when the directors of the corporation fail to bring the suit. The shareholder must make a written *demand* upon the corporation to bring the lawsuit, and the corporation either rejects it or ninety days expire without the corporation bringing the requested lawsuit.

Piercing the Corporate Veil

1. ***Limited liability of shareholders.*** Shareholders of corporations generally have *limited liability*; that is, they are liable for the debts and obligations of the corporation only to the *extent of their capital contribution* to the corporation.
2. ***Piercing the corporate veil.*** Courts can *disregard the corporate entity* and hold shareholders personally liable for the debts and obligations of the corporation if (1) the corporation has been formed without sufficient capital (*thin capitalization*) or (2) separateness has not been maintained between the corporation and its shareholders (e.g., commingling of personal and corporate assets, failure to hold required shareholders' meetings). Piercing the corporate veil is also called the *alter ego doctrine*.

BOARD OF DIRECTORS, p. 252

Rights of Directors

1. ***Board of directors.*** The board is a panel of decision makers for the corporation, the members of which are elected by the shareholders.
2. ***Policy decisions.*** The directors of a corporation are responsible for formulating the *policy* decisions affecting the corporation, such as deciding what business to engage in, determining the capital structure of the corporation, and selecting and removing top officers of the corporation.
3. ***Resolutions.*** The board of directors can adopt a resolution that approves a transaction that requires shareholder vote and recommend it to shareholders.
4. ***Right of Inspection.*** Corporate directors have an *absolute right* to have access to the corporation's books, records, facilities, premises, and any other information affecting the operation of the corporation.

Compensating Directors

Directors are usually paid an annual retainer and an attendance fee for each meeting attended.

Selecting Directors

1. ***Inside director.*** An inside director is a member of the board of directors who is also an officer of the corporation.
2. ***Outside director.*** An outside director is a member of the board of directors who is not an officer of the corporation.
3. ***Qualifications.*** There are no qualifications to serve as a director unless the articles of incorporation or bylaws prescribe qualifications.
4. ***Number of directors.*** A board of directors can consist of one or more individuals. The articles of incorporation fix the number of initial directors. This number can be amended by the articles of incorporation or bylaws.
5. ***Variable range.*** The articles of incorporation or bylaws can establish a *variable range* for the size of the board of directors. The exact number of directors within the range may be changed from time to time by the board of directors or the shareholders.

Term of Office

1. ***Annual term.*** The term of a director's office expires at the next annual shareholders' meeting following his or her election unless terms are staggered.
2. ***Staggered terms.*** If a board of directors consists of nine or more members, it may be divided into two or three *classes* (each class to be as nearly equal in number as possible), and classes can be elected to serve *staggered terms* of two or three years.
3. ***Vacancies.*** Vacancies on a board of directors can be filled by the shareholders or the remaining directors.

Meetings of the Board of Directors

1. ***Regular meeting.*** A regular meeting of the board of directors is held at the time and place scheduled in the bylaws.
2. ***Special meeting.*** A special meeting of the board of directors may be convened to discuss an important or emergency matter such as a proposed merger or a hostile takeover attempt.
3. ***Written consents.*** The board of directors may act without a meeting if all the directors sign written consents that set forth the action taken.

4. ***Conference call.*** The board of directors may meet via conference call if all the directors can hear and participate in the call.
5. ***Quorum.*** A simple *majority* of the number of directors established in the articles of incorporation or bylaws constitutes a quorum for transacting business.
6. ***Vote.*** The approval or disapproval of a *majority* of the quorum binds the entire board.
7. ***Supramajority vote.*** The articles of incorporation or bylaws may require a greater than majority of directors to constitute quorum or the vote of the board.

Committees of the Board of Directors

Unless the articles of incorporation or bylaws provide otherwise, the board of directors may create committees of its members and delegate certain powers to those committees. The most common committees are as follows:

1. ***Executive committee.*** This committee has authority to (1) act on certain matters during the interim period between board meetings and (2) conduct preliminary investigations of proposals on behalf of the board.
2. ***Audit committee.*** This committee recommends independent public accountants and supervises the audit of the financial records of the corporation by the accountants.
3. ***Nominating committee.*** This committee nominates the management slate of directors to be submitted for shareholder vote.
4. ***Compensation committee.*** This committee approves management compensation, including salaries, bonuses, stock option plans, fringe benefits, and such.
5. ***Investment committee.*** This committee is responsible for investing and reinvesting the funds of the corporation.
6. ***Litigation committee.*** This committee reviews and decides whether to pursue requests by shareholders for the corporation to sue persons who have allegedly harmed the corporation.

CORPORATE OFFICERS, p. 255

Rights of Officers

Officers. Officers are employees of the corporation who are appointed by the board of directors to manage the *day-to-day operations* of the corporation.

Removal of Officers

Unless an employment contract provides otherwise, any officer of a corporation may be removed by the board of directors.

Agency Authority of Officers

Officers and agents of the corporation have express, implied, and apparent authority to bind the corporation to contracts with third parties.

FIDUCIARY DUTY: DUTY OF OBEDIENCE, p. 258

Fiduciary Duties

Corporate directors and officers owe the fiduciary duties of trust and confidence to the corporation and its shareholders. They owe the duties of *obedience*, *care*, and *loyalty*.

Duty of Obedience

Directors and officers of a corporation have a duty to act within the authority conferred upon them by the state corporation statute, the articles of incorporation, the corporate bylaws, and the resolutions adopted by the board of directors.

FIDUCIARY DUTY: DUTY OF CARE, p. 258

Duty of Care

Corporate directors and officers have a duty to use care and diligence when acting on behalf of the corporation. This duty is discharged if they perform their duties (1) in good faith, (2) with the care that an *ordinary prudent person* in a like position would use under similar circumstances, and (3) in a manner they reasonably believe to be in the best interests of the corporation.

1. ***Negligence.*** Negligence is the failure of a corporate director or officer to exercise this duty of care when conducting the corporation's business.
2. ***Business judgment rule.*** This rule says that directors and officers are not liable to the corporation or its shareholders for honest mistakes of judgment.
3. ***Reliance on others.*** Directors and officers may rely on information and reports prepared by competent and reliable officers and employees, lawyers, public accountants, and other professionals as well as on committees of the board of directors as long as such reliance is warranted.
4. ***Dissent to directors' action.*** When an individual director opposes the action taken by the majority of the board of directors, they should register their dissent by (1) entering it in the minutes of the meeting, (2) filing a written dissent with the secretary before the adjournment of the meeting, or (3) forwarding a written dissent by registered mail to the secretary immediately following the adjournment of the meeting if the director has not attended the meeting.

FIDUCIARY DUTY: DUTY OF LOYALTY, p. 262

Duty of Loyalty

Directors and officers have a duty not to act adversely to the interests of the corporation and to subordinate their personal interests to those of the corporation and its shareholders.

Common examples of breaches of the duty of loyalty include:

1. ***Usurping a corporate opportunity.*** A director or an officer may not personally *usurp* (*steal*) an opportunity that belongs to the corporation. The corporation can acquire the opportunity from the director or officer and recover any profits made by the director or officer.
2. ***Self-dealing.*** The corporation may void any transaction with a director or an officer if it is *unfair to the corporation*. Such transactions usually involve undisclosed self-dealing by a director or officer with the corporation.
3. ***Competing with the corporation.*** Directors and officers may not compete with their corporation unless the competitive activity has been fully disclosed to the corporation and approved by a majority of disinterested directors or shareholders.
4. ***Making a secret profit.*** The corporation can sue and recover any secret profits made by an officer's or a director's breach of his or her duty of loyalty.

CRIMINAL LIABILITY, p. 264

Criminal Liability

1. ***Liability of directors and officers.*** Corporate directors and officers are *personally liable* for the crimes they commit while acting on behalf of the corporation. Criminal sanctions include fines and imprisonment.
2. ***Liability of the corporation.*** Under the law of *agency*, corporations are liable for the crimes committed by its directors and officers while acting within the scope of their authority. Criminal sanctions include monetary fines and loss of legal privileges (e.g., loss of a license).

Insurance

Corporations can purchase *directors' and officers' liability insurance (D&O insurance)* that pays the cost to defend litigation against directors and officers and pays any judgment or settlement of the lawsuit.

Indemnification

The corporation must indemnify (*pay back*) any director or officer for litigation expenses incurred in a lawsuit won by the director or officer. The corporation may indemnify a director or officer who loses a lawsuit as long as the director or officer was not adjudged liable to the corporation or did not improperly obtain personal benefit for himself or herself in the challenged transaction. Directors and officers may not be paid insurance or indemnification for intentional conduct that harmed third parties.

SARBANES-OXLEY ACT, p. 265

Sarbanes-Oxley Act of 2002

This act is a federal statute enacted by Congress to improve corporate governance rules, establish independence between public accounting firms and the public companies they audit, and eliminate conflicts of interest.

Auditing and Accounting Rules

1. ***Audit committee.*** A public company must have an audit committee that is responsible for the appointment of, payment to, and oversight of public accounting firms employed to audit the company.
2. ***Public company accounting oversight board.*** A board regulated by the SEC has the authority to adopt rules concerning auditing, accounting, independence, and ethics of public companies and public accountants.

Corporate Governance Rules

1. ***CEO and CFO certification.*** The CEO and CFO of a public company must file a statement accompanying each annual and quarterly report certifying that the signing officer has reviewed the report; that, based on the officer's knowledge, the report does not contain any untrue statement of a material fact or omit to state a material fact that would make the statement misleading; and that the financial statement and disclosures fairly present, in all material aspects, the operation and financial condition of the company. A knowing and willful violation is punishable by up to twenty years in prison and a fine of not more than $5 million.

2. ***Reimbursement of bonuses and incentive pay.*** The CEO and CFO must reimburse the company for any bonuses, incentive pay, or securities trading profits if the company is required to restate its financial statements because of material noncompliance with financial reporting requirements.
3. ***Prohibition on personal loans.*** Public companies cannot make personal loans to its directors or executive officers.
4. ***Tampering with evidence.*** It is a crime for any person to tamper with evidence to impede, influence, or obstruct any federal investigation. A violation is punishable by up to twenty years in prison and a monetary fine.
5. ***Bar from acting as an officer or a director.*** The SEC may issue an order prohibiting any person who has committed securities fraud from acting as an officer or a director of a public company.

TEST REVIEW TERMS AND CONCEPTS

Shareholders' meeting 241
Shareholder voting agreement 245
Special meeting of a board of directors 245
Special shareholders' meeting 241
Stock dividend 246
Straight (noncumulative) voting 243
Supramajority 243
Supramajority voting requirement 243
Usurping a corporate opportunity 262
Voting trust 243
Voting trust certificate 245

CASE SCENARIO REVISITED

Remember the case at the beginning of the chapters where some of the shareholders in GRG Operating, Inc. (GRG) want to remove their proxies. Can they? If a lawsuit is filed, who would win? For help with your answer, review the case *Zollar v. Smith*, 710 S.W.2d 155 (Tex. Ct. App. 1986).

PORTFOLIO EXERCISES

For the business you created at the beginning of the course, complete the following certification.

CERTIFICATION PURSUANT TO SARBANES – OXLEY ACT

I, __________, Chief Executive Officer of _____________ certify that:

1. I have reviewed this quarterly report on Form 10-Q of ______ ("the registrant") for the period ending _____ as filed with the Securities and Exchange Commission;
2. Based on my knowledge, this report does not contain any untrue statement of a material fact or omit to state a material fact necessary to make the statement made not misleading;
3. Based on my knowledge, the financial statements, and other financial information included in this report, fairly present in all material respects the financial condition, results of operations and cash flows of the registrant;
4. I have disclosed to the registrant's auditors any fraud, whether or not material, that involves management or other employees who have a significant role in the registrant's internal control over financial reporting

Date:__________________ /s/_________________.
Chief Executive Officer

WORKING THE WEB INTERNET EXERCISES

Activities

1. Find your state statute on indemnification for corporate officers and directors. Why do you think this concept was included in the statute? See www.law.cornell.edu/topics/corporations.html for an overview of corporations law with links to key primary and secondary sources.
2. Review the sample indemnification agreement at www.lawvantage.com.
3. For more coverage of the background on directors' and officers' liability, see guide.lp.findlaw.com/01topics/08corp/index.html.
4. Go to www.lawcrawler.findlaw.com. Type in the search term *piercing the corporate veil*. Note how many articles are written from the perspective of an attorney representing a small business owner against claims seeking personal assets. Note: For socially responsible investing information, see www.socialinvest.org.

CRITICAL LEGAL THINKING CASES

Case 9.1 *Shareholders' Meeting* Ocilla Industries, Inc. (Ocilla), owned 40 percent of the stock of Direct Action Marketing, Inc. (Direct Action). Direct Action was a New York corporation that specialized in the marketing of products through billing inserts. Ocilla helped place Howard Katz and Joseph Esposito on Direct Action's five-member board of directors. A dispute between Ocilla and the two directors caused Ocilla to claim that Katz and Esposito wanted excess remuneration in exchange for leaving the board at the end of their terms. As a result, no shareholders' meeting was held for one and one-half years. Under the Model Business Corporations Act, can Ocilla compel Direct Action to hold the meeting earlier? *Ocilla Indus., Inc. v. Katz*, 677 F. Supp. 1291 (E.D.N.Y. 1987).

Case 9.2 *Special Shareholders' Meeting* Jack C. Schoenholtz was a shareholder and member of the board of directors of Rye Psychiatric Hospital Center, Inc. (Rye Hospital). Four years after the hospital was incorporated, a split had developed among the board of directors concerning the operation of the facility. Three directors stood on one side of the dispute, and three directors on the other. In an attempt to break the deadlock, Schoenholtz, who owned over 10 percent of the corporation's voting stock, asked the corporation's secretary to call a special meeting of the shareholders. In response, the secretary sent a notice to the shareholders, stating that a special meeting of the shareholders would be held "for the purpose of electing directors." The meeting was held as scheduled. Some shareholders brought suit, claiming that the special shareholders' meeting was not called properly. Who wins? *Rye Psychiatric Hosp. Ctr., Inc. v. Schoenholtz*, 476 N.Y.S.2d 339 (N.Y. App. Div. 1984).

Case 9.3 *Right to Inspect Records* Helmsman Management Services, Inc. (Helmsman), became a 25 percent shareholder of A&S Consultants, Inc. (A&S), a Delaware corporation. Helmsman paid $50,000 for its interest in A&S. At the time of the stock purchase, Helmsman was also a customer of A&S, paying the company for the use of a computer software program. After making his investment, Helmsman verified A&S's billings with a periodic review of certain of A&S's books and records. Three years later, Helmsman conducted a review of

A&S's records over a six-day period. The review showed that A&S had never paid any dividends on the stock held by Helmsman and that Helmsman had never received notice of A&S's shareholder meetings. Suspecting that A&S was being mismanaged, Helmsman sent a letter to A&S, asking to inspect all of A&S's records. The letter stated several purposes for the inspection, including to (1) determine the reasons for nonpayment of dividends and (2) gain information to be used in determining how to vote in shareholders' elections. Under the Model Business Corporations Act, should Helmsman's request be honored? *Helmsman Management Serv., Inc. v. A&S Consultants, Inc.*, 525 A.2d 160 (Del. Ch. 1987).

Case 9.4 *Dividends* Gay's Super Markets, Inc. (Super Markets), was a corporation formed under the laws of the state of Maine. Hannaford Bros. Company held 51 percent of the corporation's common stock. Lawrence F. Gay and his brother Carrol were both minority shareholders in Super Markets. Lawrence Gay was also the manager of the corporation's store at Machias, Maine. One day, Lawrence was dismissed from his job. At the meeting of Super Markets's board of directors, a decision was made not to declare a stock dividend for the prior year. The directors cited expected losses from increased competition and the expense of opening a new store as reasons for not paying a dividend. Lawrence Gay claims that the reason for not paying a dividend was to force him to sell his shares in Super Markets. Lawrence sued to force the corporation to declare a dividend. Who wins? *Gay v. Gay's Super Mkts., Inc.*, 343 A.2d 577 (Me. 1975).

Case 9.5 *Duty of Loyalty* Edward Hellenbrand ran a comedy club known as the Comedy Cottage in Rosemont, Illinois. The business was incorporated, with Hellenbrand and his wife as the corporation's sole shareholders. The corporation leased the premises in which the club was located. Hellenbrand hired Jay Berk as general manager of the club. Two years later, Berk was made vice president of the corporation and given 10 percent of its stock. Hellenbrand experienced health problems and moved to Nevada, leaving Berk to manage the daily affairs of the business. Four years later, the ownership of the building where the Comedy Cottage was located changed hands. Shortly thereafter, the club's lease on the premises expired. Hellenbrand instructed Berk to negotiate a new lease. Berk arranged a month-to-month lease but had the lease agreement drawn up in his name instead of that of the corporation. When Hellenbrand learned of Berk's move, he fired him. Berk continued to lease the building in his own name and opened his own club, the Comedy Company, Inc., there. Hellenbrand sued Berk for an injunction to prevent Berk from leasing the building. Who wins? *Comedy Cottage, Inc. v. Berk*, 495 N.E.2d 1006 (Ill. App. Ct. 1986).

Case 9.6 *Duty of Loyalty* Lawrence Gaffney was the president and general manager of Ideal Tape Company (Ideal). Ideal, which was a subsidiary of Chelsea Industries, Inc. (Chelsea), was engaged in the business of manufacturing pressure-sensitive tape. Gaffney recruited three other Ideal executives to join him in starting a tape manufacturing business. The four men remained at Ideal for the two years it took them to plan the new enterprise. During this time, they used their positions at Ideal to travel around the country to gather business ideas, recruit potential customers, and purchase equipment for their business. At no time did they reveal to Chelsea their intention to open a competing business. The new business was incorporated as Action Manufacturing Company (Action).

When executives at Chelsea discovered the existence of the new venture, Gaffney and the others resigned from Chelsea. Chelsea sued them for damages. Who wins? *Chelsea Indus., v. Gaffney*, 449 N.E.2d 320 (Mass. 1983).

Case 9.7 *Indemnification* William G. Young was a director of Pool Builders Supply, Inc. (Pool Builders). Pool Builders experienced financial difficulties and was forced to file for bankruptcy. Eddie Lawson was appointed the receiver for the creditors of the corporation. Lawson believed that Young had mismanaged the corporation. Lawson filed a suit against Young and Pool Builders, alleging that Young had used Pool Builders personally to obtain money, goods, and property from creditors on the credit of the corporation. Lawson's suit also alleged that Young had attempted to convert corporate assets for his own use. Young defended the suit for himself and the corporation. At trial, the judge found insufficient evidence to support Lawson's charges, and the suit was dismissed. Young then sought to have Pool Builders pay the legal fees he had incurred while defending the suit. Can Young recover this money from the corporation? *Lawson v. Young*, 486 N.E.2d 1177 (Ohio Ct. App. 1984).

Case 9.8 *Derivative Shareholder Lawsuit* Four brothers—Monnie, Mechel, Merko, and Sam Dotlich—formed a partnership to run a heavy equipment rental business. One decade later, the company had been incorporated as Dotlich Brothers, Inc. Each brother owned 25 percent of the corporation's stock, and each served on the board of directors. During the course of its operation, the business acquired a 56-acre tract of land in Speedway, Indiana. This land was held in the name of Monnie Dotlich. Each of the brothers was aware of this agreement. The corporation also had purchased six other pieces of property, all of which were held in Monnie's name. Sam Dotlich was not informed that Monnie was the record owner of these other properties. Sam discovered this irregularity and requested that the board of directors take action to remedy the situation. When the board refused to do so, Sam initiated a lawsuit on behalf of the corporation. Can Sam bring this lawsuit? *Dotlich v. Dotlich*, 475 N.E.2d 331 (Ind. Ct. App. 1985).

Case 9.9 *Piercing the Corporate Veil* M.R. Watters was the majority shareholder of several closely held corporations, including Wildhorn Ranch, Inc. (Wildhorn). All of these businesses were run out of Watters's home in Rocky Ford, Colorado. Wildhorn operated a resort called the Wildhorn Ranch Resort in Teller County, Colorado. Although Watters claimed that the ranch was owned by the corporation, the deed for the property listed Watters as the owner. Watters paid little attention to corporate formalities, holding corporate meetings at his house, never taking minutes of those meetings, and paying the debts of one corporation with the assets of another. During August 1986, two guests of Wildhorn Ranch Resort drowned while operating a paddleboat at the ranch. The family of the deceased guests sued for damages. Can Watters be held personally liable? *Geringer v. Wildhorn Ranch, Inc.*, 706 F. Supp. 1442 (D. Colo. 1988).

BUSINESS ETHICS CASES

Case 9.10 *Business Ethics* Alfred S. Johnson, Inc. (Corporation), was incorporated by Alfred S. Johnson, who owned seventy shares of the corporation. Two employees of the corporation, James DeBaun and Walter Stephens, owned twenty and ten shares, respectively. When Johnson died ten years later, his will created a testamentary trust in which his seventy shares were placed. Johnson's will named First Western Bank and Trust Company (Bank) trustee for the trust. Several years later, Bank decided to sell the seventy shares but did not tell anyone associated with Corporation of its decision. An appraisal was obtained that valued the corporation at $326,000 as a going concern.

Three years later, Raymond J. Mattison submitted an offer to purchase the seventy shares for $250,000, payable as $50,000 in securities of companies Mattison owned and the $200,000 balance over a five-year period. Bank obtained a Dun & Bradstreet report that showed several outstanding tax liens against Mattison. Bank accepted Mattison's explanation that they were not his fault. At the time, Mattison owed Bank a judgment for fraud. Bank was also aware that Mattison owed unpaid debts and that several entities in which he was involved were insolvent. Bank did not investigate these matters. If it had, the public records of Los Angeles County would have revealed thirty-eight unsatisfied judgments against Mattison and his entities totaling $330,886, fifty-four pending lawsuits claiming damages of $373,588, and eighteen tax liens aggregating $20,327. Bank agreed to sell the seventy shares to Mattison and accepted the assets of Corporation as security for the repayment of the $200,000 balance. As part of the transaction, Bank required Mattison to agree to have Corporation give its banking business to Bank.

At the time of sale, Corporation was a successful going business with a bright future. It had cash of $76,000 and other liquid assets of over $120,000. Its net worth was about $220,000. Corporation was profitable, and its trend of earnings indicated a pattern of growth. Mattison immediately implemented a systematic scheme to loot Corporation. He (1) diverted $73,000 in corporate cash to himself and a shell company he owned; (2) caused Corporation to assign all its assets, including accounts receivable, to the shell company; (3) diverted all corporate mail to a post office box and extracted incoming checks to Corporation; (4) refused to pay corporate creditors on time or at all; (5) issued payroll checks without sufficient corporate funds; and (6) removed Corporation's books and records. One year later, hopelessly insolvent, Corporation shut down operations and was placed in receivership. At that time, its debts exceeded its assets by over $200,000. DeBaun's and Stephens's shares were worthless. They sued Bank for damages, alleging that Bank, as the majority shareholder of Corporation, had breached its fiduciary duty to the minority shareholders.

Did Bank have knowledge of the dangerous situation in which it placed Corporation? Did Bank, as the controlling shareholder of Corporation, breach its fiduciary duty to the minority shareholders? *DeBaun v. First W. Bank & Trust Co.*, 120 Cal. Rptr. 354 (Cal. Ct. App. 1975).

Case 9.11 ***Business Ethics*** Jon-T Chemicals, Inc. (Chemicals), was an Oklahoma corporation engaged in the fertilizer and chemicals business. John H. Thomas was its majority shareholder and its president and board chairman. Chemicals incorporated Jon-T Farms, Inc. (Farms), as a wholly owned subsidiary, to engage in the farming and land-leasing business. Chemicals invested $10,000 to establish Farms. All the directors and officers of Farms were directors and officers of Chemicals, and Thomas was its president and board chairman. In addition, Farms used officers, computers, and accountants of Chemicals without paying a fee, and Chemicals paid the salary of Farms's only employee. Chemicals made regular informal advances to pay Farms's expenses. These payments reached $7.5 million by January 1975.

Thomas and Farms engaged in a scheme whereby they submitted fraudulent applications for agricultural subsidies from the federal government under the Uplands Cotton Program. As a result of these applications, the Commodity Credit Corporation, a government agency, paid over $2.5 million in subsidies to Thomas and Farms. After discovering the fraud, the federal government obtained criminal convictions against Thomas and Farms. In a separate civil action, the federal government obtained a $4.7 million judgment against Thomas and Farms, finding them jointly and severally liable for the tort of fraud. Farms declared bankruptcy, and Thomas was unable to pay the judgment. Because Thomas and Farms were insolvent, the federal government sued Chemicals to recover the judgment. Was Farms the alter ego of Chemicals, permitting the United States to pierce the corporate veil and recover the judgment from Chemicals? Did Thomas act ethically in this case? *United States v. Jon-T Chemicals, Inc.*, 768 F.2d 686 (5th Cir. 1985).

ENDNOTES

1. *Meinhard v. Salmon*, 164 N.E. 545 (N.Y. 1928).

"To supervise wisely the great corporations is well; but to look backward to the days when business was polite pillage and regard our great business concerns as piratical institutions carrying letters of marque and reprisal is a grave error born in the minds of little men. When these little men legislate they set the brakes going uphill."

—Elbert Hubbard

Notebook, page 16

Corporate Acquisitions and Multinational Corporations

CHAPTER 10

CASE SCENARIO

The law firm at which you work as a paralegal represents Plant Industries, Inc. (Plant). The board of directors of Plant, under the guidance of Robert B. Bregman, the chief executive officer of the corporation, embarked on a course of action that resulted in the sale of several unprofitable subsidiaries. Bregman, without affording shareholders an opportunity to vote on the matter, engaged in a course of action to sell to Plant National (Quebec) Ltd., a subsidiary that constituted Plant's entire Canadian operations. This was a profitable subsidiary that comprised over 50 percent of Plant's assets, sales, and profits.

CHAPTER OBJECTIVES

After studying this chapter, you should be able to:

1. Describe the process of soliciting proxies from shareholders and engaging in proxy contests.
2. Define *shareholder resolution* and identify when a shareholder can include a resolution in proxy materials.
3. Describe the process for approving a merger or share exchange.
4. Define *tender offer* and describe poison pills, greenmail, and other defensive maneuvers to prevent hostile takeover.
5. Examine the use of multinational corporations in conducting international business.

PARALEGAL PERSPECTIVE

Rugina D. Poellnitz, PHP, *has been working as a paralegal for twelve years. She graduated with an associate in paralegal studies from the Center for Advanced Legal Studies, a bachelor in business administration from Louisiana Baptist University, and a postbaccalaureate in government and business from Texas Woman's University. She is currently employed as a senior paralegal of BP America Inc.'s HSSE and Regulatory groups.*

Why do you think it is important for a paralegal to understand the area of corporate acquisition? Comprehensive knowledge of corporate structure and corporate acquisitions is highly recommended for a paralegal seeking to work within a corporation despite its makeup or size.

What are the most important paralegal skills needed in your job? You must have excellent research and writing skills; exceptional organizational and time management skills; knowledge of different types of business organizations/structures; and an understanding of commercial litigation process, review of contracts/agreements, and varied governmental regulations/acts.

What is the academic background required for a paralegal entering your area of practice? The minimum required is a paralegal degree or certificate, with the most common being a paralegal degree or certificate and undergraduate degree.

How is technology involved in your job? Technology is heavily involved, from simple computer processing (creating documents, spreadsheets, and database entry), research via legal proprietary software or Google, to complex (meetings via WebEx and other media to speak to employees in international locations).

What trends do you see in your area of practice that will likely affect your job in the future? Due to increased scrutiny of companies, their shareholders, and employees, U.S. and other countries' governments are prosecuting company officers/employees and levying large fines under Foreign Corrupt Practices Act (U.S.) or similar legislation in other countries. Paralegal skills and experience are invaluable before, during, and after investigations as well as in maintenance of legal ethics and compliance programs.

What do you feel is the biggest issue currently facing the paralegal profession? I feel that the biggest issue facing the paralegal profession is inconsistency in education for paralegals. For instance, some business schools offer six- to nine-month programs for individuals without undergraduate degrees. Graduates from these programs have a difficult time securing substantive legal employment.

What words of advice do you have for a new paralegal entering your area of practice? I highly recommend that new paralegals create short- and long-term career goals, continue to work further in their education, and get involved in paralegal organizations/associations.

INTRODUCTION TO CORPORATE ACQUISITIONS AND MULTINATIONAL CORPORATIONS

During the course of its existence, a corporation may go through certain fundamental changes. A corporation must seek shareholder approval for many changes. This requires the solicitation of votes or proxies from shareholders. Persons who want to take over the management of a corporation often conduct proxy contests to try to win over shareholder votes.

Corporations often engage in acquisitions of other corporations or businesses. This may occur by friendly merger or by hostile tender offer. In defense, a corporation may erect certain barriers or impediments to a hostile takeover.

multinational corporation
A company with operations in two or more countries, generally allowing it to transfer funds and products according to price and demand conditions, subject to risks such as changes in exchange rates or political instability.

Multinational corporations conduct international business around the world. This is usually done through a variety of business arrangements, including branch offices, subsidiary corporations, and such.

This chapter discusses fundamental changes to a corporation, including the solicitation of proxies, mergers, hostile tender offers, and defensive strategies of corporations to prevent hostile takeovers. This chapter also examines the use of multinational corporations in conducting international business.

PROXY SOLICITATION AND PROXY CONTEST

Corporate shareholders have the right to vote on the election of directors, mergers, charter amendments, and the like. They can exercise their power to vote either in person or by proxy [RMBCA Section 7.22]. Voting by proxy is common in large corporations that have thousands of shareholders located across the country and around the world.

A **proxy** is a written document (often called a **proxy card**) that is completed and signed by a shareholder and sent to the corporation. The proxy authorizes another person—the proxy holder—to vote the shares at the shareholders' meeting as directed by the shareholder. The proxy holder is often a director or an officer of the corporation.

proxy
A written document signed by a shareholder that authorizes another person to vote the shareholder's shares. Also called a *proxy card*.

Federal Proxy Rules

Section 14(a) of the Securities Exchange Act of 1934 gives the Securities and Exchange Commission (SEC) the authority to regulate the solicitation of proxies.[1] The federal proxy rules promote full disclosure. In other words, management or any other party soliciting proxies from shareholders must prepare a **proxy statement** that fully describes (1) the matter for which the proxy is being solicited, (2) who is soliciting the proxy, and (3) any other pertinent information.

A copy of the proxy, the proxy statement, and all other solicitation material must be filed with the SEC at least ten days before the materials are sent to the shareholders. If the SEC requires additional disclosures, the solicitation can be held up until these disclosures are made. See Exhibit 10.1

Section 14(a)
A provision of the Securities Exchange Act of 1934 that gives the SEC the authority to regulate the solicitation of proxies.

proxy statement
A document that fully describes (1) the matter for which a proxy is being solicited, (2) who is soliciting the proxy, and (3) any other pertinent information.

Exhibit 10.1 Proxy

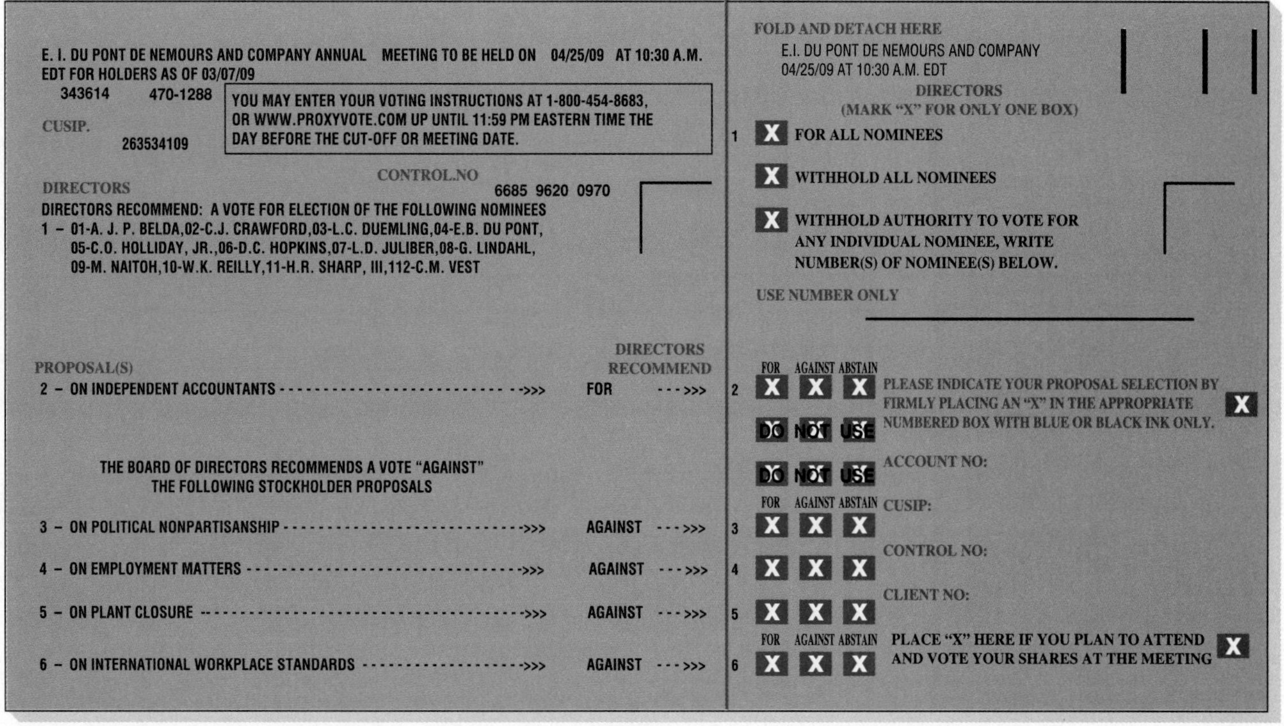

E. I. DU PONT DE NEMOURS AND COMPANY ANNUAL MEETING TO BE HELD ON 04/25/09 AT 10:30 A.M. EDT FOR HOLDERS AS OF 03/07/09

343614 470-1288

YOU MAY ENTER YOUR VOTING INSTRUCTIONS AT 1-800-454-8683, OR WWW.PROXYVOTE.COM UP UNTIL 11:59 PM EASTERN TIME THE DAY BEFORE THE CUT-OFF OR MEETING DATE.

CUSIP. 263534109

CONTROL.NO 6685 9620 0970

DIRECTORS

DIRECTORS RECOMMEND: A VOTE FOR ELECTION OF THE FOLLOWING NOMINEES

1 – 01-A. J. P. BELDA,02-C.J. CRAWFORD,03-L.C. DUEMLING,04-E.B. DU PONT, 05-C.O. HOLLIDAY, JR.,06-D.C. HOPKINS,07-L.D. JULIBER,08-G. LINDAHL, 09-M. NAITOH,10-W.K. REILLY,11-H.R. SHARP, III,112-C.M. VEST

PROPOSAL(S)	DIRECTORS RECOMMEND
2 – ON INDEPENDENT ACCOUNTANTS ------------------->>>	FOR --->>>

THE BOARD OF DIRECTORS RECOMMENDS A VOTE "AGAINST" THE FOLLOWING STOCKHOLDER PROPOSALS

3 – ON POLITICAL NONPARTISANSHIP ------------------->>>	AGAINST --->>>
4 – ON EMPLOYMENT MATTERS ------------------->>>	AGAINST --->>>
5 – ON PLANT CLOSURE ------------------->>>	AGAINST --->>>
6 – ON INTERNATIONAL WORKPLACE STANDARDS ------------------->>>	AGAINST --->>>

FOLD AND DETACH HERE

E.I. DU PONT DE NEMOURS AND COMPANY
04/25/09 AT 10:30 A.M. EDT

DIRECTORS
(MARK "X" FOR ONLY ONE BOX)

1 X FOR ALL NOMINEES

X WITHHOLD ALL NOMINEES

X WITHHOLD AUTHORITY TO VOTE FOR ANY INDIVIDUAL NOMINEE, WRITE NUMBER(S) OF NOMINEE(S) BELOW.

USE NUMBER ONLY

	FOR	AGAINST	ABSTAIN
2	X	X	X
	DO	NOT	USE
	DO	NOT	USE
3	X	X	X
4	X	X	X
5	X	X	X
6	X	X	X

PLEASE INDICATE YOUR PROPOSAL SELECTION BY FIRMLY PLACING AN "X" IN THE APPROPRIATE NUMBERED BOX WITH BLUE OR BLACK INK ONLY. X

ACCOUNT NO:

CUSIP:

CONTROL NO:

CLIENT NO:

PLACE "X" HERE IF YOU PLAN TO ATTEND AND VOTE YOUR SHARES AT THE MEETING X

CONTEMPORARY Environment

SEC PROXY RULES

The Securities and Exchange Commission (SEC), the federal administrative agency empowered to administer federal securities laws, has adopted certain rules that apply to proxy solicitation and proxy contests.

A shareholder who is not seeking proxy voting authority may engage in oral and written communications with any other shareholder without filing proxy materials with the SEC. For example, shareholders can ask each other how the corporation should be run or suggest changes. They have to register with the SEC only if they decide to solicit proxies. Shareholders who own more than $5 million of the company's securities are not covered by this rule. They must still register any written communication to shareholders with the SEC.

SEC rules require companies seeking proxies to "unbundle" the propositions set for shareholder vote so that the shareholders can vote on each separate issue. Previous proxy rules allowed companies to bundle the propositions and present them as one package for a single shareholder vote. This tactic prevented shareholders from considering the merits of individual propositions.

SEC rules require all companies to include performance charts in their annual reports. These charts must compare the company's stock performance to that of a general index of companies, such as the Standard & Poor's 500, and companies in its peer group index (e.g., retailers).

SEC rules mandate that companies provide tables in their annual reports that succinctly summarize executive compensation for the chief executive officer and its most highly compensated executives for the past three years. The tables must disclose salary, stock options, stock appreciation rights, and long-term incentive plans of these executives, including the value of each item.

Law and Ethics Questions

1. What is a proxy? Explain.
2. What is a proxy contest? Why is a proxy contest fought?
3. **Ethics** Do you think that the incumbent management has an advantage in a proxy contest? Why or why not?

Web Exercises

1. **Web** Visit the website of the Securities Exchange Commission (SEC) at www.sec.gov.
2. **Web** Use www.google.com to find an article that discusses a recent proxy contest. Who won?

Antifraud Provision

antifraud provision
Section 14(a) of the Securities Exchange Act of 1934 that prohibits misrepresentations or omissions of a material fact in the proxy materials.

Section 14(a) of the Securities Exchange Act of 1934 is an **antifraud provision** that prohibits material misrepresentations or omissions of a material fact in the proxy materials. Known false statements of facts, reasons, opinions, or beliefs in proxy solicitation materials are actionable. Violations of this rule can result in civil and criminal actions by the SEC and the Justice Department, respectively. The courts have implied a private cause of action under this provision. Thus, shareholders who are injured by a material misrepresentation or omission in proxy materials can sue the wrongdoer and recover damages. The court can also order a new election if a violation is found.

Proxy Contest

Shareholders sometimes oppose the actions taken by the incumbent directors and management. These **insurgent shareholders** may challenge the incumbent management in a **proxy contest**, in which both sides solicit proxies from the other shareholders. The side that receives the greatest number of votes wins the proxy contest. Such contests are usually held with regard to the election of directors. Management must either (1) provide a list of shareholders to the dissenting group or (2) mail the proxy solicitation materials of the challenging group to the shareholders.

insurgent shareholder
Shareholder that opposes the actions taken by the incumbent directors and management.

proxy contest
A contest in which opposing factions of shareholders and managers solicit proxies from other shareholders; the side that receives the greatest number of votes wins the proxy contest.

SHAREHOLDER RESOLUTION

At times, shareholders may wish to submit issues for a vote of other shareholders. The Securities Exchange Act of 1934 and SEC rules permit a shareholder to submit a resolution to be considered by other shareholders if (1) the shareholder has owned at least $2,000 worth of shares of the company's stock or 1 percent of all shares of the company (2) for at least one year. The resolution cannot exceed fifty words. Such **shareholder resolutions** are usually made when the corporation is soliciting proxies from its shareholders.

shareholder resolution
A resolution that a shareholder who meets certain ownership requirements may submit to other shareholders for a vote. Many shareholder resolutions concern social issues.

If management does not oppose a resolution, it may be included in the proxy materials issued by the corporation. Even if management is not in favor of a resolution, a shareholder has a right to have the shareholder resolution included in the corporation's proxy materials if it (1) relates to the corporation's business, (2) concerns a *policy issue* (and not the day-to-day operations of the corporation), and (3) does not concern the payment of dividends. The SEC rules on whether a resolution can be submitted to shareholders.

Examples: Shareholder resolutions have been presented concerning protecting the environment; reducing global warming; preventing the overcutting of the rain forests in Brazil; prohibiting U.S. corporations from purchasing goods manufactured in developing countries under poor working conditions, including the use of forced and child labor; protecting human rights; and engaging in socially responsible conduct.

Most shareholder resolutions have a slim chance of being enacted because large-scale investors usually support management. They can, however, cause a corporation to change the way it does business. For example, to avoid the adverse publicity such issues can create, some corporations voluntarily adopt the changes contained in shareholder resolutions. Others negotiate settlements with the sponsors of resolutions to get the measures off the agenda before the annual shareholders' meetings.

MERGERS AND ACQUISITIONS

Corporations may agree to friendly acquisitions or combinations of one another. This may occur through merger, share exchange, or sale of assets. These types of combinations are discussed in the following paragraphs.

merger
A situation in which one corporation is absorbed into another corporation and ceases to exist.

Merger

A **merger** occurs when one corporation is absorbed into another corporation and ceases to exist. The corporation that continues to exist is called the **surviving corporation**. The other corporation, which ceases to exist, is called the merged corporation [RMBCA Section 11.01]. The surviving corporation gains all the

surviving corporation
A corporation that acquires the assets and liabilities of another corporation by a merger or takeover.

ETHICS SPOTLIGHT

SHAREHOLDER RESOLUTION

The E. I. du Pont de Nemours and Company (DuPont), organized under the laws of the state of Delaware, is one of the largest chemical and consumer products companies in the world. DuPont has manufacturing and production facilities located in many foreign countries. Several of these countries have been criticized because child labor and forced labor are alleged to be used to produce goods in those countries.

At its annual meeting, the International Brotherhood of Teamsters General Fund, owner of shares of DuPont common stock, proposed the following shareholder resolution to the shareholders of DuPont:

Stockholder Proposal on International Workplace Standards
RESOLVED: That the Board of Directors of E. I. du Pont de Nemours and Company (Du Pont) shall adopt, implement and enforce the workplace Code of Conduct (Code) as based on the International Labor Organization's (ILO) Conventions on workplace human rights, which include:

- *No use of child labor.*
- *No discrimination or intimidation in employment.*
- *All workers have the right to form and join unions and to bargain collectively.*
- *No use of forced labor.*

Stockholder's (Teamster's) Statement in support of the proposal: *The Teamsters, in support of its proposal, provided the following statement in Du Pont's annual Proxy Statement submitted to Du Pont shareholders.*

As a global institution, Du Pont and its international operations and sourcing arrangements are exposed to sundry risks. Adoption of this proposal manages the risk of being a party to serious human rights violations in the workplace. Du Pont operates or has business relationships in a number of countries, including China, Indonesia, and Thailand, where the U.S. State Department, Amnesty International, and Human Rights Watch indicate law and public policy do not adequately protect human rights. To wit: Forced labor, illegal child labor, and violence against women.

The success of Du Pont's operations depends on consumer and governmental good will. Brand name is a significant asset. Du Pont benefits from adopting and enforcing the Code ensuring that it isn't associated with human rights violations. This protects Du Pont's brand names and its relationships with customers and the numerous governments under which Du Pont operates and with which it does business.

Position of the Board of Directors in Opposition to the Proposal
In response, Du Pont included the following statement in the Proxy Statement, recommending that Du Pont shareholders vote against the shareholder resolution.

Du Pont is committed to conducting its business affairs with the highest ethical standards, and works diligently to be a respected corporate citizen throughout the world. The company has had in place for many years an Ethics Policy, Mission Statement and Code of Business Conduct addressing many of the issues covered in the standards proposed for adoption. These corporate policies are applicable to all employees in all Du Pont businesses around the world.

The company is supportive of the general intent of the proposal and similar international workplace standards suggested by other organizations for adoption. The company reviews on an ongoing basis codes offered by other organizations, and examines its own policies and practices in light of the provisions of the proposed codes. The company also meets with advocates of codes to explore issues of mutual concern. These efforts will continue. The company therefore believes adoption of the proposed code is unnecessary.

The shareholder resolution for the adoption of international workplace standards was defeated by an overwhelming majority of DuPont shareholders at the annual meeting.

Business Ethics

1. Why do you think the International Brotherhood of Teamsters introduced this shareholder resolution? Do you think the reasons DuPont asserted for recommending that its shareholders vote against the proposal were legitimate? Explain.

rights, privileges, powers, duties, obligations, and liabilities of the merged corporation. Title to property owned by the merged corporation transfers to the surviving corporation, without formality or deeds. The shareholders of the merged corporation receive stock or securities of the surviving corporation or other consideration, as provided in the plan of merger.

Example: Corporation A and Corporation B merge, and it is agreed that Corporation A will absorb Corporation B. Corporation A is the surviving corporation. Corporation B is the merged corporation. The representation of this merger is A + B = A (see **Exhibit 10.2**).

Share Exchange

One corporation can acquire all the shares of another corporation through a **share exchange**. In a share exchange, both corporations retain their separate legal existence. After the exchange, one corporation (the **parent corporation**) owns all the shares of the other corporation (the **subsidiary corporation**) [RMBCA Section 1102]. Such exchanges are often used to create holding company arrangements (e.g., bank or insurance holding companies).

share exchange
A situation in which one corporation acquires all the shares of another corporation and both corporations retain their separate legal existence.

Example: Corporation A wants to acquire Corporation B. Assume that Corporation A offers to exchange its shares for those of Corporation B and that Corporation B's shareholders approve the transaction. After the share exchange, Corporation A owns all the stock of Corporation B. Corporation A is the parent corporation, and Corporation B is the wholly owned subsidiary of Corporation A (see **Exhibit 10.3**).

parent corporation
A corporation owning more than 50 percent of the voting shares of another corporation.

subsidiary corporation
A corporation in which another corporation, the parent, owns at least the majority of the shares and thus has control.

Required Approvals for a Merger or Share Exchange

An ordinary merger or share exchange requires (1) the recommendation of the board of directors of each corporation and (2) an affirmative vote of the majority of shares of each corporation that are entitled to vote [RMBCA Section 11.03]. The articles of incorporation or corporate bylaws can require the approval of a **supramajority**, such as 80 percent of the voting shares.

supramajority
Greater than the majority.

Exhibit 10.2 Merger

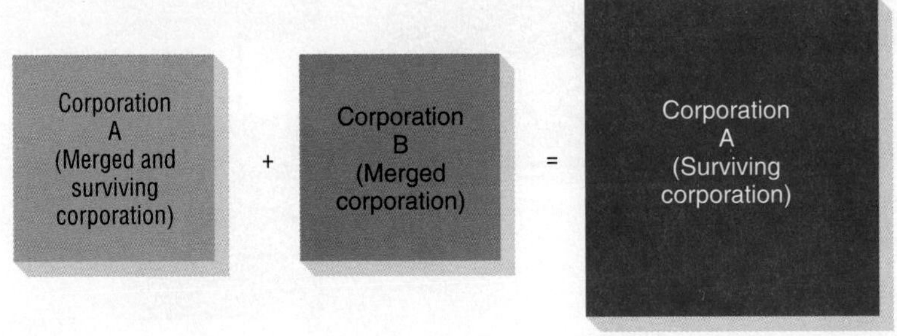

CONTEMPORARY Environment

GOOGLE TAKES OVER YOUTUBE

Sergery Brin and Larry Page, university students, founded Google in 1998 in a garage. They then built the company into a search engine, a giant of the Internet, and an advertising marketer. Chad Hurley and Steve Chen, who had left PayPal, subsequently started YouTube, a popular online video service where people watch and share original videos.

In 2006, Google acquired YouTube in a stock-for-stock transaction. The purchase price was $1.65 billion. YouTube shareholders will receive Google stock in return for their YouTube stock. Google, however, will take advantage of the YouTube brand name and operate YouTube independently. The deal keeps YouTube founders Chad Hurley and Steve Chen as well as YouTube's sixty-seven employees.

At the time of the takeover, YouTube was still unprofitable. But Google sees YouTube as being at the forefront in the online video revolution. Google believes that YouTube's video sharing site will provide marketing opportunities that will increase as viewers and advertisers migrate from television to the Internet. Google believes that the combination of the two firms will continue to build the next-generation platform for serving media worldwide.

The approval of the surviving corporation's shareholders is not required if the merger or share exchange increases the number of voting shares of the surviving corporation by 20 percent or less [RMBCA Section 11.03(g)]. The approved **articles of merger** or **articles of share exchange** must be filed with the secretary of state of the surviving corporation. The state normally issues a *certificate of merger or share exchange* to the surviving corporation after all the formalities are met and the requisite fees are paid [RMBCA Section 11.05]. See **Exhibit 10.4**.

articles of merger
A document that must be filed with the secretary of state of the surviving corporation to effectuate a merger.

articles of share exchange
A document that must be filed with the secretary of state of the surviving corporation to effectuate a share exchange.

Short-Form Merger

If the parent corporation owns 90 percent or more of the outstanding shares of the subsidiary corporation, a **short-form merger** procedure may be followed to merge the two corporations. A short-form merger procedure is simpler than an

short-form merger
A merger between a parent corporation and a subsidiary corporation that does not require the approval of the shareholders of either corporation or the approval of the board of directors of the subsidiary corporation.

Exhibit 10.3 Share Exchange

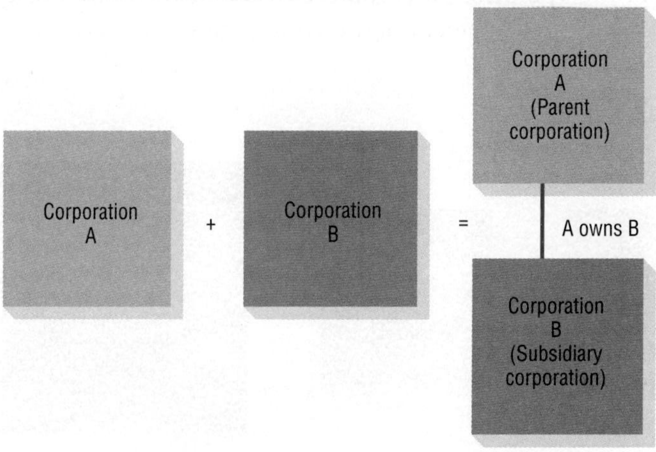

Exhibit 10.4 Articles Of Merger

Print Form

STATE OF SOUTH CAROLINA
SECRETARY OF STATE

ARTICLES OF MERGER
Corporation – Domestic
Filing Fee - $110.00

TYPE OR PRINT CLEARLY IN BLACK INK

Pursuant to S.C. Code of Laws §33-11-105, the undersigned as the surviving corporation in a merger, hereby submits the following information:

1. The name of the surviving corporation is ______________________________

2. Attached hereto and made a part hereof is a copy of the Merger (see S.C. Code of Laws, Title 33, Ch. 11). Duplicate copies of the Plan of Merger **must** be attached in order for this form to be filed.

3. Complete the following information to the extent it is relevant with respect to **each** corporation which is a party to the transaction.

(a) Name of the corporation ______________________________
Complete either (1) or (2), whichever is applicable.

(1) [ ] Shareholder approval of the merger was not required (See S.C. Code of Laws §33-11-103(h)).
(2) [ ] The Plan of Merger was duly approved by shareholders of the corporation as follows:

Voting Group	Number of Outstanding Shares	Number of Votes Entitled to be Cast	Number of Votes Represented at the meeting	Total Number of Votes Cast For AND Against*

***NOTE:** Pursuant to S.C. Code of Laws §33-11-105(a)(3)(ii), the corporation can alternatively state the total number of undisputed votes cast for the Plan Merger separately by each voting group with a statement that the number cast for the plan by each voting group was sufficient for approval by that voting group.

(b) Name of the corporation ______________________________
Complete either (1) or (2), whichever is applicable.

(1) [ ] Shareholder approval of the merger was not required (See S.C. Code of Laws §33-11-103(h)).
(2) [ ] The Plan of Merger was duly approved by shareholders of the corporation as follows:

Voting Group	Number of Outstanding Shares	Number of Votes Entitled to be Cast	Number of Votes Represented at the meeting	Total Number of Votes Cast For AND _ Against*

Exhibit 10.4 *(Continued)*

Name of Corporation ______________________

***NOTE:** Pursuant to S.C. Code of Laws §33-11-105 (a)(3)(ii) the corporation can alternatively state the total number of undisputed votes cast for the Plan of Merger separately by each voting group with a statement that the number cast for the plan by each voting group was sufficient for approval by that voting group.

4. Unless a delayed date is specified, the effective date of this document shall be the date it is accepted for filing by the Secretary of State (See S.C. Code of Laws §33-1-230(b)).
____

Date______________________

____
Name of the Surviving Corporation

____
Signature and Office

____
Type or Print Name and Office

Filing Checklist

- Articles of Merger (filed in duplicate)
- Attach a copy of the Plan of Merger
- $110.00 made payable to the South Carolina Secretary of State
- Self-Addressed, Stamped Return Envelope
- Make sure the proper individual has signed the form (Please see S.C. Code of Laws §33-1-200(f))
  Corporate forms filed with the Secretary of State should be signed by:
  (1) the Chairman of the Board of Directors, president or another of its officers
  (2) if directors have not been selected or the corporation has not been formed, by incorporators or
  (3) if the corporation is in the hands of a receiver, trustee or other court appointed fiduciary, by that fiduciary.
- Return all documents to: South Carolina Secretary of State's Office
  Attn: Corporate Filings
  P.O. Box 11350
  Columbia, SC 29211

Corporation – Domestic – Articles of Merger

Form Revised by South Carolina
Secretary of State, July 2008

Exhibit 10.4 *(Continued)*

Print Form

STATE OF SOUTH CAROLINA
SECRETARY OF STATE

ARTICLES OF SHARE EXCHANGE
Corporation – Domestic
Filing Fee - $110.00

TYPE OR PRINT CLEARLY IN BLACK INK

Pursuant to S.C. Code of Laws §33-11-105, the undersigned as the acquiring corporation in a share exchange, hereby submits the following information:

1. The name of the acquiring corporation is ____

2. Attached hereto and made a part hereof is a copy of the Plan of Share Exchange (see S.C. Code of Laws 33, Chapter 11). Duplicate copies of the Plan of Share Exchange **must** be attached in order for this form to be filed.

3. Complete the following information to the extent it is relevant with respect to **each** corporation which is a party to the transaction.

(a) Name of the corporation ____
Complete either (1) or (2), whichever is applicable.

(1) [ ] Shareholder approval of the share exchange was not required (See S.C. Code of Laws §33-11-103(h)).
(2) [ ] The Plan of Share Exchange was duly approved by shareholders of the corporation as follows:

Voting Group	Number of Outstanding Shares	Number of Votes Entitled to be Cast	Number of Votes Represented at the meeting	Total Number of Votes Cast For AND Against*

***NOTE:** Pursuant to S.C. Code of Laws §33-11-105(a)(3)(ii), the corporation can alternatively state the total number of undisputed votes cast for the Plan of Share Exchange separately by each voting group with a statement that the number cast for the plan by each voting group was sufficient for approval by that voting group.

(b) Name of the corporation ____
Complete either (1) or (2), whichever is applicable.

(1) [ ] Shareholder approval of the share exchange was not required (See S.C. Code of Laws §33-11-103(h)).
(2) [ ] The Plan of Share Exchange was duly approved by shareholders of the corporation as follows:

Voting Group	Number of Outstanding Shares	Number of Votes Entitled to be Cast	Number of Votes Represented at the meeting	Total Number of Votes Cast For AND Against*

Exhibit 10.4 *(Continued)*

Name of Corporation ______________________________

***NOTE:** Pursuant to S.C. Code of Laws §33-11-105 (a)(3)(ii) of the 1976 South Carolina Code of Laws, as amended, the corporation can alternatively state the total number of undisputed votes cast for the Plan of Share Exchange separately by each voting group with a statement that the number cast for the plan by each voting group was sufficient for approval by that voting group.

4. Unless a delayed date is specified, the effective date of this document shall be the date it is accepted for filing by the Secretary of State (See S.C. Code of Laws §33-1-230(b)).
____

Date______________________

____
Name of the Acquiring Corporation

____
Signature and Office

____
Type or Print Name and Office

Filing Checklist

- Articles of Share Exchange (filed in duplicate)
- Attach a copy of the Plan of Share Exchange
- $110.00 made payable to the South Carolina Secretary of State
- Self-Addressed, Stamped Return Envelope
- Make sure the proper individual has signed the form (Please see S.C. Code of Laws §33-1-200(f))
  Corporate forms filed with the Secretary of State should be signed by:
  (1) the Chairman of the Board of Directors, president or another of its officers
  (2) if directors have not been selected or the corporation has not been formed, by incorporators or
  (3) if the corporation is in the hands of a receiver, trustee or other court appointed fiduciary, by that fiduciary.
- Return all documents to: South Carolina Secretary of State's Office
  Attn: Corporate Filings
  P.O. Box 11350
  Columbia, SC 29211

ordinary merger because neither the approval of the shareholders of either corporation nor the approval of the board of directors of the subsidiary corporation is needed. All that is required is the approval of the board of directors of the parent corporation [RMBCA Section 11.04].

Sale or Lease of Assets

A corporation may sell, lease, or otherwise dispose of all or substantially all of its property in other than the usual and regular course of business. Such a **sale or lease of assets** requires (1) the recommendation of the board of directors and (2) an affirmative vote of the majority of the shares of the selling or leasing corporation that are entitled to vote (unless greater vote is required) [RMBCA Section 12.02]. This rule prevents the board of directors from selling all or most of the assets of the corporation without shareholder approval.

sale or lease of assets
A contract in which the seller, in consideration of the payment or promise of payment of a certain price by the buyer, transfers title and possession of the thing sold to the buyer.

Dissenting Shareholder Appraisal Rights

Specific shareholders sometimes object to a proposed ordinary or short-form merger, share exchange, or sale or lease of all or substantially all of the property of a corporation, even though the transaction received the required approvals. Objecting shareholders are provided a statutory right to dissent and obtain payment of the fair value of their shares [RMBCA Section 13.02]. This is referred to as a **dissenting shareholder appraisal right**, or an **appraisal right**. Shareholders have no other recourse unless the transaction is unlawful or fraudulent.

dissenting shareholder appraisal rights
The rights of shareholders who object to a proposed merger, share exchange, or sale or lease of all or substantially all of the property of a corporation to have their shares valued by the court and receive cash payment of this value from the corporation. Also called *appraisal rights*.

A corporation must notify shareholders of the existence of their appraisal rights before a transaction can be voted on [RMBCA Section 13.20]. To obtain appraisal rights, dissenting shareholders must (1) deliver written notice of their intent to demand payment of their shares to the corporation before the vote is taken and (2) not vote their shares in favor of the proposed action [RMBCA Section 13.23]. Shareholders must deposit their share certificates with the corporation [RMBCA Section 13.23]. Shareholders who fail to comply with these statutory procedures lose their appraisal rights.

As soon as the proposed action is taken, the corporation must pay each dissenting shareholder the amount the corporation estimates to be the fair value of their shares, plus accrued interest [RMBCA Section 13.25]. If the dissenter is dissatisfied, the corporation must petition the court to determine the fair value of the shares [RMBCA Section 13.30].

After a hearing, the court will issue an order declaring the fair value of the shares. Appraisers may be appointed to help determine this value. Court costs and appraisal fees are usually paid by the corporation. However, the court can assess these costs against the dissenters if they acted arbitrarily, vexatiously, or in bad faith [RMBCA Section 13.31].

TENDER OFFER

Recall that a merger, a share exchange, and a sale of assets all require the approval of the board of directors of the corporation whose assets or shares are to be acquired. If the board of directors of the target corporation does not agree to a merger or an acquisition, the acquiring corporation—the **tender offeror**—can make a **tender offer** for the shares directly to the shareholders of the **target corporation**. The shareholders each make an individual decision about whether to sell their shares to the tender offeror (see **Exhibit 10.5**). Such offers are often referred to as **hostile tender offers**.

tender offeror
The party that makes a tender offer.

tender offer
An offer that an acquirer makes directly to a target corporation's shareholders in an effort to acquire the target corporation.

target corporation
The corporation that is proposed to be acquired in a tender offer situation.

hostile tender offer
An offer to purchase shares made by a corporation desiring to merge with or acquire a target corporation directly to the shareholders of a target corporation.

Exhibit 10.5 Tender Offer

What passes in the world for talent or dexterity or enterprise is often only a want of moral principle.
William Hazlitt

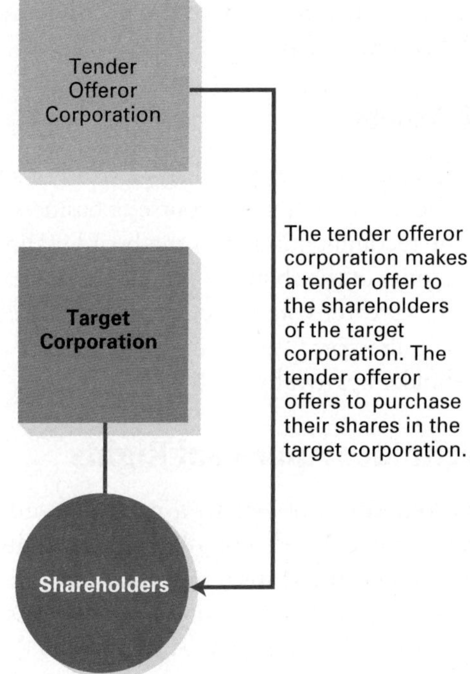

The tender offeror's board of directors must approve the offer, although the shareholders do not have to approve. The offer can be made for all or a portion of the shares of the target corporation. In a tender offer, the tendering corporation and the target corporation retain their separate legal status. However, a successful tender offer is sometimes followed by a merger of the two corporations.

Williams Act

Prior to 1968, tender offers were not federally regulated. However, securities that were issued in conjunction with such offers had to be registered with the SEC or qualify for an exemption from registration. Tender offers made with cash were not subject to any federal disclosure requirements. In 1968, Congress enacted the **Williams Act** as an amendment to the Securities Exchange Act of 1934.[2] This act specifically regulates all tender offers, whether they are made with securities, cash, or other consideration, and it establishes certain disclosure requirements and antifraud provisions.

Williams Act
An amendment to the Securities Exchange Act of 1934 made in 1968 that specifically regulates tender offers.

Tender Offer Rules

The Williams Act does not require a tender offeror to notify either the management of the target company or the SEC until the offer is made.[3] Detailed information regarding the terms, conditions, and other information concerning the tender offer must be disclosed at that time. Tender offers are governed by the following rules:

- The offer cannot be closed before twenty business days after the commencement of the tender offer.

- The offer must be extended for ten business days if the tender offeror increases the number of shares it will take or the price it will pay for the shares.
- The **fair price rule** stipulates that any increase in price paid for shares tendered must be offered to all shareholders, even those who have previously tendered their shares.
- The ***pro rata* rule** holds that the shares must be purchased on a *pro rata* basis if too many shares are tendered.

fair price rule
A rule that says any increase in price paid for shares tendered must be offered to all shareholders, even those who have previously tendered their shares.

***pro rata* rule**
A rule that says shares must be purchased on a *pro rata* basis if too many shares are tendered.

A shareholder who tenders his or her shares has the absolute right to withdraw them at any time prior to the closing of the tender offer. The dissenting shareholder appraisal rights are not available. The SEC's tender offer rules do not apply to tender offers that result in ownership of 5 percent or less of the outstanding shares of a company. These are often called mini-tender offers.

Antifraud Provision

Section 14(e) of the Williams Act prohibits fraudulent, deceptive, and manipulative practices in connection with a tender offer.[4] Violations of this section may result in the SEC bringing civil charges or the Justice Department bringing criminal charges. The courts have implied a private civil cause of action under Section 14(e). Therefore, a shareholder who has been injured by a violation of Section 14(e) can sue the wrongdoer for damages.

Section 14(e)
A provision of the Williams Act that prohibits fraudulent, deceptive, and manipulative practices in connection with a tender offer.

CONTEMPORARY Environment

LEVERAGED BUYOUTS

Many tender offerors do not have the hundreds of millions or billions of dollars necessary to purchase the stock from the shareholders of the target corporation. Instead, the tender offeror relies on the fact that the money can be raised from creditors. Many tender offers are not possible without such loans. Because of the use of borrowed money, these acquisitions are called, leveraged buyouts (LBOs).

A typical LBO works as follows. The tender offeror identifies a potential target and then contacts a large commercial bank and an investment banker. The commercial bank, for a large fee, agrees to supply some of the funds necessary to make the initial acquisition. The bank will be paid off at a later date, after the acquisition is successful.

Most of the rest of the purchase price comes from money raised by the investment banker by selling junk bonds of the acquiring firm to investors. Junk bonds are nothing more than risky bonds that pay a higher rate of interest than normal corporate bonds. Generally, the buyers are banks, pension funds, investment pools, and wealthy individuals. The investment banker is paid a huge fee by the raider for raising this money.

With this borrowed money in hand, the raider commences its hostile tender offer for the shares of the target corporation.

After the tender offer is completed, the tender offeror usually merges with the target corporation. The resulting entity is a highly leveraged corporation. The tender offeror usually sells off some of the assets to pay the bank loans, fees, and other expenses of the takeover.

Fighting a Tender Offer

crown jewel
A valuable asset of a target corporation that the tender offeror particularly wants to acquire in a tender offer.

poison pill
A corporation's defense against an unwanted takeover bid whereby shareholders are granted the right to acquire equity or debt securities at a favorable price to increase the bidder's acquisition costs.

white knight merger
A merger with a friendly party–that is, a party that promises to leave the target corporation and/or its management intact.

Pac-Man tender offer
Occurs when a corporation that is the target of a tender offer makes a *reverse tender offer* for the stock of the tender offeror.

employee stock ownership plan (ESOP) (employee benefit plan)
A type of profit-sharing plan that invests primarily in the employer's stock.

flip-over rights plan
These plans provide that existing shareholders of the target corporation may convert their shares for a greater number of the shares of an acquiring corporation.

flip-in rights plan
These plans provide that existing shareholders of the target corporation may convert their shares for a greater number of the debt securities of an acquiring corporation.

greenmail
The purchase by a target corporation of its stock from an actual or perceived tender offeror at a premium.

standstill agreement
Any agreement to refrain from taking further action; esp., an agreement by which a party agrees to refrain from further attempts to take over a corporation (as by making no tender offer) for a specified period or by which financial institutions agree not to call bonds or loans when due.

The incumbent management of the target of a hostile tender offer may not want the corporation taken over by the tender offeror. Therefore, it may engage in various activities to impede and defeat the tender offer. Incumbent management may use some of the following strategies and tactics in defending against hostile tender offers:

- **Persuasion of shareholders.** Media campaigns are often organized to convince shareholders that the tender offer is not in their best interests.
- **Delaying lawsuits.** Lawsuits may be filed, alleging that the tender offer violates securities laws, antitrust laws, or other laws. The time gained by this tactic gives management the opportunity to erect or implement other defensive maneuvers.
- **Selling a crown jewel.** Assets such as profitable divisions or real estate that are particularly attractive to outside interests—**crown jewels**—may be sold. This tactic makes the target corporation less attractive to the tender offeror.
- **Adopting a poison pill. Poison pills** are defensive strategies that are built into the target corporation's articles of incorporation, corporate bylaws, or contracts and leases. For example, contracts and leases may provide that they will expire if the ownership of the corporation changes hands. These tactics make the target corporation more expensive to the tender offeror.
- **White knight merger. White knight mergers** are mergers with friendly parties—that is, parties that promise to leave the target corporation and/or its management intact.
- **Pac-Man tender offer.** With a **Pac-Man (or reverse) tender offer**, the target corporation makes a tender offer on the tender offeror. Thus, the target corporation tries to purchase the tender offeror.
- **Issuing additional stock.** Placing additional stock on the market increases the number of outstanding shares that the tender offeror must purchase in order to gain control of the target corporation.
- **Creating an employee stock ownership plan (ESOP).** A company may create an **employee stock ownership plan (ESOP)** and place a certain percentage of the corporation's securities (e.g., 15 percent) in it. The ESOP is then expected to vote the shares it owns against the potential acquirer in a proxy contest or tender offer because the beneficiaries (i.e., the employees) have a vested interest in keeping the company intact.
- **Flip-over and flip-in rights plans.** These plans provide that existing shareholders of the target corporation may convert their shares for a greater number (e.g., twice the value) of shares of the acquiring corporation (**flip-over rights plan**) or debt securities of the target company (**flip-in rights plan**). Rights plans are triggered if the acquiring firm acquires a certain percentage (e.g., 20 percent) of the shares of the target corporation. They make it more expensive for the acquiring firm to take over the target corporation.
- **Greenmail and standstill agreements.** Most tender offerors purchase a block of stock in the target corporation before making an offer. Occasionally, the tender offeror will agree to give up its tender offer and agree not to purchase any further shares if the target corporation agrees to buy back the stock at a premium over fair market value. This payment is called **greenmail**. The agreement of the tender offeror to abandon its tender offer and not purchase any additional stock is called a **standstill agreement**.

There are many other strategies and tactics that target companies initiate and implement in defending against a tender offer.

CASE 10.1 TENDER OFFER

Paramount Communications Inc. v. QVC Network Inc., 637 A.2d 34 (Del. 1994).

Facts

In September 1993, Viacom, Inc. (Viacom), and Paramount Communications, Inc. (Paramount), announced a friendly merger agreement. Basically, Viacom was taking over Paramount. Viacom controlled national cable networks, including Showtime and The Movie Channel. Paramount's holdings included Paramount Pictures, the Simon & Schuster publishing house, Madison Square Garden, the New York Knicks basketball team, and the New York Rangers hockey team. Both sides touted the synergism of the marriage of these two companies into a media colossus.

When your ship comes in, make sure you are willing to unload it.
Robert Anthony

Five days later, QVC Network, Inc. (QVC), a rival cable operator, made a $90 per share hostile bid for Paramount that topped Viacom's merger offer. Paramount's board of directors, which did not want Paramount to be taken over by QVC, adopted the following antitakeover strategies:

1. A no-shop provision whereby the Paramount board guaranteed Viacom that it would not investigate QVC's offer or meet with QVC.
2. A lockup option that granted Viacom (but not QVC) the right to buy 23.7 million shares of Paramount at $69.14 each if a bidder other than Viacom bought Paramount.
3. An agreement to drop certain poison pill defenses as to Viacom but not as to QVC. (Thus, Viacom could pursue its acquisition of Paramount, but QVC could not.)

QVC sued Paramount in Delaware chancery court, alleging that these tactics violated the fiduciary duty of the Paramount board of directors to the corporation and its shareholders. The Delaware chancery court agreed with QVC that Paramount's defensive strategies were unlawful. Paramount appealed.

Issue

Do the defensive tactics adopted by Paramount's board of directors violate their fiduciary duties?

Court's Reasoning

The Delaware Supreme Court ruled that the "no-shop" provision was unlawful, stating that Paramount directors "had a duty to continue their search for the best value available to shareholders." The court invalidated the less than fair market value "lockup option" stock purchase plan as being an illegal transfer of corporate wealth to Viacom at the expense of Paramount shareholders.

The Delaware Supreme Court held that the poison pills Paramount had erected must be dismantled for QVC (and any other bidder) as they had been for Viacom. The court ordered that Paramount be put on the block and auctioned to the highest bidder.

Decision

The Delaware Supreme Court invalidated Paramount's no-shop provision and lockup option. The court held that once a Delaware corporation has put itself "in play," it must remove all poison pills as to all possible bidders and put itself up for auction to be purchased by the highest bidder.

Note: In February 1994, after escalating bids from both Viacom and QVC, the five-month saga ended when Viacom won the right to buy Paramount with a $10-billion-plus bid.

Case Questions

1. **Critical Legal Thinking** Can the management of a target company fight a tender offer? Explain.
2. **Business Ethics** Did the board of directors of Paramount act in their shareholders' best interests?
3. **Contemporary Business** Are many corporations safe from being taken over by a tender offer? Explain.

Business Judgment Rule

The members of the board of directors of a corporation owe a fiduciary duty to the corporation and its shareholders. This duty, which requires the board to act carefully and honestly, is truly tested when a tender offer is made for the stock of the company. That is because shareholders and others then ask whether the board's initiation and implementation of defensive measures were taken in the best interests of the shareholders or to protect the board's own interests and jobs.

business judgment rule
A rule that protects the decisions of a board of directors that acts on an informed basis, in good faith, and in the honest belief that the action taken was in the best interests of the corporation and its shareholders.

The legality of defensive strategies is examined using the **business judgment rule**. This rule protects the decisions of a board of directors that acts on an informed basis, in good faith, and in the honest belief that an action taken was in the best interests of the corporation and its shareholders.[5] In the context of a tender offer, the defensive measures chosen by the board must be reasonable in relation to the threat posed.[6]

ETHICS SPOTLIGHT

"JUST SAY NO" DEFENSE

"The corporation law does not operate on the theory that directors are obligated to follow the wishes of a majority of shares. In fact, directors, not shareholders, are charged with the duty to manage the firm."

–Judge Horsey

Time, Inc. (Time), was a publishing company that published *People*, *Money*, *Sports Illustrated*, and other magazines and newspapers; it also owned cable television and pay television channels. Warner Communications, Inc. (Warner), was a communications company that produced and sold movies, television programs, and records, and it also owns cable stations. After years of negotiations, Time and Warner agreed to a merger. Based on the agreed-upon ratio of exchange, Time shareholders were to receive $120 in stock of the new TimeWarner for each share of Time stock they owned. The shareholders' meetings to vote on the merger were set.

Paramount Communications, Inc. (Paramount), was a film production and distribution company. For years, it had been looking for an acquisition in the publishing and communications industry. Two weeks before the Time shareholders were to vote on the planned merger with Warner, Paramount announced a hostile tender offer for Time's shares at $175 per share.

Time, which was obviously going to lose the shareholder vote, canceled the proposed merger with Warner and made a friendly tender offer to acquire 50 percent of Warner's stock for $70 per share. This acquisition would make Time too big for Paramount to take over. In addition, the vote of Time shareholders would not be required. Time had other defensive maneuvers in place as well.

Paramount sued Time, alleging that the refusal of Time's management to dismantle the poison pills and put Time on the block violated their fiduciary duty. In defense, Time argued that the merger of Time and Warner was in the best interests of Time shareholders over the long run and that the long-term benefits of the combination of Time and Warner and their cultures would create synergism that would pay off in the future; Paramount's tender offer offered only one-time short-term profits.

The Delaware court applied the business judgment rule and sided with Time. The court held that the projected long-term benefits to Time shareholders justified Time management's refusal to dismantle the poison pills. The court stated: "The corporation law does not operate on the theory that directors are obligated to follow the wishes of a majority of shares. In fact, directors, not shareholders, are charged with the duty to manage the firm." Thus, incumbent management of a target corporation can "just say no" to a tender offer, as long as it can show that it is acting in the long-term interests of the shareholders. *Paramount Communications, Inc. v. Time, Inc.*, 571 A.2d 1140, **Web** 1989 Del. Lexis 917 (Supreme Court of Delaware)

Law and Ethics Questions

1. What does the "just say no" defense upheld by the Supreme Court of Delaware provide? Explain.
2. **Ethics** Is it ethical for a board of directors of a corporation to go against the wishes of its shareholders?

Web Exercises

1. **Web** Search the web to find the complete opinion of this case.
2. **Web** Visit the website of the Supreme Court of Delaware, at http://courts.delaware.gov/Courts/SupremeCourt.
3. **Web** Visit the website of TimeWarner, at www.timewarner.com.
4. **Web** Visit the website of Paramount Pictures, at www.paramount.com.
5. **Web** Use www.google.com to find an article that discusses a tender offer. Read it.

STATE ANTITAKEOVER STATUTES

Many states have enacted **antitakeover statutes** that are aimed at protecting from hostile takeovers corporations that are either incorporated in or do business within the state. Many of these state statutes have been challenged as being unconstitutional because they violate the Williams Act and the Commerce Clause and the Supremacy Clause of the U.S. Constitution.

antitakeover statutes
Statutes enacted by a state legislature that protect against the hostile takeover of corporations incorporated in or doing business in the state.

In the following case, the U.S. Supreme Court held that a state antitakeover statute was constitutional.

CASE 10.2 ANTITAKEOVER STATUTE

CTS, Corp. v. Dynamics Corp. of Am., 481 U.S. 69 (1987).

"The desire of the Indiana legislature to protect shareholders of Indiana corporations from this type of coercive offer does not conflict with the Williams Act. Rather, it furthers the federal policy of investor protection."

—Justice Powell

Facts

Indiana enacted the Control Share Acquisitions Chapter. This act covers corporations that (1) are incorporated in Indiana and have at least one hundred shareholders, (2) have their primary place of business or substantial assets in Indiana, and (3) have either 10 percent of their shareholders in Indiana or 10 percent of their shares owned by Indiana residents. The act provides that if an entity acquires 20 percent or more of the voting shares of a covered corporation, the acquirer loses voting rights to these shares unless a majority of the disinterested shareholders of the acquired corporation vote to restore such voting rights. The acquirer can request that such vote be held within fifty days after its acquisition. If the shareholders do not restore the voting rights, the target corporation may redeem the shares from the acquirer at fair market value, but it is not required to do so.

Dynamics Corporation of America (Dynamics), a Delaware corporation, announced a tender offer for one million shares of CTS Corporation, an Indiana corporation covered by the act. The purchase of these shares would have brought Dynamics's voting interest in CTS to 27.5 percent. Dynamics sued in federal court, alleging that Indiana's Control Share Acquisitions Chapter was unconstitutional. The U.S. District Court held for Dynamics. The U.S. Court of Appeals affirmed. CTS appealed.

> The usual trade and commerce is cheating all round by consent.
>
> Thomas Fuller
> *Gnomologia (1732)*

Issue

Does the Indiana Control Share Acquisitions Chapter conflict with the Williams Act or violate the Commerce Clause of the U.S. Constitution by unduly burdening interstate commerce?

Language of the U.S. Supreme Court

It is entirely possible for entities to comply with both the Williams and the Indiana acts. The statute now before the court protects the independent shareholder against the contending parties. Thus, the Indiana act furthers a basic purpose of the Williams Act, placing investors on an equal footing with the takeover bidder. The Indiana act operates on the assumption that independent shareholders faced with tender offers often are at a disadvantage. By allowing such shareholders to vote as a group, the act protects them from the coercive aspects of some tender offers. Under the Indiana act, the shareholders as a group could reject the offer although individual shareholders might be inclined to accept it. The desire of the Indiana legislature to protect shareholders of Indiana corporations from this type of coercive offer does not conflict with the Williams Act. Rather, it furthers the federal policy of investor protection.

Decision

The U.S. Supreme Court held that the Indiana Control Share Acquisitions Chapter neither conflicts with the Williams Act nor violates the Commerce Clause of the U.S. Constitution. The U.S. Supreme Court reversed the decision of the U.S. Court of Appeals.

Case Questions

1. **Critical Legal Thinking** What is a state antitakeover statute? Why would a state adopt an antitakeover statute? Explain.
2. **Business Ethics** Is it ethical for a target corporation's management to assert a state antitakeover statute?
3. **Contemporary Business** What are the economic effects of a state antitakeover statute? Whom do you think these statutes actually protect?

MULTINATIONAL CORPORATIONS

Many of the largest corporations in the world are *multinational corporations*—that is, corporations that operate in many countries. These corporations are also called **transnational corporations**. Some multinational corporations operate across borders by using branch offices, while others use subsidiary corporations.

transnational corporation
A company with operations in two or more countries, generally allowing it to transfer funds and products according to price and demand conditions, subject to risks such as changes in exchange rates or political instability.

Multinational corporations also include corporations that do business in other countries through a variety of means. This would include the use of agents, business alliances, strategic partnerships, franchising, and other arrangements.

INTERNATIONAL LAW

International Branch Office

A corporation can conduct business in another country by using a **branch office**. A branch office is not a separate legal entity but merely an office of the corporation. As such, the corporation is liable for the contracts of the branch office and is also liable for the torts committed by personnel of the branch office. There is no liability shield between the corporation and the branch office.

branch office
An offshoot, lateral extension, or division of an institution.

INTERNATIONAL LAW

International Subsidiary Corporation

A corporation can conduct business in another country by using a subsidiary corporation. The *subsidiary corporation* is organized under the laws of the foreign country. The *parent corporation* usually owns all or the majority of the subsidiary corporation. A subsidiary corporation is a separate legal entity. Therefore, the parent corporation is not liable for the contracts of or torts committed by the subsidiary corporation. There is a liability shield between the parent corporation and the subsidiary corporation.

INTERNATIONAL LAW

Exon-Florio law
Mandates the president of the United States to suspend, prohibit, or dismantle the acquisition of U.S. businesses by foreign investors if there is credible evidence that the foreign investor might take action that threatens to impair the "national security."

The Exon-Florio Law

The **Exon-Florio law** of 1988, as amended, mandates the president of the United States to suspend, prohibit, or dismantle the acquisition of U.S. businesses by foreign investors if there is credible evidence that the foreign investor might take action that threatens to impair the "national security" [50 U.S.C. 2170].

The act applies to mergers, acquisitions, takeovers, stock purchases, asset purchases, joint ventures, and proxy contests that would result in foreign control of U.S. businesses engaged in interstate commerce in the United States. The U.S. business could be a corporation, a partnership, a sole proprietorship, or another business. The size of the U.S. operation is irrelevant.

Exon-Florio and the regulations adopted thereunder do not define the term *national security*. The Treasury Department has interpreted the term broadly to include not only defense contractors but also technology and other businesses. The term *control* includes any investment exceeding 10 percent ownership in a U.S. business by a foreign investor.

When a foreign investor proposes to acquire an interest in a U.S. business, it may voluntarily notify the U.S. government of its intention. If the president of the United States finds a threat to the national security, the acquisition may be prohibited. If the foreign investor does not notify the U.S. government and completes the acquisition, it remains indefinitely subject to divestment if the president subsequently determines that the acquisition threatens the national security. The president's decision is not subject to judicial review.

CHAPTER REVIEW

PROXY SOLICITATION AND PROXY CONTEST, p. 285

Solicitation of Proxies

1. ***Proxy.*** Shareholders can exercise their rights to vote on the election of directors, mergers, charter amendments, and the like either in person or by *proxy*.
2. ***Proxy card.*** A proxy card is a written document signed by a shareholder that authorizes another person to vote the shareholder's shares.

Federal Proxy Rules

Section 14(a). This provision of the Securities Exchange Act of 1934 authorizes the *Securities and Exchange Commission (SEC)* to regulate the solicitation of proxies.

1. ***Solicitation of proxies.*** This occurs when management or others seek to obtain proxies from a corporation's shareholders.
2. ***Proxy statement.*** A proxy statement is a written document that must be given to shareholders by management and others who are soliciting shareholder proxies. The statement must fully describe (1) the matter for which the proxy is being solicited, (2) who is soliciting the proxy, and (3) any other pertinent information.
3. ***Filing with the SEC.*** Proxy statements must be filed with the SEC at least ten days before the materials are sent to shareholders.

Antifraud Provision

Section 14(a) of the 1934 Securities Exchange act prohibits misrepresentations or omissions of a material fact in proxy materials. The SEC, the U.S. Justice Department, shareholders, and others may sue the wrongdoer.

Proxy Contest

Proxy contests occur when opposing factions of shareholders and managers solicit proxies from other shareholders; the side that receives the greatest number of votes wins the proxy contest.

1. ***Opposing groups:***
   a. ***Incumbent group.*** This is the management-sponsored slate of proposed directors.
   b. ***Insurgent group.*** This is the slate of proposed directors sponsored by the group that is challenging the incumbent group.
2. ***Reimbursement of expenses.*** In a proxy contest that involves a *policy issue*, the corporation pays the incumbent management's expenses, whether they win or lose the proxy contest. If the insurgent group wins the proxy contest, the corporation must reimburse its expenses, too. If the proxy contest concerned a *personal matter*, neither side may recover its expenses from the corporation.

SHAREHOLDER RESOLUTION, p. 287

Shareholder Resolution

These resolutions are submitted by a shareholder or group of shareholders to be considered and voted by the corporation's shareholders. Most shareholder resolutions concern social issues (e.g., protection of the environment, discontinuation of the manufacture and sale of dangerous products).

1. ***Inclusion in proxy materials.*** If management does not oppose the proposal, it may be included in the proxy materials issued by the corporation. If management opposes the shareholder resolution, the SEC rules on whether the proposal must be submitted to the shareholders in the corporation's proxy materials.
2. ***Requirements.*** To be included in the corporation's proxy materials, the shareholder resolution must (1) relate to the corporation's business, (2) concern policy issues (and not the day-to-day operations of the corporation), and (3) not concern the payment of dividends.

MERGERS AND ACQUISITIONS, p. 287

Mergers and Acquisitions

Mergers, consolidations, and share exchanges are *friendly* combinations of corporations.

1. ***Merger.*** A merger occurs when one corporation is absorbed into another corporation and ceases to exist. The corporation that continues to exist after a merger is called the *surviving corporation*. The corporation that is absorbed in the merger and ceases to exist as a separate entity is called the *merged corporation*.
2. ***Consolidation.*** A consolidation occurs when two or more corporations combine to form an entirely new corporation. The new corporation is called the *consolidated corporation*.

3. ***Share exchange.*** A share exchange occurs when one corporation acquires all the shares of another corporation while both corporations retain their separate legal existence. The corporation that owns the shares of the other corporation is called the *parent corporation*. The corporation that is owned by the other corporation is called the *subsidiary corporation*.

Required Approvals for a Merger or Share Exchange

1. ***Required approvals.*** An ordinary merger or share exchange requires (1) the recommendation of the board of directors of each corporation and (2) an affirmative vote of the majority of shares of each corporation that is entitled to vote (unless a greater vote is required).
2. ***No shareholder vote required.*** The approval of the surviving corporation's shareholders is not required if the merger or share exchange increases the number of voting shares of the surviving corporation by 20 percent or less.
3. ***Articles of merger or share exchange.*** This document must be filed with the secretary of state when the merger or share exchange is completed.

Short-Form Merger

A short-form merger is a merger between a *parent corporation* and a *subsidiary corporation* where the parent corporation owns 90 percent or more of the subsidiary corporation.

Required approval.

Only the approval of the board of directors of the parent corporation is required to effectuate a short-form merger. The votes of the shareholders of either corporation and the board of directors of the subsidiary corporation are not required.

Sale or Lease of Assets

1. ***Sale or lease of assets not in the usual and regular course of business.*** This involves the sale, lease, or disposition by a corporation of all or substantially all its assets not in the usual and regular course of business.
2. ***Required approval.*** Such a sale requires (1) the recommendation of the board of directors and (2) an affirmative vote of the majority of the shares of the selling or leasing corporation that is entitled to vote (unless a greater vote is required).

Dissenting Shareholder Appraisal Rights

Shareholders who object to a proposed merger, share exchange, or sale or lease of all or substantially all the property of a corporation have a statutory right to have their shares valued by the court and receive cash payment of this value from the corporation.

1. ***Procedures.*** The corporation must notify shareholders of their appraisal rights. To obtain appraisal rights, the shareholder must (1) deliver written notice to the corporation of their intent to demand payment of their shares before the vote is taken and (2) not vote their shares in favor of the proposed action.
2. ***Fair value.*** If the shareholder does not accept the value offered by the corporation, the court will determine the *fair value* of the shares. The court may hire appraisers to assist in making this determination. Costs of this proceeding are usually borne by the corporation.

TENDER OFFER, p. 295

Tender Offer

A tender offer is an offer that an acquirer makes directly to a *target corporation's shareholders* in an effort to acquire the target corporation or control of the target corporation.

1. ***Tender offeror.*** The tender offeror is the party that makes a tender offer.
2. ***Target corporation.*** The target corporation is the corporation that is proposed to be acquired in a tender offer situation.

Williams Act

This federal statute regulates all tender offers. The Securities and Exchange Commission (SEC) is empowered to administer the Williams Act.

Tender Offer Rules

1. ***Notification.*** The tender offeror does not have to notify the SEC or the target corporation's management until the tender offer is made.
2. ***Completion.*** The tender offer cannot be closed before twenty business days after the commencement of the offer.
3. ***Extension.*** The offer must be extended for ten business days if the tender offeror increases the number of shares it will take or the price it will pay for the shares.
4. ***Fair price rule.*** This rule stipulates that any increase in price paid for shares tendered must be offered to all shareholders, even those who have previously tendered their shares.
5. ***Pro rata rule.*** This rule provides that shares must be purchased on a *pro rata* basis if too many shares are tendered.
6. ***Withdrawal rights.*** Shareholders who tender their shares have an absolute right to withdraw them at any time prior to the closing of the tender offer.

Antifraud Provision

Section 14(e). This provision of the Williams Act prohibits fraudulent, deceptive, and manipulative practices in connection with a tender offer.

Fighting a Tender Offer

The management of the target corporation often takes one or more of the following steps to try to defeat a hostile tender offer:

1. Persuade the shareholders not to tender their shares.
2. File delaying lawsuits (e.g., antitrust lawsuits).
3. Sell the *crown jewel* (e.g., a valuable asset that the tender offeror is particularly interested in acquiring).
4. Adopt *poison pills* (e.g., contract provisions that make contracts and leases expire).
5. Find a *white knight* to purchase the corporation in a friendly acquisition.
6. Conduct a *Pac-Man tender offer* (i.e., a reverse tender offer to acquire the tender offeror).
7. Issue additional stock to friendly parties.
8. Create an *employee stock ownership plan (ESOP)* and issue stock to the ESOP.
9. Adopt *flip-over* and *flip-in rights plans* that make it more expensive for the tender offeror to acquire shares.
10. Pay *greenmail* by purchasing the shares held by the tender offeror at a premium.
11. Obtain a *standstill agreement* whereby the offeror agrees not to purchase shares of the target corporation for a stipulated period of time.

12. Engage in other strategies and tactics that make it more difficult for a tender offeror to complete its tender offer.

Business Judgment Rule

This rule protects the decisions of a board of directors that acts on an *informed basis*, in *good faith*, and in the *honest belief that the action taken was in the best interests of the corporation and its shareholders*.

Tender offers

The actions of the management of a target corporation in fighting a tender offer are judged by the business judgment rule. The defensive measure must be reasonable in relation to the threat posed.

STATE ANTITAKEOVER STATUTES, p. 301

State Antitakeover Statutes

These statutes enacted by state legislatures are aimed at protecting corporations that are either incorporated in or doing business within the state from hostile takeovers.

Lawfulness.

State antitakeover statutes are lawful if they do not conflict with the federal *Williams Act* or unduly burden interstate commerce in violation of the *Commerce Clause* of the U.S. Constitution.

MULTINATIONAL CORPORATIONS, p. 303

Multinational Corporations

A multinational company is a company with operations in two or more countries, generally allowing it to transfer funds and products according to price and demand conditions, subject to risks such as changes in exchange rates or political instability.

TEST REVIEW TERMS AND CONCEPTS

Antifraud provision 286
Antitakeover statute 301
Articles of merger 290
Articles of share exchange 290
Branch office 303
Business judgment rule 300
Crown jewel 298
Dissenting shareholder appraisal right (appraisal right) 295
Employee stock ownership plan (ESOP) 298
Exon-Florio law 304
Fair price rule 297
Flip-in rights plan 298
Flip-over rights plan 298
Greenmail 298

Hostile tender offer 295
Insurgent shareholder 287
Merger 287
Multinational corporation 284
Pac-Man (or reverse) tender offer 298
Parent corporation 289
Poison pill 298
Pro rata rule 297
Proxy (proxy card) 285
Proxy contest 287
Proxy statement 285
Sale or lease of assets 295
Section 14(a) of the Securities Exchange Act of 1934 285
Section 14(e) of the Williams Act 297
Share exchange 289
Shareholder resolution 287
Short-form merger 290
Standstill agreement 298
Subsidiary corporation 289
Supramajority 289
Surviving corporation 287
Target corporation 295
Tender offer 295
Tender offeror 295
Transnational corporation 303
White knight merger 298
Williams Act 296

CASE SCENARIO REVISITED

Remember the case at the beginning of the chapter in which Robert B. Bregman, the chief executive officer of Plant Industries, Inc. (Plant), engaged in a course of action to sell off the company's entire Canadian operation? Do Plant's shareholders have to be accorded voting and appraisal rights regarding the sale of this subsidiary? What would be the shareholders' course of action if the sale went through without their approval? To help you with your answers, see *Katz v. Bregman*, 431 A.2d 1274 (Del. Ch. 1981).

PORTFOLIO EXERCISE

For the business you created at the beginning of the course, complete the following form, Form CB.

OMBAPPROVAL	
(OMB Number:	3235-0518
Expires:	June 30, 2011
Estimated average burden hours per response 0.5	

UNITED STATES
SECURITIES AND EXCHANGE COMMISSION
Washington, D.C. 20549

Form CB

TENDER OFFER/RIGHTS OFFERING NOTIFICATION FORM
(AMENDMENT NO—— .)

Please place an X in the box(es) to designate the appropriate rule provision(s) relied upon to file this Form:

Securities Act Rule 801 (Rights Offering) [ ]
Securities Act Rule 802 (Exchange Offer) [ ]
Exchange Act Rule 13e-4(h)(8) (Issuer Tender Offer) [ ]
Exchange Act Rule 14d-1(c) (Third Party Tender Offer) [ ]
Exchange Act Rule 14e-2(d) (Subject Company Response) [ ]

Filed or Submitted in paper if permitted by Regulation S-T Rule 101(b)(8) [ ]

Note: Regulation S-T Rule 101(b)(8) only permits the filing or submission of a Form CB in paper by a party that is not subject to the reporting requirements of Section 13 or 15(d) of the Exchange Act.

____

(Name of Subject Company)

____

(Translation of Subject Company's Name into English (if applicable))

____

(Jurisdiction of Subject Company's Incorporation or Organization)

____

(Name of Person(s) Furnishing Form)

____

(Title of Class of Subject Securities)

____

(CUS1P Number of Class of Securities (if applicable))

____

(Name, Address (including zip code) and Telephone Number (including area code) of Person(s) Authorized to Receive Notices and Communications on Behalf of Subject Company)

____

(Date Tender Offer/Rights Offering Commenced)

*** An agency may not conduct or sponsor, and a person is not required to respond to, a collection of information unless it displays a currently valid control number. Any member of the public may direct to the Commission any comments concerning the accuracy of this burden estimate and any suggestions for reducing this burden. This collection of information has been reviewed by OMB in accordance with the clearance requirements of 44 U.S.C. 3507.**

SEC2560 (12-08) **Persons who respond to the collection of information contained in this form are not required to respond unless the form displays a currently valid OMB control number.**

GENERAL INSTRUCTIONS

I. *Eligibility Requirements for Use of Form CB*

A. Use this Form to furnish information pursuant to Rules 13e-4(h)(8), 14d-l(c) and 14e-2(d) under the Securities Exchange Act of 1934 ("Exchange Act"), and Rules 801 and 802 under the Securities Act of 1933 ("Securities Act").

Instructions

1. For the purposes of this Form, the term "subject company" means the issuer of the securities in a rights offering and the company whose securities are sought in a tender offer.

2. For the purposes of this Form, the term "tender offer" includes both cash and securities tender offers.

B. The information and documents furnished on this Form are not deemed "filed" with the Commission or otherwise subject to the liabilities of Section 18 of the Exchange Act.

II. *Instructions for Submitting Form*

A. (1) Regulation S-T Rule 101(a)(l)(vi)(17 CFR 232.101(a)(l)(vi)) requires a party to submit the Form CB in electronic format via the Commission's Electronic Data Gathering and Retrieval system (EDGAR) in accordance with the EDGAR rules set forth in Regulation S-T (17 CFR Part 232). For assistance with technical questions about EDGAR or to request an access code, call the EDGAR Filer Support Office at (202)551-8900.

(2) If the party filing or submitting the Form CB is not an Exchange Act reporting company, Regulation S-T Rule 101(b)(8) (17 CFR 232.101(b)(8)) permits the submission of the Form CB either via EDGAR or in paper. When filing or submitting the Form CB in electronic format, either voluntarily or as a mandated EDGAR filer, a party must also file or submit on EDGAR all home jurisdiction documents required by Parts I and II of this Form, except as provided by the Note following paragraph (2) of Part II.

(3) A party may also file a Form CB in paper under a hardship exemption provided by Regulation S-T Rule 201 or 202 (17 CFR 232.201 or 232.202) When submitting a Form CB in paper under a hardship exemption, a party must provide the legend required by Regulation S-T Rule 201(a)(2) or 202(c) (17 CFR 232.201(a)(2) or 232.202(c)) on the cover page of the Form CB.

(4) If filing the Form CB in paper in accordance with a hardship exemption, you must furnish five copies of this Form and any amendment to the Form (see Part I, Item 1 .(b)), including all exhibits and any other paper or document furnished as part of the Form, to the Commission at its principal office. You must bind, staple or otherwise compile each copy in one or more parts without stiff covers. You must make the binding on the side or stitching margin in a manner that leaves the reading matter legible.

B. When submitting the Form CB in electronic format, the persons specified in Part IV must provide signatures in accordance with Regulation S-T Rule 302 (17 CFR 232.302). When submitting the Form CB in paper, the persons specified in Part IV must sign the original and at least one copy of the Form and any amendments. You must conform any unsigned copies. The specified persons may provide typed or facsimile signatures in accordance with Securities Act Rule 402(e) (17 CFR 230.402(e)) or Exchange Act Rule 12b-11(d) (17 CFR 240.12b-11(d)) as long as the filer retains copies of signatures manually signed by each of the specified persons for five years.

C. You must furnish this Form to the Commission no later than the next business day after the disclosure documents submitted with this Form are published or otherwise disseminated in the subject company's

WORKING THE WEB INTERNET EXERCISES

Activities

1. Research your own state law on antitakeover statutes. Compile examples. See **http://topics.law.cornell.edu/wex/table_corporations**.
2. What is a *phantom stock*? For a set of definitions, see **www.investopedia.com/categories/buzzwords.asp**.
3. Review your own state statutes on termination of corporations. Why do you think some lawyers advise their corporate clients who are planning to terminate to just allow the secretary of state to cause an administrative dissolution for failure to file the annual renewal application? See **http://topics.law.cornell.edu/wex/table_corporations**.
4. Find state statutes that control the distribution of corporate assets at termination for nonprofit corporations. How does this differ from the rules in for-profit corporations? See **http://topics.law.cornell.edu/wex/table_corporations**.

CRITICAL LEGAL THINKING CASES

Case 10.1 *Proxy Disclosure* Western Maryland Company (Western) was a timbering and mining concern. A substantial portion of its stock was owned by CSX Minerals (CSX), its parent corporation. The remaining shares were owned by several minority shareholders, including Sanford E. Lockspeiser. Western's stock was not publicly traded. The board of directors of Western voted to merge the company with CSX. Western distributed to the minority shareholders a proxy statement that stated that CSX would vote for the merger and recommended approval of the merger by the other shareholders. The proxy materials disclosed Western's natural resource holdings in terms of acreage of minerals and timber. It also stated real property values as carried on the company's books—that is, a book value of $17.04 per share. It included an opinion of the First Boston Corporation, an investment banking firm, that the merger was fair to shareholders; First Boston did not undertake an independent evaluation of Western's physical assets. Lockspeiser sued, alleging that the proxy materials were misleading because they did not state tonnage of Western's coal reserves, timber holdings in board feet, and actual value of Western's assets. Has Lockspeiser stated a claim for relief? *Lockspeiser v. Western Maryland Co.*, 768 F.2d 558 (4th Cir. 1985).

Case 10.2 *Proxy Contest* The Medfield Corporation (Medfield) was a publicly held corporation engaged in operating hospitals and other health care facilities. Medfield established a date for its annual shareholders' meeting, at which time the board of directors would be elected. In its proxy statement, management proposed the incumbent slate of directors. A group known as the Medfield Shareholders Committee nominated a rival slate of candidates and also solicited proxies. Medfield sent to shareholders proxy solicitation material that:

1. Failed to disclose that Medfield had been overpaid more than $1.8 million by Blue Cross and this amount was due and owing Blue Cross.
2. Failed to disclose that Medicare funds were being withheld because of Medfield's nonpayment.
3. Failed to adequately disclose self-dealing with Medfield by one of the directors who owned part of a laboratory used by Medfield.

4. Failed to disclose that Medfield was attempting to sell two nursing homes.
5. Impugned the character, integrity, and personal reputation of one of the rival candidates by stating that he had previously been found liable for patent infringement when, in fact, the case had been reversed on appeal.

At the annual meeting, the incumbent slate of directors received 50 percent of the votes cast, against 44 percent of the insurgent slate of directors. The Gladwins, who owned voting stock, sued to have the election overturned. Who wins? *Gladwin v. Medfield Corp.*, 540 F.2d 1266 (5th Cir. 1976).

Case 10.3 *Proxy Contest* The Fairchild Engine and Airplane Corporation (Fairchild) was a privately held corporation whose management proposed the incumbent slate of directors for election at its annual shareholders' meeting. An insurgent slate of directors challenged the incumbents for election to the board. After the solicitation of proxies and a hard-fought proxy contest, the insurgent slate of directors was elected. Evidence showed that the proxy contest was waged over matters of corporate policy and for personal reasons. The old board of directors had spent $134,000 out of corporate funds to wage the proxy contest. The insurgents had spent $127,000 of their personal funds in their successful proxy contest and sought reimbursement from Fairchild for this amount. The payment of these expenses was ratified by a 16-to-1 majority vote of the shareholders. Mr. Rosenfeld, an attorney who owned 25 of the 2,300,000 outstanding shares of the corporation, filed an action to recover the amounts already paid by the corporation and to prevent any further payments of these expenses. Who wins? *Rosenfeld v. Fairchild Engine & Airplane Corp.*, 128 N.E.2d 291 (N.Y. 1955).

Case 10.4 *Shareholder Resolution* The Medical Committee for Human Rights (Committee), a nonprofit corporation organized to advance concerns for human life, received a gift of shares of Dow Chemical (Dow) stock. Dow manufactured napalm, a chemical defoliant that was used during the Vietnam Conflict. Committee objected to the sale of napalm by Dow primarily because of its concerns for human life. Committee owned sufficient shares for a long enough time to propose a shareholders' resolution, as long as it met the other requirements to propose such a resolution. Committee proposed that the following resolution be included in the proxy materials circulated by management for the annual shareholders' meeting:

> *RESOLVED, that the shareholders of the Dow Chemical company request that the Board of Directors, in accordance with the law, consider the advisability of adopting a resolution setting forth an amendment to the composite certificate of incorporation of the Dow Chemical Company that the company shall not make napalm.*

Dow's management refused to include the requested resolution in its proxy materials. Committee sued, alleging that its resolution met the requirements to be included in the proxy materials. Who wins? *Medical Comm. for Human Rights v. SEC*, 432 F.2d 659 (D.C. Cir. 1970).

Case 10.5 *Dissenting Shareholder Appraisal Rights* Over a period of several years, the Curtiss-Wright Corporation (Curtiss-Wright) purchased 65 percent of the stock of Dorr-Oliver Incorporated (Dorr-Oliver). Curtiss-Wright's board of directors decided that a merger with Dorr-Oliver would be beneficial to Curtiss-Wright. The board voted to approve a merger of the two companies and to pay $23 per share to the stockholders of Dorr-Oliver. The Dorr-Oliver board and 80 percent of Dorr-Oliver's shareholders approved the merger.

The merger became effective. John Bershad, a minority shareholder of Dorr-Oliver, voted against the merger but thereafter tendered his one hundred shares and received payment of $2,300. Bershad subsequently sued, alleging that the $23 per share paid to Dorr-Oliver shareholders was grossly inadequate. Can Bershad obtain minority shareholder appraisal rights? *Bershad v. Curtiss-Wright Corp.*, 535 A.2d 840 (Del. 1987).

Case 10.6 *Tender Offer* Mobil Corporation (Mobil) made a tender offer to purchase up to forty million outstanding common shares of stock in Marathon Oil Company (Marathon) for $85 per share in cash. It further stated its intentions to follow the purchase with a merger of the two companies. Mobil was primarily interested in acquiring Marathon's oil and mineral interests in certain properties, including the Yates Field. Marathon directors immediately held a board meeting and determined to find a white knight. Negotiations developed between Marathon and United States Steel Corporation (U.S. Steel). Two weeks later, Marathon and U.S. Steel entered into an agreement whereby U.S. Steel would make a tender offer for thirty million common shares of Marathon stock at $125 per share, to be followed by a merger of the two companies.

The Marathon–U.S. Steel agreement was subject to the following two conditions: (1) U.S. Steel was given an irrevocable option to purchase ten million authorized but unissued shares of Marathon common stock for $90 per share (or 17 percent of Marathon's outstanding shares), and (2) U.S. Steel was given an option to purchase Marathon's interest in oil and mineral rights in Yates Field for $2.8 billion (Yates Field option). The Yates Field option could be exercised only if U.S. Steel's offer did not succeed and if a third party gained control of Marathon. Evidence showed that Marathon's interest in Yates Field was worth up to $3.6 billion. Marathon did not give Mobil either of these two options. Mobil sued, alleging that these two options violated Section 14(e) of the Williams Act. Who wins? *Mobil Corp. v. Marathon Oil Co.*, 669 F.2d 366 (6th Cir. 1981).

Case 10.7 *Tender Offer* The Fruehauf Corporation (Fruehauf) is engaged in the manufacture of large trucks and industrial vehicles. The Edelman group (Edelman) made a cash tender offer for the shares of Fruehauf for $48.50 per share. The stock had sold in the low $20-per-share range a few months earlier. Fruehauf's management decided to make a competing management-led leveraged buyout (MBO) tender offer for the company in conjunction with Merrill Lynch. The MBO would be funded using $375 million borrowed from Merrill Lynch, $375 million borrowed from Manufacturers Hanover Bank, and $100 million contributed by Fruehauf. The total equity contribution to the new company under the MBO would be only $25 million: $10 million to $15 million from management and the rest from Merrill Lynch. In return for their equity contributions, management would receive between 40 and 60 percent of the new company.

Fruehauf's management agreed to pay $30 million to Merrill Lynch for brokerage fees that Merrill Lynch could keep even if the deal did not go through. Management also agreed to a no-shop clause whereby they agreed not to seek a better deal with another bidder. Incumbent management received better information about the goings-on. They also gave themselves golden parachutes that would raise the money for management's equity position in the new company.

Edelman informed Fruehauf's management that it could top their bid, but Fruehauf's management did not give them the opportunity to present their offer. Management's offer was accepted. Edelman sued, seeking an injunction. Did Fruehauf's management violate the business judgment rule? Who wins? *Edelman v. Fruehauf Corp.*, 798 F.2d 882 (6th Cir. 1986).

Case 10.8 *Flip-Over Defense* Household International, Inc. (Household), was a diversified holding company with its principal subsidiaries engaged in financial services, transportation, and merchandising. The board of directors of Household adopted a forty-eight–page "Rights Plan" by a fourteen-to-two vote. Basically, the plan provided that Household common stockholders were entitled to the issuance of one irrevocable right per common share if any party acquired 20 percent of Household's shares. The right permitted Household shareholders to purchase $200 of the common stock of the tender offeror for $100. In essence, this forced any party interested in taking over Household to negotiate with Household's directors. Dyson-Kissner-Moran Corporation (DKM), which was interested in taking over Household, filed suit, alleging that this flip-over rights plan violated the business judgment rule. Who wins? *Moran v. Household Int'l, Inc.*, 500 A.2d 1346 (Del. 1985).

Case 10.9 *State Antitakeover Statute* The state of Wisconsin enacted an antitakeover statute that protects corporations that are incorporated in Wisconsin and have their headquarters, substantial operations, or 10 percent of their shares of shareholders in the state. The statute prevents any party that acquires a 10 percent interest in a covered corporation from engaging in a business combination (e.g., merger) with the covered corporation for three years unless approval of management is obtained in advance of the combination. Wisconsin firms cannot opt out of the law. This statute effectively eliminates hostile leveraged buyouts because buyers must rely on the assets and income of the target company to help pay off the debt incurred in effectuating the takeover.

Universal Foods (Universal) was a Wisconsin corporation covered by the statute. Amanda Acquisition Corporation (Amanda) commenced a cash tender offer for up to 75 percent of the stock of Universal. Universal asserted the Wisconsin law. Is Wisconsin's antitakeover statute lawful? *Amanda Acquisition Corp. v. Universal Foods*, 877 F.2d 496 (7th Cir. 1989).

BUSINESS ETHICS CASES

Case 10.10 *Business Ethics* MCA, Inc. (MCA), a corporate holding company, owned 92 percent of the stock of Universal Pictures Company (Universal) and 100 percent of the stock of Universal City Studios, Inc. (Universal City). These two subsidiaries merged pursuant to Delaware's short-form merger statute. The minority shareholders of Universal were offered $75 per share for their shares. Francis I. Du Pont & Company and other minority shareholders (Plaintiffs) rejected the offer and then perfected their dissenting shareholder appraisal rights. The appraiser filed a final report in which he found the value of Universal stock to be $91.47 per share. Both parties filed exceptions to this report.

Plaintiffs' Valuation			
Value Factor	**Value**	**Weight**	**Result**
Earnings	$129.12	70%	$90.38
Market	144.36	20	28.87
Assets	126.46	10	12.64
	Value per share		**$131.89**

Defendant's Valuation			
Value Factor	**Value**	**Weight**	**Result**
Earnings	$51.93	70%	$36.35
Dividends	41.66	20	8.33
Assets	76.77	10	7.68
	Value per share		**$52.36**

Appraiser's Valuation			
Value Factor	**Value**	**Weight**	**Result**
Earnings	$92.89	80%	$74.31
Assets	85.82	20	17.16
	Value per share		**$91.47**

The parties' ultimate disagreement was over the value of the stock. Plaintiffs submitted that the true value was $131.89 per share; the defendant said it was $52.36. The computations were as follows:

The defendant took exception to the appraiser's failure to find that, in the years prior to merger, the industry was declining, and Universal was ranked near its bottom. The defendant argued that Universal was in the business of producing and distributing feature motion pictures for theatrical exhibition. It contended that such business, generally, was in a severe decline at the time of merger and that Universal, in particular, was in a vulnerable position because it had failed to diversify, its feature films were of low commercial quality, and, unlike other motion picture companies, substantially all of its film library had already been committed to distributors for television exhibition. In short, defendant Universal was a weak "wasting asset" corporation in a sick industry with poor prospects for revival.

The shareholders saw a different company. They said that Universal's business was indeed the production and distribution of feature films, but not merely for theatrical exhibition. They argued that there was a dramatic increase in the television market for such feature films at the time of the merger. This market, they contended, gave great new value to a fully amortized film library and significantly enhanced the value of Universal's current and future productions. Thus, they painted a portrait of a well-situated corporation in a rejuvenated industry.

Did the parties act ethically in arriving at their proposed values of the company? What is the value of the minority shareholders' shares of Universal Pictures Company? *Francis I. Du Pont & Co. v. Universal City Studios, Inc.*, 312 A.2d 344 (Del. Ch. 1973).

Case 10.11 *Business Ethics* Realist, Inc. (Realist), was a Delaware corporation with its principal place of business in Wisconsin. In March 1988, Royal Business Group, Inc. (Royal), a New Hampshire corporation, acquired 8 percent of the outstanding voting stock of Realist. Royal sent a series of letters to Realist, declaring its intention to acquire all of Realist's outstanding shares at an above-market premium. Realist repulsed Royal's overtures. Unbeknownst to Royal, Realist began negotiations to acquire Ammann Laser Technik AG (Ammann), a company based in Switzerland.

Royal instituted a proxy contest and nominated two candidates for the two Realist directorships to be filed at the annual shareholders' meeting. Realist and Royal both submitted proxy statements to Realist's shareholders.

The insurgent Royal nominees prevailed. Realist announced that it had acquired Ammann. This acquisition made Realist much less attractive as a takeover target. Royal immediately withdrew its offer to acquire Realist and sued Realist to recover the $350,000 it had spent in connection with the proxy contest. Royal alleged that Realist had engaged in fraud in violation of Section 14(a) of the Securities Exchange Act of 1934 by failing to disclose its secret negotiations with Ammann in its proxy materials. The basis of Royal's complaint was that if Realist had disclosed that it intended to acquire Ammann, Royal would not have engaged in the costly proxy contest. Is Realist liable to Royal? Did Realist act unethically in seeking to acquire Ammann to thwart Royal's takeover attempt? *Royal Business Group, Inc. v. Realist, Inc.*, 933 F.2d 1056 (1st Cir. 1991).

ENDNOTES

1. 15 U.S.C. Section 78n(a).
2. 15 U.S.C. Sections 78n(d), 78n(e).
3. Section 13(d) of the Securities Exchange Act of 1934 requires that any party that acquires 5 percent or more of any equity security of a company registered with the SEC must report the acquisition to the SEC and disclose its intentions regarding the acquisition. This is public information.
4. 15 U.S.C. Section 78n(e).
5. *Smith v. Van Gorkom*, 488 A.2d 858 (Del. 1985).
6. *Unocal Corp. v. Mesa Petroleum Co.*, 493 A.2d 946 (Del. 1985).

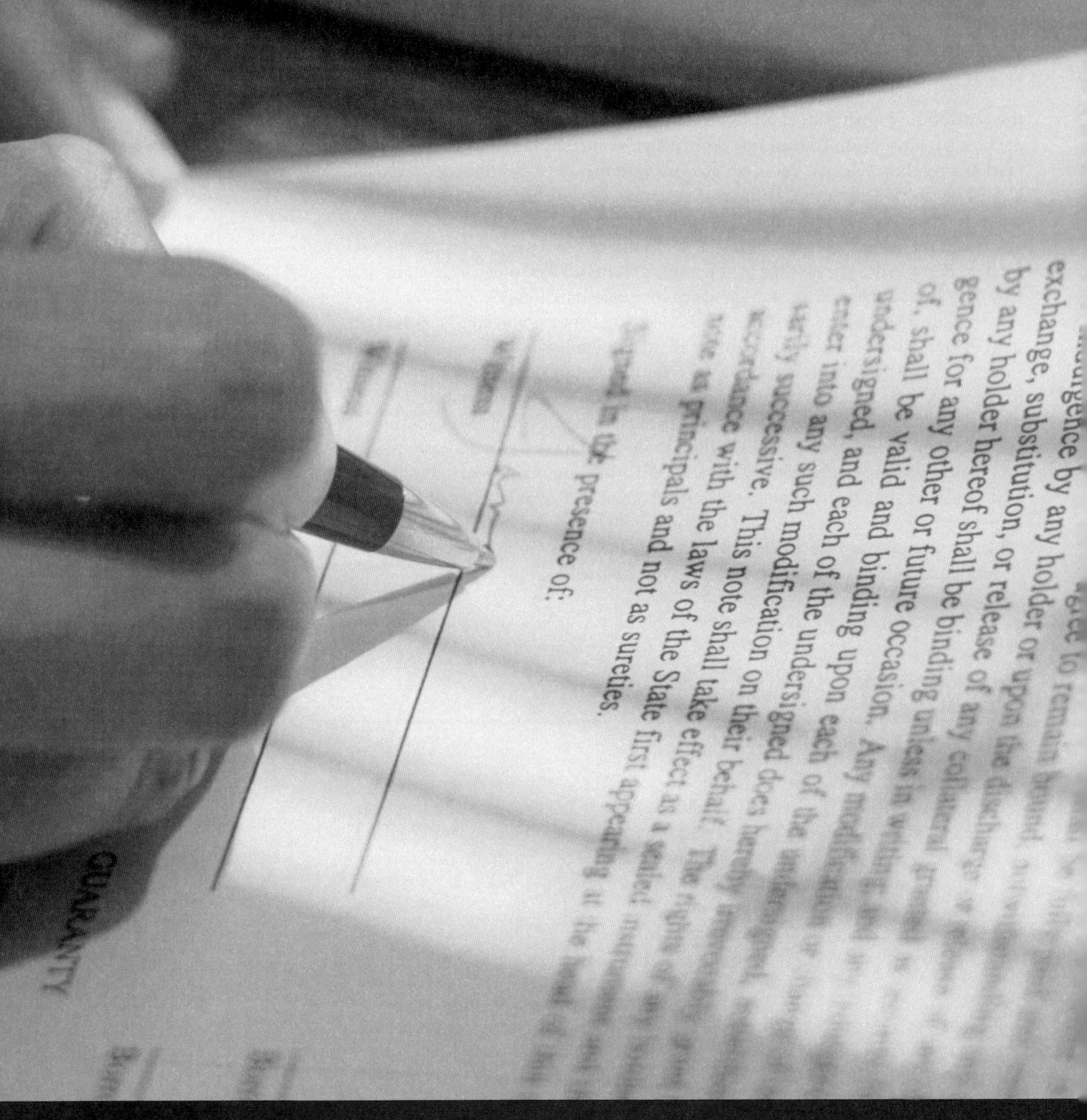

"Anyone who thinks there's safety in numbers hasn't looked at the stock market pages."

—Irene Peter

Investor Protection and Online Securities Transactions

CHAPTER 11

CASE SCENARIO

The law firm at which you work as a paralegal represents the McDonald Investment Company (McDonald). McDonald was a corporation organized and incorporated in the state of Minnesota. The principal and only place of business from which the company conducted operations was located in Rush City, Minnesota. More than 80 percent of the company's assets were located in Minnesota, and more than 80 percent of its income was derived from Minnesota. McDonald sold securities to Minnesota residents only. The proceeds from the sale were used entirely to make loans and other investments in real estate and other assets located outside the state of Minnesota. The company did not file a registration statement with the Securities and Exchange Commission (SEC).

CHAPTER OBJECTIVES

After studying this chapter, you should be able to:

1. Describe the procedure for going public and how securities are registered with the Securities and Exchange Commission.
2. Describe the requirements for qualifying for private placement, intrastate, and small offering exemptions from registration.
3. Describe insider trading that violates Section 10(b) of the Securities Exchange Act of 1934.
4. Describe the liability of tippers and tippees for insider trading.
5. Describe short-swing profits that violate Section 16(b) of the Securities Exchange Act of 1934.

PARALEGAL PERSPECTIVE

Dorothy Dansberry Roberts *is a senior paralegal with the in-house law department of The Kroger Co. in Cincinnati, Ohio. She graduated with a bachelor in paralegal studies from the University of Cincinnati and specializes in corporate/securities. She has been working as a paralegal for fifteen years.*

How or why do you think a paralegal is important in the field of investor protection? In my role as the corporate/securities paralegal at Kroger, I work on most of the company's 1933 and 1934 Act filings with the SEC. These filings include our proxy statement, 10-K, and securities offering documents. Also, I must be ready at a moment's notice to prepare and timely file Section 16 insider trading reports on behalf of our directors and officers.

What are the most important paralegal skills needed in your job? In my job, it is important to have the ability to write clearly and concisely and to have excellent listening skills. Also key are good organization, attention to detail, and the ability to multitask.

What is the academic background required for a paralegal entering your area of practice? Generally, there are no academic requirements for a paralegal entering the practice area of general corporate/securities. However, most employers giving hiring preference to paralegals with at least an associate in paralegal studies, and many prefer bachelor degrees.

My employer (The Kroger Co.) looks for paralegals with formal education. A bachelor in paralegal studies or a bachelor in another field plus a paralegal certificate is preferred.

How is technology involved in your job? Technology is key to my ability to carry out the daily responsibilities of my position. On a daily basis, I use the following technologies: Microsoft Word, Excel, and Outlook, and a matter management system developed in-house. I also use technologies developed by third-party vendors such as BowneFile 16 for Section 16 reporting, eGovDirect for submitting reports to the New York Stock Exchange, and tools developed by our registered agent (CSC) for preparation of corporate filings, project management, and electronic delivery of service of process. I also use Westlaw for research as needed.

I believe that those entering the paralegal field must have, at a minimum, a solid knowledge of computers and good typing skills to succeed. It is vital that a paralegal keep up with the latest technologies in order to remain an asset to his or her employer.

What trends do you see in your area of practice that will likely affect your job in the future? For corporate paralegals, keeping up with the latest technology will be key, as many corporate law departments move toward corporate data management systems, electronic minute books, and electronic storage of corporate records.

What do you feel is the biggest issue currently facing the paralegal profession? I believe that this is regulation, whether that is through voluntary or mandatory licensure or certification. While there is a rift between those in the legal profession as to whether some regulation of the profession should be instituted, it looks like the movement toward voluntary certification is gaining strength. It is my hope that the paralegal profession will someday become subject to mandatory regulation of some kind, with a higher educational standard being a part of that scheme.

What words of advice do you have for a new paralegal entering your area of practice? To new paralegals entering the corporate/securities area: know your way around a computer and make sure you know how to type. Come in with a basic knowledge of popular computer programs such as Word, Excel, Outlook, and PowerPoint. Perfect your writing skills, listen well, and don't be afraid to ask questions. Attorneys love follow-up, so keep them well-informed of developments in the projects they assign to you.

INTRODUCTION TO INVESTOR PROTECTION AND ONLINE SECURITIES TRANSACTIONS

Prior to the 1920s and 1930s, the securities markets in this country were not regulated by the federal government. Securities were sold to investors with little, if any, disclosure. Fraud in these transactions was common. To respond to this lack of regulation, federal and state governments enacted securities statutes to regulate the securities markets. The federal and state securities statutes are designed to require disclosure of information to investors and prevent fraud. This chapter discusses federal and state securities laws and regulations that provide investor protection, as well as the sale of securities online.

SECURITIES LAW

The federal and state governments have enacted statutes that regulate the issuance and trading in securities. The primary purposes of these acts are to promote full disclosure to investors and to prevent fraud in the issuance and trading of securities. These federal and state statutes are enforced by federal and state regulatory authorities, respectively.

DEFINITION OF SECURITY

Congress has enacted the Securities Act of 1933, the Securities Exchange Act of 1934, and several other securities statutes to regulate the issuance and sale of securities. For these federal statutes to apply, however, a **security** must first be found. Federal securities laws define securities as follows:

security
(1) An interest or instrument that is common stock, preferred stock, a bond, a debenture, or a warrant; (2) an interest or instrument that is expressly mentioned in securities acts; and (3) an investment contract.

- **Common securities.** Interests or instruments that are commonly known as securities are securities.

Examples: Common stock, preferred stock, bonds, debentures, and warrants are common securities.

LANDMARK LAW

FEDERAL SECURITIES LAWS

Following the stock market crash of 1929, Congress enacted a series of statutes designed to regulate securities markets. These federal securities statutes are designed to require disclosure to investors and prevent securities fraud. The two primary securities statutes enacted by the federal government, both of which were enacted during the Great Depression years, are as follows:

- **Securities Act of 1933**. This federal statute, enacted in 1933, primarily regulates the issue of securities by companies and other businesses. This act applies to original issue of securities, both initial public offerings (IPOs) by new public companies and sales of new securities by established companies. The primary purpose of this act is to require full and honest disclosure of information to investors at the time of the issuance of the securities. The act also prohibits fraud during the sale of issued securities. Securities are now issued online, and the 1933 act regulates the issue of securities online.
- **Securities Exchange Act of 1934**. This federal statute was enacted in 1934 to prevent fraud in the subsequent trading of securities. This act has been applied to prohibit insider trading and other frauds in the purchase and sale of securities in the after markets, such as trading on securities exchanges and other purchases and sales of securities. The act also requires continuous reporting–annual reports, quarterly reports, and other reports–to investors and the Securities Exchange Commission (SEC). Securities are now sold online and on electronic stock exchanges. The 1934 act regulates the purchase and sale of securities online.

The SEC, a federal administrative agency, enacts rules and regulations to interpret and administer federal securities laws.

- **Statutorily defined securities.** Interests or instruments that are expressly mentioned in securities acts are securities.

Examples: The securities acts specifically define preorganization subscription agreements; interests in oil, gas, and mineral rights; and deposit receipts for foreign securities as securities.

investment contract
A contract in which money is invested in a common enterprise with profits to come solely from the efforts of others; an agreement or transaction in which a party invests money in expectation of profits derived from the efforts of a promoter or other third party.

- **Investment contracts.** An **investment contract** is any contract whereby an investor invests money or other consideration in a common enterprise and expects to make a profit from the significant efforts of others. The courts apply the Howey test[1] in determining whether an arrangement is an investment contract and therefore a security. Under this test, an arrangement is considered an investment contract if there is an investment of money by an investor in a common enterprise and the investor expects to make profits based on the sole or substantial efforts of the promoter or others.

Examples: A limited partnership interest is an investment contract because the limited partner expects to make money based on the effort of the general partners. Pyramid sales schemes where persons give money to a promoter who promises them the return of their money with a promised interest or payment is an investment contract because the person who gave money to the promoter expects the promised return based on the efforts of the promoter. Investments in farm animals accompanied by care agreements have been found to be securities under this test, which is known as the Howey test.

CASE 11.1 DEFINITION OF SECURITY

SEC v. Edwards, 540 U.S. 389 (2004).

Facts

Charles Edwards was the chairman, chief executive officer (CEO), and sole shareholder of ETS Payphones, Inc. (ETS). ETS sold payphones to the public via independent distributors. The payphones were sold to buyers in a $7,000 package deal, consisting of a payphone site lease, a five-year leaseback by ETS, and an agreement whereby ETS would install the equipment at the site, arrange for connection and long-distance telephone service, collect coin revenues, and maintain and repair the payphones. Under the ETS contract, each payphone investor was guaranteed to receive $82 per month on his or her investment. ETS guaranteed to refund the full purchase price at the end of the lease. ETS enrolled over ten thousand people in the payphone program, and they invested over $300 million.

In actuality, the payphone did not generate enough revenues for ETS to make the guaranteed monthly payments. After ETS defaulted on hundreds of millions of dollars of payments to investors, it filed for bankruptcy. The Securities and Exchange Commission (SEC) brought a civil action against Edwards and ETS, alleging that the defendants had failed to register the payphone sale-and-leaseback arrangement with the SEC as a "security" prior to selling the phones to the public and had committed securities fraud. The U.S. District Court held that the payphone arrangement constituted a "security" and was therefore subject to federal securities laws. The U.S. Court of Appeals reversed, finding no security because the sale-and-leaseback provided for a fixed rate of return rather than capital appreciation or participation in the earnings of the enterprise. The SEC appealed to the U.S. Supreme Court.

Issue

Is the payphone sale-and-leaseback arrangement that guaranteed a fixed rate of return a security and therefore subject to federal securities laws?

Court's Reasoning

The U.S. Supreme Court mocked ETS's promotional brochure that stated "Opportunity doesn't always knock, sometimes it rings" by stating "And sometimes it hangs up." The Supreme Court stated that that is exactly what Edwards and ETS did to the ten thousand investors who lost $300 million on the payphone investment scheme. The Supreme Court held that Congress, by enacting federal securities laws, intended to regulate investments in whatever form they are made and by whatever name they are called. The Supreme Court stated:

> *There is no reason to distinguish between promises of fixed returns and promises of variable returns. In both cases, the investing public is attracted by representations of investment income. Moreover, investments pitched as low risk (such as those offering a guaranteed fixed return) are particularly attractive to individuals more vulnerable to investment fraud, including older and less sophisticated investors.*

The Supreme Court noted that under the reading respondent Edwards advanced, unscrupulous marketers of investments could evade the securities laws by picking a fixed rate of return to promise.

> When there is blood on the street, I am buying.
> —Nathaniel Mayer Victor Rothschild, third Baron Rothschild

Decision

The U.S. Supreme Court held that an investment arrangement that offers a fixed rate of return is a security subject to the provisions of federal securities laws. The Supreme Court reversed the decision of the Court of Appeals and remanded the case for further proceedings based on violations of securities laws and securities fraud.

Case Questions

1. **Critical Legal Thinking** If a financial arrangement that guarantees a fixed rate of return is not found to be a security, what would be the result for society? Explain.
2. **Business Ethics** Did Edwards act ethically in this case? Is there any evidence that he acted fraudulently? Explain.
3. **Contemporary Business** If Edwards had to disclose the truth about his and ETS's investment scheme, would many people have invested? Explain.

Concept Summary

Definitions of Securities

Type of Security	Definition
Common securities	Interests or instruments that are commonly known as securities, such as common stock, preferred stock, debentures, and warrants.
Statutorily defined securities	Interests or instruments that are expressly mentioned in securities acts as being securities, such as interests in oil, gas, and mineral rights.
Investment contracts	A flexible standard for defining a security. Under the Howey test, a security exists if an investor invests money in a common enterprise and expects to make a profit from the significant efforts of others.

THE SECURITIES AND EXCHANGE COMMISSION (SEC)

Securities and Exchange Commission (SEC)
The federal administrative agency that is empowered to administer federal securities laws. The SEC can adopt rules and regulations to interpret and implement federal securities laws.

rules and regulations
Adopted by administrative agencies to interpret the statutes that they are authorized to enforce.

The Securities Exchange Act of 1934 created the **Securities and Exchange Commission (SEC)** and empowered it to administer federal securities laws. The SEC is an administrative agency composed of five members who are appointed by the president. The major responsibilities of the SEC are:

- Adopting **rules** (also called **regulations**) that further the purpose of the federal securities statutes. These rules have the force of law.
- Investigating alleged securities violations and bringing enforcement actions against suspected violators. This may include a recommendation of criminal prosecution. Criminal prosecutions of violations of federal securities laws are brought by the U.S. Department of Justice.
- Regulating the activities of securities brokers and advisors. This includes registering brokers and advisors and taking enforcement action against those who violate securities laws.

EDGAR
An electronic filing and forms system used by the SEC.

The SEC has an electronic filing and forms system called **EDGAR**, where companies file required forms and information. The electronic filings on this system are viewable by the public.

PRIVATE TRANSACTIONS EXEMPT FROM REGISTRATION

exempt
1. *v.* To release from liability. 2. *adj.* Freed from a duty.

exempt transaction
A transaction involving the sale of securities that do not have to be registered with the SEC.

Certain *transactions* where securities are sold are **exempt** from registration with the SEC if they meet specified requirements. These are called **exempt transactions.** Thus, the securities sold pursuant to an exempt transaction do not have to be registered with the SEC. Exempt transactions include the *nonissuer exemption, intrastate offering exemption, private placement exemption,* and *small offering exemption.* These exempt transactions are discussed in the paragraphs that follow.

Exempt transactions that do not have to be registered with the SEC are subject to the antifraud provisions of the federal securities laws. Therefore, the issuer must provide investors with adequate information—including annual reports, quarterly reports, proxy statements, financial statements, and so on—even though a registration statement is not required.

Nonissuer Exemption

Nonissuers, such as average investors, do not have to file a registration statement prior to reselling securities they have purchased. This nonissuer exemption exists because the Securities Act of 1933 exempts from registration securities transactions not made by an issuer, an underwriter, or a dealer. For example, an investor who owns shares of IBM can resell those shares to another at any time without having to register with the SEC.

Intrastate Offering Exemption

The purpose of the **intrastate offering exemption** is to permit local businesses to raise from local investors capital to be used in the local economy without the need to register with the SEC.[2] There is no limit on the dollar amount of capital that can be raised pursuant to an intrastate offering exemption. An issuer can qualify for this exemption in only one state.

intrastate offering exemption
An exemption from registration that permits local businesses to raise capital from local investors to be used in the local economy without the need to register with the SEC.

Three requirements must be met to qualify for this exemption:[3]

1. The issuer must be a resident of the state for which the exemption is claimed. A corporation is a resident of the state in which it is incorporated.
2. The issuer must be doing business in that state. This requires that 80 percent of the issuer's assets be located in the state, 80 percent of its gross revenues be derived from the state, its principal office be located in the state, and 80 percent of the proceeds of the offering be used in the state.
3. The purchasers of the securities must all be residents of that state.

An intrastate offering can be made only in the one state in which all these requirements have been met. Rule 147 stipulates that securities sold pursuant to an intrastate offering exemption cannot be sold to nonresidents for a period of nine months.

Private Placement Exemption

An issue of securities that does not involve a public offering is exempt from the registration requirements.[4] This exemption—known as the **private placement exemption**—allows issuers to raise capital from an unlimited number of accredited investors without having to register the offering with the SEC.[5] There is no dollar limit on the securities that can be sold pursuant to this exemption.

private placement exemption
An exemption from registration that permits issuers to raise capital from an unlimited number of accredited investors and no more than thirty-five nonaccredited investors without having to register the offering with the SEC.

An **accredited investor** is:[6]

- Any natural person who has individual net worth or joint net worth with a spouse that exceeds $1 million.
- A natural person with income exceeding $200,000 in each of the two most recent years or joint income with a spouse exceeding $300,000 for those years and a reasonable expectation of the same income level in the current year.

accredited investor
An investor treated under the Securities Act of 1933 as being knowledgeable and sophisticated about financial matters, especially because of the investor's large net worth.

- A charitable organization, a corporation, a partnership, a trust, or an employee benefit plan with assets exceeding $5 million.
- A bank, an insurance company, a registered investment company, a business development company, or a small business investment company.
- Insiders of the issuers, such as directors, executive officers, or general partner of the company selling the securities.
- A business in which all the equity owners are accredited investors.

exempt security
A security that need not be registered under the provisions of the Securities Act of 1933 and is exempt from the margin requirements of the Securities Exchange Act of 1934.

nonaccredited investor
Nonaccredited investors are usually friends and family members of the insiders. They may purchase securities pursuant to a private placement exemption.

No more than thirty-five **nonaccredited investors** may purchase securities pursuant to a private placement exemption. These nonaccredited investors are usually friends and family members of the insiders. Nonaccredited investors must be sophisticated investors, however, either through their own experience and education or through representatives (e.g., accountants, lawyers, business managers). General selling efforts, such as advertising to the public, are not permitted.

Small Offering Exemption

Securities offerings that do not exceed a certain dollar amount are exempt from registration.[7] Rule 504 exempts from registration the sale of securities not exceeding $1 million during a twelve-month period. The securities may be sold to an unlimited number of accredited and unaccredited investors, but general selling efforts to the public are not permitted. This is called the **small offering exemption**.

small offering exemption
An exemption from registration that permits the sale of securities not exceeding $1 million during a twelve-month period.

Resale Restrictions

Securities sold pursuant to the intrastate, private placement, or small offering exemptions are called restricted securities because they cannot be resold for a limited period of time after their initial issue. The following restrictions apply:

- Rule 147 stipulates that securities sold pursuant to an intrastate offering exemption cannot be sold to nonresidents for a period of nine months.
- Rule 144 provides that securities sold pursuant to the private placement or small offering exemption must be held for one year from the date when the securities are last sold by the issuer. After that time, investors may sell the greater of (1) 1 percent of the outstanding securities of the issuer or (2) the average weekly volume of trading in the securities (i.e., the four-week moving average) in any three-month period. Information about the issuer must be available to the public. Generally, all restrictions are lifted after two years.

Preventing Transfer of Restricted Securities

To protect the nontransferability of restricted shares, the issuer must:

1. Require the investors to sign an *affidavit* stating that they are buying the securities for investment, acknowledging that they are purchasing restricted securities, and promising not to transfer the shares in violation of the restriction.
2. Place a *legend* on the stock certificate describing the restriction.
3. Notify the *transfer agent* not to record a transfer of the securities that would violate the restriction.

CONTEMPORARY Environment

RULE 144A: QUALIFIED INSTITUTIONAL INVESTORS

To establish a more liquid and efficient secondary market in unregistered securities, the SEC adopted Rule 144A in 1990. This rule permits "qualified institutional investors"—defined as institutions that own and invest at least $100 million in securities—to buy unregistered securities without being subject to the holding periods of Rule 144. This rule is designed to create an institutional market in unregistered securities as well as to permit foreign issuers to raise capital in this country from sophisticated investors without making registration process disclosures.

If the issuer has taken these precautions, it will not lose its exemption from registration even if isolated transfers of stock occur in violation of the restricted periods. If these precautions are not taken, the issuer may lose its exemption from registration. In that event, it has sold unregistered securities in violation of Section 5, permitting all purchasers to rescind their purchases of the securities.

■ THE SECURITIES ACT OF 1933: GOING PUBLIC

The **Securities Act of 1933** primarily regulates the issuance of securities by corporations, limited partnerships, other businesses, and individuals.[8] Section 5 of the Securities Act of 1933 requires securities offered to the public through the use of the mails or any facility of interstate commerce to be registered with the SEC by means of a registration statement and an accompanying prospectus.

Securities Act of 1933
A federal statute that primarily regulates the issuance of securities by corporations, partnerships, associations, and individuals.

CONTEMPORARY Environment

SECURITIES EXEMPT FROM REGISTRATION

Certain *securities* are exempt from registration. Once a security is exempt, it is exempt forever. It does not matter how many times the security is transferred. **Exempt securities** include the following:

- Securities issued by any government in the United States (e.g., municipal bonds issued by city governments).
- Short-term notes and drafts that have a maturity date that does not exceed nine months (e.g., commercial paper issued by corporations).
- Securities issued by nonprofit issuers, such as religious institutions, charitable institutions, and colleges and universities.
- Securities of financial institutions (e.g., banks and savings associations) that are regulated by the appropriate banking authorities.
- Securities issued by common carriers (railroads and trucking companies) that are regulated by the Interstate Commerce Commission (ICC).
- Insurance and annuity contracts issued by insurance companies.
- Stock dividends and stock splits.
- Securities issued in a corporate reorganization in which one security is exchanged for another security.

issuer
The business or party that sells securities to the public.

initial public offering (IPO)
A company's first public sale of stock; the first offering of an issuer's equity securities to the public through a registration statement.

investment bankers
Independent securities companies that assist issuers in selling securities to the public.

registration statement
A document that an issuer of securities files with the SEC that contains required information about the issuer, the securities to be issued, and other relevant information.

The business or party selling securities to the public is called the **issuer**. The issuer may be a relatively new company (e.g., Google, Inc.) selling securities to the public through an **initial public offering (IPO)**, or it may be an established company (e.g., Microsoft Corporation) selling new securities to the public. Many issuers of securities employ **investment bankers**, which are independent securities companies, to sell their securities to the public. Issuers pay a fee to investment bankers for this service.

Registration Statement

A covered issuer must file a written **registration statement** with the SEC. The issuer's lawyer normally prepares the statement, with the help of the issuer's management, accountants, and underwriters.

A registration statement must contain descriptions of (1) the securities being offered for sale; (2) the registrant's business; (3) the management of the registrant, including compensation, stock options and benefits, and material transactions with the registrant; (4) pending litigation; (5) how the proceeds from the offering will be used; (6) government regulation; (7) the degree of competition in the

INTERNATIONAL LAW

Chinese Bank Launches World's Largest IPO

In late 2006, Industrial and Commercial Bank of China (ICBC) issued shares to the public in the world's largest IPO. The bank raised over US $19 billion in a dual listing on the Hong Kong and Shanghai, China, stock exchanges. The IPO of fifty billion shares at 39 cents each was oversubscribed. The IPO made available only about 15 percent of ICBC's total shares.

One year prior to the IPO, Goldman Sachs purchased 6 percent of the bank's stock for about $3 billion. Other strategic alliance pre-IPO shares were sold to American Express, Royal Bank of Scotland, and Allianz AG of Germany. After the pre-IPO sales and IPO, the central government of China would control 72.5 percent of the bank's shares.

The IPO of China's largest bank was a tremendous success. Prior to the pre-IPO sales to strategic partners and the IPO, ICBC was a state-owned bank, meaning that the Chinese government owned and operated the bank. A few years ago, about one-third of ICBC's loans were past due, stemming from poor lending practices and corruption. Prior to the IPO, the Chinese government stepped in, infused cash into the bank, and transferred many bad loans out of the bank.

In the year prior to ICBC's IPO, two other Chinese state-owned banks, the Bank of China and China Reconstruction Bank, issued shares to the public, raising a combined $20 billion. These two Chinese IPOs rank in the world's top ten IPOs.

Web Exercises

1. **Web** Visit the website of the Industrial and Commercial Bank of China (ICBC), at www.icbc.com.cn.
2. **Web** Visit the website of the Hong Kong Stock Market, at www.hkex.com.hk.
3. **Web** Visit the website of the Shanghai Stock Market, at www.sse.com.cn.
4. **Web** Use www.google.com to find an article about a recent IPO by a foreign company in another country. Read it.

If this Form is filed to register additional securities for an offering pursuant to Rule 462(b) under the Securities Act, please check the following box and list the Securities Act registration number of the earlier effective registration statement for the same offering. ☐

If this Form is a post-effective amendment filed pursuant to Rule 462(c) under the Securities Act, check the following box and list the Securities Act registration number of the earlier effective registration statement for the same offering. ☐

If this Form is a post-effective amendment filed pursuant to Rule 462(d) under the Securities Act, check the following box and list the Securities Act registration statement number of the earlier effective registration statement for the same offering. ☐

If delivery of the prospectus is expected to be made pursuant to Rule 434, check the following box. ☐

CALCULATION OF REGISTRATION FEE

Title of Each Class of Securities to be Registered	Proposed Maximum Aggregate Offering Price (1)(2)	Amount of Registration Fee
Class A common stock, par value $0.001 per share	$2,718,281,828	$344,406.31

(1) Estimated solely for the purpose of computing the amount of the registration fee, in accordance with Rule 457(o) promulgated under the Securities Act of 1933.

(2) Includes offering price of shares that the underwriters have the option to purchase to cover over-allotments, if any.

The Registrant hereby amends this Registration Statement on such date or dates as may be necessary to delay its effective date until the Registrant shall file a further amendment which specifically states that this Registration Statement shall thereafter become effective in accordance with Section 8(a) of the Securities Act or until the Registration Statement shall become effective on such date as the Securities and Exchange Commission, acting pursuant to said Section 8(a), may determine.

Prospectus

A **prospectus** is a written disclosure document that must be submitted to the SEC along with the registration statement. A prospectus is used as a selling tool by the issuer. It is provided to prospective investors to enable them to evaluate the financial risk of an investment.

A prospectus must contain the following language in capital letters and boldface (usually red) type:

> *THESE SECURITIES HAVE NOT BEEN APPROVED OR DISAPPROVED BY THE SECURITIES AND EXCHANGE COMMISSION OR ANY STATE SECURITIES COMMISSION NOR HAS THE SECURITIES AND EXCHANGE COMMISSION OR ANY STATE SECURITIES COMMISSION PASSED UPON THE ACCURACY OR ADEQUACY OF THIS PROSPECTUS. ANY REPRESENTATION TO THE CONTRARY IS A CRIMINAL OFFENSE.*

prospectus
A written disclosure document that must be submitted to the SEC along with the registration statement and given to prospective purchasers of the securities.

Limitations on Activities During the Registration Process

Section 5 of the Securities Act of 1933 limits the types of activities that an issuer, an underwriter, and a dealer may engage in during the registration process. These limitations are divided into the following three time periods:

- **The prefiling period.** The **prefiling period** begins when the issuer first contemplates issuing the securities and ends when the registration statement is filed. During this time, the issuer cannot either sell or offer to sell the

prefiling period
A period of time that begins when the issuer first contemplates issuing securities and ends when the registration statement is filed. The issuer may not condition the market during this period.

waiting period
A period of time that begins when the registration statement is filed with the SEC and continues until the registration statement is declared effective. Only certain activities are permissible during the waiting period.

> The insiders here were not trading on an equal footing with the outside investors.
>
> Judge Waterman
> SEC v. Texas Gulf Sulphur Co., 401 F.2d 833 (2nd Cir. 1968)

ETHICS SPOTLIGHT

"PLAIN ENGLISH" DISCLOSURE IN SECURITIES OFFERINGS

Nonlawyers have always been frustrated by the legalese used by lawyers in contracts, court documents, and regulatory disclosures. There has been no wider use of arcane legal language than in prospectuses offering securities for sale to the public.

These documents, which are supposed to provide relevant information to potential investors before they invest in company stock and securities, are usually barely skimmed, let alone read, by potential investors.

The SEC decided to change this practice in 1998 when it adopted a "plain English" rule for securities offerings. Under this rule, issuers of securities must use plain English language on the cover page, in the summary, and in the risk factors sections of their prospectuses. Issuers must now use:

- Active voice
- Short sentences
- "Everyday" words
- Bullet lists for complex information
- No legal jargon or highly technical terms
- No multiple negatives

The plain English rule has required a major cultural change by issuers, underwriters, and securities lawyers, who are used to using complicated and confusing language. The SEC has stated that it will not be the "grammar police," but will instead focus on the clarity of disclosures to potential investors by issuers. The SEC hopes that its new rule will encourage issuers to use plain English throughout the entire prospectus [Rule 421(d) of Regulation C].

---

securities. The issuer also cannot *condition the market* for the upcoming securities offering. This rule makes it illegal for an issuer to engage in a public relations campaign (e.g., newspaper and magazine articles and advertisements) that touts the prospects of the company and the planned securities issue. However, sending annual reports to shareholders and making public announcements of factual matters (such as the settlement of a strike) are permissible because they are considered normal corporate disclosures.

- **The waiting period.** The **waiting period** begins when the registration statement is filed with the SEC and continues until the registration statement is declared effective.

  The issuer is encouraged to condition the market during this time. Thus, the issuer may (1) make oral offers to sell (including face-to-face and telephone conversations); (2) distribute a *preliminary prospectus* (usually called a red herring), which contains most of the information to be contained in the final prospectus except for price; (3) distribute a *summary prospectus*, which is a summary of the important terms contained in the prospectus; and (4) publish *tombstone ads* in newspapers and other publications. Unapproved writings (which are considered illegal offers to sell) as well as actual sales are prohibited during the waiting period.
- **The posteffective period.** The posteffective period begins when the registration statement becomes effective and runs until the issuer either sells all of the offered securities or withdraws them from sale. Thus, the issuer and its underwriter and dealers may close the offers received prior to the effective date and solicit new offers and sales.

  Prior to or at the time of confirming a sale or sending a security to a purchaser, the issuer (or its representative) must deliver a final prospectus (also called a statutory prospectus) to the investor. Failure to do so is a violation of Section 5. Tombtone ads are often used during this period.

The investor may rescind his or her purchase if the issuer violates any of the prohibitions on activities during these periods. If an underwriter or a dealer violates any of these prohibitions, the SEC may issue sanctions, including the suspension of securities licenses.

Sale of Unregistered Securities

Sale of securities that should have been registered with the SEC but were not violates the Securities Act of 1933. Investors can rescind their purchase and recover damages. The U.S. government can impose criminal penalties on any person who willfully violates the Securities Act of 1933.

Regulation A Offering

Regulation A permits issuers to sell up to $5 million of securities to the public during a 12-month period, pursuant to a simplified registration process. Such offerings may have an unlimited number of purchasers who do not have to be accredited investors. Issuers with offerings exceeding $100,000 must file an **offering statement** with the SEC. An offering statement requires less disclosure than a registration statement and is less costly to prepare. Investors must be provided with an offering circular prior to the purchase of securities. There are no resale restrictions on the securities.

Regulation A
A regulation that permits the issuer to sell securities pursuant to a simplified registration process.

offering statement
A document, similar to a prospectus, that provides information about a private securities offering.

Small Corporate Offering Registration (SCOR) Form

Small businesses often need to raise capital and must find public investors to buy company stock. In 1992, after years of investigation, the SEC amended Regulation A by adopting the **Small Corporate Offering Registration (SCOR) form.** The SCOR form—Form U-7—is a question-and-answer disclosure form that small businesses can complete and file with the SEC if they plan on raising $1 million or less from the public issue of securities. An issuer must answer the questions on Form U-7, which then becomes the offering circular that must be given to prospective investors.

Small Corporate Offering Registration (SCOR) form
The SCOR form–Form U-7–is a question-and-answer disclosure form that a business can complete and file with the SEC if it plans on raising $1 million or less from the public issue of securities.

Form U-7 questions are so clearly and specifically drawn that they can be answered by the issuer without the help of an expensive securities lawyer. SCOR form questions require the issuer to develop a business plan that states specific company goals and how it intends to reach them. The SCOR form is available only to domestic businesses. A SCOR form offering cannot exceed $1 million, and the offering price of the common stock or its equivalent may not be less than $5 per share. SCOR form offerings are a welcome addition for entrepreneur-owners who want to raise money through a small public offering.

Private Actions

Private parties who have been injured by violations of the Securities Act of 1933 have recourse against the violator under the following two sections:

1. **Section 12 of the Securities Act of 1933** imposes *civil liability* on any person who violates the provisions of Section 5 of the act. Violations include selling securities pursuant to an unwarranted exemption and making misrepresentations concerning the offer or sale of securities. The purchaser's remedy for a violation of Section 12 is either to rescind the purchase or to sue for damages.

Section 12
A provision of the Securities Act of 1933 that imposes civil liability on any person who violates the provisions of Section 5 of the act.

Section 11
A provision of the Securities Act of 1933 that imposes civil liability on persons who intentionally defraud investors by making misrepresentations or omissions of material facts in the registration statement or who are negligent for not discovering the fraud.

2. **Section 11 of the Securities Act of 1933** provides for *civil liability* for damages when a registration statement on its effective date misstates or omits a material fact. Liability under Section 11 is imposed on those who (1) intentionally defraud investors or (2) are negligent in not discovering the fraud. Thus, the issuer, certain corporate officers (e.g., chief executive officer, chief financial officer, chief accounting officer), directors, signers of the registration statement, underwriters, and experts (e.g., accountants who certify financial statements and lawyers who issue legal opinions that are included in a registration statement) may be liable.

due diligence defense
A defense to a Section 11 action that, if proven, makes the defendant not liable.

All defendants except the issuer may assert a **due diligence defense** against the imposition of Section 11 liability. If this defense is proven, the defendant is not liable. To establish a due diligence defense, the defendant must prove that after reasonable investigation, he or she had reasonable grounds to believe and did believe that, at the time the registration statement became effective, the statements contained therein were true and there was no omission of material facts.

Example: In the classic case *Escott v. BarChris Construction Corporation*,[9] the company was going to issue a new bond to the public. The company prepared financial statements wherein the company overstated current assets, understated current liabilities, overstated sales, overstated gross profits, overstated the backlog of orders, did not disclose loans to officers, did not disclose customer delinquencies in paying for goods, and lied about the use of the proceeds from the offering. The company gave these financial statements to its auditors, Peat, Marwick, Mitchell & Co. (Peat Marwick), who did not discover the lies. Peat Marwick certified the financial statements that became part of the registration statement filed with the SEC. The bonds were sold to the public. One year later, the company filed for bankruptcy. The bondholders sued Russo, the chief executive officer (CEO) of BarChris; Vitolo and Puglies, the founders of the business and the president and vice president, respectively; Trilling, the controller; and Peat Marwick, the auditor. Each defendant pleaded the due diligence defense. The court rejected each of the party's defenses, finding that the CEO, president, vice president, and controller were all in positions to either have created or discovered the misrepresentations. The court also found that the auditor, Peat Marwick, did not do a proper investigation and had not proven its due diligence defense. The court found that the defendants had violated Section 11 of the Securities Act of 1933 by submitting misrepresentations and omissions of material facts in the registration statement filed with the SEC.

consent order
An order issued by the SEC whereby a defendant agrees not to violate securities laws in the future but does not admit having violated securities laws in the past.

SEC Actions

The SEC may (1) issue a **consent order** whereby a defendant agrees not to violate securities laws in the future but does not admit to having violated securities laws in the past, (2) bring an action in federal district court to obtain an **injunction**, or (3) request the court to grant ancillary relief, such as *disgorgement of profits* by the defendant.

injunction
A court order commanding or preventing an action.

Criminal Liability

Section 24
A provision of the Securities Act of 1933 that imposes criminal liability on any person who willfully violates the 1933 act or the rules or regulations adopted thereunder.

Section 24 of the Securities Act of 1933 imposes *criminal liability* on any person who *willfully* violates either the act or the rules and regulations adopted thereunder.[10] A violator may be fined or imprisoned for up to five years, or both. Criminal actions are brought by the Department of Justice.

ETHICS SPOTLIGHT

SARBANES-OXLEY ACT ERECTS A WALL BETWEEN INVESTMENT BANKERS AND SECURITIES ANALYSTS

Investment banking is a service provided by many securities firms, whereby they assist companies in **going public** when issuing shares to the public and otherwise selling securities. The securities firms are paid lucrative fees for providing investment banking services in assisting companies to sell their securities and finding customers to purchase these securities. These same securities firms often provide securities analysis—providing investment advice and recommending securities listed on the stock exchanges and other securities to be purchased by the public.

In the late 1990s and early 2000s, many conflicts of interest were uncovered. Investment bankers and securities analysts of the same firm shared information, and the analysts were paid or pressured by the securities firms to write glowing reports of companies from which the investment bankers of the firm were earning fees.

Congress sought to remedy this problem by enacting Section 501 of the **Sarbanes-Oxley Act** of 2002. Section 501 established rules for separating the investment banking and securities advice functions of securities firms, thus eliminating many conflicts of interest:

- Securities firms must establish structural and institutional "walls" between their investment banking and securities analysis areas. These walls must protect analysts from review, pressure, and oversight by persons employed by the investment banking area of a securities firm.
- Securities analysts must disclose in each research report or public appearance any conflicts of interest that are known or should have been known to exist at the time of publication or public appearance.

The SEC is empowered to adopt rules to enforce the provisions of Section 501.

Business Ethics

1. Why did investment bankers of securities firms put pressure on analysts to issue positive reports on certain companies? Will the required "walls" between securities analysts and investment bankers make the analysts' information more reliable? Explain.

going public
The process of a company's selling stock to the investing public for the first time (after filing a registration statement under applicable securities laws), thereby becoming a public corporation.

Sarbanes-Oxley Act
A federal act that imposes new rules that affect public accountants. The act: created the Public Company Accounting Oversight Board (PCAOB); requires public accounting firms to register with the PCAOB; separates audit services and certain nonaudit services provided by accountants to clients; requires an audit partner of the accounting firm to supervise an audit and approve an audit report prepared by the firm and requires a second parent of the accounting firm to review and approve the audit report; and prohibits employment of an accountant by a previous audit client for certain positions for a period of one year following the audit.

THE SECURITIES EXCHANGE ACT OF 1934: TRADING IN SECURITIES

Unlike the Securities Act of 1933, which regulates the original issuance of securities, the **Securities Exchange Act of 1934** primarily regulates subsequent trading.[11] It provides for the registration of certain companies with the SEC, the continuous filing of periodic reports by these companies to the SEC, and the regulation of securities exchanges, brokers, and dealers. It also contains provisions that assess civil and criminal liability on violators of the 1934 act and rules and regulations adopted thereunder.

Securities Exchange Act of 1934
A federal statute that primarily regulates the trading in securities.

Section 10(b) and Rule 10b-5

Section 10(b) is one of the most important sections in the entire 1934 act.[12] It prohibits the use of manipulative and deceptive devices in contravention of the rules and regulations prescribed by the SEC. Pursuant to its rule-making authority, the SEC has adopted **Rule 10b-5**,[13] which provides:

> *It shall be unlawful for any person, directly or indirectly, by use of any means or instrumentality of interstate commerce or of the mails, or of any facility of any national securities exchange,*

Section 10(b)
A provision of the Securities Exchange Act of 1934 that prohibits the use of manipulative and deceptive devices in the purchase or sale of securities in contravention of the rules and regulations prescribed by the SEC.

Rule 10b-5
A rule adopted by the SEC to clarify the reach of Section 10(b) against deceptive and fraudulent activities in the purchase and sale of securities.

a. *to employ any device, scheme, or artifice to defraud,*
b. *to make any untrue statement of a material fact or to omit to state a material fact necessary in order to make the statements made, in light of the circumstances under which they were made, not misleading, or*
c. *to engage in any act, practice, or course of business that operates or would operate as a fraud or deceit upon any person, in connection with the purchase or sale of any security.*

Rule 10b-5 is not restricted to purchases and sales of securities of reporting companies.[14] All transfers of securities, whether made on a stock exchange, in the over-the-counter market, in a private sale, or in connection with a merger, are subject to this rule.[15] The U.S. Supreme Court has held that only conduct involving **scienter** (intentional conduct) violates Section 10(b) and Rule 10b-5. Negligent conduct is not a violation.[16]

scienter
Intentional conduct; scienter is required for there to be a violation of Section 10(b) and Rule 10b-5.

Section 10(b) and Rule 10b-5 require reliance by the injured party on the misstatement. However, many sales and purchases of securities occur in open-market transactions (e.g., over stock exchanges), where there is no direct communication between the buyer and the seller.

Private Right of Action

Although Section 10(b) and Rule 10b-5 do not expressly provide for a private right of action, courts have *implied* such a right. Generally, a private plaintiff may seek rescission of the securities contract or recover damages (e.g., disgorgements of the illegal profits by the defendants). Private securities fraud claims must be brought within two years after discovery or five years after the violation occurs, whichever is shorter.

SEC Actions

The SEC may investigate suspected violations of the Securities Exchange Act of 1934 and of the rules and regulations adopted thereunder. The SEC may enter into *consent orders* with defendants, seek *injunctions* in federal district court, or seek court orders requiring defendants to *disgorge* illegally gained profits.

Insider Trading Sanctions Act
A federal statute that permits the SEC to obtain a civil penalty of up to three times the illegal benefits received from insider trading.

In 1984, Congress enacted the **Insider Trading Sanctions Act,**[17] which permits the SEC to obtain a **civil penalty** of up to three times the illegal profits gained or losses avoided on insider trading. The fine is payable to the U.S. Treasury. Under the Sarbanes-Oxley Act, the SEC may issue an order prohibiting any person who has committed securities fraud from acting as an officer or a director of a public company.

civil penalty
A fine assessed for a violation of a statute or regulation.

Criminal Liability

Section 32
A provision of the Securities Exchange Act of 1934 that imposes criminal liability on any person who willfully violates the 1934 act or the rules or regulations adopted thereunder.

Section 32 of the Securities Exchange Act of 1934 makes it a criminal offense to willfully violate the provisions of the act or the rules and regulations adopted thereunder.[18] Under the Sarbanes-Oxley Act of 2002, a person who willfully violates the Securities Exchange Act of 1934 can be fined up to $5 million or imprisoned for up to twenty-five years, or both. A corporation or another entity may be fined up to $2.5 million.

Insider Trading

insider trading
A situation in which an insider makes a profit by personally purchasing shares of the corporation prior to public release of favorable information or by selling shares of the corporation prior to the public disclosure of unfavorable information.

One of the most important purposes of Section 10(b) and Rule 10b-5 is to prevent **insider trading.** Insider trading occurs when a company employee or company advisor uses material nonpublic information to make a profit by trading in the securities of the company. This practice is considered illegal because it allows insiders to take advantage of the investing public.

In the *Matter of Cady, Roberts & Co.*[19] the SEC announced that the duty of an insider who possesses material nonpublic information is to either (1) abstain from trading in the securities of the company or (2) disclose the information to the person on the other side of the transaction before the insider purchases the securities from or sells the securities to the person.

For purposes of Section 10(b) and Rule 10b-5, **insiders** are defined as (1) officers, directors, and employees at all levels of a company; (2) lawyers, accountants, consultants, and agents and representatives who are hired by the company on a temporary and nonemployee basis to provide services or work to the company; and (3) others who owe a fiduciary duty to the company.

insider
Someone who has knowledge of facts not available to the general public.

Example: The Widger Corporation has its annual audit done by its outside certified public accountants (CPAs), Young & Old, CPAs. Priscilla is one of the CPAs who conduct the audit. The audit discloses that the Widger Corporation's profits have doubled since last year, and Priscilla rightfully discloses this fact to Martha, the chief financial officer (CFO) of Widger Corporation. Both Martha and Priscilla are *insiders*. The earnings information is definitely *material*, and it is *nonpublic* until the corporation publicly announces its earnings in two days. Prior to the earnings information being made public, Priscilla and Martha buy stock in Widger Corporation at $100 per share. After the earnings information is made public, the stock of Widger Corporation increases to $150 per share. Both Priscilla and Martha are liable for insider trading in violation of Section 10(b) and Rule 10b-5 because they traded in the securities of Widger Corporation while insiders in possession of material nonpublic inside information. Martha and Priscilla could be held civilly liable and criminally guilty of insider trading in violation of Section 10(b) and Rule 10b-5.

Tipper–Tippee Liability

A person who discloses material nonpublic information to another person is called a **tipper**. A person who receives such information is known as a **tippee**. A tippee is liable for acting on material information that he or she knew or should have known was not public. The tipper is liable for the profits made by the tippee. If the tippee tips other persons, both the tippee (who is now a tipper) and the original tipper are liable for the profits made by these remote tippees. The remote tippees are liable for their own trades if they knew or should have known that they possessed material inside information.

tipper
A person who discloses material nonpublic information to another person.

tippee
A person who receives material nonpublic information from a tipper.

In the following case, the court found an insider criminally liable for insider trading and tipping.

CASE 11.2 INSIDER TRADING

***United States v. Bhagat*, 436 F.3d 1140 (9th Cir. 2006).**

"The fact that this evidence was all circumstantial does not lessen its sufficiency to support a guilty verdict."

—Judge Rawlinson

Facts

He will lie sir, with such volubility that you would think truth were a tool.
William Shakespeare
All's Well That Ends Well (1604)

Atul Bhagat worked for NVIDIA Corporation (Nvidia). Nvidia competed for a multimillion-dollar contract to develop a video game console (the Xbox) for Microsoft Corporation. Upon receiving news that Nvidia had been awarded the contract, Nvidia's chief executive officer (CEO) sent a company-wide e-mail late Sunday night, announcing the contract award. The next morning, Nvidia sent a number of follow-up e-mails, advising Nvidia employees that the Xbox information should be kept confidential and imposing a trading blackout on the purchase of Nvidia stock by employees for several days.

On Monday morning, within roughly twenty minutes after the final e-mail was sent, Bhagat purchased a large quantity of Nvidia stock. Bhagat testified that he read the e-mails roughly forty minutes after he purchased the stock. Bhagat also testified that upon learning of the trading blackout, he attempted to cancel his trade by contacting his broker, who advised him that it was too late. Bhagat could not remember what company he contacted nor the name or gender of the person with whom he spoke. However, there was no direct evidence that Bhagat read the e-mails prior to his purchase of the Nvidia stock.

Less than one-half hour after Bhagat made his purchase, his friend Mamat Gill purchased Nvidia stock. Bhagat denied having told anyone about the Xbox contract before the information was made public. There was no direct evidence that Bhagat contacted Gill prior to Gill's purchase of Nvidia stock.

The Securities and Exchange Commission (SEC) investigated Bhagat's and Gill's purchases of Nvidia stock. Subsequently, the United States brought criminal charges against Bhagat, charging him with insider trading, tipping, and obstruction of an SEC investigation. Bhagat stuck with his story regarding his purchase of Nvidia stock and denied tipping Gill about the Xbox contract. Based on circumstantial evidence, the jury convicted Bhagat of insider trading, tipping, and obstruction of an SEC investigation. Bhagat appealed.

Issue

Was Bhagat criminally guilty of insider trading, tipping, and obstruction of an SEC investigation?

Language of the Court

Insider Trading *To convict Bhagat of insider trading, the government was required to prove that he traded stock on the basis of material, nonpublic information. The government offered significant evidence to support the jury's conclusion that Bhagat was aware of the confidential X-Box information before he executed his trades. The X-Box e-mails were sent prior to his purchase. The e-mails were found on his computer. Bhagat was at his office for several hours prior to executing his trade, which provided him the opportunity to read the e-mails. Finally, Bhagat took virtually no action to divest himself of the stock, or to inform his company that he had violated the company's trading blackout. The fact that this evidence was all circumstantial does not lessen its sufficiency to support a guilty verdict.*

Tipping *To convict Bhagat of tipping Gill, the government was required to prove that the tipper, Bhagat, provided the tippee, Gill, with material, inside information, prior to the tippee's purchase of stock. Viewing the evidence in the light most favorable to the prosecution, we cannot say that no reasonable trier* *of fact could have found Bhagat guilty. Bhagat and Gill were friends, Gill purchased stock shortly after Bhagat, and Gill's purchase was his largest purchase of the year.*

Obstructing an Agency Proceeding *To convict Bhagat for obstructing an agency proceeding, the government was required to prove that an agency of the United States government was conducting a proceeding; that the defendant was aware of that proceeding; and that the defendant intentionally interfered with, or obstructed the course of, that proceeding. Sufficient evidence also supports the jury's verdict on this charge. It is undisputed that there was an SEC investigative proceeding of which Bhagat was aware. The prosecution also introduced evidence that Bhagat intentionally obstructed that proceeding by providing the SEC investigators with false information to cover up his acts of insider trading and tipping and eliminate himself as a suspect.*

Decision

The U.S. Court of Appeals upheld the U.S. District Court's judgment, finding Bhagat criminally guilty of insider trading, tipping, and obstruction of the SEC's investigation. The U.S. Court of Appeals remanded the case to the U.S. District Court for sentencing of Bhagat.

Case Questions

1. **Critical Legal Thinking** What is insider trading? Explain. What is tipping? Explain.
2. **Business Ethics** Do you think Bhagat committed the crimes he was convicted of? Why or why not?
3. **Contemporary Business** What percentage of insider trading do you think the government catches?

Misappropriation Theory

The courts have developed laws to address trading in securities by insiders who possess inside information. However, sometimes a person who possesses inside information about a company is not an employee or a temporary insider of that company. Instead, the party may be an outsider. However, an outsider's misappropriation of information in violation of their fiduciary duty violates Section 10(b) and Rule 10b-5. This rule is called the **misappropriation theory.**

misappropriation theory
The doctrine that a person who wrongfully uses confidential information to buy or sell securities in violation of a duty owed to the one who is the information source is guilty of securities fraud.

CASE 11.3 MISAPPROPRIATION THEORY U.S. SUPREME COURT CASE

United States v. O'Hagan, 521 U.S. 642 (1997).

Facts

James O'Hagan was a partner in the law firm Dorsey & Whitney in Minneapolis, Minnesota. In July 1988, Grand Metropolitan PLC (Grand Met), a company based in London, England, hired Dorsey & Whitney to represent it in a secret tender offer for the stock of the Pillsbury Company, headquartered in Minneapolis. On August 18, 1988, O'Hagan began purchasing call options for Pillsbury stock. Each call option gave O'Hagan the right to purchase one hundred shares of Pillsbury stock at a specified price. O'Hagan continued to purchase call options in August and September, and he became the largest holder of call options for Pillsbury stock. In September, O'Hagan also purchased five thousand shares of Pillsbury common stock at $39 per share. These purchases were all made while Grand Met's proposed tender offer for Pillsbury remained secret to the public. When Grand Met publicly announced its tender offer in October 1988, Pillsbury stock increased to nearly $60 per share. O'Hagan sold his Pillsbury call options and common stock, making a profit of more than $4.3 million.

The U.S. Department of Justice charged O'Hagan with criminally violating Section 10(b) and Rule 10b-5. Because this was not a case of classic insider trading because O'Hagan did not trade in the stock of his law firm's client, Grand Met, the government alleged that O'Hagan was liable under the "misappropriation theory" for trading in Pillsbury stock by engaging in deceptive conduct by misappropriating the secret information about Grand Met's tender offer from his employer, Dorsey & Whitney, and from its client, Grand Met. The district court found O'Hagan guilty and sentenced him to forty-one months in prison. The Eighth Circuit Court of Appeals reversed, finding that liability under Section 10(b) and Rule 10b-5 cannot be based on the misappropriation theory. The government appealed to the U.S. Supreme Court.

Issue

Can a defendant be criminally convicted of violating Section 10(b) and Rule 10b-5 based on the misappropriation theory?

Court's Reasoning

The U.S. Supreme Court explained that the misappropriation theory holds that a person commits fraud in connection with a securities transaction, and thereby violates Section 10(b) and Rule 10b-5, when the person misappropriates confidential information for securities trading purposes, in breach of a duty owed to the source of the information. Under this theory, a fiduciary's undisclosed, self-serving use of a principal's information to purchase or sell securities, in breach of a duty of loyalty and confidentiality, defrauds the principal of the exclusive use of that information. The Supreme Court noted that the classical theory of insider trading targets a corporate insider's breach of duty to shareholders with whom the insider transacts; the misappropriation theory outlaws trading on the basis of nonpublic information by a corporate "outsider" in breach of a duty owed not to a trading party, but to the source of the information.

The misappropriation theory comports with Section 10(b)'s language, which requires deception "in connection with the purchase or sale of any security." The Supreme Court stated that it makes no sense to hold a lawyer such as O'Hagan a Section 10(b) violator if he works for a law firm representing the target of a tender offer (e.g., if he had worked for Pillsbury), but not if he works for a law firm representing the bidder (Grand Met). The text of the statute requires no such result.

Decision

The Supreme Court held that a defendant can be criminally convicted of violating Section 10(b) and Rule 10b-5 under the misappropriation theory. The Supreme Court reversed the decision of the Court of Appeals, which held otherwise.

Case Questions

1. **Critical Legal Thinking** Should the misappropriation theory be recognized as a basis for criminal liability under Section 10(b) and Rule 10b-5? Do you agree with the Supreme Court's decision?
2. **Business Ethics** If the Supreme Court had upheld the circuit court's decision, would ethics alone be enough to prevent persons like O'Hagan from trading on secret information?
3. **Contemporary Business** Will the securities markets be more or less honest because of the Supreme Court's ruling in this case?

Aiders and Abettors

Many principal actors in a securities fraud obtain the knowing assistance of other parties to successfully complete the fraud. These other parties are known as *aiders* and *abettors*. The principal party in a securities fraud is civilly liable and criminally guilty of violating Section 10(b) and Rule 10b-5. However, whether aiders and abettors were civilly liable under Section 10(b) and Rule 10b-5 was questionable. The U.S. Supreme Court decided this issue in the following case.

CASE 11.4 Aiding and Abetting

***Stoneridge Inv. Partners, LLC v. Scientific-Atlanta, Inc.*, 552 U.S. 148 (2008).**

"There is no private right of action for aiding and abetting a Section 10(b) violation."

—Justice Kennedy

Facts

Charter Communications, Inc. (Charter), fraudulently issued financial statements that affected the value of its securities. Charter was a cable operator that provided cable service to subscribers. Charter wanted to show increased subscriber growth and cash flow. To do so, Charter obtained the knowing assistance of two companies, Scientific-Atlanta, Inc. (Scientific), and Motorola, Inc. Scientific and Motorola supplied Charter with digital cable converters—set-top boxes—that Charter's cable subscribers needed to receive cable service.

Charter entered into a fraudulent arrangement with Scientific and Motorola whereby Charter would overpay $20 for each box it purchased from Scientific and Motorola. Charter would then capitalize these payments over years rather than expense them during the current year. In addition, the parties agreed that Scientific and Motorola would repay the overpayments by purchasing advertising from Charter at higher prices than fair value. This two-part fraudulent scheme would increase Charter's revenues and profits for the year. Charter was the primary fraudulent party, and Scientific and Motorola were aiders and abettors to Charter's fraud.

Charter gave its fraudulent financial statements to its outside auditor, Arthur Andersen LLP (Andersen), to audit. During its audit of the financial statements, Andersen was fooled and did not discover Charter's fraud. Andersen certified Charter's financial statements, which Charter filed with the Securities and Exchange Commission (SEC) and made public. The fraud was discovered, and the price of Charter's stock plummeted.

Stoneridge Investment Partners, LLC, which owned stock in Charter, brought a class action civil lawsuit against Scientific and Motorola on behalf of itself and other Charter shareholders (collectively "Stoneridge"). Stoneridge relied on the ability to bring its civil action on the implied private cause of action under Section 10(b) that previous U.S. Supreme Court decisions had created. The lawsuit alleged that Scientific and Motorola—the aiders and abettors to Charter's fraud—violated Section 10(b) and Rule 10b-5 and were liable to the plaintiffs for monetary damages. The U.S. District Court dismissed Stoneridge's lawsuit. The U.S. Court of Appeals affirmed. Stoneridge appealed to the U.S. Supreme Court.

Issue

Is there an implied private civil cause of action against aiders and abettors under Section 10(b)?

Language of the U.S. Supreme Court

We conclude the implied right of action does not reach the customer/supplier companies because the investors did not rely upon their statements or representations. At most, respondents had aided and abetted Charter's misstatement of its financial results; but, there is no private right of action for aiding and abetting a Section 10(b) violation. The Section 10(b) implied private right of action does not extend to aiders and abettors.

In all events we conclude respondents' deceptive acts, which were not disclosed to the investing public, are too remote to satisfy the requirement of reliance. It was Charter, not respondents, that misled its auditor and filed fraudulent financial statements. The petitioner invokes the private cause of action under Section 10(b) and seeks to apply it beyond the securities markets—the realm of financing business—to purchase and supply contracts—the realm of ordinary business operations. The latter realm is governed, for the most part, by state law. Concerns with the judicial creation of a private cause of action caution against its expansion. The decision to extend the cause of action is for Congress, not for us. Though it remains the law, the Section 10(b) private right should not be extended beyond its present boundaries.

Decision

The U.S. Supreme Court held that there was no implied civil private right of action under Section 10(b) against aiders and abettors of securities fraud. The U.S. Supreme Court affirmed the decision of the lower court and remanded the case for further proceedings, consistent with its opinion.

Note: Although the U.S. Supreme Court held that there was no implied private cause of action under Section 10(b) against aiders and abettors (here, Scientific and Motorola), it did not disturb the implied right of plaintiffs to bring private civil actions against the primary party who commits the securities fraud (here, Charter).

Therefore, Stoneridge would have an implied civil cause of action against Charter to recover monetary damages for securities fraud in violation of Section 10(b).

Under the express right of action provided in Section 10(b), the SEC can bring civil cases against aiders and abettors, and the U.S. government can bring criminal charges against aiders and abettors. An injured party (here, Stoneridge) can bring a civil common law fraud action in state court against aiders and abettors (here, Scientific and Motorola) to recover monetary damages.

If an auditor (here, Andersen) aids and abets a primary party's securities fraud (here, Charter), the auditor would stand in the same shoes as other aiders and abettors (here, Scientific and Motorola) and not be civilly liable because the U.S. Supreme Court's decision in this case eliminated an implied civil right of action against aiders and abettors under Section 10(b). However, an injured party (here, Stoneridge) could bring a civil common law action in state court against an auditor (here, Andersen) for negligence for not discovering the fraud.

Case Questions

1. **Critical Legal Thinking** What is the difference between an *express* cause of action and an *implied* cause of action? Explain.
2. **Business Ethics** Did Charter act ethically in this case? Why do you think Scientific and Motorola participated in Charter's fraud?
3. **Contemporary Business** Why do you think Stoneridge sued Scientific and Motorola? Explain.

SHORT-SWING PROFITS

Section 16(a) of the Securities Exchange Act of 1934 defines any person who is an executive officer, a director, or a 10 percent shareholder of an equity security of a reporting company as a statutory insider for Section 16 purposes. Statutory insiders must file reports with the SEC, disclosing their ownership and trading in the company's securities.[20] These reports must be filed with the SEC and made available on the company's website within two days after the trade occurs.

Section 16(b)

Section 16(b) of the Securities Exchange Act of 1934 requires that any profits made by a statutory insider on transactions involving **short-swing profits**—that is, trades involving equity securities occurring within six months of each other—belong to the corporation.[21] The corporation may bring a legal action to recover these profits. Involuntary transactions, such as forced redemption of securities by the corporation or an exchange of securities in a bankruptcy proceeding, are exempt. Section 16(b) is a strict liability provision. Generally, no defenses are recognized. Neither intent nor the possession of inside information need be shown.

Section 16(b)
A section of the Securities Exchange Act of 1934 that requires that any profits made by a statutory insider on transactions involving short-swing profits belong to the corporation.

short-swing profits
Profits made by an insider through the sale or other disposition of corporate stock within six months after purchase.

SEC Section 16 Rules

The SEC has adopted the following rules under Section 16:

- It clarifies the definition of **officer** to include only executive officers who perform *policy-making* functions. Officers who run day-to-day operations but are not responsible for policy decisions are not included.

officers
Employees of the corporation who are appointed by the board of directors to manage the day-to-day operations of the corporation.

Examples: Policy-making executives include the chief executive officer (CEO), the president, vice presidents in charge of business units or divisions, the chief financial officer (CFO), the principal accounting officer, and the like.

- It relieves insiders of liability for transactions that occur within six months before becoming an insider.

Example: If a noninsider buys shares of a company on January 15, is hired by the company and becomes an insider on March 15, and sells the shares on May 15, there is no liability.

- It continues the rule that insiders are liable for transactions that occur within six months of the last transaction engaged in while an insider.

Example: If an insider buys shares in his company on April 30 and leaves the company on May 15, he cannot sell the shares before October 30. If he does, he violates Section 16(b).

state securities laws ("blue-sky" laws)
State securities laws are often referred to as "blue-sky" laws because they help prevent investors from purchasing a piece of the blue sky.

Concept Summary

Section 10(b) and Section 16(b) Compared

Element	Section 10(b) and Rule 10b-5	Section 16(b)
Covered securities	All securities.	Securities required to be registered with the SEC under the 1934 act.
Inside information	Defendant made a misrepresentation or traded on inside (or perhaps misappropriated) information.	Short-swing profits recoverable whether or not they are attributable to misappropriation or inside information.
Recovery	Belongs to the injured purchaser or seller.	Belongs to the corporation.

STATE SECURITIES LAWS

Most states have enacted securities laws. These laws generally require the registration of certain securities, provide exemptions from registration, and contain broad antifraud provisions. State securities laws are usually applied when smaller companies are issuing securities within that state. The Uniform Securities Act has been adopted by many states. This act coordinates **state securities laws** with federal securities laws.

State securities laws are often referred to as **"blue-sky" laws** because they help prevent investors from purchasing a piece of the blue sky. The state that has most actively enforced its securities laws has been New York. The office of the New York state attorney has brought many high-profile criminal fraud cases in recent years. The website of the Office of the New York State Attorney is www.oag.state.ny.us/home.html.

CONTEMPORARY Environment

COMMODITIES REGULATION

Commodities include grains (e.g., wheat, soybeans, oats), animals (e.g., cattle, hogs), animal products (e.g., pork bellies), foods (e.g., sugar, coffee), metals (e.g., gold, silver), and oil. A commodities futures contract is an agreement to buy or sell a specific amount and type of commodity at some future date, at a price established at the time of contracting. For example, a futures contract may be to sell 5,000 bushels of a specified grain on August 31 at $5.00 per bushel. Standardized terms are established for futures contracts (e.g., quantity and quality of the commodity, time and place of delivery). Thus, the contracts can be bought and sold on the commodities exchanges just as stocks and bonds are bought and sold on securities exchanges. Farmers, ranchers, food processors, milling companies, mineral producers, oil companies, and investors often buy and sell futures contracts.

Commodities exchanges have been established at different locations across the country where commodity futures contracts can be bought and sold by food producers, farmers, and speculators. The major commodity exchanges are:

- The Chicago Mercantile Exchange (CME)
- The Chicago Board of Trade (CBOT), now part of the CME Group
- The Commodity Exchange of New York (COMEX)
- Kansas City Board of Trade (KBOT)
- New York Mercantile Exchange (NYME), now part of the CME Group
- New York Futures Exchange (NYF)

The federal **Commodity Exchange Act (CEA)** of 1936, as amended, regulates the trading of commodity futures contracts. The **Commodity Futures Trading Commission (CFTC)**, a federal administrative agency, has the authority to regulate trading in commodities futures contracts, to adopt regulations, conduct investigations, bring administrative proceedings against suspected violators, and impose civil fines. Suspected criminal violations can be referred to the Justice Department for criminal action.

Web Exercises

1. **Web** Visit the website of the Commodity Futures Trading Commission (CFTC), at www.cftc.gov.
2. **Web** Visit the website of the Chicago Board of Trade (CBOT), at www.cbot.com.
3. **Web** Visit the website of the New York Mercantile Exchange (NYME), at www.nymex.com.
4. **Web** Use www.google.com to find the price of a futures contract for pork bellies.

Concept Review

Definitions of Securities

Type of Security	Definition
Common securities	Interests or instruments that are commonly known as securities, such as common stock, preferred stock, debentures, and warrants.
Statutorily defined securities	Interests or instruments that are expressly mentioned in securities acts as being securities, such as interests in oil, gas, and mineral rights.
Investment contracts	A flexible standard for defining a security. Under the Howey test, a security exists if an investor invests money in a common enterprise and expects to make a profit from the significant efforts of others.

(continued)

Section 10(B) and Section 16(B) Compared

Element	Section 10(b) and Rule 10b-5	Section 16(b)
Covered securities	All securities.	Securities required to be registered with the SEC under the 1934 act.
Inside information	Defendant made a misrepresentation or traded on inside (or perhaps misappropriated) information.	Short-swing profits recoverable whether or not they are attributable to misappropriation or inside information.
Recovery	Belongs to the injured purchaser or seller.	Belongs to the corporation.

CHAPTER REVIEW

DEFINITION OF SECURITY, p. 321

Definition of Security

Security. A security must be found before federal securities laws apply. A *security* is defined as:

1. ***Common securities.*** Interests or instruments that are commonly known as securities, such as common stock, preferred stock, debentures, and warrants.
2. ***Statutorily defined securities.*** Interests or instruments that are expressly mentioned in securities acts as being securities, such as interests in oil, gas, and mineral rights.
3. ***Investment contracts.*** A flexible standard for defining a security. Under the *Howey test*, a security exists if (1) an investor invests money (2) in a common enterprise and (3) expects to make a profit off the significant efforts of others.

THE SECURITIES AND EXCHANGE COMMISSION (SEC), p. 324

The Securities and Exchange Commission (SEC)

Created in 1934, the SEC is a federal administrative agency empowered to administer federal securities laws. The SEC can adopt rules and regulations to interpret and implement federal securities.

PRIVATE TRANSACTIONS EXEMPT FROM REGISTRATION, p. 324

Transactions Exempt from Registration

The following *transactions* are exempt from the SEC registration process: (1) nonissuer transactions, (2) intrastate offerings, (3) private placements, and (4) small offerings.

Nonissuer Exemption

Securities transactions *not* made by an issuer, an underwriter, or a dealer are exempt from SEC registration. This covers normal purchases of securities by investors.

Intrastate Offering Exemption

A local business can issue securities without dollar limit without registering with the SEC if the following requirements are met:

1. The issuer is a resident of the state (e.g., the corporation is incorporated in the state).
2. The issuer is doing business in the state. This requires that:
   a. 80 percent of the issuer's assets are located in the state.
   b. 80 percent of the issuer's gross revenues are derived from the state.
   c. The issuer's principal office is located in the state.
   d. 80 percent of the proceeds of the offering will be used in the state.
3. The purchasers of the securities are all residents of the state.

Private Placement Exemption

An issue of securities that does not involve a public offering is exempt from SEC registration. There is no dollar limit on the amount of securities that can be issued pursuant to this exemption. Securities can be sold to any number of *accredited investors*, but to no more than thirty-five *nonaccredited investors*.

1. ***Accredited investors.*** These include:
   a. Any natural person (including spouse) who has a net worth of at least $1 million.
   b. Any natural person who has had an annual income of at least $200,000 for the previous two years and reasonably expects to make $200,000 income in the current year.
   c. Any corporation, partnership, or business trust with total assets in excess of $5 million.
   d. Insiders of the issuers, such as executive officers and directors of corporate issuers and general partners of partnership issuers.
   e. Certain institutional investors, such as registered investment companies, pension plans, colleges and universities, and the like.

Small Offering Exemption

An offering of securities that does not exceed $1 million during a twelve-month period is exempt from SEC registration. The securities may be sold to any number of purchasers.

Resale Restrictions

1. ***Restricted securities.*** Securities sold pursuant to the intrastate, private placement, or small offering exemptions are called *restricted securities*.
2. ***Rule 147.*** This SEC rule stipulates that securities sold pursuant to an *intrastate offering exemption* cannot be sold to nonresidents for a period of nine months.
3. ***Rule 144.*** This SEC rule stipulates that securities sold pursuant to the *private placement or small offering exemption* must be held for two years; limited sales may be made between years two and three; then unlimited sales are permitted.
4. ***Preventing transfer of restricted securities.*** To prevent the illegal transfer of restricted securities, the issuer must take the following precautions:
   a. **Affidavit.** The issuer must require investors to sign an affidavit stating that they are buying the securities for investment and promising not to transfer the restricted securities until the restrictions no longer apply.
   b. **Legend.** The issuer must place a legend on the stock certificate describing the restriction.

c. ***Transfer agent.*** The issuer must appoint and notify the transfer agent not to record a transfer of the securities that would violate the restriction.

5. ***Rule 144A.*** This SEC rule permits *qualified institutional investors*—defined as institutions that own and invest at least $100 million in securities—to buy unregistered securities without being subject to the holding periods of Rule 144.

Securities Exempt from Registration

The following *securities* are exempt from the SEC registration process:

1. Securities issued by any government in the United States (e.g., municipal bonds issued by city governments).
2. Short-term notes and drafts that have a maturity date that does not exceed nine months (e.g., commercial paper issued by corporations).
3. Securities issued by nonprofit issuers, such as religious institutions, charitable institutions, and colleges and universities.
4. Securities of financial institutions (e.g., banks, savings associations) that are regulated by the appropriate banking authorities.
5. Securities issued by common carriers (e.g., railroads, trucking companies) that are regulated by the Interstate Commerce Commission (ICC).
6. Insurance and annuity contracts issued by insurance companies.
7. Stock dividends and stock splits.
8. Securities issued in a corporate reorganization where one security is exchanged for another security.

THE SECURITIES ACT OF 1933: GOING PUBLIC, p. 327

The Securities Act of 1933

This act is a federal statute that primarily regulates the *issuance* of securities by corporations, partnerships, associations, and individuals.

Registration Statement

1. ***Section 5.*** This provision of the 1933 act requires an issuer to register its securities with the SEC prior to selling them to the public if the securities or transaction does not qualify for an exemption from registration.
2. ***Registration statement.*** This is a document that an issuer of securities files with the SEC to register its securities. It must contain information about the issuer, the securities to be issued, and other relevant information.

Prospectus

A prospectus is a written disclosure document that is submitted to the SEC with the registration statement. It is distributed to prospective investors to enable them to evaluate the financial risk of the investment.

Limitations on Activities During the Registration Process

1. ***Prefiling period.*** This period begins when the issuer first contemplates issuing securities and ends when the registration statement is filed with the SEC. During this period, the issuer cannot (1) offer to sell securities, (2) sell securities, or (3) condition the market.
2. ***Waiting period.*** This period begins when the registration statement is filed with the SEC and ends when the registration statement becomes effective. During this time, the issuer cannot (1) sell securities or (2) use

unapproved writing to offer to sell the securities. The issuer may make oral offers, distribute *preliminary* and *summary prospectuses*, and publish *tombstone ads*.

3. **Posteffective period.** This period begins when the registration statement becomes effective and runs until the issuer either sells all of the offered securities or withdraws them from sale. The issuer may offer to sell and sell the securities during this period. The issuer must deliver a *final prospectus* (*statutory prospectus*) to a purchaser prior to or at the time of confirming the sale or sending the security to the purchaser.

Regulation A Offering

Regulation A. This regulation permits an issuer to sell up to $5 million of securities to the public during a twelve-month period pursuant to a simplified registration process.

Small Business Offerings

1. ***Form U-7.*** This is a question-and-answer disclosure form that a business can complete and file with the SEC to sell securities pursuant to SCOR.

Private Actions

Private parties who have been injured by a violation of the 1933 act may sue the violator to rescind the securities contract or recover damages. The plaintiff may sue under:

1. ***Section 12.*** This provision of the 1933 act imposes civil liability on any person who violates the provisions of Section 5 of the act (e.g., sells unregistered securities).
2. ***Section 11.*** This provision of the 1933 act imposes civil liability on persons who intentionally defraud investors by making misrepresentations or omissions of material facts in the registration statement or are negligent in not discovering the fraud.
   a. ***Due diligence defense.*** This is a defense to a Section 11 action that, if proven, makes the defendant not liable. It requires the defendant to have made a reasonable investigation and had reasonable grounds to believe and did believe that the statements made in the registration statement were true.

SEC Actions

The SEC may seek the following remedies:

1. ***Consent order.*** The SEC may issue a consent order whereby a defendant agrees not to violate securities laws in the future but does not admit to violating securities laws in the past.
2. ***Injunction.*** The SEC may bring an action in federal district court to obtain an injunction.
3. ***Disgorgement of profits.*** The SEC may request the court to order the defendant to disgorge illegally gained profits.

Criminal Liability

Section 24 of the 1933 act imposes criminal liability on any person who willfully violates either the act or the rules and regulations adopted thereunder. Criminal actions are brought by the U.S. Justice Department.

THE SECURITIES EXCHANGE ACT OF 1934: TRADING IN SECURITIES, p. 335

The Securities Exchange Act of 1934

This federal statute primarily regulates the *trading* of securities.

Section 10(b) and Rule 10b-5

1. ***Section 10(b).*** This provision of the 1934 act prohibits the use of manipulative and deceptive devices in the purchase or sale of securities in contravention of the rules and regulations prescribed by the SEC.
2. ***Rule 10b-5.*** This rule adopted by the SEC clarifies the reach of Section 10(b) against deceptive and fraudulent activities in the purchase and sale of securities.
3. ***Scienter.*** Only conduct involving *scienter* (intentional conduct) violates Section 10(b) and Rule 10b-5. Negligent conduct is not a violation.

Private Right of Action

Section 10(b). A private plaintiff has an *implied right* under Section 10(b) and Rule 10b-5 to sue to rescind the securities contract or recover damages from a defendant who has engaged in manipulative and deceptive practices that have caused the plaintiff injury.

SEC Actions

The SEC may enter into *consent orders* with defendants, seek *injunctions* in federal district court, or seek orders requiring defendants to *disgorge* illegally gained profits.

Criminal Liability

Section 32 of the 1934 act imposes criminal liability on any person who willfully violates the 1934 act or the rules and regulations adopted thereunder. Criminal actions are brought by the U.S. Justice Department.

Insider Trading

Insider trading occurs when an insider makes a profit by purchasing shares of the commodity prior to public release of favorable information or selling shares of the corporation prior to public disclosure of unfavorable information. Insider trading violates Section 10(b) and Rule 10b-5.

1. ***Cady, Roberts rule.*** An insider who possesses material information must either (1) abstain from trading in the securities of the company or (2) disclose the information to the person from whom the insider purchases or to whom the insider sells the securities.

Insiders

For Section 10(b) and Rule 10b-5 purposes, insiders include all employees of a company, independent contractors hired by the company on a temporary basis to provide services or work to the company, and others who owe a fiduciary duty to the company.

Tipper–Tippee Liability

1. ***Tipper.*** A tipper is a person who discloses material nonpublic information to another person.
2. ***Tippee.*** A tippee is a person who receives material nonpublic information from a tipper.

3. ***Tippee's liability.*** The tippee is liable for acting on material information received from a tipper if he or she knew or should have known that the information was not public. The tippee must disgorge profits made on the tip.
4. ***Tipper's liability.*** The tipper is liable for his or her own profits and the profits made by the tippee.

SHORT-SWING PROFITS, p. 343

Short-Swing Profits

Statutory insiders. *Section 16(a)* of the Securities Exchange Act of 1934 defines a *statutory insider* for Section 16 purposes as any person who is an executive officer, a director, or a 10 percent shareholder of an equity security of a reporting company.

Section 16(b)

1. ***Short-swing profits.*** Short-swing profits are profits made by statutory insiders on trades involving equity securities that occur within six months of each other.
2. ***Section 16(b).*** This provision of the 1934 act requires that any profits made by a statutory insider on transactions involving short-swing profits belong to the corporation.

SEC Section 16 Rules

These rules issued by the SEC clarify the persons and transactions subject to Section 16 short-swing profit rules.

STATE SECURITIES LAWS, p. 344

State Securities Laws

Most states have enacted securities laws that regulate the issuance and trading of securities. These acts are often patterned after, and are designed to coordinate with, federal securities laws. The *Uniform Securities Act,* which is a model state securities act, has been adopted by many states.

TEST REVIEW TERMS AND CONCEPTS

Accredited investor 325
Civil penalty 336
Commodity Exchange Act (CEA) 345
Commodity Futures Trading Commission (CFTC) 345
Consent order 334
Due diligence defense 334
EDGAR 324
Exempt 324
Exempt security 326
Exempt transaction 324
Final prospectus (statutory prospectus)
Going public 335
Initial public offering (IPO) 328

CASE SCENARIO REVISITED

The McDonald Investment Company was a corporation organized and incorporated in the state of Minnesota. The principal and only place of business from which the company conducted operations was located in Rush City, Minnesota. More than 80 percent of the company's assets were located in Minnesota, and more than 80 percent of its income was derived from Minnesota. McDonald sold securities to Minnesota residents only. The proceeds from the sale were used entirely to make loans and other investments in real estate and other assets located outside the state of Minnesota. The company did not file a registration statement with the SEC. Does this offering qualify for an intrastate offering exemption from registration? For help with your answer, review the case *SEC v. McDonald Inv. Co.*, 343 F. Supp. 343 (D.Minn. 1972).

PORTFOLIO EXERCISE

Go the following website: http://www.sec.gov. Access the archive of historical EDGAR documents by clicking on the *Search for Company Filings* tab and then the *Boolean and advanced searching, including addresses* link. Type the name of the company you created at the beginning of the term. View the filing detail for the first match found and print the first document. If no documents match your query, try typing in a derivative of your business name. If that does not work, try typing in "USA."

WORKING THE WEB INTERNET EXERCISES

Activities

Note: For socially responsible investing information, see **www.socialinvest.org**.

1. Using the Stanford Securities Class Action Clearinghouse site, at **securities.stanford.edu**, identify the leading sector, industry, and companies targeted in securities class action litigation.
2. Investigate the modern varieties of fraud by reading the following law review articles:
   "Internet Securities Fraud: Old Trick, New Medium," at **www.law.duke.edu/journals/dltr/ARTICLES/2001dltr0006.html**
   "Software Disclosure and Liability Under the Securities Acts," at **www.law.duke.edu/journals/dltr/ARTICLES/2001dltr0016.html**
3. Determine whether an athletic club membership can be a *security* by using the U.S. Securities & Exchange Commission site, at **www.sec.gov**.
4. Who qualifies as *accredited investors*? See Bloomberg Online Financial Market Info, at **bloomberg.com**.
5. What is Rule 144 stock? See The Motley Fool, at **www.fool.com**.
6. What constitutes insider trading? See Microsoft Investor Version 4.0, at **moneycentral.msn.com/investor/home.asp**.

CRITICAL LEGAL THINKING CASES

Case 11.1 ***Definition of Security*** Dare To Be Great, Inc. (Dare), was a Florida corporation that was wholly owned by Glenn W. Turner Enterprises, Inc. Dare offered self-improvement courses aimed at improving self-motivation and sales ability. In return for an investment of money, the purchaser received certain tapes, records, and written materials. In addition, depending on the level of involvement, the purchaser had the opportunity to help sell the Dare courses to others and to receive part of the purchase price as a commission. There were four different levels of involvement.

The task of salespersons was to bring prospective purchasers to "Adventure Meetings." The meetings, which were conducted by Dare people and not the salespersons, were conducted in a preordained format that included great enthusiasm, cheering and charming, exuberant handshaking, standing on chairs, and shouting. The Dare people and the salespersons dressed in modern, expensive clothes, displayed large sums of cash, drove new expensive automobiles, and engaged in "hard-sell" tactics to induce prospects to sign their name and part with their money. In actuality, few Dare purchasers ever attained the wealth promised. The tape recordings and materials distributed by Dare were worthless. Is this sales scheme a "security" that should have been registered with the SEC? *SEC v. Glenn W. Turner Enters., Inc.*, 474 F.2d 476 (9th Cir. 1973).

Case 11.2 ***Definition of Security*** The Farmer's Cooperative of Arkansas and Oklahoma (Co-Op) was an agricultural cooperative that had approximately 23,000 members. To raise money to support its general business operations, Co-Op sold to investors promissory notes that were payable upon demand. Co-Op offered the notes to both members and nonmembers, advertised the notes as an "investment program," and offered an interest rate higher than that available on savings accounts at financial institutions. More than 1,600 people purchased the notes, worth a total of $10 million. Subsequently, Co-Op filed for bankruptcy. A class of holders of the notes filed suit against Ernst & Young, a national firm of certified public accountants that had audited Co-Op's financial statements, alleging that Ernst & Young had violated Section 10(b) of the Securities Exchange Act of 1934. Are the notes issued by Co-Op "securities"? *Reeves v. Ernst & Young*, 494 U.S. 56 (1990).

Case 11.3 ***Transaction Exemption*** Continental Enterprises, Inc., had 2,510,000 shares of stock issued and outstanding. Louis E. Wolfson and members of his immediate family and associates owned in excess of 40 percent of those shares. The balance was in the hands of approximately five thousand outside shareholders. Wolfson was Continental's largest shareholder and the guiding spirit of the corporation, who gave direction to and controlled the company's officers. During the course of five months, without public disclosure, Wolfson and his family and associates sold 55 percent of their stock through six brokerage houses. Wolfson and his family and associates did not file a registration statement with the SEC with respect to these sales. Do the securities sales by Wolfson and his family and associates qualify for an exemption for registration as a sale "not by an issuer, an underwriter, or a dealer"? *United States v. Wolfson*, 405 F.2d 779 (2nd Cir. 1968).

Case 11.4 ***Insider Trading*** Chiarella worked as a "markup man" in the New York composing room of Pandick Press, a financial printer. Among the documents that Chiarella handled were five secret announcements of corporate takeovers. The tender offerors had hired Pandick Press to print the offers, which would later be made public, when the tender offers were made to the shareholders of the target corporations. When the documents were delivered to Pandick Press, the identities of the acquiring and target corporations were concealed by blank spaces or false names. The true names would not be sent to Pandick Press until the night of the final printing.

Chiarella was able to deduce the names of the target companies before the final printing. Without disclosing this knowledge, he purchased stock in the target companies and sold the shares immediately after the takeover attempts were made public. Chiarella realized a gain of $30,000 in the course of fourteen months. The federal government indicted Chiarella for criminal violations of Section 10(b) of the Securities Exchange Act of 1934. Is Chiarella guilty? *Chiarella v. United States*, 445 U.S. 222 (1980).

Case 11.5 *Section 10(b)* Leslie Neadeau was the president of T.O.N.M. Oil & Gas Exploration Corporation (TONM). Charles Lazzaro was a registered securities broker employed by Batemen Eichler, Hill Richards, Inc. (Bateman Eichler). The stock of TONM was traded in the over-the-counter market. Lazzaro made statements to potential investors that he had "inside information" about TONM, including that (1) vast amounts of gold had been discovered in Surinam and that TONM had options on thousands of acres in the gold-producing regions of Surinam; (2) the discovery was "not publicly known, but would be subsequently announced"; and (3) when this information was made public, TONM stock, which was then selling from $1.50 to $3.00 per share, would increase to $10.00 to $15.00 within a short period of time and might increase to $100.00 per share within a year.

The potential investors contacted Neadeau at TONM, and he confirmed that the information was not public knowledge. In reliance on Lazzaro's and Neadeau's statements, the investors purchased TONM stock. The "inside information" turned out to be false, and the shares declined substantially below the purchase price. The investors sued Lazzaro, Bateman Eichler, Neadeau, and TONM, alleging violations of Section 10(b) of the Securities Exchange Act of 1934. The defendants asserted that the plaintiffs' complaint should be dismissed because they participated in the fraud. Who wins? *Bateman Eichler, Hill Richards, Inc. v. Berner*, 472 U.S. 299 (1985).

Case 11.6 *Insider Trading* Donald C. Hoodes was the chief executive officer of the Sullair Corporation. As an officer of the corporation, he was regularly granted stock options to purchase stock of the company at a discount. On July 20, Hoodes sold six thousand shares of Sullair common stock for $38,350. On July 31, Sullair terminated Hoodes as an officer of the corporation. On August 20, Hoodes exercised options to purchase six thousand shares of Sullair stock that cost Hoodes $3.01 per share ($18,060) at the time they were trading at $4.50 per share ($27,000). Hoodes did not possess material nonpublic information about Sullair when he sold or purchased the securities of the company. The corporation brought suit against Hoodes to recover the profits Hoodes made on these trades. Who wins? *Sullair Corp. v. Hoodes*, 672 F. Supp. 337 (N.D. Ill. 1987).

BUSINESS ETHICS CASES

Case 11.7 *Business Ethics* Stephen Murphy owned Intertie, a California company that was involved in financing and managing cable television stations. Murphy was both an officer of the corporation and chairman of the board of directors. Intertie would buy a cable television station, make a small cash down payment, and finance the remainder of the purchase price. It would then create a limited partnership and sell the cable station to the partnership for a cash down payment and a promissory note in favor of Intertie. Finally, Intertie would lease the station back from the partnership. Intertie purchased more than thirty stations and created an equal number of limited partnerships, from which it received more than $7.5 million from approximately four hundred investors.

Evidence showed that most of the limited partnerships were not self-supporting but that this fact was not disclosed to investors. Intertie commingled partnership funds, taking funds generated from the sale of new partnership offerings to meet debt service obligations of previously sold cable systems; Intertie also used funds from limited partnerships that were formed but that never acquired cable systems. Intertie did not keep any records regarding the qualifications of investors to purchase the securities and also refused to make its financial statements available to investors.

Intertie suffered severe financial difficulties and eventually filed for bankruptcy. The limited partners suffered substantial losses. Did each of the limited partnership offerings alone qualify for the private placement exemption from registration? Should the thirty limited partnership offerings be integrated? *SEC v. Murphy*, 626 F.2d 633 (9th Cir. 1980).

Case 11.8 ***Business Ethics*** R. Foster Winans, a reporter for *The Wall Street Journal*, was one of the writers of the "Heard on the Street" column, a widely read and influential column in the *Journal*. This column frequently included articles that discussed the prospects of companies listed on national and regional stock exchanges and the over-the-counter market. David Carpenter worked as a news clerk at the *Journal*. The *Journal* had a conflict-of-interest policy that prohibited employees from using nonpublic information learned on the job for their personal benefit. Winans and Carpenter were aware of this policy.

Kenneth P. Felis and Peter Brant were stockbrokers at the brokerage house of Kidder Peabody. Winans agreed to provide Felis and Brant with information that was to appear in the "Heard" column in advance of its publication in the *Journal*. Generally, Winans would provide this information to the brokers the day before it was to appear in the *Journal*. Carpenter served as a messenger between the parties. Based on this advance information, the brokers bought and sold securities of companies discussed in the "Heard" column. During 1983 and 1984, prepublication trades of approximately twenty-seven "Heard" columns netted profits of almost $690,000. The parties used telephones to transfer information. *The Wall Street Journal* is distributed by mail to many of its subscribers.

Eventually, Kidder Peabody noticed a correlation between the "Heard" column and trading by the brokers. After an SEC investigation, criminal charges were brought against defendants Winans, Carpenter, and Felis in U.S. District Court. Brant became the government's key witness. Winans and Felis were convicted of conspiracy to commit securities, mail, and wire fraud. Carpenter was convicted of aiding and abetting the commission of securities, mail, and wire fraud. The defendants appealed their convictions. Can the defendants be held criminally liable for conspiring to violate and aiding and abetting the violation of Section 10(b) and Rule 10b-5 of securities law? Did Winans act ethically in this case? Did Brant act ethically by turning government's witness? *United States v. Carpenter*, 484 U.S. 19 (1987).

ENDNOTES

1. *SEC v. W.J. Howey Co.*, 328 U.S. 293 (1946).
2. Securities Act of 1933, Section 3(a)(11).
3. SEC Rule 147.
4. Securities Act of 1933, Section 4(2).
5. SEC Rule 506.
6. SEC Rule 501.
7. Securities Act of 1933, Section 3(b).
8. 15 U.S.C. Sections 77a–77aa.
9. *Escott v. BarChris Constr. Corp.*, 283 F. Supp. 643 (S.D.N.Y. 1968).
10. 15 U.S.C. Section 77x.
11. 15 U.S.C. Sections 78a–78mm.
12. 15 U.S.C. Section 78j(b).
13. 17 C.F.R.240.10b-5.
14. Litigation instituted pursuant to Section 10(b) and Rule 10b-5 must be commenced within one year after the discovery of the violation and within three years after such violation. *Lampf, Pleva, Lipkind, Prupis & Petigrow v. Gilbertson, 501 U.S. 350 (1991).*
15. The U.S. Supreme Court has held that the sale of a business is a sale of securities that is subject to Section 10(b). *See Gould v. Ruefenacht*, 471 U.S. 701(1985), where 50 percent of a business was sold, and *Landreth Timber Co. v. Landreth*, 471 U.S. 681 (1985), where 100 percent of a business was sold.
16. *Ernst & Ernst v. Hochfelder*, 425 U.S. 185 (1976).
17. 15 U.S.C. Section 78ff.
18. P.L. 98–376.
19. *In re Cady, Roberts & Co.*, 40 SEC 907 (1961).
20. 15 U.S.C. Section 781.
21. 15 U.S.C. Section 78p(b).

"It is difficult to imagine any grounds, other than our own personal economic predilections, for saying that the contract of employment is any the less an appropriate subject of legislation than are scores of others, in dealing with which this Court has held that legislatures may curtail individual freedom in the public interest."

–Justice Stone

Morehead v. New York,
298 U.S. 587 (1936).

Employment, Worker Protection, and Immigration Laws

CHAPTER 12

CASE SCENARIO

The law firm at which you work as a paralegal represents John B. Wilson (Wilson). Wilson was employed by the city of Modesto, California, as a police officer. He was a member of the special emergency reaction team (SERT), a tactical unit of the city's police department that is trained and equipped to handle highly dangerous criminal situations. Membership in SERT is voluntary for police officers. No additional pay or benefits are involved. To be a member of SERT, each officer is required to pass physical tests four times a year. One such test requires members to run two miles in seventeen minutes. Other tests call for minimum numbers of push-ups, pull-ups, and sit-ups. Officers who do not belong to SERT are not required to undergo these physical tests. One day, Wilson completed his patrol shift, changed clothes, and drove to the Modesto Junior College track. While running there, he injured his left ankle.

CHAPTER OBJECTIVES

After studying this chapter, you should be able to:

1. Explain how state workers' compensation programs work and describe the benefits available.
2. Describe employers' duty to provide safe working conditions under the Occupational Safety and Health Act.
3. Describe the minimum wage and overtime pay rules of the Fair Labor Standards Act.
4. Describe the protections afforded by the Family and Medical Leave Act
5. Explain the rules governing private pensions under the Employee Retirement Income Security Act.

PARALEGAL PERSPECTIVE

Cathy Lynn Davis, ACP, *is a paralegal with the law firm Wilkerson & Bryan, P.C., in Montgomery, Alabama. She graduated from Faulkner University with a masters in criminal justice. She has been working as a paralegal for fourteen years.*

What are the most important paralegal skills needed in your job? You must have an ability to organize cases with massive documents, computer skills, and research skills.

What is the academic background required for a paralegal entering your area of practice? There are no academic mandates, although most firms are now requiring a degree in paralegal studies from an ABA-approved institution or an advanced paralegal certification from a national paralegal association.

How is technology involved in your job? I spend a great deal of time researching online various decisions from other states and staying current with new FTC and FCC requirements for clients. I also do most, if not all, filings electronically.

What trends do you see in your area of practice that will likely affect your job in the future? One trend is the implementation of new governmental regulations that will require clients to adapt their employment and business procedures to remain current.

What do you feel is the biggest issue currently facing the paralegal profession? There is a need for a professional standard or hiring requirements.

What words of advice do you have for a new paralegal entering your area of practice? Learn from those who have gone before you. Try to find a mentor or someone you can talk to when you are not sure.

■ INTRODUCTION TO EMPLOYMENT, WORKER PROTECTION, AND IMMIGRATION LAWS

Before the Industrial Revolution, the doctrine of laissez-faire governed the employment relationship in this country. Generally, this meant that employment was subject to the common law of contracts and agency law. In most instances, employees and employers had somewhat equal bargaining power.

This changed dramatically when the country became industrialized in the late 1800s. For one thing, large corporate employers had much more bargaining power than their employees. For another, the issues of child labor, unsafe working conditions, long hours, and low pay caused concern. Both federal and state legislation were enacted to protect workers' rights. Today, employment law is a mixture of contract law, agency law, and government regulation.

Today, many high-technology and other businesses rely on employees who have been issued work visas by the U.S. government to work in the United States. These workers have to meet certain qualifications to obtain foreign guest worker visas.

This chapter discusses employment law, workers' compensation, occupational safety, overtime pay, government programs, immigration law, and other laws affecting employment.

■ WORKERS' COMPENSATION

Many types of employment are dangerous, and each year, many workers are injured on the job. Under common law, employees who were injured on the job could sue their employers for negligence. This time-consuming process placed the employee at odds with their employer. In addition, there was no guarantee that the employee would win the case. Ultimately, many injured workers—or the heirs of deceased workers—were left uncompensated.

Workers' compensation acts were enacted by states in response to the unfairness of that result. These acts create an administrative procedure for workers to receive compensation for injuries that occur on the job. First, the injured worker files a claim with the appropriate state government agency (often called the workers' compensation board or commission). Next, that entity determines the legitimacy of the claim. If the worker disagrees with the agency's findings, he or she may appeal the decision through the state court system. Workers' compensation benefits are paid according to preset limits established by statute or regulation. The amounts that are recoverable vary from state to state.

workers' compensation
Compensation paid to workers and their families when workers are injured in connection with their jobs.

Workers' Compensation Insurance

States usually require employers to purchase insurance from private insurance companies or state funds to cover workers' compensation claims. Some states permit employers to self-insure if they demonstrate that they have the ability to pay workers' compensation claims. Many large companies self-insure. Workers can sue their employers in court to recover damages for employment-related injuries if the employer does not carry **workers' compensation insurance** or does not self-insure if permitted to do so.

Employment-Related Injury

For an injury to be compensable under workers' compensation, the claimant must prove that the injury arose out of and in the course of his or her employment. An accident that occurs while an employee is actively working is clearly within the scope of this rule. Accidents that occur at a company cafeteria or while on a business lunch for an employer are covered. Accidents that happen while the employee is at an off-premises restaurant during his or her personal lunch hour are not covered. Many workers' compensation acts include stress as a compensable employment-related injury.

Exclusive Remedy

Workers' compensation is an **exclusive remedy**. Thus, workers cannot both receive workers' compensation and sue their employers in court for damages. There is one exception to this rule: If an employer intentionally injures a worker, the worker can collect workers' compensation benefits and sue the employer. Workers' compensation acts do not bar injured workers from suing responsible third parties to recover damages.

The following case involves workers' compensation issues.

CASE 12.1 WORKERS' COMPENSATION

***Medrano v. Marshall Elec. Contracting, Inc.*, 173 S.W.3d 333 (Mo. Ct. App. 2005).**

"In determining that Medrano's accidental death arose out of and in the course of his employment with MEC, the Commission relied on the mutual benefit doctrine."

—Judge Hardwick

Facts

Immar Medrano was employed as a journeyman electrician by Marshall Electrical Contracting, Inc. (MEC), in Marshall, Missouri. Medrano attended an electrician apprenticeship night class at a community college in Sedalia, Missouri. MEC paid Medrano's tuition and book fees. Attendance at the course required Medrano to drive 70 miles round-trip. One night, when Medrano was driving home from the class, a drunk driver crossed the centerline of U.S. Highway 65 and collided head-on with Medrano's automobile. Medrano died in the accident. His wife and two children filed a workers' compensation claim for death benefits against MEC. After a hearing, an administrative law judge (ALJ) denied the claim, determining that Medrano's death did not arise out of or within the course and scope of his employment. The Labor and Industrial Relations Commission (Commission) reversed the ALJ's decision, finding that Medrano was acting within the course and scope of his employment when he was killed, and awarded death benefits to Medrano's family. MEC appealed.

Issue

Was Medrano acting within the course and scope of his employment when he was killed in the automobile accident?

Language of the Court

In determining that Medrano's accidental death arose out of and in the course of his employment with MEC, the Commission relied on the mutual benefit doctrine. The doctrine holds that an injury suffered by an employee while performing an act for the mutual benefit of the employer and the employee is usually compensable. MEC argues that it received no benefit from Medrano's attendance at the apprenticeship class and, thus, the Commission erred in determining the death claim was compensable. However, our review of the entire record indicates there is substantial and competent evidence to support the Commission's finding that the classroom instruction was beneficial to Medrano and his employer.

Mike Mills, the owner and president of MEC, testified at the administrative hearing: "The training made the employees more valuable to MEC by improving the quality of service to customers." The record is sufficient to show that MEC derived substantial benefit from having its employees travel from Marshall to Sedalia to fully participate in the apprenticeship program. MEC encouraged employees to attend the classroom instruction and covered the costs of tuition. Even though employees like Medrano obtained personal benefits in formalizing their education, MEC mutually benefited from the program as a convenient way for MEC to train its employees and ultimately provide a better quality of service to its customers.

Decision

The court of appeals upheld the Commission's finding that Medrano was acting within the course and scope of his employment when he was fatally injured in the car crash. The court of appeals affirmed the Commission's award of workers' compensation death benefits to Medrano's family.

Case Questions

1. **Critical Legal Thinking** What is workers' compensation? Explain. What does the mutual benefit doctrine provide? Explain.

2. **Business Ethics** Was it ethical for MEC to argue that it did not owe workers' compensation death benefits to Medrano's surviving family?
3. **Contemporary Business** Do businesses favor workers' compensation programs? Why or why not? Do employees favor workers' compensation programs? Why or why not?

OCCUPATIONAL SAFETY

In 1970, Congress enacted the **Occupational Safety and Health Act**[1] to promote safety in the workplace. Virtually all private employers are within the scope of the act, but federal, state, and local governments are exempt. Industries regulated by other federal safety legislation are also exempt.[2] The act also established the **Occupational Safety and Health Administration (OSHA)**, a federal administrative agency within the Department of Labor that is empowered to enforce the act. The act imposes record-keeping and reporting requirements on employers and requires them to post notices in the workplace, informing employees of their rights under the act.

Occupational Safety and Health Act
A federal act enacted in 1970 that promotes safety in the workplace.

Occupational Safety and Health Administration (OSHA)
A federal administrative agency that is empowered to enforce the Occupational Safety and Health Act.

OSHA is empowered to adopt rules and regulations to interpret and enforce the Occupational Safety and Health Act. OSHA has adopted thousands of regulations to enforce the safety standards established by the act.

Specific Duty Standards

Many of the OSHA standards are **specific duty standards**. For example, OSHA standards establish safety requirements for equipment (e.g., safety guards), set maximum exposure levels for hazardous chemicals, regulate the location of machinery, establish safety procedures for employees, and the like.

specific duty standard
An OSHA standard that addresses a safety problem of a specific duty nature (e.g., requirement for a safety guard on a particular type of equipment).

PARALEGAL PERSPECTIVE

***Gia Marie Gnolfo** works with the law firm Patton & Ryan, LLC, in Chicago, Illinois. She received an associate in paralegal studies from MacCormac College. Her area of specialization is insurance defense. She has been working as a paralegal for two and a half years.*

How or why is a paralegal important to the area of employment, worker protection, and immigration? In the areas of employment, immigration, and worker protection law, a paralegal acts as a liaison to assure laborers' rights are preserved and their interests are respected.

What are the most important paralegal skills needed in your job? You must pay attention to detail, have outstanding organizational skills, and be extremely competent. You have to stay "on top of the game!"

What is the academic background required for a paralegal entering your area of practice? A certificate is required.

How is technology involved in your job? We use computers, electronic software, and transcription machines.

What trends do you see in your area of practice that will likely affect your job in the future? The insurance business is a major area of everyday life. There is so much litigation, liability, and money involved.

What do you feel is the biggest issue currently facing the paralegal profession? We will always be an essential asset to our attorney and a law firm; however we need to demand respect and appreciation for all our hard work and dedication.

What words of advice do you have for a new paralegal entering your area of practice? Stay organized, learn to prioritize, manage your time, and also pay attention. Communicate with your attorney and SMILE!

General Duty

general duty
A duty that an employer has to provide a work environment free from recognized hazards that are causing or are likely to cause death or serious physical harm to employees.

The Occupational Safety and Health Act imposes a **general duty** on an employer to provide a work environment free from recognized hazards that are causing or are likely to cause death or serious physical harm to his or her employees. This is so even if no specific regulation applies to the situation.

OSHA is empowered to inspect places of employment for health hazards and safety violations. If a violation is found, OSHA can issue a *written citation* that requires the employer to abate or correct the situation. Contested citations are reviewed by the Occupational Safety and Health Review Commission. Its decision is appealable to the Court of Appeals for the Federal Circuit. Employers who violate the act, OSHA rules and regulations, or OSHA citations are subject to both civil and criminal penalties.

ETHICS SPOTLIGHT

COMPANY VIOLATES OSHA'S SAFETY RULE

"The purpose of the safety devices listed in the regulation is to provide fall protection, and a roof cannot provide fall protection if workers must operate along the perimeter."

—Judge Thornberry

Corbesco, Inc. (Corbesco), an industrial roofing and siding installation company, was hired to put metal roofing and siding over the skeletal structure of five aircraft hangars at Chennault Air Base in Louisiana. Corbesco assigned three of its employees to work on the partially completed flat roof of Hangar B, a large single-story building measuring 60 feet high, 374 feet wide, and 574 feet long. Soon after starting work, one of the workers, Roger Matthew, who was on his knees installing insulation on the roof, lost his balance and fell 60 feet to the concrete below. He was killed by the fall.

The next day, an Occupational Safety and Health Administration (OSHA) compliance officer cited Corbesco for failing to install a safety net under the work site. The officer cited an OSHA safety standard that requires that safety nets be provided when workers are more than 25 feet above the ground. Corbesco argued that the flat roof on which the employees were working served as a "temporary floor," and therefore, it was not required to install a safety net. An administrative law judge (ALJ) of the Occupational Safety and Health Review Commission (Commission) held that Corbesco had committed a serious violation of the Occupational Safety and Health Act (Act) by failing to install a safety net at the work site. Corbesco appealed.

The U.S. Court of Appeals rejected Corbesco's argument. The Court of Appeals held that Corbesco had notice that it was required to install safety nets under its crew while they were working on the edge of a flat roof some 60 feet above a concrete floor. The Court of Appeals stated:

> *Moreover, we do not believe that the Commission has abused its discretion by determining that a flat roof cannot be a temporary floor. The purpose of the safety devices listed in the regulation is to provide fall protection, and a roof cannot provide fall protection if workers must operate along the perimeter.*

The Court of Appeals held that Corbesco had violated OSHA's rules by not providing a safety net below its employees who were working more than 25 feet above the ground.

Note: This case involves OSHA suing the company for a violation of a federal occupational safety rule. The dependents of the worker who was killed in this case can collect workers' compensation benefits because the worker was killed while on the job. *Corbesco, Inc. v. Dole*, 926 F.2d 422 (5th Cir. 1991).

Business Ethics

1. Did Corbesco act ethically in arguing that the flat roof created a temporary floor that relieved it of the duty to install a safety net?

FAIR LABOR STANDARDS ACT (FLSA)

In 1938, Congress enacted the **Fair Labor Standards Act (FLSA)** to protect workers.[3] The FLSA applies to private employers and employees engaged in the production of goods for interstate commerce. The U.S. Department of Labor is empowered to enforce the FLSA. Private civil actions are also permitted under the FLSA.

Fair Labor Standards Act (FLSA)
A federal act enacted in 1938 to protect workers. It prohibits child labor and spells out minimum wage and overtime pay requirements.

Child Labor

The FLSA forbids the use of oppressive child labor and makes it unlawful to ship goods produced by businesses that use oppressive child labor. The Department of Labor has adopted the following regulations that define lawful child labor: (1) Children under the age of 14 cannot work except as newspaper deliverers; (2) children ages 14 and 15 may work limited hours in nonhazardous jobs approved by the Department of Labor (e.g., restaurants, gasoline stations); and (3) children ages 16 and 17 may work unlimited hours in nonhazardous jobs. The Department of Labor determines which occupations are hazardous (e.g., mining, roofing, working with explosives). Children who work in agricultural employment and child actors and performers are exempt from these restrictions. Persons age 18 and older may work at any job, whether it is hazardous or not.

Minimum Wage

The FLSA establishes minimum wage and overtime pay requirements for workers. Managerial, administrative, and professional employees are exempt from the act's wage and hour provisions. The FLSA requires that most employees in the United States be paid at least the federal minimum wage for all hours worked. The federal **minimum wage** is set by Congress and can be changed. As of 2009, it was set at $7.25 per hour. The Department of Labor permits employers to pay less than the minimum wage to students and apprentices. An employer may reduce the minimum wage by an amount equal to the reasonable cost of food and lodging provided to employees.

minimum wage
The federal minimum wage is set by Congress and can be changed. As of 2009, it was set at $7.25 per hour.

There is a special minimum wage rule for tipped employees. An employee who earns tips can be paid $2.13 an hour by an employer if that amount plus the tips received equals at least the minimum wage. If an employee's tips and direct employer payment does not equal the minimum wage, then the employer must make up the difference.

Over half of the states have enacted minimum wage laws that set minimum wages at a rate higher than the federal rate. Some cities have enacted minimum wage requirements, usually called **living wage laws**, which also set higher minimum wage rates than the federal level.

living wage laws
Some cities have enacted these minimum wage requirements, which set higher minimum wage rates than the federal level.

Overtime Pay

Under the FLSA, an employer cannot require nonexempt employees to work more than forty hours per week unless they are paid **overtime pay** of one-and-a-half times their regular pay for each hour worked in excess of forty hours that week. Each week is treated separately.

overtime pay
Under the FLSA, an employer cannot require nonexempt employees to work more than forty hours per week unless they are paid overtime pay of one-and-a-half times their regular pay for each hour worked in excess of forty hours that week. Each week is treated separately.

Example: If an employee works fifty hours one week and thirty hours the next week, the employer owes the employee ten hours of overtime pay for the first week.

ETHICS SPOTLIGHT

FAIR LABOR STANDARDS ACT PAY VIOLATION

"The relevant text describes the workday as roughly the period from 'whistle to whistle.'"

–Justice Stevens

IBP, Inc., is a large producer of fresh beef, pork, and related products. At its plant in Pasco, Washington, it employs approximately 178 workers in its slaughter division and 800 line workers. All workers must wear gear such as outer garments, hardhats, earplugs, gloves, aprons, leggings, and boots. Those who use knives must wear additional protective equipment. IBP requires employees to store their equipment and tools in company locker rooms, where the workers don and doff their equipment and protective gear.

The pay for production workers is based on time spent cutting and bagging meat. Pay begins with the first piece of meat and ends with the last piece of meat. IBP pays for four minutes of clothes-changing time. IBP employees filed a class action lawsuit against IBP to recover compensation for preproduction and postproduction work, including time spent donning and doffing protective gear and time walking between the locker room and the production floor before and after their assigned shifts. The employees alleged that IBP violated the Fair Labor Standards Act (FLSA).

The U.S. District Court and the U.S. Court of Appeals held in favor of the workers. On appeal to the U.S. Supreme Court, IBP gave up on its claim for paying for the donning and doffing of protective gear but still alleged that it did not have to pay for the time spent by employees walking between the locker room and production area. The Supreme Court held against IBP. The Supreme Court stated:

> *The Department of Labor has adopted the continuous workday rule, which means that the "workday" is generally defined as the period between the commencement and completion on the same workday of an employee's principal activity or activities. The relevant text describes the workday as roughly the period from "whistle to whistle." Moreover, during a continuous workday, any walking time that occurs after the beginning of the employee's first principal activity and before the end of the employee's last principal activity is covered by the FLSA.*

The U.S. Supreme Court held that the time spent by employees walking between the locker room and the production areas of the plant was compensable under the Fair Labor Standards Act. The Supreme Court confirmed the District Court's award of $3 million to the workers. *IBP, Inc. v. Alvarez*, 546 U.S. 21 (2005).

Business Ethics

1. Did IBP act ethically in not paying the workers for the time they spent walking between the locker room and the production areas? Explain. Why do you think IBP, Inc., fought so hard against the workers' demands?

Exemptions from Minimum Wage and Overtime Pay Requirements

The FLSA establishes the following categories of exemptions from federal minimum wage and overtime pay requirements:

- ***Executive exemption.*** Executives who are compensated on a salary basis, who engage in management, have authority to hire employees, and regularly direct two or more employees.
- ***Administrative employee exemption.*** Employees who are compensated on a salary or fee basis, whose primary duty is the performance of office or nonmanual work, and whose work includes the exercise of discretion and independent judgment with respect to matters of significance.

- ***Learned professional exemption.*** Employees compensated on a salary or fee basis who perform work that is predominantly intellectual in character, who possess advanced knowledge in a field of science or learning, and whose advanced knowledge was acquired through a prolonged course of specialized intellectual instruction.
- ***Highly compensated employee exemption.*** Highly compensated employees who perform office or nonmanual work, are paid total annual compensation of $100,000 or more, and regularly perform at least one of the duties of an exempt executive, administrative, or professional employee.
- ***Computer employee exemption.*** Employees compensated either on a salary or fee basis; are employed as a computer systems analyst, computer programmer, software engineer, or other similarly skilled worker in the computer field; and are engaged in the design, development, documentation, analysis, creation, testing, or modification of computer systems or programs.
- ***Outside sales representative exemption.*** Employees whose primary duty is making sales or obtaining orders or contracts for services, who will be paid by the client or customer, and who are customarily and regularly engaged away from the employer's place of business.

ETHICS SPOTLIGHT

MICROSOFT VIOLATES FEDERAL EMPLOYMENT LAW

"It is our conclusion that Microsoft either exercised, or retained the right to exercise, direction over the services performed. This control establishes an employer–employee relationship."

—Judge Schwarzer

Microsoft Corporation is the world's largest provider of computer operating systems, software programs, and Internet browsers. The company has grown into one of the largest corporations in the United States, making one of its founders, Bill Gates, the richest person in the world. But the company was caught nickel-and-diming some of its workers. The situation was brought to light by an Internal Revenue Service (IRS) investigation.

Microsoft is headquartered in the state of Washington. In addition to having regular employees, Microsoft used the services of other workers, classified as **independent contractors** (sometimes called freelancers) and temporary agency employees (called temps). Most of these special employees worked full time for Microsoft, doing jobs that were identical to jobs performed by Microsoft's regular employees. Microsoft paid the special employees by check as outside workers. The IRS conducted an employment tax examination and determined that Microsoft had misclassified these special workers as independent contractors and that the workers in these positions needed to be reclassified as employees for federal tax purposes.

independent contractor
A person or business who is not an employee who is employed by a principal to perform a certain task on his or her behalf. "A person who contracts with another to do something for him who is not controlled by the other nor subject to the other's right to control with respect to his physical conduct in the performance of the undertaking" [Restatement (Second) of Agency].

But the IRS investigation was not the end of the story. Plaintiff Donna Vizcaino and other freelancers sued Microsoft in a class action lawsuit, alleging that they were denied employment benefits, especially employee stock options, that were paid to regular employees. Microsoft contributed 3 percent of an employee's salary to the stock option plan. The U.S. Court of Appeals agreed with the plaintiffs, citing the Internal Revenue Code, which requires such stock option plans to be available to all employees. The Court of Appeals stated, "It is our conclusion that Microsoft either exercised, or retained the right to exercise, direction over the services performed. This control establishes an employer–employee relationship." Thus, Microsoft's attempt to define certain full-time employees as freelancers and temps was rebuffed by the courts. *Vizcaino v. United States Dist. Ct.*, 173 F.3d 713 (9th Cir. 1999).

Business Ethics

1. Did Microsoft act ethically in this case? Why did Microsoft classify full-time workers as freelancers and temps? Explain.

Concept Summary

Definitions of Employment Acts

Act	Definition
Workers' compensation acts	Create an administrative procedure for workers to receive compensation for injuries that occur on the job. States usually require employers to purchase insurance from private insurance companies or state funds to cover workers' compensation claims. Some states permit employers to self-insure if they demonstrate that they have the ability to pay workers' compensation claims.
Occupational Safety and Health Act	The act imposes record-keeping and reporting requirements on employers and requires them to post notices in the workplace, informing employees of their rights under the act.
Fair Labor Standards Act (FLSA)	Forbids the use of oppressive child labor and makes it unlawful to ship goods produced by businesses that use oppressive child labor. Establishes minimum wage and overtime pay requirements for nonexempt workers. The FLSA requires that most employees in the United States be paid at least the federal minimum wage for all hours worked. Under the FLSA, an employer cannot require nonexempt employees to work more than 40 hours per week unless they are paid overtime pay of one-and-a-half times their regular pay for each hour worked in excess of 40 hours that week.

OTHER WORKER PROTECTION LAWS

In addition to the statutes already discussed in this chapter, the federal government has enacted many other statutes that regulate employment relationships. These include the Consolidated Omnibus Budget Reconciliation Act (COBRA), the Family and Medical Leave Act (FMLA), and the Employee Retirement Income Security Act (ERISA). These federal statutes are discussed in the following paragraphs.

Consolidated Omnibus Budget Reconciliation Act (COBRA)

Consolidated Omnibus Budget Reconciliation Act (COBRA)
A federal law that permits employees and their beneficiaries to continue their group health insurance after an employee's employment has ended.

The **Consolidated Omnibus Budget Reconciliation Act (COBRA)** of 1985[4] provides that an employee of a private employer or the employee's beneficiaries must be offered the opportunity to continue their group health insurance after the voluntary or involuntary termination of a worker's employment or the loss of coverage due to certain qualifying events defined in the law. The employer must notify covered employees and their beneficiaries of their rights under COBRA. To continue coverage, a person must pay the required group rate premium. Government employees are subject to parallel provisions found in the Public Health Service Act.

Employee Retirement Income Security Act (ERISA)

Employee Retirement Income Security Act (ERISA)
A federal act designed to prevent fraud and other abuses associated with private pension funds.

Employers are not required to establish pension plans for their employees. If they do, however, they are subject to the record-keeping, disclosure, and other requirements of the **Employee Retirement Income Security Act (ERISA)**.[6] ERISA is a complex act designed to prevent fraud and other abuses associated

LANDMARK LAW

FAMILY AND MEDICAL LEAVE ACT

In February 1993, Congress enacted the **Family and Medical Leave Act (FMLA)**.[5] This act guarantees workers unpaid time off from work for family and medical emergencies and other specified situations. The act, which applies to companies with fifty or more workers as well as federal, state, and local governments, covers about half of the nation's workforce. To be covered by the act, an employee must have worked for the employer for at least one year and have performed more than 1,250 hours of service during the previous twelve-month period.

Covered employers are required to provide up to twelve weeks of unpaid leave during any twelve-month period due to:

1. The birth of and care for a child
2. The placement of a child with an employee for adoption or foster care
3. A serious health condition that makes the employee unable to perform his or her duties
4. Care for a spouse, child, or parent with a serious health problem

Leave, because of the birth of a child or the placement of a child for adoption or foster care cannot be taken intermittently unless the employer agrees to such arrangement. Other leaves may be taken on an intermittent basis. The employer may require medical proof of claimed serious health conditions.

An eligible employee who takes leave must, upon returning to work, be restored to either the same or an equivalent position with equivalent employment benefits and pay. The restored employee is not entitled to the accrual of seniority during the leave period, however. A covered employer may deny restoration to a salaried employee who is among the highest-paid 10 percent of that employer's employees if the denial is necessary to prevent "substantial and grievous economic injury" to the employer's operations.

with private pension funds. Federal, state, and local government pension funds are exempt from its coverage. ERISA is administered by the Department of Labor and the IRS.

Family and Medical Leave Act (FMLA)
A federal act that guarantees workers up to twelve weeks of unpaid leave in a twelve-month period to attend to family and medical emergencies and other specified situations.

Among other things, ERISA requires pension plans to be in writing and to name a pension fund manager. The plan manager owes a fiduciary duty to act as a "prudent person" in managing the fund and investing its assets. No more than 10 percent of a pension fund's assets can be invested in the securities of the sponsoring employer.

Vesting occurs when an employee has a nonforfeitable right to receive pension benefits. First, ERISA provides for immediate vesting of each employee's own contributions to the plan. Second, it requires employers' contributions to be either (1) totally vested after five years (*cliff vesting*) or (2) gradually vested over a seven-year period and completely vested after that time.

Concept Summary

Definitions of Worker Protection Acts

Act	Definition
Consolidated Omnibus Budget Reconciliation Act	Provides that an employee of a private employer or the employee's beneficiaries must be offered the opportunity to continue their group health insurance after the voluntary or involuntary termination of a worker's employment or the loss of coverage due to certain qualifying events defined in the law.

(continued)

Family and Medical Leave Act	Guarantees workers unpaid time off from work for family and medical emergencies and other specified situations.
Employee Retirement Income Security Act	Employers that choose to establish pension plans for their employees are subject to the record-keeping, disclosure, and other requirements.

GOVERNMENT PROGRAMS

The U.S. government has established several programs that provide benefits to workers and their dependents. Two of these programs, unemployment compensation and Social Security, are discussed in the following paragraphs.

Unemployment Compensation

unemployment compensation
Payments paid under federal and state laws to assist workers who are temporarily unemployed.

Federal Unemployment Tax Act (FUTA)
A federal act that requires employers to pay unemployment taxes; unemployment compensation is paid to workers who are temporarily unemployed.

In 1935, Congress established an **unemployment compensation** program to assist workers who are temporarily unemployed. Under the **Federal Unemployment Tax Act (FUTA)**[7] and state laws enacted to implement the program, employers are required to pay unemployment contributions (taxes). The tax rate and unemployment wage level are subject to change. Employees do not pay unemployment taxes.

State governments administer unemployment compensation programs under general guidelines set by the federal government. Each state establishes its own eligibility requirements and the amount and duration of the benefits. To collect benefits, applicants must be able and available for work and seeking employment. Workers who have been let go because of bad conduct (e.g., illegal activity, drug use on the job) or who voluntarily quit work without just cause are not eligible to receive unemployment benefits.

Social Security

Social Security
A federal system that provides limited retirement and death benefits to covered employees and their dependents.

In 1935, Congress established the federal **Social Security** system to provide limited retirement and death benefits to certain employees and their dependents. The Social Security system is administered by the **Social Security Administration**. Today, Social Security benefits include (1) retirement benefits, (2) survivors' benefits to family members of deceased workers, (3) disability benefits, and (4) medical and hospitalization benefits (Medicare).

Federal Insurance Contributions Act (FICA)
A federal act that says employees and employers must make contributions into the Social Security fund.

Under the **Federal Insurance Contributions Act (FICA)**,[8] employees must make contributions (pay taxes) into the Social Security fund. An employee's employer must pay a matching amount. Social Security does not operate like a savings account. Instead, current contributions are used to fund current claims. The employer is responsible for deducting employees' portions from their wages and remitting the entire payment to the IRS.

Self-Employment Contributions Act
A federal act that says self-employed persons must pay Social Security taxes equal to the combined employer–employee amount.

Under the **Self-Employment Contributions Act**,[9] self-employed individuals must pay Social Security contributions, too. The amount of taxes self-employed individuals must pay is equal to the combined employer–employee amount.

Failure to submit Social Security taxes subjects the violator to interest payments, penalties, and possible criminal liability. Social Security taxes may be changed by act of Congress.

Concept Summary

Definitions of Employment Tax Acts

Act	Definition
Federal Unemployment Tax Act	Along with state laws enacted to implement the program, requires employers to pay unemployment contributions (taxes).
Federal Insurance Contributions Act	An employee's employer must pay a matching amount that employees pay into the social security fund.
Self-Employment Contributions Act	Self-employed individuals must pay Social Security contributions, too. The amount of taxes self-employed individuals must pay is equal to the combined employer–employee amount.

IMMIGRATION LAWS

The **Immigration Reform and Control Act of 1986 (IRCA)**[10] and the **Immigration Act of 1990**[11] are administered by the **U.S. Immigration and Customs Enforcement**. These acts make it unlawful for employers to hire illegal immigrants. Employers are required to inspect documents of prospective employees and determine that they are either U.S. citizens or otherwise qualified to work in the country (e.g., have proper work visas). Employers must maintain records and post in the workplace notices of the contents of the law. Violators are subject to both civil and criminal penalties.

Immigration Reform and Control Act of 1986 (IRCA)
A federal statute that makes it unlawful for employers to hire illegal immigrants.

H-1B Foreign Guest Worker Visa

An H-1B visa is a nonimmigrant visa that allows U.S. employers to employ in the United States foreign nationals who are skilled in specialty occupations.[12] A foreign guest worker under an H-1B visa must have a bachelor's degree or higher and have a "specialty occupation," such as engineering, mathematics, computer science, physical sciences, or medicine.

A foreign guest worker must be sponsored by a U.S. employer. Employers apply for H-1B visas for proposed foreign guest workers. The number of H-1B visas is limited, usually to fewer than 100,000 per year, so the competition is fierce to obtain such visas. H-1B visa holders are allowed to bring their immediate family members (i.e., spouse and children under 21) to the United States under the H4 visa category as dependents. An H4 visa holder may remain in the United States as long as he or she remains in legal status. An H4 visa holder is not eligible to work in the United States.

The duration of stay for a worker on an H-1B visa is three years, and this can usually be extended another three years. During this time, an employer may sponsor an H-1B holder for a green card, which if issued permits the foreign national to eventually obtain U.S. citizenship.

Concept Summary

Definitions of Immigration Acts

Act	Definition
Immigration Reform and Control Act of 1986 and the Immigration Act of 1990	These acts make it unlawful for employers to hire illegal immigrants. Employers are required to inspect documents of prospective employees

(continued)

> Poorly paid labor is inefficient labor, the world over.
> Henry George

and determine that they are either U.S. citizens or otherwise qualified to work in the country (e.g., have proper work visas). Employers must maintain records and post in the workplace notices of the contents of the law.

Concept Review

Definitions of Employment Acts

Act	Definition
Workers' compensation acts	Create an administrative procedure for workers to receive compensation for injuries that occur on the job. States usually require employers to purchase insurance from private insurance companies or state funds to cover workers' compensation claims. Some states permit employers to self-insure if they demonstrate that they have the ability to pay workers' compensation claims.
Occupational Safety and Health Act	The act imposes record-keeping and reporting requirements on employers and requires them to post notices in the workplace, informing employees of their rights under the act.
Fair Labor Standards Act (FLSA)	Forbids the use of oppressive child labor and makes it unlawful to ship goods produced by businesses that use oppressive child labor. Establishes minimum wage and overtime pay requirements for nonexempt workers. The FLSA requires that most employees in the United States be paid at least the federal minimum wage for all hours worked. Under the FLSA, an employer cannot require nonexempt employees to work more than 40 hours per week unless they are paid overtime pay of one-and-a-half times their regular pay for each hour worked in excess of 40 hours that week.

Definitions of Worker Protection Acts

Act	Definition
Consolidated Omnibus Budget Reconciliation Act	Provides that an employee of a private employer or the employee's beneficiaries must be offered the opportunity to continue their group health insurance after the voluntary or involuntary termination of a worker's employment or the loss of coverage due to certain qualifying events defined in the law.
Family and Medical Leave Act	Guarantees workers unpaid time off from work for family and medical emergencies and other specified situations.
Employee Retirement Income Security Act	Employers that choose to establish pension plans for their employees are subject to the record-keeping, disclosure, and other requirements.

Definitions of Employment Tax Acts

Act	Definition
Federal Unemployment Tax Act	Along with state laws enacted to implement the program, requires employers to pay unemployment contributions (taxes).
Federal Insurance Contributions Act	An employee's employer must pay a matching amount that employees pay into the social security fund.

Self-Employment Contributions Act	Self-employed individuals must pay Social Security contributions, too. The amount of taxes self-employed individuals must pay is equal to the combined employer–employee amount.

Definitions of Immigration Acts

Act	Definition
Immigration Reform and Control Act of 1986 and the Immigration Act of 1990	These acts make it unlawful for employers to hire illegal immigrants. Employers are required to inspect documents of prospective employees and determine that they are either U.S. citizens or otherwise qualified to work in the country (e.g., have proper work visas). Employers must maintain records and post in the workplace notices of the contents of the law.

Our children and grandchildren are not merely statistics towards which we can be indifferent.
John F. Kennedy

CHAPTER REVIEW

WORKERS' COMPENSATION ACTS, p. 360

Workers' Compensation Acts

These state statutes create an administrative procedure for workers to receive payments for job-related injuries.

1. ***Workers' compensation insurance.*** Most states require employers to carry private or government-sponsored workers' compensation insurance. Some states permit employers to self-insure.

Employment-Related Injury

To be compensable under workers' compensation, a claimant must prove that their injury arose out of and in the course of his or her employment.

Exclusive Remedy

Workers' compensation is an exclusive remedy. Thus, workers cannot sue their employers to recover damages for job-related injuries.

1. ***Exceptions to exclusive remedy rule.*** Workers may recover damages from their employers for job-related injuries if the employer:
   a. Does not provide workers' compensation.
   b. Intentionally causes the worker's injuries.
2. ***Lawsuits against third parties.*** Workers' compensation acts do not bar injured workers from suing responsible third parties to recover damages (e.g., the manufacturer of a defective machine that caused a worker's injuries).

OCCUPATIONAL SAFETY, p. 363

Occupational Safety and Health Act

This federal statute requires employers to provide safe working conditions.

1. ***Occupational Safety and Health Administration (OSHA).*** This federal administrative agency administers and enforces the Occupational Safety and Health Act.

Specific and General Duty Standards

1. ***Specific duty standards.*** These are safety standards for specific equipment (e.g., lathe) or a specific industry (e.g., mining).

> For many people like myself, it can be called the Ellis Island of the 20th century.
> Theodore H.M. Prudon
> *Describing Kennedy Airport*

2. ***General duty standards.*** These standards impose a general duty on employers to provide safe working conditions.

FAIR LABOR STANDARDS ACT (FLSA), p. 365

Fair Labor Standards Act (FLSA)

This federal statute protects workers.

Child Labor

The FLSA forbids the use of illegal child labor. The U.S. Department of Labor defines illegal child labor.

Minimum Wage and Overtime Pay Requirements

1. ***Minimum wage.*** The minimum wage is set by Congress and can be changed. The minimum wage, as of 2009, is $7.25 per hour.
2. ***Overtime pay.*** An employer cannot require employees to work more than forty hours per week unless they are paid 1.5 times their regular pay for each hour worked in excess of forty hours.

OTHER WORKER PROTECTION LAWS, p. 368

Consolidated Omnibus Budget Reconciliation Act (COBRA)

This federal statute requires an employer to offer an employee or the employee's beneficiaries the opportunity to continue health benefits (upon payment of the premium) after termination of employment due to dismissal or death.

Family and Medical Leave Act

This federal statute guarantees covered workers unpaid time off from work for the birth or adoption of a child, serious health problems of the worker, and serious health problems of a spouse, child, or parent.

Employee Retirement Income Security Act (ERISA)

This federal statute governs the establishment and administration of private pension programs to prevent fraud and other abuses.

GOVERNMENT PROGRAMS, p. 370

Unemployment Compensation

This state and federal program pays compensation to unemployed persons who meet certain qualifying standards. Employers are required to pay unemployment compensation payments to the government to fund the program. Authorized by the *Federal Unemployment Tax Act (FUTA)* and state laws.

Social Security

This federal government program provides limited retirement, disability, and medical and hospitalization to covered employees and their dependents. Employers and employees pay taxes to fund the program.

IMMIGRATION LAWS, p. 371

Immigration Reform and Control Act (IRCA)

This federal statute prohibits employers from employing illegal immigrants. Employers must require workers to prove that they are U.S. citizens or have proper work visas to work in this country.

H-1B Foreign Guest Worker Visa

An H-1B visa is a nonimmigrant visa that allows U.S. employers to employ in the United States foreign nationals who are skilled in specialty occupations.

TEST REVIEW TERMS AND CONCEPTS

CASE SCENARIO REVISITED

Remember the case at the beginning of the chapter where Wilson, a police officer employed by the city of Modesto, California, was injured while working out after his shift. What if Wilson filed a claim for workers' compensation benefits that was contested by his employer? Who wins? To help you with your answer, see *Wilson v. Workers' Compensation Appeals Bd.*, 196 Cal. App. 3d 902 (Cal. Ct. App. 1987).

PORTFOLIO EXERCISE

Emma Smith is an employee of the business you created at the beginning of the course. She has been employed with your company for three months. She has notified the company that she would like to take a leave beginning on January 1, 2010, because she has a serious health condition. Complete the following *Notice of Eligibility and Rights & Responsibilities*.

Notice of Eligibility and Rights & Responsibilities (Family and Medical Leave Act)

U.S. Department of Labor
Employment Standards Administration
Wage and Hour Division

OMB Control Number: 1215-0181
Expires: 12/31/2011

In general, to be eligible an employee must have worked for an employer for at least 12 months, have worked at least 1,250 hours in the 12 months preceding the leave, and work at a site with at least 50 employees within 75 miles. While use of this form by employers is optional, a fully completed Form WH-381 provides employees with the information required by 29 C.F.R. § 825.300(b), which must be provided within five business days of the employee notifying the employer of the need for FMLA leave. Part B provides employees with information regarding their rights and responsibilities for taking FMLA leave, as required by 29 C.F.R. § 825.300(b), (c).

[Part A – NOTICE OF ELIGIBILITY]

TO: ______________________________
Employee

FROM: ______________________________
Employer Representative

DATE: ______________________________

On ________________, you informed us that you needed leave beginning on ________________ for:

_____ The birth of a child, or placement of a child with you for adoption or foster care;

_____ Your own serious health condition;

_____ Because you are needed to care for your ____ spouse; _____child; ______ parent due to his/her serious health condition.

_____ Because of a qualifying exigency arising out of the fact that your ____ spouse; _____son or daughter; ______ parent is on active duty or call to active duty status in support of a contingency operation as a member of the National Guard or Reserves.

_____ Because you are the ____ spouse; _____son or daughter; ______ parent; _______ next of kin of a covered servicemember with a serious injury or illness.

This Notice is to inform you that you:

_____ Are eligible for FMLA leave (See Part B below for Rights and Responsibilities)

_____ Are **not** eligible for FMLA leave, because (only one reason need be checked, although you may not be eligible for other reasons):

_____ You have not met the FMLA's 12-month length of service requirement. As of the first date of requested leave, you will have worked approximately ___ months towards this requirement.

_____ You have not met the FMLA's 1,250-hours-worked requirement.

_____ You do not work and/or report to a site with 50 or more employees within 75-miles.

If you have any questions, contact ____ or view the FMLA poster located in ____.

[PART B-RIGHTS AND RESPONSIBILITIES FOR TAKING FMLA LEAVE]

As explained in Part A, you meet the eligibility requirements for taking FMLA leave and still have FMLA leave available in the applicable 12-month period. **However, in order for us to determine whether your absence qualifies as FMLA leave, you must return the following information to us by ______________________.** (If a certification is requested, employers must allow at least 15 calendar days from receipt of this notice; additional time may be required in some circumstances.) If sufficient information is not provided in a timely manner, your leave may be denied.

____ Sufficient certification to support your request for FMLA leave. A certification form that sets forth the information necessary to support your request ____**is**/____ **is not** enclosed.

____ Sufficient documentation to establish the required relationship between you and your family member.

____ Other information needed: ____

____

____

____ No additional information requested

 CONTINUED ON NEXT PAGE

If your leave does qualify as FMLA leave you will have the following **responsibilities** while on FMLA leave (only checked blanks apply):

____ Contact ______________________________ at ____________________ to make arrangements to continue to make your share of the premium payments on your health insurance to maintain health benefits while you are on leave. You have a minimum 30-day (or, indicate longer period, if applicable) grace period in which to make premium payments. If payment is not made timely, your group health insurance may be cancelled, provided we notify you in writing at least 15 days before the date that your health coverage will lapse, or, at our option, we may pay your share of the premiums during FMLA leave, and recover these payments from you upon your return to work.

____ You will be required to use your available paid ______ **sick**, _______ **vacation**, and/or ________**other leave** during your FMLA absence. This means that you will receive your paid leave and the leave will also be considered protected FMLA leave and counted against your FMLA leave entitlement.

____ Due to your status within the company, you are considered a "key employee" as defined in the FMLA. As a "key employee," restoration to employment may be denied following FMLA leave on the grounds that such restoration will cause substantial and grievous economic injury to us. We ___**have**/____ **have not** determined that restoring you to employment at the conclusion of FMLA leave will cause substantial and grievous economic harm to us.

____ While on leave you will be required to furnish us with periodic reports of your status and intent to return to work every ____________________. (Indicate interval of periodic reports, as appropriate for the particular leave situation).

If the circumstances of your leave change, and you are able to return to work earlier than the date indicated on the reverse side of this form, you will be required to notify us at least two workdays prior to the date you intend to report for work.

If your leave does qualify as FMLA leave you will have the following **rights** while on FMLA leave:

- You have a right under the FMLA for up to 12 weeks of unpaid leave in a 12-month period calculated as:

  _____ the calendar year (January – December).

  _____ a fixed leave year based on ____.

  _____ the 12-month period measured forward from the date of your first FMLA leave usage.

  _____ a "rolling" 12-month period measured backward from the date of any FMLA leave usage.

- You have a right under the FMLA for up to 26 weeks of unpaid leave in a single 12-month period to care for a covered servicemember with a serious injury or illness. This single 12-month period commenced on ______________________________________.
- Your health benefits must be maintained during any period of unpaid leave under the same conditions as if you continued to work.
- You must be reinstated to the same or an equivalent job with the same pay, benefits, and terms and conditions of employment on your return from FMLA-protected leave. (If your leave extends beyond the end of your FMLA entitlement, you do not have return rights under FMLA.)
- If you do not return to work following FMLA leave for a reason other than: 1) the continuation, recurrence, or onset of a serious health condition which would entitle you to FMLA leave; 2) the continuation, recurrence, or onset of a covered servicemember's serious injury or illness which would entitle you to FMLA leave; or 3) other circumstances beyond your control, you may be required to reimburse us for our share of health insurance premiums paid on your behalf during your FMLA leave.
- If we have not informed you above that you must use accrued paid leave while taking your unpaid FMLA leave entitlement, you have the right to have ____ **sick,** ____**vacation,** and/or ___ **other leave** run concurrently with your unpaid leave entitlement, provided you meet any applicable requirements of the leave policy. Applicable conditions related to the substitution of paid leave are referenced or set forth below. If you do not meet the requirements for taking paid leave, you remain entitled to take unpaid FMLA leave.

  ___For a copy of conditions applicable to sick/vacation/other leave usage please refer to ___________ available at: ________________________.

  ___Applicable conditions for use of paid leave:____

  ____

  ____

  ____

  ____

Once we obtain the information from you as specified above, we will inform you, within 5 business days, whether your leave will be designated as FMLA leave and count towards your FMLA leave entitlement. If you have any questions, please do not hesitate to contact:

______________________________________ at ______________________________________.

PAPERWORK REDUCTION ACT NOTICE AND PUBLIC BURDEN STATEMENT

It is mandatory for employers to provide employees with notice of their eligibility for FMLA protection and their rights and responsibilities. 29 U.S.C. § 2617; 29 C.F.R. § 825.300(b), (c). It is mandatory for employers to retain a copy of this disclosure in their records for three years. 29 U.S.C. § 2616; 29 C.F.R. § 825.500. Persons are not required to respond to this collection of information unless it displays a currently valid OMB control number. The Department of Labor estimates that it will take an average of 10 minutes for respondents to complete this collection of information, including the time for reviewing instructions, searching existing data sources, gathering and maintaining the data needed, and completing and reviewing the collection of information. If you have any comments regarding this burden estimate or any other aspect of this collection information, including suggestions for reducing this burden, send them to the Administrator, Wage and Hour Division, U.S. Department of Labor, Room S-3502, 200 Constitution Ave., NW, Washington, DC 20210. **DO NOT SEND THE COMPLETED FORM TO THE WAGE AND HOUR DIVISION.**

Page 2 Form WH-381 Revised January 2009

WORKING THE WEB INTERNET EXERCISES

Activities

1. For an overview of labor law, see "Labor and Employment Law," at **jurist.law.pitt.edu/sg_lab.htm**
2. Check the current unemployment rate at the Department of Labor, at **www.dol.gov**. Is it higher or lower than it was one year ago?

CRITICAL LEGAL THINKING CASES

Case 12.1 *Workers' Compensation* Joseph Albanese was employed as a working foreman by Atlantic Steel Company, Inc., for approximately seventeen years. His duties included supervision of plant employees. The business was sold to a new owner. One year later, after the employees voted to unionize, friction developed between Albanese and the workers. Part of the problem was caused by management's decision to eliminate overtime work, which required Albanese to go out into the shop and prod the workers to expedite the work.

Additional problems resulted from the activities of Albanese's direct supervisor, the plant manager. On one occasion, the manager informed Albanese that the company practice of distributing Thanksgiving turkeys was to be discontinued. The following year, the manager told Albanese that the company did not intend to give the workers a Christmas bonus. The plant manager also informed Albanese that he did not intend to pay overtime wages to any worker. On each occasion, after Albanese relayed the information to the workers, the plant manager reversed his own decision.

After the last incident, Albanese became distressed and developed chest pains and nausea. When the chest pains became sharper, he went home to bed. Albanese did not work thereafter. He experienced continuing pain, sweatiness, shortness of breath, headaches, and depression. Albanese filed a claim for workers' compensation based on stress. The employer contested the claim. Who wins? *Albanese's Case*, 389 N.E.2d 83 (Mass. 1979).

Case 12.2 *Occupational Safety* Getty Oil Company (Getty) operates a separation facility where it gathers gas and oil from wells and transmits them to an outgoing pipeline under high pressure. Getty engineers designed and produced a pressure vessel, called a fluid booster, which was to be installed to increase pressure in the system. Robinson, a Getty engineer, was instructed to install the vessel. Robinson picked up the vessel from the welding shop without having it tested. After he completed the installation, the pressure valve was put into operation. When the pressure increased from 300 to 930 pounds per square inch, an explosion occurred. Robinson died from the explosion, and another Getty employee was seriously injured. The secretary of labor issued a citation against Getty for violating the general duty provision for worker safety contained in the Occupational Safety and Health Act. Getty challenged the citation. Who wins? *Getty Oil Co. v. Occupational Safety & Health Review Comm'n*, 530 F.2d 1143 (5th Cir. 1976).

Case 12.3 *ERISA* United Artists is a Maryland corporation doing business in the state of Texas. United Pension Fund (Plan) is a defined-contribution employee pension benefit plan sponsored by United Artists for its employees.

Each employee has his or her own individual pension account, but Plan's assets are pooled for investment purposes. Plan is administered by a board of trustees. During a period of nine years, seven of the trustees used Plan to make a series of loans to themselves. The trustees did not (1) require the borrowers to submit written applications for the subject loans, (2) assess the prospective borrowers' ability to repay the loans, (3) specify a period in which the loans were to be repaid, or (4) call in the loans when they remained unpaid. The trustees also charged less than fair market value interest rates for the loans. The secretary of labor sued the trustees, alleging that they had breached their fiduciary duty, in violation of ERISA. Who wins? *McLaughlin v. Rowley*, 698 F. Supp. 1333 (N.D. Tex. 1988).

Case 12.4 *Unemployment Benefits* Devon Overstreet, who worked as a bus driver for the Chicago Transit Authority (CTA) for over six years, took sick leave for six weeks. Because she had been on sick leave for more than seven days, CTA required her to take a medical examination. The blood and urine analysis indicated the presence of cocaine. A second test confirmed this finding. The CTA suspended her and placed her in the employee assistance program for substance abuse for not less than thirty days, with a chance of reassignment to a nonoperating job if she successfully completed the program. The program is an alternative to discharge and is available at the election of the employee. Overstreet filed for unemployment compensation benefits. CTA contested her claim. Who wins? *Overstreet v. Illinois Dep't of Employment Sec.*, 522 N.E.2d 185 (Ill. App. Ct. 1988).

BUSINESS ETHICS CASES

Case 12.5 *Business Ethics* Jeffrey Glockzin was an employee of Nordyne, Inc. (Nordyne), which manufactured air-conditioning units. Sometimes Glockzin worked as an assembly line tester. The job consisted of attaching one of two wire leads with bare metal alligator-type clips leading from the testing equipment to each side of an air-conditioning unit. When the tester turned on a toggle switch, the air-conditioning unit was energized. Once a determination was made that the air-conditioning unit was working properly, the toggle switch would be turned off and the wire leads removed. One day, while testing an air-conditioning unit, Glockzin grabbed both alligator clips at the same time. He had failed to turn off the toggle switch, however. Glockzin received a 240-volt electric shock, causing his death. His heirs sued Nordyne for wrongful death and sought to recover damages for an intentional tort. Nordyne made a motion for summary judgment, alleging that workers' compensation benefits were the exclusive remedy for Glockzin's death. Does the "intentional tort" exception to the rule that workers' compensation is the exclusive remedy for a worker's injury apply in this case? Did Nordyne's management violate its ethical duty by not providing safer testing equipment? *Glockzin v. Nordyne, Inc.*, 815 F. Supp. 1050 (W.D. Mich. 1992).

Case 12.6 *Business Ethics* Whirlpool Corporation (Whirlpool) operated a manufacturing plant in Marion, Ohio, for the production of household appliances. Overhead conveyors transported appliance components throughout the plant. To protect employees from objects that occasionally fell from the conveyors,

Whirlpool installed a horizontal wire-mesh guard screen approximately 20 feet above the plant floor. The mesh screen was welded to angle-iron frames suspended from the building's structural steel skeleton.

Maintenance employees spent several hours each week removing objects from the screen, replacing paper spread on the screen to catch grease drippings from the materials on the conveyors, and performing occasional maintenance work on the conveyors. To perform these duties, maintenance employees were usually able to stand on the iron frames, but sometimes they found it necessary to step onto the wire-mesh screen itself. Several employees had fallen partly through the screen. One day, a maintenance employee fell to his death through the guard screen.

The next month, two maintenance employees, Virgil Deemer and Thomas Cornwell, met with the plant supervisor to voice their concern about the safety of the screen. Unsatisfied with the supervisor's response, two days later, they met with the plant safety director and voiced similar concerns. When they asked him for the name, address, and telephone number of the local OSHA office, he told them they "had better stop and think about" what they were doing. The safety director then furnished them with the requested information, and later that day, one of the men contacted the regional OSHA office and discussed the guard screen.

The next day, Deemer and Cornwell reported for the night shift at 10:45 P.M. Their foreman directed the two men to perform their usual maintenance duties on a section of the screen. Claiming that the screen was unsafe, they refused to carry out the directive. The foreman sent them to the personnel office, where they were ordered to punch out without working or being paid for the remaining six hours of the shift. The two men subsequently received written reprimands, which were placed in their employment files.

The secretary of labor filed suit, alleging that Whirlpool's actions constituted discrimination against the two men, in violation of the Occupational Safety and Health Act. Did Whirlpool act ethically in this case? Can employees engage in self-help under certain circumstances under OSHA regulations? *Whirlpool Corp. v. Marshall*, 445 U.S. 1 (1980).

ENDNOTES

1. *29 U.S.C. Sections 553, 651–678.*
2. *For example, the Railway Safety Act and the Coal Mine Safety Act regulate workplace safety of railway workers and coal miners, respectively.*
3. *29 U.S.C. Sections 201–206.*
4. *26 U.S.C. Sections 1161–1169.*
5. *29 U.S.C. Sections 2601, 2611–2619, 2651–2654.*
6. *29 U.S.C. Sections 1001 et seq.*
7. *26 U.S.C. Sections 3301–3310.*
8. *26 U.S.C. Sections 3101–3125.*
9. *26 U.S.C. Sections 1401–1403.*
10. *29 U.S.C. Section 1802.*
11. *8 U.S.C. Sections 1101 et seq.*
12. *8 U.S.C. Section 101(a)(15)(H).*

"What people have always sought is equality of rights before the law. For rights that were not open to all equally would not be rights."

–Cicero

De Officilis, Book II, Chapter XII

Equal Opportunity in Employment

CHAPTER 13

CASE SCENARIO

The law firm at which you work represents Corning Glass Works (Corning) in New York State. For years, New York law prevented females from working at night. Therefore, Corning employed male workers for night inspection jobs and female workers for day inspection jobs. Males working the night shift were paid higher wages than were females who worked the day shift. When the federal Equal Pay Act was enacted, Corning began hiring females for night shift jobs, but it instituted a "red circle" wage rate that permitted previously hired male night shift workers to continue to receive higher wages than newly hired night shift workers.

CHAPTER OBJECTIVES

After studying this chapter, you should be able to:

1. Describe the scope of coverage of Title VII of the Civil Rights Act of 1964.
2. Identify race, color, and national origin discrimination that violate Title VII.
3. Identify sex discrimination—including sexual harassment—that violates Title VII.
4. Describe the scope of coverage of the Age Discrimination in Employment Act.
5. Describe the protections afforded by the Americans with Disabilities Act.

PARALEGAL PERSPECTIVE

Laurel A. Beyer, ACP, *is an EHS (Environmental, Health, and Safety) specialist with Pall Corporation, a global corporation, in Ann Arbor, Michigan. She graduated from Madonna University with a bachelor in legal assisting. She has been working as a paralegal for sixteen years.*

How does your work in environment relate to the area of equal opportunity? Working with environmental regulations is a fast-growing opportunity for all, as environmental issues touch upon nearly every aspect of business, including equal employment opportunity.

What are the most important paralegal skills needed in your job? Organizational skills are of utmost importance as multi-tasking is a way of life for everyone in the work force these days. Keeping track of numerous projects without losing any of the details can be daunting without organization.

What is the academic background required for a paralegal entering your area of practice? A legal assisting/paralegal degree is important as it provides a well-rounded legal education. Additional classes in business or accounting are helpful as well if you find yourself working for a corporation. These will assist you in working within the business environment. Also, be sure to include contract law in your paralegal courses.

Environmental regulations are complex and involve multiple agencies. Because of this, I attend a comprehensive two-day environmental regulations class at least every two years. For the health and safety portion of the position, I also took classes and received an OSHA specialist certification in occupational health and safety through the OSHA center at Eastern Michigan University. This allows me to maintain the necessary safety training and documentation required for our group.

How is technology involved in your job? Almost everything we do involves the use of technology. Spreadsheets and databases assist in the organization and tracking of projects, and the Internet is indispensible for research. I have free e-mail subscriptions that send daily summaries of the *Federal Register* and newly enacted regulations for Michigan to my inbox.

Receiving information from co-workers all over the world entails constant e-mail correspondence. Our inboxes are filled to the brim every day, so it is important to organize these in a meaningful way to avoid losing track of items.

What trends do you see in your area of practice that will likely affect your job in the future? With the complexity of environmental issues increasing around the world, I see the need to become more familiar with the regulations of other countries as well. Networking and the Internet are the best ways to keep track of the ever-changing laws within a given field. Belonging to trade organizations and the state bar helps us to keep current.

What do you feel is the biggest issue currently facing the paralegal profession? As with any profession these days, I believe this is job security.

What words of advice do you have for a new paralegal entering your area of practice? Always maintaining a "can-do" attitude and anticipating needs before they arise can increase your value to any organization. Always remember to treat everyone with integrity. Offer assistance when you can and others will be more inclined to assist you when needed. And, last but not least, always let people know you appreciate the help they have provided.

INTRODUCTION TO EQUAL OPPORTUNITY IN EMPLOYMENT

Under common law, employers could terminate an employee at any time and for any reason. In this same vein, employers were free to hire and promote anyone they chose without violating the law. This often created unreasonable hardship on employees and erected employment barriers to certain minority classes.

Starting in the 1960s, Congress began enacting a comprehensive set of federal laws that eliminated major forms of employment discrimination. These laws, which were passed to guarantee equal employment opportunity to all employees and job applicants, have been broadly interpreted by the federal courts, particularly the U.S. Supreme Court. States have also enacted antidiscrimination laws. Many state and local governments have adopted laws that prevent discrimination in employment.

equal opportunity in employment
The right of all employees and job applicants (1) to be treated without discrimination and (2) to be able to sue employers if they are discriminated against.

This chapter discusses **equal opportunity in employment** laws.

TITLE VII OF THE CIVIL RIGHTS ACT OF 1964

Prior to the passage of major federal antidiscrimination laws in the 1960s, much discrimination in employment existed in this country. In the 1960s, Congress enacted several major federal statutes that outlawed employment discrimination against members of certain classes. These federal laws were instrumental to providing equal opportunity in employment in this country. One of the main statutes is *Title VII of the Civil Rights Act of 1964*.[1]

Scope of Coverage of Title VII

Title VII of the Civil Rights Act of 1964 applies to (1) employers with fifteen or more employees, (2) all employment agencies, (3) labor unions with fifteen or more members, (4) state and local governments and their agencies, and (5) most federal government employment. Native American tribes and tax-exempt private clubs are expressly excluded from coverage. Other portions of the Civil Rights Act of 1964 prohibit discrimination in housing, education, and other facets of life.

Title VII prohibits discrimination in hiring, decisions regarding promotion or demotion, payment of compensation and fringe benefits, availability of job training and apprenticeship opportunities, referral systems for employment, decisions regarding dismissal, work rules, and any other "term, condition, or privilege" of employment. Any employee of a covered employer, including undocumented aliens,[2] may bring actions for employment discrimination under Title VII.

Title VII prohibits two major forms of employment discrimination: disparate-treatment discrimination and disparate-impact discrimination.

Disparate-Treatment Discrimination

Disparate-treatment discrimination occurs when an employer treats a specific *individual* less favorably than others because of that person's race, color, national origin, sex, or religion. In such situations, complainants must prove that (1) they belong to a Title VII protected class, (2) they applied for and were qualified for the employment position, (3) they were rejected despite this, and (4) the employer kept the position open and sought applications from persons with the complainants' qualifications.[3]

disparate-treatment discrimination
A form of discrimination that occurs when an employer discriminates against a specific individual because of his or her race, color, national origin, sex, or religion.

Civil Rights Act of 1964
A section of a federal statute that expressly prohibits racial discrimination; it has also been held to forbid discrimination based on national origin.

Title VII of the Civil Rights Act of 1964
A title of a federal statute enacted to eliminate job discrimination based on five protected classes: *race, color, religion, sex,* and *national origin*.

LANDMARK LAW

TITLE VII OF THE CIVIL RIGHTS ACT OF 1964

After substantial debate, Congress enacted the **Civil Rights Act of 1964**. **Title VII of the Civil Rights Act** (called the **Fair Employment Practices Act**) was intended to eliminate job discrimination based on the following *protected classes: race, color, national origin, sex,* and *religion*.

As amended by the **Equal Employment Opportunity Act of 1972**, Section 703(a)(2) of Title VII provides, in pertinent part, that:

> *It shall be an unlawful employment practice for an employer*
>
> *(1) to fail or refuse to hire or to discharge any individual, or otherwise to discriminate against any individual with respect to his compensation, terms, conditions, or privileges of employment, because of such individual's race, color, religion, sex, or national origin; or*
>
> *(2) to limit, segregate, or classify his employees or applicants for employment in any way which would deprive or tend to deprive any individual of employment opportunities or otherwise adversely affect his status as an employee, because of such individual's race, color, religion, sex, or national origin.*

Example: A member of a minority race applies for a promotion to a position advertised as available at his company. The minority applicant, who is qualified for the position, is rejected by the company, which hires a nonminority applicant for the position. The minority applicant sues under Title VII. He has a *prima facie* case of illegal discrimination. The burden of proof shifts to the employer to prove a nondiscriminatory reason for its decision. If the employer offers a reason, such as saying that the minority applicant lacked sufficient experience, the burden shifts back to the minority applicant to prove that this was just a *pretext* (not the real reason) for the employer's decision.

Disparate-Impact Discrimination

disparate-impact discrimination
A form of discrimination that occurs when an employer discriminates against an entire protected class. An example would be discrimination in which a racially neutral employment practice or rule causes an adverse impact on a protected class.

Disparate-impact discrimination occurs when an employer discriminates against an entire protected *class*. Many disparate-impact cases are brought as class action lawsuits. Often, this type of discrimination is proven through statistical data about the employer's employment practices. The plaintiff must demonstrate a *causal link* between the challenged practice and the statistical imbalance. Showing a statistical disparity between the percentages of protected class employees versus the percentage of the population that the protected class makes within the surrounding community is not enough, by itself, to prove discrimination.

Example: Disparate-impact discrimination occurs when an employer adopts a work rule that is neutral on its face but is shown to cause an adverse impact on a protected class. If an employer has a rule that all applicants for an executive position must be at least 5'8" tall, this looks like a neutral rule because it applies to both males and females. However, because this rule is unrelated to the performance of an executive position and eliminates many more females than males from being hired or promoted to an executive position, it is disparate-impact sex discrimination in violation of Title VII.

Intentional Discrimination

In a case involving intentional discrimination, the offended party can recover compensatory damages. A court can award punitive damages against an employer in a case involving an employer's malice or reckless indifference to federally protected rights. The sum of compensatory and punitive damages is capped at different amounts of money, depending on the size of the employer.

Equal Employment Opportunity Commission (EEOC)

Equal Employment Opportunity Commission (EEOC)
The federal administrative agency that is responsible for enforcing most federal antidiscrimination laws.

The **Equal Employment Opportunity Commission (EEOC)** is the federal agency responsible for enforcing most federal antidiscrimination laws. The members of the EEOC are appointed by the U.S. president. The EEOC is empowered to conduct investigations, interpret the statutes, encourage conciliation between employees and employers, and bring suit to enforce the law. The EEOC can also seek injunctive relief.

To bring an action under Title VII, a private complainant must first file a complaint with the EEOC within 180 days or 300 days (depending on the state) of the alleged discrimination.[4] This time period has been strictly construed by the U.S. Supreme Court.[5] The EEOC is given the opportunity to sue the employer on the complainant's behalf. If the EEOC chooses not to bring suit, it will issue a right to sue letter to the complainant. This gives the complainant the right to sue the employer.

Remedies for Violations of Title VII

A successful plaintiff in a Title VII action can recover back pay and reasonable attorneys' fees. The courts also have broad authority to grant equitable remedies. For instance, the courts can order reinstatement, grant fictional seniority, and issue injunctions to compel the hiring or promotion of protected minorities.

RACE, COLOR, AND NATIONAL ORIGIN DISCRIMINATION

Title VII of the Civil Rights Act of 1964 was primarily enacted to prohibit employment discrimination based on *race*, *color*, and *national origin*.

Race Discrimination

Race refers to broad categories such as African American, Caucasian, Asian, and Native American. Race discrimination in employment violates Title VII.

Color Discrimination

Color refers to the color of a person's skin. Discrimination by an employer based on color violates Title VII. Color discrimination cases are not brought as often as cases involving other forms of discrimination.

National Origin or Heritage Discrimination

National origin and heritage refers to the country of a person's ancestors, cultural characteristics, or heritage. National origin or heritage discrimination would include discrimination against persons of a particular nationality (e.g., persons of Irish descent), against persons who come from a certain place (e.g., the Middle East), against persons of a certain culture (e.g., Hispanics), or against persons because of their accents. Discrimination by an employer based on a person's national origin or heritage violates Title VII.

ETHICS SPOTLIGHT

WALGREEN TO PAY $24 MILLION IN RACE DISCRIMINATION LAWSUIT

The EEOC has adopted an E-RACE Initiative to identify barriers that contribute to race and color discrimination in employment, to litigate cases involving such discrimination, and to educate the public about race and color discrimination in the workplace. With its adoption of its E-RACE Initiative, the EEOC has pursued many high-profile race and color discrimination cases. In one such case, the EEOC sued the Walgreen Company, which operates more than six thousand stores throughout the country, for engaging in race and color discrimination. The charge asserted that Walgreen systematically discriminated against African American retail management and pharmacy employees in promotions, compensation, and assignments.

The EEOC filed its complaint against Walgreen in 2007. In addition, several private lawsuits had also been filed against Walgreen, charging the same violations. Walgreen Company agreed to settle all charges—the EEOC action and the private lawsuits—by agreeing to pay $24 million to a class of thousands of African American employees and former employees nationwide. The federal court overseeing the case ruled that the consent decree is fair, reasonable, and adequate. The award is one of the largest awards obtained by the EEOC in a race and color discrimination lawsuit.

The court also issued an injunction prohibiting the Walgreen Company from engaging in similar conduct in the future. The consent decree requires Walgreen to employ outside consultants to develop standardized, nondiscriminatory store assignment and promotion standards and to review Walgreen's employment practices. The EEOC retained jurisdiction over the consent decree for five years.

An EEOC spokesperson said, "The EEOC's case is a good example of the Commission's renewed emphasis on class and systemic litigation and furthers the agency's E-RACE Initiative, which is designed to address major issues of race and color discrimination." *EEOC v. Walgreen Company* and *Tucker v. Walgreen Co.*, Civil No. 05-440-GPM and Civil No. 07-172-GPM, 2007 U.S. Dist. LEXIS 74628 (S.D. Ill. Oct. 5, 2007).

SEX DISCRIMINATION AND SEXUAL HARASSMENT

Title VII of the Civil Rights Act of 1964 prohibits job discrimination based on gender. The act, as amended, the EEOC's rules, and court decisions prohibit employment discrimination based on gender, pregnancy, and sexual orientation. In addition, sexual harassment is also prohibited.

Sex Discrimination

sex discrimination
Discrimination against a person solely because of his or her gender.

Title VII prohibits employment discrimination based on gender. Although the prohibition against **sex discrimination** applies equally to men and women, the overwhelming majority of Title VII sex discrimination cases are brought by women. Sex discrimination cases are brought where there is direct sex discrimination and *quid pro quo* sex discrimination.

Pregnancy Discrimination

Pregnancy Discrimination Act
Amendment to Title VII that forbids employment discrimination because of "pregnancy, childbirth, or related medical conditions."

In 1978, the **Pregnancy Discrimination Act** was enacted as an amendment to Title VII.[6] This amendment forbids employment discrimination because of "pregnancy, childbirth, or related medical conditions."

Sexual Harassment

sexual harassment
Lewd remarks, touching, intimidation, posting of indecent materials, and other verbal or physical conduct of a sexual nature that occurs on the job.

Sometimes managers and co-workers engage in conduct that is offensive because it is sexually charged. This is often referred to as **sexual harassment**. The U.S. Supreme Court has held that sexual harassment that creates a hostile work environment violates Title VII. Conduct such as making lewd remarks, touching, intimidation, and posting of indecent materials and other verbal or physical conduct of a sexual nature constitute sexual harassment.[7]

To determine what conduct creates a hostile work environment, the U.S. Supreme Court has stated:

> *We can say that whether an environment is "hostile" or "abusive" can be determined only by looking at all the circumstances. These may include the frequency of the discriminatory conduct; its severity; whether it is physically threatening or humiliating, or a mere offensive utterance; and whether it unreasonably interferes with an employee's work performance.*[8]

In the following case, the U.S. Supreme Court decided a hostile work environment issue.

CASE 13.1 Sexual Harassment

***Pennsylvania State Police v. Suders*, 542 U.S. 129 (2004).**

"Essentially, Suders presents a 'worse case' harassment scenario, harassment ratcheted up to the breaking point."

—Justice Ginsburg

Facts

The Pennsylvania State Police (PSP) hired Nancy Drew Suders as a police communications operator for the McConnellsburg barracks. Suders's supervisors were Sergeant Eric D. Easton, station commander at the McConnellsburg barracks, Patrol Corporal William D. Baker, and Corporal Eric B. Prendergast. Those three supervisors subjected Suders to a continuous barrage of sexual harassment that ceased only when she resigned from the force. Easton would bring up the subject of people having sex with animals each time Suders entered his office. He told Prendergast, in front of Suders, that young girls should be given instruction in how to gratify men with oral sex. Easton also would sit down near Suders, wearing Spandex shorts, and spread his legs apart. Baker repeatedly made an obscene gesture in Suders's presence that involved grabbing his genitals and shouting out a vulgar comment inviting oral sex. Baker made this gesture as many as five to ten times per night throughout Suders's employment at the barracks. Further, Baker would rub his rear end in front of her and remark "I have a nice ass, don't I?"

Five months after being hired, Suders contacted Virginia Smith-Elliot, PSP's equal opportunity officer, stating that she was being harassed at work and was afraid. Smith-Elliot's response appeared to Suders to be insensitive and unhelpful. Two days later, Suders resigned from the force. Suders sued PSP, alleging that she had been subject to sexual harassment and constructively discharged and forced to resign. The U.S. District Court held that although the evidence was sufficient for a jury to conclude that Suders's supervisors had engaged in sexual harassment, PSP was not vicariously liable for the supervisors' conduct. The U.S. District Court granted PSP's motion for summary judgment. The U.S. Court of Appeals reversed and remanded the case for trial on the merits against PSP. PSP appealed to the U.S. Supreme Court.

Issue

Can an employer be held vicariously liable when the sexual harassment conduct of its employees is so severe that the victim of the harassment resigns?

Language of the U.S. Supreme Court

To establish hostile work environment, plaintiffs like Suders must show harassing behavior sufficiently severe or pervasive to alter the conditions of their employment. The very fact that the discriminatory conduct was so severe or pervasive that it created a work environment abusive to employees because of their gender offends Title VII's broad rule of workplace equality. Beyond that, we hold, to establish "constructive discharge," the plaintiff must make a further showing: She must show that the abusive working environment became so intolerable that her resignation qualified as a fitting response. An employer may defend against such a claim by showing both (1) that it had installed a readily accessible and effective policy for reporting and resolving complaints of sexual harassment, and (2) that the plaintiff unreasonably failed to avail herself of that employer-provided preventive or remedial apparatus. This affirmative defense will not be available to the employer, however, if the plaintiff quits in reasonable response to an employer-sanctioned adverse action officially changing her employment status or situation, for example, a humiliating demotion, extreme cut in pay, or transfer to a position in which she would face unbearable working conditions.

Essentially, Suders presents a "worse case" harassment scenario, harassment ratcheted up to the breaking point. Harassment so intolerable as to cause a resignation may be effected through co-worker conduct, unofficial supervisory conduct, or official company acts. Unlike an actual termination, which is always effected through an official act of the company, a constructive discharge need not be. A constructive discharge involves both an employee's decision to leave and precipitating conduct.

Decision

The U.S. Supreme Court agreed with the U.S. Court of Appeals that Suders's case presented genuine issues of material fact concerning Suders's hostile work environment and constructive discharge claims. The Supreme Court remanded the case for further proceedings consistent with its opinion.

Case Questions

1. **Critical Legal Thinking** What is *vicarious liability*? What is *constructive discharge*? Explain.
2. **Business Ethics** Did Suders's supervisors act responsibly in this case?
3. **Contemporary Business** Do you think very much sexual harassment occurs in the workplace?

Same-Sex Discrimination

For years, it was unclear whether same-sex sexual harassment and same-sex discrimination in employment were actionable under Title VII. In 1998, in ***Omcale v. Sundowner Offshore Services, Incorporated,***[9] the U.S. Supreme Court held that same-sex harassment violated Title VII. Many state and local antidiscrimination laws outlaw same-sex discrimination and harassment in the workplace.

CONTEMPORARY Environment

EMPLOYER'S DEFENSE TO A CHARGE OF SEXUAL HARASSMENT

In two cases, *Faragher v. City of Boca Raton*, 524 U.S. 775 (1998) and *Burlington Indus., Inc. v. Ellerth*, 524 U.S. 742 (1998), female plaintiffs sued their employers, proving that their supervisors had engaged in unconsented physical touching and verbal sexual harassment. In each case, the female employee quit her job and sued her employer for sexual harassment in violation of Title VII. In *Faragher*, the employer had never disseminated to its employees a policy against sexual harassment. The U.S. District Court held in favor of the female employee. In *Burlington Industries*, the employer had disseminated its policy against sexual harassment to its employees and had put into place a complaint system that the female employee did not use. In this case, the U.S. District Court granted summary judgment to the company. After appeals, the U.S. Supreme Court accepted these two cases for review.

The U.S. Supreme Court, in both of these decisions, held that an employer is not strictly liable for sexual harassment. The Supreme Court held that an employer may raise an **affirmative defense** against liability by proving two elements:

1. The employer exercised reasonable care to prevent, and promptly correct, any sexual harassing behavior.
2. The plaintiff-employee unreasonably failed to take advantage of any preventive or corrective opportunities provided by the employer or to otherwise avoid harm.

The defendant-employer has the burden of proving this affirmative defense. In determining whether the defense has been proven, a court must consider (1) whether the employer has an antiharassment policy, (2) whether the employer had a complaint mechanism in place, (3) whether employees were informed of the antiharassment policy and complaint procedure, and (4) other factors that the court deems relevant.

affirmative Defense
A defense that raises matters not covered in the plaintiff's complaint and that will defeat the plaintiff's claim even if the plaintiff is able to prove all of the allegations in its complaint.

INTERNET LAW & ONLINE COMMERCE

E-Mails That Lead to Sexual Harassment

The use of e-mail in business has dramatically increased efficiency and information sharing among employees. Managers and workers alike can communicate with each other, send documents, and keep each other appraised of business developments. In many organizations, e-mail has replaced the telephone as the most-used method of communication, and it has eliminated the need for many meetings. This is a blessing for business. However, the downside is that e-mail has increased the exposure of businesses to sexual and racial harassment lawsuits.

E-mail often sets the social tone of an office and has been permitted to be slightly ribald. At some point, however, e-mail conduct becomes impermissible and crosses the line to actionable sexual or racial harassment. The standard of whether e-mail creates an illegal hostile work environment is the same as that for measuring harassment in any other context: The offensive conduct must be severe and cannot consist of isolated or trivial remarks and incidents. As in other harassment cases, an employer may raise a defense if it meets two required elements: (1) The employer exercised reasonable care to prevent and correct the behavior and (2) the plaintiff-employee unreasonably failed to take advantage of any preventive or corrective opportunities provided by the employer or to avoid the harm.

E-mail harassment differs from many other incidents of harassment because it is subtle and insidious. Unlike paper pin-up calendars in plain view, an employer does not readily see e-mail messages. Obscenity pulled off the Internet or scanned into a computer can be sent as an attachment to an e-mail message. Because e-mail is hidden, to detect offensive messages, employers must take action to review e-mail messages on its network. Courts have generally held that an employee does not have an expectation of privacy of e-mail. Stored e-mail is the property of the employer, which may review it freely. Employers can also use software to scan and filter e-mail messages that contain any of a predefined list of objectionable words or phrases or certain "to" or "from" headers. Employers can also use software programs to scan graphics and block X-rated pictures.

(continued)

E-mail has increased the possibility of sexual or racial harassment on the job, and it has also become a smoking gun that undermines a company's attempt to defend such cases. Therefore, employers must adopt policies pertaining to the use of e-mail by their employees and make their employees aware that certain e-mail messages constitute sexual or racial harassment and violate the law. Employers should make periodic inspections and audits of stored e-mail to ensure that employees are complying with company antiharassment policies.

RELIGIOUS DISCRIMINATION

religious discrimination
Discrimination against a person solely because of his or her religion or religious practices.

Title VII prohibits employment discrimination based on a person's religion. *Religions*, in this case, include traditional religions, other religions that recognize a supreme being, and religions based on ethical or spiritual tenets. Many **religious discrimination** cases involve a conflict between an employer's work rule and an employee's religious beliefs (e.g., when an employee is required to work on a religious holiday).

The right of an employee to practice his or her religion is not absolute. Under Title VII, an employer is under a duty to *reasonably accommodate* the religious observances, practices, or beliefs of its employees if doing so does not cause an *undue hardship* on the employer. The courts must apply these general standards to specific fact situations. In making their decisions, the courts must consider such factors as the size of the employer, the importance of the employee's position, and the availability of alternative workers.

Title VII expressly permits religious organizations to give preference in employment to individuals of a particular religion. For example, if a person applies for a job with a religious organization but does not subscribe to its religious tenets, the organization may refuse to hire that person.

DEFENSES TO A TITLE VII ACTION

Title VII and case law recognize several defenses to a charge of discrimination under Title VII. These include merit, seniority, and bona fide occupational qualification (BFOQ). These defenses are discussed in the following paragraphs.

Merit

Employers can select or promote employees based on *merit*. Merit decisions are often based on work, educational experience, and professionally developed ability tests. To be lawful under Title VII, such a requirement must be job related.

Seniority

Many employers maintain *seniority* systems that reward long-term employees. Higher wages, fringe benefits, and other preferential treatment (e.g., choice of working hours and vacation schedule) are examples of such rewards. Seniority systems provide an incentive for employees to stay with the company. Such systems are lawful if they are not the result of intentional discrimination.

bona fide occupational qualification (BFOQ)
A true job qualification. Employment discrimination based on a protected class (other than race or color) is lawful if it is *job related* and a *business necessity*. This exception is narrowly interpreted by the courts.

Bona Fide Occupational Qualification (BFOQ)

Discrimination based on protected classes (other than race or color) is permitted if it is shown to be a **bona fide occupational qualification (BFOQ)**. Thus, an employer can justify discrimination based on gender in some circumstances. To be legal, a BFOQ must be both *job related* and a *business necessity*.

As the following U.S. Supreme Court case shows, BFOQ exceptions are narrowly interpreted by the courts.

CASE 13.2 BONA FIDE OCCUPATIONAL QUALIFICATION (BFOQ)

***International Union, United Auto., Aerospace & Agric. Implement Workers of Am. v. Johnson Controls, Inc.*, 499 U.S. 187 (1991).**

"The bias in Johnson Controls' policy is obvious. Fertile men, but not fertile women, are given a choice as to whether they wish to risk their reproductive health for a particular job."

—Justice Blackmun

Facts

Johnson Controls, Inc. (Johnson Controls), manufactures batteries. Lead is the primary ingredient in the manufacturing process. Exposure to lead entails health risks, including risk of harm to a fetus carried by a female employee. To protect unborn children from such risk, Johnson Controls adopted an employment rule that prevented pregnant women and women of childbearing age from working at jobs involving lead exposure. Only women who were sterilized or could prove they could not have children were not affected by the rule. Consequently, most female employees were relegated to lower-paying clerical jobs at the company. Several female employees filed a class action suit, challenging Johnson Controls's fetal-protection policy as sex discrimination in violation of Title VII. The U.S. District Court held that the policy was justified as a bona fide occupational qualification (BFOQ) and granted summary judgment to Johnson Controls; the U.S. Court of Appeals affirmed the judgment. The plaintiffs appealed to the U.S. Supreme Court.

Issue

Is Johnson Controls's fetal-protection policy a BFOQ?

Language of the U.S. Supreme Court

The bias in Johnson Controls' policy is obvious. Fertile men, but not fertile women, are given a choice as to whether they wish to risk their reproductive health for a particular job. Johnson Controls' fetal-protection policy explicitly discriminates against women on the basis of their sex. The policy excludes women with childbearing capacity from lead-exposed jobs and so creates a facial classification based on gender.

The bona fide occupational qualifications (BFOQ) defense is written narrowly, and this Court has read it narrowly. We have no difficulty concluding that Johnson Controls cannot establish a BFOQ. Fertile women, as far as appears in the record, participate in the manufacture of batteries as efficiently as anyone else. Johnson Controls' professed moral and ethical concerns about the welfare of the next generation do not suffice to establish a BFOQ of female sterility. Decisions about the welfare of future children must be left to the parents who conceive, bear, support, and raise them rather than to the employers who hire those parents.

> Rights matter most when they are claimed by unpopular minorities.
>
> J. Michael Kirby
> *Sydney Morning Herald,*
> *November 30, 1985*

Decision

The U.S. Supreme Court held that Johnson Controls's fetal-protection policy was not a BFOQ. Instead, it was sex discrimination in violation of Title VII. The Supreme Court reversed the decision of the U.S. Court of Appeals and remanded the case for further proceedings.

Case Questions

1. **Critical Legal Thinking** What is a BFOQ? Should a BFOQ exception to Title VII liability be permitted? Why or why not?
2. **Business Ethics** Did Johnson Controls's concerns about the safety and welfare of the next generation justify its actions?
3. **Contemporary Business** Does Johnson Controls have any tort liability to children who are born injured by exposure to lead? Explain.

Concept Summary

Title VII of the Civil Rights Act

Covered employers and employment decisions	1. **Employers.** Employers with 15 or more employees for 20 weeks in the current or preceding year, all employment agencies, labor unions with 15 or more members, state and local governments and their agencies, and most federal government employment.
	2. **Employment decisions.** Decisions regarding hiring; promotion; demotion; payment of salaries, wages, and fringe benefits; dismissal; job training and apprenticeships; work rules; or any other term, condition, or privilege of employment. Decisions to admit partners to a partnership are also covered.
Protected classes	1. **Race.** A broad class of individuals with common characteristics (e.g., African American, Caucasian, Asian, Native American).
	2. **Color.** The color of a person's skin (e.g., light-skinned person, dark-skinned person).
	3. **National origin.** A person's country of origin or national heritage (e.g., Italian, Hispanic).
	4. **Sex.** A person's sex, whether male or female. Includes sexual harassment and discrimination against females who are pregnant.
	5. **Religion.** A person's religious beliefs. An employer has a duty to reasonably accommodate an employee's religious beliefs if doing so does not cause an undue hardship on the employer.
Types of discrimination	1. **Disparate-treatment discrimination.** Discrimination against a specific individual because that person belongs to a protected class.
	2. **Disparate-impact discrimination.** Discrimination in which an employer discriminates against a protected class. A neutral-looking employment rule that causes discrimination against a protected class is disparate-impact discrimination.

Defenses	1. **Merit.** Job-related experience, education, or unbiased ability test.
	2. **Seniority.** Length of time an employee has been employed by the employer. Intentional discrimination based on seniority is unlawful.
	3. **Bona fide occupational qualification (BFOQ).** Discrimination based on sex, religion, or national origin is permitted if it is a valid BFOQ for the position. Qualification based on race or color is not a permissible BFOQ.
Remedies	1. **Equitable remedy.** The court may order the payment of back pay, issue an injunction awarding reinstatement, grant fictional seniority, or order some other equitable remedy.
	2. **Damages.** The court can award compensatory damages in cases of intentional discrimination. The court can award punitive damages in cases involving an employer's malice or reckless indifference to federally protected rights.

EQUAL PAY ACT

Discrimination often takes the form of different pay scales for men and women performing the same job. The **Equal Pay Act** of 1963 protects both sexes from pay discrimination based on sex.[10] This act covers all levels of private-sector employees and state and local government employees. Federal workers are not covered, however.

Equal Pay Act
A federal statute that protects both sexes from pay discrimination based on sex. It extends to jobs that require equal skill, equal effort, equal responsibility, and similar working conditions.

The act prohibits disparity in pay for jobs that require *equal skill* (i.e., equal experience), *equal effort* (i.e., mental and physical exertion), *equal responsibility* (i.e., equal supervision and accountability), or *similar working conditions* (e.g., dangers of injury, exposure to the elements). To make this determination, the courts examine the actual requirements of jobs to determine whether they are equal and similar. If two jobs are determined to be equal and similar, an employer cannot pay disparate wages to members of different sexes.

Employees can bring a private cause of action against an employer for violating the Equal Pay Act. Back pay and liquidated damages are recoverable. In addition, the employer must increase the wages of the discriminated-against employee to eliminate the unlawful disparity of wages. The wages of other employees may not be lowered.

Civil Rights Act of 1866
A federal statute enacted after the Civil War that says all persons "have the same right . . . to make and enforce contracts . . . as is enjoyed by white persons." It prohibits racial and national origin employment discrimination.

LANDMARK LAW

CIVIL RIGHTS ACT OF 1866

The **Civil Rights Act of 1866** was enacted after the Civil War. Section 1981 of this act states that all persons "have the same right . . . to make and enforce contracts . . . as is enjoyed by white persons" [42 U.S.C. Section 1981]. This law was enacted to give African Americans, just freed from slavery, the same right to contract as whites. Section 1981 expressly prohibits racial discrimination; it has also been held to forbid discrimination based on national origin.

Employment decisions are covered by Section 1981 because the employment relationship is contractual. Although most racial and national origin employment discrimination cases are brought under Title VII, there are two reasons that a complainant would bring an action under Section 1981: (1) A private plaintiff can bring an action without going through the procedural requirements of Title VII and (2) there is no cap on the recovery of compensatory or punitive damages under Section 1981.

Criteria That Justify a Differential in Wages

The Equal Pay Act expressly provides four criteria that justify a differential in wages. These defenses include payment systems that are based on:

- Seniority
- Merit (as long as there is some identifiable measurement standard)
- Quantity or quality of product (commission, piecework, or quality control–based payment systems are permitted)
- "Any factor other than sex" (including shift differentials, i.e., night versus day shifts)

The employer bears the burden of proving these defenses.

AGE DISCRIMINATION IN EMPLOYMENT ACT

Age Discrimination in Employment Act (ADEA) of 1967
A federal statute that prohibits age discrimination practices against employees who are 40 and older.

Some employers have discriminated against employees and prospective employees based on their age. Primarily, employers have often refused to hire older workers. The **Age Discrimination in Employment Act (ADEA)**, which prohibits certain *age discrimination* practices, was enacted in 1967.[11]

The ADEA covers nonfederal employers with at least twenty employees, labor unions with at least twenty-five members, and all employment agencies. State and local government employees except those in policy-making positions are covered, as are employees of certain sectors of the federal government.

Older Workers Benefit Protection Act (OWBPA)
A federal statute that prohibits age discrimination in employee benefits.

The ADEA prohibits age discrimination in all employment decisions, including hiring, promotions, payment of compensation, and other terms and conditions of employment. The **Older Workers Benefit Protection Act (OWBPA)** amended the ADEA to prohibit age discrimination with regard to employee benefits. Employers cannot use employment advertisements that discriminate against applicants covered by the ADEA.

Protected Age Categories

Originally, the ADEA prohibited employment discrimination against persons between the ages of 40 and 65. Later, its coverage was extended to persons up to age 70. Further amendments completely eliminated an age ceiling, so the ADEA now applies to employees who are 40 and older. As a result, covered employers cannot establish mandatory retirement ages for their employees.

Because persons under 40 are not protected by the ADEA, an employer can maintain an employment policy of hiring only workers who are 40 years of age or older without violating the ADEA. However, an employer cannot maintain an employment practice whereby it hires only persons 50 years of age and older because that would discriminate against persons aged 40 to 49.

The ADEA is administered by the EEOC. Private plaintiffs can also sue under the ADEA. A successful plaintiff in an ADEA action can recover back wages, attorneys' fees, and equitable relief, including hiring, reinstatement, and promotion. Where a violation of the ADEA is found, the employer must raise the wages of the discriminated-against employee. It cannot lower the wages of other employees.

Americans with Disabilities Act (ADA)
A federal statute that imposes obligations on employers and providers of public transportation, telecommunications, and public accommodations to accommodate individuals with disabilities.

AMERICANS WITH DISABILITIES ACT

The **Americans with Disabilities Act (ADA)**,[12] which was signed into law July 26, 1990, is the most comprehensive piece of civil rights legislation since the Civil Rights Act of 1964. The ADA imposes obligations on employers and

LANDMARK LAW

AMERICANS WITH DISABILITIES ACT

Title I of the ADA prohibits employment discrimination against qualified individuals with disabilities in regard to job application procedures, hiring, compensation, training, promotion, and termination. Title I covers employers with fifteen or more employees. The United States, corporations wholly owned by the United States, and bona fide tax-exempt private membership clubs are exempt from Title I coverage.

Title I requires an employer to make reasonable accommodations to individuals with disabilities that do not cause undue hardship to the employer. **Reasonable accommodations** may include making facilities readily accessible to individuals with disabilities, providing part-time or modified work schedules, acquiring equipment or devices, modifying examination and training materials, and providing qualified readers or interpreters.

Employers are not obligated to provide accommodations that would impose an **undue burden**—that is, actions that would require significant difficulty or expense. The EEOC and the courts consider factors such as the nature and cost of accommodation, the overall financial resources of the employer, and the employer's type of operation. Obviously, what may be a significant difficulty or expense for a small employer may not be an undue hardship for a large employer.

providers of public transportation, telecommunications, and public accommodations to accommodate individuals with disabilities.

Qualified Individual with a Disability

A **qualified individual with a disability** is a person who, with or without reasonable accommodation, can perform the essential functions of the job that person desires or holds. A disabled person is someone who (1) has a physical or mental impairment that substantially limits one or more of his or her major life activities, (2) has a record of such impairment, or (3) is regarded as having such impairment. Mental retardation, paraplegia, schizophrenia, cerebral palsy, epilepsy, diabetes, muscular dystrophy, multiple sclerosis, cancer, infection with HIV (human immunodeficiency virus), and visual, speech, and hearing impairments are covered under the ADA. A current user of illegal drugs or an alcoholic who uses alcohol or is under the influence of alcohol at the workplace is not covered. However, recovering alcoholics and former users of illegal drugs are protected.

Forbidden Conduct

Title I of the ADA limits an employer's ability to inquire into or test for an applicant's disabilities. Title I forbids an employer from asking a job applicant about the existence, nature, and severity of a disability. An employer may, however, inquire about the applicant's ability to perform job-related functions. Preemployment medical examinations are forbidden before a job offer. Once a job offer has been made, an employer may require a medical examination and may condition the offer on the examination results, as long as all entering employees are subject to such an examination. The information obtained must be kept confidential.

Procedure and Remedies

Title I of the ADA is administered by the EEOC. An aggrieved individual must first file a charge with the EEOC, which may take action against the employer or

Title I of the ADA
A title of a federal statute that prohibits employment discrimination against qualified individuals with disabilities in regard to job application procedures, hiring, compensation, training, promotion, and termination.

reasonable accommodations
Title I requires an employer to make reasonable accommodations to individuals with disabilities that do not cause undue hardship to the employer. Reasonable accommodations may include making facilities readily accessible to individuals with disabilities, providing part-time or modified work schedules, acquiring equipment or devices, modifying examination and training materials, and providing qualified readers or interpreters.

undue burden
Employers are not obligated to provide accommodations that would impose an undue burden—that is, actions that would require significant difficulty or expense.

qualified individual with a disability
A person who (1) has a physical or mental impairment that substantially limits one or more of his or her major life activities, (2) has a record of such impairment, or (3) is regarded as having such impairment.

permit the individual to pursue a private cause of action. Relief can take the form of an injunction, hiring or reinstatement (with back pay), payment of attorneys' fees, and recovery of compensatory and punitive damages (subject to the same caps as Title VII damages).

AFFIRMATIVE ACTION

CONTEMPORARY Environment

AFFIRMATIVE ACTION

Title VII of the Civil Rights Act of 1964 outlawed discrimination in employment based on race, color, national origin, sex, and religion. The law clearly prohibited any further discrimination based on these protected classes. However, did the federal statute intend to grant a favorable status to the classes of persons who had been previously discriminated against? In a series of cases, the U.S. Supreme Court upheld the use of affirmative action programs to make up for egregious past discrimination, particularly based on race.

Affirmative Action Plans

Employers often adopt **affirmative action** plans, which provide that certain job preferences will be given to members of minority racial and ethnic groups, females, and other protected-class applicants when an employer makes an employment decision. Such plans can be voluntarily adopted by employers, undertaken to settle a discrimination action, or ordered by the courts.

To be lawful, an affirmative action plan must be *narrowly tailored* to achieve some *compelling interest*. Employment quotas based on a specified number or percentage of minority applicants or employees are unlawful. If a person's minority status is only one factor of many factors considered in an employment decision, that decision will usually be considered lawful.

affirmative action
A policy that provides that certain job preferences will be given to minority or other protected class applicants when an employer makes an employment decision.

Reverse Discrimination

Title VII not only applies to members of minority groups but also protects members of majority classes from discrimination. Lawful affirmative action plans have an effect on members of majority classes. The courts have held that if an affirmative action plan is based on preestablished numbers or percentage quotas for hiring or promoting minority applicants, then it causes illegal **reverse discrimination**. In this case, the members of the majority class may sue under Title VII and recover damages and other remedies for reverse discrimination. Some reverse discrimination cases are successful.

RETALIATION

Title VII of the Civil Rights Act of 1964 expressly prohibits employers from retaliating against an employee for filing a charge of discrimination or participating in a discrimination proceeding regarding race, color, national origin, sex, or religious discrimination. Acts of retaliation are also forbidden for bringing and maintaining charges of age discrimination, disability discrimination, and discrimination in violation of Section 1981 of the Civil Rights Act of 1866. Acts of retaliation include dismissing, demoting, harassing, or other methods of retaliation.

reverse discrimination
Discrimination against a group that is usually thought of as a majority.

Concept Review

Title VII of the Civil Rights Act

Covered employers and employment decisions	1. **Employers.** Employers with 15 or more employees for 20 weeks in the current or preceding year, all employment agencies, labor unions with 15 or more members, state and local governments and their agencies, and most federal government employment. 2. **Employment decisions.** Decisions regarding hiring; promotion; demotion; payment of salaries, wages, and fringe benefits; dismissal; job training and apprenticeships; work rules; or any other term, condition, or privilege of employment. Decisions to admit partners to a partnership are also covered.
Protected classes	1. **Race.** A broad class of individuals with common characteristics (e.g., African American, Caucasian, Asian, Native American). 2. **Color.** The color of a person's skin (e.g., light-skinned person, dark-skinned person). 3. **National origin.** A person's country of origin or national heritage (e.g., Italian, Hispanic). 4. **Sex.** A person's sex, whether male or female. Includes sexual harassment and discrimination against females who are pregnant. 5. **Religion.** A person's religious beliefs. An employer has a duty to reasonably accommodate an employee's religious beliefs if doing so does not cause an undue hardship on the employer.
Types of discrimination	1. **Disparate-treatment discrimination.** Discrimination against a specific individual because that person belongs to a protected class. 2. **Disparate-impact discrimination.** Discrimination in which an employer discriminates against a protected class. A neutral-looking employment rule that causes discrimination against a protected class is disparate-impact discrimination.
Defenses	1. **Merit.** Job-related experience, education, or unbiased ability test. 2. **Seniority.** Length of time an employee has been employed by the employer. Intentional discrimination based on seniority is unlawful. 3. **Bona fide occupational qualification (BFOQ).** Discrimination based on sex, religion, or national origin is permitted if it is a valid BFOQ for the position. Qualification based on race or color is not a permissible BFOQ.
Remedies	1. **Equitable remedy.** The court may order the payment of back pay, issue an injunction awarding reinstatement, grant fictional seniority, or order some other equitable remedy. 2. **Damages.** The court can award compensatory damages in cases of intentional discrimination. The court can award punitive damages in cases involving an employer's malice or reckless indifference to federally protected rights.

> Racial discrimination in any form and in any degree has no justifiable part whatever in our democratic way of life. It is unattractive in any setting but it is utterly revolting among a free people who have embraced the principles set forth in the Constitution of the United States.
>
> Justice Murphy
> *Dissenting opinion, Korematsu v. United States,* 323 U.S. 214 (1944).

> We hold these truths to be self-evident, that all men and women are created equal.
> Elizabeth Cady Stanton (1848)

CHAPTER REVIEW

TITLE VII OF THE CIVIL RIGHTS ACT OF 1964, p. 385

Title VII of the Civil Rights Act of 1964

This federal statute prohibits job discrimination based on the (1) race, (2) color, (3) religion, (4) sex, or (5) national origin of the job applicant.

Scope of Coverage of Title VII

1. ***Employers subject to Title VII.*** Employers who had fifteen or more employees for at least twenty weeks in the current or preceding year, all employment agencies, labor unions with fifteen or more members, state and local governments, and most federal agencies are subject to Title VII.
2. ***Employment decisions subject to Title VII.*** Decisions regarding hiring; promotion; demotion; payment of salaries, wages, and fringe benefits; job training and apprenticeships; work rules; and any other "term, condition, or privilege of employment" are subject to Title VII.

Forms of Title VII Actions

1. ***Disparate-treatment discrimination.*** This type of discrimination occurs when an employer treats a specific *individual* less favorably than others because of that person's race, color, national origin, sex, or religion. To be successful, complainants must prove:
   a. They belong to a Title VII protected class.
   b. They applied for and were qualified for the employment position.
   c. They were rejected despite these qualifications.
   d. The employer kept the position open and sought applicants from persons with the complainants' qualifications.
2. ***Disparate-impact discrimination.*** This type of discrimination occurs when an employer discriminates against an entire protected *class*. It may be proven by statistical data that demonstrate a causal link between the challenged practice and the statistical imbalance. *Neutral employment rules* that have an adverse impact on a protected class constitute disparate-impact discrimination.

Equal Employment Opportunity Commission (EEOC)

The EEOC is a federal administrative agency responsible for administering, interpreting, and enforcing most federal equal employment opportunity (antidiscrimination) laws.

Procedure for Bringing a Title VII Action

1. ***Complaint.*** A private complainant must file a complaint with the EEOC. The EEOC is given the opportunity to sue the employer on the complainant's behalf.
2. ***Right to sue letter.*** If the EEOC chooses not to bring suit, it will issue a *right to sue letter* that authorizes the complainant to sue the employer.

Remedies for Violations of Title VII

A successful plaintiff in a Title VII action can recover back pay, compensatory and punitive damages (subject to certain caps, based on the size of the defendant-employer), reasonable attorneys' fees, and equitable remedies such as reinstatement, fictional seniority, and injunctions.

> Legislation to apply the principle of equal pay for equal work without discrimination because of sex is a matter of simple justice.
> Dwight D. Eisenhower

RACE, COLOR, AND NATIONAL ORIGIN DISCRIMINATION, p. 387

Race, Color, and National Origin Discrimination

1. ***Race.*** Race is a broad class of individuals with common physical characteristics (e.g., African American, Caucasian, Asian, Native American).
2. ***Color.*** Color refers to the color of a person's skin (e.g., light-skinned person, dark-skinned person).
3. ***National origin or heritage.*** National origin is a person's country of origin or national heritage (e.g., Italian, Hispanic).

SEX DISCRIMINATION AND SEXUAL HARASSMENT, p. 388

Sex Discrimination

1. ***Sex.*** Sex refers to a person's sex, whether male or female.
2. ***Pregnancy.*** The *Pregnancy Discrimination Act of 1978* amended Title VII to forbid employment discrimination because of "pregnancy, childbirth, or related medical conditions."
3. ***Sexual harassment.*** Sexual harassment is lewd remarks, touching, intimidation, posting of pin-ups, and other verbal or physical conduct of a sexual nature that occurs on the job. Sexual harassment that creates a hostile work environment violates Title VII.
4. ***Sexual preference.*** Title VII applies to employment discrimination based on sexual preference.

RELIGIOUS DISCRIMINATION, p. 392

Religious Discrimination

Religious discrimination is discrimination solely because of a person's religious beliefs or practices. An employer has a duty to *reasonably accommodate* an employee's religious beliefs if doing so does not cause an *undue hardship* on the employer.

DEFENSES TO A TITLE VII ACTION, p. 392

Defenses to a Title VII Action

1. ***Merit.*** Merit includes job-related experiences, education, or unbiased employment tests.
2. ***Seniority.*** Seniority is the length of time an employee has been employed by the employer. Intentional discrimination based on seniority is unlawful.
3. ***Bona fide occupational qualification (BFOQ).*** Employment discrimination based on the sex, religion, or national origin of an applicant is permitted if it is a valid *bona fide occupational qualification (BFOQ)* for the position. To be legal, a BFOQ must be *job related* and a *business necessity*. BFOQ exceptions are narrowly interpreted by the courts.

Civil Rights Act of 1866

1. ***Section 1981 of the Civil Rights Act of 1866.*** This federal statute, enacted after the Civil War, states that all persons "have the same right . . . to make and enforce contracts . . . as is enjoyed by white persons."
2. ***Protected class.*** Section 1981 prohibits *race* and *national origin* discrimination concerning employment contracts.

> By what justice can an association of citizens be held together when there is no equality among the citizens?
>
> Cicero
> *De Re Publia De Legibus, I, xxxii, 49*

3. ***Remedies.*** A successful plaintiff can recover back pay, equitable remedies, compensatory and punitive damages, and reasonable attorneys' fees. There are no monetary caps on compensatory and punitive damages.

EQUAL PAY ACT, p. 395

Equal Pay Act

This federal statute forbids pay discrimination for the same job based on the sex of the employee performing the job. There cannot be pay disparity based on sex for jobs that require equal skill, equal effort, equal responsibility, and similar working conditions.

1. ***Criteria that justify a differential in wages.*** The Equal Pay Act stipulates that the following four criteria justify a differential in wages:
   a. Seniority
   b. Merit
   c. Quantity or quality of work (commission, piecework, or quality control–based pay systems)
   d. Any factor other than sex (e.g., night versus day shifts)

AGE DISCRIMINATION IN EMPLOYMENT ACT, p. 396

Age Discrimination in Employment Act (ADEA)

Federal statute that prohibits employment discrimination against applicants and employees who are 40 years of age or older.

1. ***Older Workers Benefit Protection Act (OWBPA).*** This federal statute amended the ADEA to prohibit age discrimination with respect to employment benefits.
2. ***Defenses.*** The same defenses that are available in a Title VII action are also available in an ADEA action.
3. ***Remedies.*** A successful plaintiff can recover back wages, attorneys' fees, and equitable relief, including hiring, reinstatement, and promotion.

AMERICANS WITH DISABILITIES ACT, p. 396

Americans with Disabilities Act of 1990 (ADA)

This federal statute imposes obligations on employers and providers of public transportation, telecommunications, and public accommodations to accommodate individuals with disabilities.

Title I of the ADA

This federal law prohibits employment discrimination against qualified individuals with disabilities.

1. ***Reasonable accommodation.*** Title I requires employers to make *reasonable accommodations* to accommodate employees with disabilities that do not cause *undue hardship* to the employer.

Qualified Individual with a Disability

A qualified individual with a disability is a person who (1) has a physical or mental impairment that substantially limits one or more of his or her major life functions, (2) has a record of such impairment, or (3) is regarded as having such impairment

Procedure and Remedies

A successful plaintiff can recover back pay, compensatory and punitive damages (subject to certain caps, based on the size of the defendant-employer), reasonable attorneys' fees, and equitable remedies, such as hiring, reinstatement, or promotion.

> All about me may be silence and darkness, yet within me, in the spirit, is music and brightness, and color flashes through all my thoughts.
>
> Helen Keller
> *The Open Door (1957)*

AFFIRMATIVE ACTION, p. 398

Affirmative Action and Reverse Discrimination

Affirmative action is a policy that provides that certain job preferences will be given to minority or other protected class applicants when an employer makes an employment decision.

1. ***Lawfulness of affirmative action plans.*** An employer may adopt a voluntary affirmative action plan that uses race or other protected class status as a "*plus factor*" in making employment decisions.
2. ***Reverse discrimination.*** Reverse discrimination is discrimination against a person who is a member of a group that is usually thought of as a majority. Very few reverse discrimination lawsuits are successful.

RETALIATION, p. 398

Retaliation

Title VII of the Civil Rights Act of 1964 expressly prohibits employers from retaliating against an employee for filing a charge of discrimination or participating in a discrimination proceeding regarding race, color, national origin, sex, or religious discrimination.

TEST REVIEW TERMS AND CONCEPTS

Affirmative action 398
Affirmative defense 391
Age Discrimination in Employment Act (ADEA) of 1967 396
Americans with Disabilities Act (ADA) 396
Bona fide occupation qualification (BFOQ) 392
Civil Rights Act of 1866 395
Civil Rights Act of 1964 385
Disparate-impact discrimination 386
Disparate-treatment discrimination 385
Equal Employment Opportunity Act of 1972 385
Equal Employment Opportunity Commission (EEOC) 386
Equal opportunity in employment 384
Equal Pay Act 395
Older Workers Benefit Protection Act (OWBPA) 396
Pregnancy Discrimination Act 388
Qualified individual with a disability 397
Reasonable accommodations 397
Religious discrimination 392
Reverse discrimination 398

CASE SCENARIO REVISITED

Remember the case at the beginning of the chapter involving the Equal Pay Act? By hiring females for night shift jobs but instituting a "red circle" wage rate that permitted previously hired male night shift workers to continue to receive higher wages than newly hired night shift workers, did Corning violate the Equal Pay Act? To help you with your answer, see *Corning Glass Works v. Brennan*, 417 U.S. 188 (1974).

PORTFOLIO EXERCISE

Harry Employee is an employee of the business you created at the beginning of the course. He has been employed with your company for over fifty years. You received the Charge of Discrimination below. What possible defenses to this charge can you raise as the employer?

WORKING THE WEB INTERNET EXERCISES

Activities

1. Review the case *Gupta v. Florida Bd. of Regents* (5/17/2000, No. 98-5392) via the Cornell Discrimination website, at **www.law.cornell.edu/topics/employment_discrimination.html**. According to the 11th Circuit Court of Appeals, is it sexual harassment to make comments to co-workers such as "You are looking very beautiful"?
2. Review Congress's statement of purpose in the ADEA. Has this law served to accomplish that purpose? See the U.S. Equal Employment Opportunity Commission site, at **www.eeoc.gov**, and the Law About . . . Employment Discrimination site, at **www.law.cornell.edu/topics/employment_discrimination.html**.
3. Find the case *PGA Tour, Inc. v. Martin* involving the ADA and a professional golfer. Do you agree with the court's decision? Try the Law About . . . Employment Discrimination site.

EEOC Form 5 (5/01)

CHARGE OF DISCRIMINATION This form is affected by the Privacy Act of 1974. See enclosed Privacy Act Statement and other information before completing this form.	Charge Presented to: ___ FEPA; X EEOC	Agency(ies) Charge No(s):

_______________ and EEOC
State or local Agency, if any

Name (*indicate Mr. Ms. Mrs.*)	Home Phone (Incl. Area Code)	Date of Birth
Harry Employee	000/000-0000	1-1-1930

Street Address	City, State and ZIP Code
1234 Main St.	Toledo, Ohio 43604

Named is the Employer, Labor Organization, Employment Agency, Apprenticeship Committee, or State or Local Government Agency That I believe Discriminated Against Me or Others. (*If more than two, list under PARTICULARS below.*)

Name	No. Employees, Members	Phone No. (Include Area Code)

Street Address	City, State and ZIP Code

Name	No. Employees, Members	Phone No. (Include Area Code)

Street Address	City, State and ZIP Code

DISCRIMINATION BASED ON (*Check appropriate box(es).*)

__ RACE __ COLOR __ SEX __ RELIGION __ NATIONAL ORIGIN

__ RETALIATION X AGE __ DISABILITY __ OTHER (Specify below.)

DATE(S) DISCRIMINATION TOOK PLACE
Earliest 1-1-2011 Latest 1-2-2011

__ CONTINUING ACTION

THE PARTICULARS ARE (*If additional paper is needed, attached extra sheet(s)*):

I have been working for over 50 years and have never received an unsatisfactory review (that I can remember). Yesterday I was fired and told I was not doing my job well. I believe I was fired because of my age.

I want this charge filed with both the EEOC and the State or local Agency, if any. I will advise the agencies if I change my address or phone number and I will cooperate fully with them in the processing of my charge in accordance with their procedures.	NOTARY – *When necessary for State and Local Agency Requirements*
I declare under penalty of perjury that the above is true and correct. 1-2-2011 (*Date*) Harry Employee (*Charging Party Signature*)	I swear or affirm that I have read the above charge and that it is true to the best of my knowledge, information and belief. SIGNATURE OF COMPLANANT Harry Employee SUBSCRIBED AND SWORN TO BEFORE ME THIS DATE (*month, day, year*)

CRITICAL LEGAL THINKING CASES

Case 13.1 ***Sex Discrimination*** The Los Angeles Department of Water and Power maintains a pension plan for its employees that is funded by both employer and employee contributions. The plan pays men and women retirees' pensions with the same monthly benefits. However, because statistically women live, on average, several years longer than men, female employees are required to make monthly contributions to the pension fund that are 14.84 percent higher than the contributions required of male employees. Because employee contributions are withheld from paychecks, a female employee takes home less pay than a male employee earning the same salary. Does this practice violate Title VII? *Los Angeles Dep't of Water & Power v. Manhart*, 435 U.S. 702 (1978).

Case 13.2 ***Hostile Work Environment*** Shirley Huddleston became the first female sales representative of Roger Dean Chevrolet, Inc. (RDC), in West Palm Beach, Florida. Shortly after she began working at RDC, Philip Geraci, a fellow sales representative, and other male employees began making derogatory comments to and about her, expelled gas in her presence, and called her derogatory names. Many of these remarks were made in front of customers. The sales manager of RDC participated in the harassment. On several occasions, Huddleston complained about this conduct to RDC's general manager. Was Title VII violated? Who wins? *Huddleston v. Roger Dean Chevrolet, Inc.*, 845 F.2d 900 (1988).

Case 13.3 ***National Origin Discrimination*** The Federal Bureau of Investigation (FBI) engaged in a pattern and practice of discrimination against Hispanic FBI agents. Job assignments and promotions were areas that were especially affected. Bernardo M. Perez, a Hispanic, brought a Title VII action against the FBI. Did the FBI violate Title VII? Who wins? *Perez v. Federal Bureau of Investigation*, 714 F. Supp. 1414 (W.D. Tex. 1989).

Case 13.4 ***Religious Discrimination*** Trans World Airlines (TWA), an airline, operated a large maintenance and overhaul base for its airplanes in Kansas City, Missouri. Because of its essential role, the stores department at the base operated 24 hours per day, 365 days per year. The employees at the base were represented by the International Association of Machinists and Aerospace Workers (Union). TWA and Union entered into a collective bargaining agreement that included a seniority system for the assignment of jobs and shifts.

TWA hired Larry Hardison to work as a clerk in the stores department. Soon after beginning work, Hardison joined the Worldwide Church of God, which does not allow its members to work from sunset on Friday until sunset on Saturday and on certain religious holidays. Hardison, who had the second lowest seniority within the stores department, did not have enough seniority to observe his Sabbath regularly. When Hardison asked for special consideration, TWA offered to allow him to take his Sabbath off if he could switch shifts with another employee-union member. None of the other employees would do so. TWA refused Hardison's request for a four-day workweek because it would have had to either hire and train a part-time worker to work on Saturdays or incur the cost of paying overtime to an existing full-time worker on Saturdays. Hardison sued TWA for religious discrimination in violation of Title VII. Did TWA's actions violate Title VII? Who wins? *Trans World Airlines v. Hardison*, 432 U.S. 63 (1977).

Case 13.5 ***Bona Fide Occupational Qualification*** At age 60, Manuel Fragante emigrated from the Philippines to Hawaii. In response to a newspaper ad,

Fragante applied for an entry-level civil service clerk job with the City of Honolulu's Division of Motor Vehicles and Licensing. The job required constant oral communication with the public, either at the information counter or on the telephone. Fragante scored the highest of 731 test takers on a written examination that tested word usage, grammar, and spelling. As part of the application process, two civil service employees who were familiar with the demands of the position interviewed Fragante. They testified that his accent made it difficult to understand him. Fragante was not hired for the position, which was filled by another applicant. Fragante sued, alleging national origin discrimination in violation of Title VII. Who wins? *Fragante v. City and County of Honolulu*, 888 F.2d 591 (9th Cir. 1989).

Case 13.6 *Age Discrimination* Walker Boyd Fite was an employee of First Tennessee Production Credit Association for nineteen years. He had attained the position of vice president–credit. During the course of his employment, he had never received an unsatisfactory review. On December 26, 1983, at age 57, Fite was hospitalized with a kidney stone. On January 5, 1984, while Fite was recovering at home, an officer of First Tennessee called to inform him that he had been retired as of December 31, 1983. A few days later, Fite received a letter stating that he had been retired because of poor job performance. Fite sued First Tennessee for age discrimination. Who wins? *Fite v. First Tenn. Prod. Credit Ass'n*, 861 F.2d 884 (6th Cir. 1988).

BUSINESS ETHICS CASES

Case 13.7 *Business Ethics* Dianne Rawlinson, 22 years old, was a college graduate whose major course of study was correctional psychology. After graduation, she applied for a position as a correctional counselor (prison guard) with the Alabama Board of Corrections. Her application was rejected because she failed to meet the minimum 120-pound weight requirement of an Alabama statute that also established a height minimum of 5 feet 2 inches. In addition, the Alabama Board of Corrections adopted Administrative Regulation 204, which established gender criteria for assigning correctional counselors to maximum-security prisons for "contact positions." These are correctional counselor positions that require continual close physical proximity to inmates. Under this rule, Rawlinson did not qualify for contact positions with male prisoners in Alabama maximum-security prisons. Rawlinson brought a class action lawsuit against Dothard, who was the director of the Department of Public Safety of Alabama. Does either the height–weight requirement or the contact position rule constitute a bona fide occupational qualification that justifies the sex discrimination in this case? Does society owe a duty of social responsibility to protect women from dangerous job positions? Or is this "romantic paternalism"? *Dothard v. Rawlinson*, 433 U.S. 321 (1977).

Case 13.8 *Business Ethics* Rita Machakos, a white female, worked for the Civil Rights Division (CRD) of the Department of Justice. During her employment, she was denied promotion to certain paralegal positions. In each instance, the individual selected was a black female. Evidence showed that the CRD maintained an institutional and systematic discrimination policy that favored minority employees over white employees. Machakos sued the CRD for race discrimination under Title VII. Who wins? *Machakos v. Attorney General of the United States*, 859 F.2d 1487 (D.C. Cir. 1988).

ENDNOTES

1. 42 U.S.C. Sections 2000e–2000e-17.
2. *EEOC v. Tortilleria "La Mejor,"* 758 F. Supp. 585 (E.D. Cal. 1991).
3. *McDonnell Douglas v. Green*, 411 U.S. 792 (1973).
4. In some states, the complaint must be filed with the appropriate state agency rather than the EEOC.
5. *Ledbetter v. Goodyear Tire & Rubber Co.*, 550 U.S. 618 (2007).
6. 42 U.S.C. Section 2000e(K).
7. *Meritor Sav. Bank v. Vinson*, 477 U.S. 57 (1986).
8. *Harris v. Forklift Sys., Inc.*, 510 U.S. 17 (1993).
9. *Omcale v. Sundowner Offshore Serv., Inc.*, 523 U.S. 75 (1998).
10. 29 U.S.C. Section 206(d).
11. 29 U.S.C. Sections 621–634.
12. 42 U.S.C. Section 12102–12118.

"International law, or the law that governs between nations, has at times, been like the common law within states, a twilight existence during which it is hardly distinguishable from morality or justice, till at length the imprimatur of a court attests its jural quality."

–Justice Cardozo

New Jersey v. Delaware, 291 U.S. 361 (1934).

International and World Trade Law

CHAPTER 14

CASE SCENARIO

The law firm at which you work as a paralegal represents August Belmont, a private banker doing business in New York City under the name August Belmont & Co. (Belmont). The Petrograd Metal Works (Petrograd), an Algerian corporation, deposited a large sum of money with Belmont. Several years ago, the Algerian government nationalized Petrograd and appropriated all its property and assets wherever situated, including the deposit account with Belmont. As a result, the deposit with Belmont became the property of the Algerian government.

Recently, the Algerian government and the United States entered into an agreement to settle claims and counterclaims between them. As part of the settlement, it was agreed that the Algerian government would take no steps to enforce claims against American nationals (including Belmont) and assigned all such claims to the United States.

CHAPTER OBJECTIVES

After studying this chapter, you should be able to:

1. Describe the U.S. government's power under the Foreign Commerce Clause and Treaty Clause of the U.S. Constitution.
2. Describe nations' court jurisdiction over international disputes.
3. Describe the functions and governance of the United Nations.
4. Describe the North American Free Trade Agreement (NAFTA) and other regional economic organizations.
5. Describe the World Trade Organization (WTO) and explain how its dispute resolution procedure works.

INTRODUCTION TO INTERNATIONAL AND WORLD TRADE LAW

international law
Law that governs affairs between nations and that regulates transactions between individuals and businesses of different countries.

International law, important to both nations and businesses, has many unique features. First, there is no single legislative source of international law. All countries of the world and numerous international organizations are responsible for enacting international law. Second, there is no single world court that is responsible for interpreting international law. There are, however, several courts and tribunals that hear and decide international legal disputes of parties that agree to appear before them. Third, there is no world executive branch that can enforce international law. Thus, nations do not have to obey international law enacted by other countries or international organizations. Because of these uncertainties, some commentators question whether international law is really law.

As technology and transportation bring nations closer together and as American and foreign firms increase their global activities, international law will become even more important to governments and businesses. This chapter introduces the main concepts of international law and discusses the sources of international law and the organizations responsible for its administration.

PARALEGAL PERSPECTIVE

***Claudia J. Taller** is a senior paralegal with the firm Squire, Sanders & Dempsey, LLP, a large firm in Cleveland, Ohio. She received her bachelor in English with a writing certificate from Kent State University and her postgraduate certificate in paralegal studies from Dyke College. She has been working as a paralegal for twenty-eight years and specializes in corporate, corporate finance, and real estate law.*

What are your thoughts about what a paralegal needs to understand in regard to international and world trade? Our global economy creates greater challenges to the paralegal in business transactions. There can be unusual requirements, language barriers, time differences, and overnight travel with passports required. However, international transaction work is a worthwhile adventure. Differences between people are broken down, and knowledge increases. It's actually pretty sensational to be involved in a deal where share certificates have Chinese characters on them, wire instructions come through with a greeting of "Buon Giorno," and you get a chance to connect with people around the globe. In reality, the world becomes smaller, more manageable, and more human as we work through the differences.

What are the most important paralegal skills needed in your job? Communication and organization are the most important skills.

What is the academic background required for a paralegal entering your area of practice?

Bachelor's degree and certification in paralegal studies are required.

How is technology involved in your job? Technology is used for business research, online forms and filing, due diligence databases, posting of information on intranet sites, and most everything else I do.

What trends do you see in your area of practice that will likely affect your job in the future? Technology allows everyone to be more efficient, and the lawyers are as adept as the paralegals in using it to do research and prepare and file forms and do due diligence. Paralegals are going to find it challenging to get work in an environment where attorneys are doing everything we do.

What do you feel is the biggest issue currently facing the paralegal profession? The legal profession is changing because clients don't want to pay the fees charged by large law firms and that will affect everyone at larger firms, from partners to secretaries.

What words of advice do you have for a new paralegal entering your area of practice? Make sure you have something to offer beyond legal expertise, such as good writing skills or creativity, that allows you to think outside the box.

THE UNITED STATES AND FOREIGN AFFAIRS

The U.S. Constitution divides the power to regulate the internal affairs of this country between the federal and state governments. On the international level, however, the Constitution gives most of the power to the federal government. Two constitutional provisions establish this authority: the Foreign Commerce Clause and the Treaty Clause.

Foreign Commerce Clause

Article I, Section 8, Clause 3 of the U.S. Constitution—the **Foreign Commerce Clause**—vests Congress with the power "to regulate commerce with foreign nations." The Constitution does not vest exclusive power over foreign affairs in the federal government, but any state or local law that unduly burdens foreign commerce is unconstitutional, as a violation of the Foreign Commerce Clause.

foreign commerce clause
A clause of the U.S. Constitution that vests Congress with the power "to regulate commerce with foreign nations."

Treaty Clause

Article II, Section 2, Clause 2 of the U.S. Constitution—the **Treaty Clause**—states that the president "shall have power, by and with the advice and consent of the Senate, to make treaties, provided two-thirds of the senators present concur."

treaty clause
A clause of the U.S. Constitution that states that the president "shall have the power . . . to make treaties, provided two-thirds of the senators present concur."

Under the Treaty Clause, only the federal government can enter into treaties with foreign nations. Under the Supremacy Clause of the Constitution, treaties become part of the "law of the land," and conflicting state or local law is void. The president is the agent of the United States in dealing with foreign countries.

Treaties and conventions are the equivalents of legislation at the international level. A **treaty** is an agreement or a contract between two or more nations that is formally signed by an authorized representative and ratified by the supreme power of each nation. **Bilateral treaties** are between two nations; **multilateral treaties** involve more than two nations. **Conventions** are treaties that are sponsored by international organizations, such as the United Nations. Conventions normally have many signatories. Treaties and conventions address such matters as human rights, foreign aid, navigation, commerce, and the settlement of disputes. Most treaties are registered with and published by the United Nations.

treaty
The first source of international law, consisting of an agreement or a contract between two or more nations that is formally signed by an authorized representative and ratified by the supreme power of each nation.

bilateral treaty
Treaty between two nations.

multilateral treaty
A compact involving many sides, persons, firms, or nations.

convention
A treaty that is sponsored by an international organization.

UNITED NATIONS

One of the most important international organizations is the **United Nations (UN)**, which was created by a multilateral treaty on October 24, 1945.[1] Most countries of the world are members of the UN. The goals of the UN, which is headquartered in New York City, are to maintain peace and security in the world, promote economic and social cooperation, and protect human rights (see **Exhibit 14.1**).

united nations (UN)
An international organization created by a multilateral treaty in 1945 to promote social and economic cooperation among nations and to protect human rights.

The UN is governed by the General Assembly, the Security Council, and the Secretariat, which are discussed in the following paragraphs.

General Assembly

The **General Assembly** is composed of all UN member nations. As the legislative body of the UN, it adopts resolutions concerning human rights, trade, finance, and economics, as well as other matters within the scope of the

general assembly
The name of the legislative body in many states; the deliberative body of the United Nations.

Exhibit 14.1 Charter of the United Nations (Selected Provisions)

Our respective Governments, through representatives assembled in the city of San Francisco, who have exhibited their full powers found to be in good and due form, have agreed to the present Charter of the United Nations and do hereby establish an international organization to be known as the United Nations.

Chapter 1. Purposes and Principles

Article 1 The Purposes of the United Nations are:

(1) To maintain international peace and security, and to that end: to take effective collective measures for the prevention and removal of threats to the peace, and for the suppression of acts of aggression or other breaches of the peace, and to bring about by peaceful means, and in conformity with the principles of justice and international law, adjustment or settlement of international disputes or situations which might lead to a breach of the peace;

(2) To develop friendly relations among nations based on respect for the principle of equal rights and self-determination of peoples, and to take other appropriate measures to strengthen universal peace;

(3) To achieve international co-operation in solving international problems of an economic, social, cultural, or humanitarian character, and in promoting and encouraging respect for human rights and for fundamental freedoms for all without distinction as to race, sex, language, or religion; and

(4) To be a centre for harmonizing the actions of nations in the attainment of these common ends.

UN Charter. Although resolutions have limited force, they are usually enforced through persuasion and the use of economic and other sanctions.

Security Council

The UN Security Council is composed of fifteen member nations, five of which are permanent members (China, France, Russia, the United Kingdom, and the United States) and ten other countries which are selected by the members of the General Assembly to serve two-year terms. The council is primarily responsible for maintaining international peace and security and has authority to use armed forces.

Secretariat

The Secretariat administers the day-to-day operations of the UN. It is headed by the **secretary-general**, who is elected by the General Assembly. The secretary-general may refer matters that threaten international peace and security to the Security Council and use his office to help solve international disputes.

secretary-general
The chief administrative officer of the United Nations, nominated by the Security Council and elected by the General Assembly.

United Nations Agencies

The UN is composed of various autonomous agencies that deal with a wide range of economic and social problems. These include the **United Nations Educational, Scientific, and Cultural Organization (UNESCO)**, the United Nations International Children's Emergency Fund (UNICEF), the International Monetary Fund (IMF), the World Bank, and the International Fund for Agricultural Development (IFAD).

United Nations Educational, Scientific, and Cultural Organization (UNESCO)
The arm of the United Nations charged with promoting the exchange of educational, scientific, and cultural enterprises among nations.

International Court of Justice (ICJ)
The judicial branch of the United Nations that is located in The Hague, the Netherlands. Only nations, not individuals or businesses, can have cases decided by this court. Also called the *World Court*.

The International Court of Justice

The **International Court of Justice (ICJ)**, also called the **World Court**, is located in The Hague, the Netherlands. It is the judicial branch of the UN. Only nations, not individuals or businesses, can have cases decided by this court. The ICJ hears cases that nations refer to it as well as cases involving treaties and the

INTERNATIONAL LAW

International Monetary Fund (IMF)

The **International Monetary Fund (IMF)**, an agency of the United Nations, was established by treaty in 1945 to help promote the world economy following the Great Depression of the 1930s and following the end of World War II in 1945. The IMF comprises more than 180 countries that are each represented on the board of directors, which makes the policy decisions of the IMF. The IMF is funded by monetary contributions of member nations, assessed based on the size of each nation's economy. The IMF's headquarters is located in Washington, DC.

The primary function of the IMF is to promote sound monetary, fiscal, and macroeconomic policies worldwide by providing assistance to needy countries. The IMF responds to financial crises around the globe. It does so by providing short-term loans to member countries to help them weather problems caused by unstable currencies, to balance payment problems, and to recover from the economic policies of past governments. The IMF examines a country's economy as a whole and its currency accounts, inflation, balance of payments with other countries, employment, consumer and business spending, and other factors to determine whether the country needs assistance. In return for the financial assistance, a country must agree to meet certain monetary, fiscal, employment, inflation, and other goals established by the IMF.

International Monetary Fund (IMF)
A UN specialized agency established to stabilize international exchange rates and promote balanced trade.

INTERNATIONAL LAW

World Bank

The **World Bank** is a United Nations agency that comprises more than 180 member nations. The World Bank is financed by contributions from developed countries, with the United States, the United Kingdom, Japan, Germany, and France being its main contributors. The World Bank has employees located in its headquarters in Washington, DC, and regional offices elsewhere throughout the world.

The World Bank provides money to developing countries to fund projects for humanitarian purposes and to relieve poverty. The World Bank provides funds to build roads, construct dams and build other water projects, establish hospitals and provide medical assistance, develop agriculture, and provide humanitarian aid. The World Bank provides outright grants of funds to developing countries for such projects, and it makes long-term low-interest-rate loans to those countries. The bank routinely grants debt relief for these loans.

World Bank
A UN specialized agency established in 1945 to provide loans that aid in economic development, through economically sustainable enterprises.

UN Charter. A nation may seek redress on behalf of an individual or a business that has a claim against another country. The ICJ is composed of fifteen judges who serve nine-year terms.

REGIONAL INTERNATIONAL ORGANIZATIONS

There are several significant regional organizations whose members have agreed to work together to promote peace and security as well as economic, social, and cultural development. The most important of these organizations are discussed in the following paragraphs.

European Union

European Union
A regional international organization that comprises many countries of western and eastern Europe and was created to promote peace and security as well as economic, social, and cultural development.

One of the most important international regional organizations is the **European Union (EU)**, formerly called the *European Community*, or *Common Market*. The EU, which was created in 1957, is composed of many countries of western and eastern Europe. Member nations are Austria, Belgium, Bulgaria, Cyprus (the Greek part), Czech Republic, Denmark, Estonia, Finland, France, Germany, Greece, Hungary, Ireland, Italy, Latvia, Lithuania, Luxembourg, Malta, the Netherlands, Poland, Portugal, Romania, Slovakia, Slovenia, Spain, Sweden, and the United Kingdom of Great Britain and Northern Ireland. The EU represents more than 500 million people and a gross community product that exceeds that of the United States, Canada, and Mexico combined.

The EU's Council of Ministers is composed of representatives from each member country, who meet periodically to coordinate efforts to fulfill the objectives of the treaty. The council votes on significant issues and changes to the treaty. Some matters require unanimity, whereas others require only a majority vote. The member nations have surrendered substantial sovereignty to the EU. The EU Commission, which is independent of its member nations, is charged to act in the best interests of the union. The member nations have delegated substantial powers to the commission, including authority to enact legislation and to take enforcement actions to ensure member compliance with the treaty.

The EU treaty creates open borders for trade by providing for the free flow of capital, labor, goods, and services among member nations. Under the EU, customs duties have been eliminated among member nations. Common customs tariffs have been established for EU trade with the rest of the world.

A single monetary unit, the **euro**, has been introduced. Not all EU countries have voted to use the euro. However, the euro can be used in all countries that comprise the Eurozone. An EU central bank, equivalent to the U.S. Federal Reserve Board, has been established to set common monetary policy.

A unanimous vote of existing EU members is needed to admit a new member. Other nonmember European countries are expected to apply for and be admitted as members of the EU. A map of the EU is shown in **Exhibit 14.2**.

North American Free Trade Agreement (NAFTA)

North American Free Trade Agreement (NAFTA)
A treaty that has removed or reduced tariffs, duties, quotas, and other trade barriers between the United States, Canada, and Mexico.

In 1990, Mexico asked the United States to set up a two-country trade pact. Negotiations between the two countries began. Canada joined the negotiations, and on August 12, 1992, the **North American Free Trade Agreement (NAFTA)** was signed by the leaders of the three countries. The treaty creates a free-trade zone stretching from the Yukon to the Yucatan, bringing together more than 400 million people in the three countries.

NAFTA has eliminated or reduced most of the duties, tariffs, quotas, and other trade barriers between Mexico, the United States, and Canada. Agriculture, automobiles, computers, electronics, energy and petrochemicals, financial services, insurance, telecommunications, and many other industries are affected. The treaty contains a safety valve: A country can reimpose tariffs if an import surge from one of the other nations hurts its economy or workers. Like other regional trading agreements, NAFTA allows the bloc to discriminate against outsiders and to cut deals among its members. NAFTA also includes special

Exhibit 14.2 Map of European Union (EU) Countries

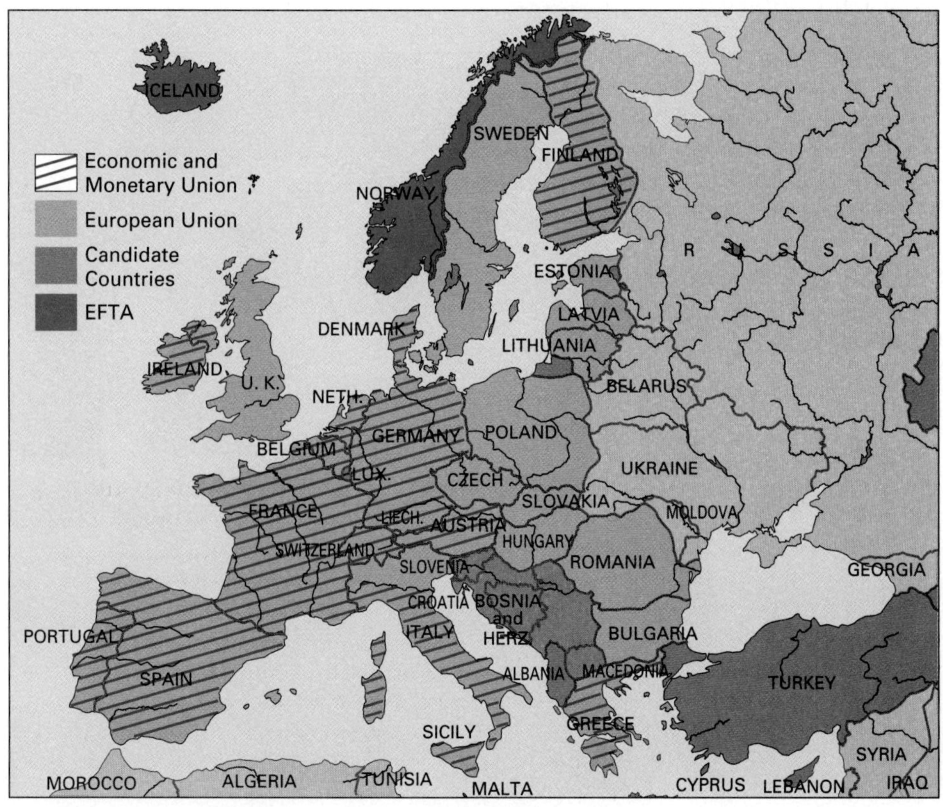

protection for favored industries that have a lot of lobby muscle. Thus, many economists assert that NAFTA is not a "free trade" pact but a *managed trade* agreement.

NAFTA forms a supernational trading region that more effectively competes with Japan and the EU. Consumers in all three countries began to pay lower prices on a wide variety of goods and services as trade barriers fell and competition increased. Critics contend that NAFTA shifted U.S. jobs—particularly blue-collar jobs—south of the border, where Mexican wage rates are about one-tenth those in the United States. Environmentalists criticize the pact for not doing enough to prevent and clean up pollution in Mexico.

A map of NAFTA countries is shown in **Exhibit 14.3**.

Association of Southeast Asian Nations (ASEAN)

In 1967, the Association of Southeast Asian Nations (ASEAN) was created. The countries that belong to ASEAN are Brunei Darussalam, Cambodia, Indonesia, Laos, Malaysia, Myanmar, Philippines, Singapore, Thailand, and Vietnam. This is a cooperative association of diverse nations.

Two of the world's largest countries, Japan and China, do not belong to any significant economic community. Although not a member of ASEAN, Japan has been instrumental in providing financing for the countries that make up that organization. China also works closely with the countries of ASEAN and is a potential member of ASEAN.

Exhibit 14.3 Map of North American Free Trade Agreement (NAFTA) Countries

Organization of the Petroleum Exporting Countries (OPEC)

One of the most well-known economic organizations is the Organization of the Petroleum Exporting Countries (OPEC). OPEC consists of oil-producing and exporting countries from Africa, Asia, the Middle East, and South America. The member nations are Algeria, Angola, Ecuador, Indonesia, Iran, Iraq, Kuwait, Libya, Nigeria, Qatar, Saudi Arabia, United Arab Emirates (UAE), and Venezuela. OPEC sets quotas on the output of oil production by member nations.

Other Regional Economic Organizations

Countries of Latin America and the Caribbean have established several regional organizations to promote economic development and cooperation. Mexico, the largest industrialized country in Latin America and the Caribbean, has entered into a free trade agreement with all the countries of Central America as well as Chile, Colombia, and Venezuela. Other regional economic organizations include countries of Central America and South America. Several regional economic communities have been formed in Africa as well.

PARALEGAL PERSPECTIVE

Joya F. Williams, CP, is a certified paralegal with one of the largest global oilfield services company, in Houston, Texas. She received an associate degree in paralegal studies from the Center for Advanced Legal Studies and specializes in corporate ethics and compliance. She has been working as a paralegal for eight years.

How do you think your work as a paralegal relates to international and world trade as they relate to business organizations? While the paralegal may not be a subject-matter expert on all areas of international and world trade, it is critical that, at a minimum, you are aware of the resources at your disposal and who to contact regarding same, so you will be an invaluable resource to the entire team.

What are the most important paralegal skills needed in your job? You must have knowledge of anticorruption policies and procedures, and Code of Business Conduct issues. You must also have the ability to provide guidance and training on anticorruption, antitrust, and Code of Business Conduct issues. Additionally an understanding and capability to process requests for approval of the third-party intermediaries; travel for government officials; meals and entertainment for government officials that require special permission as stated in the Anti-Corruption Manual; charitable contributions/community payments requested by government officials; and the ability to provide oversight and maintenance of the ethics reporting hotline [are needed].

What is the academic background required for a paralegal entering your area of practice? An associate degree in paralegal studies or a paralegal certificate from an accredited school is required, and a minimum five years of legal experience.

How is technology involved in your job? The Internet site contains all policies and procedures for an employee's review at any time. Training for mandatory courses is available online, worldwide, in many languages. SharePoint sites are created and used to view files worldwide. Reporting hotline is a web program that can be accessed from any computer, at any time and allows the employee to remain anonymous. Blackberry devices are used for communication and transmitting of files globally. Document and case management software programs are used to monitor and update large case loads.

What trends do you see in your area of practice that will likely affect your job in the future? As we move forward in the corporate environment, paralegals do not need to be in short distance from attorneys who need assistance with tasks such as legal research, case management, or administrative duties. Cases can now be managed from a distance. Best practices paralegals often find themselves responsible for document management and case management through various software programs that can be used virtually.

What do you feel is the biggest issue currently facing the paralegal profession? One of the biggest issues paralegals face is lack of adequate training. Fortunately, I had the opportunity to attend a paralegal program that equipped me with the necessary tools, proper resources, and guidance to sufficiently perform as a paralegal.

What words of advice do you have for a new paralegal entering your area of practice? You must have a strong work ethic and great communication skills. In addition, you should be dependable and possess a passion for the law to be a contributing member of any practice area. For networking opportunities, join a paralegal organization, and volunteer with the state bar in order to give back to the community. Lastly, go the extra mile and become a certified paralegal.

WORLD TRADE ORGANIZATION (WTO)

In 1995, the **World Trade Organization (WTO)** was created as part of the Uruguay Round of trade negotiations on the **General Agreement on Tariffs and Trade (GATT)**. GATT is a multilateral treaty that establishes trade agreements and limits tariffs and trade restrictions among its 150 member nations.

World Trade Organization (WTO)
An international organization of more than 130 member nations created to promote and enforce trade agreements among member nations.

The WTO is an international organization whose headquarters is located in Geneva, Switzerland. WTO members have entered into many trade agreements among themselves, including international agreements on investments, sale of goods, provision of services, intellectual property, licensing, tariffs, subsidies, and the removal of trade barriers.

INTERNATIONAL LAW

Dominican Republic–Central America Free Trade Agreement (DR-CAFTA)

After years of negotiations, the United States and several Central American countries formed the Central America Free Trade Agreement (CAFTA). The agreement originally encompassed the United States and the Central American countries of Costa Rica, El Salvador, Guatemala, Honduras, and Nicaragua. The Dominican Republic subsequently joined CAFTA, which is now commonly called Dominican Republic–Central America Free Trade Agreement (DR-CAFTA). This agreement lowered tariffs and reduced trade restrictions among the member nations. The United States has bilateral trade agreements with several other Central American countries that are not members of DR-CAFTA.

The formation of DR-CAFTA is seen as a stepping stone toward the creation of the Free Trade Area of the Americas (FTAA), which would be an ambitious free trade agreement that would encompass most of the countries of Central America, North America, and South America. The negotiation of the FTAA is difficult because of the different interests of the countries that would be members.

The WTO, which has been referred to as the "Supreme Court of Trade," has become the world's most important trade organization. The WTO has jurisdiction to enforce the most important and comprehensive trade agreements in the world among its more than 130 member nations. Many herald the WTO as a much-needed world court that can peaceably solve trade disputes among nations.

WTO Dispute Resolution

One of the primary functions of the WTO is to hear and decide trade disputes between member nations. Before the creation of the WTO, GATT governed trade disputes between signatory nations. That system was inadequate because any member nation that was found to have violated any GATT trade agreement could itself veto any sanctions imposed by GATT's governing body. The WTO solved this problem by adopting a "judicial" mode of dispute resolution to replace GATT's more politically based one.

A member nation that believes that another member nation has breached one of the trade agreements can initiate a proceeding to have the WTO hear and decide the dispute. The dispute is first heard by a three-member **WTO panel**, which issues a "panel report." The members of the panel are professional judges from member nations. The report, which is the decision of the panel, contains the panel's findings of fact and law, and it orders a remedy if a violation has been found. The report is then referred to the **WTO dispute settlement body**. This body is required to adopt the panel report unless the body, by consensus, agrees not to adopt it.

WTO panel
A body of three WTO judges that hears trade disputes between member nations and issues a "panel report."

WTO dispute settlement body
A board composed of one representative from each WTO member nation that reviews panel reports.

WTO appellate body
A panel of seven judges selected from WTO member nations that hears and decides appeals from decisions of the dispute settlement body.

There is a **WTO appellate body** to which a party can appeal a decision of the dispute settlement body. This appeals court is composed of seven professional justices selected from member nations. Appeals are limited to issues of law, not fact.

If a violation of a trade agreement is found, the panel report and appellate decision can order the offending nation to cease engaging in the violating practice and to pay damages to the other party. If the offending nation refuses to abide by the order, the WTO can order retaliatory trade sanctions (e.g., tariffs) by other member nations against the noncomplying nation.

NATIONAL COURTS AND INTERNATIONAL DISPUTE RESOLUTION

The majority of cases involving international law disputes are heard by **national courts** of individual nations. This is primarily the case for commercial disputes between private litigants that do not qualify to be heard by international courts. Some countries have specialized courts that hear international commercial disputes. Other countries permit such disputes to proceed through their regular court systems. In the United States, commercial disputes between U.S. companies and foreign governments or parties may be brought in U.S. District Court.

national courts
The courts of individual nations.

Judicial Procedure

A party seeking judicial resolution of an international dispute faces several problems, including which nation's courts will hear the case and what law should be applied to the case. Jurisdiction is often a highly contested issue. Absent an agreement providing otherwise, a case involving an international dispute will be brought in the national court of the plaintiff's home country.

Many international contracts contain a **choice of forum clause** (or **forum-selection clause**) that designates which nation's court has jurisdiction to hear a case arising out of a contract. In addition, many contracts also include a **choice of law clause** that designates which nation's laws will be applied in deciding such a case. Absent these two clauses, and without the parties agreeing to these matters, an international dispute may never be resolved.

choice of forum clause
A clause in an international contract that designates which nation's court has jurisdiction to hear a case arising out of the contract. Also known as a *forum-selection clause*.

choice of law clause
A clause in an international contract that designates which nation's laws will be applied in deciding a dispute.

Concept Summary

International Contract Clauses

Clause	Description
Forum-selection	A clause that designates the judicial or arbitral forum that will hear and decide a case.
Choice of law	A clause that designates the law to be applied by the court or arbitrator in deciding a case.

Act of State Doctrine

A general principle of international law is that a country has absolute authority over what transpires *within* its own territory. In furtherance of this principle, the **act of state doctrine** states that judges of one country cannot question the validity of an act committed by another country within that other country's own borders. In *United States v. Belmont*,[2] the U.S. Supreme Court declared, "Every sovereign state must recognize the independence of every other sovereign state; and the courts of one will not sit in judgment upon the acts of the government of another, done within its own territory." This restraint on the judiciary is justified under the doctrine of separation of powers and permits the executive branch of the federal government to arrange affairs with foreign governments.

act of state doctrine
A doctrine that states that judges of one country cannot question the validity of an act committed by another country within that other country's borders. It is based on the principle that a country has absolute authority over what transpires within its own territory.

When Kansas and Colorado have a quarrel over the water in the Arkansas River they don't call out the National Guard in each state and go to war over it. They bring a suit in the Supreme Court of the United States and abide by the decision. There isn't a reason in the world why we cannot do that internationally.

Harry S. Truman
Speech (1945)

Example: Suppose the country of North Korea outlaws the practice of all religions in that country. Paul, a Christian who is a citizen of, and living in, the United States, disagrees with North Korea's law. Paul brings a lawsuit against North Korea in a U.S. District Court located in the state of Idaho, arguing to the court that the North Korean law should be declared illegal. The U.S. District Court will apply the act of state doctrine and dismiss Paul's lawsuit against North Korea. The U.S. District Court will rule that North Korea's law is an act of that state (country) and that a U.S. court does not have authority to hear and decide Paul's case.

In the following case, the court was called upon to apply the act of state doctrine.

CASE 14.1 ACT OF STATE DOCTRINE

Glen v. Club Mediterranee, S.A.**, 450 F.3d 1251 (11th Cir 2006).**

"The act of state doctrine is a judicially-created rule of decision that precludes the courts of this country from inquiring into the validity of the public acts a recognized foreign sovereign power committed within its own territory."

—Judge Cox

Facts

Prior to the Communist revolution in Cuba, Elvira de la Vega Glen and her sister, Ana Maria de la Vega Glen, were Cuban citizens and residents who jointly owned beachfront property on the Peninsula de Hicacos in Varadero, Cuba. On or about January 1, 1959, in conjunction with Fidel Castro's Communist revolution, the Cuban government expropriated the property without paying the Glens. Also in 1959, the sisters fled Cuba. Ana Maria de la Vega Glen died and passed any interest she had in the Varadero beach property to her nephew Robert M. Glen.

In 1997, Club Mediterranee, S.A., and Club Mediterranee Group (Club Med) entered into a joint venture with the Cuban government to develop the property. Club Med constructed and operated a five-star luxury hotel on the property that the Glens had owned. The Glens sued Club Med in a U.S. District Court located in the state of Florida. The Glens alleged that the original expropriation of their property by the Cuban government was illegal and that Club Med had trespassed on their property and had been unduly enriched by its joint venture with the Cuban government to operate a hotel on their expropriated property. The Glens sought to recover the millions of dollars in profits earned by Club Med from its alleged wrongful occupation and use of the Glens' expropriated property. The U.S. District Court held that the act of state doctrine barred recovery by the Glens and dismissed the Glens' claims against Club Med. The Glens appealed.

Issue

Does the act of state doctrine bar recovery by the Glens?

Language of the Court

The act of state doctrine is a judicially-created rule of decision that precludes the courts of this country from inquiring into the validity of the public acts a recognized foreign sovereign power committed within its own territory. The doctrine prevents any court in the United States from declaring that an official act of a foreign sovereign performed within its own territory is invalid. It requires that the acts of foreign sovereigns taken within their own jurisdictions shall be deemed valid. The act of state doctrine is a product of judicial concern for separation of powers, a result of the judiciary's recognition that it is the province of the executive and legislative branches to establish and pursue foreign policy and that judicial determinations regarding the validity of the acts of foreign sovereigns might negatively affect those policies.

The validity of the Cuban government's act of expropriation is directly at issue in this litigation. The act of state doctrine is properly applied to claims, like the Glens', that necessarily require U.S. courts to pass on the legality of the Cuban government's expropriation of property within Cuba from then-Cuban citizens. Because the act of state doctrine requires the courts deem valid the Cuban government's expropriation of the real property at issue in this case, the Glens cannot maintain their claims for trespass and unjust enrichment against Club Med.

Decision

The U.S. Court of Appeals applied the act of state doctrine and affirmed the judgment of the U.S. District Court that dismissed the Glens' claim against Club Med.

Case Questions

1. **Critical Legal Thinking** What does the act of state doctrine provide? Explain.
2. **Business Ethics** Did the Cuban government act ethically when it expropriated the Glens' property? Did Club Med act ethically when it entered into a joint venture with the Cuban government to develop the property that had been expropriated from the Glens?
3. **Contemporary Business** What is the expropriation of property by a government?

Doctrine of Sovereign Immunity

One of the oldest principles of international law is the **doctrine of sovereign immunity**. Under this doctrine, *countries* are granted immunity from suits in courts in other countries. For example, if a U.S. citizen wanted to sue the government of China in a U.S. court, the citizen could not do so (subject to certain exceptions).

Originally, the United States granted absolute immunity to foreign governments from suits in U.S. courts. In 1952, the United States switched to the principle of **qualified immunity**, or **restricted immunity**, which was eventually codified in the **Foreign Sovereign Immunities Act (FSIA)** of 1976.[3] This act now exclusively governs suits against foreign nations in the United States, whether in federal or state court. Most Western nations have adopted the principle of restricted immunity. Other countries still follow the doctrine of absolute immunity.

doctrine of sovereign immunity
A doctrine that states that countries are granted immunity from suits in courts of other countries.

qualified immunity (restricted immunity)
Immunity from civil liability for a public official who is performing a discretionary function, as long as the conduct does not violate clearly established constitutional or statutory rights.

Foreign Sovereign Immunities Act (FSIA)
An act that exclusively governs suits against foreign nations that are brought in federal or state courts in the United States. It codifies the principle of *qualified, or restricted, immunity*.

> Only when the world is civilized enough to keep promises will we get any kind of international law.
> Julius Henry Cohen

Exceptions to the Sovereign Immunities Act

The FSIA provides that a foreign country is not immune from lawsuits in U.S. courts in the following situations:

- If the foreign country has waived its immunity, either explicitly or by implication
- If the action is based on a commercial activity carried on in the United States by the foreign country or carried on outside the United States but causing a direct effect in the United States

What constitutes "commercial activity" is the most litigated aspect of the FSIA. With commercial activity, the foreign sovereign is subject to suit in the United States; without it, the foreign sovereign is immune from suit in this country.

Example: The country of Cuba has state-owned enterprises. The government of Cuba wants to raise capital for these state-owned enterprises. To do so, the Cuban government sells twenty-year bonds in these companies to investors in the United States. The bondholders are to be paid 10 percent interest annually. By selling bonds to investors in the United States, the government of Cuba is involved in commercial activity in the United States. If Cuba defaults and does not pay the U.S. investors the 10 percent interest on the bonds, the bondholders can sue Cuba in U.S. court under the commercial activity exception to the doctrine of sovereign immunity to recover the unpaid interest.

Concept Summary

Act of State and Sovereign Immunity Doctrines Compared

Doctrine	Description
Act of state	A doctrine that states that an act of a government in its *own country* is not subject to suit in a foreign country's courts.
Sovereign immunity	A doctrine that states that an act of a government in a *foreign country* is not subject to suit in the foreign country. Some countries provide absolute immunity, and other countries (such as the United States) provide limited immunity.

INTERNATIONAL LAW

Jewish Law and the Torah

Torah
Judaism's most holy book; Torah refers to both Written Torah (Five Books of Moses, Prophets, Writings) and Oral Torah (Talmud).

Jewish law, which has existed for centuries, is a complex legal system based on the ideology and theology of the **Torah**. The Torah prescribes comprehensive and integrated rules of religious, political, and legal life that together form Jewish thought. Jewish law is decided by rabbis who are scholars of the Torah and other Jewish scriptures. Rabbinic jurisprudence, known as *Halakhah*, is administered by rabbi-judges sitting as the *Beis Din*, Hebrew for the "house of judgment." As a court, the *Beis Din* has roots that go back three thousand years.

Today, Jews are citizens of countries worldwide. As such, they are subject to the criminal and civil laws of their host countries. However, Jews, no matter where they live, abide by the principles of the Torah in many legal matters, such as

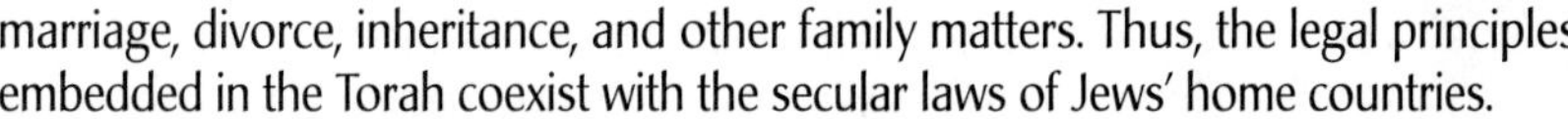

marriage, divorce, inheritance, and other family matters. Thus, the legal principles embedded in the Torah coexist with the secular laws of Jews' home countries.

Rabbinical judges tend to be actively involved in cases. True to its roots, the *Beis Din* is more a search for the truth than it is an adversarial process.

INTERNATIONAL LAW

Islamic Law and the Qur'an

Approximately 20 percent of the world's population is Muslim. Islam is the principal religion of Afghanistan, Algeria, Bangladesh, Egypt, Indonesia, Iran, Iraq, Jordan, Kuwait, Libya, Malaysia, Mali, Mauritania, Morocco, Niger, North Yemen, Oman, Pakistan, Qatar, Saudi Arabia, Somalia, South Yemen, Sudan, Syria, Tunisia, Turkey, and the United Arab Emirates. Islamic law (or *Shari'a*) is the only law in Saudi Arabia. In other Islamic countries, the *Shari'a* forms the basis of family law but coexists with other laws.

The Islamic law system is derived from the Qur'an, the **Sunnah** (decisions and sayings of the prophet Muhammad), and reasonings by Islamic scholars. By the 10th century a.d., Islamic scholars had decided that no further improvement of the divine law could be made, closed the door of *ijtihad* (independent reasoning), and froze the evolution of Islamic law at that point. Islamic law prohibits *riba*, or the making of unearned or unjustified profit. Making a profit from the sale of goods or the provision of services is permitted. The most notable consequence of *riba* is that the payment of interest on loans is forbidden. To circumvent this result, the party with the money is permitted to purchase the item and resell it to the other party at a profit or to advance the money and become a trading partner who shares in the profits of the enterprise.

Sunnah
Habit, practice, usual custom.

Today, Islamic law is primarily used in the areas of marriage, divorce, and inheritance and, to a limited degree, in criminal law. To resolve the tension between *Shari'a* and the practice of modern commercial law, the *Shari'a* is often not applied to commercial transactions.

INTERNATIONAL LAW

Hindu Law–*Dharmasastra*

Over 20 percent of the world's population is Hindu. Most Hindus live in India, where they make up 80 percent of the population. Others live in Burma, Kenya, Malaysia, Pakistan, Singapore, Tanzania, and Uganda. Hindu law is a religious law. As such, individual Hindus apply this law to themselves, regardless of their nationality or place of domicile.

Classical Hindu law rests neither on civil codes nor on court decisions but on the works of private scholars that were passed along for centuries by oral tradition and eventually were recorded in the *smitris* (law books). Hindu law–called *dharmasastra* in Sanskrit ("the doctrine of proper behavior")–is linked to the divine revelation of Veda (the holy collection of Indian religious songs, prayers, hymns, and sayings written between 2000 and 1000 B.C.). Most Hindu law is concerned with family matters and the law of succession.

After India became a British colony, British judges applied a combination of Hindu law and common law in solving cases. This Anglo-Hindu law, as it was

(continued)

My nationalism is intense internationalism. I am sick of the strife between nations or religions.

Gandhi

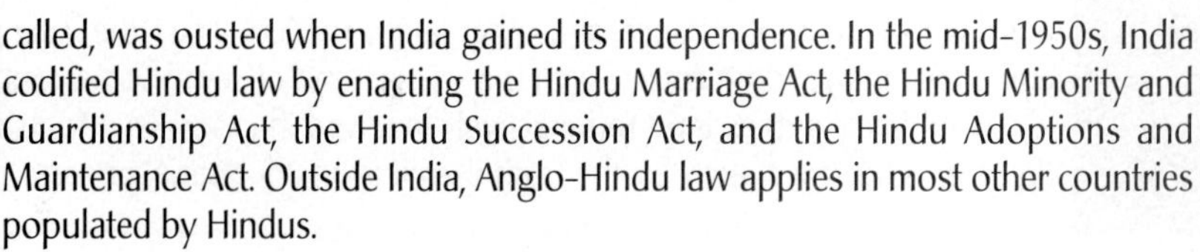

called, was ousted when India gained its independence. In the mid-1950s, India codified Hindu law by enacting the Hindu Marriage Act, the Hindu Minority and Guardianship Act, the Hindu Succession Act, and the Hindu Adoptions and Maintenance Act. Outside India, Anglo-Hindu law applies in most other countries populated by Hindus.

Concept Review

International Contract Clauses

Clause	Description
Forum-selection	A clause that designates the judicial or arbitral forum that will hear and decide a case.
Choice of law	A clause that designates the law to be applied by the court or arbitrator in deciding a case.

Act of State and Sovereign Immunity Doctrines Compared

Doctrine	Description
Act of state	A doctrine that states that an act of a government in its *own country* is not subject to suit in a foreign country's courts.
Sovereign immunity	A doctrine that states that an act of a government in a *foreign country* is not subject to suit in the foreign country. Some countries provide absolute immunity, and other countries (such as the United States) provide limited immunity.

CHAPTER REVIEW

THE UNITED STATES AND FOREIGN AFFAIRS, p. 413

The United States and Foreign Affairs

The following two provisions in the U.S. Constitution establish the federal government's authority to regulate international affairs.

1. ***Foreign Commerce Clause.*** This clause vests Congress with the power "to regulate commerce with foreign nations."
2. ***Treaty Clause.*** This clause gives the president the authority to enter into treaties with foreign nations, subject to a two-thirds vote of the Senate.

UNITED NATIONS, p. 413

The United Nations (UN)

Governance of the United Nations. The UN is an international organization headquartered in New York City. Most countries of the world are members. Its goals are to maintain peace and security in the world, promote economic and social cooperation, and protect human rights.

REGIONAL INTERNATIONAL ORGANIZATIONS, p. 415

Regional Economic Organizations

1. European Union (EU) (or Common Market)
2. African Economic Community

3. Organization of Petroleum Exporting Countries (OPEC)
4. Gulf Cooperation Council
5. Association of South East Asian Nations (ASEAN)
6. North American Free Trade Agreement (NAFTA)

THE WORLD TRADE ORGANIZATION (WTO), p. 419

World Trade Organization

The WTO is an international organization headquartered in Geneva, Switzerland. Many countries of the world are members. Its goals are to limit tariff and trade restrictions and provide a mechanism for resolving trade disputes among its member nations.

NATIONAL COURTS AND INTERNATIONAL DISPUTE RESOLUTION, p. 421

Principles of Judicial Restraint

National courts are limited by the following two principles of judicial restraint:

1. ***Act of state doctrine.*** The act of state doctrine states that judges of one country cannot question the validity of an act committed by another country *within* that other country's borders.
2. ***Doctrine of sovereign immunity.*** This doctrine states that countries are granted immunity from suits in courts in other countries. Some countries provide for *absolute immunity*, and other countries (such as the United States) provide *qualified* or *restricted immunity*. *Exceptions*: The United States provides that a foreign country is not immune from lawsuits in a U.S. court if:
   a. The foreign country has *waived* its immunity.
   b. The foreign country has engaged in *commercial activity* in the United States or outside the United States that causes a direct effect in the United States.

TEST REVIEW TERMS AND CONCEPTS

Act of state doctrine 421
Bilateral treaty 413
Choice of forum clause (forum-selection clause) 421
Choice of law clause 421
Convention 413
Doctrine of sovereign immunity 423
European Union (EU) 416
Foreign Commerce Clause 413
Foreign Sovereign Immunities Act (FSIA) 423
General Assembly 413
International Court of Justice (ICJ) (World Court) 414
International law 412
International Monetary Fund (IMF) 415
Multilateral treaty 413
National courts 421
North American Free Trade Agreement (NAFTA) 416
Qualified immunity (restricted immunity) 423

CASE SCENARIO REVISITED

Remember the case at the beginning of the chapter where Petrograd's deposit with Belmont became the property of the Algerian government and an agreement between Algeria and the United States assigned certain claims to the United States? As a result, the United States brought an action against the executors of Belmont's estate to recover the money originally deposited with Belmont by Petrograd. Who owns the money? To help you with your answer, see *United States v. Belmont*, 301 U.S. 324 (1937).

PORTFOLIO EXERCISE

Prior to the Communist revolution in Cuba, your company owned beachfront property on the Peninsula de Hicacos in Varadero, Cuba. On or about January 1, 1959, in conjunction with Fidel Castro's Communist revolution, the Cuban government expropriated the property without paying your business. In 1997, Club Mediterranee, S.A., and Club Mediterranee Group (Club Med) entered into a joint venture with the Cuban government to develop the property. Club Med constructed and operated a five-star luxury hotel on the property that your company had owned. Your company sues Club Med in a U.S. District Court located in the state of Florida arguing that the original expropriation of its property by the Cuban government was illegal and that Club Med had trespassed on its property and had been unduly enriched by its joint venture with the Cuban government to operate a hotel on their expropriated property. Your company sought to recover the millions of dollars in profits earned by Club Med from its alleged wrongful occupation and use of its expropriated property. How should the U.S. District Court rule? Explain.

WORKING THE WEB INTERNET EXERCISES

Activities

1. Go to Hieros Gamos, at **www.hg.org**. It is a huge international law site that contains laws from 230 countries in more than 50 languages. Look at the list of countries and review the legal structure of Afghanistan.

2. Survey the alternative dispute resolution (ADR) material at **www.usaid.gov**. What are some of the particular advantages to using ADR in other countries?

CRITICAL LEGAL THINKING CASES

Case 14.1 ***Act of State Doctrine*** Banco Nacional de Costa Rica is a bank wholly owned by the government of Costa Rica. It is subject to the rules and regulations adopted by the minister of finance and the central bank of Costa Rica. The bank borrowed $40 million from a consortium of private banks located in the United Kingdom and the United States. The bank signed promissory notes, agreeing to repay the principal plus interest on the loan in four equal installments due on July 30, August 30, September 30, and October 30 of the following year. The money was to be used to provide export financing of sugar and sugar products from Costa Rica. The loan agreements and promissory notes were signed in New York City, and the loan proceeds were tendered to the bank there.

The bank paid the first installment on the loan. The bank did not, however, make the other three installment payments and defaulted on the loan. The lending banks sued the bank in U.S. District Court in New York to recover the unpaid principal and interest. The bank alleged in defense that the minister of finance and the central bank of Costa Rica had issued a decree forbidding the repayment of loans by the bank to private lenders, including the lending banks in this case. The action was taken because Costa Rica was having trouble servicing debts to foreign creditors. The bank alleged that the act of state doctrine prevented the plaintiffs from recovering on their loans to the bank. Who wins? *Libra Bank Ltd. v. Banco Nacional de Costa Rica*, 570 F. Supp. 870 (S.D.N.Y. 1983).

Case 14.2 ***Forum-Selection Clause*** Zapata Off-Shore Company (Zapata) is a Houston, Texas–based American corporation that engages in drilling oil wells throughout the world. Unterweser Reederei, GMBH (Unterweser), is a German corporation that provides ocean shipping and towing services. Zapata requested bids from companies to tow its self-elevating drilling rig *Chaparral* from Louisiana to a point off Ravenna, Italy, in the Adriatic Sea, where Zapata had agreed to drill certain wells. Unterweser submitted the lowest bid and was requested to submit a proposed contract to Zapata, which it did. The contract submitted by Unterweser contained the following provision: "Any dispute arising must be treated before the London Court of Justice." Zapata executed the contract without deleting or modifying this provision.

Unterweser's deep sea tug *Bremen* departed Venice, Louisiana, with the *Chaparral* in tow, bound for Italy. While the flotilla was in international waters in the middle of the Gulf of Mexico, a severe storm arose. The sharp roll of the *Chaparral* in Gulf waters caused portions of it to break off and fall into the sea, seriously damaging the *Chaparral*. Zapata instructed the *Bremen* to tow the *Chaparral* to Tampa, Florida, the nearest port of refuge, which it did. Zapata filed suit against Unterweser and the *Bremen* in U.S. District Court in Florida, alleging negligent towing and breach of contract. The defendants asserted that suit could be brought only in the London Court of Justice. Who is correct? *M/S Bremen & Unterweser Reederei, GMBH v. Zapata Off-Shore Co.*, 407 U.S. 1 (1972).

BUSINESS ETHICS CASES

Case 14.3 *Business Ethics* Bank of Jamaica is wholly owned by the government of Jamaica. Chisholm & Co. was a Florida corporation owned by James Henry Chisholm, a Florida resident. The U.S. Export–Import Bank (Ex-Im Bank) provides financial services and credit insurance to export and import companies. The Bank of Jamaica and Chisholm & Co. agreed that Chisholm & Co. would arrange lines of credit from various banks and procure $50 million of credit insurance from Ex-Im Bank to be available to aid Jamaican importers. Chisholm & Co. was to be paid commissions for its services.

Chisholm & Co. negotiated and arranged for $50 million of credit insurance from Ex-Im Bank and lines of credit from Florida National Bank, Bankers Trust Company, and Irving Trust Company. Chisholm also arranged meetings between the Bank of Jamaica and the U.S. banks. Unbeknownst to Chisholm & Co., the Bank of Jamaica went directly to Ex-Im Bank to exclude Chisholm & Co. from the Jamaica program and requested that the credit insurance be issued solely in the name of the Bank of Jamaica. As a result, Chisholm & Co.'s Ex-Im Bank insurance application was not considered. The Bank of Jamaica also obtained lines of credit from other companies and paid them commissions. Chisholm & Co. sued the Bank of Jamaica in U.S. District Court in Miami, Florida, alleging breach of contract and seeking damages. The Bank of Jamaica filed a motion to dismiss the complaint, alleging that its actions were protected by sovereign immunity. Who wins? Did the Bank of Jamaica act ethically in trying to avoid its contract obligations? *Chisholm & Co. v. Bank of Jamaica*, 643 F. Supp. 1393 (S.D. Fla. 1986).

Case 14.4 *Business Ethics* Nigeria, an African nation, while in the midst of a boom period due to oil exports, entered into $1 billion of contracts with various countries to purchase huge quantities of Portland cement. Nigeria was going to use the cement to build and improve the country's infrastructure. Several of the contracts were with American companies, including Texas Trading & Milling Corporation (Texas Trading). Nigeria substantially overbought cement, and the country's docks and harbors became clogged with ships waiting to unload. Unable to accept delivery of the cement it had bought, Nigeria repudiated many of its contracts, including the one with Texas Trading. When Texas Trading sued Nigeria in a U.S. District Court to recover damages for breach of contract, Nigeria asserted in defense that the doctrine of sovereign immunity protected it from liability. Who wins? *Texas Trading & Milling Corp. v. Federal Republic of Nigeria*, 647 F.2d 300 (2d Cir. 1981).

ENDNOTES

1. The Charter of the United Nations was entered into force on October 24, 1945, and it was adopted by the United States on October 24, 1945 (59 Stat. 1031, T.S. 993, 3 Bevans 1153, 1976 Y.B.U.N. 1043).
2. *United States v. Belmont*, 301 U.S. 324 (1937).
3. 28 U.S.C. Sections 1602–1611.

APPENDIX A

UNIFORM PARTNERSHIP ACT (1997)

Article 1	General Provisions
Article 2	Nature of Partnership
Article 3	Relations of Partners to Persons Dealing with Partnership
Article 4	Relations of Partners to Each Other and to Partnership
Article 5	Transferees and Creditors of Partner
Article 6	Partner's Dissociation
Article 7	Partner's Dissociation When Business Not Wound Up
Article 8	Winding Up Partnership Business
Article 9	Conversions and Mergers
Article 10	Limited Liability Partnership
Article 11	Foreign Limited Liability Partnership
Article 12	Miscellaneous Provisions

UNIFORM PARTNERSHIP ACT (UPA) LOCATOR

Go to: http://www.law.upenn.edu/bll/archives/ulc/uparta/1997act_final.htm. This locator links to the Uniform Partnership Act of 1997 drafted by the National Conference of Commissioners on Uniform State Laws.

APPENDIX B

UNIFORM LIMITED PARTNERSHIP ACT (2001)

ARTICLES OF THE UNIFORM LIMITED PARTNERSHIP ACT

Article 1	General Provisions
Article 2	Formation; Certificate of Limited Partnership and Other Filings
Article 3	Limited Partners
Article 4	General Partners
Article 5	Contributions and Distributions
Article 6	Dissociation
Article 7	Transferable Interests and Rights of Transferees and Creditors
Article 8	Dissolution
Article 9	Foreign Limited Partnerships
Article 10	Actions by Partners
Article 11	Conversion and Merger
Article 12	Miscellaneous Provisions

UNIFORM LIMITED PARTNERSHIP ACT (2001) LOCATOR

Go to: http://www.law.upenn.edu/bll/archives/ulc/ulpa/final2001.pdf. This locator links to the Uniform Limited Partnership Act (2001) drafted by the National Conference of Commissioners on Uniform State Laws.

APPENDIX C

REVISED UNIFORM LIMITED LIABILITY COMPANY ACT

ARTICLES OF THE REVISED UNIFORM LIMITED LIABILITY COMPANY ACT

Article 1	General Provisions
Article 2	Formation; Certificate of Organization and Other Filings
Article 3	Relations of Members And Managers to Persons Dealing with Limited Liability Company
Article 4	Relations of Members to Each Other and to Limited Liability Company
Article 5	Transferable Interests and Rights of Transferees and Creditors
Article 6	Member's Dissociation
Article 7	Dissolution and Winding Up
Article 8	Foreign Limited Liability Companies
Article 9	Actions by Members
Article 10	Merger, Conversion, and Domestication
Article11	Miscellaneous Provisions

REVISED UNIFORM LIMITED LIABILITY COMPANY ACT LOCATOR

Go to: http://www.law.upenn.edu/bll/archives/ulc/ullca/2006act_final.pdf. This locator links to the Revised Uniform Limited Liability Company Act drafted by the National Conference of Commissioners on Uniform State Laws.

APPENDIX D

MODEL BUSINESS CORPORATION ACT (REVISED THROUGH 2002)

CHAPTERS OF THE MODEL BUSINESS CORPORATION ACT

Chapter 1	General Provisions
Chapter 2	Incorporation
Chapter 3	Purposes and Powers
Chapter 4	Name
Chapter 5	Office and Agent
Chapter 6	Shares and Distributions
Chapter 7	Shareholders
Chapter 8	Directors and Officers
Chapter 9	Domestication and Conversion
Chapter 10	Amendment of Articles of Incorporation and Bylaws
Chapter 11	Mergers and Share Exchanges
Chapter 12	Disposition of Assets
Chapter 13	Appraisal Rights
Chapter 14	Dissolution
Chapter 15	Foreign Corporations
Chapter 16	Records and Reports
Chapter 17	Transition Provisions

MODEL BUSINESS CORPORATION ACT (MBCA) LOCATOR

Go to: http://www.abanet.org/buslaw/library/onlinepublications/mbca2002.pdf. This locator links to the Model Business Corporation Act revised through 2002 adopted by the Committee on Corporate Laws of the Section of Business Law with support of the American Bar Foundation.

APPENDIX E

THE SARBANES-OXLEY ACT OF 2002

TITLES OF THE SARBANES-OXLEY ACT OF 2002

Title I	Public Company Accounting Oversight Board
Title II	Auditor Independence
Title III	Corporate Responsibility
Title IV	Enhanced Financial Disclosures
Title V	Analyst Conflicts of Interest
Title VI	Commission Resources and Authority
Title VII	Studies and Reports
Title VIII	Corporate and Criminal Fraud Accountability
Title IX	White-Collar Crime Penalty Enhancements
Title X	Corporate Tax Returns
Title XI	Corporate Fraud and Accountability

SARBANES-OXLEY ACT OF 2002 LOCATOR

Go to: http://www.law.uc.edu/CCL/SOact/soact.pdf. This locator links to the Securities Lawyer's Deskbook published by The University of Cincinnati College of Law.

APPENDIX F

SECURITIES ACT OF 1933

[AS AMENDED THROUGH P.L. 111-72, APPROVED OCT. 13, 2009]

Sections of the Securities Act of 1933

Sec. 1.	Short Title
Sec. 2.	Definitions
Sec. 2A.	Swap Agreements
Sec. 3.	Exempted Securities
Sec. 4.	Exempted Transactions
Sec. 5.	Prohibitions Relating to Interstate Commerce and the Mails
Sec. 6.	Registration of Securities and Signing of Registration Statement
Sec. 7.	Information Required in Registration Statement
Sec. 8.	Taking Effect of Registration Statements and Amendments Thereto
Sec. 8A.	Cease-and-Desist Proceedings
Sec. 9.	Court Review of Orders
Sec. 10.	Information Required in Prospectus
Sec. 11.	Civil Liabilities on Account of False Registration Statement
Sec. 12.	Civil Liabilities Arising in Connection With Prospectuses and Communications
Sec. 13.	Limitation of Actions
Sec. 14.	Contrary Stipulations Void
Sec. 15.	Liability of Controlling Persons
Sec. 16.	Additional Remedies; Limitation on Remedies
Sec. 17.	Fraudulent Interstate Transactions
Sec. 18.	Exemption From State Regulation of Securities Offerings
Sec. 19.	Special Powers of Commission
Sec. 20.	Injunctions and Prosecution of Offenses
Sec. 21.	Hearings by Commission
Sec. 22.	Jurisdiction of Offenses and Suits
Sec. 23.	Unlawful Representations
Sec. 24.	Penalties
Sec. 25.	Jurisdiction of Other Government Agencies Over Securities
Sec. 26.	Separability of Provisions
Sec. 27.	Private Securities Litigation
Sec. 27A.	Application of Safe Harbor for Forward-Looking Statements
Sec. 28.	General Exemptive Authority

SECURITIES ACT OF 1933 LOCATOR

Go to: http://www.sec.gov/about/laws/sa33.pdf . This locator links to the Securities Act of 1933 as amended through P.L. 111-72, approved October 13, 2009.

APPENDIX G

SECURITIES EXCHANGE ACT OF 1934

[AS AMENDED THROUGH P.L. 111-72, APPROVED OCT. 13, 2009]

Sections of the	Securities Act of 1934
Section 1	Short Title
Section 2	Necessity for Regulation
Section 3	Definitions and Application
Section 3A	Swap Agreements
Section 4	Securities and Exchange Commission
Section 4A	Delegation of Functions by Commission
Section 4B	Transfer of Functions with Respect to Assignment of Personnel to Chairman
Section 4C	Appearance and Practice Before the Commission
Section 5	Transactions on Unregistered Exchanges
Section 6	National Securities Exchanges
Section 7	Margin Requirements
Section 8	Restrictions on Borrowing and Lending by Members, Brokers, and Dealers
Section 9	Manipulation of Security Prices
Section 10	Manipulative and Deceptive Devices
Section 10A	Audit Requirements
Section 11	Trading by Members of Exchanges, Brokers, and Dealers
Section 11A	National Market System for Securities; Securities Information Processors
Section 12	Registration Requirements for Securities
Section 13	Periodical and Other Reports
Section 14	Proxies
Section 15	Registration and Regulation of Brokers and Dealers
Section 15A	Registered Securities Associations
Section 15B	Municipal Securities
Section 15C	Government Securities Brokers and Dealers
Section 15D	Securities Analysts and Research Reports
Section 15E	Registration of Nationally Recognized Statistical Rating Organizations
Section 16	Directors, Officers, and Principal Stockholders
Section 17	Records and Reports
Section 17A	National System for Clearance and Settlement of Securities Transactions
Section 17B	Automated Quotation Systems for Penny Stocks
Section 18	Liability for Misleading Statements

Section 19	Registration, Responsibilities, and Oversight of Self-Regulatory Organizations
Section 20	Liability of Controlling Persons and Persons Who Aid and Abet Violations
Section 20A	Liability to Contemporaneous Traders for Insider Trading
Section 21	Investigations and Actions
Section 21A	Civil Penalties for Insider Trading
Section 21B	Civil Remedies in Administrative Proceedings
Section 21C	Cease-and-Desist Proceedings
Section 21D	Private Securities Litigation
Section 21E	Application of Safe Harbor for Forward-Looking Statements
Section 22	Hearings by Commission
Section 23	Rules, Regulations, and Orders; Annual Reports
Section 24	Public Availability of Information
Section 25	Court Review of Orders and Rules
Section 26	Unlawful Representations
Section 27	Jurisdiction of Offenses and Suits
Section 27A	Special Provision Relating to Statute of Limitations on Private Causes of Action
Section 28	Effect on Existing Law
Section 29	Validity of Contracts
Section 30	Foreign Securities Exchanges
Section 30A	Prohibited Foreign Trade Practices by Issuers
Section 31	Transaction Fees
Section 32	Penalties
Section 33	Separability
Section 34	Effective Date
Section 35	Authorization of Appropriations
Section 35A	Requirements for the EDGAR system
Section 36	General Exemptive Authority

SECURITIES ACT OF 1934 LOCATOR

Go to: http://www.law.uc.edu/CCL/34Act/index.html. This locator links to the Securities Act of 1934 as amended through P.L. 111-72, approved October 13, 2009.

UNIFORM SECURITIES ACT

Go to: http://www.law.upenn.edu/bll/archives/ulc/securities/2002final.htm. This locator links to Uniform Securities Act (last revised or amended in 2005) drafted by the National Conference of Commissioners on Uniform State Laws.

GLOSSARY

abusive filing A Chapter 7 filing that is found to be an abuse of Chapter 7 liquidation bankruptcy. In such a case, the court can dismiss the case or convert the case to a Chapter 13 or Chapter 11 proceeding with the debtor's consent.

absolute priority rule A rule that says a reorganization plan is fair and equitable to an impaired class of unsecured creditors or equity holders if no class below it receives anything in the plan.

acceptance method The bankruptcy court must approve a plan of reorganization if (1) the plan is *in the best interests* of each class of claims and interests, (2) the plan is *feasible*, (3) at least one class of claims *votes to accept the plan*, and (4) each class of claims and interests is *nonimpaired*.

accommodation A shipment that is offered to the buyer as a replacement for the original shipment when the original shipment cannot be filled.

accommodation party A party who signs an instrument and lends his or her name (and credit) to another party to the instrument.

accredited investor An investor treated under the Securities Act of 1933 as being knowledgeable and sophisticated about financial matters, esp. because of the investor's large net worth.

action for an accounting A formal judicial proceeding in which the court is authorized to (1) review the partnership and the partners' transactions and (2) award each partner his or her share of the partnership assets.

act of monopolizing A required act for there to be a violation of Section 2 of the Sherman Act. Possession of monopoly power without such act does not violate Section 2.

act of state doctrine States that judges of one country cannot question the validity of an act committed by another country within that other country's borders. It is based on the principle that a country has absolute authority over what transpires within its own territory.

actual notice Notice given directly to, or received personally by, a party.

administrative agencies Agencies that the legislative and executive branches of federal and state governments establish.

administrative dissolution Involuntary dissolution of a corporation that is ordered by the secretary of state if the corporation has failed to comply with certain procedures required by law.

administrative law A body of law that governs the operation of administrative agencies.

administrative law judge (ALJ) A judge, presiding over administrative proceedings, who decides questions of law and fact concerning the case.

Administrative Procedure Act (APA) An act that establishes certain administrative procedures that federal administrative agencies must follow in conducting their affairs.

administrative subpoena An order that directs the subject of the subpoena to disclose the requested information.

adverse action A denial or revocation of credit or a change in the credit terms offered.

affirmative action Policy that provides that certain job preferences will be given to minority or other protected class applicants when an employer makes an employment decision.

affirmative warranty A statement asserting that certain facts are true.

AFL-CIO The 1955 combination of the AFL and the CIO.

after-acquired property Property that the debtor acquires after the security agreement is executed.

Age Discrimination in Employment Act of 1967 A federal act that prohibits age discrimination by employers against employees or prospective employees who are 40 years of age or older.

agency The principal–agent relationship: the fiduciary relationship "which results from the manifestation of consent by one person to another that the other shall act in his behalf and subject to his control, and consent by the other so to act."

agency by ratification An agency that occurs when (1) a person misrepresents himself or herself as another's agent when in fact he or she is not and (2) the purported principal ratifies the unauthorized act.

agency law The large body of common law that governs agency; a mixture of contract law and tort law.

agency shop An establishment where an employee does not have to join the union but must pay a fee equal to the union dues.

agent A person who has been authorized to sign a negotiable instrument on behalf of another person.

agent's duty of loyalty A fiduciary duty owed by an agent not to act adversely to the interests of the principal.

agreement of conversion Document that states the terms for converting an existing business to an LLC.

air pollution Pollution caused by factories, homes, vehicles, and the like that affects the air.

air rights parcel The air space above the surface of the earth of an owner's real property.

alien corporation A corporation that is incorporated in another country.

altered check A check that has been altered without authorization that modifies the legal obligation of a party.

alternative dispute resolution (ADR) Methods of resolving disputes other than litigation.

amendments to the constitution Besides the Bill of Rights, seventeen additions that have been added to the U.S. Constitution.

American Inventory Protection Act A federal statute that permits inventors to file a *provisional application* with the PTO, requires the PTO to issue a patent within three years in most circumstances, and provides for contested reexaminations within the PTO.

Americans with Disabilities Act (ADA) of 1990 Imposes obligations on employers and providers of public transportation, telecommunications, and public accommodations to accommodate individuals with disabilities.

annual financial statement A statement provided to the shareholders that contains a balance sheet, an income statement, and a statement of changes in shareholder equity.

annual shareholders' meeting Meeting of the shareholders of a corporation that must be held annually by the corporation to elect directors and to vote on other matters.

antecedent debt A debt that is prior in time to another transaction.

antiassignment clause A clause that prohibits the assignment of rights under the contract.

antideficiency statute A statute that prohibits deficiency judgments regarding certain types of mortgages, such as those on residential property.

antidelegation clause A clause that prohibits the delegation of duties under the contract.

antifraud provision Section 14(a) of the Securities Exchange Act of 1934, which prohibits misrepresentations or omissions of a material fact in the proxy materials.

antitakeover statutes Statutes enacted by a state legislature that protect against the hostile takeover of corporations incorporated in or doing business in the state.

antitrust laws A series of laws enacted to limit anticompetitive behavior in almost all industries, businesses, and professions operating in the United States.

apparent agency Agency that arises when a principal creates the appearance of an agency that in actuality does not exist.

apparent authority Authority of an agent that exists because the principal knowingly or negligently permits the agent to exercise it or because the principal holds the agent out as possessing it.

appellate body A panel of seven judges selected from WTO member nations that hears and decides appeals from decisions by the dispute settlement body.

appropriate bargaining unit The group that a union seeks to represent.

approval clause A clause that permits the assignment of the contract only upon receipt of an obligor's approval.

arbitration A nonjudicial method of dispute resolution whereby a neutral third party decides the case.

arbitration clause A clause contained in many international contracts that stipulates that any dispute between the parties concerning the performance of the contract will be submitted to an arbitrator or arbitration panel for resolution.

area franchise The franchisor authorizes the franchisee to negotiate and sell franchises on behalf of the franchisor.

arrearages Unpaid debts.

Article 2 and Revised Article 2 An article of the Uniform Commercial Code (UCC) that establishes rules that govern the sale of goods.

Article 2A (Leases) Article of the UCC that governs lease of goods.

Article 3 of the UCC A model code that establishes rules for the creation of, transfer of, enforcement of, and liability on negotiable instruments.

Article 3 of the UCC An article of the UCC that sets forth the requirements for negotiable instruments, including checks.

Article 4 of the UCC Establishes the rules and principles that regulate bank deposit and collection procedures.

Article 4A of the UCC An article of the UCC that establishes rules regulating the creation and collection of and liability for wire transfers.

Article 7 of the UCC An article of the UCC that provides a detailed statutory scheme for the creation, perfection, and foreclosure on common carriers' and warehouse operators' liens.

Article 9 of the UCC An article of the UCC that governs secured transactions in personal property.

articles of amendment A document filed to effectuate an amendment or change to a corporation's articles of incorporation.

articles of dissolution A document that a dissolving corporation must file with the appropriate governmental agency, usually the secretary of state, after the corporation has settled all its debts and distributed all its assets.

articles of incorporation The basic governing documents of the corporation. These documents must be filed with the secretary of state of the state of incorporation.

articles of limited liability limited partnership A written partnership agreement; document that must be filed with the secretary of state to form a limited liability limited partnership.

articles of merger A document that must be filed with the secretary of state of the surviving corporation to effectuate a merger.

articles of organization The formal document that must be filed with the secretary of state to form an LLC.

articles of partnership A written partnership agreement; document that must be filed with the secretary of state to form a limited liability partnership.

articles of share exchange A document that must be filed with the secretary of state of the surviving corporation to effectuate a share exchange.

articles of termination Document that is filed with the secretary of state that terminates the LLC as of the date of filing or upon a later effective date specified in the document.

assessment fee A fee for such things as advertising and promotional campaigns, administrative costs, and the like, billed either as a flat monthly or annual fee or as a percentage of gross sales.

assignment and delegation Transfer of both rights and duties under the contract.

attachment The creditor has an enforceable security interest against the debtor and can satisfy the debt out of the designated collateral.

attorney-in-fact Someone who is given authority through a power of attorney to do a particular nonlegal act. An "attorney in fact" need not be a member of the legal profession.

at-will LLC An LLC that has no specified term of duration.

audit committee A committee appointed by the board of an organization, especially a corporation, to oversee the financial reporting process, select an independent auditor, and receive the audit.

authorized shares The number of shares provided for in the articles of incorporation.

automatic stay The result of the filing of a voluntary or involuntary petition; the suspension of certain actions by creditors against the debtor or the debtor's property.

backward vertical merger A vertical merger in which the customer acquires the supplier.

bait and switch A type of deceptive advertising that occurs when a seller advertises the availability of a low-cost discounted item but then pressures the buyer into purchasing more expensive merchandise.

bank check A certified check, a cashier's check, or a traveler's check, the payment for which the bank is solely or primarily liable.

Bankruptcy Abuse Prevention and Consumer Protection Act of 2005 A federal act that substantially amended federal bankruptcy law. This act makes it more difficult for debtors to file for bankruptcy and have their unpaid debts discharged.

Bankruptcy Code A federal statute that establishes rules and procedures for filing bankruptcy and completing bankruptcy.

bankruptcy estate An estate created upon the commencement of a Chapter 7 proceeding that includes all the debtor's legal and equitable interests in real, personal, tangible, and intangible property, wherever located, that exist when the petition is filed, minus exempt property.

bearer paper Bearer paper is negotiated by delivery; indorsement is not necessary.

bilateral treaty Treaty between two nations.

bill of lading A document of title that is issued by a common carrier to the bailor when goods are received by the common carrier for transportation.

blank indorsement An indorsement that does not specify a particular indorsee. It creates *bearer paper*.

board of directors A panel of decision makers, the members of which are elected by the shareholders.

bona fide occupational qualification (BFOQ) Employment discrimination based on a protected class (other than race or color) is lawful if it is *job related* and a *business* *necessity*. This exception is narrowly interpreted by the courts.

bond A long-term debt security that is secured by some form of collateral.

branch office An offshoot, lateral extension, or division of an institution.

breach of a franchise agreement A breach of duty to adhere and perform under the terms of a franchise agreement.

breach of confidentiality A breach of fiduciary duty by a partner in a partnership to keep information confidential.

breach of the duty of care A failure to exercise care or to act as a reasonable person would act.

building codes State and local statutes that impose specific standards on property owners to maintain and repair leased premises.

business judgment rule A rule that protects the decisions of the board of directors, who act on an informed basis, in good faith, and in the honest belief that the action taken was in the best interests of the corporation and its shareholders.

buy-and-sell agreement An agreement that requires selling shareholders to sell their shares to the other shareholders or to the corporation at the price specified in the agreement.

buyer in the ordinary course of business A person who in good faith and without knowledge that the sale violates the ownership or security interests of a third party buys the goods in the ordinary course of business from a person in the business of selling goods of that kind. A buyer in the ordinary course of business takes the goods free of any third-party security interest in the goods.

bylaws A detailed set of rules adopted by the board of directors after the corporation is incorporated that contains provisions for managing the business and the affairs of the corporation.

case brief A summary of each of the following items of a case: (1) case name and citation, (2) key facts, (3) issue presented, (4) holding of the court, and (5) court's reasoning.

causation A person who commits a negligent act is not liable unless his or her act was the cause of the plaintiff's injuries. The two types of causation that must be proven are (1) *causation in fact (actual cause)* and (2) *proximate cause (legal cause)*.

causation in fact or actual cause The actual cause of negligence. A person who commits a negligent act is not liable unless causation in fact can be proven.

C corporation A corporation whose income is taxed through it rather than through its shareholders.

certificate of authority A document authenticating a notarized document that is being sent to another jurisdiction.

certificate of cancellation A document that is filed with the secretary of state upon the dissolution of a limited partnership.

certificate of dissolution A document issued by a state authority (usually the secretary of state) certifying that the named person has been duly elected.

certificate of interest A document that evidences a member's ownership interest in an LLC.

certificate of limited liability limited partnership A document that is filed by an LLLP with the secretary of state's office to organize under state law.

certificate of limited partnership A document that two or more persons must execute and sign that makes the limited partnership legal and binding.

certificate of registration 1. *Copyright*. A U.S. Copyright Office document approving a copyright application and stating the approved work's registration date and copyright registration number. 2. *Trademarks*. A document affirming that the U.S. Patent and Trademark Office has allowed and recorded a trademark or service mark.

chain of distribution All manufacturers, distributors, wholesalers, retailers, lessors, and subcomponent manufacturers involved in a transaction.

chain-style franchise The franchisor licenses the franchisee to make and sell its products or distribute services to the public from a retail outlet serving an exclusive territory.

changing conditions defense A price discrimination defense that claims prices were lowered in response to changing conditions in the market for or the marketability of the goods.

Chapter 11 A bankruptcy method that allows reorganization of the debtor's financial affairs under the supervision of the bankruptcy court.

Chapter 13 A rehabilitation form of bankruptcy that permits the courts to supervise the debtor's plan for the payment of unpaid debts by installments.

Chapter 7 liquidation bankruptcy The most familiar form of bankruptcy; the debtor's nonexempt property is sold for cash, the cash is distributed to the creditors, and any unpaid debts are discharged.

choice of forum clause Clause in an international contract that designates which nation's court has jurisdiction to hear a case arising out of the contract. Also known as a forum-selection clause.

choice of law clause Clause in an international contract that designates which nation's laws will be applied in deciding a dispute.

civil penalty A fine assessed for a violation of a statute or regulation.

Civil Rights Act A federal statute that prohibits racial discrimination in the transfer of real property.

Civil Rights Act of 1866 A section of a federal statute that expressly prohibits racial discrimination; it has also been held to forbid discrimination based on national origin.

Clean Air Act A federal statute enacted to assist states in dealing with air pollution.

closely held corporation A corporation owned by one or a few shareholders.

closing The finalization of a real estate sales transaction that passes title to the property from the seller to the buyer.

codicil A separate document that must be executed to amend a will. It must be executed with the same formalities as a will.

C.O.D. shipment A type of shipment contract where the buyer agrees to pay the shipper cash upon the delivery of the goods.

coinsurance clause A clause that permits an owner who insures his or her property to a certain percentage of its value to recover up to the face value of the policy.

collateral Security against repayment of the note that lenders sometimes require; can be a car, a house, or other property.

collateral contract A promise where one person agrees to answer for the debts or duties of another person.

collective bargaining The act of negotiating contract terms between an employer and the members of a union.

collective bargaining agreement The resulting contract from a collective bargaining procedure.

"coming and going" rule A rule that says a principal is generally not liable for injuries caused by its agents and employees while they are on their way to or from work.

Commerce Clause A clause of the U.S. Constitution that grants Congress the power "to regulate commerce with foreign nations, and among the several states, and with Indian tribes."

common carrier A firm that offers transportation services to the general public. The bailee owes a *duty of strict liability* to the bailor.

common stock A type of equity security that represents the *residual* value of the corporation.

common stock certificate A document that represents the common shareholder's investment in the corporation.

common stockholder A person who owns common stock.

community property A form of ownership where each spouse owns an equal one-half share of the income both spouses earned during the marriage and one-half of the assets acquired by this income during the marriage.

competing with a corporation A way in which a corporate officer or director can breach his or her duty of loyalty.

competing with the partnership A way in which a partner in a partnership can breach his or her duty of loyalty.

competing with the principal A way in which an agent can breach his or her duty of loyalty.

conditioning the market (gun-jumping) The act of unlawfully soliciting the public's purchase of securities before the SEC approves a registration statement.

confirmation The bankruptcy court's approval of a plan of reorganization.

conglomerate merger A merger that does not fit into any other category; a merger between firms in totally unrelated businesses.

consent order An order issued by the SEC whereby a defendant agrees not to violate securities laws in the future but does not admit having violated securities laws in the past.

Consolidated Omnibus Budget Reconciliation Act (COBRA) Federal law that permits employees and their beneficiaries to continue their group health insurance after an employee's employment has ended.

constructive notice Usually written notice to a third party that is put into general circulation, such as in a newspaper.

Consumer Product Safety Act (CPSA) A federal statute that regulates potentially dangerous consumer products and created the Consumer Product Safety Commission.

Consumer Product Safety Commission (CPSC) An independent federal regulatory agency empowered to (1) adopt rules and regulations to interpret and enforce the Consumer Product Safety Act, (2) conduct research on safety, and (3) collect data regarding injuries.

consumer protection laws Federal and state statutes and regulations that promote product safety and prohibit abusive, unfair, and deceptive business practices.

contingency-fee basis A contractual arrangement whereby an attorney agrees to represent the client, with the compensation to be a percentage of the amount recovered for the client.

continuation of a general partnership Occurs when surviving or remaining partners exercise their right to continue the partnership after dissolution.

contract in restraint of trade A contract that unreasonably restrains trade.

convention An agreement or compact, especially one among nations; a multilateral treaty.

conversion of personal property A tort that deprives a true owner of the use and enjoyment of his or her personal property by taking over such property and exercising ownership rights over it.

convertible preferred stock Permits preferred stockholders to convert their shares into common stock.

cooperative A form of co-ownership of a multiple-dwelling building where a corporation owns the building and the residents own shares in the corporation.

co-ownership When two or more persons own a piece of real property. Also called *concurrent ownership.*

copyright infringement When a party copies a substantial and material part of the plaintiff's copyrighted work without permission. A copyright holder may recover damages and other remedies against the infringer.

Copyright Revision Act of 1976 Federal statute that (1) establishes the requirements for obtaining a copyright and (2) protects copyrighted works from infringement.

corporate citizenship A theory of responsibility that says a business has a responsibility to do good.

corporate seal A design containing the name of the corporation and the date of incorporation that is imprinted by the corporate secretary using a metal stamp on certain legal documents.

corporate criminal liability Criminal liability of corporations for actions of their officers, employees, or agents.

corporation A fictitious legal entity that (1) is created according to statutory requirements and (2) is a separate taxpaying entity for federal income tax purposes.

cost justification defense A defense in Section 2(a) action that provides that a seller's price discrimination is not unlawful if the price differential is due to "differences in the cost of manufacture, sale, or delivery" of the product.

cost of supplies A franchise fee involving the payment for supplies purchased from the franchisor.

counteroffer A response by an offeree that contains terms and conditions different from or in addition to those of the offer. A counteroffer terminates an offer.

Court of Appeals for the Federal Circuit A court of appeals in Washington, DC, that has special appellate jurisdiction to review the decisions of the Claims Court, the Patent and Trademark Office, and the Court of International Trade.

court of chancery A court administering equity; a court that proceeds according to the forms and principles of equity; a court of equity as distinguished from a common-law court.

covenant not to compete A contract that provides that a seller of a business or an employee will not engage in a similar business or occupation within a specified geographical area for a specified time following the sale of the business or termination of employment. Also called a *noncompete clause.*

covenant of good faith and fair dealing Under this implied covenant, the parties to a contract are not only held to the express terms of the contract but are also required to act in "good faith" and deal fairly in all respects in obtaining the objective of the contract.

covenant of quiet enjoyment A covenant that says that a landlord may not interfere with the tenant's quiet and peaceful possession, use, and enjoyment of the leased premises.

cram down method A method of confirmation of a plan of reorganization where the court forces an impaired class to participate in the plan of reorganization.

credit report Information about a person's credit history that can be secured from a credit bureau.

creditor–debtor relationship Created when a customer deposits money into the bank; the customer is the creditor and the bank is the debtor.

creditors' committee The creditors holding the seven largest unsecured claims are usually appointed to the creditors' committee. Representatives of the committee appear at bankruptcy court hearings, participate in the negotiation of a plan of reorganization, assert objections to proposed plans, and so on.

critical legal thinking The process of specifying the issue presented by a case, identifying the key facts in the case and applicable law, and then applying the law to the facts to come to a conclusion that answers the issue presented.

cross-complaint Filed by the defendant against the plaintiff to seek damages or some other remedy

crossover worker A person who does not honor a strike who either (1) chooses not to strike or (2) returns to work after joining the strikers for a time.

crown jewel A valuable asset of the target corporation that the tender offeror particularly wants to acquire in the tender offer.

cruel and unusual punishment A clause of the Eighth Amendment that protects criminal defendants from torture or other abusive punishment.

cumulative preferred stock Stock that provides any missed dividend payments must be paid in the future to the preferred shareholders before the common shareholders can receive any dividends.

cumulative voting A shareholder can accumulate all of his or her votes and vote them all for one candidate or split them among several candidates.

custom The second source of international law, created through consistent, recurring practices between two or more nations over a period of time that have become recognized as binding.

damages for accepted nonconforming goods A buyer or lessee may accept nonconforming goods and recover the damages caused by the breach from the seller or lessor or deduct the damages from any part of the purchase price or rent still due under the contract.

"danger invites rescue" doctrine Doctrine that provides that a rescuer who is injured while going to someone's rescue can sue the person who caused the dangerous situation.

d.b.a. (doing business as) The abbreviation usually precedes a person's or business's assumed name. It signals that the business may be licensed or incorporated under a different name.

debenture A long-term unsecured debt instrument that is based on the corporation's general credit standing.

debtor The borrower in a credit transaction.

debtor-in-possession A debtor who is left in place to operate the business during the reorganization proceeding.

debt securities Securities that establish a debtor–creditor relationship in which the corporation borrows money from the investor to whom the debt security is issued.

declaration of duties If the delegatee has not assumed the duties under a contract, the delegatee is not legally liable to the obligee for nonperformance.

decree of dissolution A decree entered by a court that judicially dissolves a corporation on a specific date.

decree of judicial dissolution A decree that may be granted to a partner whenever it is not reasonably practical to carry on the business in conformity with a limited partnership agreement.

default Failure to make scheduled payments when due, bankruptcy of the debtor, breach of the warranty of ownership as to the collateral, and other events defined by the parties to constitute default.

defective formation Occurs when (1) a certificate of limited partnership is not properly filed, (2) there are defects in a certificate that is filed, or (3) some other statutory requirement for the creation of a limited partnership is not met.

deficiency judgment A judgment that allows a secured creditor to successfully bring a separate legal action to recover a deficiency from the debtor. Entitles the secured creditor to recover the amount of the judgment from the debtor's other property.

derivative action (derivative lawsuit) A suit by a beneficiary of a fiduciary to enforce a right belonging to the fiduciary; especially a suit asserted by a shareholder on the corporation's behalf against a third party (usually a corporate officer) because of the corporation's failure to take some action against the third party.

Digital Millennium Copyright Act (DMCA) A federal statute that prohibits unauthorized access to copyrighted digital works by circumventing encryption technology or the manufacture and distribution of technologies designed for the purpose of circumventing encryption protection of digital works.

directors' and officers' liability insurance Insurance that protects directors and officers of a corporation from liability for actions taken on behalf of the corporation.

direct price discrimination Price discrimination in which (1) the defendant sold commodities of like grade and quality (2) to two or more purchasers at different prices at approximately the same time, and (3) the plaintiff suffered injury because of the price discrimination.

disability insurance Insurance that provides a monthly income to an insured who is disabled and cannot work.

discharge Actions or events that relieve certain parties from liability on negotiable instruments. There are three methods of discharge: (1) payment of the instrument; (2) cancellation; and (3) impairment of the right of recourse.

discharge in bankruptcy A real defense against the enforcement of a negotiable instrument; bankruptcy law is intended to relieve debtors of burdensome debts, including negotiable instruments.

disclosure statement A statement that must contain adequate information about the proposed plan of reorganization that is supplied to the creditors and equity holders.

dishonored Occurs when an instrument has been presented for payment and payment has been refused.

disparate-impact discrimination Occurs when an employer

discriminates against an entire protected class. An example would be where a facially neutral employment practice or rule causes an adverse impact on a protected class.

disparate-treatment discrimination Occurs when an employer discriminates against a specific individual because of his or her race, color, national origin, sex, or religion.

disposition of collateral If a secured creditor repossesses collateral upon a debtor's default, he or she may sell, lease, or otherwise dispose of it in a commercially reasonable manner.

disposition of goods A seller or lessor who is in possession of goods at the time the buyer or lessee breaches or repudiates the contract may in good faith resell, release, or otherwise dispose of the goods in a commercially reasonable manner and recover damages, including incidental damages, from the buyer or lessee.

dispute settlement body A board comprised of one representative from each WTO member nation that reviews panel reports.

dissension When an individual director opposes the action taken by the majority of the board of directors.

dissenting shareholder appraisal rights Shareholders who object to a proposed merger, share exchange, or sale or lease of all or substantially all of the property of a corporation have a right to have their shares valued by the court and receive cash payment of this value from the corporation.

dissolution of a general partnership The change in the relation of the partners caused by any partner ceasing to be associated in the carrying on of the business.

distributional interest A member's ownership interest in an LLC that entitles the member to receive distributions of money and property from the LLC.

distribution of property *Nonexempt property* of the bankruptcy estate must be distributed to the debtor's secured and unsecured creditors pursuant to the statutory priority established by the Bankruptcy Code.

distributorship franchise The franchisor manufactures a product and licenses a retail franchisee to distribute the product to the public.

dividend A distribution of profits of the corporation to shareholders.

dividend preference The right to receive a fixed dividend at stipulated periods during the year (e.g., quarterly).

division of markets When competitors agree that each will serve only a designated portion of the market.

doctrine of sovereign immunity States that countries are granted immunity from suits in courts of other countries.

doctrine of strict liability in tort A tort doctrine that makes manufacturers, distributors, wholesalers, retailers, and others in the chain of distribution of a defective product liable for the damages caused by the defect irrespective of fault.

document of title An actual piece of paper, such as a warehouse receipt or bill of lading, that is required in some transactions of pick up and delivery.

domain name A unique name that identifies an individual's or company's website.

domestic corporation A corporation in the state in which it was formed.

domestic limited partnership A limited partnership in the state in which it was formed.

Dominican Republic–Central America Free Trade Agreement The agreement that modified the Central America Free Trade Agreement (CAFTA) formed by the United States and several Central American countries lowering tariffs and reducing trade restrictions after the addition of the Dominican Republic.

double taxation Taxing the same thing twice for the same purpose by the same taxing authority during identical taxation periods.

Dram Shop Act Statute that makes taverns and bartenders liable for injuries caused to or by patrons who are served too much alcohol.

Drug Amendment to the FDCA An amendment that gives the FDA broad powers to license new drugs in the United States.

dual agency Occurs when an agent acts for two or more different principals in the same transaction.

dual-purpose mission An errand or other act that a principal requests of an agent while the agent is on his or her own personal business.

due diligence defense A defense to a Section 11 action that, if proven, makes the defendant not liable.

durable power of attorney A power of attorney that remains in effect during the grantor's incompetency.

duty not to willfully or wantonly injure The duty an owner owes a trespasser to prevent intentional injury or harm to the trespasser when the trespasser is on his or her premises.

duty of accountability A duty that an agent owes to maintain an accurate accounting of all transactions undertaken on the principal's behalf.

duty of care The obligation we all owe each other not to cause any unreasonable harm or risk of harm.

duty of loyalty A duty that directors and officers have not to act adversely to the interests of the corporation and to subordinate their personal interests to those of the corporation and its shareholders.

duty of notification An agent's duty to notify the principal of information he or she learns from a third party or other source that is important to the principal.

duty of obedience A duty that directors and officers of a corporation have to act within the authority conferred upon them by the state corporation statute, the articles of incorporation, the corporate bylaws, and the resolutions adopted by the board of directors.

duty of ordinary care The duty an owner owes an invitee or a licensee to prevent injury or harm when the invitee or licensee steps on the owner's premises.

duty of performance An agent's duty to a principal that includes (1) performing the lawful duties expressed in the contract and (2) meeting the standards of reasonable care, skill, and diligence implicit in all contracts.

duty of reasonable care The duty that a reasonable bailee in like circumstances would owe to protect the bailed property.

duty of slight care A duty not to be grossly negligent in caring for something in one's responsibility.

duty of strict liability A duty that common carriers owe that says if the goods are lost, damaged, destroyed, or stolen, the common carrier is liable even if it was not at fault for the loss.

duty of utmost care A duty of care that goes beyond ordinary care that says common carriers and innkeepers have a responsibility to provide security to their passengers or guests.

duty to compensate A duty that a principal owes to pay an agreed-upon amount to the agent either upon the completion of the agency or at some other mutually agreeable time.

duty to cooperate A duty that a principal owes to cooperate with and assist the agent in the performance of the agent's duties and the accomplishment of the agency.

duty to defend An insurer owes a duty to defend an insured against a lawsuit involving a risk covered by the policy. This duty includes providing a lawyer and paying court costs and deposition fees.

duty to indemnify A duty that a principal owes to protect the agent for losses the agent suffered during the agency because of the principal's misconduct.

duty to inform A duty a partner owes to inform his or her co-partners of all information he or she possesses that is relevant to the affairs of the partnership.

duty to notify An agent's duty to notify a principal of information that is important to the principal.

duty to perform An agent's duty to a principal that includes (1) performing the lawful duties expressed in the contract and (2) meeting the standards of reasonable care, skill, and diligence implicit in all contracts.

duty to reimburse A duty that a principal owes to repay money to the agent if the agent spent his or her own money during the agency on the principal's behalf.

e-commerce The sale of goods and services by computer over the Internet.

EDGAR An electronic filing and forms system used by the SEC.

electronic funds transfer system (EFTS) Computer and electronic technology that makes it possible for banks to offer electronic payment and collection systems to bank customers. E-banking and e-money consist of: (1) automated teller machines (ATMs); (2) point-of-sale terminals; (3) direct deposit and withdrawal; (4) online banking; and (5) debit cards.

electronic mail (e-mail) Electronic written communication between individuals using computers connected to the Internet.

elements of a bailment The following three elements are necessary to create a bailment: (1) personal property, (2) delivery of possession, and (3) a bailment agreement.

e-mail and web contracts Contracts that are entered into by e-mail and over the World Wide Web.

Employee Retirement Income Security Act (ERISA) A federal act designed to prevent fraud and other abuses associated with private pension funds.

employee stock ownership plan (ESOP) (employee benefit plan) A type of profit-sharing plan that invests primarily in the employer's stock.

employer–employee relationship A relationship that results when an employer hires an employee to perform some form of physical service.

employer lockout Act of the employer to prevent employees from entering the work premises when the employer reasonably anticipates a strike.

endorsement An addition to an insurance policy that modifies it.

engagement A formal entrance into a contract between a client and an accountant.

entrepreneur A person who forms and operates a new business either by himself or herself or with others.

Environmental Impact Statement (EIS) A document that must be prepared for all proposed legislation or major federal action that significantly affects the quality of the human environment.

Environmental Protection Agency (EPA) An administrative agency created by Congress in 1970 to coordinate the implementation and enforcement of the federal environmental protection laws.

environmental protection laws Federal and state statutes and regulations that limit levels of pollution and require the cleanup of hazardous waste sites.

Equal Access to Justice Act A federal act that protects persons from harassment by federal administrative agencies.

Equal Credit Opportunity Act (ECOA) A federal statute that prohibits discrimination in the extension of credit based on sex, marital status, race, color, national origin, religion, age, or receipt of income from public assistance programs.

equal dignity rule A rule that says that an agent's contracts to sell property covered by the Statute of Frauds must be in writing to be enforceable.

Equal Employment Opportunity Commission (EEOC) The federal administrative agency responsible for enforcing most federal antidiscrimination laws.

equal opportunity in employment The right of all employees and job applicants (1) to be treated without discrimination and (2) to be able to sue employers if they are discriminated against.

Equal Pay Act of 1963 Protects both sexes from pay discrimination based on sex; extends to jobs that require equal skill, equal effort, equal responsibility, and similar working conditions.

equity securities Representation of ownership rights to the corporation. Also called *stocks*.

escheats A doctrine that states that if a person dies without a will and has no surviving relatives, his or her property goes to the state.

estate pour autre vie A life estate measured in the life of a third party.

estop To stop or bar; impede.

EU Commission A commission charged to act in the best interests of the European Union in enacting legislation and taking enforcement actions to enforce the treaty.

euro The official currency of most countries in the European Union.

European Union (Common Market) Comprises many countries of western Europe; created to promote peace and security plus economic, social, and cultural development.

exclusive agency contract A contract a principal and agent enter into that says the principal cannot employ any agent other than the exclusive agent.

exclusive license A license that grants the licensee exclusive rights to use informational rights for a specified duration.

exempt 1. *v.* To release from liability. 2. *adj.* Freed from a duty.

exempt property Property that may be retained by a debtor pursuant to federal or state law; debtor's property that does not become part of the bankruptcy estate.

exempt security A security that need not be registered under the provisions of the Securities Act of 1933 and is exempt from the margin requirements of the Securities Exchange Act of 1934.

exempt transaction A transaction involving the sale of securities that do not have to be registered with the SEC.

Exon-Florio law Mandates the president of the United States to suspend, prohibit, or dismantle the acquisition of U.S. businesses by foreign investors if there is credible evidence that the foreign investor might take action that threatens to impair the "national security."

express agency An agency that occurs when a principal and an agent expressly agree to enter into an agency agreement with each other.

express authorization A stipulation in the offer that says the acceptance must be by a specified means of communication.

express power (enumerated power) A political power specifically delegated to a governmental branch by a constitution.

extradition Sending a person back to a country for criminal prosecution.

extreme duress Extreme duress, but not ordinary duress, is a real defense against enforcement of a negotiable instrument.

failure to provide adequate instructions A defect that occurs when a manufacturer does not provide detailed directions for safe assembly and use of a product.

failure to warn A defect that occurs when a manufacturer does not place a warning on the packaging of products that could cause injury if the danger is unknown.

Fair Credit and Charge Card Disclosure Act An amendment to the TILA that requires disclosure of certain credit terms on credit card and charge card solicitations and applications.

Fair Credit Reporting Act (FCRA) An amendment to the TILA that protects a consumer who is the subject of a credit report by setting out guidelines for credit bureaus.

Fair Debt Collection Practices Act (FDCPA) A federal act that protects consumer-debtors from abusive, deceptive, and unfair practices used by debt collectors.

Fair Housing Act A federal statute that makes it unlawful for a party to refuse to rent or sell a dwelling to any person because of his or her race, color, national origin, sex, or religion.

Fair Labor Standards Act (FLSA) A federal act enacted in 1938 to protect workers; prohibits child labor and establishes minimum wage and overtime pay requirements.

fair price rule A rule that says any increase in price paid for shares tendered must be offered to all shareholders, even those who have previously tendered their shares.

fair use doctrine A doctrine that permits certain limited use of a copyright by someone other than the copyright holder without the permission of the copyright holder.

Family and Medical Leave Act A federal statute that guarantees covered workers unpaid time off from work for the birth or adoption of a child, serious health problems of the workers, and serious health problems of a spouse, child, or parent.

family farmer An individual, a corporation, or a partnership that engages in farming operations and meets the requirements for filing for a Chapter 12 proceeding.

family fisherman An individual, a corporation, or a partnership that engages in commercial fishing operations and meets the requirements for filing for a Chapter 12 proceeding.

federal administrative agencies Administrative agencies that are part of the executive or legislative branch of government.

Federal Arbitration Act (FAA) A federal statute that provides for the enforcement of most arbitration agreements.

Federal Dilution Act of 1995 A federal statute that protects famous marks from dilution.

Federal Insurance Contributions Act (FICA) A federal act that says employees and employers must make contributions into the Social Security fund.

Federal Patent Statute of 1952 Federal statute that establishes the requirements for obtaining a patent and protects patented inventions from infringement.

Federal Reserve System A system of twelve regional Federal Reserve banks that assist banks in the collection of checks.

Federal Trade Commission (FTC) Federal administrative agency empowered to enforce the Federal Trade Commission Act and other federal consumer protection statutes.

Federal Unemployment Tax Act (FUTA) A federal act that requires employers to pay unemployment taxes; unemployment compensation is paid to workers who are temporarily unemployed.

fictitious business name statement (certificate of trade name) A statement that most states require businesses operating under a trade name to file.

fiduciary duty Duty of loyalty, honesty, integrity, trust, and confidence owed by directors and officers to their corporate employers.

fiduciary relationship A relationship in which one person is under a duty to act for the benefit of another on matters within the scope of the relationship.

final prospectus A final version of the prospectus that must be delivered by the issuer to the investor prior to or at the time of confirming a sale or sending a security to a purchaser.

final settlement Occurs when the payor bank (1) pays the check in cash, (2) settles for the check without having a right to revoke the settlement, or (3) fails to dishonor the check within certain statutory time periods.

finance lease A three-party transaction consisting of the lessor, the lessee, and the supplier.

financing statement A document filed by a secured creditor with the appropriate government office that constructively notifies the world of his or her security interest in personal property.

fixed amount of money A negotiable instrument must contain a promise or order to pay a fixed amount of money.

flip-in rights plan These plans provide that existing shareholders of the target corporation may convert their shares for a greater number of the debt securities of an acquiring corporation.

flip-over rights plan These plans provide that existing shareholders of the target corporation may convert their shares for a greater number of the shares of an acquiring corporation.

floating lien A security interest in property that was not in the possession of the debtor when the security agreement was executed; includes *after-acquired property*, *future advances*, and *sale proceeds*.

Food and Drug Administration (FDA) Federal administrative agency that administers and enforces the federal Food, Drug, and Cosmetic Act (FDCA) and other federal consumer protection laws.

Food, Drug, and Cosmetic Act (FDCA) A federal statute enacted in 1938 that provides the basis for the regulation of much of the testing, manufacture, distribution, and sale of foods, drugs, cosmetics, and medicinal products.

foreclosure Legal procedure by which a secured creditor causes the judicial sale of the secured real estate to pay a defaulted loan.

foreign commerce clause A clause of the U.S. Constitution that vests Congress with the power to "regulate commerce with foreign nations."

foreign corporation A corporation in any state or jurisdiction other than the one in which it was formed.

foreign limited partnership A limited partnership in all other states besides the one in which it was formed.

Foreign Sovereign Immunities Act Exclusively governs suits against foreign nations that are brought in federal or state courts in the United States; codifies the principle of qualified or restricted immunity.

foreseeability standard A rule that says that an accountant is liable for negligence to third parties who are foreseeable users of the client's financial statements. It provides the broadest standard for holding accountants liable to third parties for negligence.

formal will A will that meets the requirements of the Statute of Wills.

forum-selection clause Contract provision that designates a certain court to hear any dispute concerning nonperformance of the contract.

forward vertical merger A vertical merger in which the supplier acquires the customer.

four legals Four notices or actions that prevent the payment of a check if they are received by the payor bank before it has finished its process of posting the check for payment.

franchise Established when one party licenses another party to use the franchisor's trade name, trademarks, commercial symbols, patents, copyrights, and other property in the distribution and selling of goods and services.

franchise agreement An agreement that the franchisor and the franchisee enter into that sets forth the terms and conditions of the franchise.

franchisee One who is granted a franchise.

franchisor One who grants a franchise.

Freedom of Information Act A federal act that gives the public access to documents in the possession of federal administrative agencies. There are many exceptions to disclosure.

fresh start The goal of federal bankruptcy law: To discharge the debtor from burdensome debts and allow him or her to begin again.

frolic and detour When an agent does something during the course of his employment to further his own interests rather than the principal's.

FTC franchise rule A rule set out by the FTC that requires franchisors to make full presale disclosures to prospective franchisees.

FTC notice A notice required to be placed on the cover of a franchisor's required disclosure statement to prospective franchisers.

fully disclosed agency An agency in which a contracting third party knows (1) that the agent is acting for a principal and (2) the identity of the principal.

fully disclosed principal A principal whose identity is known to the third party.

funding a living trust To fund a living trust, the grantor transfers title to his or her property to the trust.

future goods Goods not yet in existence (ungrown crops, unborn stock animals).

General Agreement on Tariffs and Trade (GATT) A multiparty international agreement—signed originally in 1948—that promotes international trade by lowering import duties and providing equal access to markets. More than 150 nations are parties to the agreement.

general assembly The name of the legislative body in many states; the deliberative body of the United Nations.

general corporation statues Enacted by states to permit corporations to be formed without the separate approval of the legislature.

general duty A duty that an employer has to provide a work environment "free from recognized hazards that are causing or are likely to cause death or serious physical harm to his employees."

general government regulation Government regulation that applies to many businesses and industries collectively (e.g., antidiscrimination laws).

generally accepted accounting principles (GGAPs) Standards for the preparation and presentation of financial statements.

generally accepted auditing standards (GAASs) Standards for the methods and procedures that must be used to conduct audits.

generally known dangers A defense that acknowledges that certain products are inherently dangerous and are known to the general population to be so.

general partners Partners in a limited partnership who invest capital, manage the business, and are personally liable for partnership debts, Persons liable for the debts and obligations of a general partnership. Also known simply as partners.

general partnership An association of two or more persons to carry on as co-owners of a business for profit [UPA Section 6(1)]. Also known as an ordinary partnership.

general power of attorney A power of attorney that authorizes an agent to transact business for the principal.

general principles of law The third source of international law, consisting of principles of law recognized by civilized nations. These are principles of law that are common to the national law of the parties to the dispute.

general-purpose clause A clause often included in the articles of incorporation that authorizes the corporation to engage in any activity permitted corporations by law.

generic name A term for a mark that has become a common term for a product line or type of service and therefore has lost its trademark protection.

genuineness of assent The requirement that a party's assent to a contract be genuine.

going public The process of a company's selling stock to the investing public for the first time (after filing a registration statement under applicable securities laws), thereby becoming a public corporation.

good faith Honesty in fact in the conduct or transaction concerned. The good faith test is subjective.

good faith purchaser for value A person to whom good title can be transferred from a person with voidable title. The real owner cannot reclaim goods from a good faith purchaser for value.

good faith subsequent lessee A person to whom a lease interest can be transferred from a person with voidable title. The real owner cannot reclaim the goods from the subsequent lessee until the lease expires.

goods Tangible things that are movable at the time of their identification to the contract.

good title Title that is free from any encumbrances or other defects that are not disclosed but would affect the value of the property.

government contractor defense A defense that says a contractor who was provided specifications by the government is not liable for any defect in the product that occurs as a result of those specifications.

government-owned (public) corporation A corporation whose shares are traded to and among the general public.

grace period A period of time after the actual expiration date of a payment but during which the insured can still pay an overdue premium without penalty.

greenmail The purchase by a target corporation of its stock from an actual or perceived tender offeror at a premium.

group boycott When two or more competitors at one level of distribution agree not to deal with others at another level of distribution.

guest statute Statute that provides that if a driver of a vehicle voluntarily and without compensation gives a ride to another person, the driver is not liable to the passenger for injuries caused by the driver's ordinary negligence.

hardship discharge A discharge granted if (1) the debtor fails to complete the payments due to unforeseeable circumstances, (2) the unsecured creditors have been paid as much as they would have been paid in a Chapter 7 liquidation proceeding, and (3) it is not practical to modify the plan.

Hart-Scott-Rodino Antitrust Improvement Act Requires certain firms to notify the FTC and the Justice Department in advance of a proposed merger. Unless the government challenges the proposed merger within thirty days, the merger may proceed.

hazardous waste Solid waste that may cause or significantly contribute to an increase in mortality or serious illness or pose a hazard to human health or the environment if improperly managed.

horizontal merger A merger between two or more companies that compete in the same business and geographical market.

horizontal restraint of trade A restraint of trade that occurs when two or more competitors at the same *level of distribution* enter into a contract, combination, or conspiracy to restrain trade.

hostile tender offer An offer to purchase shares made by a corporation desiring to merge with or acquire a target corporation directly to the shareholders of a target corporation.

Immigration Reform and Control Act of 1986 (IRCA) A federal statute that makes it unlawful for employers to hire illegal immigrants.

implied agency An agency that occurs when a principal and an agent do not expressly create an agency, but it is inferred from the conduct of the parties.

implied authorization Mode of acceptance that is implied from what is customary in similar transactions, usage of trade, or prior dealings between the parties.

implied exemptions Exemptions from antitrust laws that are implied by the federal courts.

implied powers Powers beyond express powers that allow a corporation to accomplish its corporate purpose.

implied warranties The law *implies* certain warranties on transferors of negotiable instruments. There are two types of implied warranties: transfer and presentment.

implied warranty of authority An agent who enters into a contract on behalf of another party impliedly warrants that he or she has the authority to do so.

implied warranty of fitness for a particular purpose A warranty that arises where a seller or lessor warrants that the goods will meet the buyer's or lessee's expressed needs.

implied warranty of fitness for human consumption A warranty that applies to food or drink consumed on or off the premises of restaurants, grocery stores, fast-food outlets, and vending machines.

implied warranty of habitability A warranty that provides that the leased premises must be fit, safe, and suitable for ordinary residential use.

implied warranty of merchantability Unless properly disclosed, a warranty is implied when sold or leased goods are fit for the ordinary purpose for which they are sold or leased, and other assurances.

imposter A person who impersonates a payee and induces a maker or drawer to issue an instrument in the payee's name and to give it to the imposter.

imposter rule A rule that says if an imposter forges the indorsement of the named payee, the drawer or maker is liable on the instrument and bears the loss.

imputed knowledge Knowledge attributed to a given person, especially because of the person's legal responsibility for another's conduct.

inaccessibility exception A rule that permits employees and union officials to engage in union solicitation on company property if the employees are beyond reach of reasonable union efforts to communicate with them.

incidental authority Authority needed to carry out actual or apparent authority.

incidental beneficiary A party who is unintentionally benefited by other people's contracts.

incorporation by reference When integration is made by express reference in one document that refers to and incorporates another document within it.

incorporator The person or persons, partnerships, or corporations that are responsible for incorporation of a corporation.

indenture agreement A contract between the corporation and the holder that contains the terms of a debt security.

independent contractor A person or business who is not an employee who is employed by a principal to perform a certain task on his behalf. "A person who contracts with another to do something for him who is not controlled by the other nor subject to the other's right to control with respect to his physical conduct in the performance of the undertaking" [Restatement (Second) of Agency].

indirect price discrimination A form of price discrimination (e.g., favorable credit terms) that is less readily apparent than direct forms of price discrimination.

inferior performance Occurs when a party fails to perform express or implied contractual obligations that impair or destroy the essence of the contract.

inherently dangerous activity An activity that can be carried out only by the exercise of special skill and care and that involves a grave risk of serious harm if done unskillfully or carelessly.

initial license fee A lump-sum payment for the privilege of being granted a franchise.

initial public offering (IPO) A company's first public sale of stock; the first offering of an issuer's equity securities to the public through a registration statement.

injunction A court order commanding or preventing an action.

innocent misrepresentation A false statement that the speaker or writer does not know is false; a misrepresentation that, although false, was not made fraudulently.

Insecticide, Fungicide, and Rodenticide Act A federal statute that requires pesticides, herbicides, fungicides, and rodenticides to be registered with the EPA; the EPA may deny, suspend, or cancel registration.

INS Form I-9 A form that must be filled out by all U.S. employers for each employee; states that the employer has inspected the employee's legal qualifications to work.

inside director A member of the board of directors who is also an officer of the corporation.

insider Someone who has knowledge of facts not available to the general public.

insider trading When an insider makes a profit by personally purchasing shares of the corporation prior to public release of favorable information or by selling shares of the corporation prior to the public disclosure of unfavorable information.

Insider Trading Sanctions Act of 1984 A federal statute that permits the SEC to obtain a civil penalty of up to three times the illegal benefits received from insider trading.

instrument Term that means *negotiable instrument.*

insurable interest A person who purchases insurance must have a personal interest in the insured item or person.

insurance A means for persons and businesses to protect themselves against the risk of loss.

insured The party who pays a premium to a particular insurance company for insurance coverage.

insurer The insurance company.

insurgent shareholder Shareholder that opposes the actions taken by the incumbent directors and management.

intangible property Rights that cannot be reduced to physical form such as stock certificates, certificates of deposit, bonds, and copyrights.

intellectual property rights Intellectual property rights, such as patents, copyrights, trademarks, trade secrets, trade names, and domain names are very valuable business assets. Federal and state laws protect intellectual property rights from misappropriation and infringement.

intended beneficiary A third party who is not in privity of contract but who has rights under the contract and can enforce the contract against the obligor.

intentional misrepresentation (fraud or deceit) A harmfully and deceptive statement of fact.

intermediate scrutiny test Test that is applied to classifications based on protected classes other than race (e.g., sex, age).

International Court of Justice The judicial branch of the United Nations that is located in The Hague, the Netherlands. Also called the *World Court.*

international law Law that governs affairs between nations and that regulates transactions between individuals and businesses of different countries.

International Monetary Fund A UN specialized agency established to stabilize international exchange rates and promote balanced trade.

in transit A state in which goods are in the possession of a bailee or carrier and not in the hands of the buyer, seller, lessee, or lessor.

intrastate offering exemption An exemption from registration that permits local businesses to raise capital from local investors to be used in the local economy without the need to register with the SEC.

invasion of the right to privacy A tort that constitutes the violation of a person's right to live his or her life without being subjected to unwarranted and undesired publicity.

investment bankers Independent securities companies that assist issuers in selling securities to the public.

investment contract A contract in which money is invested in a common enterprise with profits to come solely from the efforts of others; an agreement or transaction in which a party invests money in expectation of profits derived from the efforts of a promoter or other third party.

involuntary petition A petition filed by creditors of the debtor; alleges that the debtor is not paying his or her debts as they become due.

irrevocable agency An agency that the principal cannot terminate.

issued shares Shares that have been sold by the corporation.

issuer The business or party that sells securities to the public.

joint and several liability Liability that may be apportioned either among two or more parties or to only one or a few select members of the group, at the adversary's discretion. Thus, each liable party is individually responsible for the entire obligation, but paying party may have a right of contribution and indemnity from nonpaying parties.

joint liability Liability shared by two or more parties.

joint venture A voluntary association of two or more parties (natural persons, partnerships, corporations, or other legal entities) to conduct a single or isolated project with a limited duration.

judicial decisions and teachings The fourth source of international law, consisting of judicial decisions and writings of the most qualified legal scholars of the various nations involved in the dispute.

judicial dissolution Occurs when a corporation is dissolved by a court proceeding instituted by the state.

jurisdiction The authority of a court to hear a case.

key-person life insurance Life insurance purchased and paid for by a business that insures against the death of owners and other key executives and employees of the business.

Lanham Trademark Act (as amended) Federal statute that (1) establishes the requirements for obtaining a federal mark and (2) protects marks from infringement.

lapse of time An offer terminates when a stated time period expires. If no time is stated, an offer terminates after a reasonable time.

lease fees Payment for any land or equipment leased from the franchisor, billed either as a flat monthly or annual fee or as a percentage of gross sales or other agreed-upon amount.

legal entity (legal person) Legal existence; an entity other than a natural person that can function legally, sue, be sued, act through agents, etc.

license A contract that transfers limited rights in intellectual property and informational rights. Grants a person the right to enter upon another's property for a specified and usually short period of time.

licensee The party who is granted limited rights in or access to intellectual property or informational rights owned by the licensor.

licensee's damages Monetary damages that a licensee may recover from a licensor who breaches a contract.

licensing An arrangement where a party that owns trademarks and other intellectual property (the *licensor*) contracts to permit another party (the *licensee*) to use these trademarks and intellectual property in the distribution of goods, services, software, and digital information.

licensing agreement Detailed and comprehensive written agreement between the licensor and licensee that sets forth the express terms of their agreement.

licensing statute Statute that requires a person or business to obtain a license from the government prior to engaging in a specified occupation or activity.

licensor The owner of intellectual property or informational rights who transfers rights in the property or information to the licensee.

licensor's damages If a licensee breaches a contract, the licensor may sue and recover monetary damages from the licensee caused by the breach.

life insurance A form of insurance in which the insurer is obligated to pay a specific sum of money upon the death of the insured.

limited duty of care A member or manager of an LLC is not liable to the LLC for injuries caused to the LLC by his or her ordinary negligence. The ordinarily negligent member or manager and the LLC on whose behalf the member or manager was acting when the negligent act occurred are liable to the injured third party.

limited liability Members are liable for the LLC's debts, obligations, and liabilities only to the extent of their capital contributions. Liability that shareholders have only to the extent of their capital contribution. Shareholders are generally not personally liable for debts and obligations of the corporation.

limited liability company (LLC) A hybrid form of business that has the attributes of both partnerships and corporations.

limited liability company codes State statutes that regulate the formation, operation, and dissolution of limited liability companies.

limited liability limited partnership (LLLP) A special type of limited partnership that has both general partners and limited partners where both the general and limited partners have limited liability and are not personally liable for the debts of the LLLP.

limited liability of limited partners The limited liability of limited partners of a limited partnership only up to their capital contributions to the limited partnership; limited partners are not personally liable for the debts and obligations of the limited partnership.

limited liability of shareholders A general rule of corporate law that provides that generally shareholders are liable only to the extent of their capital contributions for the contracts and debts of their corporation and are not personally liable for the contracts and debts of the corporation.

limited liability partnership (LLP) A special form of partnership where all partners are limited partners and there are no general partners.

limited partners Partners in a limited partnership who invest capital but do not participate in management and are not personally liable for partnership debts beyond their capital contribution.

limited partnership A special form of partnership that is formed only if certain formalities are followed. It has both general and limited partners.

limited partnership agreement A document that sets forth the rights and duties of the general and limited parties; the terms and conditions regarding the operation, termination, and dissolution of the partnership; and so on.

liquidation preference The right to be paid a stated dollar amount if the corporation is dissolved and liquidated.

Magnuson–Moss Warranty Act A federal statute that regulates express full and limited warranties made by sellers and lessors.

manager-managed LLC An LLC that has designated in its articles of organization that it is a manager-managed LLC.

mark The collective name for trademarks, service marks, certification marks, and collective marks that all can be trademarked.

market extension merger A merger between two companies in similar fields whose sales do not overlap.

material alteration A partial defense against enforcement of a negotiable instrument by an HDC. An HDC can enforce an altered instrument in the original amount for which the drawer wrote the check.

maximizing profits A theory of social responsibility that says a corporation owes a duty to take actions that maximize profits for shareholders.

McCarran-Ferguson Act A federal statute that gave the regulation of insurance to the states.

means test A new test added by the 2005 act that applies to debtors who have family incomes that exceed the state's median income for families of the same size.

Medicinal Device Amendment to the FDCA An amendment enacted in 1976 that gives the FDA authority to regulate medicinal devices and equipment.

meeting of the creditors A meeting of the creditors in a bankruptcy case that must occur not less than ten days nor more than thirty days after the court grants an order for relief.

meeting the competition defense A defense provided in Section 2(b) that says a seller may lawfully engage in price discrimination to meet a competitor's price.

member An owner of an LLC.

member-managed LLC An LLC that has not designated that it is a manager-managed LLC in its articles of organization.

merchant A person who (1) deals in the goods of the kind involved in the transaction or (2) by his or her occupation holds himself or herself out as having knowledge or skill peculiar to the goods involved in the transaction.

Merchant Court The separate set of courts established to administer the "law of merchants."

merger Occurs when one corporation is absorbed into another corporation and ceases to exist.

Miranda rights A warning that must be read to a criminal suspect before he or she is interrogated by the police or other government officials.

misappropriation theory The doctrine that a person who wrongfully uses confidential information to buy or sell securities in violation of a duty owed to the one who is the information source is guilty of securities fraud.

misuse A defense that relieves a seller of product liability if the user abnormally misused the product. Products must be designed to protect against foreseeable misuse.

mobile sources Sources of air pollution such as automobiles, trucks, buses, motorcycles, and airplanes.

Model Business Corporation Act (MBCA) A model act drafted in 1950 that was intended to provide a uniform law for regulation of corporations.

Model Nonprofit Corporation Act A model act governing the formation, operation, and termination of not-for-profit corporations.

money A "medium of exchange authorized or adopted by a domestic or foreign government" [UCC 1-201(24)].

monopoly power The power to control prices or exclude competition measured by the market share the defendant possesses in the relevant market.

multilateral treaty A compact involving many sides, persons, firms, or nations.

multinational corporation A company with operations in two or more countries, generally allowing it to transfer funds and products according to price and demand conditions, subject to risks such as changes in exchange rates or political instability.

municipal corporation A city, town, or other local political entity formed by charter from the state and having the autonomous authority to administer the state's local affairs; especially a public corporation created for political purposes and endowed with political powers to be exercised for the public good in the administration of local civil government.

National Ambient Air Quality Standards (NAAQS) Standards for certain pollutants set by the EPA that protect (1) human beings (primary) and (2) vegetation, matter, climate, visibility, and economic values (secondary).

national courts The courts of individual nations.

National Environmental Policy Act (NEPA) A federal statute enacted in 1969 that mandates that the federal government consider the adverse impact a federal government action would have on the environment before the action is implemented.

National Labor Relations Board (NLRB) A federal administrative agency that oversees union elections, prevents employers and unions from engaging in illegal and unfair labor practices, and enforces and interprets certain federal labor laws.

negligence A tort related to defective products in which the defendant has breached a duty of due care and caused harm to the plaintiff. Failure of a corporate director or officer to exercise the duty of care while conducting the corporation's business. Negligence in which the accountant breaches the duty of reasonable care, knowledge, skill, and judgment that he or she owes to a client when providing auditing and other accounting services to the client. Also known as accountant malpractice.

nonaccredited investor These investors are usually friends and family members of the insiders. They may purchase securities pursuant to a private placement exemption.

nonconvertible preferred stock A security (bond or preferred stock) that may be exchanged by the owner for another security, esp. common stock from the same company at a fixed price on a specified date.

noncumulative preferred stock Preferred stock that must receive dividends in full before common shareholders may receive any dividend.

nonparticipating preferred stock Preferred stock that does not give the shareholder the right to additional earnings—usually surplus common-stock dividends—beyond those stated in the preferred contract.

nonprice vertical restraints Restraints of trade that are unlawful under Section 1 of the Sherman Act if their anticompetitive effects outweigh their procompetitive effects.

nonprofit corporation A corporation that is formed to operate charitable institutions, colleges, universities, and other not-for-profit entities.

nonredeemable preferred stock Preferred stock that is not redeemable.

North American Free Trade Agreement (NAFTA) An international treaty that creates a regional free-trade zone consisting of the United States, Canada, and Mexico.

note An instrument that evidences the borrower's debt to the lender; debt security with a maturity of five years or less.

note and deed of trust An alternative to a mortgage in some states.

not-for-profit corporation A corporation organized for some purpose other than making a profit.

notice of a shareholder's meeting A corporation is required to give the shareholders written notice of the place, day, and time of annual and special meetings.

notice of dissolution The dissolution of a partnership terminates the partners' actual authority to enter into contracts or otherwise act on behalf of the partnership. A notice of dissolution must be given to certain third parties.

novation The substitution by mutual agreement of one debtor for another or of one creditor for another, whereby the old debt is extinguished.

Nuclear Waste Policy Act of 1982 A federal statute that says the federal government must select and develop a permanent site for the disposal of nuclear waste.

nuncupative will Oral will that is made before a witness during the testator's last illness. Also called a *dying declaration* or *deathbed will*.

Nutrition Labeling and Education Act A federal statute that requires food manufacturers and processors to provide nutritional information on most foods and prohibits them from making scientifically unsubstantiated health claims.

Occupational Safety and Health Act A federal act enacted in 1970 that promotes safety in the workplace.

Occupational Safety and Health Administration (OSHA) A federal administrative agency that is empowered to enforce the Occupational Safety and Health Act.

offering statement A document, similar to a prospectus, that provides information about a private securities offering.

officers Employees of the corporation who are appointed by the board of directors to manage the day-to-day operations of the corporation.

Older Workers Benefit Protection Act (OWBPA) A federal act that prohibits age discrimination in employee benefits.

"on them" item A check presented for payment by the payee or holder where the depository bank and the payor bank are not the same bank.

"on us" item A check that is presented for payment where the depository bank is also the payor bank. That is, the drawer and payee or holder have accounts at the same bank.

operating agreement An agreement entered into among members that governs the affairs and business of the LLC and the relations among members, managers, and the LLC.

order for relief The filing of either a voluntary petition, an unchallenged involuntary petition, or a grant of an order after a trial of a challenged involuntary petition.

ordinary bailments (1) Bailments for the sole benefit of the bailor, (2) bailments for the sole benefit of the bailee, and (3) bailments for the mutual benefit of the bailor and bailee.

organizational meeting A meeting that must be held by the initial directors of the corporation after the articles of incorporation are filed.

outside director A member of the board of directors who is not an officer of the corporation.

outstanding shares Shares of stock that are in shareholder hands.

overtime pay Under the FLSA, an employer cannot require nonexempt employees to work more than forty hours per week unless they are paid overtime pay of one-and-a-half times their regular pay for each hour worked in excess of forty hours that week. Each week is treated separately.

P.A. (professional association) A group of professionals organized to practice their profession together, although not necessarily in corporate or partnership form.

Pac-Man tender offer Occurs when a corporation that is the target of a tender offer makes a *reverse tender offer* for the stock of the tender offeror.

palming off Unfair competition that occurs when a company tries to pass one of its products as that of a rival.

panel A panel of three WTO judges that hears trade disputes between member nations and issues a "panel report."

parent corporation A corporation owning more than 50 percent of the voting shares of another corporation.

partially disclosed principal A principal whose existence—but not actual identity—is revealed by the agent to a third party.

participating preferred stock Stock that allows the stockholder to participate in the profits of the corporation along with the common stockholders.

partnership agreement A written agreement that partners sign. Also called *articles of partnership.*

partnership at will A partnership with no fixed duration.

partnership for a term A partnership with a fixed duration.

part performance A doctrine that allows the court to order an oral contract for the sale of land or transfer of another interest in real property to be specifically performed if it has been partially performed and performance is necessary to avoid injustice.

Patent and Trademark Office (PTO) A federal administrative agency that reviews patent applications and grants patents.

patent infringement Unauthorized use of another's patent. A patent holder may recover damages and other remedies against a patent infringer.

perfection by possession of the collateral If a secured creditor has physical possession of the collateral, no financing statement has to be filed; the creditor's possession is sufficient to put other potential creditors on notice of his or her secured interest in the property.

perfection of a security interest Establishes the right of a secured creditor against other creditors who claim an interest in the collateral.

permanent trustee A legal representative of the bankruptcy debtor's estate, usually an accountant or lawyer; elected at the first meeting of the creditors.

per se rule A rule that is applicable to those restraints of trade considered inherently anticompetitive. Once this determination is made, the court will not permit any defenses or justifications to save it.

personal guarantee Where a creditor may require a partner to personally guarantee the repayment of the loan in order to extend credit.

personal liability The kind of responsibility for the performance of an obligation that exposes the personal (not just business) assets of the person to the payment of the obligation.

picketing The action of strikers walking in front of the employer's premises carrying signs announcing their strike.

piercing the corporate veil A doctrine that says if a shareholder dominates a corporation and uses it for improper purposes, a court of equity can disregard the corporate entity and hold the shareholder personally liable for the corporation's debts and obligations.

plan of reorganization A plan that sets forth a proposed new capital structure for the debtor to have when it emerges from reorganization bankruptcy. The debtor has the exclusive right to file the first plan of reorganization; any party of interest may file a plan thereafter.

plant life and vegetation Real property that is growing in or on the surface of the land.

point sources Sources of water pollution such as paper mills, manufacturing plants, electric utility plants, and sewage plants.

poison pill A corporation's defense against an unwanted takeover bid whereby shareholders are granted the right to acquire equity or debt securities at a favorable price to increase the bidder's acquisition costs.

possession A lease grants the tenant *exclusive possession* of the leased premises for the term of the lease or until the tenant defaults on the obligations under the lease.

Postal Reorganization Act An act that makes the mailing of unsolicited merchandise an unfair trade practice.

posteffective period The period of time that begins when the registration statement becomes effective and runs until the issuer either sells all of the offered securities or withdraws them from sale.

pour-over will A will that is necessary to distribute any of the grantor's property not in the living trust at the time of the grantor's death.

power of attorney An express agency agreement that is often used to give an agent the power to sign legal documents on behalf of the principal.

powers of an LLC An LLC has the same powers as an individual to do all things necessary or convenient to carry on its business or affairs

preferential lien Occurs when (1) a debtor gives an unsecured creditor a secured interest in property within ninety days before the filing of a petition in bankruptcy, (2) the transfer is made for a preexisting debt, and (3) the creditor would receive more because of this lien than it would as an unsecured creditor.

preferential transfer Occurs when (1) a debtor transfers property to a creditor within ninety days before the filing of a petition in bankruptcy, (2) the transfer is made for a preexisting debt, and (3) the creditor would receive more from the transfer than it would from Chapter 7 liquidation.

preferential transfer to an insider A transfer of property by an insolvent debtor to an "insider" within one year before the filing of a petition in bankruptcy.

preferred stock A type of equity security that is given certain preferences and rights over common stock.

preferred stock certificate A document that represents a shareholder's investment in preferred stock in the corporation.

preferred stockholder A person who owns preferred stock.

prefiling period A period of time that begins when the issuer first contemplates issuing the securities and ends when the registration statement is filed. The issuer may not condition the market during this period.

Pregnancy Discrimination Act Amendment to Title VII that forbids employment discrimination because of "pregnancy, childbirth, or related medical conditions."

premium The money paid to the insurance company for insurance coverage.

pretrial hearing A hearing before the trial in order to facilitate the settlement of a case. Also called a *settlement conference*.

price-fixing Occurs where competitors in the same line of business agree to set the price of the goods or services they sell: raising, depressing, fixing, pegging, or stabilizing the price of a commodity or service.

principal A person who authorizes an agent to sign a negotiable instrument on his or her behalf. The party who employs another person to act on his or her behalf.

principal–agent relationship An employer hires an employee and gives that employee authority to act and enter into contracts on his or her behalf.

priority The order in which conflicting claims of creditors in the same collateral are solved.

private corporation A corporation formed to conduct privately owned business.

private placement exemption An exemption from registration that permits issuers to raise capital from an unlimited number of accredited investors and no more than thirty-five nonaccredited investors without having to register the offering with the SEC.

Private Securities Litigation Reform Act of 1995 A federal statute that limits a defendant's liability to its proportionate degree of fault.

probability of a substantial lessening of competition If there is a probability that a merger will substantially lessen competition or create a monopoly, the court may prevent the merger under Section 7 of the Clayton Act.

process of certification The accepting bank writes or stamps the word certified on the ordinary check of an account holder and sets aside funds from that account to pay the check.

processing plant franchise The franchisor provides a secret formula or process to the franchisee, and the franchisee manufactures the product and distributes it to retail dealers.

products liability The liability of manufacturers, sellers, and others for the injuries caused by defective products.

professional agent A person with considerable skill in his or her field.

professional corporation (P.C.) A corporation formed by lawyers, doctors, or other professionals.

professional malpractice The liability of a professional who breaches his or her duty of ordinary care.

professional malpractice insurance Insurance that insures professionals against liability for injuries caused by their negligence. Also known as malpractice insurance.

profit corporation A corporation created to conduct a business for profit that can distribute profits to shareholders in the form of dividends.

promissory note A two-party negotiable instrument that is an unconditional written promise by one party to pay money to another party.

promissory warranty Stipulates that the facts will continue to be true throughout the duration of the policy.

promoter A person or persons who organize and start the corporation, negotiate and enter into contracts in advance of its formation, find the initial investors to finance the corporation, and so forth.

promoter's contracts A collective term for such things as leases, sales contracts, contracts to purchase property, and employment contracts entered into by promoters on behalf of the proposed corporation prior to its actual incorporation.

proof of claim A document required to be filed by unsecured creditors that states the amount of their claim against the debtor.

pro rata rule A rule that says shares must be purchased on a *pro rata* basis if too many shares are tendered.

prospectus A written disclosure document that must be submitted to the SEC along with the registration statement and given to prospective purchasers of the securities.

provisional credit Occurs when a collecting bank gives credit to a check in the collection process prior to its final settlement. Provisional credits may be reversed if the check does not "clear."

proxy The written document that a shareholder signs authorizing another person to vote his or her shares at the shareholders' meetings in the event of the shareholder's absence.

proxy card A written document signed by a shareholder that authorizes another person to vote the shareholder's shares.

proxy contest When opposing factions of shareholders and managers solicit proxies from other shareholders, the side that receives the greatest number of votes wins the proxy contest.

proxy statement A document that fully describes (1) the matter for which the proxy is being solicited, (2) who is soliciting the proxy, and (3) any other pertinent information.

public corporation A corporation formed to meet a specific governmental or political purpose.

publicly held corporation A corporation that has many shareholders and whose securities are often traded on national stock exchanges.

purchase money security interest An interest a creditor automatically obtains when it extends credit to a consumer to purchase consumer goods.

purchasing property The most common method of acquiring title to personal property.

qualified immunity (restricted immunity) Immunity from civil liability for a public official who is performing a discretionary function, as long as the conduct does not violate clearly established constitutional or statutory rights.

qualified individual with a disability A person who (1) has a physical or mental impairment that substantially limits one or more of his or her major life activities, (2) has a record of such impairment, or (3) is regarded as having such impairment.

quorum The required number of shares that must be represented in person or by proxy to hold a shareholders' meeting. The RMBCA establishes a majority of outstanding shares as a quorum. The number of directors necessary to hold a board of directors meeting or transact business of the board.

Racketeer Influenced and Corrupt Organizations (RICO) Act Federal statute that authorizes civil lawsuits against defendants for engaging in a pattern of racketeering activities.

ratification The act of a minor after the minor has reached the age of majority by which he or she accepts a contract entered into when he or she was a minor. When a principal accepts an agent's unauthorized contract.

rational basis test Test that is applied to classifications not involving a suspect or protected class.

Rawls's social contract A moral theory that says each person is presumed to have entered into a social contract with all others in society to obey moral rules that are necessary for people to live in peace and harmony.

reaffirmation agreement An agreement entered into by a debtor with a creditor prior to discharge, whereby the debtor agrees to pay the creditor a debt that would otherwise be discharged in bankruptcy. Certain requirements must be met for a reaffirmation agreement to be enforced.

real defense A defense that can be raised against both holders and HDCs.

reasonable accommodations Title I requires an employer to make reasonable accommodations to individuals with disabilities that do not cause undue hardship to the employer. Reasonable accommodations may include making facilities readily accessible to individuals with disabilities, providing part-time or modified work schedules, acquiring equipment or devices, modifying examination and training materials, and providing qualified readers or interpreters.

reclamation The right of a seller or lessor to demand the return of goods from the buyer or lessee under specified situations.

recovery of damages A seller or lessor may recover damages measured as the difference between the contract price (or rent) and the market price (or rent) at the time and place the goods were to be delivered, plus incidental damages, from a buyer or lessee who repudiates the contract or wrongfully rejects tendered goods.

recovery of goods from an insolvent seller or lessor A buyer or lessee who has wholly or partially paid for goods before they are received may recover the goods from a seller or lessor who becomes insolvent within ten days after receiving the first payment; the buyer or lessee must tender the remaining purchase price or rent due under the contract.

recovery of lost profits If the recovery of damages would be inadequate to put the seller or lessor in as good a position as if the contract had been fully performed by the buyer or lessee, the seller or lessor may recover lost profits, plus an allowance for overhead and incidental damages, from the buyer or lessee.

recovery of the purchase price or rent A seller or lessor may recover the contracted-for purchase price or rent from the buyer or lessee (1) if the buyer or lessee fails to pay for accepted goods, (2) if the buyer or lessee breaches the contract and the seller or lessor cannot dispose of the goods, or (3) if the goods are damaged or lost after the risk of loss passes to the buyer or lessee.

redeemable preferred stock Stock that permits the corporation to buy back the preferred stock at some future date.

registered agent A person or corporation that is empowered to accept service of process on behalf of the corporation.

registration statement Document that an issuer of securities files with the SEC that contains required information about the issuer, the securities to be issued, and other relevant information.

regular meeting of a board of directors A meeting held by the board of directors at the time and place established in the bylaws.

Regulation A A regulation that permits the issuer to sell securities pursuant to a simplified registration process.

regulatory statute A licensing statute enacted to protect the public.

rejection of nonconforming goods If the goods or the seller's or lessor's tender of delivery fails to conform to the contract, the buyer or lessee may (1) reject the whole, (2) accept the whole, or (3) accept any commercial unit and reject the rest.

relevant geographical market A relevant market that is defined as the area in which the defendant and its competitors sell the product or service.

relevant product or service market A relevant market that includes substitute products or services that are reasonably interchangeable with the defendant's products or services.

relief from stay May be granted in situations involving depreciating assets where the secured property is not adequately protected during the bankruptcy proceedings; asked for by a secured creditor.

religious discrimination Discrimination against a person solely because of his or her religion or religious practices.

rent An agreed upon amount the tenant pays the landlord for the leased premises.

renunciation of authority The express or tacit abandonment of a right without transferring it to another.

replacement workers Workers who are hired to take the place of striking workers. They can be hired on either a temporary or permanent basis.

replevin An action by a buyer or lessor to recover scarce goods wrongfully withheld by a seller or lessor.

repossession A right granted to a secured creditor to take possession of the collateral upon default by the debtor.

resale price maintenance A *per se violation* of Section 1 of the Sherman Act; occurs when a party at one level of distribution enters into an agreement with a party at another level to adhere to a price schedule that either sets or stabilizes prices.

Resource Conservation and Recovery Act (RCRA) A federal statute that authorizes the EPA to regulate facilities that generate, treat, store, transport, and dispose of hazardous wastes.

respondent superior A rule that says an employer is liable for the tortious conduct of its employees or agents while they are acting within the scope of its authority.

restricted securities Securities that were issued for investment purposes pursuant to the intrastate, private placement, or small offering exemption.

retention of collateral If a secured creditor repossesses collateral upon a debtor's default, he or she may propose to retain the collateral in satisfaction of the debtor's obligation.

revenue-raising statute A licensing statute with the primary purpose of raising revenue for the government.

reverse discrimination Discrimination against a group that is usually thought of as a majority.

Revised Article 3 A comprehensive revision of the UCC law of negotiable instruments that reflects modern commercial practices.

Revised Model Business Corporation Act (RMBCA) A revision of the MBCA in 1984 that arranged the provisions of the act more logically, revised the language to be more consistent, and made substantial changes in the provisions.

Revised Uniform Limited Partnership Act (RULPA) A 1976 revision of the ULPA that provides a more modern, comprehensive law for the formation, operation, and dissolution of limited partnerships.

revocation of authority Termination of authority.

rider A separate document that will modify an existing insurance policy.

right of first refusal An agreement that requires a selling shareholder to offer his or her shares for sale to the other parties to the agreement before selling them to anyone else.

right of inspection A right that shareholders have to inspect the books and records of the corporation.

right of survivorship A joint tenant's right to succeed to the whole estate upon the death of the other joint tenant.

right to cover The right of a buyer or lessee to purchase or lease substitute goods if a seller or lessor fails to make delivery of the goods or repudiates the contract or if the buyer or lessee rightfully rejects the goods or justifiably revokes their acceptance.

right to cure A licensor has the right to cure a contract under certain conditions.

right to die A personal liberty protected by the U.S. Constitution.

right to dispose of goods The right to dispose of goods in a good faith and commercially reasonable manner. A seller or lessor who is in possession of goods at the time the buyer or lessee breaches or repudiates a contract may in good faith resell, release, or otherwise dispose of the goods in a commercially reasonable manner and recover damages, including incidental damages from the buyer or lessee.

right to participate in management A situation in which, unless otherwise agreed, each partner has a right to participate in the management of a partnership and has an equal vote on partnership matters.

right to reclaim goods The right of a seller or lessor to demand the return of goods from the buyer or lessee under specified situations.

right to recover goods from an insolvent seller or lessor The right of a buyer or lessee who has wholly or partially paid for goods before they are received to recover the goods from a seller or lessor who becomes insolvent within ten days after receiving the first payment; the buyer or lessee must tender the remaining purchase price or rent due under the contract.

right to recover the purchase price or rent A seller's or lessor's right to recover the contracted-for purchase price or rent from the buyer or lessee (1) if the buyer or lessee fails to pay for accepted goods, (2) if the buyer or lessee breaches the contract and the seller or lessor cannot dispose of the goods, or (3) if the goods are damaged or lost after the risk of loss passes to the buyer or lessee.

right to reject nonconforming goods or improperly tendered goods A situation in which a buyer or lessee rejects goods that do not conform to the contract. If the goods or the seller's or lessor's tender of delivery fails to conform to the contract, the buyer or lessee may (1) reject the whole, (2) accept the whole, or (3) accept any commercial unit and reject the rest.

right to stop delivery of goods in transit The right of a seller or lessor to stop delivery of goods in transit if he or she learns of the buyer's or lessee's insolvency or if the buyer or lessee repudiates the contract, fails to make payment when due, or gives the seller or lessor some other right to withhold the goods.

right to withhold delivery A seller's or lessor's right to refuse to deliver goods to a buyer or lessee upon breach of a sales or lease contract by the buyer or lessee or the insolvency of the buyer or lessee.

Robinson-Patman Act Section 2 of the Clayton Act is commonly referred to by this name.

royalty fee Compensation for the use of property, expressed as a percentage of the receipts or as an account per unit produced; a payment made to an author or composer by a licensee, copyright holder, or assignee for each copy of his or her work sold; a payment made to an inventor for each article sold under his or her patent.

Rule 10b-5 A rule adopted by the SEC to clarify the reach of Section 10(b) against deceptive and fraudulent activities in the purchase and sale of securities.

rule of reason A rule that holds that only unreasonable restraints of trade violate Section 1 of the Sherman Act. The court must examine the pro- and anticompetitive effects of the challenged restraint.

rules and regulations Adopted by administrative agencies to interpret the statutes that they are authorized to enforce.

Sabbath law A law that prohibits or limits the carrying on of certain secular activities on Sundays.

Safe Drinking Water Act A federal statute enacted in 1974 and amended in 1986 that authorizes the EPA to establish national primary drinking water standards.

sale The passing of title from a seller to a buyer for a price. Also called a *conveyance*.

sale on approval A type of sale in which there is no actual sale unless and until the buyer accepts the goods.

sale or lease of assets A contract in which the seller, in consideration of the payment or promise of payment of a certain price by the buyer, transfers title and possession of the thing sold to the buyer.

sale or return A contract that says that the seller delivers goods to a buyer with the understanding that the buyer may return them if they are not used or resold within a stated or reasonable period of time.

sale proceeds The resulting assets from the sale, exchange, or disposal of collateral subject to a security agreement.

Sarbanes-Oxley Act A federal act that imposes new rules that affect public accountants. The act: created the Public Company Accounting Oversight Board (PCAOB); requires public accounting firms to register with the PCAOB; separates audit services and certain nonaudit services provided by accountants to clients; requires an audit partner of the accounting firm to supervise an audit and approve an audit report prepared by the firm and requires a second parent of the accounting firm to review and approve the audit report; and prohibits employment of an accountant by a previous audit client for certain positions for a period of one year following the audit.

scienter Means international conduct. Scienter is required for there to be a violation of Section 10(b) and Rule 10b-5.

S corporation A corporation whose income is taxed through its shareholders rather than through the corporation itself. Only corporations with a limited number of shareholders can elect S-corporations tax status under Subchapter S of the Internal Revenue Code.

search warrant A warrant issued by a court that authorizes the police to search a designated place for specified contraband, articles, items, or documents. The search warrant must be based on probable cause.

secondary boycott picketing A type of picketing where unions try to bring pressure against an employer by picketing his or her suppliers or customers.

"secondary meaning" When an ordinary term has become a brand name.

secretary-general The chief administrative officer of the United Nations, nominated by the Security Council and elected by the General Assembly.

secret profits Partners may not make secret profits from partnership business.

Section 1 of the Sherman Act Prohibits *contracts*, *combinations*, and *conspiracies* in restraint of trade. Prohibits tying arrangements involving goods, services, intangible property, and real property.

Section 2 of the Sherman Act Prohibits the act of monopolization and attempts or conspiracies to monopolize trade.

Section 2(a) of the Robinson-Patman Act Prohibits direct and indirect price discrimination by sellers of a commodity of a like grade and quality where the effect of such discrimination may be to substantially lessen competition or to tend to create a monopoly in any line of commerce.

Section 2(b) of the Robinson-Patman Act A defense that provides that a seller may lawfully engage in price discrimination to meet a competitor's price.

Section 3 of the Clayton Act Prohibits tying arrangements involving sales and leases of goods.

Section 5 of the FTC Act Prohibits *unfair and deceptive* practices.

Section 7 of the Clayton Act A section that provides that is it unlawful for a person or business to acquire the stock or assets of another "where in any line of commerce or in any activity affecting commerce in any section of the country, the effect of such acquisition may be substantially to lessen competition, or to tend to create a monopoly."

Section 7 of the NLRA A law that gives employees the right to join together and form a union.

Section 8(a) of the NLRA A law that makes it an unfair labor practice for an employer to interfere with, coerce, or restrain employees from exercising their statutory right to form and join unions.

Section 8(b) of the NLRA A law that prohibits unions from engaging in unfair labor practices that interfere with a union election.

Section 10(b) A provision of the Securities Exchange Act of 1934 that prohibits the use of manipulative and deceptive devices in the purchase or sale of securities in contravention of the rules and regulations prescribed by the SEC.

Section 11 A provision of the Securities Act of 1933 that imposes civil liability on persons who intentionally defraud investors by making misrepresentations or omissions of material facts in the registration statement or who are negligent for not discovering the fraud.

Section 11(a) A section of the Securities Act of 1933 that imposes civil liability on accountants and others for (1) making misstatements or omissions of material facts in a registration statement or (2) failing to find such misstatements or omissions.

Section 12 A provision of the Securities Act of 1933 that imposes civil liability on any person who violates the provisions of Section 5 of the act.

Section 14(a) Provision of the Securities Exchange Act of 1934 that gives the SEC the authority to regulate the solicitation of proxies.

Section 14(e) A provision of the Williams Act that prohibits fraudulent, deceptive, and manipulative practices in connection with a tender offer.

Section 16(a) A section of the Securities Exchange Act of 1934 that defines any person who is an executive officer, a director, or a 10 percent shareholder of an equity security of a reporting company as a *statutory insider* for Section 16 purposes.

Section 16(b) A section of the Securities Exchange Act of 1934 that requires that any profits made by a statutory insider on transactions involving *short-swing profits* belong to the corporation.

Section 18(a) A section of the Securities Exchange Act of 1934 that imposes civil liability on any person who makes false or misleading statements in any application, report, or document filed with the SEC.

Section 24 A section of the Securities Act of 1933 that makes it a criminal offense for any person to (1) willfully make any untrue statement of material fact in a registration statements filed with the SEC, (2) omit any material fact necessary to ensure that the statements made in the registration statement are not misleading, or (3) willfully violate any other provision of the Securities Act of 1933 or rule or regulation adopted thereunder.

Section 32 A provision of the Securities Exchange Act of 1934 that imposes criminal liability on any person who willfully violates the 1934 act or the rules or regulations adopted thereunder.

Section 32(a) A section of the Securities Exchange Act of 1934 that makes it a criminal offense for any person willfully and knowingly to make or cause to be made any false or misleading statement in any application, report, or other document required to be filed with the SEC pursuant to the Securities Exchange Act of 1934 or any rule or regulation adopted thereunder.

Section 552 of the Restatement (Second) of Torts A rule that says that an accountant is liable only for negligence to third parties who are members of a limited class of intended users of the client's financial statements. It provides a broader standard for holding accountants liable to third parties for negligence than does the ultramares doctrine.

section of the country A division of the country that is based on the relevant geographical market; the geographical area that will feel the direct and immediate effects of the merger.

secured transaction A transaction that is created when a creditor makes a loan to a debtor in exchange for the debtor's pledge of personal property as security.

Securities Act of 1933 A federal statute that primarily regulates the issuance of securities by corporations, partnerships, associations, and individuals.

Securities and Exchange Commission (SEC) Federal administrative agency that is empowered to administer federal securities laws. The SEC can adopt rules and regulations to interpret and implement federal securities laws.

Securities Exchange Act of 1934 A federal statute that primarily regulates the trading in securities.

security (1) An interest or instrument that is common stock, preferred stock, a bond, a debenture, or a warrant; (2) an interest or instrument that is expressly mentioned in securities acts; and (3) an investment contract.

security agreement The agreement between the debtor and the secured party that creates or provides for a security interest.

self-dealing If the directors or officers engage in purchasing, selling, or leasing of property with the corporation, the contract must be fair to the corporation; otherwise, it is voidable by the corporation. The contract or transaction is enforceable if it has been fully disclosed and approved.

Self-Employment Contributions Act A federal act that says self-employed persons must pay Social Security taxes equal to the combined employer-employee amount.

seller's or lessor's cancellation A seller or lessor has the right to cancel a sales or lease contract if the buyer or lessee rejects or revokes acceptance of the goods, fails to pay for the goods, or repudiates the contract in part or in whole.

service mark A mark that distinguishes the services of the holder from those of its competitors.

sex discrimination Discrimination against a person solely because of his or her gender.

sexual harassment Lewd remarks, touching, intimidation, posting pinups, and other verbal or physical conduct of a sexual nature that occurs on the job.

share exchange When one corporation acquires all the shares of another corporation and both corporations retain their separate legal existence.

shareholder A person who owns shares of stock in a corporation or joint-stock company.

shareholder resolution A resolution submitted by a shareholder to other shareholders provided he or she meets certain requirements set out in the Securities Exchange Act of 1934 and SEC rules adopted thereunder. The SEC determines if a shareholder proposal qualifies to be submitted to other shareholders for vote.

shareholder voting agreement Agreement between two or more shareholders agreeing on how they will vote their shares.

short-form merger A merger between a parent corporation and a subsidiary corporation that does not require the vote of the shareholders of either corporation or the board of directors of the subsidiary corporation.

short-swing profits Profits made by an insider through the sale or other disposition of corporate stock within six months after purchase.

Small Corporate Offering Registration (SCOR) Form The SCOR Form—Form U-7—is a question-and-answer disclosure form that businesses can complete and file with the SEC if they plan on raising $1 million or less from the public issue of securities.

small offering exemption For the sale of securities not exceeding $1 million during a twelve-month period.

social host liability Rule that provides that social hosts are liable for injuries caused by guests who become intoxicated at a social function. States vary as to whether they have this rule in effect.

Social Security Federal system that provides limited retirement and death benefits to covered employees and their dependents.

sole proprietor An owner; one who runs a business.

sole proprietorship A form of business where the owner is actually the business; the business is not a separate legal entity.

sources of international law Those things that international tribunals rely on in settling international disputes.

special bailees Includes common carriers, warehouse companies, and innkeepers.

special meeting of a board of directors A meeting convened by the board of directors to discuss new shares, merger proposals, hostile takeover attempts, and so forth.

special power of attorney A power of attorney that limits the agent's authority to only a specified matter.

special shareholders' meetings Meetings of shareholders that may be called to consider and vote on important or emergency issues, such as a proposed merger or amending the articles of incorporation.

specific duty An OSHA standard that addresses a safety problem of a specific duty nature (e.g., requirement for a safety guard on a particular type of equipment).

specific government regulation Government regulation that applies to a specific industry (e.g., telecommunications laws).

stakeholder interest A theory of social responsibility that says a corporation must consider the effects its actions have on persons other than its stockholders.

standstill agreement Any agreement to refrain from taking further action; esp., an agreement by which a party agrees to refrain from further attempts to take over a corporation (as by making no tender offer) for a specified period or by which financial institutions agree not to call bonds or loans when due.

state action exemptions Business activities that are mandated by state law are exempt from federal antitrust laws.

state antitakeover statutes Statutes enacted by state legislatures that protect corporations incorporated in or doing business in the state from hostile takeovers.

statement of disassociation A document filed with the secretary of state that gives constructive notice that a member has disassociated from an LLC.

stationary sources Sources of air pollution such as industrial plants, oil refineries, and public utilities.

statute of repose A statute that limits the seller's liability to a certain number of years from the date when the product was first sold.

statutory exemptions Exemptions from antitrust laws that are expressly provided in statutes enacted by Congress.

stock dividend Additional shares of stock paid as a dividend.

stopping delivery of goods in transit A seller or lessor may stop delivery of goods in transit if he or she learns of the buyer's or lessee's insolvency or if the buyer or lessee repudiates the contract, fails to make payment when due, or gives the seller or lessor some other right to withhold the goods.

straight voting Each shareholder votes the number of shares he or she owns on candidates for each of the positions open.

strategic alliance An arrangement between two or more companies in the same industry whereby they agree to ally themselves to accomplish a designated objective.

strict liability standard Common law duty that says innkeepers are liable for lost, damaged, or stolen goods of guests even if they were not at fault for the loss.

strict or absolute liability Standard for imposing criminal liability without a finding of *mens rea* (intent).

strict scrutiny test Test that is applied to classifications based on race.

strike A cessation of work by union members in order to obtain economic benefits or correct an unfair labor practice.

subfranchisor One who grants a franchise

subject matter jurisdiction Jurisdiction over the subject matter of a lawsuit.

subrogation If an insurance company pays a claim to an insured for liability or property damage caused by a third party, the insurer succeeds to the right of the insured to recover from the third party.

subsidiary corporation A corporation in which another corporation, the parent, owns at least the majority of the shares and thus has control.

Sunnah Habit, practice, usual custom.

supramajority Greater than the majority.

supramajority voting requirement A requirement that a greater than majority of shares constitutes a quorum of the vote of the shareholders.

surety The third person who agrees to be liable in a surety arrangement.

surety arrangement An arrangement where a third party promises to be *primarily* liable with the borrower for the payment of the borrower's debt.

surviving corporation A corporation that acquires the assets and liabilities of another corporation by a merger or takeover.

taking possession A method of acquiring ownership of unowned personal property.

target corporation The corporation that is proposed to be acquired in a tender offer situation.

tax A charge, usually monetary, imposed by the government on persons, entities, transactions, or property to yield public revenue.

tenant in partnership A special legal status that exists only in a partnership. Upon the death of a partner, the deceased partner's right in specific partnership property vests in the remaining partner or partners; it does not pass to the deceased partner's heirs or next of kin.

tender offer An offer that an acquirer makes directly to a target corporation's shareholders in an effort to acquire the target corporation.

tender offeror The party that makes a tender offer.

termination The ending of a corporation that occurs only after the winding-up of the corporation's affairs, the liquidation of its assets, and the distribution of the proceeds to the claimants.

termination by acts of the parties An agency may be terminated by the following acts of the parties: (1) mutual agreement, (2) lapse of time, (3) purpose achieved, and (4) occurrence of a specified event.

termination by impossibility When agency relationship terminates because a situation arises that makes its fulfillment impossible.

termination by operation of law An agency is terminated by operation of law, including: (1) death of the principal or agent, (2) insanity of the principal or agent, (3) bankruptcy of the principal, (4) impossibility of performance, (5) changed circumstances, and (6) war between the principal's and agent's countries.

termination statement A document filed by the secured party that ends a secured interest because the debt has been paid.

term LLC An LLC that has a specified term of duration.

tippee The person who receives material nonpublic information from a tipper.

tipper A person who discloses material nonpublic information to another person.

Title I Title I of the ADA requires an employer to make reasonable accommodations to employees with disabilities that do not cause undue hardship to the employer.

Title I of the Landrum-Griffin Act Referred to as labor's "bill of rights" that gives each union member equal rights and privileges to nominate candidates for union office, vote in elections, and participate in membership meetings.

Title III of the ADA A title of the ADA that prohibits discrimination on the basis of disability in places of public accommodation operated by private entities.

Title VII of the Civil Rights Act of 1964 (Fair Employment Practices Act) Intended to eliminate job discrimination based on five protected classes: *race, color, religion, sex,* or *national origin.*

Torah Judaism's most holy book; Torah refers to both Written Torah (Five Books of Moses, Prophets, Writings) and Oral Torah (Talmud).

tort A wrong. There are three categories: (1) intentional torts, (2) unintentional torts (negligence), and (3) strict liability.

tortfeasor A person who has committed a tort; a wrongdoer.

Toxic Substances Control Act A federal statute enacted in 1976 that requires manufacturers and processors to test new chemicals to determine their effect on human health and the environment before the EPA will allow them to be marketed.

trade dress Federal protection of the look and feel of a product, a product's packaging, or a service establishment.

trademark A distinctive mark, symbol, name, word, motto, or device that identifies the goods of a particular business.

trademark infringement Unauthorized use of another's mark. The holder may recover damages and other remedies from the infringer.

trademark or service mark A distinctive mark, symbol, name, word, motto, or device that identifies the goods or services of a particular franchisor.

trade name A name used in trade to designate a particular business.

trade secret A product formula, pattern, design, compilation of data, customer list, or other business secret. An idea that makes a franchise successful but that does not qualify for trademark, patent, or copyright protection.

transnational corporation A company with operations in two or more countries, generally allowing it to transfer funds and products according to price and demand conditions, subject to risks such as changes in exchange rates or political instability.

traveler's check A form of check sold by banks and other issuers. Traveler's checks are issued without a named payee. The purchaser fills in the payee's name when he or she uses the check to purchase goods or services.

treasury shares Shares of stock repurchased by the company itself.

treaties The first source of international law, consisting of agreements or contracts between two or more nations that are formally signed by an authorized representative and ratified by the supreme power of each nation.

treaty A compact made between two or more nations.

treaty clause The constitutional provision giving the president the power to make treaties, with the advice and consent of the Senate.

trespass to land A tort that interferes with an owner's right to exclusive possession of land.

trespass to personal property A tort that occurs whenever one person injures another person's personal property or interferes with that person's enjoyment of his or her personal property.

trial briefs Documents submitted by the parties' attorneys to the judge that contain legal support for their side of the case.

tying arrangement A restraint of trade where a seller refuses to sell one product to a customer unless the customer agrees to purchase a second product from the seller.

ultramares doctrine A rule that says that an accountant is liable only for negligence to third parties who are in privity of contract or in a privity-like relationship.

***ultra vires* act** An act by a corporation that is beyond its express or implied powers.

unauthorized signature A signature made by a purported agent without authority from the purported principal.

undisclosed agency An agency in which a contracting third party does not know of either the existence of the agency or the principal's identity.

undisclosed principal One who acts through an agent at a time when a third party has no notice that the agent is acting for a principal.

undue burden Employers are not obligated to provide accommodations that would impose an undue burden—that is, actions that would require significant difficulty or expense.

unemployment compensation Payments paid under federal and state laws to assist workers who are temporarily unemployed.

unfair advantage theory A theory that holds that a merger may not give the acquiring firm an unfair advantage over its competitors in finance, marketing, or expertise.

unfair competition Competition that violates the law.

Uniform Commercial Code (UCC) Comprehensive statutory scheme that includes laws that cover aspects of commercial transactions.

Uniform Computer Information Transactions Act (UCITA) Model state law that creates contract law for the licensing of information technology rights.

Uniform Franchise Offering Circular (UFOC) A uniform disclosure document that requires the franchisor to make specific presale disclosures to prospective franchisees.

Uniform Limited Liability Company Act (ULLCA) A model act that provides comprehensive and uniform laws for the formation, operation, and dissolution of LLCs.

Uniform Limited Partnership Act (ULPA) A model law promulgated in 1916 for adoption by state legislatures to govern the relationship between the partners of a limited partnership.

Uniform Partnership Act (UPA) Model act that codifies partnership law. Most states have adopted the UPA in whole or part.

unilateral refusal to deal A unilateral choice by one party not to deal with another party. This does not violate Section 1 of the Sherman Act because there is not concerted action.

union shop An establishment where an employee must join the union within a certain number of days after being hired.

unissued shares Shares of a corporation that have been authorized but are not outstanding.

unit A single thing of any kind; a fixed quantity.

United Nations An international organization created by a multilateral treaty in 1945 to promote social and economic cooperation among nations and to protect human rights.

United Nations Educational, Scientific, and Cultural Organization (UNESCO) The arm of the United Nations charged with promoting the exchange of educational, scientific, and cultural enterprises among nations.

United States Copyright Office A federal administrative agency where copyrights may be registered.

unlimited liability General partners have unlimited personal liability for the debts and obligations of the limited partnership.

unsecured credit Credit that does not require any security (collateral) to protect the payment of the debt.

usurping a corporate opportunity A director or officer steals a corporate opportunity for himself or herself.

usurp the opportunity To steal an opportunity for oneself.

vertical merger A merger that integrates the operations of a supplier and a customer.

vertical restraint of trade A restraint of trade that occurs when two or more parties on *different levels of distribution* enter into a contract, combination, or conspiracy to restrain trade.

vicarious liability Being responsible because someone else is responsible; indirect legal responsibility (e.g., an employer is liable for the negligence of its employee).

voidable transfer An unusual payment or transfer of property by the debtor on the eve of bankruptcy that would unfairly benefit the debtor or some creditors at the expense of other creditors. Such transfer may be avoided by the bankruptcy court.

voluntary dissolution A corporation that has begun business or issued shares can be dissolved upon recommendation of the board of directors and a majority vote of the shares entitled to vote.

voluntary petition A petition filed by the debtor; states that the debtor has debts.

voting trust An agreement between stockholders and a trustee whereby the rights to vote the stock are transferred to the trustee.

voting trust certificate A certificate issued by a voting trustee to the beneficial holders of shares held by the voting trust.

waiting period A period of time that begins when the registration statement is filed with the SEC and continues until the registration statement is declared effective. Only certain activities are permissible during the waiting period.

warehouse company A bailee engaged in the business of storing property for compensation. Owes a *duty of reasonable care* to protect the bailed property.

warehouse receipt A document of title that is issued by a warehouse company to the bailor when goods are received by the warehouse company for storage.

warranties of quality Seller's or lessor's assurance to buyer or lessee that the goods meet certain standards of quality. Warranties may be expressed or implied.

warranty of fitness for a particular purpose A warranty that arises when a seller or lessor warrants that the goods will meet the buyer's or lessee's expressed needs.

waste Occurs when a tenant causes substantial and permanent damage to the leased premises that decreases the value of the property and the landlord's reversionary interest in it.

white-collar crimes Crimes usually involving cunning and deceit rather than physical force.

white knight merger Mergers with friendly parties—that is, parties that promise to leave the target corporation and/or its management intact.

Williams Act An amendment to the Securities Exchange Act of 1934 made in 1968 that specifically regulates all tender offers.

winding-up and liquidation The process by which a dissolved corporation's assets are collected, liquidated, and distributed to creditors, shareholders, and other claimants.

wire fraud The use of telephone or telegraph to defraud another person.

withholding delivery The act of the seller or lessor purposefully refusing to deliver goods to the buyer or lessee upon breach of the sales or lease contract by the buyer or lessee or the insolvency of the buyer or lessee.

workers' compensation acts Acts that compensate workers and their families if workers are injured in connection with their jobs.

work-related test A test to determine the liability of a principal; if an agent commits an intentional tort within a work-related time or space, the principal is liable for any injury caused by the agent's intentional tort.

World Bank A UN specialized agency established in 1945 to provide loans that aid in economic development through economically sustainable enterprises.

World Court Located in The Hague, the Netherlands, this is the judicial branch of the UN. Only nations, not individuals or businesses, can have cases decided by this court.

World Trade Organization (WTO) An international organization of more than 130 member nations created to promote and enforce trade agreements among member nations.

written order A stop-payment order that is good for six months after the date it is written.

wrongful disassociation Occurs when a member withdraws from (1) a term LLC prior to the expiration of the term or (2) an at-will LLC when the operating agreement eliminates a member's power to withdraw.

wrongful dissolution When a partner withdraws from a partnership without having the right to do so at that time.

wrongful eviction A violation of the covenant of quiet enjoyment.

wrongful termination The termination of an agency contract in violation of the terms of the agency contract. The nonbreaching party may recover damages from the breaching party. Termination of a franchise without just cause.

WTO appellate body A panel of seven judges selected from WTO member nations that hears and decides appeals from decisions of the dispute settlement body.

WTO dispute settlement body A board composed of one representative from each member nation that reviews panel reports.

WTO panel A body of three WTO judges that hears trade disputes between member nations and issues a "panel report."

CASE LISTING

DeBaun v. First W. Bank & Trust Co., 120 Cal. Rptr. 354 (Cal. Ct. App. 1975). 279

Dothard v. Rawlinson, 433 U.S. 321 (1977). 407

Dotlich v. Dotlich, 475 N.E.2d 331 (Ind. Ct. App. 1985). 278

Dunkin' Donuts of Am., Inc. v. Middletown Donut Corp., 495 A.2d 66 (N.J. 1985). 220

Duval v. Midwest Auto City, Inc., 425 F. Supp. 1381 (D. Neb. 1977). 70

Dwinnell's Cent. Neon v. Cosmopolitan Chinook Hotel, 587 P.2d 191 (Wash. Ct. App. 1978). 129

Edelman v. Fruehauf Corp., 798 F.2d 882 (6th Cir. 1986). 315

8 *Brookwood Fund v. Bear Stearns & Co.*, 539 N.Y.S.2d 411 (N.Y. App. Div. 1989). 127

EEOC v. Tortilleria "La Mejor," 758 F. Supp. 585 (E.D. Cal. 1991). 408

Ernst & Ernst v. Hochfelder, 425 U.S. 185 (1976). 357

Escott v. BarChris Constr. Corp., 283 F. Supp. 643 (S.D.N.Y. 1968). 357

Faragher v. City of Boca Raton, 524 U.S. 775 (1998). 390

Fite v. First Tenn. Prod. Credit Ass'n, 861 F.2d 884 (6th Cir. 1988). 407

Fragante v. City and County of Honolulu, 888 F.2d 591 (9th Cir. 1989). 407

Franklin Life Ins. Co. v. Commonwealth Edison Co., 451 F. Supp. 602 (S.D. Ill. 1978). 204

Francis I. Du Pont & Co. v. Universal City Studios, Inc., 312 A.2d 344 (Del. Ch. 1973). 316

Franklin Life Ins. Co. v. Commonwealth Edison Co., 451 F. Supp. 602 (S.D. Ill. 1978). 204

Gay v. Gay's Super Mkts., Inc., 343 A.2d 577 (Me. 1975). 277

General Electric Credit Corps v Stover, 708 S.W. 2d 355 (Ct. App. Mo. 1986). 108

Geringer v. Wildhorn Ranch, Inc., 706 F. Supp. 1442 (D. Colo. 1988). 278

Getty Oil Co. v. Occupational Safety & Health Review Comm'n, 530 F.2d 1143 (5th Cir. 1976). 378

Gilroy v. Conway, 391 N.W.2d 419 (Mich. Ct. App. 1986). 103

Ginn v. Renaldo, Inc., 359 S.E.2d 390 (Ga. Ct. App. 1987). 22

Gladwin v. Medfield Corp., 540 F.2d 1266 (5th Cir. 1976). 313

Glen v. Club Mediterranee, S.A., 450 F.3d 1251 (11th Cir 2006). 422

Glidden Co. v. Department of Labor and Indus., 700 A.2d 555 (Pa. Commw. Ct. 1997). 70

Glockzin v. Nordyne, Inc., 815 F. Supp. 1050 (W.D. Mich. 1992). 379

Goodman v. Darden, Doman & Stafford Assoc., 670 P.2d 648 (Wash. 1983). 205

Gould v. Ruefenacht, 471 U.S. 701(1985). 357

Green v. Jackson, 674 S.W.2d 395 (Tex. Ct. App. 1984). 47

Grinder v. Bryans Road Bldg. & Supply Co., 432 A.2d 453 (Md. 1981). 46

Handley v. Ching, 627 P.2d 1132 (Haw. Ct. App. 1981). 203

Hankin v. Hankin, 493 A.2d 675 (Pa. 1985). 103

Harris v. Forklift Sys., Inc., 510 U.S. 17 (1993). 408

Hayes v. Tarbenson, Thatcher, McGrath, Treadwell & Schoonmaker, 749 P.2d 178 (Wash. Ct. App. 1988). 101

Helmsman Management Serv., Inc. v. A&S Consultants, Inc., 525 A.2d 160 (Del. Ch. 1987). 277

Hilgendorf v. Hague, 293 N.W.2d 272 (Iowa 1980). 25

Hilton v. Eckersley, 119 Eng. Rep. 781 (Q.B. 1855). 106

Holiday Inns, Inc. v. Shelburne, 576 So. 2d 322 (Fla. Dist. Ct. App. 1991). 218

Huddleston v. Roger Dean Chevrolet, Inc., 845 F.2d 900 (1988) 406

Husted v. McCloud, 436 N.E.2d 341 (Ind. Ct. App. 1982). 101

Hutchinson Baseball Enter., Inc. v. Commissioner of Internal Revenue, 696 F.2d 757 (10th Cir. 1982). 202

IBP, Inc. v. Alvarez, 546 U.S. 21 (2005). 366

Iota Management Corp. v. Boulevard Inv. Co., 731 S.W.2d 399 (Mo. Ct. App. 1987). 24

International Union, United Auto., Aerospace & Agric. Implement Workers of Am. v. Johnson Controls, Inc., 499 U.S. 187 (1991). 393

Jacobson v. Stern, 605 P.2d 198 (Nev. 1980). 204

Johnson v. Rogers, 763 P.2d 771 (Utah 1988). 44

Jones v. H.F. Ahmanson & Co., 460 P.2d 464 (Cal. 1969). 204

KFC Corp. v. Marion-Kay Co., 620 F. Supp. 1160 (S.D. Ind. 1985). 237

Katz v. Bregman, 431 A.2d 1274 (Del. Ch. 1981). 309

Kawasaki Shop of Aurora, Inc. v. Kawasaki Motors Corp., 544 N.E.2d 457 (Ill. App. Ct. 1989). 235

Keating v. Goldick, No. 00C-10-223 WCC, No. 01C-11-027 WCC, 2004 Del. LEXIS 102, at *1 (Super Ct. April 6, 2004). 10

Edward A. Kemmler Memorial Foundation v. Mitchell, 584 N.E.2d 695 (Ohio 1992). 89

Kentucky Fried Chicken Corp. v. Diversified Container Corp., 549 F.2d 368 (5th Cir. 1977). 235

King v. Bankerd, 492 A.2d 608 (Md. 1985). 24

Koehlke v. Clay Street Inn, Inc., No. 2002-A-0108, 2003 Ohio LEXIS 4819 (Ct. App. Sept. 30, 2003). 69

Korematsu v. United States, 323 U.S. 214 (1944). 399

Kosters v. Seven-Up Co., 595 F.2d 347 (6th Cir. 1979). 234

Estate of Krempasky, 501 A.2d 681 (Pa. Super. Ct. 1985). 25

Lampf, Pleva, Lipkind, Prupis & Petigrow v. Gilbertson, 501 U.S. 350 (1991). 357

Landreth Timber Co. v. Landreth, 471 U.S. 681 (1985). 357

Lange v. National Biscuit Co., 211 N.W.2d 783 (Minn. 1973). 48

Largey v. Radiotelephone, Inc., 136 Cal. App. 3d 660 (Cal. Ct. App. 1982). 47

Lawson v. Young, 486 N.E.2d 1177 (Ohio Ct. App. 1984). 278

Ledbetter v. Goodyear Tire & Rubber Co., 550 U.S. 618 (2007). 408

Libby-Broadway Drive-In, Inc. v. McDonald's Sys., Inc., 391 N.E.2d 1 (Ill. App. Ct. 1979). 232

Libra Bank Ltd. v. Banco Nacional de Costa Rica, 570 F. Supp. 870 (S.D.N.Y. 1983). 429

Lockspeiser v. Western Maryland Co., 768 F.2d 558 (4th Cir. 1985). 312

M/S Bremen & Unterweser Reederei, GMBH v. Zapata Off-Shore Co., 407 U.S. 1 (1972). 429

Machakos v. Attorney General of the United States, 859 F.2d 1487 (D.C. Cir. 1988). 407

Mackay v. Douglas, 14 L.R.-Eq. 106 (1872). 72

Venezio v. Bianchi, 508 N.Y.S.2d 349 (N.Y. App. Div. 1986). 47

Vernon v. Schuster, 688 N.E.2d 1172 (Ill. 1997). 60

Virginia Partners, Ltd. v. Day, 738 S.W.2d 837 (Ky. Ct. App. 1987). 124

Vizcaino v. United States Dist. Ct., 173 F.3d 713 (9th Cir. 1999). 367

Vohland v. Sweet, 435 N.E. 2d 860 (Ind. Ct. App. 1982). 77

Washington Steel Corp. v. TW Corp., 465 F. Supp. 1100 (W.D. Pa. 1979). 47

Whirlpool Corp. v. Marshall, 445 U.S. 1 (1980). 380

Wickham v. Southland Corp., 213 Cal. Rptr. 825 (Cal. Ct. App. 1985). 236

Wilson v. Church, 11 Ch. D. 576 (1879). 267

Wilson v. Workers' Compensation Appeals Bd., 196 Cal. App. 3d 902 (Cal. Ct. App. 1987). 375

Zollar v. Smith, 710 S.W.2d 155 (Tex. Ct. App. 1986). 275

Zuckerman v. Antenucci, 478 N.Y.S.2d 578 (N.Y. App. Div. 1984). 88

SUBJECT INDEX

D

E

G

Q

R

S

W